HIGH AVAILABILITY
NETWORKING
WITH CISCO

HIGH AVAILABILITY NETWORKING WITH CISCO

VINCENT C. JONES

ADDISON–WESLEY

Boston   San Francisco   New York   Toronto   Montreal
London   Munich   Paris   Madrid   Capetown
Sydney   Tokyo   Singapore   Mexico City

Many of the designations used by manufacturers and sellers to distinguish their products are claimed as trademarks. Where those designations appear in this book, and Addison-Wesley was aware of a trademark claim, the designations have been printed with initial capital letters or in all capitals.

The author and publisher have taken care in the preparation of this book, but make no expressed or implied warranty of any kind and assume no responsibility for errors or omissions. No liability is assumed for incidental or consequential damages in connection with or arising out of the use of the information or programs contained herein.

The publisher offers discounts on this book when ordered in quantity for special sales. For more information, please contact:

Pearson Education Corporate Sales Division
One Lake Street
Upper Saddle River, NJ 07458
(800) 382-3419
corpsales@pearsontechgroup.com

Visit AW on the Web: www.awl.com/cseng/

Library of Congress Cataloging-in-Publication Data

Jones, Vincent C., 1947–
    High availability networking with Cisco / Vincent C. Jones.
        p.   cm.
    ISBN 0-201-70455-2
        1. Computer networks.   2. Computer network architectures.   3. Routers (Computer networks)   I. Title.

TK5105.5 .J66 2000
004.6—dc21   00-048509

ISBN 0-201-70455-2
Text printed on recycled paper
1 2 3 4 5 6 7 8 9—MA—0403020100
First printing, December 2000

Contents

Acknowledgments

This book would not have been possible without the help of many people. First and foremost was my wife, Sona, without whose loving support this book would never have materialized.

My daughter, Kohar, was also instrumental in ensuring that my writing was coherent and intelligible, sacrificing many hours reviewing and commenting on drafts so that the technical reviewers could concentrate on technical issues.

Karen Gettman at Addison-Wesley deserves credit for initially convincing me to make the effort to write this book. Thanks also to Beth Burleigh Fuller of Booksmiths Unlimited and the folks at Stratford Publishing Services for their work on the production of this book.

Then there is the international army of people who reviewed chapters for technical content and presentation, shared their favorite configuration tricks, and otherwise helped make this book what it is. These include Hansang Bae, Gaurav Banga, Fabio Bellini, Johnny Chen, Ray Chester, Nigel Clarke, Matt Douhan, Curt Freemyer, Peter E. Fry, Andreas Plesner Jacobsen, Siraz K. Kureshi, Ronald B. Leask, Mark R. Lindsey, Barry Margolin, Nazir Mohamed, William B. Norton, Kacheong Pong, Dr. Robert C. Raciti, Linda M. Richman, Ivan Rogers, Glen S. Rosen, Jesper Skriver, Alan Strassberg, David Strom, Kenneth Tarnawsky, Walter Weiss, and Richard Wright.

Preface

This book explores and discusses a wide range of potential approaches to improving network availability, allowing you to choose those most appropriate for your organization and its unique needs and constraints. The goal is to show how to achieve higher network availability both in theory and in practice. In economic terms, this means pushing the design to the point at which the cost of eliminating further unavailability exceeds the cost to the organization of the losses due to downtime.

While the theoretical aspects apply to networks of all sizes and technologies, the example solutions provided focus on the needs of moderate sized extended corporate networks using IP version 4 and stable, moderate performance technologies such as Frame Relay, ISDN, and Ethernet—not because these technologies are fundamentally more or less reliable than others, but because they tend to be the networks that have grown to the point of being critical to the day-to-day operations of the organization without a staff of dedicated network designers and architects to provide optimization and support.

HOW TO USE THIS BOOK

This book is written for those looking for design techniques to cost effectively improve network availability. The reader is assumed to be knowledgeable in the fundamentals of large network design and comfortable going to other references for more details on specific protocols and functions.

The basic approach of this book is divide and conquer. Each chapter attacks a general need of high availability network design, from defining what high availability really means and requires in the first chapter to the final chapter's discussion of the essential commitment to a full range of network management capabilities. Within each chapter, the general need is broken down into specific requirements. Within each specific requirement, the problem being addressed and possible solutions are first discussed on a general theoretical level. Wherever practical, one or more specific scenarios are defined and example solutions implemented, typically using Cisco routers.

Please read through the example implementations even if you never expect to touch a Cisco system. The examples and their accompanying discussions serve to flesh out the theoretical framework, showing typical adjustments required to get the theory presented to actually work in a real world environment. Many of these adjustments have nothing to do with Cisco but rather reflect limitations in the current implementations of network protocols. Technical managers and others will find this book's survey of all aspects of high availability network design invaluable. There are a vast array of considerations which should be part of any design and tunnel vision can be costly. It is very easy (and common) to implement point solutions which in the process of eliminating one weakness introduce other modes of failure. Choosing the best solution is rarely possible without a system-wide perspective.

Network implementors in a Cisco environment will find this book a cookbook of Cisco solutions that they can modify and install in their own network. These readers should still pay attention to the theoretical discussions preceding each example so they can identify modifications necessary to fit their unique environment.

It is essential for all to keep in mind that high availability is not just a design parameter, it is also an executive management commitment to funding adequate resources, staffing and training for the life of the network. At the same time, even though this book focuses on enhancing the availability of the network, we must always keep our sense of perspective. From the user's viewpoint, it is immaterial whether it is the network, the server, the software or the client platform which fails. Cost effective availability improvement needs to be balanced across all causes of failure to ensure that the resources required are applied where they will have the most impact on the bottom line.

This is much easier to say than it is to do, as few organizations even know what their current availability is or keep any statistics on the causes of failure. Even fewer organizations have proceeded to the stage of analyzing their bottom line costs for various failure modes. But higher network availability remains indisputably important. Fortunately, it is never too late to start on the road to higher availability.

CHAPTER BY CHAPTER

Chapter 1, Reliability and Availability, introduces the theory and technology of high availability networks. First the stage is set with the potential cost of network downtime for mundane production as well as "must run" networks. The mathematical basis behind predicting availability, different approaches to providing higher availability, and the availability challenges unique to computer networks form the core of the chapter. The chapter ends with the need to provide physical diversity in multiply connected WANs and LANs, setting the stage for the rest of the book.

High availability is not an automatic result of adding redundant links and components to a network. Adding redundancy adds complexity to the network, which must be recognized and utilized. *Chapter 2, Bridging and Routing,* starts out with a quick review of network terminology, then surveys the available layer two bridging approaches (simple learning, SR and TST) and popular layer three routing protocols for IP (static, RIP, OSPF, Integrated IS-IS, EIGRP, and BGP), briefly discussing how each works and the strengths and weaknesses of each. Along the way, parameter tuning which may be appropriate to speed up response to failures is explored and examples provided.

Chapter 3, Multihomed Hosts, extends the availability benefits of redundant connectivity all the way to the end system in an IP network. Starting with the simple step of adding a second NIC to an end system, the challenges presented in supporting applications when the server (or client) has two IP addresses are explored. Then two approaches to giving the two NICs the appearance of a single IP address (proprietary and via routing) are examined, with full configuration examples for the latter. The chapter concludes with a discussion of server cluster terminology, techniques and limitations.

Dial backup is a popular alternative to installing additional "permanent" links. In *Chapter 4, Dial Backup for Permanent Links,* the first of two dedicated to dial backup, three different dial backup approaches are introduced, distinguished by how the router determines the need to place a call. After exploring the underlying assumptions behind each and how those assumptions affect their suitability for various applications, a basic "how to" for IP dial backup is provided. Using examples of ISDN dial backup applied to leased lines, Frame Relay, and DSL, the critical factors requisite to successful implementation are highlighted.

Chapter 5, Advanced Dial Backup, extends the general concepts introduced in Chapter 4 to meet the specific needs of a range of requirements. It starts with the challenge of using asynchronous modems rather than ISDN, then moves on to explore techniques for combining multiple dial links to provide higher bandwidth. After a brief look at providing IPX support, the chapter concludes with how to use BGP with generic dial-on-demand routing to provide dial backup driven by routing table changes without the limitations associated with Cisco's proprietary dialer watch facility.

Chapter 6, Multiple Routers at a Single Site, focuses on eliminating the router as a single point of failure from the viewpoint of preventing end-systems at a location from being isolated from the rest of the WAN. Starting with solutions to the limitations inherent in the IP concept of a default gateway, the chapter then explores how to provide a second router without doubling the WAN communications costs by getting one router to provide dial backup for a link on another router. It then finishes with how to configure the routers on a physically extended LAN so that even if the LAN is split in two by a failure, IP systems on both halves of the LAN can still communicate with the outside world.

Chapter 7, Hub-and-Spoke Topology, explores the unique requirements of hub and spokes networks. Hub and spoke is a popular topology for HQ data center and other applications because it allows major simplifications in the routing structure, but it can also introduce complications. The chapter starts with a discussion on how to get around limitations on the number of peers supportable on a single router and how to scale a hub-and-spoke design to handle an arbitrary number of spokes without requiring the spoke routers to maintain more than a handful of routes each. The focus then shifts to configuring dial-on-demand routing so that a spoke router can dial any of several routers at the hub without concern for which answers. Finally, critical considerations when the hub expands to actually be multiple sites, such as a primary and backup data center, are explored.

Chapter 8, Connecting to Service Providers, looks at the special considerations that apply when connecting with networks outside our control. The challenge is split into two levels: connecting to well-defined, relatively trustworthy external networks and connecting to the Internet. For the former, the focus is on solving the problem of redundant connectivity using floating static routes driven by an IGP. For the latter, the focus is on the limits of static routing and how to make the most of BGP for both multiple connections to a single ISP and redundant connections to multiple ISPs.

Any time we can't trust the "other network," we should firewall it. The problem is that a firewall not only blocks traffic from the "bad guys," it also blocks desirable traffic such as routing information. *Chapter 9, Connecting Through Firewalls,* focuses on how firewalls are integrated into a network and the various ways traffic can be routed to the appropriate firewall. Starting with an example of a fully redundant network with no firewall failover capability, it looks at different ways to provide useful redundancy for the firewalls without sacrificing security.

Many organizations also use DLSw to support IBM SNA communications. *Chapter 10, IBM SNA and DLSw,* looks at the challenges of supporting DLSw in a fully redundant manner, starting with Token Ring LAN support where support of redundant DLSw links is automatic. Then the challenge of providing working redundant fallback in support of Ethernet attached devices is addressed. The chapter ends with how to implement high availability redundant DLSw in a firewalled environment.

Chapter 11, Disaster Recovery Considerations, scales the survey of high availability design techniques to consider continued operations in the event of a site-wide or regional disaster. The cost of full scale disaster recovery combined with fundamental weaknesses in the IPv4 protocol suite means every solution is a compromise. The chapter looks at some of the key considerations in planning for disaster recovery with little or no service interruption, some of the potential failure modes that need to be designed around, and the use of commercially available load sharing approaches to implement high availability disaster recovery.

Chapter 12, Management Considerations, finishes the book with a look at network management. In a network design with redundant capabilities for high availability, network management is not an option. It is essential that faults be found and fixed as quickly as possible, even though they may have no immediate impact on network functionality. Surveying the technical and management skills and discipline required to run a high availability network, the chapter focus on the critical roles of network monitoring, configuration management, and total quality control.

An extensive glossary is also included in recognition of the huge range of acronyms and technical terms required in a book covering as wide a variety of concerns as this one.

PRODUCT DISCLAIMER

For those of you not using Cisco products, I apologize for the exclusive use of Cisco routers in the router configuration examples provided. I strongly encourage you to continue reading regardless, as many of the challenges and tradeoffs discussed as part of the Cisco configuration apply to routers and switches from other vendors as well. Even though the terminology, command syntax, and feature sets differ, the underlying protocols are based on the same standards and the same set of constraints.

For those of you who are using Cisco products, I have tried to indicate in each configuration the oldest version of Cisco IOS that the particular configuration can be expected to run on. In indicating a minimum IOS, I ignored interim release trains (such as 11.1 and 11.3) and all releases prior to 11.0. My assumption is that in a network requiring maximum availability, only mainstream IOS releases that are actively supported and in General Distribution status will be of interest.

This book reflects techniques I have used over the years to help my clients minimize the impact of failure on network operations. Almost all the examples are extracted from working configurations that have been proven in production environments, then adapted and sanitized for publication. As a service to readers, all the example configurations are available on the Networking Unlimited, Inc., Web site at *http://www.networkingunlimited.com.* All feedback is welcome.

Reliability and Availability

Network failures and the weather have a lot in common. As Mark Twain was fond of saying, "Everybody talks about the weather, but nobody does anything about it." The fact that we cannot control the weather or its effects, however, does not mean that we have to ignore them. In alpine regions, we build our roofs to shed snow rather than collapse under the load. In the tropics, we include windows that can be left open for ventilation even as the rain comes pouring down. And in river valleys, we build outside the flood plain. Networking is like the weather—we can identify our most likely and highest impact failure modes and plan accordingly.

Networks share many characteristics with computer systems, and all techniques used to improve the reliability of computer systems apply to the networks that support them. For this reason, we typically see networking equipment installed in the computer room so that it can share the physical security and controlled environment already in place to protect the primary computing resources.

Networking deals with the vagaries of unreliable links. As a result, networking protocols are carefully designed to deal with virtually any failure imaginable and can provide communications despite failed hardware, failed links, or incorrect configurations. The apocryphal network protocol designer, accused of being paranoid in design by including antidotes to everything that possibly could go wrong, responded quite honestly: "Paranoia is imagining 'they' are out to get you. When 'they' really are out to get you, it is called 'doing the right thing.'"

The challenge in networking is recognizing that any failure mode that can occur eventually occurs, no matter how improbable. The critical question is not "if," but "when." That is, *when* the failure occurs, can the network design and operation handle it? If the answer is "no," it is time to do the probability and impact analysis to determine if the price of the fix will outweigh the losses when the failure occurs.

In this chapter, we start with a brief discussion of the importance of high network availability, focusing on the risks and benefits that can help justify the expense of making significant improvements. We follow with the theory of reliability and availability and how they are related and how they are different. We conclude the chapter with a discussion of how the developed theory applies to typical computer networks and the issues in the design of wide area networks (WANs) and local area networks (LANs).

THE NEED FOR NETWORK AVAILABILITY

The outage began at 3 P.M. Monday and continued through the evening. The situation affected not only business-to-business data communications but also a wide swath of the consumer economy. Bank ATM machines, travel agency orders, and credit card transactions were disrupted.[1]

The El Niño storms damaged a large, heavily traveled bridge over a river in central California. Fiber from at least two carriers was contained in a single conduit that runs through the bridge. When the river crested, both carriers' connectivity was lost. Some customers, believing they had purchased multiple services that ran on separate fiber paths, were surprised to discover that these services were actually run across the same fiber.[2]

These are just two examples of the kind of widely publicized events that demonstrate the challenge of network availability. Downtime translates into lost money for businesses. For example, recent studies have claimed that network downtime costs can run as high as $6 million per hour for retail brokerage applications. But you do not have to be a high-profile New York City brokerage house or Internet commerce server to suffer real losses due to network downtime.

Computer networking has matured well beyond the point where simply getting communications to occur at all is considered a major accomplishment. Network availability has joined throughput and delay as a key network performance metric, and downtime becomes an increasingly critical problem for computer users. This is not because computers and the networks they utilize are becoming less reliable. If anything, the opposite is true. The challenge is that users are demanding greater and greater availability. As businesses and other organizations become more dependent on computers and support networks for their ongoing operations, it becomes more critical for hardware and software failures not to interfere with those operations.

Whether cost is measured in terms of lost information, lost productivity, lost revenues, customer dissatisfaction, or technical support costs, downtime impacts the bottom line. Investment in a networking infrastructure that reduces that downtime can yield a positive return on investment (ROI).

In many ways, the biggest challenge we face is determining the real cost of downtime because in many organizations, downtime costs are difficult-to-measure soft costs. Ideally, we would like to establish an annual cost of downtime for every system and then measure the benefits obtained by mitigating each problem that could have caused a system to fail. We can then select among the various available options to improve availability based upon cost, effort, and impact.

The importance of determining the cost of downtime is frequently underestimated by the technically minded. The best technical design in the world does not help if those with the solution cannot get the required buy-in from management. Since information technology in general, and network infrastructure in particular, is frequently viewed as a cost center with no profit potential for the organization, management is understandably reluctant to increase those costs. While the technical elegance of the solution may be lost on management, a high ROI based on the cost of downtime versus the cost of eliminating that downtime gets positive attention every time.

Defining Network Availability

While we may all agree on the desirability of high network availability, we must be careful any time we see informal terms such as *high availability* and *fault tolerant* used to describe different degrees of availability. These are context-dependent marketing terms rather than technical specifications and carry as much meaning as other marketing terms such as *lo-cal* and *extra rich*, which is to say, no meaning at all. For example, Hewlett-Packard defines a *high availability server* as one that is working in excess of 99% of the scheduled working time and a *fault tolerant* server as one that can provide uptime in excess of 99.999%.[3] IBM, on the other hand, defines high availability as 99.7% and considers fault tolerant to be a design methodology rather than an availability level.[4]

This confusion is not surprising. A device that is down an average of 8 hours a year would be considered 99.9% available on a 24-hour-a-day, 7-day-a-week (24 × 7) basis, but only 99.6% available if measured against and within a 40-hour work week. Then again, if all failures occurred outside of working hours and we were measuring against the same 40-hour work week, the availability would be 100%.

There can also be a major difference in business impact between a system that fails once a year for an entire 8-hour work day with no services available, and the same eight hours of downtime randomly distributed over the course of the year with no individual failure lasting longer than 5 minutes. Both reflect 99.9% availability, but the former would probably have the CEO pounding the desk of the MIS manager while the latter might not even be noticed. At the other extreme, if the individual failures averaged 2 seconds each, that 99.9% available system would be failing approximately every 33 minutes, making it nearly impossible for a task requiring one hour of uninterrupted access to complete.

Similarly, there can be a major difference between scheduled and unscheduled downtime. The frustration level of users will be much lower if they can accurately predict when they will be inconvenienced and have confidence that they will be able to resume their activities on schedule.

A Web merchant, for example, may not see the lesser penalty from scheduled rather than unscheduled downtime because one of the site's selling features is the convenience of ordering whenever desired without regard to any concept of normal business hours. Nevertheless, a savvy Web merchant faced with the prospect of scheduled downtime would schedule it for the slowest period possible and then work extra hard to provide an interim coverage solution so that the downtime would not be noticed by customers, even though it meant significant extra work for the Information Systems (IS) staff. As we shall see, one of the keys to higher availability is having that interim solution in place to cover the unscheduled, as well as the scheduled, downtime.

The impact of unscheduled downtime may even be affected by the ability to predict its duration. For example, if it is known that a downtime incident will be of extended duration, less convenient workarounds (such as transferring data entry operators to a location that is still operational) may be activated sooner, thereby reducing the overall impact of the failure.

DETERMINING AVAILABILITY REQUIREMENTS

Designing and implementing significant improvements in network availability is rarely trivial. Developing appropriate solutions can involve considerable time, effort, and expense, and their scope will usually extend well beyond the traditional limits of network design to include computing services platforms, application design, operating procedures, and user training. Successful solutions must match the business requirements and make appropriate tradeoffs among cost, recovery speed, and the scope of outages covered.

For most businesses, the main business requirement is high availability of application functionality, for which the network is just one more weak link in the chain of systems that must be operational for applications to function. At the same time, the network is typically dependent on the general support infrastructure in place for computing services such as power, management procedures, and physical access controls, making it next to impossible to make the network much more reliable than the systems it is supporting. Maintaining a business perspective ensures that the limited resources available are applied where they will have the most impact on the bottom line.

Although we would always like to develop an availability solution that exactly matches the business requirements, it is rarely possible. Many business requirements are tradeoffs themselves, and some may even be mutually exclusive. No matter what, the more stringent the requirements, the more expensive the solution. Thus we will need to balance how fast we can recover from any particular failure with the range of failures we need to protect against and the costs we are willing to incur to provide that protection. The key to making appropriate tradeoffs is to recognize that failures will occur and the only question is when and how often. We can then decide on appropriate levels of protection commensurate with the risk and expected losses. But we must also recognize that no matter what is done, 100% availability is impossible to achieve, and the closer we strive to get to perfection the higher the costs.

As an example of tradeoffs, consider the issue of power supplies. Few would consider foregoing the cost of an uninterruptible power supply to tide over the surges, droops, and brief outages endemic in commercial power sources, but providing motor-generators and a two-week supply of fuel to support continued operations in the event of a major regional disaster is another story. Although it may be the most cost effective way to provide power in such an unusual event, it does nothing to support continued availability of communications links, water, building access, and many other related concerns that are also essential to continued operation. To have all these needs met, a remote disaster recovery site may be a more appropriate solution. Then again, the organization may decide that the cost of adequate protection is too high, accept the exposure, and hope that their insurance will cover enough of the losses to keep them solvent.

One of the disadvantages of designing for high availability is that when a failure finally does force downtime, the resulting outage will typically be very difficult to fix because all the easy problems have already been taken care of in the design. It may even seem that the better the design, the more severe and prolonged the outage when one does occur. What we are overlooking, of course, is the fact that a less well designed system would be brought down by the same failure for at least the same amount of time, would be no less difficult to restore to operation, and would have suffered numerous other failures in the meantime that the high availability design would have survived without incident.

Except in rare circumstances in which there is already a high availability infrastructure in place, a high availability network design should also include:

- Additional communications, networking, and network management resources

- Additional computing and infrastructure resources

- Development and testing of new procedures

Clearly, improving availability requires considerable resources to accomplish significant goals. Attempts to improve availability without regard to the needs of the business are rarely cost effective. You must look at the business impact of unplanned outages before you can develop an effective design. For example, switching from asynchronous modem dial backup to ISDN backup for a link to reduce the downtime from 45 seconds to 5 seconds may make the network downtime statistics look better, but if the end users' applications still crash, resources have been expended but the business requirement has still not been met.

Unplanned outages usually have a financial impact in three ways. The first category of financial impact due to unplanned outages is lost work time by users. Think of people who need systems for their work and who are less productive for as long as the network is down. They might have to repeat certain parts of their work when the system becomes available again. Or work overtime to make up for the outage.

The second category of financial impact is lost transactions. If the system serves customer transactions online, the customer is not likely to wait for the network to come up again. While some customers might try to repeat their online transaction at a later time, others will take their business to competitors and might never come back. In addition, transactions in progress may end in an inconsistent state, leading to further customer dissatisfaction.

A third category of financial impact is lost system capacity. Work that was in progress is interrupted by the outage and thus needs to be repeated after service is restored. At that time, the work will be competing for system capacity with other work. This added work load may require additional system and network capacity.

Even in smaller computer networks, the sum of the three categories of financial impact can amount to a substantial figure. Quantifying the cost of downtime is fundamental to planning for higher availability. After all, we always want to keep Courtney's Law in mind: "Never spend more money fixing a problem than tolerating it will cost you."[5]

Measurable costs and issues involved in tolerating a problem include

Number and duration of outages

Number of users affected

Loss of productive time or overtime per user

Transaction rate and average turnover value per transaction

System capacity and time required for workload repetition

The required improvements in availability can then be documented in service level objectives. These should define, for each application service supported:

Hours of service

Maximum and minimum response time

Maximum number of outages per time interval

Maximum duration of any single outage

Minimum interval between outages

For network design purposes, you must translate application service level objectives into network service level objectives. For instance, the hours of service determine what time slots, if any, are available for routine maintenance and other scheduled downtime. The maximum acceptable response time will need to be allocated between application software, systems software, and communications support to determine minimum bandwidth and maximum network delay parameters. The minimum response time gives us a point beyond which there is no benefit to improving performance for this application. In addition, the maximum number of outages per time interval combined with the maximum single outage duration gives the lower limit on the required availability. (The minimum interval between outages simply means that if two outages occur close together, they will be considered a single extended outage.)

Network design is driven also by the communications protocols used to support the applications. In general, network applications are driven by time-outs and retransmissions at various layers of the OSI reference model. If network service can be restored before the protocols used by the application declare the communications to be down, the service impact will be a performance degradation rather than a service outage. These numbers can range widely, from a few hundred milliseconds for classic IBM systems network architecture (SNA) physical unit-to-physical unit communications to over a minute for the Transmission Control Protocol (TCP).

Different failure modes can have different impacts. For example, while the TCP time-out and retransmit algorithm may tolerate a gap in service of several minutes, a single report to the end system to communicate that the destination address is no longer valid (as may occur between the time a routing protocol detects failure of a link and when it completes determination of a new route to get around that failed link) may cause the application to immediately terminate the TCP connection even if the gap in service is only milliseconds in duration. Depending on the application and how it is programmed, this could result in the loss of any work in progress and might even require the user to manually restart the application.

As part of our network design, we must always be aware of the potential for minor disruptions at the network level to have major impact on user processes and the application availability they perceive. As we will see in Chapter 2, Bridging and Routing, we can sometimes avoid problems by tuning protocol parameters. But at other times, we may find it necessary to change our design to use an entirely different protocol, topology, or approach.

AVAILABILITY MEASUREMENT AND REPORTING

While the availability requirements per application may be easy to define even if the costs are not, it does not tell us why we have an availability problem. Before we can improve availability, we need to know our current availability. This requires a two pronged attack that starts with an *availability management analysis* to measure the current systems availability and examine the causes of past failures. This analysis looks at historic problem reporting data. Organizations that have not taken availability seriously may lack adequate records, thus eliminating the historical perspective and limiting the data sample to recent recall.

Outage analysis is based on data regarding system unavailability for a time frame that reflects normal operations. The process can be time consuming, but the insight provided can be invaluable. A structured approach such as the following is highly recommended.

1. Gather data from all available sources such as the problem management database, system logs, operator logs, help desk records, trouble ticket databases, and phone bills (if already using dial backup).

2. Analyze the major causes of unavailability such as hardware, access line, and service provider network failures, and power, software, configuration, procedure, documentation, and human errors.

3. Differentiate between unavoidable problems and outage times, and partially or totally avoidable problems and outage times.

4. Categorize the outages into significant and less significant occurrences. Less important outages might not be worthy of further study unless they recur or indicate a trend.

5. Identify the root cause of each outage. This is rarely the documented cause of the problem, as it frequently includes process or procedural problems.

6. Identify any secondary problems that contributed to the duration or frequency of outages.

7. Review the existing recovery procedures and support structures for their currency and effectiveness.

All findings and recommendations resulting from the outage analysis should be documented in a detailed report. This report should include:

The number of outages analyzed and their timeframe

A quantification of the avoidable outage time

Areas that need special focus

The expected level of improvement

For maximum management impact for your report, you should tie the findings back to the business case by discussing not only the avoidable outage times but also the lost business or expenses that could have been avoided. Highlight this business case for improving availability in the executive summary. Remember to include illustrations and graphs highlighting areas that require enhancement or a new focus and trends that deserve further analysis.

Once you know the problems, you can perform a component failure impact analysis to determine potential causes of future unplanned outages and their impact. This is done by looking at the current configuration and identifying its potential single points of failure. In addition, if extended service hours are required, an analysis of service downtime caused by system maintenance should be performed. However, unless the requirement is for zero scheduled downtime, this is usually more of a problem for computer systems design than it is for network design. But we do need to be careful of the maintenance needs of our network management support systems and their databases to avoid getting caught trying to unravel a problem, with no available tools.

When a network component fails, it stops transporting data correctly. This might cause some network users to be cut off or the entire network to crash, or it might have no user-visible impact. When a network crashes, it is unable to transport data for any users or applications. All end users lose access to networked application services. While uncommon in large networks, network crashes do occur, usually due to procedural errors that introduce invalid configuration or routing information into the network that is then propagated by the routing protocol.

On the other hand, network meltdown can also occur in what appears to be a stable network when design errors allow an unforeseen component failure to force the network into an unstable state. For example, it is possible to outgrow an extended LAN built around transparent Spanning-Tree switches so that when an active inter-switch link fails, the network is too loaded with production traffic to allow the Spanning-Tree algorithm to converge on a new topology and restore connectivity.

With a partial network failure, only some end users or applications are affected. For example, only the users in a particular office on a single LAN segment are disconnected or only SNA connectivity is lost while TCP/IP and IPX continue without incident. Partial failures are much more common and need to be carefully evaluated because although the effects of a partial failure may not be widespread on the network, the impact on the business workflow can vary widely depending on the function of the affected end users. For example, if a branch office is cut off from headquarters, the only impact may be a loss of e-mail and the need to phone or fax critical messages for the duration of the outage. But if that branch office is dependent on that link for accepting and satisfying customer orders, the financial impact could be dramatic.

At the same time, with large enough networks, it must be recognized that some classes of components, such as end user workstations and low speed WAN links, will always have some failed members. This simply represents the normal state of the system. Even if the individual links were 99.9% available individually, on the average, at any instant in time one out of every thousand would be in a failed state.

Another critical part of component analysis is how the failure of a component can be detected. While loss of some components will be painfully obvious, in a network already designed to provide reasonable availability, operations can continue with no visible impact through a wide range of component failures. Even when there is an impact on operations, it is not always obvious which of the many related components is actually causing the failure. Sometimes we know by tracing data through the network and seeing where we lose touch with it. Sometimes, the component may be smart enough to send us a message that it is about to fail or the components that must communicate with the failed component may indicate their inability to communicate with the failed device. Of course, such indicators might leave us guessing which device is faulty—the device being complained about or the device doing the complaining.

One common way of detecting failure is waiting until users complain, a technique derisively called "using the scream-o-meter." This approach is inadequate and becomes more so as we improve the availability designed into a network because in a properly designed network with redundant components, the end users will not detect a problem until all backup components and links are down as well. We will explore this issue in the next section of this chapter.

MATHEMATICS OF RELIABILITY AND AVAILABILITY

A network that is always available is available 100% of the time, regardless of how we measure "the time." Once we move away from the unattainable 100% mark, however, the "time" gets a lot fuzzier. If a system must be 99% available, what does that really mean? We know that 1% of the time the network will not be able to carry traffic in support of applications, but we do not know the following:

How often the network can be down

How long the network can be down

Whether we care if the network is down

The time frame of the measurement

If the network is scheduled to be up continuously (24 × 7) and we are measuring over a one-year time frame, 99% availability translates into 87 hours and 40 minutes of downtime. If the network is required only 8 hours a day, 5 days a week, 99% availability translates into 20 hours and 48 minutes of downtime. This does not sound too bad until we realize that if the 20 hours is tallied only during working hours, the downtime equates to 2.5 working days of unavailability and unlimited

TABLE 1-1.   *Required Availability and Associated Allowed Downtime*

AVAILABILITY	24 × 7 DOWNTIME	SINGLE SHIFT DOWNTIME
90%	36.5 days	25 working days
99%	87 hr, 40 min	20.8 hr (2.5 working days)
99.9%	8 hr, 45 min	2 hr, 5 min
99.99%	52.6 min	12.5 min
99.999%	5 min, 15 sec	75 sec
99.9999%	31.6 sec	7.5 sec

downtime outside of working hours. Further complicating the issue is the fact a 40-hour work week implies no communications with other time zones, no telecommuters working off-hours, no Internet phones or messaging services, no flexible working hours, and no overtime or special events.

Table 1-1 summarizes the allowable downtime per year for various levels of availability.

In determining the acceptable level of availability, consider the maximum duration of any single downtime incident. While 99% availability might be acceptable "on the average," if all downtime occurred in a single incident and the business went bankrupt as a result, we would have to change our requirements. Obviously, we need to know not only the average requirement, but also the limits on single incidents before the business is severely impacted.

MTBF AND MTTR

Availability can be fully characterized by two simple numbers: the Mean Time Between Failures (MTBF) and the Mean Time To Repair (MTTR). The MTBF defines the length of time, on the average, that a system is expected to function failure free. The MTTR defines the length of time, on the average, required to get the system working again when it does fail. Taken together, the availability is simply the time the system is avalable (the MTBF) divided by the total time of the measurement (the sum of MTBF and MTTR) or

$$\text{Availability} = \frac{\text{MTBF}}{\text{MTBF} + \text{MTTR}} \cdot 100\%$$

Now that we know what MTBF and MTTR are, let's apply the knowledge. Consider that we buy a new car at midnight on January 1 to start the new year. On February 15, we have a flat tire that takes us 1 hour to repair (unplanned outage). On

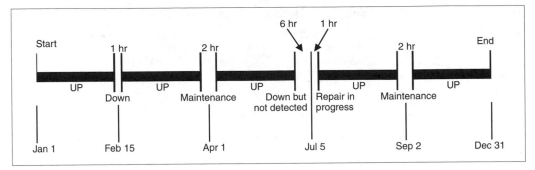

FIGURE **1-1.** *MTBF and MTTR for a new car*

April 1, we take it into the shop for 2 hours for an oil change (scheduled maintenance). On July 5, we discover that we left the headlights on and need to wait 1 hour for a jump start (an unplanned but very preventable outage). Finally, on September 2, we have the oil changed again during another 2 hours of scheduled downtime. The car then works without incident until the start of the next year.

Figure 1-1 shows our car experience. The heavy line indicates when the car was fully functional (state was up), and the blank portions indicated downtime, whether unplanned or scheduled. (Note that the downtime charged against our July dead battery is 7 hours, not 1 hour. Even though we did not need to use the car from the time the battery died on the night of July 4 until the morning of July 5, the car was down and not useable for a full 7 hours.) If we add up the hours, the car was available 8,748 hours and unavailable for 12 hours over the course of the full year, for an average availability of 99.6%.

$$\text{Availability} = \frac{\text{Uptime}}{\text{Uptime} + \text{Downtime}} \cdot 100\% = \frac{8,748}{8,748 + 12} \cdot 100\% = 99.86\%$$

Similarly, over the period of one year (8,760 hours), we had four failures (two planned and predictable, two unplanned) and 8,748 hours free of failure, so the mean time between failures was

$$\text{MTBF} = \frac{8,748}{4} = 2,187 \text{ hours}$$

The calculation of the MTTR might be considered unfair by some, because we include in the repair time not just the time required for unscheduled repairs (1 hour for the flat tire and 5 minutes for the dead battery), but also all time the system was unavailable for operations. This includes

1 hour for the flat tire on February 15

5 minutes for the jump start on July 5

55 minutes for the mechanic to show up on July 5

6 hours for the dead battery that we did not know about

4 hours for the scheduled maintenance

This yielded

$$\text{MTTR} = \frac{1:00 + 2:00 + 6:00 + 0:55 + 0:05 + 2:00}{4} = \frac{12}{4} = 3 \text{ hours}$$

Our example illustrates a number of critical considerations in calculating availability. For instance, consider our flat tire experience. It was properly classified as an unpredictable, unavoidable failure. However, the downtime should have been 15 minutes rather than 1 hour. The other 45 minutes of downtime was due to a lack of training (we had never had to change a flat tire before).

As another example, some might argue that it is unfair to charge as downtime the time the car sat idle with a dead battery that we did not know about because we did not need to go anywhere. While it is true that the impact on our productivity was only 1 hour, if the car had been needed at any time during those 6 hours, it would have failed us. By that line of reasoning, we should count only our time behind the wheel going from one location to another as uptime. In addition, if we are not going to use in our calculations time that the car is unavailable and unneeded, we should not count time as uptime either. In this case, we could repeat this exercise based on 10-hour working days or 1-hour commutes, whatever is more appropriate.

Along the same lines, time spent waiting for the mechanic to arrive is counted as part of repair time even though the repair work did not start until the mechanic arrived. Indeed, if you asked the manufacturer for a MTTR for dead batteries, it would be on the order of a few minutes, not a full hour. But in the real world, what we care about is availability for functional use. Downtime—whether due to negligence, acts of God, or poor planning—is still downtime. In the same way, when evaluating networking products and alternatives, we need to consider not only the time required to make the repair, but also the time required to discover that a problem exists, determine what component is at fault, dispatch repair, wait for parts, and restore configurations and databases to normal operation.

We approach network component availability as we did the car example. Our sample network is a medium-sized (approximately 100 locations) network in New York City using 56-Kbps Frame Relay links. The router logs for a full calendar year were analyzed for indications of link failures. For each link, the time spent in the up state and in the failed state was totaled over the entire year and a count was made of the number of times each link failed. Any periods of up time lasting less than three minutes were considered part of downtime. Listing 1-1 summarizes statistics for a sample of these links.

When we look at this real example, we can see why we must be very careful when looking at statistical averages. For example, our calculated average availability of 99.16% would not prepare us for over two weeks of downtime afflicting Location 8. In addition, although averages allow us to work with the statistics, they can hide underlying properties of the raw data. For instance, plotting a scattergram of the date and time of each detected failure versus the location (the first 50 days of the year are plotted in Figure 1-2) reveals several patterns. The calculated MTBF of 132 hours and MTTR of 1.12 hours for this collection of links hides the fact that many of the failures came in bunches. Some lines were marginal, failing intermittently over time. These failures show up as a horizontal line in the scattergram. Failures could also be due to failures inside the carrier's Frame Relay network that brought down all links passing through a particular switch or trunk. These failures show up as a vertical line. The strong and frequent vertical patterns in

Link	Frame Drops	Total Up Time		Total downtime		MTBF (hr)	MTTR (hr)
Location-01	8	364 d	19:13:13		03:55:34	1094.4	0.5
Location-02	41	364 d	04:59:36		18:09:11	213.1	0.4
Location-03	13	364 d	20:00:16		03:08:31	673.5	0.2
Location-04	36	364 d	18:47:23		04:21:24	243.1	0.1
Location-05	52	364 d	07:11:29		15:57:18	168.1	0.3
Location-06	11	364 d	09:58:07		13:10:40	795.0	1.2
Location-07	22	364 d	22:15:54		00:52:53	398.1	0.04
Location-08	10	350 d	03:30:16	14 d	19:38:31	840.3	35.6
Location-09	16	364 d	16:22:49		06:45:58	547.0	0.4
Location-10	30	364 d	18:03:08		05:05:39	291.8	0.2
Location-11	51	361 d	08:22:55	3 d	14:45:52	170.0	1.7
Location-12	65	361 d	18:27:14	3 d	04:41:33	133.5	1.2
Location-13	0	364 d	23:08:47		--none--	8760.0	N/A
Location-14	9	364 d	22:12:50		00:55:57	973.1	0.1
Location-15	14	363 d	08:18:42		38:50:05	622.8	2.8
Location-16	73	362 d	16:09:55		54:58:52	119.2	0.8
Location-17	83	362 d	10:55:58		60:12:49	104.8	0.7
Location-18	53	364 d	03:27:23		19:41:24	164.8	0.4
Location-19	17	364 d	13:59:42		09:09:05	514.7	0.5
Location-20	50	364 d	09:25:26		13:43:21	174.9	0.3

LISTING 1-1.   *Sample extract from analysis of one year of 56 Kbps frame relay use*

Figure 1-2 clearly indicate the presence of many common points of failure shared by multiple links.

IMPROVING AVAILABILITY THROUGH HIGHER RELIABILITY

Should we decide that our car was not available enough, there are two approaches we could use to improve its availability. We could improve the reliability of the car so that it failed less often (increasing its MTBF) and returned back to service quicker (decreasing its MTTR). Or we could get a second car so that when the first one failed, we could fall back on the other. In the real world, achieving maximum availability usually requires combining both approaches.

There are a number of ways we could improve the availability of our original car, and many tradeoffs are possible even in this simplistic example. For example, we could add a training regimen so that we would be prepared for common road hazards like changing a tire. This would have reduced the downtime suffered for that event to 15 minutes. We could shift our scheduled maintenance to a higher priced specialty shop that provides an oil change in 15 minutes rather than requiring a two hour block of time for their scheduling convenience.

As for our dead battery incident, we could carry jumper cables in the trunk and learn how to use them ourselves, eliminating the wait for a mechanic. A better

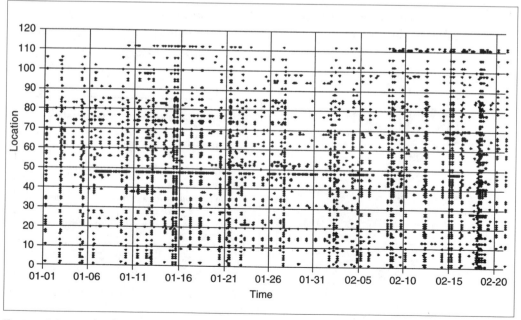

FIGURE 1-2. *Fifty days of Frame Relay failures*

approach would be to drive a car with a headlight reminder chime that we could hear so as not to leave the lights on in the first place.

We now have enough information for an *outage analysis* as defined earlier. Figure 1-3 shows that we have identified four outages (all that occurred with this system) and determined that of 12 hours of downtime suffered, all but 45 minutes were avoidable. A *component failure impact analysis* would look at other potential failures and what could be done to minimize their impact. For example, even though we did not have a failure from running out of gas, a checklist before starting to drive should include checking gauges, headlights, taillights, and turn signals and verifying that the headlights are on, the seat belt is engaged, the mirrors are adjusted, and so on.

While the report would note that we should have done a lot better this past year given our experience to date, it should note also that we were probably lucky, as there were no major repairs requiring extended time in the repair shop (which we would expect as the car got older), and the car was not involved in any accidents. Nor, for that matter, was the car towed by the police for illegal parking, but that too is an avoidable outage with proper procedures.

The bottom line is that our availability experience should have been 99.99% rather than 99.86%. Note that the improvement came primarily from reducing the MTTR, which dropped from 3 hours to only 15 minutes, as the MTBF was only improved from 2,187 hours to 2,919.75 (three outages totaling 45 minutes per year rather than four totaling 12 hours for the year).

Despite the availability improvement by fixing our procedures and training levels, the component failure impact analysis should note that we are at significant risk for a catastrophic downtime event (commonly known as a car accident), which

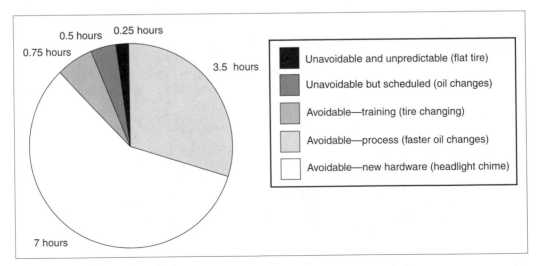

FIGURE 1-3. *Outage analysis summary*

could render the vehicle down for days or even weeks. This could be considered a classic example of the need for a disaster recovery plan.

As in the world of computers, we have several choices for dealing with the risk. We could live with the risk, we could have a hot standby spare (a second car in the garage, ready to go), or we could have a backup plan (such as a rental car agreement guaranteeing availability of a replacement vehicle within four hours). Each has its own costs, risks, and benefits. The second car, for example, is not only expensive if it is not otherwise used, but also needs to be regularly tested to ensure that it will work when needed. On the other hand, it makes routine maintenance of the primary vehicle easier because there is no downtime while the primary vehicle is being serviced. We will look more closely at these possibilities in the next section when we discuss our second approach to improving availability, adding redundancy.

Before we move on to redundancy, however, let's take a look at what conclusions we could draw from our New York City Frame Relay network example. A closer examination of the raw data shows that a relatively small number of lines were contributing to a large proportion of the detected failures. These lines included several lines that seemed to routinely fail, indicating that they were never really getting properly fixed, which in turn indicated that the root cause of the failures either had not been found or if found, was not being fixed.

With our new data in hand, we went back to the carrier to determine what was really wrong with the specific lines. For example, one of them turned out to have an improperly mounted punch-down block in the basement of the building, which was allowing vibrations to wiggle the wires, working them loose and leading to intermittent faiures. Another was traced to a bad cable in the street, which was subsequently replaced (previous repairs had just moved the problem link from one bad twisted-pair in the cable to another).

We also superimposed weather records on the data. This showed that several links appeared sensitive to flooding, as they would tend to fail following periods of heavy rain or melting snow. By presenting this data to the carrier, we were able to get the leaks in the cables repaired and eliminate more predictable failures. The analysis also confirmed our assumption that the majority of link failures were in the "last mile" of the 56-Kbps links and that defining (and paying for) redundant permanent virtual circuits was not cost effective.

IMPROVING AVAILABILITY THROUGH REDUNDANCY

Availability is a statistic that lets us predict the probability a system will be usable when required. That system, however, consists of components and connections, each of which has its own availability statistics and a specific impact on the usability of the system when it is not available. In terms of our car, some components, such as engine and brakes, are essential, and if they fail, the car is down. Others are superfluous, such as the ash tray (at least for non-smokers) and the radio. Some, such as head-lights and windshield wipers, are only needed under certain conditions and might (or might not) cause downtime. Many, such as mirrors, brake lights, and horn, while not exactly essential, do significantly increase the probability of future downtime by raising the probability of disastrous events when they are not functional.

The key to predicting the availability of systems is to know the availability of the components comprising the system and how each contributes to the functional state of the system. Consider the system in Figure 1-4 where each component, A, B, and C, must function for the system to be available. Like a series circuit in electricity, all three components must work for the system to work. Note that to simplify the calculations, we express availability as a probability relative to unity rather than as a percentage. If working with percentages, we would need to divide the availability number by 100.

Since all three components need to be functional for the system to be available, we can calculate the overall availability as the product of the individual availabilities with[6]

$$\text{Availability}_{\text{Overall}} = \text{Availability}_A \cdot \text{Availability}_B \cdot \text{Availability}_C$$

$$= 0.99 \cdot 0.97 \cdot 0.98 = 0.94 \ (94\%)$$

The overall system availability deteriorates rapidly as we add more components. Consider the network link in Figure 1-5, which consists of a router, a CSU/DSU, a point-to-point T1 link, another CSU/DSU, and finally another router. Note that while we include the cables connecting the routers to the CSU/DSUs, we ignore details of how the T1 link is provided by our carrier. One of the advantages of working with availability statistics is that once we finish a calculation, we can treat the entire combination as a "black box" and hide the details.

Calculating the availability of this link from router to router, we get an overall availability of

$$\text{Availability}_{\text{Overall}} = \text{Avail}_{\text{Router}} \cdot \text{Avail}_{\text{Cable}} \cdot \text{Avail}_{\text{CSU/DSU}} \cdot \text{Avail}_{\text{T1 Link}} \cdot \text{Avail}_{\text{CSU/DSU}} \cdot \text{Avail}_{\text{Cable}} \cdot \text{Avail}_{\text{Router}}$$

$$= 0.999 \cdot 0.9999 \cdot 0.9995 \cdot 0.98 \cdot 0.995 \cdot 0.9999 \cdot 0.999 \cdot 100\% = 97.7\%$$

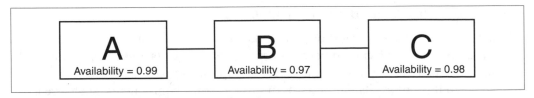

FIGURE 1-4.   *Simple serial availability*

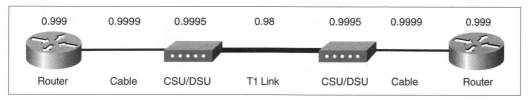

| 0.999 | 0.9999 | 0.9995 | 0.98 | 0.9995 | 0.9999 | 0.999 |
| Router | Cable | CSU/DSU | T1 Link | CSU/DSU | Cable | Router |

FIGURE 1-5. *Availability of a point-to-point T1 link*

Higher availability can be attained by adding redundancy. Going back to our simple block diagram of Figure 1-4, we add a new block D, as in Figure 1-6. This provides the same functionality as block B, but with an availability of only 0.95. Even though block D is not that reliable by itself, we need only block B or block D to be available in order for our overall system to be available. In probability terms, we are now concerned only with the probability that both block B and block D are unavailable, which is

$$\text{Availability}_{B+D} = 1 - (\text{Unavailability}_B \cdot \text{Unavailability}_D)$$

$$= 1 - ((1 - \text{Availability}_B) \cdot (1 - \text{Availability}_D))$$

$$= 1 - ((1 - 0.97) \cdot (1 - 0.95)) = 1 - (0.03 \cdot 0.05) = 1 - 0.0015 = 0.9985 \ (99.85\%)$$

Once we have the availability of the parallel blocks B and D, we can then calculate the serial availability of the system in Figure 1-7, in which the combination of blocks B and D becomes a single block B+D with the availability of the two in parallel, as shown:

$$\text{Availability}_{\text{Overall}} = \text{Availability}_A \cdot \text{Availability}_{B+D} \cdot \text{Availability}_C$$

$$= 0.99 \cdot 0.9985 \cdot 0.98 = 0.969 \ (96.9\%)$$

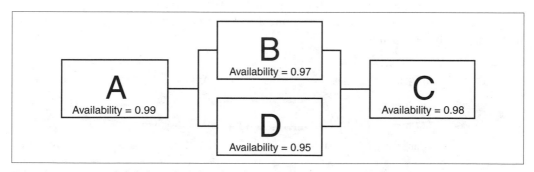

FIGURE 1-6. *Availability with redundant components*

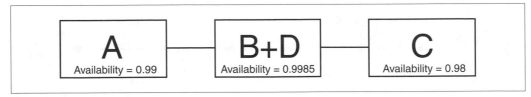

FIGURE 1-7. *Reduction of the redundant components of Figure 1-6 to a single, more reliable equivalent component*

By isolating and combining parallel and serial combinations of components and treating the availability of the resulting combined components as individual components of richer functionality, we can determine the availability of arbitrarily complex combinations of components.

Before proceeding further, we need to emphasize a critical limitation to enhancing availability by adding redundancy. The formula for parallel functionality applies *only* if the two blocks in parallel have no common failure modes. Failure to recognize this crucial limitation can lead to severe miscalculations and false expectations.

Consider again the network link example in Figure 1-5. Should we decide that an overall availability of 97.7% is not enough, simply adding another T1 link, as in Figure 1-8, is not going to have the desired impact. If we blindly apply the availability formulas, we would calculate a composite availability of 97.88% for each T1, combined availability of 99.96% for the two in parallel, and an overall router-to-router availability of 99.75%. While the mathematics are correct, the conclusion is wrong.

Our conclusion is wrong because although the picture shows parallel, independent paths, there are many failure modes common between the two paths. More than likely, the CSU/DSUs and the router at each site share common power sources. A technician working near the router could just as easily unplug both cables instead of only one cable, when grabbing anything convenient to avoid falling. And, most importantly, it is extremely likely that the two T1 links share carrier facilities en route. Unless we have gone to great effort and expense to ensure diverse routing, many of the failures that could take down one line will take down both lines. Street work, for example, that severs the cable carrying one T1 will interrupt all signals in the cable, including the other T1 line.

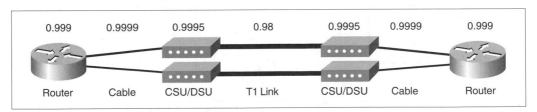

FIGURE 1-8. *Ineffective redundant serial links*

To mitigate failure risk, diversity must be maintained from end to end, starting with the local loops and including the local carrier offices, regional concentration centers for long distance communications, and common long haul links (the long distance companies tend to be each other's best customers as they buy and sell bandwidth to reduce the costs of installing underutilized bandwidth). In our example, our reliability needs might be better served by installing a 95% available private microwave between the two sites rather than the allegedly 98% available second T1. That way, we could potentially achieve a real availability of 99.69% (assuming we could control our local failure dependencies between the two paths).

NEED FOR TESTING

When a component is not in continuous use, the availability is no longer a function of MTBF and MTTR only. The problem is that the MTTR includes not only the time required to make repairs, but also the time required to determine that a repair is required. For example, if we use an uninterruptible power supply (UPS) to improve network availability and the only time we check to see if it works is when the power fails, the availability of the UPS is no longer determined by

$$\text{Availability} = \frac{\text{MTBF}}{\text{MTBF} + \text{MTTR}}$$

Since repair will not be initiated until it is too late, the MTTR used in the formula is meaningless. Rather than determining the system availability, the MTTR merely determines how long we have to wait to get running again, assuming that the power does not come back on in the meantime.

Instead of looking at component availability, we should consider the probability that the UPS might have failed at any time since the last time it was known to be good. Assuming that the probability of component failure is a constant (which is the same assumption made in all the formulas in this chapter), the probability that a component will work when we need it is given by

$$\text{Probability}_{\text{Still Functional}} = e^{-\lambda \cdot \tau}$$

where τ is the time elapsed since last known to be functional and λ is the failure rate.

MTBF, which is measured in units of time per unit failure, and λ, which is measured in units of failures per unit of time, are related by

$$\text{MTBF} = \frac{1}{\lambda}$$

This relationship between λ and MTBF allows us to calculate the probability that a component will still work after time τ by using

$$\text{Probability}_{\text{Still Functional}} = e^{-\frac{\tau}{\text{MTBF}}}$$

The relationship between λ and MTBF is used also by manufacturers to derive the MTBF figures that are occasionally found in their data sheets. After all, if a vendor waited until they had enough experience with the product to publish an MTBF based on failure experience in customer use, the product would be obsolete long before the data could be published. Vendors may instead use predictive analysis, where the MTBF is calculated based on the components making up the system.

Note that predictive metrics do not apply to software, as the probability of failure in software is neither random with time nor a constant probability. The probability of software failure is 100% whenever the sequence that triggers a failure occurs and is 0% at all other times.

In our analysis, we also have to be careful that there are not additional failure mechanisms that are activated by idleness. For example, returning to our new car example, assume that we put the spare car in the garage where we can find it when needed. Three months later, when we need it, the probability that it will start is zero because the battery will have lost its charge. This failure mechanism has nothing to do with MTBF or the probability of the car breaking. Rather it is a function of the design of the car and the assumption by the designers that it will be regularly used. Communications lines exhibit similar properties, as lines that have been down for an extended period are routinely deactivated by service providers.

The bottom line is that if a function is not continuously exercised in normal operations, it needs to be tested on a routine basis if there is to be any expectation that it will work when required. Figure 1-9 graphically demonstrates this relationship. Although initially the probability of correct functioning is 100%, it drops rapidly with time. By the time we have reached the MTBF interval, the probability the device is still functional is down to less than 37%.

Now that we are convinced that testing is not optional, the question to answer is how often we need to test. This can be determined from Table 1-2, which lists the interval between tests (in units of MTBF) required to ensure various minimum probabilities of success should the box be needed. It should be noted that these probabilities are also the probability that the test will pass. The equivalent test intervals for a typical MTBF of one year (8,270 hours) and 25,000 hours are also included to provide a sense of perspective.

The theory discussed so far applies to hardware failures; we need also to be wary of software and configuration errors getting introduced. Even with strict configuration management, large networks are constantly evolving as new sites and new

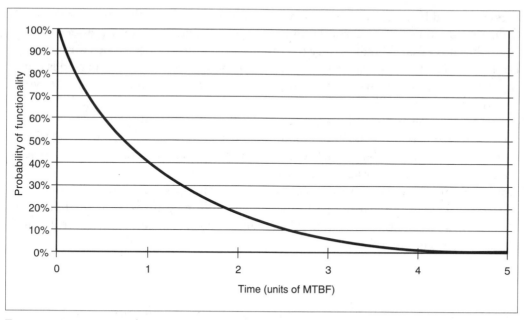

FIGURE 1-9. *Impact of not testing standby device readiness*

TABLE 1-2. *Maximum Test Intervals Required to Maintain an "Availability" Level*

NUMBER OF NINES	PROBABILITY STILL ALIVE	$\dfrac{\tau}{\text{MTBF}}$	TEST INTERVAL MTBF = 1 YEAR	TEST INTERVAL MTBF = 25,000 HR
8	0.99999999	1.00×10^{-8}	0.32 sec	0.90 sec
7	0.9999999	1.00×10^{-7}	3.16 sec	9.00 sec
6	0.999999	1.00×10^{-6}	31.56 sec	90 sec
5	0.99999	1.00×10^{-5}	5.25 min	15 min
4	0.9999	1.00×10^{-4}	52.6 min	2:30
3.5	0.9995	5.00×10^{-4}	4:23	12:30
3	0.999	1.00×10^{-3}	8:46	25:01
2.5	0.995	5.01×10^{-3}	43:56	5.22 days
2	0.99	0.0101	3.67 days	10.47 days
1.5	0.95	0.0513	18.73 days	53.43 days
1	0.9	0.105	38.48 days	109.75 days
0.5	0.5	0.693	253.17 days	1.98 yr

services are added. It is rarely practical to perform full scale testing of all probable failure modes on every link, router and switch every time a new user is added to a LAN, but it is essential that proper operation of the network design be continuously confirmed. The time to verify that the routing protocols perform as expected is during controlled tests, not when their proper operation is required to keep the network functional during a crisis.

Much of this testing will occur naturally as a side effect of daily operations in a well-managed network. The key is to not only detect routine failures, but also to go a step further and verify that the network response was as designed. It also makes sense that whenever possible, tests should be designed so that they can be performed without impacting normal operations. That way, they can be executed frequently and automatically without fear of disrupting service. This maximizes the probability that the network will continue working when failures occur. Remember, in the real world, the question is not *whether* a failure will occur, but how frequently.

FUNCTIONAL AVAILABILITY

Given the fact that most failures will affect only a subset of users or applications, it is generally more productive to look at functional availability than at overall availability. This is particularly true when the time comes to decide between alternatives based on their value to the organization. The goal of functional availability is to bridge the gap between the applications and business processes determined in the *business impact analysis* and the mathematics of reliability and availability.

Consider the business scenario in Figure 1-10, in which we have a small office with four users and two services, order entry, and e-mail. We know that some failures have far more impact on the business than others. To determine the functional availability of each service, we take the total time each "unit" of service could be available and subtract the time each unit is not available. For example, assume that during the course of the year, each unit could be in use for 2,080 hours. Further assume that user 3's workstation dies for 2 days (16 working hours), the e-mail server dies for 2 days (16 working hours), and the hub dies for 2 days (16 working hours).

From the viewpoint of the functional availability of the order entry process, if there were no failures of any components, we would have a total of four units functioning 2,080 hours each or a total of 8,320 possible hours of functional availability. The failure of user 3's workstation, however, causes the loss of one functional unit for 16 hours for a net loss of 16 hours of functional availability. The failure of the e-mail server has no impact on the order entry system. However, the failure of the hub prevents all four users from functioning, so its 16-hour failure translates into 64 hours of less functional availability. Adding the numbers, we can calculate the functional availability for the order entry process as

$$\text{Functional Availability}_{\text{Order Entry}} = \frac{4 \cdot 2{,}080 - 16 \cdot 1 - 4 \cdot 0 - 4 \cdot 16}{4 \cdot 2{,}080} = \frac{8{,}320 - 80}{8{,}320} = \frac{8{,}240}{8{,}320} = 0.990$$

or 99.0%. Similarly, for the e-mail function, we calculate the functional availability as

$$\text{Functional Availability}_{\text{E-mail}} = \frac{4 \cdot 2{,}080 - 16 \cdot 1 - 4 \cdot 1{,}624 \cdot 16}{4 \cdot 2{,}080} = \frac{8{,}320 - 144}{8{,}320} = \frac{8{,}176}{8{,}320} = 0.983$$

or 98.3%.

We can then develop a matrix like that in Table 1-3 to summarize the relative impact of any particular component device failure. In this table, we find that only one component affects all services for all users—the LAN hub. What we see also is that although the impact of changing the availability of the workstations and that of the hub is technically the same (because the unavailability of the workstations when multiplied by the number of workstations yields the same number of lost user hours as the unavailability of the hub multiplied by the number of users affected by the loss of the hub), the impact on operations is not the same. When we lose a workstation, the

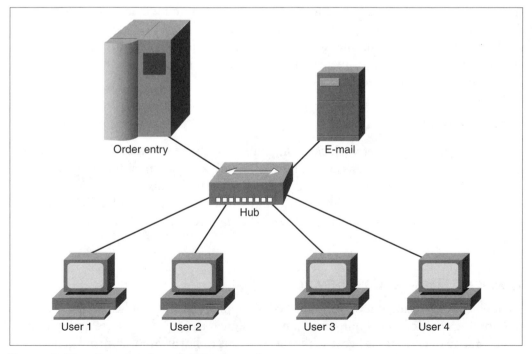

FIGURE 1-10. *Functional availability example*

TABLE 1-3. *Relative Impact of Different Device Failures*

DEVICE	NUMBER OF DEVICES	NUMBER OF USERS AFFECTED	SERVICES AFFECTED
Workstation	4	1	All
Hub	1	All	All
E-mail server	1	All	E-mail
Main server	1	All	Order entry
WS to hub link	4	1	All
E-mail server to hub link	1	All	E-mail
Main server to hub link	1	All	Order entry

office can continue to function, albeit with reduced efficiency because there is one less order taker, but when we lose the hub, nobody can work and orders (and income) are lost.

This imbalance in importance may apply even if the hub is significantly more available than the individual workstations, because the cost of a hub failure shutting down operations could be far greater than the cost of running in a degraded mode. After all, the former shuts down the revenue stream whereas the latter merely makes for lower efficiency. Again, functional availability lets us focus on the impact of component failures and specify a metric that takes into account the differing importance of various components and functions.

NETWORK VULNERABILITIES

There are many ways a network can fail, and although we will tend to focus on those unique to networking, such as communications link failures, most failure modes are identical to those in any high availability application for computers. An understanding of the various modes of failure is essential when calculating availability because only those failures that are independent of other failures can be alleviated by adding redundancy.

CLASSICAL HARDWARE CONSIDERATIONS

Reliability engineering is a well-established discipline that also applies to hardware networking components. Equipment can be designed to provide high reliability under a wide range of conditions because the mechanisms of hardware failure are generally well understood. Back in the 1950s, the Advisory Group for the Reliability of Electronic Equipment (AGREE) discovered that the failure rate of electronic components and systems follows the classical "bathtub" curve shown in Figure 1-11. The bathtub

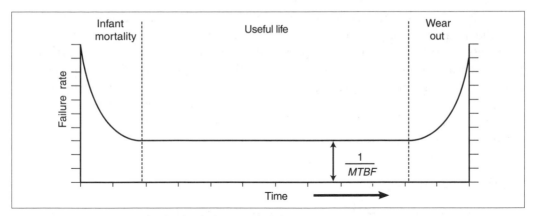

FIGURE 1-11. *Classic "bathtub" failure probability*

reliability curve has three clearly defined time periods: infant mortality, useful life, and wear out.

In the infant mortality phase, we see a (hopefully) brief initial period of a high failure rate. This rate rapidly declines. Failures occurring during the infant mortality phase are not random. Rather, they are parts that were defective in manufacture or assembly and that are failing under operational stress. High reliability manufacturers will "burn-in" their products before shipping to get through this phase in the factory rather than at the customer's site. It is called "burn-in" because the time required to weed out infant mortality failures can be shortened significantly by increasing the stress by running at elevated temperatures.

Once the defective units are weeded out, we enter the useful life period. During the useful life, failures will be random. Reliability figures cited by manufacturers usually apply to this portion of the product life cycle, where the goal is to minimize the failure frequency to lower the bottom of the bathtub as much as possible. But we must use care at this stage because the failure frequency and the duration of the useful life are independent factors and a failure frequency that corresponds to a MTBF of 200 years does not imply that the useful life of the product in service is 200 years. Rather, it means that the instantaneous probability of random failure while we are in the useful life period is the same as if we had an MTBF of 200 years. The actual useful life may be much shorter.

At the end of the useful life period, we enter the wear out mode. The steadily rising failure rate reflects the devices' components wearing out at the end of their life span. As they wear out, less stress is required to cause failure and the failures are no longer randomly distributed. Note that the useful life period is rarely a constant, as many wear out mechanisms are affected by the stresses applied during the useful life. Generally, a device constantly running at the high end of its rated temperature range will reach the wear out stage much sooner than the same device running at lower temperatures.

When applied to situations requiring high availability, we clearly want to be past the infant mortality stage before installing any hardware in the field. If necessary, we can leave the unit running in the test lab to weed out early failures rather than just making sure it still works after being shipped and immediately boxing it back up for deployment. However, we also need to be aware of the other end of the lifecycle. When the time comes, we will need to proactively replace units in the field with new, burned-in units before our functional availability is degraded by the increasing failure rate of the worn out components.

Software Considerations

Failures caused by software defects, on the other hand, follow a very different pattern. Any defects are in the software from the beginning and are present in all devices running that code, just waiting to be triggered. As a result, software defects tend to appear in bursts as the operating conditions change and the defect is exposed. The nature of software defects makes it essential to determine the cause of any anomalous behavior observed during normal operation that could be an indicator of faulty software or configuration.

Note that with software defects, we cannot distinguish between defects in the software provided by the manufacturer and errors in the configuration we have applied to the device. High availability requires strict configuration management of all hardware and software so that all changes are tested and verified before being put into production. Shotgun changes in an attempt to get the network back online after a collapse may bring immediate relief, but they also open up the network to future problems if the changes are not analyzed and the root causes of the initial failure determined.

The nature of software errors puts us at risk of catastrophic failure when exposure of a specific defect takes down all systems running a particular software release or depending upon a specific capability. This can put us in a quandary of deciding between the ease of maintenance and support of a single vendor's platform running the same software release everywhere and the diversity of using multiple vendors and multiple software releases within vendors.

Using multiple vendors is not a guarantee of fewer problems because we have to contend with incompatibilities between vendors and between different releases from the same vendor. In addition, the difficulty of testing and qualifying new software releases increases exponentially with the number of features used and other versions that we must test against. Consequently, we may find that despite the potential of catastrophic defect exposure, availability is improved by standardizing on just a few platforms running a single software release that is limited enough to be within our ability to adequately test. This is particularly the case if the alternative is settling for a cursory testing of a wide range of platforms and multiple software releases that leads to frequent, preventable failures in the field.

SITE INFRASTRUCTURE

Site infrastructure includes such support services as the electrical power required to run the equipment, any air conditioning or ventilation required to prevent overheating, and physical security to protect the equipment from tampering, disconnection, or theft.

Electrical power is required to keep the equipment running. Power problems typically arise in one of three different ways: surges and noise that interfere with proper equipment operation, brief sags and interruptions that cause systems to reboot, and extended losses of all power. Surges and electrical noise on the power lines can cause operating errors, shorten the life of equipment, and in extreme cases, even destroy the electronics. While this level of power problem can be handled with quality surge protection, it is usually more cost effective to extend the protection to include sags and brief outages by using UPS.

The challenge in designing UPS protection lies in determining how many UPSs should be used and how long they must provide power. Putting all devices on one large UPS reduces costs and is more efficient, but it also means that a power protection failure will shut down the entire site. For locations that support critical operations or that may be commonly subjected to extended power outages, additional power backup in the form of emergency generators may be required. The battery-based UPSs are then used to cover the gap between power failure detection and bring the emergency generators online. In this case, we also need to consider continuation of air conditioning and other longer term infrastructure requirements.

High availability infrastructure requirements go beyond obvious needs to include protection from accidents (such as by securing all cables so that they cannot be accidentally disconnected), avoidance of premature failure due to airborne contamination (particularly metal particles from mechanical work), and prevention of mistakes due to inaccurate documentation (such as shutting off power to critical devices because the breakers are not correctly labeled).

Realistically, a network node cannot be any more reliable than the infrastructure it depends on. For example, investing in components with redundant power supplies does little good if both are fed from the same power source and the related breaker is turned off to service another piece of equipment. These are considerations that are well known for large computer data centers, but frequently neglected at satellite locations where the "data center" consists of a few pieces of networking gear locked in a closet.

Data collected by The Uptime Institute[7] reveals that more than half of all site infrastructure failures are directly related to human activity. More important, their data indicate that 80% of those human-caused failures could have been prevented if proper procedures had been followed. This does not mean that you must lock up the equipment and throw away the key; their data showed that good maintenance programs pay for themselves with an average of four outages prevented for each outage caused. Rather, it means that defining and enforcing appropriate procedures to correctly and safely perform work around active networking equipment must be part of the network design.

Appropriate procedures cover such requirements as personal accountability, who is allowed access to equipment spaces, and who is authorized to approve work. It also includes who needs to be notified of the work (both in the planning stages and during execution), who to contact if anything goes wrong, work rules for inside the computer room and other equipment areas, proper documentation of the work to be done (including tracking of its progress to ensure that no steps are skipped), and proper documentation of the work so that it reflects "as built." Last, it includes the requirement that at least two fully qualified people work together to perform any tasks that could impact uptime—one to do the work and one to check that the correct work is being done and being done correctly.

No matter what, you must remember that bad things will happen. If all network equipment is in the same rack, a single accident could take down the entire network at the site. If all equipment is in the same room, an isolated event such as a small fire or loss of air conditioning could still take down the entire site. Obviously, when designing for maximum reliability, physical diversity of all components is essential. While the probability of failure due to accidents and such is typically small, the repair time can be quite lengthy, virtually guaranteeing that when something happens, even moderate availability goals will not be met. By splitting the site network infrastructure among multiple, physically separate equipment rooms, the size of the "event" required to take down the entire site network becomes much larger, not only reducing the probability of occurrence even further, but also ensuring that when a large enough event does occur (and note that the conditional is *when*, not *if*), so few users will be left functional that the loss of network access will not be significant.

COMMUNICATIONS LINKS

Communications links have traditionally been the weak link of networking. Signal cables, even though they are totally passive, are a frequent cause of failure. In the world of local area networks, it is not unusual for 90% of the LAN failures to be traced to connector failure. This is not surprising because the connectors absorb the majority of the stress every time users rearrange their offices or a personal computer or laptop is relocated or reconnected. Indeed, one of the initial reasons for the popularity of 10BaseT networking was the functional availability improvement resulting from the limitation of the impact of a failed user connection to only the user with the bad connector, rather than the entire network segment.

Backbone network cables are normally not subject to the abuse that end-user cabling must withstand, but they still fail. Construction workers seem to have an uncanny ability to select the most critical cables to cut while they are working. Keeping the failure modes independent means that backup cables must be "physically diverse" from the cables that they are backing up. This is not always easy. For example, there may not be a second set of cable risers available in a high rise building. Again, the key is to balance the protection improvement with the cost of providing the additional protection.

WAN links are different from other network components. First and foremost, they are owned and maintained by the carrier and offered to us as a black box capability. This makes it very difficult to determine aspects such as diversity of routing because even a carefully planned diverse route could be eliminated at any time by a maintenance action to get around problems associated with that route or to take advantage of the availability of new, lower cost (to the service provider) routes. Without the visibility into the internal workings of the carrier's network, we would not even be aware of these changes until such time as that route fails, taking both of our supposedly diverse links down with it.

Another characteristic of WAN links is that they have two very distinct failure modes. While a cable cut or hardware failure can instantly stop all communications, copper-based WAN communications links frequently die gradually, providing plenty of warning of impending total failure. In traditional voice communications, this deterioration may come in the form of gradually increasing noise or static on the line. In digital communications, it comes in the form of a gradually increasing bit error rate, leading to increasingly frequent and increasingly longer line outages.

Normally, monitoring the long term quality of a line will yield a pattern like that in Figure 1-12, where the line gradually deteriorates until service is called, at which point, the line is tested and restored, and the cycle repeats itself. The two keys to line quality maintenance are the dotted horizontal lines in the graph. When service is required, the carrier will repair the link until it meets the higher quality standard, which is the minimum quality level acceptable for a completed repair. The lower dotted line represents the minimum quality level acceptable in a line in service, and repairs will only be made if the quality is less than this lower level.

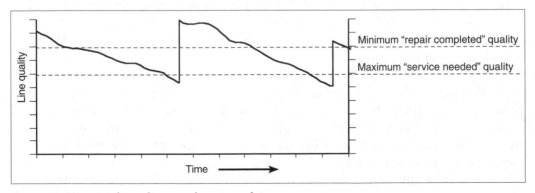

FIGURE 1-12. *Link quality as a function of time*

What does not show in the graph (but can be critical) is that on many links, the customer must call and request service before repair action is initiated. Routine carrier monitoring of link quality is usually only automatic on high-speed links. This means that it is up to us to detect that the line has deteriorated to the point where service is required. The good news is that if we are routinely monitoring line performance, there is no reason we should not be able to get the line repaired before it begins to significantly impact network performance. This can have a particularly significant impact on the availability of low speed lines such as analog, ISDN, and 56/64 Kbps services.

SECURITY

While normally not considered a part of network availability, adequate network security is essential to avoid downtime due to denial of service attacks, the need to recover from corrupted data, or the cleansing of systems that are victims of viruses or hacked software. This can be hard for networkers who concentrate on getting the network to provide adequate connectivity. Security, as a result, has frequently been shunted aside as too difficult, counterproductive, or merely an application concern.

While this attitude toward security might have been forgivable in the past when successful networking was a novelty, now that network availability directly impacts the organization's profitability and possibly even its very existence, security can no longer be ignored. Having said that, please note that this book is about network design for high availability and not about network security. Thus, we will not discuss security other than to point out that if security is neglected, high availability will not be possible.

Note that concern about security is not limited to networks attached to the Internet. Indeed, most companies make the mistake of only providing protection against external attacks, leaving their applications vulnerable to insider attacks that can result in even greater financial loss. As has been proven time and again, security must be designed into the network, the operating systems, the applications, and the processes themselves to be cost effective. While the network cannot protect the entire organization, failure to include protection as part of the network design leaves the organization unnecessarily exposed.

Firewalls are an example of planned protection and can be used between functional units to simplify enforcement of application security requirements that might be necessary to protect the privacy of personnel information in the payroll department or trade secrets in the R&D laboratory. Like watertight compartments on a warship, they can prevent a single breech from sinking the entire ship and limit the damage to a well-specified area.

Another example is the use of priority queuing to provide traffic isolation. This not only isolates various traffic classes from each other, but also can reduce the impact of denial of service attacks and routing loops on core network services. This can be particularly effective for protecting services, such as routing and network management, that are essential for maintaining network stability.

DESIGNING FOR HIGHER NETWORK AVAILABILITY

Network availability can be improved at many levels, and one of the challenges is maintaining a balanced approach so that the most cost effective improvements are made first. The task can be likened to a hunt for single points of failure with the goal of eliminating those with the largest impact at the lowest possible cost.

From the network design viewpoint, the challenge in eliminating single points of failure is to provide redundancy that will not only still be functional when needed, but also will be automatically put into service to carry the load. That is, the networking protocols must be capable of detecting the failed component and reconfiguring and rerouting traffic through the remaining components. This can get tricky because one of the challenges facing all network protocols is the need to tolerate minor failures yet still detect when the minor failures have become major failures.

In the next chapter, we will discuss some of the available networking protocols, how they work, and how to tune them to better support high availability networking. Before we get to the protocols, however, we will spend just a little more time talking about the links that connect the nodes of the network and some of the challenges the links present.

WAN COMMUNICATIONS DIVERSITY

WAN communications links are the bane of networking, and providing redundancy free of common failure modes requires much effort. The challenge with WAN links is not the distance they cover, but the fact that their provisioning and service are generally not under our control. Instead, we must depend on the telephone company or other service providers to keep them working. Even when competitive service providers are used, we are frequently still dependent on the local telephone company for providing "the last mile," which is the copper or fiber link connecting our building to the nearest telephone central office.

Traditionally, providing physical diversity for a site's network access has required contracting with the local telephone company to provide service from the distribution system of a second central office. This is not the typical foreign exchange service, which is provisioned by using another local loop to the same local central office that is then tied to a central office trunk connecting to the foreign central office. Foreign exchange service provided this way results in even less reliability than two links to the same local central office!

True physical diversity requires that the telephone company extend the service area of the second central office to include our location. This is usually a very expensive proposition (as we may be the only user of the extended cable plant), particularly if services must be installed underground and digging is required. Careful attention must be paid to the physical provisioning to ensure that physical diversity is maintained at all points. For example, it does little good to pay for physical diversity from the phone company and then run both lines in the same conduit once they are inside the building. A second service entrance must be provided to maintain the physical diversity from end to end.

Equally important, it is not sufficient to merely ensure that adequate physical diversity is part of the *initial* provisioning. It is easy for diversity to be lost as services are rerouted during emergency repairs or routine maintenance to improve service efficiency. Detecting this loss of physical diversity can be very difficult. If we are lucky, we will have outstanding communications with the carrier's operations personnel and be kept in the loop on all repair and maintenance actions affecting our lines. However, this is not only rare, it still provides no guarantees, because changes may be made that affect routing of a communications link and those changes might not be recognized as such by the field personnel or others in the chain of information flow. However, we can monitor our links and look for trends. For instance, loss of diversity can sometimes be identified by looking for common timing patterns in minor disturbances (the classic "things that go bump in the night" errors and the noise bursts that randomly occur on all lines).

There are now also alternatives available, at least in some locations, that allow for network service delivery independent of the local telephone infrastructure. In many areas of the United States, cable television service providers are getting into the networking business. While the service was originally designed around the needs of Web surfing consumers, cable service providers in some areas are recognizing that their cable bandwidth can also be sold to business customers in need of more reliable bandwidth.

A Metropolitan Area Networks (MAN) service, usually based on redundant fiber loops and protection switching, can also be effective. In some very high demand areas, such as New York City, alternate service providers have pulled their own communications cables under the streets to provide alternate local loops. Of course, we must watch the physical paths utilized to ensure that the redundant paths really are physically diverse and not all routed down the same street, allowing one backhoe to sever them all.

Wireless networking provides another potential path for linking to alternate service providers. Services available in some areas are capable of bypassing the telephone company's local loop and supporting data rates up to several Mbps to fixed sites. Microwave or infrared point-to-point links are available at speeds up to

45 Mbps. However, these are usually limited to line-of-sight distances and typically require us to have "roof rights" on our building to place the antennas. Microwave normally also requires a license allocating the RF spectrum used, which may not be available in locations in which competing users have beaten us to the available allocations.

Satellite links are also regaining popularity, as users discover that although satellite communications have their own set of problems (such as rain fade, sight angles, and antenna size for high bandwidth), these problems are generally independent of those that affect terrestrial links, making them an excellent choice for alternate links in which diversity of failure modes is critical to providing high availability. However, care must be taken when using satellite links because of the speed of light link delays (250 ms, one way). This frequently requires adjusting link level parameters to prevent timeouts and may be incompatible with applications that cannot handle the half-second round trip response time.

In addition to consideration of the physical link used, the network service used to provide end-to-end connectivity also will impact reliability. Although it is easier to provision a network with one service type, whether Frame Relay, ATM, or other, there are benefits to using multiple services. Once inside the WAN cloud, links and switches are usually dedicated so that a failure affecting Frame Relay service may not affect ISDN service or ATM. Again, it is essential to get "under the covers" of the service provider to determine if we are really getting useful diversity for the effort we must exert to utilize alternative services. More and more service providers are putting all their data services, such as X.25, Frame Relay, and ATM, over a common ATM backbone to reduce costs and improve performance. The trend is to expand the range of services running on that common core to include voice as well as data services.

Consequently, it may be necessary to forego some quantity discounting and spread our traffic across multiple service providers. But even then we are not guaranteed diversity. There is extensive cross selling of services between the major service providers to reduce the costs of servicing less populous areas, so although we may be contracting with Sprint and AT&T for diverse service to a site, both may actually be sharing bandwidth on the same MCI/WorldCom fiber link. This problem is not limited to rural areas in the middle of nowhere. Older practitioners will remember the Illinois Bell Hinsdale central office fire on Sunday, May 8, 1988. This single event shut down virtually all communications services provided to 35,000 homes and 13,000 businesses in the western Chicago suburbs. In addition to the affected local phone lines, the site was the primary switching center for long distance access to the area, so even those facilities that still had local phone service were cut off from the rest of the world.[8] Again, remember that getting the details required to determine if we actually have the diversity we need can be daunting and subject to change as new deals are negotiated between carriers and internal routes change.

INTERNAL DIVERSITY

If diversity is not maintained once inside the facility, the external link diversity will be wasted. For example, if all the links enter the building through the same service entrance or share a common conduit to the computer room, or if all network hardware is mounted in the same rack, we still have critical single points of failure. The only difference is that the common failure mode is now in our domain, but that makes no difference to network users, who only care that the network is down.

In many organizations, implementing internal diversity is as much a political challenge as it is a technical one. When the responsibility for dealing with failure crosses organizational boundaries, there is a real temptation to optimize the design of our portion of the network to minimize the downtime chargeable to our unit rather than to optimize the overall design for maximum functional availability.

Consider the dual router configuration for the small site in Figure 1-13. This is a typical configuration in which the need for redundancy has been driven by WAN unreliability. The problem is that even though the WAN connectivity is fully redundant, the LAN still has multiple single points of failure. Even though hubs are simple devices that rarely fail, the fact remains that they do fail—and without redundancy the users are isolated until repairs can be made. Unless the routers used are

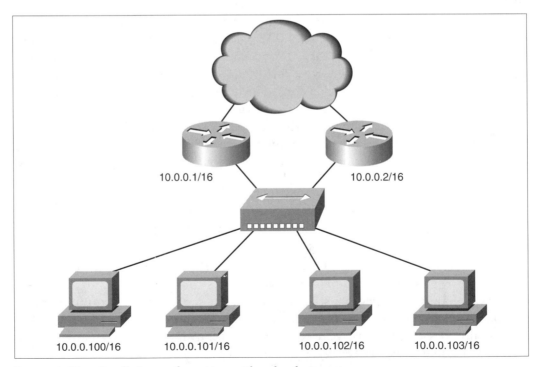

FIGURE 1-13. *Small site configuration with redundant routers*

10.0.0.1/16   10.0.0.2/16

10.0.0.100/16   10.0.0.101/16   10.0.0.102/16   10.0.0.103/16 significantly less reliable than the hub, there is relatively little gain in availability with end-user systems as compared to a single router solution with the same connectivity.

We can eliminate most of the single points of failure by splitting the one large LAN into multiple smaller LANs, as in Figure 1-14. That way, the loss of a hub would only affect the users connected to that hub. For example, if the left hub died, only the users on the 10.1.0.0 subnetwork would be affected. Depending on the applications, production might be maintainable by simply moving users to a system connected to the still functional 10.2.0.0 subnetwork. The user in the center illustrates how it is possible to connect a critical user or server to both subnetworks. We will discuss techniques for accomplishing this in Chapter 3, Multihomed Hosts.

Note that this more robust configuration has only a minor impact on the cost of the LAN, as only a few more hub ports are required to support the redundant router connections and multihomed hosts. On the other hand, it does have a significant impact on the cost of the WAN, as the routers must be faster and more expensive to support the additional LAN connections, particularly if there is substantial LAN-to-LAN traffic. Network design and maintenance is also more complex, as the single site now consumes addresses from three independent subnetworks rather than one, and routing tables on routers throughout the network are increased from the single entry for the site to two plus the number of multihomed hosts. More

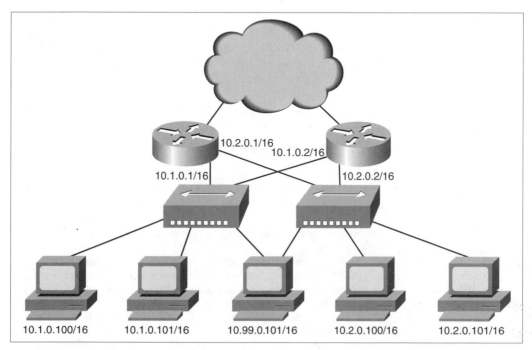

FIGURE 1-14. *Robust site configuration with redundant routers*

important, the introduction of a second router introduces new failure modes and the required protection adds significant complexity to the network design. All these factors tend to increase the cost of the WAN, while the LAN administrator gets all the credit for the reduction in downtime risk.

WRAP-UP

Everyone wants higher network availability, but providing it cost effectively can require significant effort because the cost and effort increase dramatically for each "nine" added to the target level of availability. The first step is to determine what availability is currently being provided and the cost to the organization of the failures that have already occurred or that can be predicted.

Using the mathematics of reliability and availability, we can then identify weak areas in the network design and the impact of improving the reliability and adding appropriate redundancy to the current network structure. Based on the needs of the organization, we can then select which improvements to make based on their cost and the payback to the organization in terms of avoided downtime costs.

Networks share many of the availability and reliability concerns of other computing resources, and the techniques used to improve data center availability are directly applicable. However, networks also introduce availability considerations that are unique to networking, such as dependence on communications links that may not be under our control, as well as others, such as political turf issues, that are exacerbated by the nature of networking. Our job is to identify the vulnerabilities and the requirements that apply to our environment and effectively maximize the useful availability of the network.

NOTES

1. *Network World Magazine*, 14 April 1998, in a story about an AT&T frame relay outage, reprinted with permission.
2. *Network Magazine*, August 1998, reprinted with permission.
3. Hewlett-Packard. "Intel-Based Multi-Server System High Availability." June 1999.
4. IBM. *Continuous Availability Systems Design Guide*. Redbook SG24-2085-00. December 1998.
5. William H. Murray, as quoted by Andy Briney. Information Security. October 1999. Page 55, reprinted with permission.
6. Mathematicians may note that we ignore the probability of two or more components failing at the same time. The difference only becomes significant when dealing with multiple components whose individual availability is less than 80% or so, and ignoring the difference allows us to easily scale the calculations to arbitrarily complex systems of components. In engineering, we call this a safe approximation because the error is on the conservative side. In this example, we calculated the availability as 0.94109 whereas strictly correct probability theory, which subtracts out the probabilities of any two failing at the same time and then correcting for all three failing at the same time, would give the answer

as 0.94209, a difference of only 0.001 or about 0.1% in this example. More important, the higher the availability of the individual components, the smaller the error in both absolute and relative terms.

7. Computersite Engineering and The Uptime Institute. "Site Uptime Procedures and Guidelines for Safely Performing Work in an Active Data Center." December 1999. (www.uptime.com)

8. *Los Angeles Times.* May 14, 1988. Home Edition. Part 1, Page 1. *New York Times.* May 26, 1988. Late City Final Edition. Section A, Page 1.

Bridging and Routing

Although we want to make our individual components as reliable as possible, the only way to improve the availability of functions provided by inherently unreliable components is to make them redundant. Availability improves only to the extent that the modes of failure of the parallel components are independent and unrelated. In this chapter, we assume that we have adequate failure independence in our individual components and will look at the protocols required to allow network communications to continue despite component failures.

There are a wide range of choices available for networking protocols, and within each network architecture, there are typically more choices to be made in terms of bridging and routing protocol selections. We will start with the OSI reference model definitions of connectivity and see how the various protocols interact to allow communications. We will then look at the specifics of the bridging and routing protocols most commonly used in TCP/IP networks. The emphasis in each will be on what they are designed to accomplish, critical assumptions in their design, how they can influence network availability, and how we can tune their parameters to minimize the downtime associated with failure recovery.

BASIC CONNECTIVITY DEFINITIONS

The International Organization for Standardization's Open Systems Interconnection reference model (commonly called the ISO OSI model) defines the basic terminology used in any modern discussion of networking protocols and connectivity. Ask most networkers about the OSI reference model and they respond with the seven layer stack in Figure 2-1, which is the protocol stack the OSI reference model defines for a normal end system. However, this seven layer protocol stack is actually only a small part of the overall conceptual model defined in ISO 7498, the international standard that defines the OSI reference model.

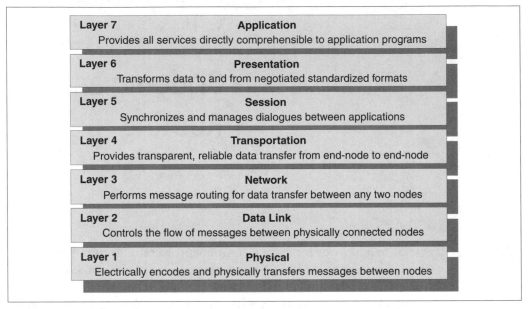

FIGURE 2-1. *OSI reference model protocol stack*

CONNECTIVITY IN THE OSI REFERENCE MODEL

While originally intended to define a framework for development of protocol standards (the OSI protocol suite), the OSI reference model provides a vendor- and protocol-independent set of definitions that can be used to discuss any network architecture from IBM Systems Network Architecture (SNA) to the Internet Architecture Standard (IAS) that is more commonly referred to as TCP/IP.

In real-world networks, you are rarely blessed with a physical link between every pair of end systems that you desire to communicate. Instead, the actual communications must pass through one or more intermediaries, as shown in Figure 2-2. These inbetween devices have different names depending on which layer of the OSI reference model they use to provide their connectivity.

The OSI reference model defines four classes of intermediary devices: *repeater, bridge, intermediate system,* and *protocol conversion gateway.* Routers are a class of intermediate systems that happen to provide routing as well as relaying functionality.

Repeaters provide connectivity by regenerating the electrical signals at the Physical layer, as in Figure 2-3. Other than restoring signal strength and timing, they provide no further function. The repeater function is rarely visible as a distinct, separate component except in Ethernet and similar Carrier Sense Multiple Access with Collision Detection (CSMA/CD) networks. Even in Ethernet class networks, they are not always called repeaters when labeling the boxes. For example, in 10BaseT Ethernet, they are called concentrators or may be a function provided by a hub.

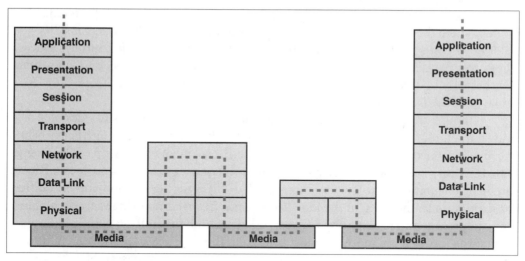

FIGURE 2-2. *The "real" OSI reference model*

Repeaters operate at the bit level and have no knowledge of or impact on framing (how the bits are organized) or addressing (where they are going). Although the media might be different on either side, the data rate and the order and meaning of bits must be identical on both sides of a repeater. In particular, a repeater cannot be used to connect 10-Mbps Ethernet to 100-Mbps Ethernet, nor can it be used to connect any kind of Ethernet to any kind of Token Ring.

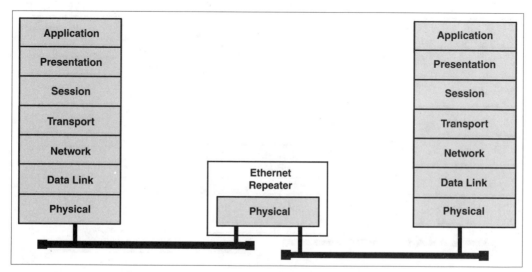

FIGURE 2-3. *OSI reference model repeater architecture*

Bridges provide their connectivity at the data link layer of the OSI reference model, where they can take advantage of the addressing information in *Link Protocol Data Units* (LPDUs, or frames) to provide filtering and simple routing services. They are a popular means of extending the physical limits of LAN technologies such as Ethernet and Token Ring, and they operate at the *Medium Access Control* (MAC) sublayer of the Data Link layer, as illustrated in Figure 2-4.

Although the physical media and signaling can differ on opposite sides of a bridge, the Link layers must match. For example, although bridges can efficiently and effectively connect 10BaseT and 100BaseT Ethernet segments or 4-Mbps Token Rings with 16-Mbps Token Rings, using bridges to interconnect Ethernet and Token Rings can be problematic due to the variations, such as bit ordering within bytes and different maximum frame sizes, in the Link layer usage. Translating bridges are available that can provide interoperability between Ethernet and Token Ring LANs, but those that do the job well are more than just bridges in the OSI reference model definition because of the additional functions, such as segmentation and reassembly, that are provided.

The OSI reference model defines intermediate systems as the boxes that provide connectivity at the network layer as shown in Figure 2-5. The OSI reference model also defines the term *router* to describe those intermediate systems that also perform a routing function (choosing from among multiple available paths) in addition to relaying (forwarding). Note how the Network layer is split into sublayers to allow the use of different network technologies for the underlying connectivity. Note also that just as there could be repeaters between an end system and a bridge, there can be

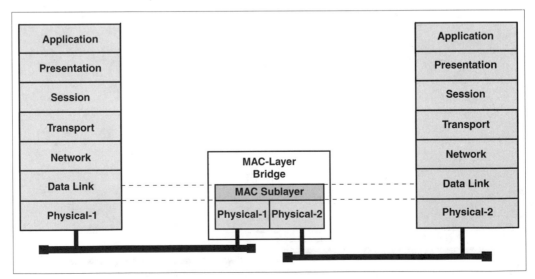

FIGURE 2-4. *OSI reference model bridge architecture*

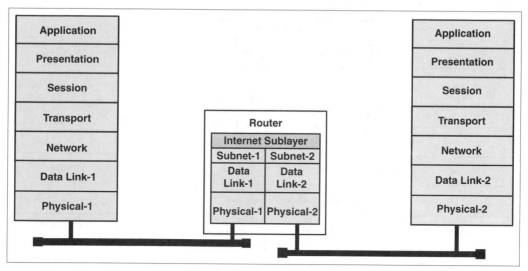

FIGURE 2-5.   *OSI reference model intermediate system architecture*

repeaters and bridges between end systems and intermediate systems as well as more than one intermediate system between two end systems.

In TCP/IP lexicon, the intermediate systems were originally called gateways, and the terminology continues to linger. If it is essential to use the old terminology, the only way to avoid confusion is to always insist on qualifying the term *gateway* with a modifier. So if you are referring to a legacy TCP/IP router, it would be called an *Internet gateway* to distinguish it from a *protocol conversion gateway,* which we discuss next.

If the protocols do not match by the time the top of the Network layer is reached, the OSI reference model mandates a seven-layer protocol conversion gateway, as in Figure 2-6, because the OSI reference model defines only end-system-to-end system functionality above the Network layer. With a protocol conversion gateway between them, the networks on either side are totally independent because the end systems on either network can see only as far as the protocol conversion gateway. Although the use of protocol conversion gateways can theoretically allow us to connect any system to any other system, from a practical viewpoint, the results are rarely satisfactory for services that are performance-sensitive or that require more than rudimentary capabilities.

Because of our concern with improving network availability, we will concentrate on bridges and routers. Repeaters, due to their function, provide no opportunity for standard box-level redundancy. Protocol conversion gateways require applications to support any redundant capabilities, which is again outside the scope of the network design.

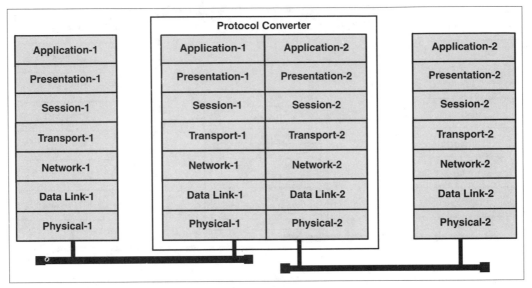

FIGURE 2-6. *OSI reference model protocol conversion gateway architecture*

A bridge with more than two interfaces is frequently called a switch. Be very careful of the term *switch,* as it is a marketing term with no value as a specification. It is usually best to ignore what the box is called and determine its function and capabilities from its specifications. As a general rule, a layer-2 switch is a bridge. However, it might be a store-and-forward bridge, which can introduce significant delays as each frame must be received before it is processed and sent on its way, or it might be a cut-through bridge, which pauses only long enough to ensure that a collision is not likely (at least 40 µseconds for 10-Mbps 802.3 or Ethernet) before processing the frame and forwarding it on as required.

Cut-through switching is essential for minimizing store-and-forward delays, but it is practical only between interfaces running at the same speed. If the inbound interface is faster than the outbound interface, the performance gain is minimal as the delay will be dominated by the serialization time for the outbound frame. If the inbound interface is slower, transmission must be delayed until the entire frame is received to ensure that the output does not run out of frame to send before the frame finishes arriving.

Because the term *switch* has come to be associated with higher performance, it has become a popular marketing term, and we now see layer-2, layer-3 and layer-4 switches being advertised. A layer-2 switch is usually a multiport bridge. A layer-3 switch is usually a wire speed router, with only LAN interfaces and a minimal set of capabilities. A layer-4 switch is a layer-3 switch that uses information from layer 4 (such as ports or application protocol identification) to drive forwarding decisions.

Along the same lines, the term *hub* describes the location of a box rather than how it enables connectivity. Although not technically correct, we will use the term *hub* in this book when referring to the physical device used to connect the network interfaces on multiple systems to form a LAN. However, we will use the term *hub* only when from the viewpoint of the network design under discussion, it does not matter what speed the network is running at, what MAC protocol is being used, or whether the device is an 802.3 concentrator, an 802.5 multistation access unit, or a layer-2 switch.

We need to always be wary of the influence of marketing on terminology. The boxes providing bridging or routing functionality may be called almost anything, and it is essential to identify how the connectivity is actually being provided regardless of the label on the box. As we have already seen, the term switch can legitimately be used to refer to connectivity at any layer of the OSI reference model. We will also find that a gateway could be a router, but it could also be a protocol conversion gateway. One vendor called their bridges "protocol independent routers" while others have called their protocol conversion gateway offerings "bridges."

The key at all layers and with all modes of connectivity is the ability of the protocols involved to detect failures and to provide communications despite failures. We will come back to these issues in a bit, but first a discussion on connectivity and topology.

NETWORK TOPOLOGIES

A critical adjunct to the protocol architecture of the network is the physical topology, or the pattern used to connect the various pieces. We call the various pieces of equipment networked together the nodes, and we call the communications lines connecting them the links. How the nodes are connected by the links determines the topology, while the topology determines which nodes must make forwarding decisions to select from multiple paths (decision nodes) and which have no choice of path (simple nodes). The various combinations possible are illustrated in Figure 2-7. Each topology has its advantages and disadvantages. Except for the bus topology, all may be found in routed, bridged, and cell-switched infrastructures.

The hierarchical tree, Figure 2-7(a), is the classic layout for connecting terminals to central host systems. Forwarding decisions are simplified by the regular nature of the topology, and top-down, host-to-terminal relationships are easily implemented. Where costs are an issue, optimization of node and link provisions for full connectivity is easily calculated. However, this simplicity breaks down if redundant connectivity is required.

The mesh, Figure 2-7(b), is the standard topology for WANs when high availability is more important than low cost because it enables redundant links with a minimum of unnecessary redundancy. This is the only topology in which the forwarding

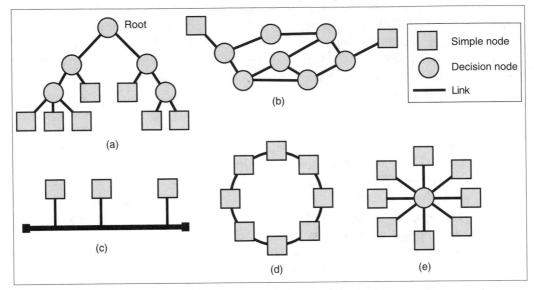

FIGURE 2-7. *Network topologies: (a) hierarchical tree, (b) mesh, (c) bus, (d) ring, and (e) star*

decisions are non-trivial. It is the topology most often used to implement WAN services from X.25 packet-switched networks to the most advanced asynchronous transfer mode (ATM) networks. Because the actual internal connections will vary with implementation and user needs, the whole mesh is often replaced in diagrams with a general networking cloud. This reinforces the transparency of the network internals and focuses the designer on the services provided rather than on the details of how it is provided.

The bus structure, Figure 2-7(c), is the most common topology for LANs. Since each system is directly linked to all other systems, there is no need for routing. This simplifies network implementation. Because all transmissions are received by all systems, broadcast and multicast capabilities are easily and efficiently provided. At the same time, because adding users does not add to the bandwidth available, expansion capability is finite as each user added competes for the fixed capacity of the medium. This limitation has been addressed in modern LANs by using bridges in the form of layer-2 switches and by raising the data rate of the LAN (where once 10 Mbps was considered a high-speed LAN, today we see gigabit LANs handling the traffic).

The ring structure, Figure 2-7(d), is also popular for LANs, although that popularity is waning due to the cost premium associated with IBM Token Ring (IEEE 802.5) and Fiber Distributed Data Interface (FDDI) installations. The performance benefits theoretically possible from ring networks have never been relevant to the average user. Meanwhile, Ethernet speed increases and low-cost layer-2 switches have made those technical advantages much less significant even in most of those applications in which they used to be relevant.

The star topology in Figure 2-7(e), also known as a hub and spoke, uses a central switching node to connect an end node to any other end node. Putting all the intelligence required to route from node to node in the central node allows for efficient implementation, but it comes at the price of irreparable loss of the network any time the central switch is unavailable. This topology is most common in Private Branch Exchange (PBX) networks and public telephone service provisioning.

When looking at real networks, there are two other critical topological factors to keep in mind. First of all, we need to distinguish between the physical topology and the logical topology. The physical topology reflects how the wires are run in the building, and in a modern LAN installation based on twisted pair wiring, the topology is invariably a star. However, on that star, the electrical signals may interact as a bus in the case of Ethernet or as a ring in the case of Token Ring. From the viewpoint of the protocols, the fact that the physical topology is a star is irrelevant; what matters is the logical topology, which dictates how the devices communicate. Similarly, a physical mesh topology of transparent Spanning-Tree bridges will be logically pruned to a hierarchical tree to eliminate forwarding loops. On the other hand, from the viewpoint of availability, the physical topology is very relevant because it has a direct impact on the vulnerability of the network to physical damage and on the location of single points of failure.

Today's networks are almost never a pure topology. Instead they blend the different topologies to gain the benefits each has to offer at different levels. For example, the ubiquitous 10BaseT Ethernet LAN, which is physically a star and logically a bus, will also be a single node from the viewpoint of the topology of the bridges and switches that connect the individual LAN segments in the facility. That topology might be a star (if using a collapsed backbone architecture), a hierarchical tree (if using simple learning bridges), or a mesh (if using redundantly connected source routing or transparent Spanning-Tree bridges). While these distinctions may seem pedantic, they can be critical when optimizing the functional availability of the network.

MULTIPLE CONNECTIONS VERSUS SINGLE CONNECTIONS

We worry about the network topology because it directly impacts the degree of connectivity in the network, both in terms of the direct reliability of the communications media and the availability of redundant capabilities. In a simple bus or ring topology, a single cable failure will take down all systems on the LAN segment. In a star topology, on the other hand, that single cable failure will affect only the one end system at the end of the cable.

To get around this failure sensitivity, most LANs today are physically wired in a star configuration, with each link a home run back to the local wiring closet from the end system location being serviced. Equipment in the wiring closet will then connect the individual links into the desired logical topology. By including in that equipment the ability to detect link failure, failed links can be automatically isolated from the rest of the LAN and their functional availability impact limited to a single end system.

This detection capability can be as simple as the electromechanical relays in an IBM Token Ring multistation access unit, which are powered from the end system so that a disconnect, power down, or cable cut will isolate the failed system and remove it from the ring. The detection capability could also be in the form of an IEEE 802.3 concentrator (repeater) that is required to automatically disable any port that suffers 30 consecutive collisions to allow the rest of the network to continue functioning. It could also be a layer-2 switch with a dedicated store and forward bridge port linking each end system to the rest of the LAN.

The challenge in detection is that the more failure modes the hub is designed to handle, the more complex the implementation and the more likely it is for the hub rather than the cables that are being protected to be the cause of failure. We see the same situation in hierarchical tree WANs, in which more complex (and more expensive) access devices are used to provide dial backup for the point-to-point links.

Once we reach the limits of the reliability of the components, we need to turn to redundancy. FDDI uses dual counter-rotating rings, as shown in Figure 2-8, so that if a node or a link fails, the nodes on either side of the failure can loop the rings around and keep communications flowing (albeit with only half the bandwidth). Depending on the nature of the applications being supported, this might require that we size the network so that the capacity requirements never exceed 50%.

The more common way to achieve redundancy in connectivity is through the use of an appropriately configured mesh topology. Figure 2-9 illustrates how we commonly use a mesh network to link multiple LAN segments. Even though the LAN

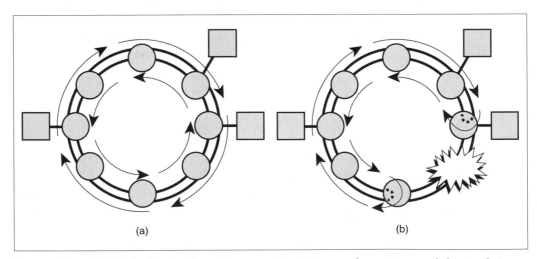

(a)   (b)

FIGURE 2-8. *FDDI dual-redundant ring operation: (a) normal operation and (b) ring being restored after a failure is detected*

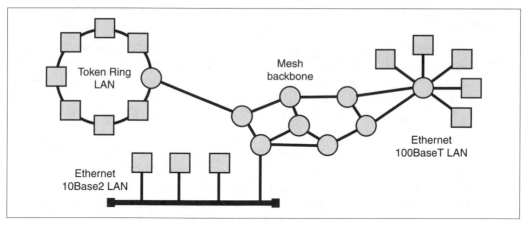

FIGURE 2-9. *Mesh backbone connecting multiple LAN segments*

segments themselves have single points of failure, those failure points will at most affect a single LAN segment. Redundancy in the critical connectivity between the LAN segments prevents isolated failures in the backbone mesh network from affecting more than one LAN.

Note that we deliberately neglect to indicate whether the redundancy is provided by bridges, routers, or other means. We will get to those considerations later in this chapter when we discuss protocol capabilities and selection. At this stage, all we care about is that there are no single points of failure in the backbone that could affect more than a single LAN segment. As the network grows in size, we will continue to add layers to the hierarchy and thus provide another level of connectivity to interconnect multiple meshed LAN segments. We will then interconnect those large networks of networks to create even larger networks.

We see a tradeoff even at this level. Notice that there are two links into the backbone for the 100BaseT Ethernet and only one for the the Token Ring and the 10Base2 Ethernet. This implies that either the availability requirements for the 100BaseT network are higher than for the other two networks, or its component reliability is lower. Alternatively, it could simply mean that due to the environment and location of the other two LANs, the addition of a second link that is sufficiently independent in its failure modes to significantly add to availability is too costly for the current value of the incremental availability to the organization.

Detecting Failure

The other key to effective utilization of redundancy is the ability to detect link or component failure and reroute traffic over the remaining connectivity. This is not as easy as it might seem because failures are not always an all-or-nothing proposition, and even the best of communications links are never perfect. As a result, there is a tradeoff to be made between declaring a good link to be down and allowing a bad link to remain in service. Compounding the challenge is the need for all components involved to agree on the state of a (potentially) failed component or link. The growth of networking protocols in the early years was frequently spurred by network collapses and failures due to the overlooking of rare failure modes.

Consider a link with a bit error rate (BER) of 10^{-6}. This BER means that on average, every million bits (10^6 bits) delivered will have one bit incorrect. However, since networks communicate in protocol data units ranging in size from less than 64 octets to over 18,000 octets, this translates into one bad frame or packet out of every 2,000 (for small protocol data units) or one out of every seven for giant frames. On an Ethernet network where the maximum transmission unit is 1,500 data octets, we would typically see one out of every 80 frames fail to be delivered. While this would be considered unacceptable on a LAN, where the protocols are designed around the assumption that at most one frame in 10,000 will be incorrect, on an analog dial-up link, a raw bit error rate of 10^{-6} would be considered close to perfection.

The normal technique to detect link failure is to periodically exchange hello packets of some sort between the components at either end. These could be transparent Spanning-Tree frames in a bridged environment or routing updates or keepalives between routers. If for some period no hello packets are received, the link is considered to be down. The challenge for protocol designers is that these hello packets do not carry useful data and are strictly overhead while the network is running under normal (that is, link up) conditions. Consequently, there is a strong desire to minimize the size and number of hello packets, and routing protocols typically default so that they consume only a few percent of the available bandwidth.

This usually means that it takes anywhere from 30 seconds to several minutes to detect that a link or peer component has failed (unless we are lucky and the Physical layer reports loss of the link). While this level of responsiveness is excellent compared with waiting for a service technician to locate and repair a line problem, if the goal is five nines (99.999%) availability (where the total downtime budget for the year is only five minutes), a single link failure could consume the majority of the downtime budget for the year. When we examine the details of specific protocols later in this chapter, we will also examine what parameters we may be able to adjust to speed up recovery from link failures. The tradeoff is that in order to speed up recovery, we typically need to increase the percentage of bandwidth "wasted" on routing overhead and risk routing instability if we fail to consider all factors or make any errors in configuration.

Simply exchanging hello packets more frequently and waiting less time before declaring a link down isn't the answer either. In a worst case scenario, a link could fail so that small packets, such as hello packets, are relatively unaffected while larger packets, which would be used by applications, suffer from an unacceptably high failure rate. This is not a hypothetical situation. It is a natural consequence of supporting reasonably large frames on a link that develops a high bit error rate. Consider a link with a bit error rate of 10^{-4}. Hello packets that are 64 octets in length would have a probability of failure of

$$\text{Probability}_{\text{Failure}} = \text{Number of Bits} \cdot \text{Bit Error Rate} = 64 \text{ Octets} \cdot 8 \, \frac{\text{Bits}}{\text{Octet}} \cdot 10^{-4} = 0.0512 \, (5\%)$$

If we required three consecutive missed hellos to declare the link down (the minimum recommended value in most routing protocols), the link would generally be considered up, and when it did get declared down, it would quickly recover.

At that same time, 1,500 octet packets, as might be used for a file transfer or screen update on a network tuned for maximum Ethernet performance, would have an average of 1.2 bits incorrect in each packet, a per packet probability of failure that is high enough that applications would not only slow down, but also drop their connections, freeze, or otherwise fail completely.

In a conventional network, manual intervention by network operations staff to force the link down completely might be acceptable. But again, in a high availability network, we need to automatically detect this class of failure and react quickly. Our first thought might be to use maximum-sized packets for the hello exchanges. But that is not an adjustable parameter in many protocols. What we really want is a protocol that monitors the link quality as seen by data. While our routing protocols may not provide this function, the point-to-point protocol (PPP; *See* RFC 1661) does. If we use PPP for the link protocol rather than a vendor proprietary protocol, we can enable link quality monitoring (defined by RFC 1989) and ensure that the link remains at an adequate performance level, as judged by the current ability to transfer data frames as well as the ability to exchange routing hello packets.

Quoting from RFC 1989:

There are many different ways to measure link quality, and even more ways to react to it. Rather than specifying a single scheme, Link Quality Monitoring is divided into a "mechanism" and a "policy." PPP fully specifies the "mechanism" for Link Quality Monitoring by defining the Link-Quality-Report (LQR) packet and specifying a procedure for its use.

PPP does NOT specify a Link Quality Monitoring "policy"—how to judge link quality or what to do when it is inadequate. That is left as an implementation decision . . .[1]

By enabling PPP link quality monitoring and defining a policy of declaring the link down if the quality is not high enough, we can mitigate the situation in which the routing protocol succeeds over a marginal link inadequate for production traffic.

On a Cisco router, enabling link quality monitoring is a two-step process, as can be seen in Listing 2-1. First we have to configure the interface to use PPP encapsulation rather than the default Cisco proprietary HDLC implementation (the encapsulation *ppp* line). Then we need to configure the PPP on the interface to use link quality monitoring (the *ppp quality* 90 line). This line both turns on the periodic exchange of link quality report packets as defined by the PPP standard and defines the policy.

Cisco routers have a very simplistic policy for using the statistics reported by the link quality report packets. The number specifies what percentage of sent and received packets must be successful to consider the link up. This is calculated by comparing the number of packets sent during the reporting period with the number of good packets reports as received by the PPP peer and similarly comparing the number of packets reported sent by the peer with the number known to have been received error free. In this example, we declare the link down if less than 90% of the packets sent and received are successful.

This approach is not perfect, as the protocol overhead of PPP is higher than the default HDLC implementation used by most vendors, both in terms of CPU cycles used and the number of overhead bits sent over the link. It also does not fully automate the correction of the problem, as it is still necessary for network management to recognize that the link is being shut down and to initiate appropriate diagnostic and repair actions. It also does not prevent a high link BER from impacting network performance, because once the link is declared down, PPP will initiate negotiations to bring it back up. Since these negotiations are based on the exchange of relatively small frames, they are likely to succeed on a marginal link and allow its return to service, at which point the larger frames start flowing, the error rate climbs, and it gets taken back out of service again.

On the other hand, this cycling will be very noticeable, and by setting the minimum link quality fairly high as is done in this example, the problem can be detected and corrective action initiated before the link deteriorates to the point where applications are failing rather than just slowing down for frequent retransmissions.

```
version 11.0
!
interface Serial2/0
  description T1 link we do not trust
  ip address 10.0.0.1 255.255.255.252
  encapsulation ppp
  ppp quality 90
!
end
```

LISTING 2-1. *Configuring PPP link quality monitoring*

Note that we also need to balance our setting of the keepalive interval with anticipated traffic as well as desired detection delay, since a single bad packet could cause a reported failure rate of 100% if there were no other traffic at the time. This potential for PPP link quality monitoring to exaggerate the failure rate due to a quantization error can significantly diminish the utility of the function. On the positive side, when traffic is low enough that we have to worry about quantization errors, it is also probably low enough that dropping the link is not going to cause major traffic disruption.

BRIDGING FOR HIGHER AVAILABILITY

Today's local area networks are all designed around the standards defined by the Institute for Electrical and Electronic Engineers (IEEE) 802 Committee. IEEE 802 networks have three layers under the Network layer rather than the two in the OSI reference model. This is not a violation of the OSI reference model (Figure 2-10(a)), because the model explicitly acknowledges the expectation that layers will be sliced and diced to match reality. The MAC layer of the IEEE 802.1 architecture (Figure 2-10(d)) has properties and functions from both the Physical layer and the Data Link layer, so the OSI reference model assigns it to the Data Link layer (Figure 2-10(b)). However this has lead to confusion because the IEEE 802 numbering scheme puts the Logical Link Control (LLC) under 802.2 while the MAC and Physical layers are standardized by the specific LAN and MAN technology groups, such as 802.3 and 802.5, and share the same numeric designation.

Efforts to reduce the confusion by moving the Medium Access Control sublayer down to the Physical layer, as in Figure 2-10(c), have met with mixed success. While

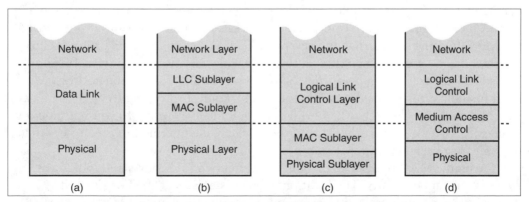

FIGURE 2-10. *Mapping of IEEE 802.1 layers to sublayers of the OSI reference model: (a) OSI reference model, (b) official mapping of IEEE layers to OSIRM sublayers, (c) less confusing mapping of IEEE layers to OSIRM sublayers, and (d) functional mapping*

it does reduce confusion over the numbering, the bridging function of an IEEE 802 MAC layer bridge is very clearly a Data Link layer function and should not be confused with Physical layer repeaters. Keep in mind that this is strictly an argument of terminology. Whatever OSI layer the IEEE 802 MAC layer is assigned to has no impact on how the MAC functions or how the network as a whole transports data.

While not all LAN standards are IEEE 802 standards, all popular general purpose LAN standards have been designed following the 802.1 architecture guidelines, simplifying their interconnection and minimizing unnecessary incompatibilities. For example, FDDI was developed under the auspices of the American National Standards Institute (ANSI), but shares common Medium Access Control mechanisms with the IEEE 802.5 Token Ring standards, and both use identical LLC (IEEE 802.2).

CLASSIC BRIDGING

One of the critical limitations of LAN protocols is the need to assume in their design an upper limit on the number of systems on the LAN and the maximum distance between any two end systems. To maximize performance and maintain high efficiency while supporting typical upper level protocols at a reasonable cost usually means that the LAN will be very local. For example, Ethernet and IEEE 802.3 limit the collision domain to 2,500 m maximum when running at 10 Mbps to allow timely and reliable detection of collisions, a critical requirement for efficient operation of a CSMA/CD protocol. The collision domain allowed at higher data rates is proportionally smaller in dimension. Similarly, the maximum number of systems in a single IEEE 802.5 Token Ring is strictly limited by the need to control clock skew (the specific limit depends upon the data rate and the media used).

The challenge is that as we outgrow the limits of the LAN topology, it is not cost effective to migrate to a new topology. Rather, we need a means of expanding the LAN to interconnect multiple independent LAN segments or rings. Looking at the MAC framing of Ethernet and several IEEE-802 compliant LAN protocols in Figure 2-11, we see that even though there are wide variations in the structure and fields in a frame, every frame includes a 48-bit source and destination address, which must be unique across the domain of the organization. By keeping track of the location of systems on the network, a bridge can provide forwarding for those frames of interest to systems on the other side of the bridge while filtering out any frames that are only locally significant.

A simple MAC bridge can be built by taking two LAN ports and looking at every frame on both ports. The location of end systems as defined by their MAC addresses can be automatically learned by examining the source address of every incoming frame. Every time a new address is seen coming in an interface, it can be added to the table of addresses for that interface. Then the destination address can be checked to determine what to do with the frame.

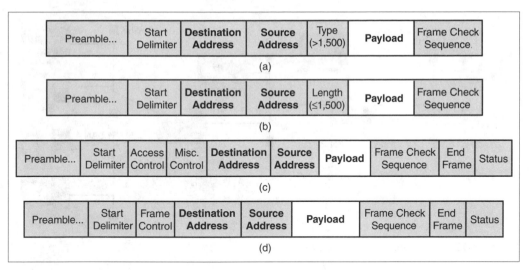

FIGURE 2-11. *LAN MAC framing: (a) Ethernet, (b) IEEE 802.3, (c) IEEE 802.5, and (d) FDDI*

If the destination is an address that is known to be on the LAN connected to the interface on which the frame arrived, the frame can be discarded because it has already been seen by the destination and the bridge is not needed. If the destination address is associated with a different interface, the frame will be sent out in that interface so that it can be picked up by the destination. If the destination is not recognized as being associated with any interface, as will happen if the destination has yet to send a frame or if the destination is a broadcast or multicast address, then the bridge will send the frame out every interface other than the one from which it arrived.

The basic operation of transparent learning bridges is illustrated in Figure 2-12 with a classic two port bridge on the left and a three port bridge on the right. From the viewpoint of each bridge, systems on the far side of the other bridge are indistinguishable from those local on the LAN. The forwarding tables on each bridge are fully populated in this illustration, as would be the case if all systems were active on the network. Operation of the multiport bridge on the right is slightly more complex than the original two-port bridge. Whereas the two-port bridge needs to determine only that the destination is not known to be on the incoming port before forwarding a frame out the other side, the three-port bridge must then check the forwarding tables on each of its other ports to determine out which port to send the frame. If the destination is not found on any port, then it must be flooded out every port except the one through which it entered.

Each address's entry in the forwarding tables also has a timeout associated with it, so that if the source address is not detected in an incoming packet for a given period of time, the address in the table will cease to be used. That way, if a system

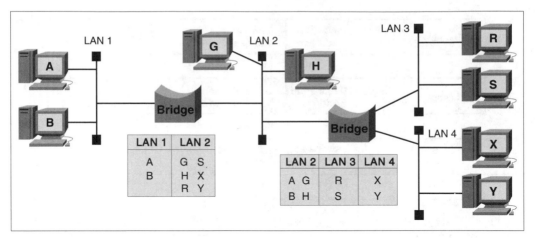

FIGURE 2-12. *Learning bridge operation*

attached to a LAN on one interface is moved to a LAN on another interface, the bridge will automatically update its tables to provide connectivity.

The beauty of a classic learning bridge is that its operation is totally transparent to the communicating devices because the frame is addressed directly to the destination. At the same time, the bridge reduces traffic levels by keeping local traffic local. One of the keys to successful LAN design with bridges is to place the bridges where they will have the greatest impact on reducing unneeded interLAN traffic. Bridges can also help stabilize the extended LAN by isolating many LAN problems (such as excessive collisions, noise, or high local traffic levels) to only the LANs on the one interface, preventing problems on one LAN segment from affecting other LAN segments.

On the other hand, the transparent operation of the bridge is also its major weakness. The Link layer protocols used by the sender and the receiver must be identical for communications to occur. If the sender is using IP in Ethernet encapsulation, so must the receiver. Similarly, if the sender is using IP in IEEE 802.2 Subnetwork Access Protocol (SNAP) encapsulation, the destination must also understand the SNAP encapsulation. The bridge will not convert between Ethernet and SNAP encapsulations. The same situation can occur with IPX traffic. All users must be configured to use (or automatically capable of supporting) the same encapsulation, whether that is Ethernet, 802.2 SNAP, 802.2 LLC, or raw 802.3.

While simple learning bridges make it easy to expand a LAN, they are generally unacceptable in a high availability design because they require a singly connected topology in order to function. There are two solutions available for this dilemma: source route bridging that is associated with IEEE 802.5 Token Ring networks and transparent Spanning-Tree bridging that is designed to be independent of LAN technology and is generally associated with Ethernet, IEEE 802.3, and all other LAN technologies, except for Token Ring.

TOKEN RING SOURCE ROUTE BRIDGING

When IBM introduced their Token Ring networking architecture in 1985, they were caught in a bind. One of the features of Token Ring was the use of the address-recognized and frame-copied flags that were part of the trailer on each frame going around the ring. By using these flags, the sending system would know immediately if the destination address it was using was a valid address (the address-recognized flag would be set) and if the destination had successfully read the frame as it went by on the ring (the frame-copied flag would be set). There was no need to wait for a time-out to recover from two very common failure modes.

The problem was that these flags were not useful if standard transparent bridging was used. It would have been extremely difficult with the technology then available for a transparent bridge to check its forwarding tables to see if it had an entry for the destination address before the frame passed it by. More importantly, no matter how good the technology, if transparent bridging were attempted, the flags would no longer be useful. No matter how the bridge responded to incoming frames, it could be wrong.

For example, not setting the address-recognized flag would discourage the sender from continuing the communication and prevent sessions from being established with systems on the other side of the bridge. Setting the address-recognized flag would return the wrong error message if the address turned out not to exist on the other side of the bridge either. Similar problems arise with the frame-copied flag, resulting in either excessive retransmissions (if it is not set) or long delays (if it is set and the frame cannot be delivered after all). The basic problem is that these flags, while leading to very efficient feedback between sender and receiver when on the same ring, are too low-level to allow use beyond the scope of a single ring.

The IBM solution to this dilemma was to introduce source route bridging. Source route bridging puts the burden of determining the correct path through the network on the end systems communicating rather than on the bridges. Before sending a frame, the end system determines the desired route through all intervening bridges and LANs to get to the destination end system. This route is then inserted into the header of the frame before it is placed on the ring.

Source routing provides a number of benefits for bridging. It makes the implementation of the bridge very simple, as there is no need for the bridge to keep track of systems on the attached networks. The bridge does not even need to look at all packets. It just sits on the LAN waiting for a frame to go by that has its identification in the routing information field. When a frame goes by addressed to the bridge, it can set the address-recognized and frame-copied fields correctly, based on the ability of the bridge to recognize itself in the routing information field. There is no danger of confusing the system that placed the frame on the ring because all end systems and bridges are aware of the presence of the source route and the local significance of the status flags. Since the routing information field also includes the next LAN on the path, the bridge immediately knows, with no need to search through forwarding tables with potentially thousands of entries, which ring to place the frame on next.

Source route bridging provided many advantages for the Token Ring environment in addition to making the implementation of bridges very easy. Since the end systems were responsible for determining routes and not the bridges, there was no problem providing redundant bridges between rings or multiple simultaneous paths between end systems. As a result, bridged networks could be designed without the constraint of bridges as critical, single points of failure.

The challenge in source route bridging is for the end systems to determine the best route. Most of the route determination algorithms depend on broadcast propagation to find routes between arbitrary end systems. While these algorithms have the advantage of being simple to implement and are generally robust, they do have problems scaling to very large networks. In a high availability design, this should not be a major issue because routing should be in effect at the Network layer long before the individual LANs become too large for effective bridging.

While not a problem for Token Ring implementations that had no installed base at introduction, the requirement for source routing capable software on the end systems was a major problem for Ethernet and other popular LAN architectures that already had an installed base at the time Token Ring and source routing were released. Because of the impossibility of retrofitting the installed base of users, the introduction by IBM of source route bridges for Token Ring created a major marketing problem for Ethernet vendors such as Digital Equipment Corporation (DEC).

TRANSPARENT SPANNING-TREE BRIDGING

Prior to the introduction of Token Ring's source route bridging, the limitation of learning bridges to a singly connected topology was simply accepted. If the single points of failure intrinsic in such a design were unacceptable, then the only choice was to either install routers or use bridges implementing a proprietary routing protocol. The former was slow, expensive, and only worked with protocol architectures that were routable. The latter required committing to a single vendor and could be very expensive if the wrong vendor was chosen and it became necessary to replace all connectivity components.

The answer was the development of transparent Spanning-Tree (TST) bridges. Transparent Spanning Tree works by having the bridges communicate with one another, then disabling redundant connectivity so that the working bridge topology becomes a minimal Spanning Tree connecting all LAN segments. Once the Spanning-Tree algorithm has run and all loops are removed from the working topology, the bridges can function as classical transparent learning bridges using the remaining active ports. Since all calculations and protocol exchanges are handled strictly by the bridges, there are no hardware or software changes required on any end systems, making transparent Spanning Tree fully compatible with the preexisting installed base of Ethernet systems.

The transparent Spanning-Tree algorithm is based on the exchange of Bridge Protocol Data Units (BPDUs) and functions as follows:

All bridges claim to be the root bridge and broadcast BPDUs so indicating.

The bridge with the lowest identifier (which includes the globally unique MAC address to ensure that there will be no ties) becomes the root bridge.

Each bridge that connects to a LAN segment serviced by the root bridge broadcasts on all other LAN segments their cost metric to reach the root bridge.

On each LAN segment, the bridge with the lowest cost path to the root bridge remains active and all other bridges deactivate that port.

In the event of a tie in the cost calculation, the bridge with the lowest identifier wins.

The minimal Spanning Tree continues to be built using the same algorithm until all LAN segments have exactly one path to the root bridge.

Until the minimal Spanning Tree is completed, no bridges can forward traffic (the standard algorithm calls for 30 seconds free of port status changes before a bridge can start forwarding traffic from or to any specific port). As a result, when a failure occurs that requires renegotiation of the Spanning Tree, the network will be logically disconnected until the new topology is settled. The larger and more complex the network, the longer it takes to run the algorithm to completion and the more likely it is that failures will occur, thus requiring renegotiation.

The problem is that the transparent Spanning-Tree algorithm specified for general use must be very conservative to eliminate the potential of introducing loops in the active topology, no matter what topology is actually used for physical connectivity. An enhanced standard algorithm defined by IEEE 802.1w provides for *rapid reconfiguration* by placing constraints on the topology that can be physically used. Its use would permit almost immediate recovery from link failures. The draft standard was still in the balloting process when this book was written, so it is not known when products will become available implementing rapid reconfiguration.

Although not of concern from an availability viewpoint but potentially important from a cost effectiveness viewpoint, the redundant bridges and links that are not part of the negotiated Spanning Tree are not useful for carrying traffic. This is normally not a major issue for LANs, but when remote bridges over WAN links are involved, it can be a significant cost factor.

Transparent Spanning-Tree bridges are sometimes used to interconnect Token Ring networks, but the results are rarely satisfactory. Like simple learning bridges, they do not support the address-recognized and frame-copied flags in the IEEE 802.5 frame trailer. Unless there are end systems on the Token Ring that do not support source routing, source routing bridges are a better solution for Token Ring environments.

While it is theoretically possible to bridge between Token Ring and Ethernet-like networks, we can expect problems due to the many link level differences, such as the bit ordering within addresses, Token Ring expectations of source routing support, and different maximum frame sizes supported. Translating bridges are available that can handle the incompatibilities, but it is usually much easier to just use routers rather than bridges. At the Network layer, only the payload in the LAN frame is passed from one LAN to the other, eliminating any dependence upon special cases and specific software releases for proper operation.

SWITCHED LAN DESIGN

Today's LANs are generally designed around multiport switches rather than discrete bridges, but the design principles are the same. The challenge for the designer is that whereas classic LAN design guidelines have focused on maximum end-to-end bandwidth at minimum cost, we need to modify that focus so that it rests on end-to-end functional availability. This could mean using four 50-port hubs rather than one large 200-port hub, but we must also be careful that the choices made contribute to availability. For example, that 200-port "Enterprise" hub may have redundant power supplies, cooling fans, switch fabrics and switch processors, built-in error detection and reporting, and have a device MTBF of 200,000 hours, yielding a superior functional availability even though four times the number of users are affected when it does fail.

While high reliability components can help availability, they are not sufficient by themselves to provide high availability. Network elements are not stand-alone devices but components of a network system whose internal operations and system-level interactions are governed by software and configuration parameters. Each component of the network system also resides in a physical environment that provides electrical power, environmental control, and human operators. Weaknesses in any of these softer aspects of the network has the potential to cause failures that prevent attaining the high availability expected from high reliability components.

When designing a high availability switched LAN, we can look at classic WAN design experience for guidance. The key is to design the LAN so that there are no single points of failure from end to end. This is much more difficult than it sounds because the end users on the LAN are almost always singly connected. The usual compromise is to leave individual PCs and workstations singly connected and only provide redundant paths from the wiring closet back to the servers. Critical users and servers then use multiple Network Interface Cards (NICs) to connect to the LAN.

By meeting the need for high availability through redundancy in the network design and topology rather than depending on high reliability devices, we can reduce our dependence on perfection in the far harder to control soft failure arena. The network elements providing the redundancy can be physically diversified, reducing the potential of physical environment problems disrupting communications. Similarly, because there are multiple, independent paths, maintenance work and software upgrades are more easily implemented without interrupting production.

Consider the classic switched Ethernet design in Figure 2-13(a), which connects user systems to a common server in the computer room. Assuming all links and devices are 99.95% available, the network availability seen by the user between workstation X and the server is about 99.75%. Adding a fourth switch and dual homing the server, as in Figure 2-13(b), raises the network availability as seen by the user at X to 99.90%, with almost all unavailability due to the remaining single points of failure in the access line and first floor switch. And if we dual home the user as well as the server as is done for the user at Z, the network availability increases to better than 99.999%.

While the improvement in calculated availability may be dramatic, we must be careful not to get overconfident. For example, our calculations assume that the switch over to an alternate route happens instantaneously, which we know is not going to be true. If these are Token Ring networks using source route bridging, we are also assuming that they have retained knowledge of alternate paths and we will

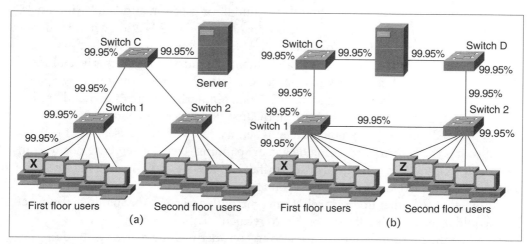

FIGURE 2-13. *Higher availability through redundant design*

not be faced with a mini broadcast storm as every user system affected by the outage rediscovers all available routes. In bridged networks in particular, it is crucial to keep the topologies simple and compact to minimize the impact of route recalculation. Under these conditions, a typical Token Ring network using LLC type 2 (LLC2) for end-to-end error control would suffer an interruption on the order of a few seconds, short enough that it would probably not even be noticed by the user.

On the other hand, if these are Ethernet networks and the failure is one that requires a new Spanning Tree to be negotiated, the gap in service will be 40 to 50 seconds and would be quite noticeable to an active user, even if the higher level protocols were able to pick up where they left off once the new Spanning Tree was running. This is a severe enough impact that switch vendors have introduced proprietary extensions to the transparent Spanning-Tree protocols to improve recovery speeds.

Enhancements to the IEEE standard are in progress and should be considered when they appear in commercial products. Until then, proprietary solutions remain the only choice. For example, we could split the LAN into multiple virtual LANs (VLANs) and use per-VLAN Spanning Trees. Another modification we could consider would be disabling Spanning-Tree convergence safeties.

Not all switches offer the ability to run the Spanning-Tree algorithm independently on each defined VLAN and doing so increases the overhead traffic on trunks supporting multiple VLANs. Splitting the network into multiple VLANs also introduces the requirement to provide routing between the VLANs, significantly increasing the configuration complexity. But by running the Spanning-Tree algorithm independently on each VLAN and judiciously selecting the Spanning-Tree root and cost parameters for each VLAN, we can both optimize the Spanning Tree for users on each VLAN and reduce the number of users impacted by any single link or switch failure.

For example, continuing with the network in Figure 2-13(b), we could put the first floor users on one VLAN and the second floor users on another. By making Switch C the root for the Spanning Tree on the first floor VLAN and Switch D the root for the Spanning Tree on the second floor VLAN, both floors could use optimal routes to a dedicated port on the server when all systems are functioning properly. Failure of Switch C or the uplink to that switch would force VLAN 1 to negotiate a new Spanning Tree but would have no impact on VLAN 2. Similarly, failure of Switch D or its link to Switch 2 would have no impact on the first floor users and would force only VLAN 2 to recalculate its Spanning Tree. In neither case would all users be affected. This also has the benefit of reducing delays in Spanning-Tree convergence due to competition for bandwidth from heavy user traffic. Failure of Switch 1 on the first floor or Switch 2 on the second floor would disconnect all users on that floor who were not dual homed to the other floor as well. However, with a per-VLAN Spanning Tree, neither would force the other floor's VLAN to recalculate its Spanning Tree.

If we take this approach, we do need to consider routing as well as bridging issues. For example, it makes a major difference in the network design if the server supports VLANs on its interfaces because otherwise, second floor users would be forced to go through a router to take advantage of the remaining connectivity. The implementation of dual-homed users would also be very different, as the two interfaces would now be on independent subnetworks and the protocols used by network interface card vendors to provide automatic failover would not function.

We could avoid some of these issues by using a bridge between the VLANs. Taking this option requires using a different Spanning-Tree protocol on the bridge between the VLANs to avoid creating a single Spanning Tree of the combined VLANs. For example, if the IEEE Spanning-Tree protocol was used on the switches, the DECnet Spanning-Tree protocol could be used between the VLANs. Generally, this is not a good approach to use as it also nullifies many of the advantages of using VLANs, such as broadcast traffic isolation. Sometimes, however, there is no choice, as when dealing with protocols which can not be routed.

Disabling the safety features built into the Spanning-Tree protocol can also significantly speed up convergence after a failure. The Spanning-Tree protocol was designed for robust, plug-and-play operation in bridged networks with arbitrary complexity (with many loops) and many hops (up to seven) between bridges. By constraining ourselves to a simpler, more structured connectivity environment, we can safely short-circuit many of the safeguards built into the Spanning-Tree protocol to permit much faster convergence, reducing the failure recovery time in our redundantly configured LAN. For example, Cisco defines three shortcut modes of operation that can be applied to any specific port on a switch, *UplinkFast, BackboneFast* and *PortFast*.

With *UplinkFast,* each VLAN is configured with an uplink group of ports, including the root port that is the primary forwarding path to the designated root bridge of the VLAN and one or more secondary ports that are blocked. When a direct uplink fails, *UplinkFast* unblocks the highest priority secondary link and begins forwarding traffic without going through the Spanning-Tree listening and learning states. Bypassing listening and learning reduces the fail-over time after uplink failure to approximately the BPDU hello interval of 1 to 5 seconds.

UplinkFast, or its equivalent from other vendors, should be used only on switches at the periphery of the Spanning Tree (those we commonly call *access switches* or *tier one switches*). Stability requires that the network be configured such that any failure that could cause the normal uplink to cease to be the preferred path to the root bridge will cause the preferred secondary uplink that is being activated to be the designated path to the (potentially new) root bridge after convergence of the Spanning-Tree protocol. While *UplinkFast* would work for our example LAN in Figure 2-13(b), we would be better off modifying the redundancy to eliminate the cross-linking at the access switches. The dual star topology in Figure 2-14 would allow us to increase the size of the LAN to handle a large number of access switches and assign individual users on each access switch to an appropriate VLAN rather than the VLAN per-access switch we had used.

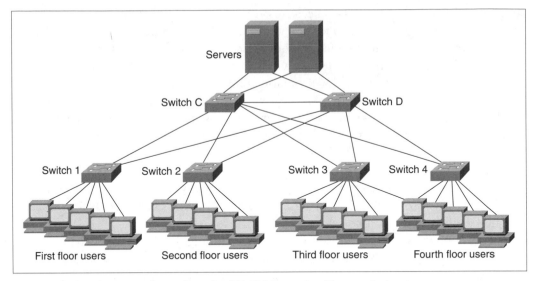

FIGURE 2-14. *Structured topology for VLAN Spanning-Tree optimization*

By defining multiple VLANs on each access switch, half with Switch C as the root bridge and half with Switch D as the root bridge, we can retain the simplicity and multivendor support of Spanning Tree while still getting load sharing on our uplinks. Multiple switches at any single location should be connected as if they were at independent locations, to avoid introducing loops. Cross connects at the access level are possible, but the cost savings are usually negated by the complexity of ensuring that no loops are introduced that could cause *UplinkFast* to be unsuitable.

The *BackboneFast* feature accelerates Spanning-Tree convergence after the failure of non-directly-connected (indirect) network links. Under normal Spanning-Tree operations, when a switch is notified of an indirect link failure, it waits for its forwarding table to age out before beginning the process of listening and learning to determine the new topology. With *BackboneFast,* the switch immediately proceeds to the listening/learning state on its blocked ports without waiting for the max age timer to expire, reducing the convergence time by the max age setting (typically 20 seconds). In the configuration of Figure 2-14, this feature does not contribute to Spanning-Tree recovery performance as indirect links are only used for backup access. It is safe to turn it on in this configuration, even though it does not directly contribute, and would be useful if implementing cross-links at the access level or more than two switches at the server support level.

The *PortFast* feature effectively turns off Spanning Tree on a port that is dedicated to an end system or concentrator with no potential for being part of a bridged loop. *PortFast* allows the switch port to begin forwarding as soon as the end system is connected, again bypassing the listening and learning states and eliminating up to

30 seconds of delay before the end system can begin sending and receiving traffic. This mode of operation is frequently required to allow end systems that have just been powered on to retrieve setup information from over the network. It would also be essential on the links to dual-homed user B if the technology used for dual homing kept the redundant interface in an inactive state until needed.

We will temporarily ignore the challenge of providing transparent dual homing for the user and server systems and wait to address that topic in the next chapter. Before that, we need to look at how we can expand our bridged LANs with routers.

ROUTING FOR HIGHER AVAILABILITY

Routing is required to scale networks to support large numbers of users or to efficiently span long distances. Before we look at the specifics of protocols used to provide routing, we first need to review some of the terminology used to describe routing implementations.

ROUTING FUNDAMENTALS

The OSI reference model recognizes three distinct classes of protocols essential to routing traffic from one end system to another: directory services, end-system-to-intermediate-system routing, and intermediate-system-to-intermediate-system routing.

Directory services allow an end system to translate a system or service name into the appropriate parameters required to establish communications through the network. In the world of TCP/IP, for example, we have the Domain Name System (DNS), which allows translation of domain names into the IP address associated with that domain name. While we will ignore directory services for now, we will come back to it in Chapter 11, Disaster Recovery Considerations, where we discuss its role in routing traffic to a disaster recovery site when the primary service has failed.

End-system-to-intermediate-system (ES-IS) routing serves a dual function. For the end system, it defines where to send a packet on the local subnetwork so that it can be delivered to the desired ultimate destination, which may or may not reside on the same subnetwork and may or may not share a common Data Link layer protocol with the originator. It also defines how an intermediate system can determine what end systems it can reach on the physical subnetworks to which that intermediate system attaches. As we shall see in Chapter 3, Multihomed Hosts, and again in Chapter 6, Multiple Routers at a Single Site, the simplistic nature of the ES-IS protocols in the TCP/IP protocol suite creates multiple challenges to providing high service availability.

Intermediate-system-to-intermediate-system (IS-IS) routing protocols are used by routers in their communications with each other to determine the best currently available route to a router serving the end system specified by the network address in the packet. Intermediate-system-to-intermediate-system routing protocols are further divided into intradomain routing protocols and interdomain routing protocols. Although most people think of the distinction between the two as being based on the size of the network, the critical factor is the ability to share routing metrics rather than the number of end systems, routers, or physical subnetworks serviced.

In an intradomain routing protocol, the route metrics used to define the "goodness" of any specific route are shared by all systems in the routing domain. This allows intradomain routing to accurately distinguish between alternate routes and reliably identify the best route or routes available.

In interdomain routing, the routing protocol can no longer assume that the metrics used to describe route quality from one routing domain can be compared to the metrics used in a different routing domain. This can make selection of a "best" route an interesting challenge. In addition, the routing process must consider if administrative policies define a route as acceptable before choosing it as "best." *Acceptable* is then defined in terms of existence of a route that meets all policies applicable to the packet being routed, such as "data from source X may not be carried through domain Y" or "data of type Z should always use this route, if available."

In effect, while intradomain routing combines individual physical subnetworks into a large homogeneous network, interdomain routing combines the networks defined by independent routing domains into an even larger, but potentially less efficiently routed, network of networks. In the TCP/IP world, a routing domain is called an Autonomous System (AS), an intradomain routing protocol is called an Interior Gateway Protocol (IGP), and an interdomain routing protocol is called an Exterior Gateway Protocol (EGP). Intradomain routing protocols commonly found in TCP/IP networks today include the open standards Routing Information Protocol (RIP; *See* RFC 1058), RIP version 2 (RIPv2; *See* RFC 2453), Open Shortest Path First routing protocol version 2 (OSPF; *See* RFC 2328), Integrated IS-IS (RFC 1195, an extension of the OSI link-state IS-IS protocol, ISO 10589), and the Cisco-proprietary Interior Gateway Routing Protocol (IGRP) and Enhanced-IGRP (EIGRP) routing protocols. The only common interdomain routing protocol is the Border Gateway Protocol (BGP; *See* RFC 1771). Be careful in reading the TCP/IP literature, as the term EGP is used to refer both to the general concept of an interdomain routing protocol and to an early protocol for providing interdomain routing, the RFC 904 Exterior Gateway Protocol (EGP).

Other protocol architectures generally include only intradomain routing protocols in their definitions. This is not as big a limitation as it might seem, as modern intradomain routing protocols such as Novell's NetWare Link Services Protocol (NLSP) can scale to handle thousands of subnetworks and tens of thousands of users. While we make frequent use of BGP throughout the examples in this book, we only need the interdomain routing capabilities of BGP in Chapter 8, Connecting to Service Providers. The rest of the time we are taking advantage of other properties of the BGP protocol.

In the realm of intradomain routing protocols, there are additional distinctions that can be drawn. Generally, all intradomain routing protocols belong to one of two classes of routing protocols: distance-vector or link-state. In the early days of networking, virtually all networks that used dynamic routing used a distance-vector protocol. As the processing power of routers grew through the years, it became practical to implement link-state protocols where each router maintains a complete map of the state of all links in the network rather than limiting its view to just the links to its neighbors.

Link-state algorithms (also known as shortest-path-first algorithms) flood routing information to all nodes in the internetwork. Each router maintains a database reflecting the state of all links between all of its peers. Then, when a link changes state, only the changes need to be communicated, minimizing the network bandwidth consumed by the routing protocol in large networks. Some popular link-state protocols are TCP/IP OSPF, OSI IS-IS, and Novell NLSP. Distance-vector algorithms (also known as Bellman-Ford algorithms) call for each router to send all or some portion of its routing table, but only to its neighbors. In essence, link-state algorithms send small updates everywhere, while distance-vector algorithms send large updates, but only to neighboring routers. Some popular distance-vector protocols are TCP/IP RIP and RIPv2, Novell IPX RIP, and Cisco's IGRP.

Because they converge more quickly, link-state algorithms are less prone to routing loops than distance-vector algorithms. Link-state algorithms will consistently calculate the same routes regardless of the order in which updates are received and can be mathematically guaranteed to converge under all steady state conditions. These factors enhance their popularity in large networks. On the other hand, link-state algorithms require more CPU power and memory than distance-vector algorithms. Link-state algorithms, therefore, can be more expensive to implement and support.

Despite their differences, both algorithm types can perform well in most circumstances. Specific implementations of each have their own strengths and weaknesses. The bad reputation of distance-vector algorithms is largely due to the use of early protocol designs, such as the original TCP/IP RIP, which were pushed far past their design limits in environments for which they were not suited, leading to poor performance and unstable operation. This could be considered the networking equivalent to complaining that Microsoft Windows 1.1 does not run Office 2000. Cisco's IGRP, also a pure distance-vector protocol, was the only stable, robust routing protocol suitable for very large TCP/IP network domains until the introduction of Integrated IS-IS in 1990.

Cisco's EIGRP, which uses the Diffusing-Update Algorithm (DUAL) developed at SRI International by Dr. J. J. Garcia-Luna-Aceves, is a modified distance-vector algorithm that gets around many of the limitations of classic distance-vector protocols by having each router keep copies of each neighbor's routing tables as well as its own. That way, when a route is lost, an alternate route, if one exists that can be guaranteed to be loop free, can be immediately utilized. This provides many of the fast convergence advantages of a link-state protocol while retaining much of the computational simplicity of a distance-vector protocol, allowing lower cost routers to support more peers than would be practical with OSPF or other true link-state protocols.

STATIC ROUTING

Before we start our tour through some available dynamic routing protocols, we will review the concept of static routing. In static routing, the routing decision is made by the network administrator, who programs each device with the appropriate next hop information for all required addresses. While frequently looked down upon as an inferior routing mechanism, static routing does have its place. For example, it is very common to include a static "route of last resort" or default gateway so that if a packet needs to be routed to a destination that is not known to the dynamic routing protocol, it can be forwarded toward a router that may have better information.

In many network environments, we use the concept of conditional static routes to simplify and enhance network operation. A conditional static route is simply a static route that is active if and only if the target of the route is known. If the target is known, the static route based on that target will be used, otherwise an alternate route, if any, will be used. This allows static routing to be used in conjunction with dynamic routing to provide many of the benefits of dynamic routing without incurring the overhead. Conditional static routes are also used to define a fall back route, such as a dial-on-demand backup, should a primary route fail.

Most router vendors enhance this mechanism to provide floating static routes by including a concept of route "goodness," which can be attached to each static route. That way, we can prioritize which static routes will be used under which conditions. By also defining a "goodness" metric to each dynamic routing protocol, it is possible to select a route based on how the route is learned and override routes learned from less-desirable sources with static routes. This is done while still allowing the use of preferred routes that are learned dynamically. We will make extensive use of floating static routes when implementing dial-backup solutions.

Floating static routes are also useful in environments in which we need the link status detection provided by a dynamic routing protocol (such as on a Frame Relay or ATM network where communications can be lost even though our link to the service provider is still up) but otherwise still want the security or efficiency of a static route. They are also useful when communicating through a firewall where we dare not trust any routing advertisements received from systems on the other side of the firewall other than as a means to determine if the firewall is functional.

Consider the network environment pictured in Figure 2-15, where the router at Corporate Site A will normally learn routes to Corporate Site B from the OSPF

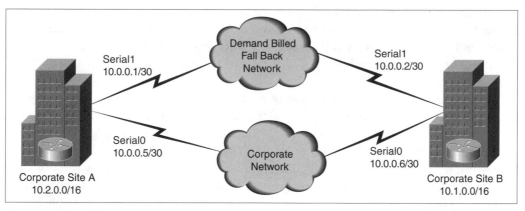

FIGURE 2-15. *Floating static routes*

protocol running over the preferred network. Our challenge is that although we want full connectivity through the fall back network, because it is demand billed, we only want to use it if no other route is available. Perhaps even more important, we do not want to pay for the overhead traffic that a dynamic routing protocol would require if run between the two sites over the fall back network.

On a Cisco router, the single floating static route in Listing 2-2 would suffice to direct traffic through the demand billed network only if there were no route through the preferred network. Note that unlike a dynamic routing protocol, there is no overhead traffic required to maintain route status. However, should an addressing change be introduced at Corporate Site B, all sites configured like Corporate Site A will need to be manually updated with the new routing information, whereas the dynamic routing information will be automatically updated.

The key in Listing 2-2 is in the final parameter, the *150* at the end of the *ip route* statement, which states that this route should only be used if there are no known routes with "goodness" less than 150. Cisco calls the "goodness" metric *administrative distance* with allowable values from 1 to 255, with lower values being preferred. Nortel calls the "goodness" metric *route preference* with allowable values from 1 to 16,

```
version 11.0
!
hostname SiteA
!
ip route 10.1.0.0 255.255.0.0 10.0.0.2 150
!
end
```

LISTING 2-2. *Floating static route will use fall back network only if required*

with higher values being preferred. Since the *administrative distance* for routes learned through OSPF is 110, which is less that 150, any time a route to 10.1.0.0/16 is known through OSPF, it will be used and the static route will be ignored. However, as soon as the OSPF learned route is no longer available, the static route will float to the top and take over.

One challenge with static routing is the potential for delays when a floating static route needs to be activated. Cisco routers, for example, only check for changes to static routes during per-minute processing and when an interface goes down or comes up. If a dynamic routing protocol adds or deletes a route from the routing tables and there is no accompanying interface state change, static routes will not change until the next execution of per-minute processes. This can result in an added delay of up to a full minute before the required floating static route is available for use and communications are restored.

RIP ROUTING

Routing Information Protocol (RIP) could be considered the mainstay of small TCP/IP networks. It has a long history of successful use starting with its original incarnation as the Xerox protocol, GWINFO, for use with the Xerox Networking Services (XNS) protocol suite. It was adapted to Internet Protocol and released as the *routed* program shipped with Berkeley Standard Distribution (BSD) Unix in 1982.

RIP itself evolved as an Internet routing protocol and the various versions in use formally united in RFC 1058, published in 1988, which also tried to unify the many enhancements devised to avoid slow convergence in everyday use. Other protocol suites use modified versions of RIP, including the AppleTalk Routing Table Maintenance Protocol (RTMP) and the Banyan VINES Routing Table Protocol (RTP), which are based on the Internet Protocol (IP) version of RIP. The IPX RIP used in Novell NetWare networks is a direct descendant of the Xerox protocol, with all the fixes found from IP experience folded in.

The IP version of RIP has been updated with the RIP version 2 specification to provide support for variable length subnetwork masking, a simple authentication mechanism, and other improvements essential in today's TCP/IP networks. However, the original version still remains in wide use.

RIP is a distance-vector protocol that uses hop count as its metric and ensures stability through specifying a small metric (16) as infinity, limiting its use to networks where the longest route is 15 hops or less. While the use of split horizon with poison reverse and triggered updates are now part of the protocol, there are still situations where "counting to infinity" is required to detect the loss of a route. These issues and how RIPv2 gets around them are discussed in detail in RFC 1058 (and repeated in RFC 2453), so we will not discuss them here further.

Default parameters for the IP version specify broadcasting the full routing table every 30 seconds (the update interval) and declaring a peer router as down if no broadcasts are heard for 180 seconds (the route *timeout* timer). Should a peer be declared down due to a lack of updates received, all destinations that are routed through that peer are flagged as unreachable and their metric is set to infinity (16) in the routing table for an additional 120 seconds (the route *garbage-collection* timer). At this time, the route is removed from the routing table and forgotten. If an advertisement is received for the destination while the garbage-collection timer is running, the garbage-collection timer is cleared and the new route inserted in the table. Some implementations of RIP will replace any routes that have reached at least half the *timeout* timer value with equal cost routes received from a different source rather than waiting until the current route has been declared invalid before accepting an alternate route. This eliminates unnecessary downtime when multiple routes of equal cost are in place (the RIP protocol supports only one route to any destination at any one time).

Depending on the implementation, the route *timeout* and *garbage-collection* timers may be specified as a multiple of the update interval rather than as a time period. The default values (recommended by the RFCs) of 30 seconds, 180 seconds, and 120 seconds, respectively, would then translate to 30 seconds, three update intervals, and two update intervals.

Cisco routers deviate from the RFC specifications in their implementation of RIP, implementing route holddown in addition to split horizon, poison reverse, and triggered updates to further enhance routing stability. Taking the place of the update, route timeout and garbage-collection timers specified by the RFC, Cisco's implementation of RIP uses the parameters update time, invalid time, and holddown time. The update time is the interval between transmissions of normal routing updates (routing changes, such as a link going up or down that trigger an update will reset this timer). The invalid time specifies how long a time can pass before a route is declared invalid due to no updates being received. The route then enters holddown where the destination is flagged as inaccessible and advertised as unreachable. Unlike the *garbage-collection* timer wait defined in the RFCs, any routing updates regarding this destination are ignored while in the holddown state. The holddown time then specifies how long to stay in the holddown state before flushing the destination from the routing tables and allowing updates that indicate routes to the destination to be entered into the routing table once again.

Cisco routers default these times to 30 seconds, 180 seconds, and 180 seconds, respectively. However, should the route be lost due to exceeding the invalid time, the actual holddown interval is reduced to 60 seconds. Cisco routers also define a fourth parameter, the *flush time*, which determines how long a route can stay in the routing tables without an update; that parameter defaults to 240 seconds. Therefore, the use of default timers can require up to 4 minutes for recovery from loss of a link even when an alternate path is already available.

Clearly, RIP is an inappropriate routing protocol for a high availability network where it is unacceptable for a loss of a link to result in minutes of downtime. However, RIP is useful in a number of scenarios in which the need is for a simple routing protocol with minimal processing overhead, such as determining if a specific link is functional or allowing end systems to dynamically locate available routers. Under these limited conditions, we can often reduce the contents of routing updates to a minimum of routing information. By keeping the routing updates very small and their scope extremely limited, we can safely modify the timers from their default values to speed up response to link outages without creating excessive overhead traffic or sacrificing routing stability.

Cisco routers allow adjustment of the RIP timers using the *timers basic* configuration statement. Listing 2-3 shows the RIP configuration used on a Cisco router that reduces the recovery time from link failure to a maximum of 10 seconds. It also disables holddown to eliminate dropped connections due to ICMP destination unreachable responses to data packets routed while the destination is in holddown. The *timers basic* line sets the update interval to three seconds and the invalid time to 10 seconds, allowing a little slack so that two lost and one delayed updates will not drop the link. The setting of zero for the holddown time allows alternate routes to be accepted from the first update received after the link is declared down.

A configuration like this one would not be appropriate for general purpose routing in which there was any potential for routing loops. In a tightly controlled topology with predictable changes where there is no danger of encountering problematic cases, short circuiting unneeded safeties is normally safe. We also need to rigorously document our assumptions that made the short cuts possible so that future revisions to the network do not result in introducing instability. Good documentation can be as important as good design in a high availability network, a topic we will come back to in Chapter 12, Management Considerations.

As a general rule, unless there is a need to work with systems that support only the original RIP (version 1), we always want to use RIP version 2 even if we do not

```
version 11.2
!
router rip
version 2
timers basic 3 10 0 10
network 192.168.1.0
!
end
```

LISTING 2-3. *Adjustment of RIP timers to minimize response time to link failure*

initially require its additional functionality. Because the extra information carried by RIP version 2 update packets uses reserved fields already in the RIP version 1 update packet definition, there is no savings in bandwidth consumption from using the older, less-capable protocol version.

OSPF ROUTING

Development of the Open Shortest Path First (OSPF) routing protocol standard for IP networks began in 1988, as the limitations of RIP made it increasingly unsuitable for the larger, more heterogeneous networks being put into service by the mid-1980s. OSPF was derived from several research efforts, including Bolt, Beranek, and Newman's (BBN's) SPF algorithm developed in 1978 for the ARPANET, Dr. Radia Perlman's research on fault-tolerant broadcasting of routing information (published in 1988), BBN's work on area routing (published in 1986), and an early version of OSI's Intermediate System-to-Intermediate System (IS-IS) routing protocol, which in turn was largely based on work at DEC for DECnet routing. The SPF algorithm, which forms the basis of all modern link-state protocols, is also referred to as the Dijkstra algorithm, for the person credited with its creation.

OSPF operates within a routing hierarchy and scales by dividing the routing domain into multiple areas that attach to a common backbone area (area 0). Figure 2-16 illustrates part of a network showing the area 0 backbone and three areas. Note that area 100 is singly connected to the backbone with a single point of failure in router H, even though both the area and the backbone are each multiply connected. We would probably consider that situation unacceptable unless communications between area 100 and the rest of the network did not share the high availability requirements of other communications.

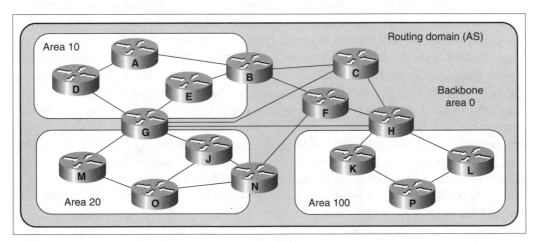

FIGURE 2-16. *OSPF area hierarchy*

Link-state advertisements (LSAs) containing information on attached interfaces, metrics used, and other variables are sent to all other routers in the same hierarchical area. As each router accumulates link-state information, it uses the SPF algorithm to calculate the shortest path to each destination subnetwork. Although all routers share the same link-state database, each will calculate its own view of the topology with itself as the root of the shortest path tree.

Routers with multiple interfaces can participate in multiple areas. These routers are called *area border routers* (ABR) and maintain separate topological databases for each area. Each area's topology is invisible to routers outside the area. By keeping area topologies separate, routing traffic is reduced, as is the computational burden of calculating the shortest path tree.

This partitioning into areas results in two different types of OSPF routing, depending on whether the source and destination are in the same or different areas: intraarea routing occurs when the source and destination are in the same area, and interarea routing occurs when they are in different areas. Any time the routing protocol has converged, which is to say, any time the network topology and status are stable, intraarea routing in OSPF is guaranteed to be optimal.

Interarea routing, on the other hand, will be a tradeoff between the level of hiding of route information implemented on area border routers and the routing burden imposed on all routers in an area. There are many optimizations possible in configuring an OSPF network that permit different degrees of hiding of route information across area boundaries in an effort to minimize the computational and bandwidth overhead of the protocol.

However, we must weigh the performance impact of propagating detailed routing information with the potential for suboptimal routing if we hide too much. For example, one popular optimization is to configure area border routers to simply inject a default route into each non-backbone area rather than summaries of all routes that can be reached through the backbone. However, consider the impact of this approach on even the small, simple network of Figure 2-16. If all links have the same cost metric, packets from router A in area 10 to router M in area 20 would be sent to router B because it is the closest area border router to router A, even though router G would be a better area border router for accessing area 20. From router B, there are two equal paths to area 20, B-C-G and B-F-N. Depending on the specific assignment of IP subnetworks inside area 20 and the degree of summarization configured on the area border routers for area 20, we may or may not have knowledge in the backbone on any preference between area border routers for the subnetwork we are trying to reach. But in this case, the computational savings gained by route summarization could be costly in terms of performance as packets that follow the former path would be delivered directly to router M from router G while those which follow the latter path would encounter still more delay as they are routed through router O. Return packets from router M to router A, on the other hand, would all follow the optimal route M-G-D-A.

While OSPF is the most powerful intradomain routing protocol in the IP arsenal and can scale to efficiently handle large internetworks with thousands of routers and tens of thousands of individual networks in a single routing domain, it will only scale effectively if the network is designed and implemented to scale efficiently. It can really pay when setting up the network to ensure not only that adequately redundant connectivity is established, but also that routing will be reasonably optimal, especially for high traffic and performance sensitive communicators. This same requirement also applies when using BGP or other interdomain routing protocols to route between autonomous systems.

The OSPF backbone area is responsible for distributing routing information between areas as well as for carrying all traffic between areas. It consists of all area border routers, networks not wholly contained in any area, and their attached routers. Since all communications between areas must flow through the backbone area, it is essential that the backbone area remain fully connected at all times. If necessary, virtual routes may be defined between area border routers serving the same area to provide or restore backbone connectivity. On the other hand, if a non-backbone area should be split, the backbone will automatically provide communications between all pieces that still include an area border router with connectivity to the backbone. Clearly, even in normal availability OSPF networks, the backbone should be designed for high availability.

The Cisco Internetwork Design Guide specifies the following four critical guidelines to minimize performance and stability problems in OSPF routed networks.

- *The number of routers in an area*—OSPF uses a CPU-intensive algorithm. The number of calculations that must be performed given n link-state packets is proportional to $n \log n$. As a result, the larger and more unstable the area, the greater the likelihood for performance problems associated with routing protocol recalculation. Generally, an area should have no more than 50 routers. Areas with unstable links should be smaller.

- *The number of neighbors for any one router*—OSPF floods all link-state changes to all routers in an area. Routers with many neighbors have the most work to do when link-state changes occur. In general, any one router should have no more than 60 neighbors.

- *The number of areas supported by any one router*—A router must run the link-state algorithm for each link-state change that occurs for every area in which the router resides. Every area border router is in at least two areas (the backbone and one area). In general, to maximize stability, one router should not be in more than three areas.

- *Designated router selection*—In general, the designated router and backup designated router on a local-area network (LAN) have the most OSPF work to do. It is a good idea to select routers that are not already heavily loaded with CPU-intensive activities to be the designated router and backup designated router. In addition, it is generally not a good idea to select the same router to be the designated router on many LANs simultaneously.[2]

While it is possible to implement stable and successful networks that exceed these guidelines, doing so increases the potential for problems and reduces the CPU cycles available for other useful activities. When it comes to maximizing the availability of the network by minimizing the time required to react to communications failures, there are four significant adjustable time intervals defined in the OSPF specification (*See* RFC 2328). These intervals, their definitions, and the RFC-suggested values when running on a LAN are summarized in Table 2-1.

Of these parameters, the largest impact will normally come from adjusting the *Hello Interval* and the corresponding *Router Dead Interval*. These two parameters determine how long it will take to detect a link failure that has not caused the link to fail at the Physical or Data Link layer. All routers running OSPF on a subnetwork must configure these parameters to the same value or OSPF will not establish a neighbor relationship across the subnetwork. However, each subnetwork is configured independently, so a router with both slow and fast links can optimize the values for each link.

The 40 second *Router Dead Interval* is the key, but since it is generally not a good idea to reduce it to less than three times the *Hello Interval,* we usually need to reduce the *Hello Interval* as well. Fortunately, the OSPF hello packets are relatively small, 48 octets plus an additional four octets for each additional neighbor identified on the subnetwork, so increasing their frequency is usually not a big issue from the viewpoint of network overhead. Nor is the processing of hello packets a major concern. However, we do want to ensure that the interval is long enough to avoid the danger of declaring the link down unnecessarily, as there is significant processing and traffic loading associated with flooding the network with link-state updates when any link changes state and having all affected routers run the SPF algorithm to determine new routes (and repeating the process a few seconds later after the link is discovered to not be down after all).

Decreasing *Rxmt Interval* is usually not important, as it only comes into play when link-state updates are lost in transit. At the same time, it must be long enough

TABLE 2-1.   *OSPF Parameters that Influence Downtime Due to Link or Router Failure*

INTERVAL NAME	USAGE	TYPICAL VALUE (SECONDS)
Hello Interval	The length of time between the hello packets that the router sends on the interface	10
Router Dead Interval	The length of time before the router's neighbors will declare it down because they stop hearing the router's hello packets	40 (4 × Hello Interval)
Rxmt Interval	Delay before retransmitting a link update that has not been acknowledged	5
MinLS Interval	The minimum time between changes to the status of any specific link	5

to allow round trip propagation of the update and delayed acknowledgments. We need to be careful adjusting the retransmit interval because failure to make a corresponding adjustment to the acknowledgment delay on neighbor systems could result in excessive retransmissions. Since many routers do not provide a parameter for adjusting the acknowledgment delay but rather set it based on the retransmit delay, we need to make sure that all routers in a neighbor relationship are configured with the same value for retransmit interval.

MinLS Interval is only important if the link is unstable to the extent that its status is flapping. The mechanism used to ignore a link-state change that comes too soon on the heels of a prior change to the same link is to silently discard the update, so there exists the potential that the update could be ignored for a period approaching the sum of the minimum link-state interval plus the retransmit interval. On the other hand, a flapping link is extremely processor-intensive if it causes constant reexecution of the SPF algorithm, so we should carefully evaluate the benefit to be gained by reducing this timer below the default 5 seconds. We would probably gain more uptime by addressing the need to identify marginal BER links that are good enough to pass hello packets but not good enough to support production traffic.

Listing 2-4 illustrates how these parameters are controlled on Cisco routers. Notice that while the Hello Interval and Router Dead Interval are reduced to 3 seconds

```
version 11.0
!
interface Serial1/0.1 point-to-point
 description Frame relay (CIR 1500) OSPF timer example
 ip address 10.0.0.1 255.255.255.252
 ip ospf authentication-key ijklmnop
 ip ospf hello-interval 3
 ip ospf dead-interval 10
 bandwidth 1500
 frame-relay interface-dlci 500 IETF
!
interface Serial1/1
 description Point-to-point T1 OSPF timer example
 ip address 10.0.0.5 255.255.255.252
 ip ospf authentication-key qrstuvw
 ip ospf hello-interval 10
 ip ospf dead-interval 40
 bandwidth 1500
!
end
```

LISTING 2-4. *Modifying OSPF timers for faster response to link failure*

and 10 seconds respectively on interface Serial1/0.1, they are left at the default values of 10 seconds and 40 seconds on interface Serial1/1.

Serial1/0.1 is a Frame Relay link. Frame Relay, like ATM, X.25, Ethernet and other network-based connectivity, can fail in ways that, while remaining up at the Data Link and Physical layers, render the link incapable of carrying traffic. Hence it is imperative that this mode of failure be detected quickly since it can be expected to occur frequently.

Serial1/1, on the other hand, is a point-to-point leased line. Since the link level runs end-to-end over this link, there is little danger of undetected failure other than excessive BER. As a result, we leave the Hello Interval and Dead Router Interval at their default values because there is very low probability that speeding them up will detect problems any faster. From a failure detection point of view, we could even slow them down with values in excess of the default, but the overhead at the default rate is low enough that there is little to be gained.

Cisco supports further tuning of the CPU load when running OSPF by allowing the addition of delays before running the SPF algorithm. By default, Cisco routers impose a 5-second delay before running the SPF algorithm when an incoming link-status change mandates a recalculation of the routing data base. This allows time for all link-state changes associated with the failure event to arrive so that all changes required can be calculated at once. Then, after an SPF calculation has been completed, there is by default a 10-second moratorium before the SPF algorithm will be run again. This means that there could be an added delay of up to 10 seconds before responding to the second of two unrelated but nearly simultaneous failures.

Normally a delay of 10 seconds is not going to be noticed, but because it could be in addition to any delay in detecting the failure, we may want to tune these parameters as well. These commands are illustrated in Listing 2-5, where we adjust all the timers to ensure that response to a Serial1/0.1 failure never exceeds 15 seconds.

In this case, we have not only increased the frequency of hello exchanges over the link, but also have decreased the retransmit interval for faster recovery from lost update packets being sent over the link. The *timers spf* statement in the router section of the configuration then modifies the initial SPF delay and minimum interval between SPF algorithm runs to 3 seconds and 5 seconds, respectively. So, in our worst case failure scenario, it could take us up to 10 seconds to detect failure of the Frame Relay link and even if that event occurred shortly after an SPF algorithm calculation, the maximum wait before the SPF algorithm could be run again would be, at worst, an additional 5 seconds.

We also have adjusted Rxmt Interval downward slightly in the *ip ospf retransmit-interval 3* line in Listing 2-5. If the network is well-connected with multiple alternate routes between routers, this is usually unnecessary. However, if there are only two independent paths between the two routers and we are reporting failure of one of them, we want to minimize the delay in getting the message across that we need to

```
version 11.0
!
interface Serial1/0.1 point-to-point
 description Frame relay (CIR 1500) - 2nd OSPF timer example
 ip address 10.0.0.1 255.255.255.252
 ip ospf hello-interval 3
 ip ospf dead-interval 10
 ip ospf retransmit-interval 3
 bandwidth 1500
 frame-relay interface-dlci 500 IETF
!
router ospf 1234
 timers spf 3 5
 network 10.0.0.0 0.0.0.3 area 0.0.0.10
! other interfaces go here
!
end
```

LISTING 2-5. *Modifying Cisco OSPF parameters for faster response to multiple link failures*

send all traffic down this remaining link, even if the link is in poor condition and dropping packets. We do need to be careful in adjusting this parameter and make sure that we do not reduce it to the point where we are causing unnecessary retransmissions due to the time required to return and process acknowledgments. Significant retransmission levels should be a sign that the link needs repair rather than a configuration decision.

EIGRP ROUTING

Cisco's proprietary Enhanced Interior Gateway Routing Protocol (EIGRP) is a popular routing protocol in networks made up of all Cisco routers. Its popularity is due to a number of factors. It is backwards compatible with the original Cisco Interior Gateway Routing Protocol (IGRP), which made it the obvious upgrade path for existing Cisco-based IGRP networks. It also provides the response speed and bandwidth utilization efficiency of a link-state protocol without the associated intense CPU loading and strict hierarchical design requirements. Of course, there are always trade-offs and the use of EIGRP requires more than just a commitment to Cisco for all routing products. In particular, even though EIGRP can easily scale to handle very large networks with minimal planning and does not suffer from the stability and potential slow recovery problems associated with RIP, careful attention must be paid to the network design if the full benefits of the protocol are to be attained. To see why, we first need to discuss how EIGRP functions.

EIGRP implements a modified distance-vector algorithm called the Diffusing Update Algorithm (DUAL). DUAL uses the concept of *feasible successors* to allow EIGRP to converge very quickly. Each EIGRP router stores a copy of its neighbors' distance-vector routing tables. This allows the router to utilize a new route to a destination instantly if another feasible route is known. This route is called a *feasible successor* to the previous route and if one is available, recovery from a link failure is simultaneous with its detection. We will return to this concept of feasible successors because the availability of feasible successors is the key to rapid recovery from link failures in an EIGRP network.

If no feasible successor is available based on the routing information previously learned from its neighbors, a router running EIGRP must find a new route to that destination. To do so it enters the *active* state and sends a query to each of its neighbors, asking for an alternate route to the destination. These queries propagate until an alternate route is found. Routers that are not affected by a topology change remain *passive* and do not need to be involved in the query and response.

A router using EIGRP receives full routing tables when it first establishes neighbor relationships with each neighbor. Thereafter, only changes to the routing tables are sent and those to only the neighbor routers that are affected by the change. A *successor* is a neighboring router that is currently being used for packet forwarding, that provides the least cost route to the destination, and that is not part of a routing loop. *Feasible successors* are routers that have routes to the destination that could be used in case the existing route fails. Feasible successors provide paths that are not least-cost but can be guaranteed not to introduce routing loops.

It is the determination that a neighbor router has a route that cannot possibly be a routing loop through this router that allows EIGRP to quickly recover from typical failures. To perform this determination, the router maintains a topology table with a list of all routes (destination networks) advertised by neighbors, the calculated cost of getting to each network, and each neighbor's cost of getting to each network.

The route metric to any particular destination is determined by adding the cost advertised by each neighbor to the cost of reaching that neighbor. These costs are initially determined when the protocol is in the *active* state and seeking all loop free paths to the destination. Once a set of loop free paths have been determined, the algorithm can transition from the *active* to the *passive* state. This transition is critical because it establishes the baseline used to determine the *successors* to be used for current routing and the metric to be used in the future for selecting *feasible successors* should the current successors cease to be useable.

The metric for the best route available to a destination when the DUAL algorithm transitions from the *active* state to the *passive* state is entered into the topology table for that destination network as the *feasible distance* (FD). The neighbor (or neighbors) that have routes with this metric (as measured by the local router) are the current *successors* and will be used for routing traffic to the destination. (As is the case with OSPF on Cisco routers, the mode of load sharing will depend on the route caching policy configured and may be per-packet or per-destination address.) Successor routers will continue to be used for the destination as long as at least one of them is available.

Should all the successor routers fail (or raise the costs of their routes to the destination even though they are still reachable) so that no successors remain providing a route with the best available local metric, a feasible successor is sought. A feasible successor is any neighbor whose advertised cost to reach the destination (not including our cost to reach the neighbor) is less than the feasible distance. Since the neighbor's cost is less than our cost, we can be sure that the route the neighbor is advertising does not loop through us (because if it did, the cost would be at least our feasible distance even if the neighbor considered the cost to reach us as zero). Note that even though our cost to reach the destination is now higher, the feasible distance does not change. That way, we are protected from a neighbor that is slow to update its routing tables.

Each topology-table entry for a destination will always be in one of two states: active or passive. A destination is in the passive state when the router has at least one successor or feasible successor, and it is in the active state when the router is performing a recomputation to identify a successor because none is available. As long as feasible successors are available, a destination never has to go into the active state, and the alternate path can be put into service immediately.

A recomputation occurs when a destination has no feasible successors. The router initiates the recomputation by sending a query packet to each of its neighboring routers. The neighboring router can send a reply packet, indicating it has a feasible successor for the destination, or it can send a query packet, indicating that it is participating in the recomputation. While a destination is in the active state, a router cannot change the destination's routing-table information. After the router has received a reply from each neighboring router, the topology-table entry for the destination returns to the passive state, and the router can select a successor.

While the destination is in the active state, the route is in holddown mode and any traffic for that destination will generate a destination unreachable response (or the equivalent for protocols other than IP). Depending on the size and connectivity of the network, this could take tens of seconds. Any TCP/IP applications that react to receipt of a destination unreachable by terminating their TCP connections will have a problem. Depending on the application, the impact on the user's productivity could be all out of proportion with the severity of the routing problem.

Our challenge then is to ensure that under normal conditions, we always have at least one feasible successor to seamlessly back up each primary route. This is not always easy because unlike OSPF where the only requirement before using an alternate route is that it exist (the SPF algorithm ensures there are no routing loops), EIGRP will reject valid routes merely because their metric is too high to guarantee that they are loop free based on the simplistic feasible distance test.

Consider the simple two sites with redundant routers and redundant links network in Figure 2-17. While by appearances this configuration should provide uninterrupted, albeit lower, performing service in the event the primary T1 link should fail and would do so if we were using OSPF as our routing protocol, the results with EIGRP would be quite different if we followed standard network design guidelines for maximum efficiency.

By default, EIGRP calculates a metric for each link based on the bandwidth and delay associated with the link. The published default delay for LANs is 1 ms while that for serial links is 20 ms, but if the design depends on the default values, it pays to do a reality check because switched 100BaseT delay, for example, defaults to 0.1 ms rather than 1 ms. Similarly, the Cisco command reference states that the default metric is calculated as

$$\text{Metric} = \text{Delay (in tens of microseconds)} \cdot 256 + \frac{256 \cdot 10^{10}}{\text{Bandwidth (in bits/second)}}$$

which we can translate to more reasonable units as

$$\text{Metric} = \text{Delay (in milliseconds)} \cdot 25,600 + \frac{2,560,000}{\text{Bandwidth (in Mbits/second)}}$$

However, what is not mentioned is that the formula only applies to a single link. The metric calculation used when routing only adds the delays of each link. The bandwidth contribution is tracked separately and only that of the slowest link along

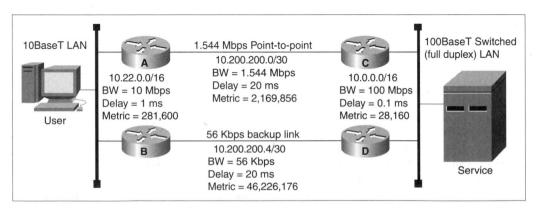

FIGURE 2-17. *Feasible successor network*

the path contributes to the overall metric. So, the metric for a destination that is not directly attached is

$$\text{Metric} = \text{Total Path Delay (in milliseconds)} \cdot 25{,}600 + \frac{2{,}560{,}000}{\text{Bandwidth of Slowest Link (in Mbps)}}$$

As a result, although EIGRP will favor a 1.544-Mbps link over a 1.500-Mbps link connecting two LANs, it will not favor the 1.544-Mbps link over even a 64-Kbps link if another hop on the path is a 56-Kbps link. When designing a network where this could be a factor, it is essential to override the default delays with values that will force routing along the desired paths.

Returning to our original example of Figure 2-17, where concatenation of slow routes is not a factor, we can see that the metric calculated by EIGRP for the 10-Mbps user LAN would be

$$\text{Metric} = 1 \text{ ms} \cdot 25{,}600 + \frac{2{,}560{,}000}{10 \text{ Mbps}} = 25{,}600 + 256{,}000 = 281{,}600$$

and the metric for the T1 link between Router A and Router C would be

$$\text{Metric} = 20 \text{ ms} \cdot 25{,}600 + \frac{2{,}560{,}000}{1.544 \text{ Mbps}} = 512{,}000 + 1{,}657{,}856 = 2{,}169{,}856$$

Checking the entries in the EIGRP topology table by using the *show ip eigrp topology* command (Listing 2-6) shows that the metrics calculated by Router A match the expected values.

Turning our attention to Router C in Listing 2-7, we see the expected entry for the route to the user LAN 10.22.0.0/16 through the Serial1 and Router A whose metric is the sum of the serial link plus the delay portion of the metric for the user LAN. What we do not see in the listing is any mention of the alternate path to the user LAN through Router D because even though Router D has a loop-free path to the user LAN, it is not a feasible successor. To see why, we need to look at the EIGRP topology table in Router D.

Router D, like Router C, has two possible routes to the user LAN 10.22.0.0/16. Table 2-2 summarizes all possible routes to the user LAN 10.22.0.0/16 and their associated metrics for each of the four routers. For Router A and Router B, the user LAN is a connected network, so there is no possibility of a feasible successor existing. On Router D, the best available path is the route D-->C-->A, with metric 2,198,016, so the value 2,198,016 becomes the FD for destination 10.22.0.0/16. Router B is also advertising a route to 10.22.0.0/16 to Router D, and while it is a much costlier route from the viewpoint of Router D, the cost of the route once we reach Router B

```
RouterA> show ip eigrp topology
IP-EIGRP Topology Table for process 1

Codes: P - Passive, A - Active, U - Update, Q - Query, R - Reply,
       r - Reply status
 •
 •
 •
P 10.22.0.0/16, 1 successors, FD is 281600
        via Connected, Ethernet0
P 10.200.200.0/30, 1 successors, FD is 2169856
        via Connected, Serial1
 •
 •
 •
```

LISTING 2-6.   *Excerpt from the EIGRP topology table for Router A in Figure 2-17*

is only 281,600, which is less than the FD for the destination of 2,198,016, so Router B is a *feasible successor* for that destination. If anything should happen to disrupt the route through Router C, Router D could immediately start using the route through Router B.

Router C, on the other hand, has a preferred route only slightly better than that of Router D and sets its FD to the metric for that route of 2,195,456. Router D is also advertising a route to 10.22.0.0/16 to Router C, and not only is it a much costlier route from the viewpoint of Router C, the cost of the route once we reach

```
RouterC> show ip eigrp topology
IP-EIGRP Topology Table for process 1

Codes: P - Passive, A - Active, U - Update, Q - Query, R - Reply,
       r - Reply status
 •
 •
 •
P 10.22.0.0/16, 1 successors, FD is 2195456
        via 10.200.200.2 (2195456/281600), Serial1
P 10.200.200.0/30, 1 successors, FD is 2169856
        via Connected, Serial1
 •
 •
 •
```

LISTING 2-7.   *Excerpt from the EIGRP topology table for Router C in Figure 2-17*

TABLE 2-2.   *Available Routes to 10.22.0.0/16 and Their Associated EIGRP Metrics*

ROUTER (FEASIBLE DISTANCE)	PATH	ROUTE METRIC	NEIGHBOR'S ROUTE METRIC	ROUTE STATUS
A (281,600)	Ethernet0	281,600	Directly connected	Directly connected
B (281,600)	Ethernet0	281,600	Directly connected	Directly connected
C (2,195,456)	C -->A	2,195,456	281,600	Successor
	C-->D-->B	46,254,336	46,251,776	Potential loop
D (2,198,016)	D-->B	46,251,776	281,600	Feasible successor
	D-->C-->A	2,198,016	2,195,456	Successor

Router D is still 46,251,776, which is not less than the FD for the destination of 2,195,456. This means that we can not be certain that the route being advertised by Router D does not include the route that Router C is advertising through Router A, so Router D cannot be considered a *feasible successor* for the destination.

Should anything happen to disrupt the route through Router A, Router C has no *feasible successor* and must go into active state to query all its remaining neighbors for an alternate route to 10.22.0.0/16. In this particular case, Router D does have a *feasible successor* for destination 10.22.0.0/16 that does not include a direct link to Router C, so it can return that information to Router C, which can then return to passive state with a new route and a new feasible distance.

In this example scenario, the time spent by Router C in the active state is probably measured in milliseconds. However, we must remember that Router C is also probably the default gateway for the server (after all, it has a T1 link to the outside compared to Router D's 56-Kbps link) and while it is in active state, any packets received that are destined to the user LAN will elicit a destination unreachable response with a possibly severe impact on the application program.

Unfortunately, there does not appear to be a general solution for the challenge of ensuring availability of feasible successors. The key is that as long as we are aware of the potential for problems, we can often find specific workarounds for a specific critical need.

For example, the simplest solution might be to just make Router D the default gateway rather than Router C. However, we will see later on, that approach will not protect us from a problem that takes out Router C rather than a link attached to it. One of our challenges in high availability design will always be the critical need to examine all aspects of failure and be wary of solving one weakness at the expense of inadvertently creating another.

One solution is to take advantage of the distance-vector nature of EIGRP and adjust the metrics on each router interface to force the routing we really want while maintaining availability of feasible successors for all critical paths. This takes advantage of the fact that unlike OSPF, there is no need for every router in the network to have a consistent image of the network path costs. This allows us to adjust parameters so that paths have different costs depending on the direction they are traversed.

Once we have resolved the feasible successor problem, we can turn our attention back to the common routing protocol challenge of speeding up the response to failure by speeding up the detection of failures. In theory, we do this the same way for EIGRP that we did for OSPF. That is, we increase the frequency of hello packets and decrease the time we are willing to wait to see a neighbor's hello packet before declaring the link down. As always, we must make the tradeoff between speed of response to failure and unproductive overhead traffic carried over limited bandwidth links. Listing 2-8 shows an EIGRP configuration for an ATM link providing detection of a down, but not out, path in 5 seconds or less, ensuring continued service at the Application level as long as there is a *feasible successor* when the link fails.

The statement *ip hello-interval eigrp 99 1* in Listing 2-8 sets the interval between hello packets sent on this interface for the EIGRP process 99 to 1 second. This is the fastest supported rate. The *ip hold-time eigrp 99 4* statement then sets the time allowed by the EIGRP running as process 99 to pass without receiving a hello packet before declaring the neighbor unreachable. From the viewpoint of link failure

```
version 11.2
!
interface ATM3/0.1 point-to-point
 ip unnumbered Loopback1
 ip hello-interval eigrp 99 1
 ip hold-time eigrp 99 4
 bandwidth 1544
 ipx delay 7
 no ip directed-broadcast
 pvc 3/1
 !
!
router eigrp 99
 network 10.0.0.0
 no auto-summary
 eigrp log-neighbor-changes
!
end
```

LISTING 2-8. *EIGRP tuning for 5-second worst-case detection of link failure*

detection, the EIGRP hold time is equivalent to the OSPF *Router Dead Interval* parameter.

It is essential to keep in mind that adjusting timers for quicker failure detection should only be considered in the context of an overall network design for higher availability. There are good reasons for the defaults being as slow as they are, and the benefits from speeding them up usually only become significant when the network is already performing at or near the five nines level of availability.

Integrated IS-IS Routing

Integrated IS-IS is a modification of the OSI IS-IS routing protocol that can be used for network protocols other than OSI Connectionless Network Protocol (CLNP). IS-IS is a link-state routing protocol developed from the same roots as OSPF. Indeed, many of the differences between the two are due to lessons learned from early deployments of IS-IS while OSPF was being developed. IS-IS specifies a two-level routing protocol consisting of level 1 areas connected by a level 2 intradomain backbone.

When used for OSI routing, the network address consists of a hierarchical address consisting of a routing domain, the IS-IS routing area (only meaningful within the specified domain), the end system identifier, and the network service access point (specifying the transport protocol to get the packet). There is no concept of a network identifier portion in the network address. Every level 1 router in an area learns the best path to every end system in the area.

If a destination is not in the same area as a level 1 router, it will be routed to the nearest level 2 router for delivery to the correct area or external domain through the level 2 backbone. The level 2 routers will then forward the packet to the nearest level 2 router serving the destination area (or providing access to the outside domain). Once the packet is received by a level 1 router in the destination area, it will be routed by the best available path to any level 1 routers that can directly communicate with the end system specified.

Integrated IS-IS adds several fields to standard IS-IS packets to allow IS-IS to support IP routing. These fields allow the level 1 routers to inform each other of the reachability of IP network addresses with subnetwork masks from each router. Because IP addresses do not include an area field, assigning network addresses so that they can be summarized by level 2 routers is a critical part of scaling support for a large IP network using Integrated IS-IS.

From an availability viewpoint, network design with Integrated IS-IS is virtually identical to network design with OSPF. This should not be surprising as the two protocols are virtually identical in philosophy, sharing common roots.

Integrated IS-IS use is common among large Internet service providers. There are a number of reasons for this popularity, although some of them are historical. In particular, IS-IS is the only scalable routing protocol defined for routing OSI CLNP packets, a common service requirement through the early 1990s. Integrated IS-IS was the first commercially available, open-standard routing protocol that was stable enough and scalable enough to run a large commercial network, providing service providers an alternative to Cisco IGRP and other proprietary, single-vendor solutions for their rapidly growing networks.

Today, Integrated IS-IS provides not only the rapid response of a link-state routing protocol, but also the ability to tune most performance parameters to fit a wide range of application environments. While the goal normally is to minimize bandwidth and CPU overhead, the knowledgeable designer can adjust the tradeoffs between response time and overhead to achieve any level of desired performance for the protocol. For example, we can adjust the lifetime of advertisements sent out in link state packets (LSPs) to force the refresh of all link-state information at any interval between 1 and 65,535 seconds using the *max-lsp-lifetime* configuration command. Our biggest challenge is that many of these adjustments are very slow to get documented, making them unnecessarily difficult to utilize.

An Integrated IS-IS enhancement introduced in Cisco IOS 12.0T train (*isis hello-interval minimal*) permits tuning the exchange of hello packets so that unreported link failures can be detected in 1 second. Listing 2-9 shows the configuration of a Frame Relay link using Integrated IS-IS routing that will reroute around normal Frame Relay link failures within 1½ seconds. If downtime is to be avoided at all costs and there are sufficient CPU cycles and link bandwidth available, Integrated IS-IS is currently the recovery speed champion.

```
version 12.1
!
hostname Router_2
!
interface Loopback0
 ip address 10.0.0.1 255.255.255.255
!
interface Serial1/0
 no ip address
 encapsulation frame-relay
 frame-relay lmi-type ansi
! WARNING: See the note in the text re: broadcasts
 frame-relay broadcast-queue 256 256000 200
!
interface Serial1/0.32 point-to-point
 bandwidth 1984
 ip unnumbered Loopback0
 ip router isis
                                              (continued)
```

```
  frame-relay interface-dlci 32
  isis circuit-type level-2-only
  isis metric 11 level-2
  isis hello-interval minimal
  no isis hello padding
  isis lsp-interval 10000
 !
router isis
  redistribute connected
  passive-interface Loopback0
  net 49.4321.0000.0a00.0001.00
  is-type level-2-only
  metric-style wide
  set-overload-bit on-startup 30
  max-lsp-lifetime 65535
  lsp-refresh-interval 65000
  spf-interval 1 1 10000
  prc-interval 1 1 10000
  lsp-gen-interval 1 1 10000
  no hello padding point-to-point
  log-adjacency-changes
  display-route-detail
 !
ip classless
 !
end
```

LISTING 2-9. *Integrated IS-IS tuning for 1½-second link failure detection and recovery*

We do more adjusting than essential to illustrate some of the currently undocumented parameter settings that are popular in an Integrated IS-IS environment. For example, the *max-lsp-lifetime* and *lsp-refresh-interval* commands make no contribution to the response time to link failure. Rather, they minimize the number of background recalculations when the network is stable.

The key configuration line for fast link-failure detection is the *isis hello-interval minimal* in the interface configuration. This line sets the hello-interval to whatever value is required so that the number of hello packets that must be missed to detect link failure (specified by the *isis hello-multiplier* parameter) will be sent every second. Since the default value of the hello-multiplier is three, we will be sending three IS-IS hello packets out the link every second. We also minimize link overhead by reducing the size of each hello packet with the line *no isis hello padding* and by only enabling level-2, interarea routing exchanges.

Because these packets are broadcast and we send three each second on each PVC, we will usually need to increase the broadcast queue. If the hello broadcasts do not get through, the PVCs will be declared down due to a lack of broadcast buffers. This will disrupt service far more than the few seconds we are trying to shave off of detecting link failure.

We also limit the transmission of link-state updates over the link to no more frequently then every 10 seconds using the line *isis lsp-interval 10000.* This reduces the impact of unstable lines elsewhere in the network, a major consideration when designing with hair-trigger detection of link status.

Further down, under *router isis,* we also adjust the allowed frequency of running the IS-IS routing calculations. It does little good to detect a link-state change in 1 second if we then wait 5 seconds before allowing the link-state algorithm to run. We do this in the lines *spf-interval 1 1 10000, prc-interval 1 1 10000,* and *lsp-gen-interval 1 1 10000,* which adjust the allowed frequency of shortest-path-first calculations, partial route calculations, and link-state packet release, respectively.

For each of these three commands, the first number is the minimum number of seconds between any two successive executions, the second number is the initial wait in milliseconds before starting an execution following detection of a need to execute (unless we must delay due to the first or last parameters), and the third number is the wait in milliseconds before successive execution of the algorithm or action for the same cause.

We set the first two intervals at their minimum possible values of 1 second and 1 millisecond, respectively, to minimize delays in propagating updates. To keep the CPU requirements under control if a route starts to flap, we set the third parameter to 10 seconds.

Note that earlier IOS releases accept only a single parameter for the *spf-interval* and *lsp-gen-interval* commands and do not recognize the *prc-interval* command. Like the *minimal* parameter on the *hello-interval,* these are enhancements to allow finer tuning of the Integrated IS-IS protocol.

One quirk of the Integrated IS-IS protocol is that even though we are not supporting OSI routing, we still must define an OSI network address for IS-IS to use in routing exchanges (the *net 49.4321.0000.0a00.0001.00* line). OSI network addresses are built on a hierarchical structure consisting of a routing domain, routing area, host ID, and NSAP selector. In this example, we use an Authority and Format ID (AFI) of 49 to specify that this is a locally defined address format.

Remember that the host ID portion of the address (the six octets preceding the last octet of the address) must be unique across the routing domain. In this case, we used the common convention of converting the local IPv4 address 10.0.0.1 to hexadecimal (*0a00.0001*) and padding it with leading zeroes to get a six octet host ID of *0000.0a00.0001.* The two octets before the host ID (*4321*) are the IS-IS area number.

Other features of Integrated IS-IS that are illustrated here, although not essential for high-speed error detection and recovery, are the lines *metric-style wide* and *set-overload-bit on-startup 30*. The former is another new feature, which expands the range of metric values permitted for level-2 links, allowing finer tuning of routing decisions. Use *metric-style narrow* if interoperating with routers running IOS 12.0 or earlier. The latter prevents this router from being used for transit traffic until it has been up for 30 seconds. This reduces the impact of lines coming to life after a reboot, allowing all changes to be combined in a single update cycle once the router is stable.

Although not required, we turn on *log-adjacency-changes* so that we an keep track of any instability or other problems detected in the lines. We also turn on *display-route-detail* to include the LSP number that originated the route when we used *show ip route*.

BGP ROUTING

Unlike the other routing protocols we have been discussing so far, which are all intradomain routing protocols, the Border Gateway Protocol (BGP) is designed to be an interdomain ("interautonomous system" in IP parlance) routing protocol. The primary function of a BGP speaking system is to exchange network reachability information with other BGP systems so that destinations outside a routing domain can be found and accessed. This network reachability information includes information on the list of ASs that must be traversed to reach the destination.

The current version of BGP, defined in RFC 1771, is BGP-4, which provides a range of mechanisms for supporting classless interdomain routing, including support for advertising an IP prefix, eliminating network classes, and aggregating routes, including AS paths.

BGP performs three types of routing: interautonomous system routing, intraautonomous system routing, and pass-through autonomous system routing. Interautonomous system routing occurs between two or more BGP routers in different autonomous systems. Peer routers in these systems use BGP to maintain a consistent view of the internetwork topology. When used in this mode, we frequently refer to the protocol as Exterior BGP (EBGP). We will use EBGP routing to provide high availability connectivity to the Internet through one or more internet service providers. For more information, see Chapter 8, Connecting to Service Providers.

Intraautonomous system routing occurs between two or more BGP routers located within the same AS. Peer routers within the same AS can use BGP to maintain a consistent view of the domain topology. When used in this mode, we frequently refer to the protocol as Interior BGP (IBGP). IBGP can also be used to determine which router will serve as the connection point for specific external autonomous systems. The BGP protocol instance running on a router may provide intraautonomous system routing services, interautonomous system routing services, or both at the same time. In addition to its use as a routing protocol, we will also use IBGP as a tightly controlled source of traffic to force dialing of backup links in Chapter 5, Advanced Dial Backup, and propagate routing information through firewalls with minimal impact on security in Chapter 9, Connecting through Firewalls.

Pass-through AS routing occurs between two or more BGP peer routers that exchange traffic across an AS that does not run BGP. In a pass-through AS environment, the BGP traffic neither originates within the AS nor is destined for an end system within that AS. BGP must interact with whatever intradomain routing protocol is being used to transport IP traffic through that AS.

As with any routing protocol, BGP maintains routing tables, transmits routing updates, and bases routing decisions on routing metrics. However, unlike intradomain routing protocols, BGP is unable to assume that metrics received from different sources are comparable in any way, as each routing domain can and will define its own routing metrics. Consequently, the primary function of a BGP system is to exchange network-reachability information with other BGP systems. This information is used to construct a graph of AS connectivity from which routing loops can be pruned and with which AS-level policy decisions can be enforced. BGP is neither a distance-vector protocol nor a link-state protocol. Rather, it is a path-vector protocol in a class by itself.

Each BGP router maintains a routing table that lists all feasible paths to a particular network. For EBGP, each path will be in the form of an ordered list of ASs that must be traversed to reach the AS containing the destination network. Routers do not routinely refresh the BGP routing table. Instead, routing information received from peer routers is retained until either an incremental update is received or the peer is determined to be no longer reachable through an absence of hello-message exchanges.

BGP devices exchange routing information upon initial data exchange and after incremental updates. When a router first connects to the network, BGP routers exchange their entire BGP routing tables. Similarly, when the routing table changes, routers send the portion of their routing table that has changed. BGP routers do not send regularly scheduled routing updates, and BGP routing updates advertise only one path to any specific network address/prefix length combination.

BGP uses a single routing metric to determine the best path to a given network. This metric consists of an arbitrary unit number that specifies the degree of preference of a particular link. The BGP metric typically is assigned to each link by the network administrator. The value assigned to a link can be based on any number of criteria, including the number of ASs through which the path passes, the stability, the speed, the delay, and the cost.

Routers running the BGP protocol are called BGP speakers. Messages between BGP speakers are exchanged using a Transmission Control Protocol (TCP) connection.

Four BGP message types are defined: open message, update message, notification message, and keep-alive message.

The open message opens a BGP communications session between peers and is the first message sent by each side after the TCP connection is established. Open messages are confirmed with a keep-alive message and must be acknowledged before updates, notifications, and routine keep-alives can be exchanged.

An update message provides routing updates to other BGP speakers, allowing routers to construct a consistent view of the network topology. Updates are also sent using TCP to ensure reliable delivery. Update messages can add new routes to the routing table or withdraw routes that are no longer valid. Both actions may be included in a single update.

A notification message is sent when an error condition is detected. Notifications are used to close an active session and inform the other speakers of the reasons for closing the session.

The keep-alive message notifies BGP peers that a device is active. Keep-alives are sent often enough to keep the sessions from expiring and can serve a purpose similar to that of hello packets in OSPF and EIGRP. However, unlike typical intradomain protocols, the keep-alive packets for BGP are carried over the error-controlled channel provided by the TCP connection between each pair of BGP speakers.

The challenge with BGP is that it is designed foremost for stability and flexibility. Performance is a secondary consideration. As a result, the protocol has an incredible range of configuration and filtering options to allow routing decisions based on every consideration from type of service required to who is asking for service. Consequently, it is quite easy to make minor mistakes in configuration that prevent routing from working correctly. For example, one common mistake is subnetting a public IP address assignment and forgetting to include a summary route that exactly matches the BGP network statement.

BGP can sometimes seem downright recalcitrant since it has stability requirements that will cause it to refuse to route under conditions that would be considered perfectly normal for an intradomain routing protocol. For example, default interdomain peering can only be established between two routers on the same subnetwork. That is, the routers in the two different ASs must be physically attached and correctly configured before EBGP will even start. While this requirement can be overridden, doing so without a complete understanding of the consequences can lead to unstable routing.

Similarly, IBGP will not even attempt to establish a peer relationship unless the destination address of the peer is explicitly in the local router's routing table. A default route will not work even if it points in the correct direction. The key is to remember that BGP is designed to allow routers that do not really trust each other to communicate well enough to allow communications to occur. As a result, the protocol never assumes that unspecified parameters will default to compatible values. Critical parameters such as hello interval and dead time are exchanged as part of the open packet exchange and if the parameters are not set compatibly, the speakers will refuse to establish a peer relationship or exchange routes.

While BGP may seem unwieldy and inefficient, we need to remember that this is the protocol that allows the millions of systems on the Internet to communicate with one another regardless of what intradomain or interior gateway protocol is being used to route the networks that support either end system or any of the intervening transit networks.

ROUTED NETWORK DESIGN

A strong routing protocol is essential to building a high availability network. High availability in a world of low-reliability communications links mandates a network topology providing complete redundancy for all links. Achieving adequate redundancy without excessive complexity means using a structured design. A good design will provide a backup for every link and every network device between any two end systems. By cleanly separating the primary and backup paths, we gain a number of potential advantages.

The first advantage is that the network elements providing redundancy can be kept physically separated from the primary network elements, reducing the probability of common failure modes in physical services and environment.

The second advantage is that maintenance activities in one path do not affect most operations in the alternate path. That way, problems with software bugs, configuration errors, upgrades, or other activities can be carried out in one path while the other continues to support production traffic.

The third advantage is that with redundancy in the network, individual component reliability is no longer as crucial to network availability. This can have a net impact of reducing the cost of providing a given level of availability.

The last advantage is that load sharing between primary and backup paths may be possible, which can reduce costs or enhance performance under normal operating conditions. This can be particularly significant when approaching the capacity of high-cost links, as it may be more cost effective to add a third path rather than upgrade the existing paths to the next level of performance.

Figure 2-18 shows a structured, fully redundant network design combining bridging and routing for a large building or campus network. This is similar in concept to the small, switched LAN design in Figure 2-14, but has been expanded with a layer of routing functionality between the user access switches and the server switches. While only a single user and a single server are illustrated, the structure assumes large numbers of both in multiple locations, but all are assumed to be close enough to reach using LAN technologies.

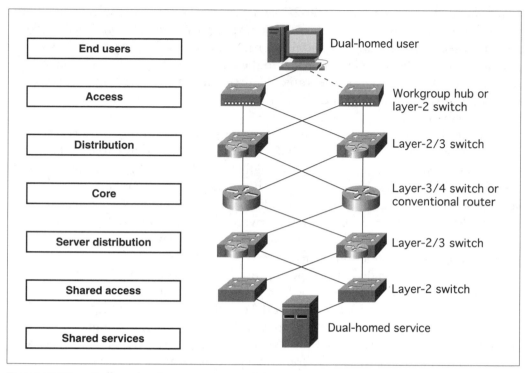

End users

Access

Distribution

Core

Server distribution

Shared access

Shared services

Dual-homed user

Workgroup hub or
layer-2 switch

Layer-2/3 switch

Layer-3/4 switch or
conventional router

Layer-2/3 switch

Layer-2 switch

Dual-homed service

FIGURE 2-18.   *Fully redundant campus topology*

Shared services and end users are topologically identical, and local services are often found on end user subnetworks to keep local traffic out of the core routers. We split them out here to more clearly show the alternate paths that are available for the primary communications path between client and server. High-performance services are also more likely to be on higher speed LANs in order to support large numbers of users.

Keep in mind that we are only showing a small fraction of the total campus network in Figure 2-18. Each pair of core layer-3/4 switches will typically support at least 10 pairs of distribution switches, depending on data rates, traffic levels, and performance requirements. Similarly, each pair of layer-2/3 switches at the distribution layer will support from 5 to 20 pairs of access switches (more for personal computer users, less for high performance servers). Finally, each access layer-2 switch supports a similar number of end systems. The bottom line is that a single pair of high-performance core switches may suffice for a campus network with several thousand users. Smaller sites may combine the distribution and access switches into a single combined level.

Remember to take the terms *layer-2/3 switch* and *layer-3/4 switch* with a grain of salt. From the viewpoint of the core, both are just a means of obtaining router functionality. For example, the layer-2/3 switches may be conventional switches with routers attached or routing modules installed. Similarly, *layer-3/4 switch* is a marketing term used to sell a router optimized for routing between local area networks, playing off the cachet currently attached to the buzzword "switch." The specific hardware used will depend on the traffic requirements, the protocol support requirements, the environment, the vendor preferences, and what is available at the best price when needed.

A speedy response to failures mandates a full-powered routing protocol, so we would usually use OSPF (or EIGRP if a Cisco-only core and distribution layers). When using OSPF, the campus would normally be configured as a single area but not area zero. That way, when the time comes to expand to include other sites (and consequently other OSPF areas), we can establish an independent backbone area zero dedicated to providing communications between all areas and would only need to modify the configuration of the routing in the core layer, leaving the distribution layer routing configuration untouched.

To handle an extended organization, we connect the individual campuses at the core layer. This may involve replacing or augmenting the core layer-3/4 switches with high performance conventional routers if the switches do not provide all the features we need to build our WAN. To provide physical diversity in the communications connecting geographically distributed sites, we would make sure that each pair of core routers connects to at least two different, independent remote sites. Depending on the distances involved and the anticipated traffic levels, we might see anywhere from a single low-speed link to each of two remote sites (one on each core router) to multiple links on each core router to provide direct routing for common high-density traffic flows. The important factor at the WAN level is that we build the connectivity so that the topology remains fully connected not only if a network device or link fails, but also if a service provider or an entire site fails (as would happen in a fire, an extended power outage, or another major disaster).

In a geographically large network, we would want to ensure that each site not only connects to at least two different sites, but also that those sites are at least 100 miles apart. In other words, we would work to not only provide resilience for loss of a site, but also for loss of an entire region. Sometimes even 100 miles is not enough to avoid susceptibility to a common disaster if the two sites share a common hazard. For example, there have been times when hundreds of miles of the Mississippi River basin have flooded. So we must use common sense in addition to applying rules of thumb when designing our network.

WRAP-UP

In designing high availability networks, we frequently depend on redundancy in the network topology so that link and component failures can be covered by other links and components. Redundancy can only provide continued service in the face of failure when the networking protocols can detect the failures and identify and use any remaining paths to keep the traffic flowing.

At the Link layer of the OSI reference model, we use source route bridging (for Token Ring networks) and transparent Spanning-Tree bridging (for Ethernet and related CSMA/CD networks) to link multiple LANs to provide more reliable local connectivity. The bridging function may also be called layer-2 switching.

At the Network layer of the OSI reference model, we call the protocols routing protocols and the devices that implement them routers. Some routers may be called layer-3 switches, layer-4 switches, or layer-3/4 switches. Because of the wide range of requirements for network designs, there are many routing protocols available. In the world of TCP/IP, the five most important routing protocols are RIPv2, OSPF, EIGRP, integrated IS-IS, and BGP. Each has its strengths and each suffers from significant weaknesses. A well-designed network will often use more than one, each being used where its strengths are most needed and each avoided where its weaknesses could interfere with stability, performance, or availability.

NOTES

1. Simpson, W. "PPP Link Quality Monitoring," *RFC 1989*. Daydreamer. August 1996.
2. *Cisco Internet Design Guide,* http://www.cisco.com/univercd/cc/td/doc/cisintwk/idg4. These materials have been reproduced by Addison-Wesley, Inc. with the permission of Cisco Systems, Inc. COPYRIGHT © 2000 CISCO SYSTEMS, INC. ALL RIGHTS RESERVED.

C H A P T E R   3

Multihomed Hosts

While the technology to implement a high availability network using a multiple-connected mesh of dedicated links is well-developed in modern routers and switches and their associated routing and bridging protocols, the same can not be said of the computers and other end systems that depend on the network. The typical end user or network server continues to use a single NIC to connect to the network. The higher the availability of the network infrastructure, the more likely that this single point of failure will become the weak link in the network design.

As the application increases in importance, the potential for single points of failure in normally reliable components such as LAN cables, hubs, switches, and NICs becomes increasingly unacceptable. This is particularly true when considering the server side of the application, as any failure that makes a server inaccessible will affect all of that server's clients. If the application is important enough, the server will need to be replicated, as the hardware and software running the application also are a potential single point of failure. However, for many applications, there is a middle ground where a single LAN attachment is not good enough, yet the application cannot justify server replication or redundant end systems. After all, very few users want to have two workstations on their desk.

As we can see from Figure 3-1, there are several critical single points of failure in a typical end system LAN connection. From top to bottom, these include the LAN access device or "hub" in the wiring closet, the specific port on that access device, the cable plant connecting the end system to the LAN access device (including building wiring, patch panels or outlets, patch cables at each end, and all associated connectors), and the network interface in the end system. If the LAN access device is not a dedicated port-per-user switch, we would also have additional single points of failure in the uplink from the user's LAN access device to the switch or other device that does provide the multiple connections to the rest of the LAN. Again, we need to consider the entire path making up the uplink, including any intervening singly connected

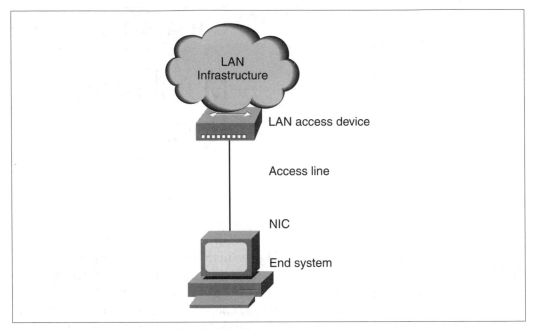

FIGURE 3-1. *Singly connected end system*

devices that make up the path, along with the switch or router that provides the multiple connections into the redundantly connected part of the network.

In this chapter, we will examine approaches that allow us to extend the multiply connected design of our high availability network all the way to the end systems on the network, effectively eliminating all single points of failure normally associated with network access. We will start by examining the impact of simply adding a second NIC to the end system. We will then look at techniques we can use to hide the fact that there are two NICs from external systems so that both appear to the outside world to have the same network address. We will conclude the chapter by addressing appropriate solutions for when the end system is providing a critical network service and we can no longer ignore the fact that the end system is also a single point of failure.

TWO NETWORK INTERFACES WITH INDEPENDENT ADDRESSES

The initial approach we might consider is simply to install a second network interface in the critical system, as in Figure 3-2. Indeed, many servers in the field already have multiple network interfaces installed to get around bandwidth limitations. That way, if a NIC died or a cable failure disrupted our normal communications path, we would still have network access through the second network interface. The problem

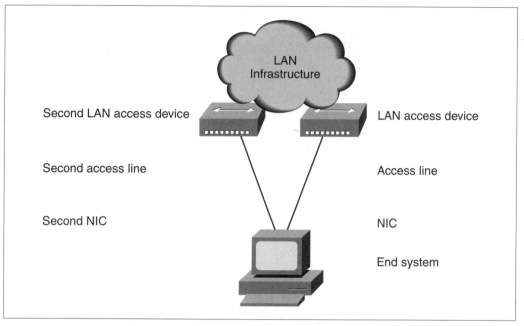

FIGURE 3-2. *Two network interfaces on one end system*

with this approach is that the ability of the second network link to fill in for a failed primary link will depend upon the network protocol architecture in use. In an OSI network, for example, both interfaces would share a common Network Service Access Point (NSAP) identifier, and communications would occur over whichever interface provided the optimal path for the specific sender and receiver. Other than the routers in the network, no other systems would even be aware of the topological details of how this end system was actually attached to the network.

In the world of TCP/IP, on the other hand, the end system would be a classic IP multihomed host and each interface would be assigned its own IP address. All other network devices would see the dual-attached end system as two independent and unrelated end systems. As a result, unless the applications could be programmed to understand that both addresses referred to the same end system, all access would be lost as soon as the IP address being used to address this end system became unavailable.

If the end system were an interactive client, this behavior might still be considered acceptable. This assumes the user could simply restart whatever applications were interrupted and use the remaining LAN connection to continue operations. It also assumes that the end system can detect the failed LAN connection and continue to use only the functional LAN connection, a potentially difficult assumption to satisfy. The difficulty of this task depends upon a number of factors, not the least of which are the networking capabilities of the operating system running on the end system. As we shall see, it also depends on how the other end system involved is attached to the network.

If the application uses domain names rather than IP addresses to identify the server, we could include both IP addresses in the DNS servers. But this assumes that the clients will automatically try the second address returned by a DNS lookup if the first IP address fails. Even in applications such as Web publishing, where the capabilities have been refined in support of load sharing needs and when hardware appliances are available to test each IP address assigned to a service and use only functioning addresses in response to DNS queries, there is the constant challenge of inappropriate behavior on the part of clients and intermediary DNS servers that do not properly honor DNS lifetime settings.

IMPACT OF NETWORK CONNECTION FAILURE

To understand the full impact of network connection failure, we must first look at connectivity variations. When a multihomed end system goes to send a packet, the destination will either be on the same subnetwork as one of the system's LAN interfaces or on a subnetwork that can be reached through a router directly accessible to the sending system. While the details of network connectivity will vary, there are generally only four cases that need to be considered. When a failure of any kind occurs, we need to consider whether the LAN interface associated with the failure is the LAN interface that would normally have been used to forward the packet to reach the destination and whether we are sending directly to the ultimate destination or sending indirectly through a router.

There are also two modes of LAN connection failure we need to consider: those in which the end system is aware that the LAN connection is down and those in which the end system believes that the LAN connection is still functional. This gives us a total of eight possible combinations, which are summarized in Table 3-1.

TABLE 3-1. *Impact of LAN Connection Failure Based on Route to Destination*

DESTINATION ROUTE	DETECTED FAILURE	UNDETECTED FAILURE
1—Same subnetwork as failed interface	Unreachable	Unreachable
2—Same subnetwork as functional interface	OK	OK
3—Indirectly routed through failed interface	Maybe	Unreachable
4—Indirectly routed through functional interface	OK	OK

The inability to reach any system on the same subnetwork as the failed interface is an implementation decision, not a fundamental flaw in the definition of IP. However, unlike many routers, including Cisco's, which will deactivate all routing entries for a failed interface from the routing tables to allow learning alternate routes to the same subnetworks, virtually all host IP implementations continue to associate the failed interface with the configured subnetworks, making it impossible to reach them. The safest way to avoid this limitation is to configure the network so that all server end systems are on different physical networks than any client end systems. That way, a destination will never be unreachable because the LAN interface connected to its subnetwork is down. On the other hand, it also means that every packet must be processed by a router (or a layer-3 switch).

Once we eliminate the first two rows of the table, we can attack row three. For maximum availability, we need to do two things: we need to convert the "Maybe" in row three to an "OK" and we need to ensure that any LAN connectivity failure will be detected so we can stay out of the "Unreachable" column.

The former depends upon the IP implementation on the end system. On many computers, all we need to do is configure two default gateways. As long as there is a default gateway defined that can be reached through whichever LAN interface is still functional, we will have connectivity. Just be aware that there are some TCP/IP protocol stack implementations that can be configured only with a single default gateway and others that refuse to change their default gateway selection once one of the configured entries has been used successfully. And as already mentioned, some IP implementations do not even check if an interface is functional before sending traffic through it.

Reliably detecting LAN connectivity failure is not as easy. The problem is that we cannot depend on the network interface to report failure. After all, the failure may not be in our network interface or the link to which it attaches but within the LAN infrastructure or in the connectivity between the LAN infrastructure and the router connecting us with the rest of the organization. Detecting link failure requires us to determine whether we can communicate with the appropriate default gateway (router) through that interface. This is a normal function of the exchange of hello packets in a routing protocol, which leads us to the conclusion that the best way to detect whether a network interface can function as a path to outside destinations is to run a routing protocol through the interface between our system and whomever we need to communicate with on the attached LAN.

RIP is commonly used for this purpose, even if more sophisticated routing protocols are used between routers for lower overhead, faster convergence, and higher stability. In the context of an end system simply determining the availability of routers on a LAN, it is hard to surpass the simplicity of RIP. When using RIP for this purpose, the end systems frequently will listen for RIP broadcasts from routers and not send any broadcasts of their own. After all, as an end system, the only networks they know how to reach are the networks they are on, and we certainly do not want them forwarding packets from one network to another. This mode of operation is called *passive RIP*.

As long as our routers use RIP to advertise only a default route for passive RIP end systems, there is no problem using RIPv1, despite its lack of support for variable length subnetwork masks (VLSM). However, unless the use of RIPv1 is essential due to inadequate support of RIPv2 on systems that must be supported, we should use RIPv2 whenever possible to facilitate support of active routing by multi-homed systems.

Passive RIP is frequently used to avoid the limitations of assigning a default gateway when configuring the end system, as it automatically allows the end system to detect what routers are available on the LAN to reach outside destinations, and possibly even to pick the best router available for any particular destination. For the sake of efficiency and security, particularly when using RIPv1, which does not support authentication or VLSM, the routers are normally configured to ignore the contents of incoming RIP packets. Similarly, unless there are significant variations in connectivity between routers on the LAN, it is usually enough to just advertise the default route.

The configurations on the end system will depend on the end system operating system and version. On the router side of the LAN, Listing 3-1 is one possible configuration for a Cisco router to provide RIPv1 broadcasts for local end systems. In this example, RIP is used only to advertise availability of a default gateway to end systems on the LAN attached to *interface Ethernet0*. The routing protocol used for production traffic in this example is OSPF, but any other routing protocol except RIP could have been used.

```
version 11.0
!
interface Ethernet0
 description LAN connection to local systems
 ip address 10.10.0.1 255.255.0.0
!
interface Serial0
 description WAN connection to everyone else
 ip address 10.1.2.1 255.255.255.252
!
router ospf 154
! Statements to control the "real" routing go here
!
router rip
! Generate and control RIP broadcasts to local users
```

(continued)

```
  redistribute static
  passive-interface Serial0
  network 10.0.0.0
  distribute-list 2 out Ethernet0
  distribute-list 1 in Ethernet0
  !
ip route 0.0.0.0 0.0.0.0 Serial0
access-list 1 deny any
access-list 2 permit 0.0.0.0
  !
end
```

LISTING 3-1.   *Passive RIP configuration using RIPv1*

In Listing 3-1 the line *router rip* enables the RIP protocol on the router. The lines that follow the *router rip* statement then define how RIP should be configured. *Redistribute static* tells RIP to include all static routes defined in its routing updates. In this case, there is only one static route defining a default route, *ip route 0.0.0.0 0.0.0.0 Serial0*. As long as the serial interface is up, this router will have a default route to advertise. There is no problem if other static routes were needed for other purposes, because we need to filter all extraneous routes from the RIP advertisements regardless.

The next line, *passive-interface Serial0,* tells RIP not to broadcast advertisements out the serial interface where they would waste bandwidth. We need to do this because the following line, *network 10.0.0.0,* tells RIP that all interfaces that have addresses assigned in the class A network 10.0.0.0 should have RIP routing enabled on them. It also tells RIP to include the subnetworks defined by those interfaces in the RIP routing tables to be advertised, which we do not want (nor would they be useful, as RIPv1 cannot handle VLSM).

In this example, the inability to advertise subnetwork masks correctly is moot, as we tell RIP to include only the default route in advertisements broadcast out the Ethernet0 interface with the line *distribute-list 2 out Ethernet0.* This line in turn refers to the filter defined by access-list 2. On Cisco routers, every access list is interpreted as if there were a deny everything line added at the end. So the single line *access-list 2 permit 0.0.0.0* says that only routing entries that refer to the address 0.0.0.0 (the default route) should be included in routing updates.

The final RIP configuration line, *distribute-list 1 in Ethernet0,* is not essential, but highly recommended. This line tells RIP to apply the filter defined by access list number 1, *access-list 1 deny any,* to any routing advertisements received on the Ethernet0 interface. Since access list 1 says to deny everything, we will ignore any RIP advertisements on the LAN, preventing any misconfigured (or malicious) systems on the LAN from corrupting our production routing tables. Unlike *access-list* filters applied to live traffic, there is very little CPU overhead associated with applying filters to routing advertisements.

Listing 3-2 is a configuration that provides identical functionality except that it uses RIPv2 rather than RIPv1. The only change is the addition of the line *version 2* under *router RIP,* which tells RIP to use version 2 of the protocol rather than version 1. Unlike the previous example, this example will not run under IOS 11.0 because the earliest general distribution IOS release with RIPv2 capability is IOS 11.2.

If there were other routers on the same LAN with significantly different connectivity, we might want to inform passive RIP end systems of all routes rather than simply confirming the existence of this router. In that case, the default route definition and static redistribution could have been replaced with the RIP configuration in Listing 3-3.

```
version 11.2
!
interface Ethernet0
 description LAN connection to local systems
 ip address 10.10.0.1 255.255.0.0
!
interface Serial0
 description WAN connection to everyone else
 ip address 10.1.2.1 255.255.255.252
!
router ospf 154
! Statements to control the "real" routing go here
!
router rip
! Generate and control RIPv2 multicasts to local users
 version 2
 redistribute static
 passive-interface Serial0
 network 10.0.0.0
 distribute-list 2 out Ethernet0
 distribute-list 1 in Ethernet0
!
ip route 0.0.0.0 0.0.0.0 Serial0
access-list 1 deny any
access-list 2 permit 0.0.0.0
!
end
```

LISTING 3-2. *Passive RIP configuration using RIPv2*

```
version 11.2
!
router rip
 network 10.0.0.0
 version 2
 redistribute ospf 154 metric 1
 distribute-list 1 in Ethernet0
 passive-interface Serial0
!
end
```

LISTING 3-3. *RIP redistribution of dynamic routes from OSPF*

In this case, we do not limit the routes advertised in LAN RIP broadcasts and instead import the routes to redistribute from the "real" interior gateway protocol, OSPF. Because we are merely redistributing routes into RIP rather than using RIP as the network routing protocol, there is no routing benefit to redistributing full routes because all routing metrics are lost in the redistribution process. If routing efficiency depends on the end systems picking specific routers for specific destinations, the configuration becomes much more complex.

Generally, if the network topology is complex enough to make the choice of gateway by the end system significant, it is too complex to route efficiently with any version of RIP, making it impractical to simply use RIP as the overall network routing protocol. On the other hand, routing protocols suitable for a complex network are not suitable for end systems. EIGRP is Cisco-proprietary and generally unavailable except on Cisco platforms. OSPF is computationally intensive and the number of OSPF peers safely supportable on any single router is limited, making it a poor choice if more than a few dozen end systems need the capability.

Route maps can be used to improve routing efficiently by translating the key network routing protocol metrics in our environment into appropriate "hop counts" in the RIP advertisements. For example, if we wanted any destinations not in our OSPF routing domain to be least desired, destinations on the 16-bit subnetworks 10.5.0.0, 10.6.0.0, and 10.7.0.0 to be most preferred, and all other destinations to be in between, we could add the route map in Listing 3-4 to our configuration (and similar corresponding route maps to all other routers serving these end systems).

Cisco uses the concept of route maps to control route distribution between routing protocols. With this example, when redistributing routes learned by OSPF into RIP, RIP will apply *route-map 5* to each route to determine how it should be imported. Route maps are applied in ascending order of weight, so a route being considered for import will be checked first to see if it matches any condition under *route-map 5 permit 20*. Routes that match all *match* clauses under this route-map weight

```
version 11.2
.!
router rip
 version 2
 timers basic 5 15 15 50
 redistribute ospf 154 route-map 5
 network 10.0.0.0
 distribute-list 99 in Ethernet0
 !
route-map 5 permit 20
 match route-type external
 set metric 10
 !
route-map 5 permit 30
 match ip address 1
 set metric 1
 !
route-map 5 permit 40
 match ip address 2
 set metric 5
 !
access-list 1 permit 10.5.0.0 0.0.255.255
access-list 1 permit 10.6.0.0 0.0.255.255
access-list 1 permit 10.7.0.0 0.0.255.255
access-list 2 permit any
access-list 99 deny any
 !
end
```

LISTING 3-4. *Controlling redistributed routes using route maps*

would be processed as specified by the route map. This map checks if the route is OSPF-type external in the line *match route-type external*. If it is, the redistribution is permitted and the *set metric 10* clause causes RIP to advertise it with a metric of 10 (remember that 16 is infinity in RIP). Once a route matches a route map, no further checking is performed.

The second route map, with weight 30, checks for routes to addresses specified in access list 1. Be careful with Cisco access lists, as they use wild card masks. This can be confusing if you are used to working with IP subnetwork masks. Matches here get their RIP metric set to 1. The third route-map segment compares the address to access-list 2, which will match anything. So any routes that do not satisfy any of the prior route-map segments will still be distributed by RIP but with their metric set to 5.

In addition to the route maps for setting metrics on the RIP advertisements, we made an unrelated modification to the RIP timers. By setting the update interval to 5 seconds, we can adjust RIP on the end system to declare the LAN interface to be down any time we do not receive an update for 15 seconds, a much more reasonable time-out than the default. This, of course, assumes that the timers on the RIP implementation are adjustable. However, even if some end systems are not adjustable, setting the update frequency short will not hurt. It will just waste bandwidth on the LAN if none of the end systems adjust their timers to take advantage of it.

If the size of RIP update packets is small (as would be the case if only advertising a default route), we could shrink the update interval to the minimum, which on Cisco routers is 1 second. Since a heavily loaded router may be a few seconds slow, we might want to be less aggressive adjusting the end systems and wait about 5 seconds before declaring the link to be down rather than using the rule of thumb time-out of three times the update interval.

By implementing a routing protocol, even one as simplistic as RIP, an end system can quickly detect loss of network connectivity and automatically start using its remaining network interface(s) to communicate with all systems except those on the failed LAN segment. The only time a LAN failure is not detected is when it only affects transmissions from the end system without affecting the ability of the end system to receive RIP broadcasts. If this was considered an unacceptable risk, a routing protocol that tests for bidirectional exchange of hello packets, such as OSPF or BGP, would need to be used. As we shall see in the next section, there are other, far more significant shortcomings to this approach when used on servers rather than clients.

APPLICATION RECOVERY REQUIREMENTS

While adding a simple routing protocol to the two interfaces helps the end system send packets to external systems, it suffers from two critical weaknesses. First of all, as we already saw, it typically does nothing to help the end system reach other end systems on the same IP subnetwork as the disconnected interface, even if the LAN is otherwise fully functional. This is a fundamental limitation of the IP protocol, as all systems on the same physical network (as determined by the source and destination IP addresses and the source subnetwork mask) are assumed to be directly reachable, and most network implementations will assume that if the LAN is down, all addresses in the same subnetwork are unreachable. As discussed earlier, this first weakness can be overcome by configuring clients and servers on separate subnetworks so that they must always communicate through a router (or layer-3 switch), even if both are connected to the same physical LAN. This workaround will increase our hardware costs and will impact high-performance applications due to the added delay on every packet exchange.

The second weakness is not as easily resolved. Even if a particular network route is no longer valid, the systems we are communicating with have no way to determine that they should shift to the network address associated with a remaining functional interface (assuming that when the connection was established, it was with the IP address of the network interface that was no longer useable). The basic problem is that with our two addresses, we look like two independent systems and it is up to the application to recognize that the two addresses are equivalent. As a general rule, applications today do not have that degree of intelligence.

At best, the application may use some form of directory services, such as DNS, to provide a name-to-address mapping. This allows us to use DNS load sharing software or a load sharing appliance to associate a still functional address with the name used to access us. However, the original connection will still be lost and a new connection will need to be established. Even then, it assumes that the remote client and all DNS servers between the remote client and our system respect DNS address lifetimes, rather than use cached results from previous lookups.

On the other hand, if the end system is the client rather than the server, so that the communications are initiated from us rather than to us, this address memory is not a problem because we will automatically use the correct address when establishing the new connection through the remaining interface. As long as the application can automatically reestablish communications, the solution may be satisfactory. For example, if the application is Web browsing, the page loading at the time of the failure will freeze, but hitting the Reload button will transparently establish a new connection using the remaining interface's IP address and thus successfully load the page.

Clearly the acceptability of this solution will depend on the application and on the delays involved and the quantity of work lost by terminating and restarting the specific transaction or application. If the typical transaction takes several minutes to perform, the delay due to a restart becomes much more significant. More important, if the application could be left in a potentially inconsistent state (such as might occur in a database update if both ends were not permitted to completely time out), the results of continuing could be catastrophic and we should not consider this approach.

If the end system is a server that is contacted by client systems rather than a client which initiates all connections, this is generally not a useful approach unless the client application can be implemented to understand that the server has multiple addresses and each should be tried in turn. Realistically, if the client application is this intelligent, it would probably be able to handle two independent servers, which is a far superior, albeit more costly, approach to improving server availability.

TWO NETWORK INTERFACES WITH ONE IP ADDRESS

Clearly, we would prefer the end system be known to other end systems by a single network address rather than by one address for each network connection. This challenge can be attacked either at the LAN interface or through network routing. Good solutions exist for both approaches.

SMART NETWORK INTERFACE CARDS

LAN hardware vendors have recognized this weakness for a long time and many provide proprietary solutions. The basic scheme uses two interface cards on the end system and customized drivers so that the two (or more) NICs appear to the end system operating system as well as to the outside world as a single network interface. While normally targeted at load sharing, most vendors' implementations provide transparent link backup as well. Often referred to as "port trunking," and properly referred to as "link aggregation," each vendor markets the capability under their own trademark (3Com Dynamic Access, Bay Multi-Link Trunking, Cabletron SmartTrunk, Cisco Fast EtherChannel, and so on). We will look at two popular vendor solutions, one from Intel and the other from 3Com.

Intel introduced their Adapter Fault Tolerance (AFT) feature in 1996. Two or more Intel PRO/100 or PRO/1000 server adapters are installed in the server and AFT is configured in the driver. If there are any problems with a cable, NIC, switch port, or hub port along the primary link, the secondary link takes over. The operating system driver detects link problems by exchanging MAC-level probe frames between the adapters. The frequency of probe frames and the number of missed frames before declaring a link to be down are adjustable. Default values lead to a switch over from the primary to the backup link in approximately 30 seconds, but systems can be configured so that the switch over can occur within 2 to 3 seconds.

3Com calls their solution Dynamic Access. Like the Intel AFT feature, 3Com's provides load balancing and the ability to combine up to eight NICs in a single "virtual NIC" definition. The traffic distribution works independently for inbound and outbound traffic.

A hashing algorithm distributes traffic sent by the server across the grouped NICs. As each client connects to the server, the algorithm determines which NIC the client will communicate with for the duration of that connection. One NIC in the group is designated the primary, while the other NICs in the group are designated secondary. If a cable were disconnected from one of the secondary NICs, the load-balancing software reruns the hashing algorithm without the failed NIC, and clients are reassigned to the remaining NICs.

If the primary NIC connection fails, the load-balancing software allows one of the secondary NICs to assume the role of the primary, including its MAC address and any configured multicast groups. Then, a hashing algorithm is run to redistribute the converted secondary's original clients to functional group members.

Traffic from client to server (receive traffic) is distributed by using a round-robin assignment of client connection requests to server NICs in the group. Each new connection between the server and client is assigned to a new server NIC within the group by means of a connection-based algorithm with each server NIC used on a rotating basis. If a single client has multiple connections to the server, inbound traffic from each connection will shift in a round-robin fashion to the next NIC in the load-balancing group.

If one of the connections fails, the receive load-balancing function communicates with the clients to cause them to direct their transmit traffic (the server's receive traffic) to an alternate NIC. While this temporarily disrupts load balancing, it does keep the network traffic flowing despite link failure.

There are two key weaknesses to all these approaches. The first weakness is temporary: all vendor-specific solutions are proprietary. Depending on the solution chosen, this could lock in a single vendor for all LAN interfaces that need to cooperate. Being dependent on a specific vendor also limits the applicability of the solution to only those operating systems (and only the specific versions of those operating systems) that the vendor chooses to support, which may not include those supported by all required applications. This issue will decline in importance as products implementing the IEEE 802.3ad link-aggregation standard become widely available.

The second critical weakness is more fundamental in nature. Link aggregation approaches only protect against faults in the link being aggregated. That is, the protection is limited to the network interface on the end system, the cable plant, and the port on the hub, or the switch servicing the end system. Connectivity problems that do not cause the LAN interface on the end system to lose communications with the hub (such as failure of the LAN interface on the router leading to the outside world) are not detected and therefore would continue to disrupt communications. Full protection requires all links in the LAN to be aggregated.

Because these solutions all work at the Data Link layer of the OSI reference model, their protection is limited to failures that are isolated to individual LAN access cables, ports, and interfaces. Any mode of failure that takes down the entire LAN would be fatal. Many solutions on the market are even more restrictive and require that all physical cables in any one aggregate link terminate on the same concentrator or switch, leaving that box as a single point of failure as well.

On the other hand, unlike the Network layer approaches we will look at next, these Data Link layer approaches provide protection for locally connected systems, minimizing the disruption of common LAN failures and allowing high performance client-server connections with no intervening routers adding delay. They are also an excellent way to get more bandwidth in a LAN connection without moving up to the next level of speed technology, an option that is not always available due to the installed cable plant. Other than financial considerations, there is also nothing preventing us from implementing both approaches.

ANATOMY OF A NOVELL SERVER

A Network layer solution to this challenge has been implemented in the world of IPX by Novell servers since the early days of personal computers. Those of you who have been exposed to Novell server configuration may have wondered why an IPX network number is required not only for each LAN interface, but also for the server itself. The reason for the extra IPX network address is the Novell solution to the problem of servicing multiple LAN connections with a single address.

In Figure 3-3, we look inside a Novell NetWare server and its network interfaces and see that logically a Novell server is not just a NetWare server, but also an IPX router. By hiding the server behind a router, all NetWare clients refer to the server by its one unique address and connect by sending packets to the router that provides the best path to the server. For local users, this is always going to be the router built into the server. While originally intended to allow a single server to service multiple LANs, it also provides the transparency of access for external users that we have been seeking.

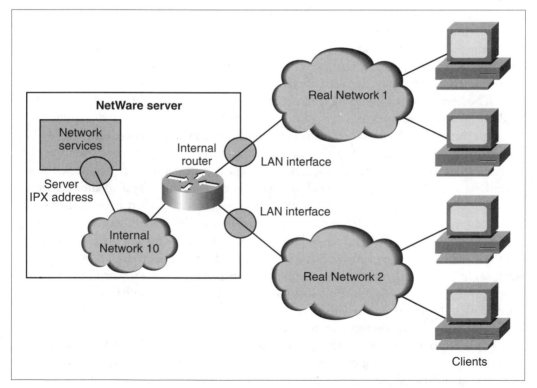

FIGURE 3-3. *Logical structure of a Novell NetWare IPX server*

We can take an equivalent approach with IP by defining a loopback port to provide a network address that is not on any existing subnetwork and by running a routing protocol on the host end system to advertise that address to the real routers on the network. Whereas before the routers were configured to ignore the contents of any routing packets received from end systems, now they need to accept those advertisements and distribute them throughout the network. Clearly, care must be taken when implementing this approach to protect the network from malicious end systems, either by running a routing protocol that includes authentication, or by filtering the routing packets at the router so that only acceptable information is processed.

Care must also be taken to ensure that the end system is not asked to carry transit traffic. While it may be possible to ensure this simply by proper configuration of the routing protocol on the end system, security again dictates that the routing infrastructure be configured to enforce the restriction.

As is the case with a Novell server, this approach typically will not work for communications to devices that are on the attached LAN that failed. The problem for local clients is that while the local client has no problems sending packets to the server through any routers on the LAN, since it is routing toward the internal network number, the reverse may not be possible. If the server does not detect that the LAN interface is down (and on some TCP/IP implementations, even if it *does* detect that the LAN interface is down), the server will attempt to send any responses to the client out the interface that is identified as the LAN that the client is on.

The behavior of IP sending a packet to an IP address identified as being on a directly attached subnetwork, which is to assume that the packet can be delivered through the attached interface and any available alternate routes are ignored, will be a constant challenge for us. In this case, it is also the reason it is not sufficient to turn on a routing protocol on the end system and expect operations to continue without defining an address on a subnetwork not associated with any physical subnetwork.

For clients that are on any subnetworks other than the failed LAN, communications will continue unaffected by the failure other than a brief pause in communications while the failure is detected and revised routes are propagated. Depending on the sensitivity of the routing protocol, this could be a long enough gap to be noticeable or it could even be long enough to cause connections to drop. For example, the generic UNIX example using *routed* to implement the RIP routing protocol with default parameter values can require 3 to 4 minutes before a link is declared down and alternate routing takes over.

This approach is not as effective on end systems that are clients because the source address used during connection setup will still be that of the interface rather than the loopback address. As a result, behavior for end systems that initiate the communications session will be identical to the scenario already discussed about two interfaces with two independent IP addresses.

TABLE 3-2. *Impact of Various Classes of Failure*

INITIATOR	CLIENT LOCATION	CONNECTION ORIENTATION	IMPACT OF FAILURE
Client	Local LAN	Continuous	Communications lost until LAN operation is restored
Client	Local LAN	Transaction	Communications lost until LAN operation is restored
Client	Routed	Continuous	Transparent fallback to the working LAN with no impact other than delay during switch over
Client	Routed	Transaction	Transparent fallback to the working LAN with no impact other than delay during switch over
Server	Local LAN	Continuous	Communications lost until LAN operation is restored
Server	Local LAN	Transaction	Communications lost until LAN operation is restored
Server	Routed	Continuous	Connection broken; reconnect successful using working LAN link
Server	Routed	Transaction	Transactions in progress lost; transparent fallback to working LAN for subsequent transactions

The behavior can be seen by considering the various modes of possible application use and network failure. There are actually only three critical factors that are material: first, either the dual homed system or the external end system initiates the exchange; second, either the external end system is on one of the access subnetworks or it is on a subnetwork not directly connected to the dual homed system; and third, either the application is connection-oriented or it is connectionless. We do not need to consider the case in which the access link that fails is not on the preferred route to the external end system, because failure of a link not being used for communications has no impact on the communications. That leaves us with eight possible combinations, and the impact of each is summarized in Table 3-2.

CONFIGURATION EXAMPLE: GENERIC UNIX USING *ROUTED*

This example is intended more for illustration than for practical application. While it works, it is slow to react to network changes and lacks support of flexible subnetwork assignments. It is included because it can be easily configured on any workstation or server with a TCP/IP protocol stack that supports IP forwarding, the ability to define multiple loopback ports (or alias multiple IP addresses on a single loopback port), and the Berkeley *routed* program. In other words, it will work on virtually any

UNIX platform released in the past 20 years, including look-alikes such as Linux, as well as many non-UNIX platforms.

It should be noted that the performance limitations associated with this example are due to the minimal *routed* implementation of RIPv1 capabilities assumed rather than to limitations in the platform or approach. After we examine this simple implementation, we will look at a practical implementation using OSPF for the end system routing protocol that has been tuned to respond much more quickly to network problems.

The hardware configuration in Figure 3-4 is used for this example. Since many versions of *routed* only implement support for basic version 1 RIP, all subnetworks of an IP network class must use the same subnetwork mask. We get around this limitation by assigning all 16-bit prefix LAN subnetworks from the private class A network 10.0.0.0 and by using an address from the private class C network 192.168.1.1 for the server global address.

When implementing any of these designs, we need to make sure that the loopback address used for global addressing (192.168.1.1 in this example) is defined as an

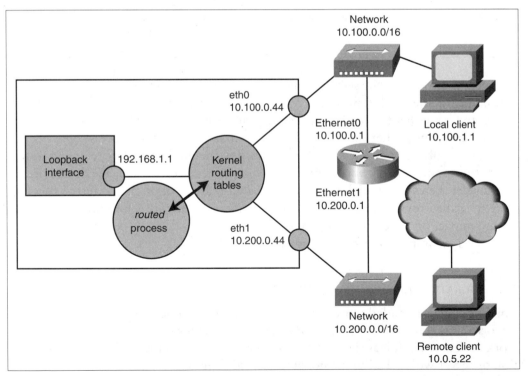

FIGURE 3-4. *Dual homed server with a single IP address*

addition to the standard loopback address of 127.0.0.1 rather than as a replacement. Many applications and services depend on the use of the hard configured address of 127.0.0.1 to signify the local system. Although the specific command required to install a network interface will vary from system to system, it will typically use some form of the *ifconfig* command, as in Listing 3-5.

```
root# ifconfig lo:0 inet 192.168.1.1 netmask 255.255.255.255
```

LISTING 3-5. *Typical* ifconfig *command to add an arbitrary loopback port*

Use the *ifconfig* command with no parameters to determine what loopback interfaces are already defined on the system. For example, in many Linux distributions, the loopback port is called *lo*, and additional IP addresses are assigned using aliases that are named *lo:0, lo:1, lo:2,* and so on.

The *routed* daemon will normally ignore loopback addresses because they traditionally are only significant to the local system. We get around this by defining a static route to the loopback address so that *routed* has something it considers worth advertising. Most implementations of *routed* use the file */etc/gateways* to define local configuration. So, we need to add the line in Listing 3-6 to the *gateways* file.

```
net 192.168.1.1 gateway 127.0.0.1 metric 1 active
```

LISTING 3-6. *UNIX* /etc/gateways *added line for dual homing with RIP*

This line serves two purposes. First, it instructs *routed* to insert a path in the kernel routing table to forward incoming packets addressed to our "single" IP address 192.168.1.1 to the real loopback port. Second, because the route installed looks to *routed* like a path to an external network, it will include the network 192.168.1.0 in RIP broadcasts it generates on the LAN interfaces. Note that we need this route in addition to defining a loopback port with the same address. Otherwise, when a packet comes in addressed to 192.168.1.1, it will be forwarded to the loopback port where it will be discarded because the loopback port does not recognize the address.

So now that the end system is configured to advertise its internal address, we can configure the routers on the real LANs to accept those advertisements and make the global address reachable from everywhere in the network. To keep this configuration simple, we will use just a single router with two Ethernet interfaces. In a real world environment, we would probably want at least two routers to provide redundancy in that arena. While the router configuration excerpt in Listing 3-7 looks very similar to those already discussed when configuring for multihomed systems identified by their LAN IP addresses, there are two critical changes.

```
version 11.0
!
interface Ethernet0
description Primary LAN for servers
 ip address 10.100.0.1 255.255.0.0
!
interface Ethernet1
description Second LAN for server access redundancy
 ip address 10.200.0.1 255.255.0.0
!
! Statements to define links to other networks & routers
!
router ospf 154
 redistribute rip metric 12 subnets route-map rip2ospf
! Statements to control the "real" routing go here.
! Could use EIGRP or other routing protocol instead—
! Just change the metric defined for RIP routes to match.
!
router rip
 redistribute static
 passive-interface Serial0
 network 10.0.0.0
 distribute-list 2 out Ethernet0
!
ip route 0.0.0.0 0.0.0.0 Serial0
access-list 2 permit 0.0.0.0 0.0.0.0
access-list 3 permit 192.168.1.0 0.0.0.255
!
route-map rip2ospf permit 25
 match ip address 3
!
end
```

LISTING 3-7. *Dual homed server support using RIP*

First, the access lists regulating the RIP router process listening to the LANs must
be opened up to accept advertisements from all dual homed servers that are to be supported. Second, the global IP address learned through RIP from the dual homed server
must be redistributed into the real routing protocol so that external systems will know
how to reach the server. Access-list 3 prevents OSPF (or whatever routing protocol is
being used between routers) from advertising any addresses learned from RIP other
than the one for the logical address of the server we wish to advertise.

CONFIGURATION EXAMPLE: PRACTICAL LINUX SERVER USING *GATED*

The simple *routed* implementation described in the previous section is good for developing an understanding of the theoretical approach. But the potential for delays of up to 4 minutes before recovering from a simple network failure, combined with the wastefulness of fixed subnetwork masks, make it impractical for production applications. Good responsiveness can be attained by installing a routing daemon that supports RIPv2 and provides the ability to adjust the timers to allow faster recovery. Response to failure within 5 seconds can be achieved easily with RIPv2 using an update interval of one second, an invalid interval of 4 seconds, and no holddown.

Unfortunately, the support of TCP/IP and routing protocols in particular varies widely across the spectrum of all server operating systems from Windows to mainframes, as well as between versions of the same operating system and various vendors' UNIX releases. Despite the variations, it is still instructive to look at what can be done in a specific operating environment to make this approach much more responsive. Here we will look at a near-production quality example and in the process review the tradeoffs made in the design. (A "full production quality" design would use multiple routers, which would only detract from the discussion at this point.)

First we replace the simplistic *routed* routing daemon with a routing daemon that understands modern, high performance routing protocols. This allows us to tune the network to recover from failure in seconds rather than minutes. In this example we use Linux and the publicly available *GateD* version 3.5 (www.gated.merit.edu) so that we can use OSPF rather than RIP as the routing protocol between the real routers and the dual homed systems. We use OSPF rather than RIPv2 to detect one-way faults. Unlike RIP and RIPv2, OSPF hello exchanges include acknowledgment of receipt of hello multicast packets from all other OSPF neighbors on that network segment. Consequently, a failure that allowed RIP broadcasts to be sent but not received would be detected rather than creating a black hole.

The Linux side of the configuration is very similar to the simple configuration already discussed. In this configuration, the same loopback address is assigned. The primary difference is that *GateD* gets its configuration from the file */etc/gated.conf* rather than */etc/gateways* and uses different syntax and keywords, as can be seen in Listing 3-8.

The OSPF timers on the LAN segments are modified to reduce the time required to detect LAN link failure and change over to alternate routes. These should be adjusted to match the LAN bandwidth and processing power available. Just make sure that the same settings are used on all systems on the LAN. This can sometimes be tricky as none of the software writers seem to like the parameter names used in RFC 2328 where OSPF is defined, so they all make up their own.

```
rip no { } ;
ospf yes {
   area 123 {
       interface all {
           enable ;
           retransmitinterval 2 ;
           transitdelay 1 ;
           hellointerval 3 ;
           routerdeadinterval 10 ;
           } ;
       stubhosts {
           192.168.1.1 cost 5 ;
           } ;
       } ;
   } ;
```

LISTING 3-8. GateD *configuration for Linux dual homed server using OSPF*

Regardless of how they are set, all routers (and other systems) running OSPF on the same physical network segment must use the same settings for OSPF on that segment or they will not exchange routes. On Cisco routers, they are adjusted as part of the interface configuration, as can be seen in the configuration excerpt in Listing 3-9. We also want to make certain that OSPF selects real routers, and not end systems, to be the Designated Router and Backup Designated Router for the LAN.

Using OSPF to speed recovery does introduce scaling challenges, as the dual homed systems must now maintain routing information for the entire OSPF area. This not only consumes significant CPU power on the systems, it also limits the number of "real" adjacencies the routers can handle before running out of power. In a small network with only a few dozen sites to support, we could make the WAN area zero and assign a unique area to each location supporting multihomed servers. The problem with this approach is that the entire OSPF routing architecture would need to be redesigned when the organization grew too large to tie all sites with dual homed servers to area zero.

Another way to achieve scaling for large networks would be to use EIGRP for the organization network rather than OSPF and then redistribute the local OSPF-learned routes into EIGRP. While not sufficient justification by itself, convenience in supporting dual homed hosts might be one more factor in favor of running a proprietary routing protocol. Alternatively, we could run BGP with our dual homed hosts and redistribute that into the real network routing.

The easiest solution, if we are willing to sacrifice the ability to detect the occasional one-way communications failure, is to run RIPv2 on the dual homed systems with the timers set to low values and redistribute the RIPv2 routes into OSPF. We just

```
version 11.0
!
interface Ethernet0
description Primary LAN for servers
 ip address 10.100.0.1 255.255.0.0
 ip ospf dead-interval 10
 ip ospf hello-interval 3
 ip ospf retransmit-interval 2
 ip ospf transmit-delay 1
!
interface Ethernet1
 description Second LAN for server access redundancy
 ip address 10.200.0.1 255.255.0.0
 ip ospf dead-interval 10
 ip ospf hello-interval 3
 ip ospf retransmit-interval 2
 ip ospf transmit-delay 1
!
! Statements to define links to other networks & routers
!
router ospf 1
! Statements to control the "real" routing go here.
 network 10.100.0.0 0.0.255.255 area 123
 network 10.200.0.0 0.0.255.255 area 123
!
```

LISTING 3-9.   *Router configuration for dual homed server using OSPF*

need to be careful to minimize the number of routes known to RIP in order to keep the RIP update overhead at a reasonable level.

Another approach is to take advantage of the ability of Cisco routers to run multiple OSPF processes and redistribute the dual homed host routes learned by the local OSPF process into the OSPF process used to support the organizational network. Running multiple instances of OSPF is not commonly done because of the CPU-intensive nature of the protocol; however, if the local topology is simple (and there is no reason it should not be), the CPU overhead is fairly minimal for a reasonable number of servers. Just be sure to keep an eye on the CPU utilization.

TWO SYSTEMS WITH ONE IP ADDRESS

Real redundancy requires more than just two LAN connections. It requires completely redundant systems so that when one system fails, there remains another to take its place. This presents multiple challenges for both the network and the application designer, for it is not enough for the network to provide transparent access to the system. It is also essential that both systems mirror the same data and that one can complete any transaction started on the other. The full requirements for synchronization tend to be very application-specific.

Consider a Web server. If the server is serving fixed information or even database lookups, there is no problem duplicating the information in a second server and instituting a policy of updating both at the same time. If the same Web server is modified to start executing electronic commerce transactions, however, the problem becomes immensely more difficult, as we now have to keep the data on both servers consistent despite failures in clients, communications, and either server.

Equally important to consider is the degree of physical diversity desired. At one end of the scale is a critical application server for a local workgroup, where we simply want to avoid loss of work in progress or interruptions in customer service. If the building loses power, however, nobody is going to care about the server as long as it stays up longer than their workstation. On the opposite end of the spectrum are the needs for disaster recovery and service distribution for global service providers, where some downtime might be acceptable as long as service can be quickly restored when a primary service center is unable to function. The goal might be not only disaster recovery, but also load sharing and performance optimization by providing service from the nearest servers.

Server Clusters

As we build more and more redundancy into the server system, from dual power supplies and fans to multiple network interfaces, the logical next step is to replace the single box server with a cluster of servers. This is also a popular way to provide additional server capacity without resorting to forklift upgrades. Because there are no useful applicable standards for clustering for high availability and any appropriate solution will critically depend upon the applications that must be supported and the conditions under which they must continue to be provided, there are many possible solutions from which to choose. While the detailed operating system and server software requirements to implement a computer cluster are beyond the scope of this book, we still need to look at how clusters work to see how they impact the network design.

There are three critical but separable logical components making up an application server: the network access, the application process, and the application datastore. Up to this point, we have looked at adding redundancy to the network access portion but have left ourselves with single points of failure in the computer and data storage functions. The various approaches to clustering differ in how they implement and control redundancy in the systems behind the network interface. The key to successful clustering is that while the application process may be easily duplicated, it is essential that the application data remain consistent at all times and for all accessing processes. Figure 3-5 shows how dual application processors share a common datastore. The variations between clustering approaches are in how they monitor the status of the various pieces, the level of dedication of each piece to specific processes, and how redundancy in the datastore is handled while maintaining data consistency.

Looking at the server processing piece, there are two general cases: passive backup server or parallel active servers. In the former architecture, the secondary server sits idle in the background monitoring the status of the primary server and serves only if failure of the primary server is detected. This approach is easy to implement, but costs can get high because the secondary server is not available to support normal processing demands. Novell Systems Fault Tolerant (SFT) Level III is a classic example of this approach.

With parallel active servers, both servers are used for processing application tasks with either able to back up the other should a failure occur. This mode of operation, which is also called "active/active," can reduce costs as the number of servers increases because there is no need to provide a dedicated secondary server to back up each active server. On the other hand, the startup costs are frequently higher because of the increased complexity of the software. There may also be performance issues if the servers remaining after a failure are unable to handle the load.

Parallel active server architectures can be further subdivided based on how they handle the sharing of the common application data. The three common approaches, in order of increasing complexity, are the "duplicate everything" approach, the "share nothing" approach, and the "share everything" approach.

In the duplicate everything approach, each server has its own datastore and active data is continuously copied from server to server. This is the approach used in products like Vinca, Marathon, and NSI Double Take. It provides an extra degree of safety because all data storage as well as all data processing components are

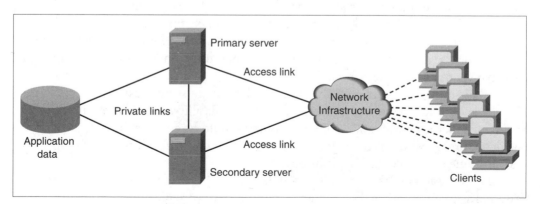

FIGURE 3-5. *Shared datastore server cluster*

duplicated. On the down side, there is high network and server overhead required to maintain the data mirrors on each server. There is also the potential for loss of transactions in progress at the time of failure, depending upon the latency in the data mirroring and whether intermediate results are maintained in local memory or in the shared data store. However, the biggest challenge with this approach is the challenge of maintaining mirror consistency any time both servers are shut down.

Extreme care must be taken to ensure that the server with the up-to-date disk image is the first to start. This is normally not a problem when servers are brought up or down for maintenance because then it is simply a matter of adhering to proper procedures. The problem arises when an uncontrolled outage, such as an extended power failure, occurs that affects both servers and the order of start up does not match the order of shut down. Again, there is no problem configuring UPS and servers to sequence the shutdown and restart correctly under normal conditions. The problem lies in preventing the situation where a server happens to be down when the power goes off but is "fixed" by the cycling of power. If the server with the out-of-date data store recovers first, it will resume processing with the out-of-date data. Upon completion of the first transaction, which may be as mundane as logging the failure of the other server, its datastore becomes the more current of the two. Consequently, when the second server comes on line it will determine that it has the out-of-date data and update its copy to match that of the active server, erasing all transactions which occurred while the other server was down.

While the probability of such a failure is low, the consequences are so severe that most organizations will disable the ability to automatically recover from double faults and require manual intervention. For example, only the primary server may be configured to "autostart" after a power failure, with the secondary server configured to wait for an operator to give it the command, just in case.

In the "share nothing" approach, both servers are connected to the same disks, but each server has exclusive control over its portion of the common data store. In the event of server failure, the secondary server will take over control of the primary server's disk space, locking the primary server out. This approach eliminates the challenge of maintaining consistency between disk images, and eliminates any backend network or server overhead keeping multiple copies up to date. This is the approach used by Microsoft Cluster Server.

While the software complexity is reduced, the data store must be carefully designed and implemented to provide adequate availability. At a minimum, disk mirroring or other fault tolerant RAID technology should be considered mandatory for the datastore. After all, if the data store associated with an application fails, no server can continue to service that application.

The suitability of this approach will depend upon the sensitivity to data store failure. Keep in mind that if drive mirroring is used to provide hardware redundancy with independent data stores, the data store effectively becomes a "duplicate everything" server system for the primary and secondary application servers, and the same care to guard against data inconsistency and incorrect updating of mirrors must be exercised.

Though the "share everything" approach is similar to the "share nothing" approach in that a common data store is used by both servers, the difference rests in the fact that in the former, all servers can access all the data all the time. Of course this isn't really true; the locking of data at the datastore level in "share nothing" is moved down to the smallest data unit consistent with the applications. While this approach has significant impact on the efficiency and scalability of clustered applications, particularly large databases, it really has negligible impact on the availability of the server. This approach, as exemplified in Oracle Parallel Server and Sun Cluster Architecture, is most common in the UNIX server arena where the motivation has been to maximize scalability as well as availability.

SERVER CLUSTER CONSIDERATIONS

When implementing server clusters for high availability, there are a number of networking issues which must be addressed. The network used inside the cluster to provide internal communications is normally dictated by the cluster solution chosen and is irrelevant. How the systems in the cluster attach to the access network can be critical. Of particular importance are any assumptions made in the design of the cluster about how to detect access network failures and provide a single system image to the outside world.

As might be expected, there are as many approaches to this problem as there are cluster solution software providers. Many solutions are environment specific; some work only with Windows using NetBIOS over IP, others work only with TCP/IP connections, some require matching proprietary client software, and others may work only with local clients on the same physical LAN. It is critical that the access network and the cluster software cooperate, or at least not interfere with each other.

Consider, for example, a server cluster for Windows SMB clients that uses a lead system that answers NetBIOS name requests with the IP address of the next available server in the cluster. The problem with this approach, of course, is its inability to transparently recover from loss of a server. The client must start over with a new name request to receive a new IP address.

A similar approach for generic IP connectivity is to use DNS and configure the server name with all IP addresses for each server. That way, each time a connection was made, the name server would return a different preferred address and traffic would get distributed. The problem with this approach is that from the viewpoint of the network, it is not a single system image, but a server farm. We will investigate server farm solutions and their challenges in the next section of this chapter.

Which approach is appropriate for any specific application will, of course, depend on the application. We also need to be careful that we continue to balance the failure risks so that we do not wind up with an ineffective solution such as a bulletproof server cluster accessed through a network with multiple single points of failure. The techniques described earlier in this chapter for providing continued network access remain a viable part of the solution, but extreme care must be taken that the approach used by the server cluster to detect failure and control the switch over of services is compatible with the approach used to provide continued network access in the face of network failure.

For example, many cluster solutions assume that the network interfaces on all members of the cluster are on the same LAN so that keep-alive frames can be sent at the MAC level without burdening any router on the LAN with keep-alive traffic. This is essential if two physical interfaces are to provide redundancy for serving the same IP address. If we were to provide redundancy for the primary server by routing through multiple interfaces to an advertised loopback address, loss of an interface could cause the secondary server to take over servicing that interface and leave us with both the primary and the secondary servers acting as the active server. While this might even work under stable conditions, a failure elsewhere in the network could result in packets originally routed to one server being delivered to the other midway through a transaction, with potentially disastrous results.

SERVER FARMS

Another popular approach is to move the challenge of making multiple servers look like a single system out of the server domain and into independent load-sharing capabilities that are inserted between the clients and the servers, as in Figure 3-6. This

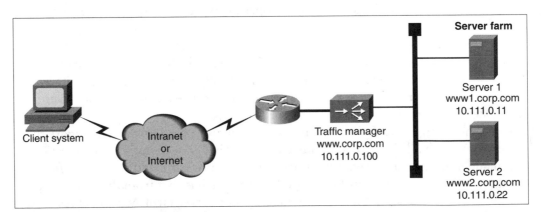

FIGURE 3-6. *Load sharing using a traffic management appliance*

approach has been driven by the needs of high capacity e-commerce Web sites that are too heavily loaded to run on any single server or cluster server.

Hardware vendors have stepped up to the challenge and a number of dedicated products are available commercially to provide load sharing of TCP/IP services. As might be expected, they tend to be targeted to the needs of e-commerce Web sites, but many of the techniques used are suitable for other applications as well. Typical Internet traffic management (ITM) products in this class include the Cisco LocalDirector, the F5 BIG/ip, and the RadWare Web Server Director (WSD).

These boxes sit between the access network and the individual servers and redirect incoming service requests to the optimum available server. This can include monitoring the number of open connections on each server, the traffic level to and from the server, and properties of the server, such as status and capacity. It is also essential that the traffic manager monitor transactions and remove any servers that stop responding from the ranks of active servers.

There are three basic approaches used by Internet traffic managers for load sharing of IP traffic: dynamic DNS, HTTP redirection, and network address proxy. All three approaches suffer from one critical problem: state information on a failed server is lost when the server fails, forcing the application to back up and restart. If state information is critical to success of the application, the application may need to be redesigned so that the client can bring the backup server up to speed. This is not always easy, particularly when the application is one that we do not control or influence. It also may not be safe, as some Web merchants learned the hard way when unethical shoppers discovered they could adjust the prices stored in hidden fields in their Web shopping carts to treat themselves to unofficial discounts.

As mentioned in the beginning of this chapter, dynamic DNS is a good solution for load sharing but can be problematic as a mechanism for shifting traffic away from a dead server. The problem is two-fold. First, by setting the lifetime on DNS responses to short values, we create significant additional DNS traffic because every connection request issues a fresh DNS query. Even if we have no problems handling the traffic load, the extra round trip slows down the application. More important, unless we completely control the environment from client all the way to the traffic manager DNS server, we can expect to encounter DNS caches that ignore the lifetime settings on our responses and continue to send the client to the IP address of a dead server.

Consequently, while DNS traffic management is good for load sharing, it is not the best solution for enhancing availability in this application. However, in Chapter 11, when we expand the problem domain to multiple sites and return to load sharing techniques to implement disaster recovery, we will come back to DNS. We do this not because the problems with its use are resolved, but because the alternatives are even more flawed.

HTTP redirection is another technique used for load balancing in Web server farms. The traffic manager responds to the initial page request with an HTTP response telling the Web browser to get the data from a different server. While HTTP redirection works well for load sharing, its applicability to high availability is limited. Even if the application is Web-centric and is unaffected by the extra round trip delay on the initial page request that triggers the redirect, the approach is limited. Once a browser is redirected to a specific server, there is no mechanism to change that browser's server should the server develop a problem.

The third alternative is network address proxy. By delivering all packets addressed to the official IP address of the server to the load sharing system, it can translate the IP address used by the outside world to access the Web site to the real IP address of an available server. The selected server then performs the requested operation and responds, with all packets in the response channeled back through the load sharing system. There the source and destination addresses in the responses from the server get translated back to the IP addresses originally used in the client's request.

This technique allows the traffic manager to transparently connect clients with arbitrary servers, using whatever algorithms are desired to determine which server handles which requests and which servers are no longer capable of providing services. From the viewpoint of the application, the traffic manager does not exist. However, it may be expensive because unlike dynamic DNS and HTTP redirection, the traffic manager must touch every packet to and from every server in the farm in order to adjust the IP addresses in each. At the same time, because the traffic manager's network address translation requires the traffic manager to maintain the state of every active translation, the traffic manager becomes a single point of failure unless it is designed to share state information with a backup traffic manager and a backup traffic manager is installed and configured.

Eliminating the single point of failure in the address proxy traffic manager requires more than just adding a second traffic manager, as is evident in the minimal redundant configuration in Figure 3-7. The specific network connectivity and protocol requirements will depend on the traffic manager used and exactly how it operates.

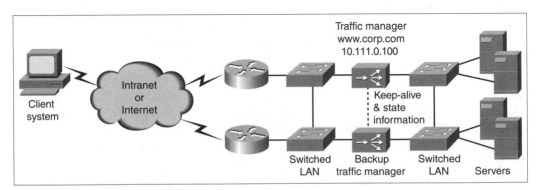

FIGURE 3-7. *Traffic management with no single points of failure*

Some translate both client and server addresses so that the responses from the servers will be routed back to the traffic manager while others only modify the server address. The former are more flexible in placement but must do more work on every packet. The latter must be installed so that at some point there is only a single path available from the server back to the client and they are in that single path. Adding to the confusion, some are inserted in the network as if they were bridges while others behave more like firewalls.

Some traffic managers place such severe constraints on the network design that even though the traffic manager is redundant, single points of failure are mandated in the network surrounding the traffic manager to allow the traffic manager to perform its function. While the traffic manager vendors brag about their abilities to detect slow or dysfunctional servers, it can be very hard to determine how other problems (such as traffic manager, router, or switch failure) are detected. When and how the backup traffic manager takes over the role of the primary can also impact the network infrastructure required to support traffic manager redundancy.

There are also variations in the sharing of state information and the ability of the backup traffic manager to handle traffic for other services while in standby mode. Extreme care in product selection and system integration are mandatory, as many of the traffic management appliances that are billed as providing redundant solutions have had the necessary synchronization and switchover mechanisms added to an original design which lacked them, with varying levels of success.

On the positive side, if the need is for high performance and high capacity beyond what can be obtained from any single server, traffic managers provide a way to expand capacity. Whether we are designing network availability enhancements to a server farm or designing a server farm as a means of enhancing network availability of a service, understanding the working details of the specific traffic manager used to implement the server farm is critical.

INTELLIGENT CLIENTS

Server farms are not the only way to provide redundancy through the use of multiple, unrelated servers. The best solution from the network design viewpoint is to use enhanced client software that is aware of the existence of alternative servers and knows to go to a backup server if there are any problems reaching the primary server. As might be expected, this is easier for some applications than for others. For example, there is the challenge of configuring all the clients in large installations in such a way as to distribute the workload across all available servers. More important and fundamental is the decision of whether the client or the server is responsible for ensuring database integrity in the event of an interrupted transaction.

With the client software in control of retries, there is a significantly increased potential for partially completed transactions because the client can switch to a backup server while the primary server is merely temporarily inaccessible rather than down. Whereas the primary and secondary servers can be tightly and redundantly coupled, which minimizes the potential of the active server being declared down by the backup while the active server remains alive, the coupling between the client and the active server is much more tenuous and prone to failure.

In applications in which the same transaction can be safely executed multiple times, such as Web browsing or non-locking database queries, mistakes made by enhanced client software in identifying a down server are not important, making the enhanced client software a highly desirable feature for high availability. On the other hand, if the transaction would have a different value if repeated, such as a database update that sets a value based on its current value, the data inconsistencies introduced by an enhanced client could reduce overall functional availability rather than improve it.

Probably the greatest limitation on putting the burden for recovery on the client is that in many applications, we do not have the option of specifying the client, and the client software that is mandated does not have the capability. For example, in the world of Web servers, very few Web masters have control over what browsers will be used against their servers, particularly those Web sites that are accessed by the general public.

WRAP-UP

Providing network access to an end system with no single points of failure is non-trivial in an IP environment if transparency of addressing is to be maintained. We looked at a range of solutions from simply adding a second NIC on a different IP network to installing a traffic management appliance in front of a server farm.

We determined that while there is no magic solution that meets all needs, there are a wide variety of potential solutions that can meet the needs of specific applications. As is typical of most network design questions, we need to make tradeoffs. The best approach for end system availability enhancement will depend upon the application, the requirements, and the budget.

For server-oriented end systems, a cluster solution is the only way to provide non-stop services, but the benefits must exceed the costs. If a cluster cannot be justified, two interfaces serving a single IP address can keep network failures from causing server outages. Servers that must support many local users may be best off using solutions that implement link aggregation at the NIC level. Servers capable of running a routing protocol can provide multihomed access to their services while retaining a single IP address identity.

For end-user, client-oriented end systems, the only two solutions that provide real benefit in a TCP/IP environment are two interfaces with two IP addresses and two "intelligent" interfaces that emulate a single interface. The former is an order of magnitude cheaper but only useful if the applications in use can cleanly recover from disconnection.

Dial Backup for Permanent Links

Many networks can ill afford the down time associated with dependence on a single full-time link. The productivity loss and inconvenience this causes may not, however, be enough to justify the cost of duplicating that link with enough physical redundancy to make a worthwhile availability improvement.

A popular approach under these constraints is to use dial backup instead of a second permanent line. Dial backup that is only occasionally used normally costs far less than a second permanent, physically diverse, full-time link. When implemented properly, dial backup can significantly improve network operational availability. On the other hand, if not properly designed, managed, and maintained, dial backup may provide only the illusion of protection. To garner potential benefits, it is essential to understand not only how to implement dial backup, but also what is required to manage a network dependent upon dial backup.

We normally associate dial backup with Integrated Services Digital Networks (ISDN) lines and analog modems over switched voice-grade telephone lines (commonly referred to as POTS, for Plain Old Telephone Service). But the critical design requirements apply to any technology that provides bandwidth on demand, including Switched Virtual Circuits (SVC) over X.25 packet switches, Frame Relay, or Asynchronous Transfer Mode (ATM).

In this chapter, we will first look at some of the critical considerations in designing a dial backup solution, such as the ability to obtain adequate bandwidth, techniques to deal with inadequate backup bandwidth, and reasons why it is essential to frequently and routinely test all dial backup links. We will then look at three common techniques that a router can use to recognize the need to initiate a dial backup connection (*backup interface, dialer watch,* and dial-on-demand) and examine the strengths and weaknesses of each approach. Finally, we will illustrate each of the three approaches with working Cisco router configurations providing useful ISDN dial backup capabilities.

In Chapter 5, we will continue with a discussion and examples of more specialized dial backup features, such as using analog modems over conventional dialed telephone links and using multilink PPP to provide higher bandwidth. We will also look at the implications of routing IPX along with IP. Chapter 5 will conclude with a general approach to dial backup, with no dependency on proprietary router capabilities, that provides the ability to dial any specific backup link based on the status of any other links, including other dial backup links.

We will return in future chapters to build on these dial backup capabilities to satisfy specific requirements. In Chapter 6, we will look at the challenge of using dial backup on one router to back up a link on a different router. In Chapter 7, we will look at how we can configure dial backup so that it is not dependent upon the router being called. Finally, in Chapter 8, we will look at using dial backup when connecting with outside service providers.

GENERAL CONSIDERATIONS

Design of a dial backup solution entails a number of critical concerns, starting with the ability to obtain adequate bandwidth. We will look at some typical bandwidth considerations and see why it is often reasonable to use a much lower speed link for backup than would be considered acceptable for the primary link. We will then look at the theory and practice of dial backup testing, an essential habit if the dial backup solution is to contribute to network availability. The rest of the chapter will look at the mechanics of configuring a router to place a dial backup call whenever it is needed—but only when needed and only for as long as needed.

Before we get into the details, remember that network management is not optional. Regardless of what form it comes in, redundancy will not keep your network running if a second failure occurs before you have learned about the first. Even if you do not consider your network a high availability system, if you plan to use dial backup then plan to install at least rudimentary network monitoring first. If you are not continually monitoring, you will not discover link problems (assuming no one complains about network response times) until 2 months later, when you're faced with outrageous phone bills because you did not realize that several of your sites were running full time on their ISDN backup links.

GETTING ADEQUATE BANDWIDTH ON DEMAND

The first question that must be answered when considering a dial backup solution is whether adequate bandwidth can be obtained at a reasonable cost. Generally, when we think of dial backup links we think of Plain Old Telephone Service (POTS) using an analog modem or of Integrated Services Digital Network (ISDN). Those are the technologies we will focus on in the next two chapters. However, any network service—such as X.25, frame relay or cell relay—that offers the option of demand-billed, switched virtual circuits could also be considered. In this case we would need to make sure that the network was designed and provisioned so that the necessary switched virtual circuits would be accessible when needed.

Table 4-1 summarizes some of the various media and methods that could be considered for use in a dial backup scenario. The available bandwidth numbers may seem low; they reflect the bandwidth that can generally be relied upon, rather than the best the link is capable of providing under ideal circumstances.

While services such as Frame Relay and cell relay are clearly superior technologies when high data rates are required, extreme care must be exercised before choosing them for the dial backup medium. One of the key requirements for high availability is independence of failure modes. Unless the switched virtual circuits used for dial backup are accessed over different local loops and use different service providers for their infrastructure, there is a high probability that when the primary permanent virtual circuits fail, the backup switched virtual circuits will not be

TABLE 4-1. *Media Capabilities for Dial Backup*

BANDWIDTH	MEDIA	BENEFITS	DRAWBACKS
10 Kbps	Cell phone with Analog modem	Immune to local loop problems.	Highest cost per bps and least bandwidth of any option.
25 Kbps	POTS with V.90 Modem	Widely available. Modems can adapt to very poor line conditions.	Slow to connect. Poor line conditions may force speed to as low as 2 Kbps.
56 Kbps	ISDN BRI 1 B channel	Simple and fast connection. 64 Kbps if local calls.	Less tolerant of poor line conditions (all or nothing).
100 Kbps	ISDN BRI 2 B channels	Full capacity of the BRI line.	Requires multilink PPP to combine B-channels.
512 Kbps	X.25 SVC	Not channelized like ISDN. Widely available at lower data rates.	Per packet delivery delays tend to be high.
1.2-2 Mbps	ISDN PRI	Number of channels used can adapt to traffic up to all 23 or 30 B-channels.	Multilink PPP capability to combine channels is limited.
2 Mbps	Frame Relay SVC	Excellent match with typical LAN requirements.	Hard to get adequate diversity. Savings versus a PVC may be minimal.
43 Mbps	Cell relay (ATM) SVC	Only practical way to get very high data rates.	Very limited availability. Lack of usage standards. High cost.

available either. Nor is it adequate to simply use X.25 to backup Frame Relay, or Frame Relay to backup cell relay.

Most major service providers today have combined their data service networks so that all traffic is carried over the same asynchronous transfer mode (ATM) cell relay backbone. Consequently, a major failure has a high probability of affecting multiple data service offerings. POTS or ISDN may not share the same degree of vulnerability only because many local and regional carriers have not yet fully integrated their legacy voice networks into their data networks.

Another challenge facing dial backup for high-data-rate connections is the current cost structure in the data communications marketplace, wherein the majority of the cost of a data communications link is in the local access loops. As a result, the availability benefits gained by an adequately diverse backup loop may not justify the additional complexity in the network design and the cost of the loop itself. At high data rates, it is usually more cost-effective to work with the service provider to provision redundant full-time high-speed access.

We must recognize that it can be very difficult to get a service provider to provide and maintain route diversity in network services, regardless of our willingness to pay the extra costs involved. As discussed in Chapter 1, even if we can obtain diverse routing initially, service providers tend to groom their systems and combine links that were once diverse to reduce their costs and take advantage of service improvements. Using two service providers is not sufficient to guarantee route diversity, as bandwidth sharing is very common in the industry—particularly when locations outside of major metropolitan areas are involved.

We must also recognize that even if a dial backup link is insufficient to support application traffic, it may still be desirable to support network management and other administrative traffic. Availability of a dial backup link could reduce the delay in determining that the loss of communications with a site is due to service provider failure rather than a problem at the site, reducing the downtime before service is restored.

COPING WITH BACKUP BANDWIDTH LIMITATIONS

Many designers overlook the potential of backing up higher-speed links with "undersized" dial links. Major savings are possible because, while the primary links must be sized to provide desired levels of service, the backup links often can be sized to provide only the minimum acceptable level of service. Similarly, while the primary links are sized to handle all traffic, it may be reasonable to limit the dial backup links to support important traffic only. Combining both factors frequently leads to the conclusion that a low-cost Basic Rate Interface (BRI) ISDN link providing only two 64-Kbps B-channels is sufficient to back up a 1.544 or 2.048 Mbps leased line.

The key, as in every aspect of network design, is to have a good understanding of the real network requirements from the user perspective. In a multiprotocol network, it may be reasonable only to support certain services while running over dial backup. For example, the dial backup may only support IPX routing and leave the IP users disconnected. That way, users could still access critical personal computer services, while Web surfing would be cut off. Conversely, if adequate server performance were impossible over the dial backup link, and the applications were not mission critical, it might make sense to support only IP traffic. Usually, it is more effective to implement the filtering with priority queuing so that unimportant traffic will be shunted aside to make room for productive traffic, rather than be completely disconnected. This allows for the support of less-critical applications at reduced service levels using any idle bandwidth leftover after servicing mission-critical traffic.

When taking the reduced-service-level approach to bandwidth allocation, be aware that different router vendors use different terminology to describe and configure their queuing priorities. For example, Cisco supports several queuing prioritization modes and uses the term *priority queuing* to describe the mode wherein one service has absolute priority over another. Configuration in this mode means lower-priority traffic can be cut off completely if there is enough higher-priority traffic to consume all available bandwidth. Since this mode of prioritization can render the network useless for lower-priority protocols, it is usually more desirable to use a prioritization scheme wherein the lower-priority data streams are guaranteed some percentage, albeit a small one, of the available bandwidth.

Be careful when using bandwidth allocation modes, however, as they can have the undesirable side effect of wasting bandwidth. For example, if the low-priority traffic is given 10% of the available bandwidth, some priority queuing implementations will limit the low-priority traffic to 10% even if the 90% reserved for high-priority traffic is not being used. Most effective from the user viewpoint but most difficult to implement from the vendor viewpoint are priority schemes (*custom queuing* in the Cisco vernacular) in which the bandwidth allocations are treated as minimum guarantees and any idle bandwidth is available for whatever priority has traffic to send.

Even if priority queuing can provide the required bandwidth allocations, we still need to be careful if working with delay-sensitive protocols. Consider an environment in which the priority application is Voice-Over-IP (VOIP) and the background low-priority application is Web browsing. VOIP sends one packet every 20 ms and can only function if the delivery delay is 100 ms or less. Meanwhile, the Web browser will try to use the largest frame size possible when downloading an image or other page content in order to maximize efficiency and performance.

This is not a conflict on a 1.544-Mbps link, where the time required to transmit a typical 1,500-byte Web data packet is less than 8 ms. But when the same 1500-byte frame is sent over a 64-Kbps ISDN B-channel, the link will be consumed for 188 ms. Consequently, every time a low-priority frame is sent, the high-priority application will be hit with an unacceptable delay, even though the compressed voice data stream may need only 15 Kbps of the 64 Kbps available.

There are numerous ways we can resolve this conflict. For example, in an IP-only environment we could adjust the Maximum Transfer Unit (MTU) size on the dial backup link to 600 bytes so that the maximum wait for any single frame would be 75 ms. However, this would cause any larger IP packets with the Do Not Fragment (DF) bit set to be discarded, with the potential of breaking any of the many applications that use DF improperly. Alternatively, we could use multilink PPP and enable packet fragmentation and interleaving so that the fragmentation of the larger packets would be invisible to the IP layer. However, this capability is not available on all PPP implementations and can be sensitive to line noise and other link imperfections. Yet another approach would be to bring up two dial backup links and dedicate one to delay-sensitive traffic and the other to bulk traffic. But that doubles our minimum connection cost and requires the implementing of policy routing to separate the data streams.

Clearly, the correct solution requires a clear understanding of which applications are mission critical and which are expendable, and what their service requirements are in terms of delay and bandwidth. It also requires political astuteness to ensure that all users buy in to the reduced service levels and understand that the alternative to reduced service is no service. Most important, it requires clearly documenting the trade-offs made and continued open communications with applications providers and users. This is necessary to ensure that as the application mix changes, the access priorities on the dial backup links change to match.

Finally, remember that just as load balancing can be used to allow multiple permanent links to carry more traffic than a single link, load balancing can be used to support multiple logical dial backup links. When we reach multilink PPP's limits to combine multiple dial connections into a single logical link, we can use multiple logical links in parallel and load balance at the packet level. This should only be done as a last resort, however—it limits our ability to minimize costs by dynamically adjusting the number of dial connections in the multilink PPP bundle to match the applied load. We will come back to the issues that must be addressed to make this practical in the next chapter.

THE NEED FOR CONSTANT TESTING

Dial backup also presents a major challenge to network management. As discussed in Chapter 1, link availability for intermittently used links is no longer a constant function of the Mean Time Between Failure (MTBF) and the Mean Time To Repair (MTTR). Instead, we have to consider the probability that the link will have failed at any time since the last time it was last tested or otherwise known to be good, which is strictly a function of the MTBF and the time τ since last tested.

To get a feel for the impact of not testing, consider a backup link with a predicted availability of 99.98% based on a MTBF of 2 years and a MTTR of 4 hours. If we last tested the link yesterday, the probability that it will work today, 24 hours later, is

$$\text{Probability Still Functional} = e^{-\frac{\tau}{\text{MTBF}}} = e^{-\frac{24 \text{ hours}}{2 \text{ years}}} = e^{-\frac{24 \text{ hours}}{17532 \text{ hours}}} = e^{-0.001369} = 0.9986$$

or 99.86%, which is probably acceptable. Stretching out the testing to once a week yields

$$\text{Probability Still Functional} = e^{-\frac{\tau}{\text{MTBF}}} = e^{-\frac{7 \text{ days}}{2 \text{ years}}} = e^{-\frac{7 \text{ days}}{730.5 \text{ days}}} = e^{-0.009582} = 0.9905$$

or a 99.05% probability at the end of the week that the link will still be functional, which is probably still acceptable.

On the other hand, if we have not tried the link in the last 6 months, the probability that it will work when we need it is only

$$\text{Probability Still Functional} = e^{-\frac{\tau}{\text{MTBF}}} = e^{-\frac{6 \text{ months}}{2 \text{ years}}} = e^{-\frac{6 \text{ months}}{24 \text{ months}}} = e^{-0.25} = 0.7788$$

or 77.88%. In other words, about one time out of every four that we try to switch over to dial backup, we will be unable to connect and communications will be lost.

If we do not test at all, and it has been 5 years since the last use, the probability that the line still works will have dropped to

$$\text{Probability Still Functional} = e^{-\frac{\tau}{\text{MTBF}}} = e^{-\frac{5 \text{ years}}{2 \text{ years}}} = e^{-2.5} = 0.0821$$

or less than 10%, and we might as well not have bothered to install dial backup in the first place.

In order to achieve high availability using dial backup, we must routinely and frequently test all standby components that might be called into operation to replace a failed system. From a pragmatic viewpoint, this means that testing must be automated and nonintrusive. Even if tests cannot be automated to the extent that they require with no human intervention—other than following up on reported problems—they should be automated to minimize the effort and skill required to execute them. Otherwise they will be postponed while more immediate needs are addressed.

Even if the tests cannot be fully automated, they must be designed so that they can be performed without impacting normal operations. If at all possible, there should be no service disruption associated with testing, regardless of test outcome. Otherwise we will face the same dilemma with dial backup testing that we face with uninterruptible power supply testing. Any test that has the potential to disrupt normal operation when it succeeds in uncovering a failure is far too dangerous for routine—let alone automated—execution.

Remember, in the real world the question is not whether failures will occur, but rather how frequently they will occur. We want to design our dial backup implementation so that it can be fully tested without impact on normal operation (including the ability to support continued operation should the primary link fail while the test is in progress). Testing requirements will frequently compel us to choose a dial backup approach that is not the easiest to configure or the most efficient to operate.

We also need to do more than just check for the presence of a "dial tone" on the ISDN interface once a week, although even that is better than no testing at all. Nor is it enough to verify that calls can be placed from the source router to the appropriate interface on the target router or routers. We really need to confirm that the dial backup link will provide useful communications between the end-systems depending on it. This can be critical in an operational network, because not all dial backup failures are due to faulty phone lines.

For example, one client lost two-thirds of his backup capability over a period of 3 weeks despite daily testing of all lines. Unbeknownst to him, a software defect in the router firmware had disabled the routing protocol on two of his three Primary Rate Interface (PRI) ISDN lines. Even though calls were still being answered and authenticated, the routing protocol had stopped setting up peer relationships with the routers at the other end of the incoming calls. While the floating static routes at the dialing router correctly forwarded traffic into the core, and syslog entries appeared normal, the core never learned a route for sending responses back to the calling site. As a result, useful communications were impossible.

The problem was only discovered when routine analysis of the system logs uncovered one remote site placing an extended, continuous series of short duration calls. Since this was not the correct response to a failed Frame Relay link (the ISDN backup was designed to dial up and stay connected continuously until Frame Relay service was restored), the situation was investigated and the problem uncovered. The nightly ISDN tests were revised to allow testing not just of establishment of a PPP session, but also of end-system-to-end-system IP connectivity.

DIAL BACKUP APPROACHES

When implementing dial backup capabilities on a router or other networking device, we must choose between two fundamental philosophies. Either the call can be triggered by detection of a failure, which indicates the need to dial a specific destination, or the call can be triggered by the presence of a packet with a destination address that is associated with a path through a dialed link.

The former mode of operation tends to vary widely among router vendors, as there are many different definitions of failure that can be used to identify the need to place a backup call. The most common is the loss of a physical interface. This is not surprising when we consider that the normal application of dial backup is as a means to recover from the failure of a permanent link. Since there is no common name for this mode of backup, we will refer to it by the Cisco command used to enable it, *backup interface.* (We are already using the Nortel name, *dial backup,* to refer to the general concept of backing up a permanent link with a dialed link.)

Instead of loss of an interface, we can use loss of a destination from the routing tables to trigger the backup call. By triggering the call based on a destination that can only be learned over an interface via the routing protocol, we can be assured that a backup call will be placed any time a primary link degrades to the point that routing exchanges fail—regardless of the up or down status of the protected interface. Again, there is no common name for this mode of operation, so we will refer to it by the Cisco command name *dialer watch.*

The mode of operation wherein the call is triggered by the association of a destination with the dial link is commonly called *dial-on-demand.* Dial-on-demand is normally associated with the configuration of a router at a remote site that connects part-time, only placing a call when there is user traffic and automatically dropping the call when no longer needed. Its use for forcing a backup call is not a primary design consideration in most router implementations but rather an alternative use of a commonly available capability.

Each approach has its advantages and disadvantages, which we will address in the sections to follow. The availability of specific capabilities and the terminology used to describe those capabilities as implemented on any specific router platform will vary from router vendor to router vendor. Because there are no standards defining dial backup capabilities, or even standardized terminology for discussing the concepts, we will use the terminology used in current Cisco documentation rather than invent our own.

DIALING DRIVEN BY INTERFACE STATUS DOWN (CISCO *BACKUP INTERFACE*)

Using the failure of one interface to trigger the activation of another is probably the most common method of providing dial backup on routers today. On Cisco routers, this capability is enabled using the *backup interface* command set. The equivalent function on Nortel routers is called *Dial Backup Service.* This approach is easy to configure and it works. However, there are some significant limitations that we need to be aware of when designing this type of backup solution.

While *backup interface* works well, it does suffer from one critical weakness—failure of the primary link must be detected by the router before the backup call will be placed. On a typical leased-line point-to-point connection, this is rarely a problem, as most link layer protocols used over a point-to-point link can be configured to exchange periodic keep-alive frames (Breath of Life [BofL] frames on Nortel). This allows for the reliable detection of link failures that are not reflected in a physical layer report, such as the CSU/DSU's dropping the Data Carrier Detect (CD) or Data Set Ready (DSR) interface signals.

This weakness can become problematic if the physical interface links to a network service rather than directly to the remote router. For example, an interface configured to use Frame Relay communicates at the physical and link layers to a Frame Relay service provider rather than directly to the remote router. As a result, a failure inside the Frame Relay network or at the link to the remote router may not cause the local link to the frame relay network to fail. The link used to trigger the backup call remains up even though the link is not useable for end-to-end communications; this results in a loss of communications until either the local link fails or network service is restored.

The challenge of backing up services such as Frame Relay can be seen in the option offered by Nortel to support dial backup of the link to the Frame Relay cloud, as well as end-to-end dial backup of permanent virtual circuits through the Frame Relay cloud. While dial backup to the cloud can be a low-cost method of enhancing the availability of an unreliable local loop, we will not consider it further because it does not provide protection from failures inside the Frame Relay cloud or at the other end of the logical links. In a high-availability network, we should only consider using dial backup to the cloud if we also have other paths that do not go through the cloud to protect us from cloud failures.

The need to detect interface failure means we generally cannot use the *backup interface* approach when taking advantage of low-cost Digital Subscriber Line (DSL) connections where the interface used to connect to the local DSL access device is an Ethernet LAN. The problem is that the Ethernet interface on the router will always be up regardless of the state of the DSL link.

Sometimes we can get around the difficulty of detecting interface failure by using a link protocol that includes the exchange of keep-alive frames such as RFC 1661 Point-to-Point Protocol (PPP). For Frame Relay networks, Cisco introduced an end-to-end keep-alive function (*frame-relay end-to-end keepalive*) in IOS Release 12.0(5)T. As IOS 12.1 matures and stabilizes, this function will enable *backup interface* to be used over Frame Relay networks with the same degree of confidence that is currently reserved for dial backup driven by a routing protocol.

The need to detect interface failure before activating the backup link also means that *backup interface* can only be used if the backup link and the link being backed up are on the same router. The *backup interface* approach is not suitable if we wish to improve availability by using independent routers for the primary and backup links.

Testing an implementation based on the *backup interface* approach can also be problematic. Since the primary link must fail in order to activate the backup link, operational testing is clearly disruptive, particularly if the test determines that the backup is not working correctly.

Non-disruptive testing of the dial link portion of the backup path is possible, but requires dynamically adjusting the router configuration to allow a call to be placed while the primary link is still functional. The operational configuration must then be restored when the test is completed. While automated testing is possible, the difficulty of doing it safely usually forces us to consider an alternate approach to dial backup, unless we need capabilities specific to the *backup interface* approach.

DIALING DRIVEN BY ROUTING TABLE ENTRY MISSING (CISCO *DIALER WATCH*)

To get around the limitations of the *backup interface* approach, Cisco introduced the *dialer watch* feature in IOS version 12.0. *Dialer watch* provides the ability to force up a backup connection whenever a specified address is not in the router's routing table. There is no equivalent capability in Nortel routers, at least in BayRS releases through 14.10.

The usage constraints of this approach are quite severe even in the Cisco version, but given its potential, we can expect to see functionality and availability expand with time. In the meantime, we will discuss how to get most of the functionality desired from *dialer watch* using standard, widely available dial-on-demand functionality.

The IOS 12.0 and 12.1 releases of *dialer watch* only work with IP addresses. Addresses in other protocol architectures cannot be used to trigger *dialer watch* calls. However, the backup links can be configured to support whatever protocols are desired, as long as the triggering can be from IP. A much more critical limitation is that *dialer watch* is only supported for addresses learned through the Cisco proprietary IGRP and EIGRP routing protocols.

The requirement to use IGRP and EIGRP as the routing protocol is not as severe as it first appears. We can sometimes get around the restriction and use our preferred routing protocol for real routing by redistributing the watched routes into EIGRP on the router used to place the call. That way, only the router placing the call must be a Cisco router. However, we must be sure that the dialing router can never learn the watched route via the dial link, or the connection will be unstable. We also need to be careful because this is not a documented workaround. Consequently, it should be tested thoroughly before being placed into production and before any changes are made to the IOS release running on the watching router.

A safer approach for supporting open routing protocols is to use dial-on-demand routing.

DIALING DRIVEN BY BEST ROUTE TO DESTINATION (DIAL-ON-DEMAND)

While *dialer watch* is an easy way to get the functionality we need in a Cisco proprietary environment, it is not a solution for everyone. Those using other vendors' routers and even those using Cisco but unwilling (or unable) to run the most recent IOS release can achieve similar results with conventional dial-on-demand and with creative definitions of addresses and route filters. With a little extra effort, we can achieve functionality equivalent to that of *dialer watch* with any current IOS release, using standard routing protocols, and in mixed-vendor environments.

Dial-on-demand capability is available from virtually all router vendors who provide routers with asynchronous or ISDN interfaces. Cisco calls the facility *Dial-on-Demand Routing* (DDR). The equivalent facility on Nortel routers is called *Dial-on-Demand Service*. We will find that while its use for dial backup requires more work than approaches designed to provide that capability, it is worth the extra effort. It easily supports automated, nondisruptive testing, reducing the overall effort required to implement a total solution.

All we need in addition to a dial-on-demand capability is support for floating static routes, or the equivalent, so that we can avoid using dial links when better routes are available.

The key is to define floating static routes that direct normal traffic through the dial backup links only when the primary links cannot be used. This is easiest if the calling router can use a default route for all traffic, but if the routing protocol can handle advertisement filters, almost any topology can be used. The critical requirement is ensuring that traffic to an appropriate destination (one we can configure to bring up the dial backup link) will always be available to force the link up when needed.

It is necessary to define the floating static routes used to drive dial-on-demand backup so that the backup links are not dialed when they are not actually needed. There must be careful definition of primary link default routes tied to destinations that can only be learned through our dynamic routing protocol. That way, as long as a primary link is up, we will have a default route to use that does not invoke the dial backup link. Note that we must use target addresses for these default routes that can only be learned from the dynamic routing protocol. If we use addresses on connected networks, we are back to the *backup interface* mode of operation, wherein the link must be physically down before a call will be placed.

The primary advantage of using dial-on-demand for link backup is the ease of testing the backup link. A call can be placed merely by explicitly addressing a packet to the address used to force up the link. In fact, our challenge is usually the oppo-site. We may need to filter routing updates to prevent network management systems and other applications that try to send data to all detected addresses from inadver-tently bringing up or keeping up the dial link when it is not needed for backup communications.

The primary disadvantage of using dial-on-demand for link backup is the dependence on floating static routes. This is not a problem with typical dial backup network topologies, which tend to be fairly simple. But as the connectivity gets more complex, the configuration burden can grow significantly. However, in practical terms, it is also true that by the time the connectivity gets too complex for controlling dial-on-demand, the network has usually outgrown the use of dial backup for anything other than management and control anyway. No matter how complex the network, a default route of last resort that forces up an emergency dial link to headquarters or the network control center can still be helpful and is easily implemented.

Choosing a Dial Backup Approach

Typical of most network decisions, the choice of *backup interface, dialer watch,* or dial-on-demand to implement link backup is not always clear. Each has advantages and each has limitations. All three are essentially identical in terms of the speed with which they respond to a failure. Both *dialer watch* and dial-on-demand are able to respond to any failure that can be detected by the routing protocol. Whether a particular feature of an approach is an advantage or a disadvantage will frequently depend upon the application.

The most critical factors we should consider, aside from the ability to detect failures and the implementation complexity, are product availability, call stability, testability, and link performance.

In terms of product availability, the *dialer watch* approach is a new capability and currently only available on Cisco routers running one of the latest IOS releases (12.0 or later). Support is limited to IGRP- and EIGRP-routed IP networks. If we need to work with OSPF, IS-IS, RIP, BGP or any other Internet standard routing pro-tocol for IP, or are not running IP on our network, the *backup interface* and dial-on-demand approaches are the only supported alternatives.

In terms of call stability, *backup interface* will prompt the link to dial when the primary fails, but it does not otherwise monitor the backup link to ensure that it stays up. *Dialer watch* will keep the dial link activated until the addresses being watched can be reached via a route other than through the dial interface. If there is very little traffic, this could mean that the link is being kept up unnecessarily. Dial-on-demand requires traffic to keep the link up, so if there is insufficient traffic the link may drop when it should be up. On the other hand, as long as there is "interesting" traffic, dial-on-demand will also automatically redial to keep the link up if required.

Looking at the other side of the coin, only dial-on-demand allows us to drop the backup link if there is no traffic, allowing potentially significant cost savings. However, this advantage is usually moot in a high-availability network, in which the time required to initiate dial-on-demand sessions would have too much impact on availability. Dial-on-demand can also lead to substantial additional configuration complexity. It may require configuring both routers to dial each other, unless we can guarantee that traffic calling for use of the dial backup link will always be initiated from one site.

Non-disruptive testing of the backup link when using *backup interface* requires going into configuration mode on the calling router, removing the *backup interface* command from the running configuration, verifying that the backup link comes up correctly, then restoring all *backup interface* commands defined on the interface. (All *backup interface*-associated configurations on an interface, such as *backup load* and *backup delay* statements, are automatically removed when the no *backup interface* command is issued.) This is not only a cumbersome procedure, but also a risky one. It requires that the tester have the ability to reconfigure the router and there is nothing to prevent him or her from adjusting other parameters except the integrity of the operator or script writer.

It is also possible to test *backup interface* by downing the primary and waiting for the backup link to restore communications. However, this mode of testing disrupts production traffic, particularly if the test uncovers a problem with the backup link.

Testing the backup link when using dial-on-demand or *dialer watch* merely requires logging into the remote router and sending a packet to the address used to force a dial-on-demand call at the command prompt. Executive mode is not required, nor is production traffic affected while the testing occurs, even if the testing is automated and executed while the backup link is already carrying production traffic. With an appropriate selection of test addresses, it is often practical to test the backup link directly from end-systems, without logging into any routers.

Dialer watch has the advantage of being compatible with *backup interface*. This means the backup line can be used not only for backup, but also for bandwidth augmentation. The ability to use the backup line for bandwidth augmentation is lost when using dial-on-demand. This consideration is becoming less and less important as the disparity between normal link data rates and backup link data rates continues to grow, reducing the contribution of the backup link to overall network performance.

Regardless of the specific implementation approach selected—be it *backup interface, dialer watch,* or dial-on-demand routing—dial backup can significantly improve network availability at a low incremental cost. While the difficulty of link testing when using *backup interface* usually rules out that approach, both *dialer watch* and dial-on-demand are viable alternatives for high-availability networking.

If it can be used in your environment, *dialer watch* is easier to configure and implement than dial-on-demand. On the other hand, dial-on-demand can be used in many environments in which *dialer watch* is not supported, and test support is usually easier to add. The optimal approach to use, as always, will depend upon the network architecture, user requirements, and typical and worst-case traffic flows.

BASIC ISDN DIAL BACKUP

The wide-ranging utility of dial backup is reflected in the fact that the *backup interface* command set has been an integral part of Cisco IOS since the days of 2,400 bps modems. Over the years, its implementation has been refined to provide better control over the backup link and more flexibility in its usage. The basic concept is elegantly simple. The *backup interface* command allows the network designer to assign one interface to be activated any time a specified interface goes down. For example, the code segment in Listing 4-1 sets Serial 1 as the backup line for Serial Interface 0.

The impact is equivalent to issuing the *shutdown* command to interface serial 1, except that any time Serial Interface 0 fails, Serial Interface 1 is enabled (until Serial 0 returns to the up state, at which time Serial 1 is shut down again). Originally, when the backup interface was triggered, all that the router would do was raise the data terminal ready (DTR) signal to the attached modem. It was up to the modem to place a call to restore connectivity. With the release of IOS 9.0, *dialer in-band* was introduced, allowing the router to control a "smart" modem using chat scripts. IOS 10.0 introduced support for ISDN dial backup.

As might be expected, there is more to the *backup interface* command than just the ability to turn one interface up or down based on the status of another interface. There are also commands to adjust how long to wait before enabling the backup interface (to avoid placing unnecessary calls when the primary connection drops for just a brief time) and how long to wait before taking down the backup interface after the primary interface returns to normalcy (to prevent downtime if the primary link requires multiple tries to reestablish itself, another common phenomenon).

```
version 11.0
!
interface serial 0
 backup interface Serial1
!
end
```

LISTING 4-1. *Backup interface command*

CONFIGURATION EXAMPLE: DIAL BACKUP USING
CISCO *BACKUP INTERFACE*

To see the benefits and shortcomings of the *backup interface* approach, we need only look at a few examples of typical usage. To minimize configuration complexity, we will assume the network consists of two sites, New York and Chicago. These are connected by a 56-Kbps dedicated link backed up with an ISDN line, as shown in Figure 4-1.

Assuming we want New York to initiate the ISDN call, the router configurations would look like those in Listings 4-2 and 4-3. Recognize that, in a real configuration, we would also need to include configuration entries for security, management, and other services. While we show OSPF routing in this example, there is no routing protocol dependency when using *backup interface;* we just as easily could have used any other routing protocol, such as EIGRP, RIPv2, or even static routes.

The primary reason for the popularity of the *backup interface* approach is evident in the listings. It will become even more evident as we look at examples of other approaches and at the additional complexity that comes with controlling the dial link and preventing unwanted calls. The BRI interface is effectively shut down by the *backup interface* command referencing it. All we need is to set up the backup link so that it will always dial as soon as it is enabled. In this case, the *dialer-list 1* line is set up so that every routing hello packet would trigger it if the *backup interface* command were not keeping it down.

The configuration for the Chicago router in Listing 4-3 follows the same pattern but is even simpler. Since it will be receiving the call rather than placing it, we can leave the ISDN interface active at all times and do not include a *backup interface* command on Serial 0. The one constraint is that we must not have a *backup interface* command pointing to the BRI interface on any other interfaces

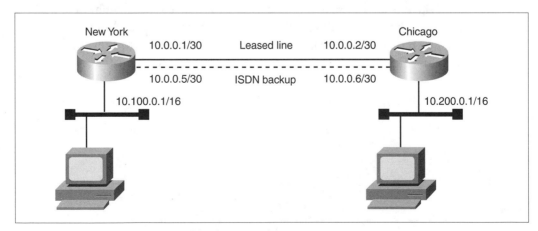

FIGURE 4-1. *Simple example of backup interface*

```
version 11.0
!
hostname NewYork
!
username Chicago password Secret1
ip subnet-zero
isdn switch-type basic-ni1
!
interface Ethernet0
 ip address 10.100.0.1 255.255.0.0
!
interface Serial0
 ip address 10.0.0.1 255.255.255.252
 backup interface BRI0
!
interface BRI0
 ip address 10.0.0.5 255.255.255.252
 encapsulation ppp
 isdn spid1 21255512120101
 isdn spid2 21255512340101
 dialer map ip 10.0.0.6 name Chicago speed 56 broadcast
   ➥ 13125551212
 dialer-group 1
 ppp authentication chap
!
router ospf 1
 network 10.0.0.0 0.0.0.7 area 10
 network 10.100.0.0 0.0.255.255 area 10
!
ip classless
!
dialer-list 1 protocol ip permit
!
end
```

LISTING 4-2. *Calling router using backup interface commands*

on this router. Otherwise we risk having the interface disabled when the New York router tries to dial in.

In this configuration, Chicago is in a passive role and has no responsibility for link recovery beyond being able to receive an ISDN call from New York. We remove the phone number from the *dialer map* statement pointing to the New York router, preventing the Chicago router from attempting to dial. Note that Chicago could

```
version 11.0
!
hostname Chicago
!
username NewYork password Secret1
ip subnet-zero
isdn switch-type basic=ni1
!
interface Ethernet0
 ip address 10.200.0.1 255.255.0.0
!
interface Serial0
 ip address 10.0.0.2 255.255.255.252
!
interface BRI0
ip address 10.0.0.6 255.255.255.252
encapsulation ppp
isdn spid1 31255512120101
isdn spid2 31255512340101
dialer map ip 10.0.0.5 name NewYork speed 56 broadcast
dialer-group 1
ppp authentication chap
!
router ospf 1
network 10.0.0.0 0.0.0.7 area 10
network 10.200.0.0 0.0.255.255 area 10
!
ip classless
!
dialer-list 1 protocol ip permit
!
end
```

LISTING 4-3. *Called router using backup interface commands*

serve as a dialing target for other locations using *backup interface* simply by our adding more dialer maps to the ISDN interface definition.

Compared to a dial-on-demand router configuration, these configurations are remarkably simple. There are no access lists required to define interesting traffic and no static routes or proprietary tricks required to identify what is on the other end of the dial link. That is because there is no need to control the state of the link. The *backup interface* command keeps the dial link shut down when not needed and activates the ISDN link when interface Serial 0 fails, without regard to traffic flow requirements. The routing protocol in use then handles the rest.

CONFIGURATION EXAMPLE: CISCO *BACKUP INTERFACE* Options

Before we move on to the other two approaches to dial backup, we'll discuss several very useful capabilities available with the *backup interface* approach. We will show how Cisco does it; other vendors, such as Nortel, provide similar capabilities using different command and parameter names.

We can minimize dial backup operational costs by pausing a few seconds before dialing whenever the primary link drops. This allows us to ignore the clock slips and other transient errors that often occur on long-distance links. At the same time, we do not want to wait too long, as this extends the down time suffered if a call is required. Ideally, we should optimize the delay based on operational experience with the link, but a delay on the order of 5 to 10 seconds is normally sufficient and should have only minor impact on functional availability. Indeed, if we cannot afford to wait a few extra seconds to recover, we probably should not be using dial backup.

Along the same lines, we normally do not want to release the backup link the instant the primary link returns to service. It is very common for lines to bounce when being restored after an outage, and we usually do not want to trust a failed link until it appears stable. As a general rule, we want to wait at least 90 seconds before declaring the primary link ready and releasing the backup link.

On a Cisco router, we would configure a 5-second delay before activating the backup link, and a 90-second delay before releasing the backup link, by adding the statement *backup delay 5 90* after the *backup interface* statement.

If we were using asynchronous dial backup rather than ISDN, we would increase the delay before releasing a call to make up for the 30- to 60-second delay associated with setting up an analog modem call. A value on the order of five minutes is typically more appropriate, unless cost constraints are severe.

Some vendors extend the *backup interface* approach to allow the use of the backup link for bandwidth augmentation as well as for failure recovery. On Cisco routers, the *backup interface* command is extended using the *backup load* option. So if we added the statement *backup load 60 10* to the configuration of interface Serial 0 on the New York router, then when the traffic load (either inbound or outbound) on Serial 0 exceeded 60% of its configured bandwidth, the ISDN line would be activated. It would stay activated until the total load carried by both Serial 0 and BRI0 dropped below 10% of their combined capacity.

This ability to add bandwidth on demand can be quite useful even if the network does not need to use *backup interface* to provide failed line restoral. With more recent IOS releases, we can also get around the constraint that each backup interface can only back up a single primary interface, by using dialer profiles rather than the physical interface for the backup interfaces. For example, if New York had a leased line to Atlanta as well as to Chicago, we could back up both and provide bandwidth augmentation for the link to Chicago by using the configuration in Listing 4-4 for New York.

```
version 11.2
hostname NewYork
!
username Chicago password Secret1
username Atlanta password Secret2
ip subnet-zero
isdn switch-type basic-ni1
!
interface Ethernet0
 ip address 10.100.0.1 255.255.0.0
!
interface Serial0
 ip address 10.0.0.1 255.255.255.252
 bandwidth 56
 backup delay 5 120
 backup interface Dialer0
 backup load 75 20
!
interface Serial1
 ip address 10.0.0.9 255.255.255.252
 backup delay 10 90
 backup interface Dialer1
!
interface BRI0
 no ip address
 encapsulation ppp
 isdn spid1 21255512120101
 isdn spid2 21255512340101
 dialer pool-member 10
 ppp authentication chap
!
interface Dialer0
 ip address 10.0.0.5 255.255.255.252
 encapsulation ppp
 bandwidth 56
 dialer remote-name Chicago
 dialer string 13125551212 class isdn56
 dialer pool 10
 dialer-group 1
 ppp authentication chap
!
```

(*continued*)

```
interface Dialer1
 ip address 10.0.0.13 255.255.255.252
 encapsulation ppp
 bandwidth 56
 dialer remote-name Atlanta
 dialer string 14045551212 class isdn56
 dialer pool 10
 dialer-group 1
 ppp authentication chap
!
router ospf 1
 network 10.0.0.0 0.0.0.15 area 10
 network 10.100.0.0 0.0.255.255 area 10
!
ip classless
!
map-class dialer isdn56
 dialer isdn speed 56
!
dialer-list 1 protocol ip permit
!
end
```

LISTING 4-4. *Backup interface with bandwidth augmentation and shared BRI*

Chicago remains unchanged and Atlanta is identical to Chicago, aside from the local variances in IP addresses, New York password, and Service Profile ID (SPID) numbers. This approach will not work with IOS releases prior to 11.2 because the *dialer profiles* capability required to map multiple backup interfaces onto the same physical interface was not introduced until IOS 11.2. Dialer profiles also require a *dialer-group* definition of "interesting" traffic, even though the presence of "interesting" traffic is not used to control dialing. The *dialer-list 1 protocol ip permit* line specifies that any IP traffic presented to the interface should bring up the link. Normally, this would cause OSPF hello exchanges to bring up the link, but the *backup interface* command overrides the dialer-list and keeps the link down until needed.

Two other noteworthy choices in this example configuration are the definition of dialer class *isdn56* and the wide range between the load levels used to trigger and release bandwidth augmentation calls. Since long-distance ISDN calls may be carried on a voice trunk rather than a 64-Kbps clear-data channel, we force the call to be placed at 56 Kbps rather than 64 Kbps to maximize the probability that the first attempt will succeed.

A wide range between the initiate call and terminate call threshold levels for load augmentation (75% versus 20% in this example) is recommended to minimize flapping of the dial backup line. Keep in mind that the initiation threshold is determined by traffic on the primary link only, while the termination threshold uses the sum of the traffic on both the primary and backup links. We must also explicitly state the bandwidth of the primary and backup links in order to calculate the traffic thresholds. The error caused by using default bandwidth values would be minor on the ISDN link—64 Kbps instead of 56 Kbps would be used for 100%. But the default bandwidth on Serial 0 would be 1,544 Kbps, and load augmentation would never kick in because loading on the primary link could never exceed 3.6%.

The values in this example were selected to minimize line usage by bringing up the ISDN link for load augmentation only when the primary link is heavily loaded. This would be appropriate for applications that are not delay sensitive. When supporting delay-sensitive traffic, it might be more appropriate to bring up the ISDN line as soon as loading exceeded 50% (at this point, queuing delays would only be doubling the no-load delay) rather than waiting until the queuing delays were four times the no-load values. Of course, the exact point chosen would also depend on how much delay was acceptable and on the tenability of the added cost of the long distance call.

CONFIGURATION EXAMPLE: DIAL BACKUP USING *DIALER WATCH*

In Figure 4-2, we modify the example network of Figure 4-1 by connecting our two sites via a Frame Relay network rather than a point-to-point leased line, while

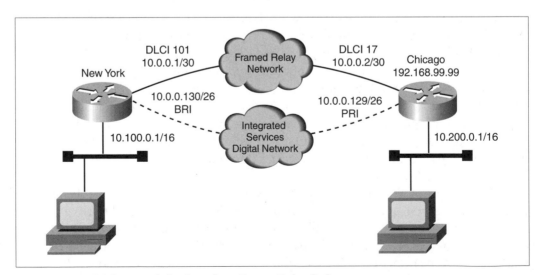

FIGURE 4-2. Dialer watch *backup for a Frame Relay link*

continuing to use ISDN for dial backup. While this configuration is simpler than most real networks, it is sufficient to demonstrate the theory and implementation of *dialer watch* backup functionality.

Dialer watch provides a number of crucial improvements over the conventional *backup interface* examples in the previous section. Backup initialization is linked to the dynamic routing protocol, rather than to a specific interface or static route entry. Therefore, both primary and backup interfaces can be any interface type and can be used across multiple interfaces and multiple routers.

Dialer watch also improves on the *backup interface* redial functionality, allowing it to dial indefinitely if the secondary backup line does not initially connect or does not stay connected. This provides much more reliable backup in cases of intermittent media difficulties or flapping interfaces, situations that can cause problems when only *backup interface* is used.

The primary advantage of *dialer watch,* compared to dial-on-demand backup, is that it does not rely on the presence of "interesting" packets to trigger dialing. The link is brought up whenever the watched routes are not in the routing tables from a source other than the backup link. This allows us to use *dialer watch* even though other links are still active, providing optimal routing to other locations.

There are a few key points to note in the configuration of the calling (New York) router in Listing 4-5. First, there is no benefit to using the *backup interface* command on the Frame Relay link. If the Frame Relay link goes down at the physical level, all routes learned through that interface will immediately be purged from the local routing table, triggering *dialer watch* to dial.

```
version 12.0
!
hostname NewYork
!
username Chicago password Secret1
ip subnet-zero
isdn switch-type basic-ni1
!
ip host TestISDN 192.168.0.99
ip host CallISDN 10.0.0.6
!
interface Ethernet0
 ip address 10.100.0.1 255.255.0.0
!
```

(continued)

```
interface Serial0
 no ip address
 encapsulation frame-relay
!
interface Serial0.1 point-to-point
 ip address 10.0.0.1 255.255.255.252
 bandwidth 56
 frame-relay interface-dlci 101 broadcast
!
interface BRI0
 ip address 10.0.0.130 255.255.255.192
 bandwidth 56
 delay 5000
 encapsulation ppp
 no keepalive
 dialer watch-disable 150
 ! Dialer map for calling Chicago
 dialer map ip 10.0.0.129 name Chicago speed 56 broadcast
   ➥ 13125551212
 ! Dialer map for dialer watch
 dialer map ip 10.200.0.0 name Chicago speed 56 broadcast
   ➥ 13125551212
 dialer watch-group 5
 dialer-group 1
 isdn spid1 21255512120101
 isdn spid2 21255512340101
 ppp authentication chap
!
router eigrp 1
 network 10.0.0.0
 no auto-summary
!
ip classless
ip route 0.0.0.0 0.0.0.0 10.200.0.1
ip route 192.168.0.0 255.255.255.0 Null0
!
access-list 100 deny   eigrp any any
access-list 100 permit ip any any
!
dialer watch-list 5 ip 10.200.0.0 255.255.0.0
dialer-list 1 protocol ip list 100
!
end
```

LISTING 4-5. Dialer watch *calling router configuration*

In a production environment, we would usually watch a loopback interface address on the Chicago router rather than the Ethernet subnetwork. That way, we would not dial the ISDN link unnecessarily just because there was a LAN problem at the core. For this example, we keep the configuration simple by having *dialer watch* keep track of the IP address of the Ethernet network in Chicago and minimizing the number of networks and addresses defined.

Since we are no longer disabling the BRI interface with a *backup interface* command, we now have to prevent dialing with access-list 100 when not needed. The access-list 100 and its assignment to the dialer prevent the EIGRP multicasts, which are always being generated by the ISDN interface, from bringing up the link. The EIGRP multicasts are not actually blocked, as we need the routing protocol to function over the ISDN link. Rather, the *dialer-list* definition identifies them as "not interesting" and therefore not worthy of bringing up or keeping up the ISDN link. Any other IP traffic is defined as "interesting" and causes dialing. If there are other sources of broadcast or multicast traffic, such as personal computers running Windows and using NetBIOS over TCP/IP, we would need to include their broadcasts in the definition of "not interesting."

For the same reason, we adjust the EIGRP routing metric on the backup link (using the statement *delay 5000* to override the default delay of 2000 used by Cisco for serial and ISDN links) so that, when both are up, the primary link will be preferred by the routing protocol. If the dial backup link could be considered better than or equal to the primary link, traffic would never stop flowing through the backup link once it came up. The dial link would remain connected forever, regardless of the state of primary link. Note that we only need to control the flow of traffic from New York to Chicago, as returning packets have no impact on the New York decision to keep the backup link up.

We also need to make sure that the *dialer watch-group* and the *dialer-group* are assigned different group numbers. These two classes of groups appear to share a common group identifier in IOS 12.0, preventing proper functioning if both are given the same numerical value.

The router configuration for Chicago in Listing 4-6 could be a duplicate of the configuration used to illustrate the *backup interface* example, with support for Frame Relay added. Nothing special needs to be done to support *dialer watch* at the called end of the dial connection. However, we will assume Chicago is a central router serving many locations and upgrade it to use an ISDN Primary Rate Interface (PRI) line. This will enable it to receive calls from up to 23 locations simultaneously. We will keep the configuration comprehensible by limiting the configuration of other locations to comments showing where the additional configuration lines would go. Support for additional sites would parallel that for the New York router. Note that since *dialer watch* is not running on the receiving router, this router is not required to run IOS 12.0 or later versions of IOS.

```
version 11.0
!
hostname Chicago
!
username NewYork password Secret1
!names and passwords for other remotes go here
!
isdn switch-type primary-dms100
controller T1 0
 framing esf
 linecode b8zs
 pri-group timeslots 1 24
!
interface Loopback99
 description Test address for backup link testing
 ip address 192.168.0.99 255.255.255.255
!
interface Ethernet0
 ip address 10.200.0.1 255.255.255.0
!
interface Serial0
 no ip address
 encapsulation frame-relay
!
interface Serial0.1 point-to-point
 ip address 10.0.0.2 255.255.255.252
 bandwidth 56
 frame-relay interface-dlci 17
!
! Frame Relay links to other sites go here
!
interface Serial0:23
 ip address 10.0.0.129 255.255.255.192
 encapsulation ppp
 bandwidth 56
 delay 5000
 no keepalive
 dialer idle-timeout 300
 dialer map ip 10.0.0.130 name NewYork speed 56 broadcast
! Dialer maps for other sites go here
 dialer-group 1
 ppp authentication chap
 !                                                    (continued)
```

```
router eigrp 1
 network 192.168.0.99
 network 10.0.0.0
 distribute-list 99 out Serial0.1
! Block test address on other frame relay links here
 no auto-summary
!
ip classless
!
access-list 99 deny 192.168.0.99
access-list 99 permit any
access-list 100 deny   eigrp any any
access-list 100 permit ip any any
!
dialer-list 1 protocol ip list 100
!
end
```

LISTING 4-6.   Dialer watch *called router configuration*

Similarly, there is no requirement that all calling routers use *dialer watch,* as there is nothing in the Chicago router configuration that is specific to that capability. Some calling routers could use *backup interface,* some could use *dialer watch,* and some could use dial-on-demand. However, only those using *dialer watch* or dial-on-demand would be able to take advantage of the support added for dial link testing.

Note that this sample configuration, adapted from a production environment, includes several features not found in the examples published on Cisco's web site. These include: a full definition of "interesting" traffic on the router receiving the call, the overstated delay on the PRI link, and the definition of Loopback 99. By defining a consistent view of "interesting" traffic, we protect ourselves from the situation wherein the remote system thinks the link is up and running even though routing has failed, and the remote site is not receiving traffic from the core. In this case, a series of calls all exactly 5 minutes (300 seconds) long is a clear indication that the ISDN link is not working properly, even though it appears to be coming up correctly from the viewpoint of the remote site.

The *delay 5000* line on the PRI interface prevents the continued use of the ISDN link when the primary link is functioning properly. Since dialer interfaces are always up, we do not want to have to wait until the backup link drops and the routing protocol times out before switching over to the primary link for traffic to New York. Since both the primary link and this backup link are 56-Kbps links, we fudge on the backup link to minimize the impact on routing decisions when the network is running normally.

Loopback 99 is defined, then filtered out of all EIGRP advertisements except the ISDN interface. It serves no function relative to normal network communications. Its purpose is to simplify ISDN link testing. It provides a target that can be pinged from the other side of the ISDN link (after the ISDN link is brought up by pinging the dial-on-demand trigger address). This will only succeed if the routing protocol is exchanging routes across the ISDN link. Without the Loopback 99, the only way to be sure the ISDN link is working would be to shut down the Frame Relay link, wait for the ISDN link to come up, and then communicate between end systems from LAN to LAN. This mode of testing is clearly not appropriate while production traffic is present. We therefore provide a non-destructive mode of testing, executable at any time, that provides high confidence that the ISDN link is capable of carrying production traffic.

When adapting system names, passwords, SPID numbers, ISDN switch types, and dialer map phone numbers to another application environment, make sure that all user names and passwords are consistently defined. Both pairs of routers on a dial link must agree on the other's name and password. Double check, because even though the Challenge Handshake Authentication Protocol (CHAP) is not case sensitive on the system name, the dialer maps can be. Case mismatches can result in strange failures that are difficult to track down.

As mentioned earlier, the *speed 56* keyword in the dialer map is highly recommended for inter-LATA ISDN calls, unless a premium long distance provider is being used. The default is the full 64-Kbps ISDN bandwidth, which is frequently unavailable on long-distance calls and may not always be available even on local calls. Specifying *speed 56* ensures that the link will come up whether or not the connection can support a 64-Kbps clear channel.

CONFIGURATION EXAMPLE: DIAL BACKUP USING DIAL-ON-DEMAND

Continuing the New York-to-Chicago example of Figure 4-2, we will explore how to achieve equivalent dial backup protection, without the limitations of *dialer watch*, by using dial-on-demand. "Interesting" packets to destinations known to be at the other end of the dial link are used by dial-on-demand to bring up the dial link (and to keep it up). We need to ensure two conditions for success: first, that the primary link is considered a better path to outside destinations so that when it is up no attempt is made to send packets via the dial up link. Second, the dial backup link must be recognized as an available path any time the primary link is down. This is not always as easy as it sounds, but it can usually be done with judicious configuration of floating static routes.

Minimizing potential delay in placing the backup call can require effort. If the routing protocol uses holddown for stability, there may also be a dead period before the old route is removed from the routing table and the replacement route using the dial link can be activated. Then, if there is no "interesting" traffic present to force up the backup link, there may be an additional delay before dialing is activated.

We can eliminate holddown delays by using a routing protocol that does not require them. If we do not have a choice of routing protocol, we can at least minimize the holddown delays using the techniques discussed in Chapter 2.

We can minimize the probability that no "interesting" traffic will be present by including a logging specification in the dialing router's configuration to a remote syslog server. That way, even if there happens to be a pause in normal traffic at the same time that the primary link fails, the syslog entries reporting the change can force the ISDN link up immediately, minimizing the delays seen when normal data traffic resumes. Note that the syslog server does not actually need to exist, as the attempt to send a report will be enough to bring up the link.

In many environments, we can also depend upon status polls from network management systems to devices at the calling site to keep the link up once it is dialed in. If there is no guaranteed source of "interesting" traffic, we would have to create one. Ways to do this using BGP or RIPv2 are presented in the next chapter.

As in the *dialer watch* example, we define "interesting" as any packets other than routing protocol exchanges (access list 100). If there are other sources of broadcasts or multicasts, those too would need to be declared "not interesting."

The time-out before the link is dropped should also be given some thought. Set too long, it wastes money by keeping up an ISDN link after the link is required. Set too short, the time-out may cause the link to drop while there is still traffic to be carried or when the primary link flaps on the way back up. The 170-second value used in this example was chosen because the local telephone company bills a flat rate for the first 3 minutes. This value allows the link to be tested at minimum cost, yet keeps it up as long as practical to minimize the potential of premature drops.

We will make this example a little more interesting by replacing the New York end of the Frame Relay link with a lower-cost, higher-speed Digital Subscriber Line (DSL), as shown in Figure 4-3. The impact of this change on the ISDN backup configuration is negligible. But the primary link configuration is completely different at both ends. The New York router now interacts with the Chicago router as if it were another router on a local Ethernet LAN. Meanwhile, the Chicago router frame relay configuration must be adjusted to communicate with the New York router through the services of the DSL bridge on the New York LAN.

Unlike in an end-to-end Frame Relay network, where most failures would eventually be detected by the PVC going down, there is no way that *backup interface* could even be considered in this environment. The Ethernet 1 interface on the New York router will always be up, as long as the hub it plugs into is working. The state of the DSL network or the Frame Relay network will never be detectable by the New York router interface. If we want dial backup to function in this environment, we must use either *dialer watch* or dial-on-demand.

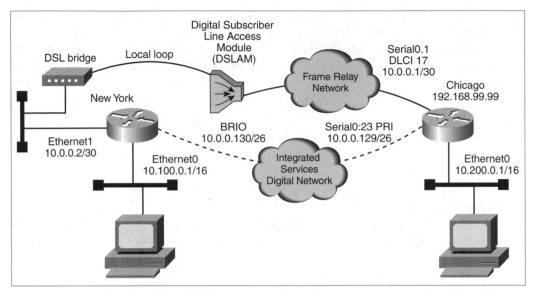

FIGURE 4-3. Dialer watch *backup for a frame relay link*

The Chicago router must implement the other half of a remote bridge. This allows it to connect with the New York LAN through the DSL bridge across the frame relay PVC. Remote bridging PPP would be used for this purpose. While theoretically we could bridge the New York LAN directly onto the Chicago LAN and let a different router handle the routing chores, that would not be a scalable approach. Instead, we use a Bridge Group Virtual Interface (BVI) on the Chicago router. The BVI links the bridge group used to enable remote bridging over the Frame Relay link with router services that expect to be configured on a physical interface. We then apply the routing configuration required to route packets to and from the New York router to the BVI interface that connects to the New York DSL bridge.

Returning our attention to dial backup considerations, we find a few critical changes between Listing 4-7 and the *dialer watch* example we just looked at. The key change is the addition of an alternate default route using a floating static route through the ISDN dialer map address for the Chicago router. When the primary DSL-to-frame relay link is up, the default route through the Ethernet address of the Chicago router is learned through routing protocol. This route has a lower administrative distance (90 for EIGRP, 110 for OSPF) so that the dial backup floating static route will be ignored. However, whenever the primary link fails, the dynamic routing protocol will detect the absence of hello packets and remove its routing table entry for 10.200.0.0/16. The dial backup floating static route now floats to the top because it has the shortest administrative distance and its path—via 10.0.0.6—is always up.

```
version 11.0
!
hostname NewYork
!
username Chicago password Secret1
ip subnet-zero
isdn switch-type basic-ni1
!
ip host TestISDN 192.168.0.99
ip host CallISDN 10.0.0.6
!
interface Ethernet0
 description LAN for local users
 ip address 10.100.0.1 255.255.0.0
!
interface Ethernet1
 description LAN for DSL access to Chicago
 ip address 10.0.0.1 255.255.255.252
 bandwidth 384
 delay 2000
!
interface BRI0
 description Dial backup for DSL link to Chicago
 ip address 10.0.0.130 255.255.255.192
 encapsulation ppp
 bandwidth 56

 delay 5000
 no keepalive
 isdn spid1 21255512120101
 isdn spid2 21255512340101
 dialer idle-timeout 170
 dialer map ip 10.0.0.129 name Chicago speed 56 broadcast
   ➡ 13125551212
 dialer hold-queue 10
 dialer-group 1
 ppp authentication chap
!
router eigrp 1
 network 10.0.0.0
 no auto-summary
 eigrp log-neighbor-changes
```

(*continued*)

```
!
ip classless
ip route 0.0.0.0 0.0.0.0 10.200.0.1
ip route 0.0.0.0 0.0.0.0 10.0.0.6 150
ip route 192.168.0.0 255.255.255.0 Null0
!
access-list 100 deny    eigrp any any
access-list 100 permit ip any any
!
logging 10.200.0.123
!
dialer-list 1 protocol ip list 100
!
end
```

LISTING 4-7. *Dial-on-demand backup calling router configuration*

The next packet to the Chicago LAN or any other unknown destination triggers the dial-on-demand.

The floating static routes at the New York end are the key to successful backup using dial-on-demand. They are the way the New York router knows that the dial link can be used to reach Chicago until the backup link comes up and routing tables can be exchanged. This configuration assumes that all traffic leaving New York must be routed through Chicago, regardless of the final destination. That is a valid assumption unless we are using dial backup behind multiple primary links, a much less common situation. In later chapters, we will explore ways to ensure that appropriate traffic will always be present to trigger dial-on-demand in other topologies.

The bandwidth and delay statements added to the Ethernet1 and ISDN interface definitions are not needed to ensure that all traffic to the core will flow over the DSL link when it is functional. However, with them set at the actual values, better routes to the core will be correctly identified and used by the routing protocol, and network monitoring tools will be able to correctly calculate link loading. In general, we only want to provide misleading link metrics in situations where we must force routing across what would normally be a slower link, as we did in the preceding *dialer watch* example. If we were running OSPF rather than EIGRP, we would adjust link metrics using *ip ospf cost* statements rather than *delay* statements in order to get the routing protocol to make the desired routing decisions.

Just as when we used *dialer watch*, the decision here to switch to the backup link is unrelated to the status of the interfaces at either end. Whenever the routing protocol is unable to exchange hello packets through the Frame Relay network, the dial backup link will be activated. Ideally, we would like to use a routing protocol such as OSPF or Integrated IS-IS. These verify that the exchange of hello packets is working in both directions, rather than just listening for them the way EIGRP or RIPv2 does. This way, we could also recover from an asymmetric failure blocking traffic flow from New York to Chicago but allowing packets from Chicago to reach New York. However, for the sake of this example, we have already introduced enough complications by changing the New York link to DSL.

The ISDN portion of the configuration of the Chicago side in Listing 4-8 is unchanged from that in the *dialer watch* example in Listing 4-6.

```
version 11.2
!
hostname Chicago
!
username NewYork password Secret1
!
isdn switch-type primary-dms100
controller T1 0
 framing esf
 linecode b8zs

 pri-group timeslots 1 24
!
interface Loopback99
 description Test address for backup link testing
 ip address 192.168.0.99 255.255.255.255
!
interface Ethernet0
 description Local users and services
 ip address 10.200.0.1 255.255.255.0
!
interface Serial0
 description Shared frame relay Link
 no ip address
 encapsulation frame-relay IETF
!
interface Serial0.1 point-to-point
 description PVC to New York DSL bridge
 bandwidth 384
 frame-relay interface-dlci 17
 bridge-group 5
 bridge-group 5 spanning-disabled
```

(continued)

```
!
interface Serial0.2 point-to-point
 description Example of a PVC to another DSL bridge
 bandwidth 384
 frame-relay interface-dlci 18
 bridge-group 6
 bridge-group 6 spanning-disabled
!
interface Serial0:23
 description Dial backup (answer only)
 ip address 10.0.0.129 255.255.255.192
 encapsulation ppp
 bandwidth 56
 delay 5000
 no keepalive
 dialer idle-timeout 300
 dialer map ip 10.0.0.130 name NewYork speed 56 broadcast
 dialer-group 1
 ppp authentication chap
!

interface BVI5
 description IP link to New York Router (frame & DSL)
 ip address 10.0.0.2 255.255.255.252
 bandwidth 384
 delay 2000
!
interface BVI6
 description Example of another IP link
 ip address 10.0.0.9 255.255.255.252
 bandwidth 384
 delay 2000
!
router eigrp 1
 network 192.168.0.99
 network 10.0.0.0
 distribute-list 99 out BVI5
 distribute-list 99 out BVI6
 no auto-summary
!
ip classless
!
```

(*continued*)

```
access-list 99 deny 192.168.0.99
access-list 99 permit any
access-list 100 deny    eigrp any any
access-list 100 permit ip any any
!
dialer-list 1 protocol ip list 100
!
bridge irb
bridge 5 protocol ieee
 bridge 5 route ip
bridge 6 protocol ieee
 bridge 6 route ip
!
end
```

LISTING **4-8.** *Dial-on-demand called router configuration*

As was mentioned earlier, the same dial backup configuration can be used on the called router to support dial-on-demand, *dialer watch,* and *backup interface* callers. On the other hand, even though we are still using Frame Relay to reach New York, the whole logic of the primary linkage is changed because of the DSL bridge at the New York end of the link.

In order to communicate with the DSL bridge, we enable integrated routing and bridging (the Cisco name for the ability to route a given protocol between routed interfaces and bridge groups) with the *bridge irb* statement. We define a bridge group on the router for the link using the statement *bridge 5 protocol ieee.* We then enable the bridged virtual interface to route IP packets to the New York router using the statement *bridge 5 route ip* under *bridge 5 protocol ieee.*

We want each remote router to be on an independent link so that it does not see the other's broadcasts. We therefore define a Frame Relay subinterface for New York and tie its PVC to Bridge Group 5. The extra statement *bridge-group 5 spanning-disabled* turns off Spanning-Tree protocol (STP) exchanges on the link. We have no other bridged links to New York, and the STP frames would merely consume bandwidth for no purpose. Using this approach, each DSL site would require definition of a unique bridge group, bridged virtual interface, and Frame Relay subinterface.

Interface BVI5 is automatically associated with Bridge Group 5 by virtue of its interface number, so it is effectively an interface on the DSL access Ethernet LAN in New York. We enable routing on the interface by assigning it an IP address. Note that while we use a /30 subnetwork here for consistency with the preceding dial backup examples, we would normally use a slightly larger subnetwork. This would allow access to the network management services on the 10BaseT hub used to connect the New York router with the New York DSL bridge. Theoretically, this limits us to 255 DSL connections, the maximum number of bridge groups possible. However, on routers that were not designed for DSL bridging, we usually run out of CPU cycles first.

When designing the configuration, it is critical to remember that the interface to New York is not the Frame Relay subinterface, but rather the bridged virtual interface. For example, our EIGRP filter for dial link testing under *router eigrp* 1 is applied to *BVI5* rather than *Serial0.1*. Similarly, it is the bandwidth and delay statements under *interface BVI5* that control route preference, not those under *interface Serial0.1*. The latter bandwidth statement merely keeps link usage report percentages correct.

WRAP-UP

Dial backup is a popular technique for improving availability in singly connected networks. There will still be brief service interruptions while the backup link is dialed, but dialing around service problems can greatly reduce the impact of WAN service problems. Of course, we still need to guard against common causes of failure, such as a back hoe digging up the street or shared service provider facilities. But many of the common problems associated with access lines and public network services can be easily circumvented at a low cost, making dial backup a practical step even when an application does not justify the cost of fully redundant communications.

In this chapter, we looked at the three most popular approaches to providing dial backup: *backup interface*, wherein we place a call because another interface on the router has reported a failure; *dialer watch*, wherein we place a call because a route being watched is no longer in the routing table; and dial-on-demand, wherein we place a call because the dial link has become the preferred route to a destination. We then looked at a simple scenario involving two routers, one in New York and one in Chicago, with a single permanent link and a single dial backup link between them. We examined how each mode of dial backup could be configured on Cisco routers to provide the required functionality. In the process, we explored some of the unique benefits and limitations of each approach.

In the beginning of the chapter, we also identified the critical need for network monitoring and management in a dial backup environment, including the need to frequently test dial backup links to ensure that they will work when needed. Along the way, we looked at some of the ways we could improve the testability of our designs so that we could maintain a high probability of dial backup's working correctly when needed. In the process, we concluded that while the *backup interface* approach can make implementation much simpler, the impact on testing makes it our last-resort choice, to be avoided if at all possible.

The powerful *dialer watch* capability would have been our preferred approach for dial backup, but it currently suffers from several severe limitations. It is only available on Cisco routers in recent IOS releases, preventing its use on older IOS releases with proven stability. It also only supports Cisco's proprietary routing protocols IGRP and EIGRP, making it unsuitable for mixed-vendor environments and other networks designed around open standards. Of lesser concern in today's TCP/IP-dominated networking world, it only supports IP.

The dial-on-demand approach to dial backup, while more cumbersome than the approaches designed specifically for this purpose, comes out on top by process of elimination. In forthcoming chapters, we will look at other scenarios and concentrate on how we can satisfy their dial backup needs using a generic dial-on-demand approach. Those who are in a position to take advantage of the Cisco proprietary *dialer watch* approach can easily adapt the presented dial-on-demand solutions to the use of *dialer watch*.

Advanced Dial Backup

In the previous chapter, we looked at the concept of dial backup and how we could use generic dial-on-demand capabilities to reliably enhance the availability of permanent links. Our solutions were limited to providing IP support over a single ISDN B-channel. We also required either a reliable source of traffic to appropriate destinations to trigger dial-on-demand or the use of Cisco's proprietary *dialer watch* capability. This was necessary unless we could be certain that all normal modes of communication failure would be detected at the link level.

In this chapter, we will look at each of these constraints in turn, starting with examples of dial backup using asynchronous links across the public switched telephone (voice) network (PSTN), highlighting configuration issues unique to the medium. We will then look at techniques to combine multiple ISDN 64-Kbps links to provide greater bandwidth, building to an ISDN dial backup solution providing 2.5 Mbps of useful bandwidth on demand. Then we will diverge from IP and look at the challenge faced when dial backup needs to support IPX. We will discuss how IP-driven dial-on-demand can be used to minimize the complexity of the IPX configuration, allowing IPX users to take advantage of our various IP-based tricks.

We will finish the chapter by showing how we can use Border Gateway Protocol (BGP) to force any desired dial-on-demand backup link to connect without depending upon specific user traffic patterns. This produces the functional equivalent of Cisco's proprietary *dialer watch* capability without its limitations. We will demonstrate the capability of the approach with two examples. One is a configuration that provides the ability to implement a second level of dial backup to back up a dial backup link. The other is a configuration wherein two serial links on one router are backed up by a single BRI interface on the same router. This allows all production traffic to be dynamically routed with no dependency on user traffic to initiate the backup calls.

DIAL BACKUP OVER ASYNCHRONOUS LINKS

All our examples of dial backup so far have assumed the use of ISDN lines. ISDN lines have several properties which make them well suited for backup purposes, including the ability to connect quickly, reasonable monthly costs, and predictable data rates. However, there are times when we want or need to use analog voice circuits provided by a public switched telephone network (or POTS) rather than take advantage of ISDN. ISDN service, while widely available, is not universally available, so we may not have the choice of selecting ISDN. If our bandwidth needs are minimal, we may decide that the added cost of ISDN service is not cost effective, particularly if the applications we need to support would not be adversely affected by the 30- to 60-second delay while a POTS line connects and the modems negotiate.

The use of POTS versus ISDN is transparent from the viewpoint of *dialer watch* or dial-on-demand routing backup. At the dialer level of configuration, both media have the same requirements, such as availability of suitable traffic to force the link up. However, there are additional capabilities we will want to add to improve performance and allow the configuration to be tuned to suit the hardware available. Most of the differences are due to the lack of a consistent standard protocol for handling asynchronous lines and modems rather than to any logical differences in the functioning of POTS and ISDN lines. Both link technologies support the same Point-to-Point Protocol (PPP) link technology, making their differences at the physical layer transparent to the network once the link is established.

GENERAL DIFFERENCES BETWEEN POTS AND ISDN

There are two fundamental differences between POTS-based backup links and ISDN-based backup links. The first is the speed of connection and the second is the lack of standardization in connection controls. Both factors tend to make the configuration of POTS dial backup more complex than the equivalent ISDN functionality.

When initially connecting, analog modems that are used over POTS lines require both more time to dial and more time to determine line characteristics and establish digital communications at the maximum possible data rate. It can generally be safely assumed that a local ISDN call will be connected and PPP options will be negotiated at the link layer within 1 or 2 seconds. Depending upon the speed of the authentication mechanism used, they could be ready to carry traffic almost immediately thereafter. Analog modems, on the other hand, must wait for a dial tone, dial the desired number, and, finally, wait for the remote modem to answer the phone. With Touch Tone, or dual-tone multifrequency (DTMF), dialing and a U.S. standard ring pattern of 1 second on, 6 seconds off, we should expect an average delay of about 5 seconds just to get the line up between the two modems. In other words, an analog connection is just getting started with the modem-to-modem link setup and modulation parameter negotiations when the ISDN link is already carrying productive traffic.

Once the POTS link is connected, the modems need to determine what capabilities each has and negotiate the best mode of operation available given the connection quality of the phone call and what each modem can handle. After they have settled on a compatible set of signaling standards, high-speed modems must execute an initial training session to establish the actual line conditions for this call and configure themselves accordingly. Only then can they start to provide a digital data link between the two sites so that a PPP link can be negotiated router to router, authentication can be performed, and productive traffic can be carried. Depending upon the modems involved, we should allow at least 30 seconds to get the link up and running and 45 seconds or longer for long-distance and international calls. More time is also needed when mixing modem families because several modulation and error protection protocols might need to be tried before agreement can be reached.

On Cisco routers, only 30 seconds is allowed by default for a dialed connection to complete. While this is more than adequate for matching modems making local calls, more time can be allocated by using the interface configuration command dialer *wait-for-carrier-time*. The time-out must be set long enough for the worst-case call from that interface. But we do not want to set the time-out any higher than required, as that would delay the retry when a call silently fails.

In the meantime, the traffic which initially caused the link to be dialed would normally be discarded as undeliverable. To prevent these initial packets from being lost, we want to queue them up until the link comes up and then send them. The configuration line to do this on a Cisco router is *dialer hold-queue*. When configuring a hold queue (which can be up to 100 packets long), we need to weigh how much memory is reserved for this function against the maximum number of packets likely to be seen. If we use this command, we may also need to increase the time-out on the hold-queue to allow time for the connection to establish. Cisco's default timeout of 30 seconds is too short for less than ideal modem-to-modem connections to complete before the held packets are discarded. While the time-out modifier is not mentioned in the Cisco command references, the line *dialer hold-queue xxx timeout yyy* can be used to set the hold-queue on an interface to *xxx* packets and hold them for *yyy* seconds before discarding them.

The other major challenge with asynchronous communications is the lack of standardization in both the physical layer communications between router and modem and the command languages used to control various vendors' modems. This requires us to configure data rates, handshaking, number of stop bits, and so on just to allow the router to exchange data with the modem. Once we can communicate with the modem, we need to issue the correct commands (*chat scripts* in the Cisco world) to initialize the modem. Only then will it properly handshake for flow control, answer the phone as required, respond to and assert the appropriate RS-232 signal lines, and dial the desired phone number on demand.

There is wide variation among modem command languages and requirements—based not only upon the modem vendor but even varying from model to model within a single vendor's product line. Scripts that work for one modem may not work for another. This increases the initial challenge of getting a POTS-based link functional, and when a modem fails and must be replaced with a different model it is often necessary to reconfigure the router.

CISCO IMPLEMENTATION CONSIDERATIONS

Further confusing the issue when dealing with Cisco routers (not that other vendors are any less confusing) is the variety of interface and platform dependencies that affect asynchronous link configuration. Unlike the ISDN support—a serial interface if connecting to a 23B+D or 30B+D Primary Rate Interface (PRI), or a BRI interface if connecting to an ISDN 2B+D Basic Rate Interface—the definition of an interface for asynchronous communications on most platforms is split between the line definition and interface Async configuration.

There is actually logic behind this function split. The line definition controls the communications between the router and the local modem. The line definition provides the Async interface with the ability to use a specific modem without regard to the specifics of router-to-modem command syntax, or of asynchronous communications parameters like data rate and number of stop bits. The Async interface definition then controls how the modem will be used to provide communications across the analog link. This includes both local functions—such as dialing a number—and end-to-end functions—such as data encapsulation, peer authentication, and protocol support. The key point is that all configuration specific to the make and model of the attached modem can be confined to the line definition.

Dialer interfaces, on the other hand, define a unified interface that can control multiple Async or ISDN interfaces, treating the combination of lines as a single resource. This can be used to simplify a configuration by moving common configuration items from the Async interface to the dialer interface. It also serves the far more critical function of allowing multiple lines to be treated as a rotary group so that when a call needs to be placed, any available Async interface can be used.

Another area in which configuration can get confusing is the location and attachment of the physical modem. External modems can be attached to dedicated asynchronous ports, to the Auxiliary port, or, on some routers, to the serial ports. Internal modems are available with dedicated analog interfaces or with digital interfaces that dynamically connect to individual channels on a T1, E1, BRI, or PRI interface. Each is configured differently even though they may be providing identical functionality.

Adding to the potential for confusion is Cisco's default assumption that asynchronous links will be used to connect with dial-in end-systems, such as personal computers, rather than to other routers. As a result, features that are enabled by default on other ports, such as routing exchanges, need to be explicitly enabled on asynchronous ports.

Care must also be exercised when using the Auxiliary port to support communications. The Auxiliary port was originally designed to support emergency management access rather than network traffic. As a result, its maximum data rate is limited to 38,400 bps in router models introduced before 1998. More important, even on newer models in which the data rate can be higher, the port is still serviced by the processor on a character-by-character basis. This makes it a potential major drain on CPU resources.

CONFIGURATION EXAMPLE: EXTERNAL MODEM ON THE AUX PORT TO A PRI WITH DIGITAL MODEMS

Despite its limitations, asynchronous dial backup can be very useful when not much bandwidth is needed and the connection setup delays can be tolerated—particularly if costs must be minimized and usage is expected to be minimal. When digital service is not available, whether because of line limitations or failures, or simply because there is not enough time to get service installed, analog connections using an available voice phone line can save the day. It can also be useful to have analog modem communications configured, but not physically connected, just so they're available in case they're needed. Even though service restoration in this case may require a visit to the site to deliver and connect a modem and find an available phone line, the job can be done by any available technician as no configuration changes will be needed on the router.

For the configuration example shown in Figure 5-1, we use an external V.90 modem attached to the Auxiliary port on the New York router to dial into an ISDN PRI serviced by digital modems on the Chicago router. This provides us with up to 33.6 Kbps from New York to Chicago and up to 52 Kbps from Chicago to New York, depending on line conditions. Realistically, we should not plan on seeing much more than 28.8 Kbps to Chicago and 44 Kbps to New York, as the maximum data rates require near-perfect line conditions, which almost never occur. Depending upon the data being sent, we may be able to attain higher throughput by enabling V.42bis compression on the modems.

Then again, if New York is using an older router, such as a Cisco 2500, the data rate on the AUX port is limited to 38.4 Kbps, regardless of line conditions or negotiated data compression.

The essential parts of the New York router configuration are shown in Listing 5-1. To minimize distraction, we only show those portions of the configuration

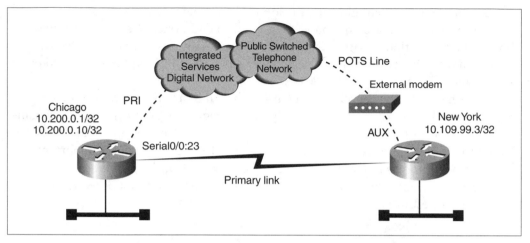

FIGURE 5-1. *Backup from AUX port with external modem to PRI with digital modems*

required to support the dial backup function. All other interfaces, including the link being backed up, as well as all management and control aspects of the configuration are not shown.

There are a few aspects of the configuration of the calling router that are not always clear in the Cisco documentation. While the use of IP unnumbered is not required, when we do choose to have it we use a loopback port for the IP address. Many people use the LAN interface address instead, since if the LAN is down on a single LAN port router and all users are LAN connected, there is no need to place a dial backup call. While this conserves IP addresses and may even save a little money by avoiding fruitless calls, it has one major disadvantage. If the

```
version 11.0
!
hostname NewYork
!
username Chicago password SharedSecret
!
chat-script courier-reset ABORT ERROR "" "at" "" "at&f" OK
 ➥ "atl1m1&b1&h1&r2&c1&d2&m5&k1s0=2" OK
chat-script courier-dial ABORT ERROR ABORT "NO " ABORT BUSY ""
 ➥ "at" OK "at dt \T" TIMEOUT 90 CONNECT \c
!
interface Loopback2
 description IP address for Async Dialer
                                                    (continued)
```

```
  ip address 10.109.99.3 255.255.255.255
 !
interface Async65
 ip unnumbered Loopback2
 encapsulation ppp
 bandwidth 33
 delay 15000
 async default routing
 async mode interactive
 dialer in-band
 dialer idle-timeout 300
 dialer map ip 10.200.0.10 name Chicago broadcast 13125551234
 dialer hold-queue 10 timeout 60
 dialer-group 1
 ppp authentication chap
 !
router eigrp 1
 network 10.0.0.0
 no auto-summary
 !
ip host CallAsync 10.200.0.10
ip classless
ip route 0.0.0.0 0.0.0.0 10.200.0.1 150
ip route 0.0.0.0 0.0.0.0 10.200.0.10 160
ip route 10.200.0.10 255.255.255.255 Async65
access-list 102 deny   eigrp any any
access-list 102 permit ip any any
 !
dialer-list 1 protocol ip list 102
 !
line aux 0
 password secret
 script startup courier-reset
 script dialer courier-dial
 script reset courier-reset
 login
 modem InOut
 transport input all
 speed 115200
 flowcontrol hardware
 !
end
```

LISTING 5-1. *Asynchronous dial backup configuration on calling router*

primary link goes down and we do not receive a call, we will not know whether the problem is with the dial backup circuit or with the Ethernet. Using a loopback address, even if the Ethernet and the primary link go down, we are able to contact the router and determine the extent of the problem. For the same reason, we configure the Auxiliary port to receive calls—we can try then to dial in to determine why we have lost contact.

The *async default routing* command tells the router to enable routing on this interface. This is a common oversight, since only asynchronous interfaces default to routing disabled rather than routing enabled when their IP addresses are included under a routing protocol.

The definition of *ip host CallAsync* simplifies testing. Logging into the router and executing the command *ping CallAsync* will automatically place a call no matter what other connectivity is available. Thus we can quickly verify that the link works correctly at the physical level, without disturbing any other communications in place.

We also extend the time-out on the hold-queue so that the packets that brought up the link initially will still be there when the link finally comes up.

To allow us to dial in for emergency management, as well as support dial-on-demand routing, we add the command *async mode interactive* to the Async interface definition. We have the modem configuration chat script execute not only when placing a call, but also upon start-up of the router and every time the asynchronous link resets (the lines *script startup courier-reset* and *script reset courier-reset* under *line aux 0* do this).

The modem chat script (*chat-script courier-reset*) contains a number of optional selections beyond those mandatory to set up the modem for dial-on-demand routing. The initial expect-send pair (*"" "at"*) lets the modem detect the speed of the link between the router and the modem. The second expect-send pair (*"" "at&f"*) sets the modem to a known state. It is not important whether the first *at* is recognized; all we care about is whether the reset to hardware default takes place. The third expect-send pair modifies the default configuration to get the configuration we really want. The details of that command are provided in Table 5-1. Note that the specific commands used will vary from modem to modem; this particular example was written for a 3COM/US Robotics Courier modem, model V.Everything. The key is to configure the modem so that it will do three things: use 1) the Request to Send (RTS) and Clear to Send (CTS) lines, allowing for bidirectional flow control with the router; 2) personal-computer-style hardware handshaking hang up and return to command state any time the Data Terminal Ready (DTR) line is dropped by the router; and 3) assert the Data Carrier Detect (DCD) line while connected and only while connected.

The remaining configuration parameters used are not mandatory, but I have found them to be useful. Turning on the speaker while dialing, though potentially annoying in a data center environment, can be a critical trouble-shooting tool when

TABLE 5-1. *Courier V.Everything Modem Setup for Dial-on-Demand Routing*

COMMAND	FUNCTION	COMMENT
at	Start of command string	Tell the modem a command follows
l1	Speaker volume low	No need to be noisy
m1	Speaker on until handshake complete	Helps trouble shooting if we can tell what the modem is doing
&b1	DTE data rate fixed at the rate used by the last "at" command	Router-to-modem link should run at highest mutual rate
&h1	Hardware handshake on and XON/XOFF handshake off for transmitting data to the modem	XON/XOFF handshaking is not supported on the Auxiliary port
&r2	Hardware handshake on and XON/XOFF handshake off for receiving data from the modem	Many modems use a single command for both directions
&c1	DCD follows real carrier detect	Lets the modem inform the router when the line drops
&d2	Hang up on DTR drop and reset modem. Only answer calls when DTR is asserted	Lets the router force the modem to hang up and go back to command state
&m5	Disconnect if error protection cannot be negotiated	If the connection is too poor to support error protection, hang up and try again
&k1	Use compression if available	Make the most of the limited bandwidth available
s0=2	Autoanswer on the second ring	Allows calling in from a terminal for emergency management

you're on the phone with the remote site, trying to get them back on the air. A nontechnical person with access to the router area can tell you if the modem is getting a dial tone, dialing a number, or getting an intercept message without touching any of the equipment.

If we plan to abort the connection attempt upon receiving an error message from the modem, we may need to configure the modem to generate unambiguous error messages that we can detect. (Many modems, like the Couriers, do so by default.) This allows us to set a longer time-out on connection attempts without being unduly delayed by busy signals and such. In this example, it is not a major issue, but it can have a major impact on down time if there are multiple numbers that can be called.

In a controlled environment where we know the modems we will be calling, there is no excuse for not using modem-level error detection and recovery. Error protection does increase frame delivery delay slightly because each frame must be completely received by the remote modem before its contents can be verified. Only then can the modem start to deliver the frame to the destination router. But error protection also improves the useful bandwidth of the dial link by almost 20%; with it, there is no longer a need to send start and stop bits as part of the data stream. Unless there is a need to communicate with modems that do not support error protection, its use should be mandatory. As long as both modems share support for either the MMP4 or the V.42 error protection standard, the only other time error protection will be refused is when the connection quality is so poor that it cannot support the protocol negotiation. If the connection is that bad, it will not be able to support useful traffic either.

Modem data compression, on the other hand, is desired but not required. Usually, if the link is good enough to support error protection it will be good enough to support data compression. An inability to negotiate data compression is usually an indication that there are modem compatibility issues; dropping the call to place it again will rarely help.

Unless it is inadvisable due to security considerations, I also like to configure the modem to autoanswer. That way, if a site is down and it is not calling in correctly, we can place a call to the site and see if we can communicate with the router that way. Frequently, this is the reason there is a modem attached to the router in the first place, and we are simply using what is already available to enhance network availability.

The chat script *courier-dial* is used to do the actual dialing. The ABORT traps allow us to recover and schedule redial without waiting a full 90 seconds for the attempt to time out. The "OK" "atdt \T" tells the modem to dial the number provided by the dialer map. The "CONNECT" "\c" says to wait until the modem replies with a connect message before returning control of the physical interface to the asynchronous link interface. The "\c" is a command to the chat-script to send nothing and to continue on.

The line *dialer-list 1 protocol ip list 102* specifies that any IP traffic other than routing hellos (EIGRP in this example) should bring up the link. The floating static route *ip route 0.0.0.0 0.0.0.0 10.200.0.10 160* makes the dial link the default route any time the primary link goes down. In this case, the destination 10.200.0.1 is a route normally learned via the primary link. Any address that will always be removed from the routing table when the primary link is down can be used. We also require that it always be in the routing tables when the primary link is up. So it is safer to use a loopback interface address rather than an IP address associated with a physical network, which could go down.

The line *ip route 10.200.0.10 255.255.255.255 Async65* ties the IP unnumbered address of the asynchronous interface on the router we are calling to our local asynchronous interface. This is a standard part of dial-on-demand routing, as otherwise, we would not know how to reach the target in our backup default route. Note that a dialer interface such as Async65 is always up—even when not connected (a *show interface* will give the interface status as *up (spoofing)*. We cannot, therefore, add any floating static default routes to use in case the default route through the Async65 interface does not connect. There are several ways to work around this fundamental limitation of dial-on-demand routing. We will discuss two of them in the final section in this chapter, on techniques for providing dial backup for dial-on-demand links. In Chapter 7, we will show a third approach that is useful for hub-and-spokes configurations. In the meantime, Listing 5-2 shows us what is required at the other end of the link to configure the Chicago router to receive our analog calls using an ISDN PRI interface with digital modems.

```
version 11.2
!
hostname Chicago
!
username NewYork password SharedSecret
!Other calling routers and their passwords go here
!
controller T1 0/0
 framing esf
 linecode b8zs
 pri-group timeslots 1-24
!
interface Loopback10
 description Actual target for all remote dialins
 ip address 10.200.0.10 255.255.255.255
!
interface Serial0/0:23
 description PRI for remote router dial-in
 no ip address
 encapsulation ppp
 dialer pool-member 1
 isdn switch-type primary-dms100
 isdn incoming-voice modem
 ppp authentication chap
!
interface Group-Async1
 description Digital Modems in slot 2
 no ip address
 encapsulation ppp
 async mode dedicated
```

(continued)

```
  dialer in-band
  dialer pool-member 11
  ppp authentication chap
  group-range 65 94
!
interface Dialer11
 ip unnumbered Loopback10
 encapsulation ppp
 bandwidth 33
 delay 15000
 no peer neighbor-route
 no peer default ip address
 dialer remote-name NewYork
 dialer pool 11
 dialer-group 1
 ppp authentication chap
!
router eigrp 1
 network 10.0.0.0
!
ip classless
access-list 100 deny    eigrp any any
access-list 100 permit ip any any
dialer-list 1 protocol ip list 100
!
end
```

LISTING 5-2.   *Asynchronous dial configuration on router being called*

This is a significantly more complex configuration, and not just because we are using dialer profiles rather than legacy dialer maps. First, we have to configure the T1 controller (*controller T1*) providing the physical attachment to our ISDN PRI. Then, we have to configure the D-channel on the PRI line so that we can support the 23 B-channels it provides (*interface Serial0/0:23*). Two key statements in this configuration are *isdn incoming-voice modem,* which directs any incoming calls identified as voice calls to an available digital modem, and *ppp authentication chap,* which allows the serial interface to determine who is calling so that the call can be associated with the correct dialer profile.

The *interface Group-Async1* definition is a shorthand way of applying the same configuration to multiple asynchronous interfaces—in this case, the 30 digital modems installed in slot two of the router. Finally, we have the dialer profile (*interface Dialer11*), which tells the router how to handle this particular user. If we trace a call from the calling New York router through this router, we can see how all the pieces fit together.

On the calling router in New York, all traffic is normally routed via routes learned from the primary link(s) to the rest of the network. Any destination not in the routing tables will use the default route, which will be through the primary link with the lowest metric for access to the IP address 10.200.0.1. When all primary links are down, two things happen. First, the target of the default route, 10.200.0.1, is removed from the routing tables, so the default route is no longer valid. The router looks for an alternative, and finds the default route via 10.200.0.10. This route was previously ignored because it has a higher administrative distance than the default route through 10.200.0.1. The destination 10.200.0.10 is always in the routing table because there is a static route that links it with the interface Async65. Async65 is always up, even when the modems are not connected.

The first packet needing to go to a destination that used to be known from the routing protocol running over the primary links (now unknown) will instead take the path specified by the active default route. All traffic (other then EIGRP keepalives) is considered useful because of the dialer group definition tied to access list 102. Dial-on-demand routing, therefore, will dial the number given by the dialer map in *interface Async65* that connects to the address 10.200.0.10. The modem will be dialed using the chat script specified by the *script dialer* statement under *line aux 0*.

As the call comes in on the Chicago router, it is announced on the D-channel as an incoming voice call and assigned to an available B-channel. The serial interface directs it, as a voice call, to connect to an available digital modem. This establishes modem-to-modem communications with the modem on the calling router in New York. Once the modems do their work—probing the line and negotiating the highest possible speed, error protection, and data compression—each modem asserts DCD to inform the asynchronous interface that it can now start to use the link. The line *async mode dedicated* causes the Chicago router to immediately start negotiating point-to-point protocol (PPP) parameters to bring up an IP channel over the link. As soon as PPP establishes that communications are possible, it starts the Challenge Handshake Authentication Protocol (CHAP) as specified by *ppp authentication chap*.

As part of the CHAP protocol, the routers learn each other's identity, and the Chicago router can scan all its dialer profiles to find the one assigned to caller *New York*. The call is then bound to *interface Dialer11,* and the parameters specified there are applied to the connection. The line *no peer neighbor-route* overrides the default behavior of PPP to automatically insert a route to the other end of the PPP link into the routing tables. (This would be necessary to communicate with a caller, such as a personal computer, that does not support routing protocols on dial links.) Since this is a router-to-router link on which both sides will be exchanging routing information, there is no need to insert a duplicate route. This is not an issue on the New York router because the route is already in the routing tables from the static route that allowed us to place the call in the first place.

Similarly, the *no peer default ip address* statement says that the remote system will provide an IP address for its end of the link, and we do not have to provide it as part of PPP link setup negotiations. The *dialer pool 11* statement ties the dialer to specific physical line resource pools, so that in a more complex environment we can allocate different services to different line priorities and ensure that a line will be available for critical services. Finally, the *dialer-group 1* statement connects this PPP connection with the definition of "interesting" traffic in *dialer-list 1 protocol ip list 100,* while the *delay 15000* statement ensures that traffic will flow via the primary link when it returns to life. The dial link can then time out and drop the call.

COMBINING CHANNELS FOR HIGHER BANDWIDTH

One of the primary limitations of classical dial backup is the limited bandwidth available on an analog voice channel or an ISDN B-channel. There are two primary approaches to linking multiple calls to increase available bandwidth: Multilink Point-to-Point Protocol (Multilink PPP or MLP, also MP and MPPP) and equal cost path load sharing. Each has unique benefits and limitations. We will look at both approaches and then show how we can combine them to use all the bandwidth in two ISDN PRIs for a single logical backup connection.

MULTILINK PPP

Multilink PPP is defined in RFC 1990. It provides load balancing across multiple serial links, multivendor interoperability, packet fragmentation, and packet resequencing. When it is used with dial-up links, additional links can be added or excess links dropped based on levels of inbound and outbound traffic.

Multilink PPP is designed to bundle arbitrary numbers of individual links running at arbitrary speeds into a single logical link. However, you need to be careful when mixing and matching links. Optimizing for speed variations and other link performance differences is not required by the protocol specification, and not every vendor's implementation works efficiently. Particularly in mixed vendor environments, it is safest to bundle only identical or very similar links, such as ISDN B-channels or T1 leased lines.

While multilink PPP can be used to provide load sharing across multiple point-to-point links, we will focus on its application to dial backup. We will use it to combine multiple asynchronous modem links or ISDN B-channels on Basic Rate Interfaces (BRIs) or Primary Rate Interfaces (PRIs). Because of the way multilink PPP ensures packets are delivered in order, we should try to avoid using multilink PPP on analog connections unless the line quality is consistently very good. If the modems on just one POTS line in a multilink bundle need to pause and retrain, all communications across all lines in the multilink PPP bundle will be delayed.

Even with high-quality analog lines, there are strict limits on the number of asynchronous interfaces it makes sense to combine. A Cisco guideline for using multilink PPP with default parameters is to never combine more than three asynchronous interfaces using V.34 modems into a single channel bundle. Even then, packets might be dropped occasionally if large bursts of short frames occur.

Multilink PPP is much more suitable for ISDN and other quality digital channels. Cisco has not published any guidelines on how many ISDN channels can be safely combined before router performance or transfer efficiency starts to suffer. But Nortel limits bundle size to 30 lines, enough to use all B-channels on a 2.048 Mbps E1-based PRI. The maximum number of lines practical to use in a single multilink PPP bundle may be more or less than 30; it will depend on the amount of memory available, the number of individual lines and bundles configured and in use, the speed of the lines available, the packet sizes, and the traffic patterns.

CONFIGURATION EXAMPLE: MULTILINK PPP WITH ASYNCHRONOUS MODEMS

To see how multilink PPP can be used to combine analog links, we will consider the scenario in Figure 5-2. The asynchronous dial-in server in New York, originally installed to provide dial-in access for local branch offices, is configured to also provide 100 Kbps of emergency communications with Chicago using up to three of its POTS lines.

To configure multilink PPP on asynchronous interfaces, we configure the asynchronous interfaces to support PPP encapsulation and multilink PPP. Then we

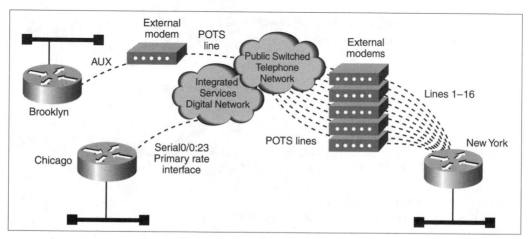

FIGURE 5-2. *Multilink PPP using analog modems and POTS*

configure a dialer interface to match and add bandwidth on demand with *dialer load-threshold*. The excerpts from the New York router's configuration in Listing 5-3 show configuration requirements to provide support for both individual remote sites dialing in using a single asynchronous line (as defined by the Virtual Template). They also show a multilink PPP backup connection to Chicago (Dialer 22). Not shown are additional dialers defined for other purposes or any other connectivity. Use care if implementing this example verbatim, as some IOS releases will not use the Virtual Template definition if there is exactly one dialer defined. If necessary, simply add an extra dialer for a non-existent user.

```
version 12.0
!
hostname NewYork
!
aaa new-model
aaa authentication login default local
aaa authentication login console enable
aaa authentication login vty local
aaa authentication login dialin local
aaa authentication ppp default local
aaa authentication ppp dialin if-needed local
!
username Brooklyn password secret1
username Bronx password secret2
username Manhattan password secret3
username Queens password secret4
username StatenIs password secret5
! . . .
username Chicago password SharedSecret
ip host CallChicago 10.200.0.10
!
interface Loopback20
 description Address for async router dialins
 ip address 10.200.0.20 255.255.255.255
!
interface Loopback25
 description Address for emergency link to Chicago
 ip address 10.200.0.25 255.255.255.255
!
interface Virtual-Template1
 description dial-in by local routers
 bandwidth 33
```

(continued)

```
 delay 15000
 ip unnumbered Loopback20
 no ip route-cache
 ip tcp header-compression passive
 no keepalive
 no peer neighbor-route
 no peer default ip address
 ppp authentication chap
!
interface Group-Async1
 description Async interfaces in Dialer Pools
 no ip address
 encapsulation ppp
 no ip route-cache
 async default routing
 async mode dedicated
 dialer in-band
 dialer pool-member 100
 pulse-time 3
 ppp authentication chap ms-chap pap
 group-range 1 13
!
interface Group-Async2
 description Async interfaces reserved for backup to Chicago
 no ip address
 encapsulation ppp
 no ip route-cache
 async default routing
 async mode dedicated
 dialer in-band
 dialer pool-member 22 priority 100
 pulse-time 3
 ppp authentication chap
 ppp multilink
 group-range 14 16
!
interface Dialer22
 description Dial OUT to Chicago
 ip unnumbered Loopback25
 encapsulation ppp
 no ip route-cache
 bandwidth 33
 delay 15000
```

(continued)

```
  no keepalive
  dialer remote-name Chicago
  dialer string 13125551234
  dialer hold-queue 10
  dialer load-threshold 50 either
  dialer pool 22
  dialer-group 1
  ppp authentication chap
  ppp multilink
!
router eigrp 1
 network 10.0.0.0
 no auto-summary
!
ip classless
ip route 0.0.0.0 0.0.0.0 10.200.0.1 150
ip route 0.0.0.0 0.0.0.0 10.200.0.10 160
ip route 10.200.0.10 255.255.255.255 Dialer22
access-list 102 deny    eigrp any any
access-list 102 permit ip any any
!
dialer-list 1 protocol ip list 102
!
line 1 16
 modem InOut
 modem autoconfigure type usr_courier
 transport preferred none
 transport input all
 speed 115200
 flowcontrol hardware
!
end
```

LISTING 5-3.   *Multilink PPP using asynchronous modem links*

A few items essential for multilink PPP support on the physical interface (*interface Group-Async2*, in this example) include the following:

- Specify *no ip address*; protocol support is controlled by the logical (Dialer22) interface.

- The encapsulation must be PPP and authentication must be performed to identify the dialer profile to bind to.

- Dial-on-demand routing must be enabled (using the *dialer in-band* statement).

- The physical interface must be part of a rotary group using either *dialer pool* (for dialer profiles) or a *dialer rotary-group* assignment (legacy DDR).

- *PPP multilink* must be specified in order to negotiate multilink controls during the initial PPP link negotiations.

On the logical interface (*interface Dialer22*, in this example), multilink PPP support mandates include the following:

- There must be specification of *ip unnumbered* to negotiate support for the IP protocol.

- The *dialer load-threshold* command must appear in order to control bandwidth on demand.

- *Encapsulation ppp, ppp authentication chap*, and *ppp multilink* must appear here as well as in the physical interface definitions.

Setting the *dialer load-threshold* can be tricky. Because the 5-minute running average is used to calculate the load, the link bundle can be slow to respond to changes in load. To minimize this effect—and to ensure that additional links will be called into play, even if a poor connection limits the speed of the initial connection—the 100% bandwidth value is set low (33 Kbps in this example) and the threshold is set even lower (only 50/255 of 33 Kbps per active link). Even so, an overloaded link can remain unassisted for almost a full minute before another call is initiated.

The *aaa* statements and the definitions of *interface Virtual-Template1* and *interface Group-Async1* are for local router dial-in support and are not required for multilink PPP operation.

At the Chicago end of the connection, the configuration is identical to that already discussed in Listing 5-2, except that we need to add the statement *ppp multilink* to the configuration of *interface Group-Async1* and *interface Dialer1*.

CONFIGURATION EXAMPLE: BRI TO BRI MULTILINK PPP

To enable multilink PPP on a single Integrated Services Digital Network (ISDN) Basic Rate Interface (BRI) or Primary Rate Interface (PRI), the requirements are similar, but we are not required to define a dialer rotary group separately. This is because all B-channels in an ISDN interface are a dialer rotary group by default. However, we do have to define either dialer rotary groups (when using legacy dialing) or dialer pools

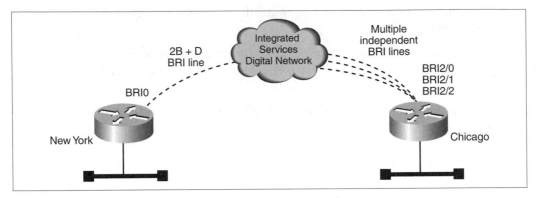

FIGURE 5-3. *Multilink PPP using one or more ISDN BRI lines*

(when using dialer profiles) to combine multiple BRIs. Consider the scenario in Figure 5-3. We have a router with a single BRI interface in New York requiring a 100-Kbps backup connection to the router in Chicago, which is equipped with multiple BRI interfaces.

To show that either flavor of Cisco dialer can be used, we will configure legacy dialing on the New York end and dialer profiles on the Chicago end. Listing 5-4 looks at the multilink PPP setup for the single BRI on the New York router.

```
version 11.0
!
hostname NewYork
!
username Chicago password NYsecret
isdn switch-type basic-ni1
!
interface Loopback1
 ip address 192.168.100.10.255.255.255.255
!
interface BRI0
 ip unnumbered Loopback1
 encapsulation ppp
 bandwidth 56
 no keepalive
 isdn spid1 21255512340000
 isdn spid2 21255512350000
 dialer idle-timeout 120
 dialer map ip 10.100.0.2 name Chicago speed 56 broadcast
    ➡ 13125551111
```
(continued)

```
    dialer map ip 10.100.0.2 name Chicago speed 56 broadcast
      ➡ 13125552222
    dialer map ip 10.100.0.2 name Chicago speed 56 broadcast
      ➡ 13125553333
    dialer hold-queue 10
    dialer load-threshold 100 either
    dialer-group 1
    ppp authentication chap
    ppp multilink
   !
   router ospf 123
    network 192.168.100.10 0.0.0.0 area 99
    !other networks to support go here
   !
   ip host TestISDN 10.100.0.2
   ip classless
   ip route 0.0.0.0 0.0.0.0 10.0.0.1 150
   ip route 0.0.0.0 0.0.0.0 10.100.0.2 160
   ip route 10.100.0.2 255.255.255.255 BRI0
   access-list 102 deny    ospf any any
   access-list 102 permit ip any any
   !
   dialer-list 1 protocol ip list 102
   !
   end
```

LISTING 5-4.   *Multilink PPP using a single BRI and legacy dialing*

The IP address 10.0.0.1 used for the preferred default route is a loopback port on the Chicago router. It is learned through the dynamic routing protocol running across the primary link to Chicago, which the multilink PPP connection is backing up. This must be a different IP address than the ISDN target address used to bring up the backup link. If we try to use the same IP address for both, the backup path through the ISDN interface will always be used, because the router will always choose a connected path to a destination over a learned path.

Other than the *ppp multilink* statement and its corresponding *dialer load-threshold* setting, this configuration is identical to the ISDN BRI dial backup in the previous chapter. The difference is that we now get 112 Kbps of bandwidth from our dial backup link rather than only 56 Kbps.

If we are using multilink PPP and we want all the links in a multilink bundle to remain connected indefinitely, we should set the *dialer idle-timeout* to a very high value. The special cases where *dialer-load threshold 1* would keep all links in a rotary group connected indefinitely and *dialer-load threshold 2* would keep two links connected indefinitely are only supported in IOS 11.0 and earlier versions.

One feature of this configuration having nothing to do with multilink PPP is the use of multiple dialer maps to provide the equivalent of a physical rotary configuration for the target ISDN BRI lines. By configuring each BRI as a rotary within the two channels it provides, we produce the equivalent of six numbers in the dialing rotation. Other sites calling the Chicago router would use similar configurations, but they would rotate the order of the dialer maps to call their preferred line first.

The Chicago configuration in Listing 5-5 is a little more complex because it is using dialer profiles to support calls from four different sites on three BRI lines. We prefer not to restrict callers to any specific line. That way, even if one of the Chicago BRI lines is down, remote sites are still able to connect (assuming there is at least one free B-channel available).

```
version 11.2
!
hostname Chicago
!
username NewYork password NYsecret
username LosAngeles password LAsecret
username Portland password Psecret
username Evanston password Esecret
isdn switch-type basic-ni1
!
interface Loopback1
 description Target Address for Default Routes on Remotes
 ip address 10.0.0.1 255.255.255.255
!
interface Loopback2
 description Target Address for ISDN Dialing
 ip address 10.100.0.2 255.255.255.255
!
interface BRI2/0
 no ip address
 encapsulation ppp
 isdn spid1 31255511110101
 isdn spid2 31255511120101
 dialer pool-member 2
 ppp authentication chap
 ppp multilink
!
```

(continued)

```
interface BRI2/1
 no ip address
 encapsulation ppp
 isdn spid1 31255522220101
 isdn spid2 31255522230101
 dialer pool-member 2
 ppp authentication chap
 ppp multilink
!
interface BRI2/2
 no ip address
 encapsulation ppp
 isdn spid1 31255533330101
 isdn spid2 31255533340101
 dialer pool-member 2
 ppp authentication chap
 ppp multilink
!
interface Dialer2
 description dial-in from New York
 ip unnumbered Loopback2
 encapsulation ppp
 no peer default ip address
 dialer remote-name NewYork
 dialer pool 2
 dialer-group 1
 ppp authentication chap
 ppp multilink
!
interface Dialer3
 description dial-in from Los Angeles
 ip unnumbered Loopback2
 encapsulation ppp
 no peer default ip address
 dialer remote-name LosAngeles
 dialer pool 2
 dialer-group 1
 ppp authentication chap
 ppp multilink
!
interface Dialer4
 description dial-in from Portland
 ip unnumbered Loopback2
```

(continued)

```
 encapsulation ppp
 no peer default ip address
 dialer remote-name Portland
 dialer pool 2
 dialer-group 1
 ppp authentication chap
 ppp multilink
!
interface Dialer5
 description dial-in from Evanston
 ip unnumbered Loopback2
 encapsulation ppp
 no peer default ip address
 dialer remote-name Evanston
 dialer pool 2
 dialer-group 1
 ppp authentication chap
 ppp multilink
!
router ospf 123
 network 10.0.0.1 0.0.0.0 area 99
 network 10.100.0.2 0.0.0.0 area 99
 ! other networks to support go here
!
ip classless
access-list 102 deny    ospf any any
access-list 102 permit ip any any
!
dialer-list 1 protocol ip list 102
!
end
```

LISTING 5-5. *Multilink PPP using multiple BRIs and dialer profiles*

The duplication of the *encapsulation ppp, ppp authentication chap,* and *ppp multilink* lines in both the *interface BRI* sections and the *interface Dialer* sections is deliberate and essential. The specification under *interface BRI* determines what facilities will be supported on that physical interface, while the specification under *interface Dialer* specifies which of the modes supported by the physical interface will be used by the logical dialer.

The challenge is that an incoming call must be identified by the BRI interface before it can be bound to a dialer interface to invoke the desired dialer profile for the connection. The only two mechanisms available for this function, assuming there is a choice of profiles, are calling number identification (which ties the caller to a specific phone number) and PPP authentication. To minimize configuration complexity, we use the CHAP authentication to identify the caller and select the correct dialer profile.

But this means that all PPP link properties, which include not only authentication but also multilink usage, must be negotiated before the call can be assigned to the correct dialer. Therefore, these properties need to be configured twice. There are also some confusing special cases involved with setting up a dialer profile configuration. For example, if there is only one dialer profile defined, the call is passed to the dialer profile before PPP negotiations are started. This can cause other possible bindings, such as a virtual template, to be ignored.

The load-threshold is not set on the incoming multilink PPP dialers on this router. That is because this router has no way to place a call for those bundles, so there is no need to measure and respond to traffic loading. We do, however, configure the *dialer-list* to keep the link up only if there is "interesting traffic"—just in case there is a failure in the routing protocol, configuration, or software.

We do have a challenge in that if all four remote sites need to call in simultaneously, and the first three have already consumed two B-channels each, the fourth site will be locked out. We would like to reserve B-channels for specific sites, which would seem to be an ideal application of the min-link qualifier available on the Cisco *dialer pool-member* statement. Unfortunately, that feature is only honored when outgoing calls are being placed, so it does not help us here. Instead, we try to minimize the potential for occurrence by setting a high threshold in the *dialer load-threshold* commands on the calling routers.

This is a common trade-off when dial backup is configured, as normally very few sites will require a dial link at the same time. But there are scenarios in which every site might be trying to dial in, such as a catastrophic failure in the network service used for the primary links. As always, we would have to weigh the cost of providing all the links that might possibly be required against the probability of and potential loss from such an event. In this case, the cost is merely the procurement of a fourth BRI line at Chicago—but when designing a large network, we could be talking about multiple PRI lines, additional interfaces, or even additional routers to handle the load.

LOAD SHARING OF EQUAL COST LINKS

Multilink PPP is limited in the number of ISDN B-channels that can be combined into a single bundle. The maximum useful size of any one bundle is at most one PRI. If we need to go faster, we need to either change technologies or find another approach to combining individual channels. If we are using a routing protocol that can cope with multiple equal routes between the two locations involved, we can expand the effective bandwidth of ISDN by load sharing across multiple PPP bundles.

Load sharing is a common technique for permanent links and can also be used for dial backup links. It can present, however, a number of critical tradeoffs. First, we must resolve the design issues faced when implementing aggregate permanent links. The first question is whether load sharing should be on a per-packet basis or on a per-destination basis. This often requires making a critical choice between balancing the loading on each link and keeping the processor utilization on the router at acceptable levels.

In the Cisco world, the traditional way to load share on a per-packet basis is to force the router to use process-switching rather than fast-switching by applying the *no ip route-cache* command to the interfaces. This forces the router to route each packet individually, allowing packets to any one destination to be distributed across all available routes. Fast-switching (enabled by default or reinstated by using one of the *ip route-cache* commands) caches the routing decision for the first packet to a destination and uses that path for all subsequent packets to the same destination.

The primary drawback of process-switching is its CPU consumption. Because of this, the maximum number of packets per second that can be process-switched on any router platform is much less than the number that can be fast-switched. Table 5-2 gives some typical performance numbers from Cisco's sales guides. On a typical router, the impact of using process-switching versus using the default method of fast-switching is an order of magnitude.

TABLE 5-2. *Cisco Router Performance with Process-Switching versus Fast-Switching*

ROUTER PLATFORM	PROCESS-SWITCHING (PACKETS/SECOND)	FAST-SWITCHING (PACKETS/SECOND)
1600	600	4,000
1700	1,500	8,400
2500	800	4,400
2600	1,500	15,000
3620	2,000	16,000
3640	4,000	40,000
MC3810	2,000	10,000
4000	1,800	14,000
4500	5,000	40,000
4700	7,000	50,000
7000-RP	2,500	30,000
7200-NPE300	20,000	300,000
7500-RSP2	10,000	150,000
7500-RSP4	20,000	300,000

If fast-switching is enabled on the interfaces, the processor load will be minimal, but all packets to a specific destination will use the same link (or multilink PPP bundle). This can be critical if we are supporting a high bandwidth application wherein all packets are addressed to the same server address, as we lose the benefits of spreading the load across multiple links.

To solve the dilemma of whether to fast-switch or process-switch, Cisco introduced an alternative called Cisco Express Forwarding (CEF). One of the key features of CEF is the ability to do per-packet load distribution at fast-switching forwarding rates. As that capability is implemented on more platforms, and the IOS releases which support it stabilize, the decision of whether to use per-packet or per-destination load balancing will become one of which works best for the applications being supported, rather than which the router can handle.

When process-switching is used to extend the capability of ISDN-based dial backup, the capacity penalty for process-switching must be carefully watched. Under worst-case loading, each T1 PRI could carry over 4,000 packets per second in each direction. This is 8,000 packets per second for the router to process per PRI. This worst-case packet rate could be considered pathological. But should traffic ever approach these levels, any router sized to handle only a few Mbps of data in fast-switching mode would be overwhelmed.

The primary challenge in aggregating multiple multilink PPP bundles for load sharing lies in getting all the individual bundles to dial. The *backup interface* command only supports assigning a single interface to the backup role, so it is not useful even if we could depend on it to detect link failure. Similarly, our standard approach using dial-on-demand routing cannot be guaranteed to bring up more than a single link. Once the first bundle comes up and routes are learned, there will be no further traffic to force the other desired bundles to initiate. As a result, if any of the bundles should fail to connect on the first try, they may never try again.

What we would like to do is use *dialer watch* with multiple dialer profiles, one for each multilink PPP bundle. By using a different watched address for each multilink PPP bundle and only allowing that address to be propagated over the primary full-time link and the one backup bundle (Figure 5-4), we could reliably force an arbitrary number of multilink PPP bundles to be initiated and maintained. Unfortunately, the implementation of *dialer watch,* at least in IOS 12.0 and 12.1, restricts its use to legacy dialer configurations, so we have no way to identify more than one source/destination pairing of names. So when using *dialer watch* we cannot establish more than one multilink PPP bundle, because we lack the means to distinguish each bundle.

We could force dial-on-demand to function by using two real subnetworks for the selective advertisements. But using production network addresses rather than loopback interface addresses would mean that if we were forced onto ISDN backup, and for any reason not all of the multilink PPP bundles could be established, then at least one production network would be unreachable—even though a working backup link existed.

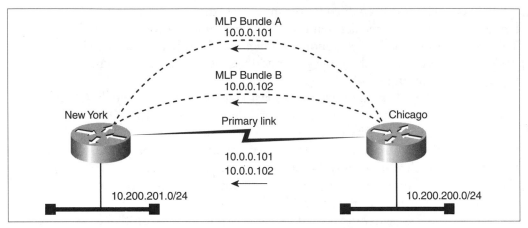

FIGURE 5-4. *Aggregating multilink PPP bundles*

The solution is to use dial-on-demand with dialer profiles and configure a routing protocol to generate the necessary trigger traffic. While EIGRP, RIP, and OSPF normally exchange routing information or hello packets using a broadcast or a multicast address, some implementations include extensions to allow the specification of neighbors by IP addresses (as is done by default with BGP).

In our configuration example, we will use RIP version 2 (RIPv2) to generate the traffic that will force up dial-on-demand. RIPv2 has a number of advantages for this application. It requires very little in the way of router resources to run; it will generate UDP routing update packets to any address we care to specify, and as frequently as we want (up to once per second); it will continue to send these update packets at the same rate regardless of whether or not it receives a response; and it can be heavily filtered to minimize the size of the packets required to transmit the updates.

CONFIGURATION EXAMPLE: 2.5 MBPS ISDN DIAL BACKUP

In this example configuration, we will set up the route advertisements of the loopback ports on the target Chicago router as diagrammed in Figure 5-4. We will also configure RIPv2 on the New York router to generate a reliable source of traffic for each of those addresses. Anytime the primary link fails, the RIPv2 update packets will force the dialing of the initial link in each bundle. We define a separate loopback port on the Chicago router for each multilink PPP bundle we wish to support. Then we control the routing advertisements for each address so that they can only be learned at the New York router if either the primary link is up or the associated multilink PPP bundle is connected. With EIGRP, we would filter the advertisements being sent by Chicago with *distribute-list out interface* statements under *router eigrp*. But in this example we are using OSPF as our routing protocol, and it does not support the filtering of individual routes in link-state advertisements on a per-interface basis.

Instead, we must filter the advertisements in New York with *distribute-list in interface* statements.

As long as the primary link is up and functioning, the New York router will route the RIPv2 update packets to both trigger addresses over the primary link, and no calls will be placed. When the primary link fails, however, both addresses will disappear from the New York router's routing tables. Each trigger address will then activate a different floating static route; the route will vector the trigger address via its own dialer interface. Each dialer in turn will set up a multilink PPP bundle to the Chicago router using different source host names (NewYorkA and NewYorkB using the *ppp chap hostname* command) and different destination router names (ChicagoA and ChicagoB respectively, using the *dialer remote-name* command). As long as all bundles have the same routing metrics for all routes except the trigger addresses, link aggregation will take over and the traffic load will be shared across all channels of all bundles.

Note that it is not required that the primary link to Chicago actually terminate on the New York router. As long as OSPF has a route to the Chicago target addresses, the floating static routes that activate the dial backup will remain inactive.

Just to be safe, we define different loopback addresses for each bundle's *ip unnumbered* IP address. We also define a unique loopback address for RIP to advertise. We then need to enable RIP on this address and every interface that might be used to send directed RIPv2 updates. Passive-interface commands are then used to disable all RIPv2 multicasts. Listing 5-6 shows all the relevant portions of the New York router configuration.

```
version 11.2
!
hostname NewYork
!
username ChicagoA password SecretA
username ChicagoB password SecretB
!
interface Loopback0
 description IP address for RIP to advertise
 ip address 10.0.0.100 255.255.255.255
!
interface Loopback1
 description Source IP address for bundle A to Chicago
 ip address 10.100.0.1 255.255.255.255
!
interface Loopback2
 description Source IP address for bundle B to Chicago
 ip address 10.100.0.2 255.255.255.255
!
```

(continued)

```
interface Serial0/0:23
 description ISDN PRI for MLP bundle A
 no ip address
 encapsulation ppp
 no ip route-cache
 dialer pool-member 1
 isdn switch-type primary-dms100
 ppp authentication chap
 ppp chap hostname NewYorkA
 ppp multilink
!
interface Serial0/1:23
 description ISDN PRI for MLP bundle B
 no ip address
 encapsulation ppp
 no ip route-cache
 dialer pool-member 2
 isdn switch-type primary-dms100
 ppp authentication chap
 ppp chap hostname NewYorkB
 ppp multilink
!
interface Dialer1
 description MLP bundle A
 ip unnumbered Loopback1
 encapsulation ppp
 no ip route-cache
 dialer remote-name ChicagoA
 dialer string 18885551111
 dialer hold-queue 10
 dialer load-threshold 10 either
 dialer pool 1
 dialer-group 1
 ppp authentication chap
 ppp chap hostname NewYorkA
 ppp multilink
!
interface Dialer2
 description MLP bundle B
 ip unnumbered Loopback2
 encapsulation ppp
 no ip route-cache
 dialer remote-name ChicagoB
 dialer string 18885552222
```

(continued)

```
 dialer hold-queue 10
 dialer load-threshold 10 either
 dialer pool 2
 dialer-group 1
 ppp authentication chap
 ppp chap hostname NewYorkB
 ppp multilink
!
router rip
 version 2
 timers basic 10 10 10 10
 passive-interface Dialer1
 passive-interface Dialer2
 ! Set any other interfaces in 10.0.0.0/8 to passive.
 network 10.0.0.0
 neighbor 10.0.0.101
 neighbor 10.0.0.102
 distribute-list 4 out
 no auto-summary
!
router ospf 1
 network 10.100.0.1 0.0.0.0 area 1234
 network 10.100.0.2 0.0.0.0 area 1234
 distribute-list 1 in Dialer1
 distribute-list 2 in Dialer2
!
ip classless
ip route 10.0.0.101 255.255.255.255 10.0.0.1 190
ip route 10.0.0.102 255.255.255.255 10.0.0.2 190
ip route 10.0.0.1 255.255.255.255 Dialer1
ip route 10.0.0.2 255.255.255.255 Dialer2
!
access-list 1 deny 10.0.0.102
access-list 1 permit any
access-list 2 deny 10.0.0.101
access-list 2 permit any
access-list 4 10.0.0.100
access-list 102 deny   ospf any any
access-list 102 permit ip any any
!
dialer-list 1 protocol ip list 102
!
end
```

LISTING 5-6. *Aggregated multilink PPP dial backup links—calling router*

We use a separate dialer pool for each bundle so that each can be independently limited to the desired maximum number of B-channels. We also set up the dialer pools to keep each bundle on its own PRI. This is not required for small bundles, but when the bundles are large, we want to minimize the possibility that a line disturbance will affect any more bundles than it absolutely has to. We also set a low *dialer load-threshold* to force up links fairly quickly when the path is loaded, yet still allow calls to be dropped when the bandwidth is not needed.

The *no ip route-cache* lines in each dialer disable the default fast-switching. This allows load balancing to occur on a per-packet, rather than a per-destination, basis. If Cisco Express Forwarding were supported by the platform and IOS version, we would have configured it to enable per-packet load balancing.

If there happens to be an adequate range of destinations so that per-packet load balancing is not required, then fast-switching could be enabled using the *ip route-cache* command on each interface. But test carefully, as some dialer implementations perform poorly with fast-switching. Per-destination load balancing should also be selected if the alternate paths have different delays (or variable delays), and per-packet load balancing could introduce a significant probability of out-of-order packet delivery. This often has a more adverse impact on performance than the loss of efficiency in the load balancing. Since fast-switching is the default, this will only be necessary if fast-switching is disabled with a *no ip route-cache* command. Fast-switching may also need to be turned back on if CPU loading is too high, regardless of our desire for per-packet load balancing.

Normal and backup operation can be examined by looking at the floating static routes towards the end of the configuration extract. Normally, the two addresses being continuously sent RIPv2 UDP updates are known via the production routing protocol (OSPF in this case) running over the primary link, which is unfiltered and carries all routes. When the primary link fails, the floating static routes float to the top, and each of the target addresses forces up its associated multilink PPP bundle. For example, 10.0.0.101 is routed via 10.0.0.1, which is always reachable via the static route pointing it to Dialer1.

We reduce the delay in bringing up the ISDN links by changing the RIP timers from their default update interval of 30 seconds down to 10 seconds, using the statement *timers basic 10 10 10 10*. The first number is the update timer. The remaining numbers (invalid, holddown, and flush intervals) can be set to any legal value, as we are not using RIP for routing. Setting them all to 10 is acceptable to the router but would cause instability if we were actually exchanging routes. We set them all to the same value for two reasons: first, to remind us to ensure that the instance of RIP running is never used for routing purposes; and second, to remind us that we can modify the update interval as needed without wasting time in calculating appropriate values for the other intervals.

The final critical configuration lines are the access lists applied to the routing protocols to control which routes are learned over which links. Route advertisements received via *interface Dialer1*, for example, will ignore any mention of target 10.0.0.102. This way, *interface Dialer1* will only be considered a potential path to 10.0.0.101. RIPv2 updates to that address will be able to get through, while those to 10.0.0.102 will still need to travel via *interface Dialer2*, forcing that interface to dial a call if it has not already. Any other dialers configured (only *interface Dialer2* in this example, but there could be more if more bandwidth were needed) similarly must filter incoming advertisements to allow only their unique target address and none of the target addresses used for other backup links.

Normally, we try to put any routing distribution lists on the sending router to minimize the number of routes propagated. We would do that here if we were using EIGRP rather than OSPF. Cisco's OSPF implementation allows the filtering of inbound OSPF routing advertisements only on a per-interface basis, and even those are not allowed under all conditions. For example, an area border router may silently ignore any distribution lists applied to routing advertisements. We also need to ensure that the filters are not overridden by route summarization or other configuration options.

Turning our attention to Listing 5-7, we can see the configuration required for the Chicago router to be called. Aside from the extra loopback interfaces defined to provide targets for the RIPv2 UDP update packets, our example looks like a standard multilink PPP configuration for a site receiving calls from two different routers, NewYorkA and NewYorkB. The only strange part is the use of a different IP address for each dialer—but we know this is because NewYorkA and NewYorkB are really the same router.

```
version 11.2
!
hostname Chicago
!
username NewYorkA password SecretA
username NewYorkB password SecretB
!
interface Loopback1
 description Source IP address for bundle A from New York
 ip address 10.0.0.1 255.255.255.255
!
interface Loopback2
 description Source IP address for bundle B from New York
 ip address 10.0.0.2 255.255.255.255
!
```
(continued)

```
interface Loopback101
 description Target IP address for bundle A triggers
 ip address 10.0.0.101 255.255.255.255
!
interface Loopback102
 description Target IP address for bundle B triggers
 ip address 10.0.0.102 255.255.255.255
!
interface Serial0/0:23
 description ISDN PRI for NewYorkA
 no ip address
 encapsulation ppp
 no ip route-cache
 dialer pool-member 1
 isdn switch-type primary-dms100
 ppp authentication chap
 ppp chap hostname ChicagoA
 ppp multilink
!
interface Serial0/1:23
 description ISDN PRI for New YorkB
 no ip address
 encapsulation ppp
 no ip route-cache
 dialer pool-member 1
 isdn switch-type primary-dms100
 ppp authentication chap
 ppp chap hostname ChicagoB
 ppp multilink
!
interface Dialer1
 description MLP bundle A
 ip unnumbered Loopback1
 encapsulation ppp
 no ip route-cache
 dialer remote-name NewYorkA
 dialer pool 1
 dialer-group 1
 no peer default ip address
 ppp authentication chap
 ppp chap hostname ChicagoA
 ppp multilink
!
```

(continued)

```
interface Dialer2
 description MLP bundle B
 ip unnumbered Loopback2
 encapsulation ppp
 no ip route-cache
 dialer remote-name NewYorkB
 dialer pool 1
 dialer-group 1
 no peer default ip address
 ppp authentication chap
 ppp chap hostname ChicagoB
 ppp multilink
!
router ospf 1
 network 10.0.0.1 0.0.0.0 area 1234
 network 10.0.0.2 0.0.0.0 area 1234
 network 10.0.0.101 0.0.0.0 area 1234
 network 10.0.0.102 0.0.0.0 area 1234
 !
ip classless
access-list 102 deny    ospf any any
access-list 102 permit ip any any
 !
dialer-list 1 protocol ip list 102
 !
end
```

LISTING 5-7. *Aggregated multilink PPP dial backup links—called router*

We determine the multilink PPP bundle for each incoming call by the pseudonym used by the calling router. Careful testing is in order here, as not all IOS releases that support dialer profiles handle *ppp chap hostname* correctly. Check the system logs to ensure that the correct names are applied to the ISDN call records. Although both PRIs are in the same dialer pool, each will handle calls for only one of the two multilink PPP bundles from New York, as the New York dialers for each bundle use a different phone number to place their calls.

SUPPORTING IPX ALONG WITH IP

Many networks must also support the IPX protocol suite, usually (but not always) to support Novell NetWare servers. IPX in general and Novell NetWare servers in particular impose their own set of unique requirements on the routers. IPX uses the same routing philosophy as IP, wherein each physical network is identified by a network number and the individual systems on the network are identified by the host ID. Unlike IP, however, IPX always uses 32 bits for the network ID and 48 bits for the host ID. While this makes for a larger address space, it also makes it impractical to aggregate addresses in routing advertisements, as there is no concept of a subnetwork mask.

The major challenge with IPX is that, while IP can be dynamically routed using RIP or OSPF (or IGRP or EIGRP if using Cisco routers), IPX routing choices are RIP or NetWare Link State Protocol (NLSP; or EIGRP on Cisco) only. Although IPX appears to have two out of three routing protocols in common with IP, the reality of the situation is that there is virtually no sharing possible. The standard RIP used for IPX is very different from that used for IP, to the extent that we will refer to it as IPXRIP to prevent confusion. The situation with EIGRP is slightly better, as both IP and IPX can share the same EIGRP process. But even then the routing databases are separately maintained, so the only significant savings is in the reduced number of hello packets.

Acceptance of EIGRP as a routing protocol for IPX has been limited. Acceptance was initially poor due to defects in EIGRP's implementation of IPX routing—these continued to plague the offering for the first few years. Early adopters were primarily those who had no choice but to utilize a proprietary product to get the efficiency and very large IPX network sizes that EIGRP made possible. By the time EIGRP had stabilized to the point where it was ready for trouble-free production use, Novell had introduced NLSP, providing the equivalent of OSPF routing capability for IPX without the market limitations inherent in using a single router vendor's proprietary product.

The desirability of running a single routing protocol rather than several has not been lost on Novell, and newer releases of NetWare can run over pure IP with no IPX support required. However, many of us still support legacy equipment that will need IPX support for years to come, so a look at what it takes to provide dial backup for IPX is in order.

CONFIGURATION EXAMPLE: IPX DIAL BACKUP WITH IPXRIP

Before we look at supporting both IPX and IP, let us look at an IPX-only dial backup scenario. Since *dialer watch* does not support IPX, we must use dial-on-demand for our dial backup (unless we are lucky enough to be in an environment where we could rely on *backup interface*). Since there is normally a permanent link in place, we can make a number of simplifying assumptions in our IPX support scenario. In particular, we can assume that local clients and servers will have already learned about available services (via the Novell Service Advertisement Protocol [SAP]), and that we do not need to emulate this availability—or the exchange of watchdog packets—while the links are not up.

We do need to know some IPX network numbers that can be used to force the dial backup link up when the primary link fails. These should be the IPX network numbers used by the servers if the remote site is providing server services, or the IPX network numbers used to identify the LANs at the other site if the servers are local and we are calling the client site.

The basic philosophy of the dial backup is identical to what we have discussed so far, except that the protocol is IPX rather than IP, so we have to use IPX configuration commands. We must also be much more concerned with performance issues with IPX, as the LAN-oriented protocols which must typically be supported are much more sensitive to delay. Consider the simple scenario in Figure 5-5. We have two sites, one with a Novell NetWare server, the other with a single client, connected by a primary link that is backed up by an ISDN link.

Normally, when supporting Novell we configure the client site to call the server site. This reflects the request/response architecture of typical Novell NetWare services, wherein the client initiates almost every interaction. Unlike a classical dial-on-demand IPX configuration, in which we would try to minimize the time spent with the line active, here we are trying to replace a full-time link. We make no attempt to filter out SPX watchdog packets or any other non-essential traffic that would help to keep the backup link alive when the primary link is down. Looking first at the Chicago router at the server site, we have the configuration shown in Listing 5-8.

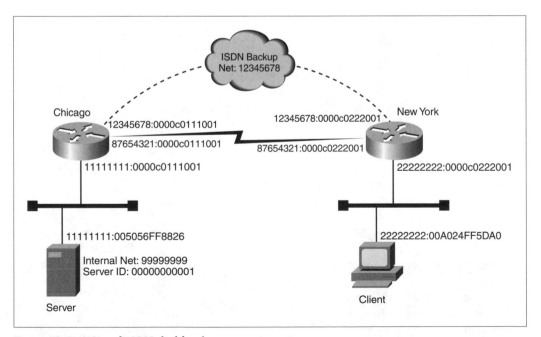

FIGURE 5-5.   *Simple IPX dial backup scenario*

```
version 11.0
!
hostname Chicago
!
username NewYork password secret
ipx routing 0000.c011.1001
isdn switch-type basic-ni1
!
interface Ethernet0
 no ip address
 ipx network 11111111 encapsulation SAP
 ipx output-rip-delay 55
 ipx output-sap-delay 55
!
interface Serial0
 no ip address
 ipx delay 7
 ipx network 87654321
 ipx output-rip-delay 200
 ipx output-sap-delay 200
 ipx sap-interval 5
!
interface BRI0
 no ip address
 encapsulation ppp
 no keepalive
 ipx network 12345678
 ipx delay 30
 ipx output-rip-delay 200
 ipx output-sap-delay 200
 ipx sap-interval 5
 isdn spid1 31255511110000
 isdn spid2 31255511120000
 dialer idle-timeout 300
 dialer map ipx 12345678.0000.c022.2001 name NewYork
  ➥ broadcast
 dialer hold-queue 10
 dialer-group 1
 ppp authentication chap
!
access-list 902 deny 1
access-list 902 deny 4
access-list 902 permit -1
```

(*continued*)

```
!
dialer-list 1 protocol ipx list 902
!
end
```

LISTING 5-8.   Called router configuration for simple IPX dial backup

In this example we use standard IPXRIP and assign IPX network numbers to all interfaces. While this is not required, it keeps dialer configuration much simpler if static MAC addresses are assigned as part of the *ipx routing* command. That way, if a router needs to be replaced in the field, we do not need to reconfigure all the routers that might be calling it so that their dialer maps and floating static routes match the new Ethernet MAC address. We also insert a larger gap between multiple packet RIP and SAP advertisements to minimize their impact on production traffic. Similarly, we stretch out the interval between full SAP updates to further reduce the overhead.

Access-list 902 prevents RIP and SAP advertisements, which are broadcast out of every link supporting IPX, from bringing up the dial link when it's not needed. Any other broadcast services in use—such as NetBIOS—should be added to the filter. As is the case with IP, here the dialer filter does not block the traffic listed as *deny*. Rather, it ignores the presence of denied traffic when deciding when to bring up the link and when to drop it.

The client-side router configuration (Listing 5-9) is more interesting, because this is the router that is responsible for placing and maintaining the call. Floating static routes in IPX must be identified as floating static, and we do not have the luxury of fine gradations in weight that are available in IP floating static routes.

```
version 11.0
!
hostname NewYork
!
username Chicago password secret
ipx routing 0000.c022.2001
isdn switch-type basic-ni1
!
interface Ethernet0
 no ip address
 ipx network 22222222 encapsulation SAP
 ipx output-rip-delay 55
 ipx output-sap-delay 55
!
```

(continued)

```
interface Serial0
 no ip address
 ipx delay 7
 ipx network 87654321
 ipx output-rip-delay 200
 ipx output-sap-delay 200
 ipx sap-interval 5
!
interface BRI0
 no ip address
 encapsulation ppp
 no keepalive
 ipx network 12345678
 ipx delay 30
 ipx output-rip-delay 200
 ipx output-sap-delay 200
 ipx sap-interval 5
 isdn spid1 21255512340000
 isdn spid2 21255512430000
 dialer idle-timeout 300
 dialer map ipx 12345678.0000.co11.1001 name Chicago broadcast
 ➥ 13125551111
 dialer hold-queue 10
 dialer-group 1
 ppp authentication chap
!
access-list 902 deny 1
access-list 902 deny 4
access-list 902 permit -1
!
ipx route 11111111 12345678.0000.c011.1001 floating-static
ipx route 99999999 12345678.0000.c011.1001 floating-static
!
dialer-list 1 protocol ipx list 902
!
end
```

LISTING 5-9.   *Calling router configuration for simple IPX dial backup*

Most of the New York router's configuration is a mirror image of the Chicago router's. In particular, the *ipx output-rip-delay, ipx output-sap-delay* and *ipx sap-interval* must all match those on the Chicago router end of each link. Indeed, other than those addressing changes to match the location, the only lines that differ are the dialer map and the floating static routes.

As is the case with *ip dialer maps,* the *ipx dialer map* on the New York router must have a phone number included so it can dial the Chicago router. If we had clients and servers at both locations, we would configure both routers to dial each other. However, we would need to use care in handling the situation in which both routers happen to dial and connect at the same time.

The keys to correct operation are the definition of floating static routes (the *ipx route* statements) on the New York router and the control of route selection by *ipx delay.* The keyword *floating-static* tells the router to ignore the static route if the network specified (11111111 and 99999999 in this example) is known through a dynamic routing protocol. When the primary link fails and the destination is removed from the routing table, the corresponding floating static route will be inserted in its place. Note that we define routes both to the LAN and to the internal network on the server. Theoretically, the static route to the LAN is not necessary if we are only using Novell NetWare services. However, it is included here just in case there are any client-to-client applications.

The *ipx delay* statements serve the same function as the delay statements used with EIGRP when configuring dial-on-demand routing backup for IP. IPXRIP routes on the basis of minimum delay. The choice of delays—seven for permanent and 30 for ISDN—used in this example have nothing to do with the actual delays on the links. The intent is that in a larger network, where there are multiple routers and paths, we choose a path that requires more LAN or permanent link hops over a path that keeps the ISDN line active.

The correct values to use for delay will depend upon the specific constraints on network performance. The values in this example are based on the assumption that if there is any permanent connectivity available, the dial backup should not be used. In other words, we apply the same criteria for keeping the line up that we used for bringing it up in the first place. What is essential is that IPX use the primary link any time primary and dial backup are up at the same time.

CONFIGURATION EXAMPLE: DIAL BACKUP WITH OSPF FOR IP AND RIP FOR IPX

Simultaneous support for both IP and IPX, even when EIGRP is used for routing both, is done in the mode of ships passing in the night. That is, neither protocol has any knowledge or awareness of the other, and each must independently determine the optimal route to use through the network. As a result, it is quite common when line problems occur for one protocol to be affected more than the other, as each routing protocol converges at its own speed. This is most apparent in older networks in which OSPF or EIGRP is used to route the IP traffic, while the IPX is left to be handled by IPXRIP.

However, the fact that the IP and the IPX routing protocols do not communicate with one another does not mean that we cannot take advantage of the higher performance available in one routing protocol to benefit the lesser performance of another. In this example configuration, we let IP take care of bringing up the backup link so that by the time IPXRIP discovers there is a problem with the primary link, the backup link is already up, known as an alternate route, and ready to take over.

By letting IP handle the dialing chores, we can greatly simplify the IPX configuration. We can leave just enough in place so that normal IPX traffic will force up the link, most of the time, if there is insufficient IP traffic to do the job. This allows us to take a broad-brush approach to defining "interesting" IPX traffic. If we ignore traffic that should bring up the link, the penalty is minor because IP will bring the link up anyway. In an application in which IPX traffic will never be present (or useful) in the absence of IP traffic, we could further simplify the configuration by not defining any IPX traffic as "interesting."

The key to reasonable response time for IPXRIP is to change the update interval timer. The default value of 60 seconds means it could take up to 4 minutes to detect that the primary link has failed and move traffic over to the backup link. Reducing the update interval timer is only practical on low-speed links if the network is small enough or the routing simple enough that the number of IPX routes to be exchanged can be kept to a small number. Otherwise the routing overhead can be excessive. It is also essential when adjusting the IPXRIP update timer to a nondefault value that all devices attached to that interface are configured for the new value—otherwise, IPXRIP will fail.

To minimize the percentage of available bandwidth wasted, we only adjust the update timer on the higher-speed primary link. We can set the IPXRIP update interval to the minimum value allowed on Cisco routers—10 seconds—rather than the default 60 seconds. This reduces the worst-case detection and holddown time required for IPXRIP to 40 seconds. By the time IPXRIP is ready to accept the higher-cost route through the ISDN backup link, that link will already be up and ready for use because of the response of the IP routing protocol.

On Cisco routers, the IPXRIP update interval must be adjusted with care, or strange results can occur. The problem is that the granularity of the update timer is determined by the shortest interval set on any of the interfaces in the router. To avoid problems, all interfaces must be configured to an integral multiple of the shortest update interval used on any interface on that router. The default value of 60 seconds must also be considered unless all interfaces have explicitly set values.

As an example of what can be done to hasten IPX recovery, we will take the IPX dial backup configuration we just did and combine it with the IP-only multilink PPP configuration we did earlier in this chapter. We will focus on the configuration of the calling New York router, as the configuration of the called router does not contribute to our understanding. Listing 5-10 provides the configuration statements essential to support dial backup, again leaving out all routing, security, and management configuration statements.

```
version 11.0
!
hostname NewYork
!
username Chicago password secret
!
ipx routing 0000.0c01.0105
isdn switch-type basic-ni1
!
interface Loopback0
 description Management & OSPF IP
 ip address 192.168.0.1 255.255.255.255
!
interface Serial0
 ip unnumbered Loopback0
 bandwidth 1544
 ipx delay 7
 ipx network 12345678
 ipx output-rip-delay 200
 ipx output-sap-delay 200
 ipx sap-interval 5
 ipx update-time 10
!
interface BRI0
 ip unnumbered Loopback0
 encapsulation ppp
 bandwidth 56
 ipx delay 30
 ipx network 87654321
 ipx output-rip-delay 200
 ipx output-sap-delay 200
 ipx sap-interval 5
 isdn spid1 21255512340000
 isdn spid2 21255512350000
 dialer idle-timeout 170
 dialer map ip 10.100.0.2 name Chicago speed 56 broadcast
  ➡ 13125551111
 dialer map ip 10.100.0.2 name Chicago speed 56 broadcast
  ➡ 13125552222
 dialer map ip 10.100.0.2 name Chicago speed 56 broadcast
  ➡ 13125553333
 dialer map ipx 87654321.0000.C011.1001 name Chicago speed
  ➡ 56 broadcast 13125551111
```

(continued)

```
   dialer map ipx 87654321.0000.C011.1001 name Chicago speed
    ➡ 56 broadcast 13125552222
   dialer map ipx 87654321.0000.C011.1001 name Chicago speed
    ➡ 56 broadcast 13125553333
   dialer hold-queue 10
   dialer load-threshold 200 either
   dialer-group 1
   ppp multilink
   ppp authentication chap
 !
 router ospf 123
  network 192.168.0.1 0.0.0.0 area 4321
 !Add local networks here
 !
 ip classless
 ip route 0.0.0.0 0.0.0.0 10.100.0.1 150 ! Chicago via frame
 ip route 0.0.0.0 0.0.0.0 10.100.0.2 160 ! Chicago via ISDN
 ip route 10.100.0.2 255.255.255.255 BRI0
 access-list 102 deny    ospf any any
 access-list 102 permit ip any any
 access-list 902 deny 1
 access-list 902 deny 4
 access-list 902 permit -1
 !
 ipx route 11111111 87654321.0000.c011.1001 floating-static
 ipx route 99999999 87654321.0000.c011.1001 floating-static
 !
 dialer-list 1 protocol ipx list 902
 dialer-list 1 protocol ip list 102
 !
 end
```

LISTING 5-10. *IPX dial backup driven by IP OSPF routing*

Before we get to the IPX behavior, let's quickly review how the IP dial backup works. The key to IP communications recovery is in the hierarchy of floating static routes defining the default path. The preferred route is via a loopback address on the Chicago router, known only through the routing protocol running between the two routers. With unnumbered serial links, this could be the address used for the far side of the link—but it is safer to use a dedicated loopback address, just in case there is a problem with the routing protocol's setting up a proper neighbor relationship. If the primary link fails, this address will not be known to the routing protocol and the backup static route will float to the top. The backup static route points to an address on the other end of the ISDN link, which the New York router knows it can reach because of the static route pointing to BRI0. Any packets then will be routed to the BRI0 interface, and the ISDN backup call will be placed.

Whether we are running OSPF or EIGRP as our IP routing protocol, the behavior will be the same. If the serial interface fails hard, the dial backup will be initiated immediately. If the serial interface failure prevents communications but does not cause a hardware or link layer indication of failure, the routing protocol will detect that the destination is unreachable because hello packets will cease to arrive. Either way, all learned routes will be removed from the routing table and only the target address for the ISDN link will remain a candidate.

Configuration of the permanent link is arbitrary except for the *bandwidth, ipx delay,* and *ipx update-time* statements. Because dial-on-demand dialer interfaces are always reported to be up, whether or not they are connected, the *bandwidth* and *ipx delay* must be set so that the primary link will always be preferred over the backup link for both IP and IPX. If necessary, the metric for OSPF that is usually set based on the link bandwidth can be overriden using an *ip ospf cost* statement on the backup interface. Otherwise, when the backup link is released, traffic flow will be blocked until the loss of the route is detected by the associated routing protocol.

Note that in newer IOS releases, the syntax of the commands *ipx update-time* and *ipx sap-interval* has been changed to *ipx update interval rip* and *ipx update interval sap,* respectively. The SAP interval is expressed in seconds rather than minutes, as in earlier IOS releases. This is not a problem when an older configuration is migrated to a newer IOS release, as the newer IOS releases recognize the old syntax and translate it to the new syntax automatically. However, the new syntax will not be recognized if an older IOS release happens to be used with a configuration saved with the new syntax. If this occurs, the IPX update interval will revert to the default value on one end of the link, and IPXRIP at the other end will cycle the link up and down as it times out, waiting for the updates that should be arriving every 10 seconds.

Also, always double-check the dialer map statements to make sure that the names used in the dialer maps exactly match the host name configured on the router at the other end of the link. For example, in some IOS releases the IPX dialer maps are case sensitive, while the IP dialer maps are not. This can be very confusing to troubleshoot because IP works and IPX does not, even though the dialer maps used to place the call are configured identically.

BGP-DRIVEN DIAL BACKUP

One critical requirement for successful use of dial-on-demand for backup purposes is having "interesting" traffic present at the router with the backup line to force the dial. When there is only one permanent and one dial link, it is usually easy to configure the routers so that any normal traffic, which frequently includes the syslog's reporting that the primary link has gone down, will force the link up. But if we want to provide dial backup for more than one permanent link, or implement a second level of dial backup just in case, it is no longer a given that there will be appropriate traffic to trigger the dialing.

Consider an application in which we want to provide dial backup for dial backup. The easy solution is to use IOS 12.0 and *dialer watch*. We simply define two unique loopback port addresses at the target site, then define filters to advertise them both over the primary link, only one of them over the preferred dial link, and neither of them over the secondary dial link. Then we set up a *dialer watch* on the preferred dial link for the address only advertised over the primary link and a *dialer watch* on the secondary dial link for the address advertised over both the primary and the preferred dial links. This is a trivial extension to the normal use of *dialer watch*.

On the other hand, there are many networks for which the use of *dialer watch* is not an option. We may be using OSPF rather than EIGRP for network routing, or we may be unwilling or unable to upgrade to IOS 12.0. Even without the ability to use *dialer watch,* there may be a need to use two levels of backup. With a little extra effort, *dialer watch* can be emulated using any IOS release that supports dial-on-demand routing. It can also be emulated, with the appropriate vendor specific modifications, on any vendor's routers that support dial-on-demand-like capability, advertisement filtering for the interior gateway protocol in use, and Border Gateway Protocol (BGP). This approach can be used to force dialing to occur anytime we cannot guarantee the presence of appropriate traffic to force up a link.

What we do is set up a pair of loopback addresses on the target router(s) with restricted advertising—the same as when we use *dialer watch* to do the job. But instead of depending upon *dialer watch* to force up the link, we configure a BGP peering between the two routers. Hierarchical floating static routes are configured to use the BGP keepalive exchanges to force the preferred link and normal dial-on-demand routing to force the backup link.

CONFIGURATION EXAMPLE: DIAL BACKUP FOR DIAL BACKUP (IP AND IPX)

To see how this works in action, we will look at the scenario in Figure 5-6. We have two routers with three possible links between them—the primary dedicated link, an ISDN backup line, and an asynchronous modem connection to backup the ISDN line. On the calling end, we will use a small office router configuration with a single BRI line and an asynchronous modem on the Auxiliary port. On the called end, we will use a data center router configuration with an ISDN PRI line for supporting

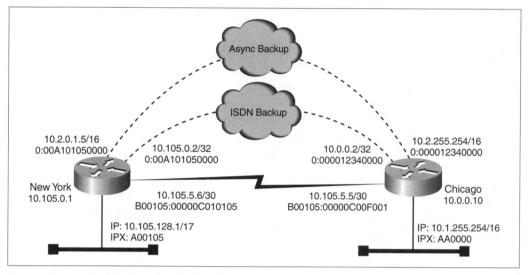

FIGURE 5-6. *Dial backup for dial backup example*

many dial-in connections. But we will support the asynchronous connection on the
Auxiliary port to illustrate how we can dial into a port that also needs to support
interactive network management access.

In a production configuration, each of these links would be served by a separate router at the target location. For this example, however, the required configuration is shown as being all on one router, and only the configuration for the one
remote site is included. (We would not normally use an ISDN PRI line to back up a
single ISDN BRI site.) Similarly, the use of IP unnumbered and IPXWAN (the IPX
equivalent) is not required for this example to work, but, as we will discuss in
Chapter 7, it is frequently mandated by scalability considerations. We also show
the primary link as being Frame Relay, even though there are no known protocol
dependencies.

We will start Listing 5-11 with the calling router in New York. This example
configuration should be considered the minimum to get ISDN and asynchronous dial
support of IP and IPX, not a fully optimized configuration ready for implementation.
Many commands useful when supporting IPX are not shown, such as filters suppress-
ing advertisement of unnecessary addresses and services and spacing out RIP and
SAP updates over the slow WAN links. Nor is this example adequate for an IPX-only
environment. For instance, if there is no outbound IP traffic present at the Primary
router when the Frame Relay link dies, it will never attempt to bring up the asynchronous link. Indeed, as you can see from the dialer maps, IPX traffic is incapable of
bringing up the dial link on this router, as only IP traffic is defined as "interesting"
to the dialer.

```
version 11.0
!
hostname NewYork
!
username Chicago password NYsecret
!
ipx routing 0000.0c01.0105
ipx internal-network A10105
isdn switch-type basic-ni1
chat-script courier ABORT ERROR ABORT "NO " ABORT BUSY "" "at"
 ➥ "" "at&f" OK "atl1m1&b1&h1&r2&c1&d2&m5&k1s0=2" OK "at dt \T"
 ➥ TIMEOUT 90 CONNECT \c
chat-script target-login TIMEOUT 10 Password-\r-Password
 ➥ InSecure "Chicago>" "ppp 10.2.1.5"
!
interface Loopback1
 description Source IP address for BGP
 ip address 10.105.0.1 255.255.255.255
!
interface Loopback2
 description Source IP address for ISDN backup
 ip address 10.105.0.2 255.255.255.255
!
interface Ethernet0
 description Local user network(s)
 ip address 10.105.128.1 255.255.128.0
 ipx network A00105 encapsulation sap
!
interface Serial0
 description Primary links
 no ip address
 encapsulation frame-relay
!
interface Serial0.17 point-to-point
 description PVC to Chicago
 ip address 10.105.5.6 255.255.255.252
 bandwidth 56
 delay 2000
 ipx delay 7
 ipx network B00105
 frame-relay interface-dlci 17
!
```

(continued)

```
interface BRI0
 description Preferred backup path
 ip unnumbered Loopback2
 encapsulation ppp
 bandwidth 56
 delay 5000
 no keepalive
 ipx ipxwan 0 unnumbered NewYork
 ipx delay 30
 isdn spid1 80055512120101
 isdn spid2 80055512130101
 dialer idle-timeout 170
 dialer map ipx 0.0000.1234.0000 name Chicago speed
 ➥ 56 broadcast 18775551234
 dialer map ip 10.0.0.2 name Chicago speed 56 broadcast
 ➥ 18775551234
 dialer hold-queue 10
 dialer-group 1
 ppp authentication chap
!
interface Async1
 description Last resort backup path
 ip address 10.2.1.5 255.255.0.0
 encapsulation ppp
 bandwidth 33
 delay 15000
 ipx ipxwan 0 unnumbered NewYork
 ipx delay 30
 async default routing
 async mode interactive
 dialer in-band
 dialer idle-timeout 300
 dialer map ipx 0.0000.1234.0000 name Chicago broadcast
 ➥ 18885559999
 dialer map ip 10.2.255.254 name Chicago modem-script courier
 ➥ system-script target-login broadcast 18885559999
 dialer hold-queue 10 timeout 60
 dialer-group 1
 ppp authentication chap
!
router eigrp 1
 network 10.0.0.0
!
```

(continued)

```
router bgp 99
 network 10.105.0.1 mask 255.255.255.255
 timers bgp 10 120
 neighbor 10.0.0.10 remote-as 99
 neighbor 10.0.0.10 update-source Loopback1
!
! Routing for Production Traffic
! Use frame relay if available
ip route 0.0.0.0 0.0.0.0 10.0.0.1 150
! Otherwise use ISDN if available
ip route 0.0.0.0 0.0.0.0 10.0.0.3 155
! If all else fails, try Asynchronous dial
ip route 0.0.0.0 0.0.0.0 10.2.255.254 160
! Routing for BGP Keepalives
! Use frame relay if available
ip route 10.0.0.10 255.255.255.255 10.0.0.1 150
! Otherwise force up ISDN
ip route 10.0.0.10 255.255.255.255 10.0.0.2 160
! ISDN dial address
ip route 10.0.0.2 255.255.255.255 BRI0
! Asynchronous dial address
ip route 10.2.0.0 255.255.0.0 Async1
access-list 102 deny   eigrp any any
access-list 102 permit ip any any
!
dialer-list 1 protocol ip list 102
!
line aux 0
 password mumble
 script dialer courier
 login
 modem InOut
 transport input all
 speed 38400
 flowcontrol hardware
!
end
```

LISTING 5-11.   *IP and IPX dial backup for dial backup—calling router (New York) configuration*

The *hostname* and *username* statements provide the identification and pass-words to be used for CHAP authentication. We must be careful here to be consistent among the definition of the *hostname* and any *username* or *dialer map* statements that reference the *hostname*. Even though most functions are not case sensitive, some, such as IPX dialer maps, are. Since this sensitivity (or lack thereof) is not always documented, it is best to simply ensure that all references are identical. Note also that while the *username* must match the remote *hostname*, the password must match (also case sensitive) the password in the *username* statement on the remote system identifying the local *hostname*.

The *ipx routing* command turns on IPX so that Novell NetWare can be supported on the network. The MAC address definition is not mandatory, as we are using IPXWAN on the dial-up links. As a result, it only affects the IPX network address used to identify this end of the Frame Relay link. On the other hand, the IPX internal network assignment (*ipx internal-network A10105*) is critical, as it becomes part of the IPX host address when this router is identified using IPXWAN. We will discuss how this address mapping is done when we get to the *dialer map ipx* statements.

The *chat-script courier* statement is a combination of the chat scripts we used in the first example in this chapter for dialing with a 3COM/USR Courier V.Everything modem. The second chat script, *target-login*, however, is new. Unlike a modem setup or dial chat script, this is a system chat script used to set up communications at the system-to-system level once the modems have established a communications link at the physical level and before starting PPP link setup negotiations. We start by setting a 10-second time-out and then looking for the router password prompt (created by the *password* setting on the target router's Auxiliary port). The construction *Password-\r-Password* is a Cisco syntax feature that says to look for the string terminated by the first hyphen (the *Password:* prompt). If this is found, it proceeds to the next token (sending the string *InSecure* in this case); otherwise, it sends the string up to the second hyphen (\r says to send a carriage return) and tries again, this time looking for the string that ends this token.

In other words, when the modems connect, we look for a password prompt. If we do not see a password prompt within 10 seconds, we request one by sending a carriage return. If we still do not get a password prompt, the script fails and we reset the link. However, if at any point we get a password prompt (whether or not we sent a carriage return), we continue by sending our password *InSecure*. Note that this password is carried in the chat script as clear text, regardless of any settings for password encryption in the global configuration. That is why we use different passwords for this login and the CHAP authentication that will follow. Even though this password is displayed in clear text as part of the router configuration, it is also your first line of defense against hackers dialing in on the modem line. It should be a strong password. The enable password on the target router should be similarly strong and closely guarded—something that will not be weakened even if the login and CHAP passwords are compromised.

If you are using authentication services that require a user name as well as a password, the system chat script would be modified by replacing *Password-\r-Password* with *Username-\r-Username MyName Password*, substituting the appropriate name for *MyName*. This should be seriously considered even though it is not shown here.

In our other examples, we did not touch on the ability to log in to the target router when dialing into the Auxiliary port. In this case, however, we are trying to preserve our ability to use the Auxiliary port for emergency router access. We cannot shut down hackers by not giving them a login prompt without denying ourselves the access we desire.

Once we receive the router prompt *Chicago>* we tell the Chicago router that we want to establish a PPP connection on the link using the IP address 10.2.1.5 at our end of the link. We then unconditionally turn control over to PPP to negotiate the link parameters for IP and IPX. There is no need to check for a correct response, as any failure at this stage would be the result of a configuration error, and there is no way to automatically recover from that.

The configuration of the *Loopback, Ethernet,* and *Serial* interfaces are all standard, so we will skip ahead to the ISDN configuration for interface *BRI0.* This too we have seen before, at least up to the line starting *ipx ipxwan.* IPXWAN is a Novell standard protocol for serial links that provides IPX functionality equivalent to IP unnumbered. The link is assigned an IPX network number of 0. The host ID is determined by taking the internal network number of the router for the first 32 bits of the 48 bit host ID and tacking on 16 bits of zero. This can be seen in the IPX dialer map, where the internal network ID *1234* of the Chicago router translates into the remote IPX address 0:0000.1234.0000.[1] Beyond that, the configuration of the ISDN communications under interface BRI0 is standard.

Moving down to the *interface Async1,* we deviate from standard practice by assigning a large address space to the asynchronous link. Aside from showing how to assign an IP address as part of the connection sequence, there is no justification for this flagrant waste of IP address space. In particular, defining a real IP subnetwork for the backup link rather than using IP unnumbered makes it difficult to scale the solution to handle multiple dial-in servers.

The *async default routing* line is required to enable routing exchanges over the link, while the *async mode interactive* allows us to dial into the modem for router access in an emergency. The former is mandatory; the latter is optional. If dial-in access is not needed, the *modem InOut* line configuration of the Auxiliary port should be changed to *modem callout* and the modem script changed to disable rather than enable auto-answer.

If IPX traffic is considered important, we should add the appropriate *access-list* and *dialer-list* statements to define IPX traffic as "interesting" to dial-on-demand. We would also want to change the routing protocol used for IPX to something that responds more quickly than IPXRIP. We could then duplicate the *modem-script* and *system-script* commands on the IP dialer map onto the IPX dialer map statement to allow IPX packets to initiate a backup call across the asynchronous link.

Note that we again extend the time-out on the *dialer hold queue* to allow time for the connection to be completed. The default time-out of 30 seconds is rarely long enough to allow setup of a long-distance modem connection. We also use the same *dialer-list* assignment (*dialer-group 1*) for both ISDN and asynchronous dialers. Since both interfaces must handle and respond to the same data traffic, this allows us to use a common *dialer-list* for defining "interesting" and "uninteresting" traffic.

The *router eigrp 1* section is there to support routing. We could just as easily be using OSPF or any other full-powered interior routing protocol that supports selective filtering of advertisements.

The *router bgp 99* section, on the other hand, is used to support dial backup rather than routing. Normally BGP is used for routing between management domains (we will look at some considerations related to that use in Chapter 8). In this application, however, we use it as an easily controlled source of IP packets that can be addressed to an arbitrary host address. This is unlike EIGRP, OSPF, RIP, or other interior gateway protocols that normally depend on multicast or broadcasts. We also take advantage of the fact that BGP will only establish a connection to a destination that is explicitly in the routing tables. If BGP is required to support real routing, consider using RIPv2 instead, as we did for bringing up multiple multilink PPP bundles earlier in this chapter (or consider *dialer watch* if it is useable in your environment).

Looking at the individual lines defining BGP usage, we start with a network statement telling BGP to advertise only the local loopback interface. This minimizes the size of the BGP routing updates and routing tables. There is no need to advertise all local subnetworks, as we are not using BGP to perform any actual routing functions. The next line, *timers bgp 10 120*, determines how quickly our dial backup will be triggered and how long we will attempt to place a call before we stop making continuous tries. The former number is the number of seconds between hello packets and determines the maximum dead time between possible trigger packets. The latter number is the delay before a peer is considered unreachable, which translates into how long we can be confident that BGP will continue to send hello packets at the configured rate.

The two *neighbor* lines are repeated for each router for which we desire forcing traffic to be generated. The first specifies that we are using BGP as an interior gateway protocol. The second keeps the source address in the BGP packets constant as we shift from using one interface to another.

The weighting of the floating static routes is critical to successful operation. The static routes must have a higher administrative distance specified than that used by the interior routing protocol. The other key is the Chicago router's filtering of its locally defined loopback addresses so that only certain loopback targets are advertised over any specific link. (This filtering might need to be done on the New York router if we were using a routing protocol other than EIGRP.) Under normal conditions, all traffic flows via Frame Relay. When the Frame Relay link goes down, the 10.0.0.1 target is no longer reachable, and the router looks for an alternative default route. Since the target address 10.0.0.3 is only advertised over ISDN, it will not be available and the only useable target will be 10.2.255.254 via the asynchronous link. Under the rules of dial-on-demand routing, dial links are always connected (whether physically connected or not), so the floating static route through the asynchronous port is activated and the first non-local packet to be routed initiates an analog call.

So far, this is just standard asynchronous dial backup as presented in the first example in this chapter. The single difference is the extra floating static route that only comes into play when ISDN is connected and the primary link is down. To bring up the ISDN link, we need traffic addressed to the ISDN target address of 10.0.0.2. This is where BGP comes into play. Since the peer address 10.0.0.10 is not advertised over any links from the target router, the only way we can establish a BGP peering is via static routes, of which we define only two.

The preferred route is via the Frame Relay target address so that when Frame Relay is up, BGP will exchange keepalive packets using the primary link. However, whenever the primary route disappears, we immediately fall back to the floating static route through the "always available" target address used for ISDN (that is why we need two ISDN target addresses, one to be used only when ISDN is up, the other to use at any time to bring ISDN up). As a result, even if we are currently carrying all production traffic through the asynchronous backup link, we will still continuously try to bring up the ISDN link with BGP's attempts to exchange keepalive messages. Be aware that once the link is declared down by BGP, the ISDN retries will be based on attempts to reestablish a TCP connection, not on the routine exchange of keep-alive packets, and retries will occur periodically rather than continuously. Some people may consider this a benefit and others a defect.

Finally, the access lists define "interesting" traffic for the dialer lists. Here we use the minimum required to prevent continuous dialing caused by EIGRP multicasts or RIP or SAP broadcasts. Similarly, we use our standard configuration for a slow Auxiliary port.

Before we discuss the individual functions configured on the data center router Chicago, keep in mind that normally these functions would be distributed across two or more routers to eliminate the Chicago router as a single point of failure. Since dial target routers often serve many remotes, it is quite possible that all functions will be on any single target router but that their use will be distributed across multiple remotes. It is also possible to make multiple target routers look and behave like a single router for dial backup purposes, further enhancing redundancy without adding significant complexity to the remote router configurations. We will discuss these modifications in the context of a hub-and-spokes topology in Chapter 7.

In Listing 5-12, we turn our attention to the configuration details on the router Chicago, which is the target of all these calls. The only features unique to the support of multiple levels of dial backup in this router's configuration—as opposed to the support of multiple remote routers with a conventional single level of backup—are the extra loopback addresses, the advertisement filters defined for EIGRP, and the configuration of BGP in addition to the production routing protocol.

```
version 11.0
!
hostname Chicago
!
username NewYork password NYsecret
! Define other locations and passwords here...
ipx routing 0000.0C00.F001
ipx internal-network 1234
isdn switch-type primary-dms100
chat-script courier ABORT ERROR ABORT "NO " ABORT BUSY "" "at"
  ➡ "" "at&f" OK "atl1m1&b1&h1&r2&c1&d2&m5&k1s0=2" OK
!
controller T1 0
 framing esf
 linecode b8zs
 pri-group timeslots 1-24
!
interface Loopback1
 description Primary target for frame relay users
 ip address 10.0.0.1 255.255.255.255
!
interface Loopback2
 description IP Address for ISDN Unnumbered
 ip address 10.0.0.2 255.255.255.255
!
interface Loopback3
 description Routing target for ISDN users
 ip address 10.0.0.3 255.255.255.255
!
interface Loopback10
 description Routing target for BGP keepalives
 ip address 10.0.0.10 255.255.255.255
!
interface Ethernet0
 ip address 10.1.255.254 255.255.0.0
 ipx network AA0000 encapsulation sap
!
interface Serial0
 description Frame Relay (T1)
 no ip address
 encapsulation frame-relay
!
! Subinterfaces to support other sites go here
!
```

(continued)

```
interface Serial0.105 point-to-point
 description PVC to router New York
 ip address 10.105.5.5 255.255.255.252
 bandwidth 56
 delay 2000
 ipx delay 7
 ipx network B00105
 frame-relay interface-dlci 105
!
interface Serial0:23
 ip unnumbered Loopback2
 encapsulation ppp
 bandwidth 56
 delay 5000
 no keepalive
 ipx ipxwan 0 unnumbered Chicago
 ipx delay 20
 dialer idle-timeout 300
 dialer map ipx 0.00A1.0105.0000 name NewYork speed
   ➥ 56 broadcast
 dialer map ip 10.105.0.2 name NewYork speed 56 broadcast
! Dialer maps to support other sites go here
 dialer-group 1
 ppp authentication chap
!
interface Async1
 ip address 10.2.255.254 255.255.0.0
 encapsulation ppp
 bandwidth 33
 delay 15000
 ipx ipxwan 0 unnumbered Chicago
 ipx delay 30
 async default routing
 async dynamic address
 async mode interactive
 peer default ip address 10.2.99.99
 dialer in-band
 dialer idle-timeout 300
 dialer map ipx 0.00A1.0105.0000 name NewYork broadcast
 dialer map ip 10.2.1.5 name NewYork broadcast
! Dialer maps to support other sites go her
 dialer-group 1
 ppp authentication chap
 pulse-time 3
```

(continued)

```
!
router eigrp 1
 network 10.0.0.0
 distribute-list 10 out Async1
 distribute-list 11 out Ethernet0
 distribute-list 12 out Serial0.25
 distribute-list 13 out Serial0:23
 no auto-summary
!
router bgp 99
 network 10.0.0.10 mask 255.255.255.255
 timers bgp 10 120
 neighbor 10.105.0.1 remote-as 99
 neighbor 10.105.0.1 update-source Loopback10
!
ip classless
access-list 10 deny   10.0.0.0 0.0.0.255
access-list 10 permit any
access-list 11 deny   10.0.0.0 0.0.0.255
access-list 11 permit any
access-list 12 permit 10.0.0.1 0.0.0.0
access-list 12 deny   10.0.0.0 0.0.0.255
access-list 12 permit any
access-list 13 permit 10.0.0.2 0.0.0.0
access-list 13 permit 10.0.0.3 0.0.0.0
access-list 13 deny   10.0.0.0 0.0.0.255
access-list 13 permit any
!
dialer-list 1 protocol ipx permit
dialer-list 1 protocol ip permit
!
line aux 0
 login
 password InSecure
 script startup courier
 script reset courier
 modem InOut
 transport input all
 stopbits 1
 speed 38400
 flowcontrol hardware
!
end
```

LISTING 5-12. *IP and IPX dial backup for dial backup—called router (Chicago) configuration*

The extra loopback interfaces provide us with the additional addresses required to support multilevel dial-on-demand. In the same way, BGP must be configured so that it responds to the BGP protocol exchanges from remote routers. This allows for maintainance of a steady exchange of hello packets to force up links when required. The unique contribution of the target router is the filtering of address advertisements in the routing protocol used for production routing (EIGRP in this example).

The advertisement filters on the access lines are set up to allow all "real" addresses to be advertised while blocking all target addresses except those specifically delegated to that link (10.0.0.1 on the frame relay link, access-list 12, and 10.0.0.2 and 10.0.0.3 on the ISDN link, access-list 13). This is appropriate for a mesh configuration, but be aware that there are better ways to handle large hub-and-spoke networks, in which exchanging full routing tables will consume unnecessary bandwidth. The goal should be to advertise as few addresses as possible while maintaining maximum capability to utilize alternate routes.

The use of BGP for routing as well as for dial backup support should not be attempted on the same router. While it is theoretically possible to combine the two functions, the potential for introducing mistakes is just too high. If BGP routing functions must be supported on either the calling or the target router, consider modifying this approach to use RIPv2-directed neighbors rather than BGP.

Note the inclusion of an advertisement filter on the local Ethernet port, in addition to those on the links to the remotes. This prevents the remote router from learning routes to the trigger addresses via connections that may be available through other routers. Just use care when setting up this filter so as not to block a loopback address used to identify the real router to network management. In this case, we dedicated the subnetwork 10.0.0.0/24 to artificial target addresses, blocking all advertisements of addresses in this range by default.

CONFIGURATION EXAMPLE: DIAL BACKUP FOR MULTIPLE PRIMARY LINKS

We can use a similar approach to provide dial backup for multiple serial links, without depending upon default routes or other dial-on-demand tricks. Consider the environment in Figure 5-7: we have the Los Angeles site connected by leased lines to New York and Chicago as part of a general mesh topology. Even though the Los Angeles router has full routing tables from both the Chicago router and the New York router, we want to bring up the appropriate ISDN backup line any time either serial link fails.

The key, as before, is to block the routing advertisements for the BGP target addresses on all links except the link being protected. In this case, the Chicago router uses the loopback address 10.111.0.10 for its BGP peering and the loopback address 10.111.0.1 for a dial-on-demand target for the Los Angeles router. The Chicago router then completely blocks the BGP address so that it is not included in any advertisements

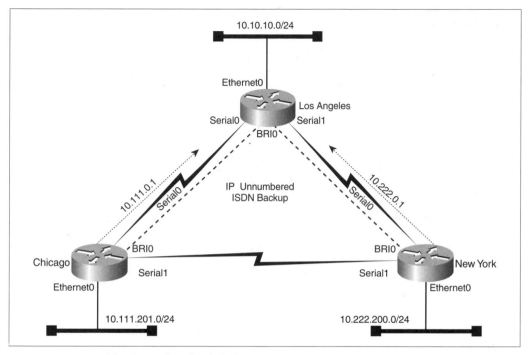

FIGURE 5-7. *Dial backup of multiple links*

to any other routers. As a result, the only way that the Los Angeles router can set up the BGP peering is by using the links defined by its local floating static routes. In the same way, the New York router defines the BGP target 10.222.0.10 and the steering target 10.222.0.1 and blocks them so that the only advertisement that escapes is the 10.222.0.1 steering target out the serial link to the Los Angeles router.

The basic operation is straightforward. If the serial link between the Chicago and Los Angeles routers is up, then the Los Angeles router receives routing advertisements for 10.111.0.1 and sends its BGP keepalives to 10.111.0.10 via the primary link. Any time that specific serial link fails, for whatever reason, the Los Angeles router will stop receiving advertisements for 10.111.0.1. As soon as 10.111.0.1 is removed from its routing table, the next available route to 10.111.0.10 will float to the top and subsequent keepalives will be routed to 10.111.0.2, bringing up the ISDN link to the Chicago router. The serial link between Los Angeles and New York is protected the same way, using the advertisements for 10.222.0.1 that are sent by the New York router only over the serial link to Los Angeles.

To see how this is done, we look first at the configuration of the Chicago router in Listing 5-13. This is just a standard ISDN target (call-accepting) configuration with a few critical bells and whistles to force the Los Angeles router to rely on its floating static routes to reach the BGP address.

```
version 11.0
!
hostname Chicago
!
username LosAngeles password secretCLA
ip subnet-zero
isdn switch-type basic-ni1
!
interface Loopback0
 description Target for BGP peering via primary links
 ip address 10.111.0.1 255.255.255.255
!
interface Loopback2
 description Source IP address for dial backup
 ip address 10.111.0.2 255.255.255.255
!
interface Loopback10
 description Source address for BGP peers
 ip address 10.111.0.10 255.255.255.255
!
interface Ethernet0
 description Local user network
 ip address 10.111.201.1 255.255.255.0
!
interface Serial0
 description Primary link to Los Angeles
 ip address 10.0.0.2 255.255.255.252
 bandwidth 128
 delay 2000
!
interface Serial1
 description Link to New York
 ip address 10.0.0.9 255.255.255.252
 bandwidth 128
 delay 2000
!
interface BRI0
 description Dial backup from Los Angeles
 ip unnumbered Loopback0
 encapsulation ppp
 bandwidth 128
 delay 3000
 no keepalive
```

(continued)

```
  isdn spid1 87755512340101
  isdn spid2 87755512990101
  dialer idle-timeout 300
  dialer map ip 10.10.0.1 name LosAngeles broadcast
  dialer-group 1
  ppp authentication chap
  ppp multilink
 !
router eigrp 1
 network 10.0.0.0
 distribute-list 10 out BRI0
 distribute-list 10 out Ethernet0
 distribute-list 11 out Serial0
 distribute-list 10 out Serial1
 no auto-summary
 !
router bgp 99
 network 10.111.0.10 mask 255.255.255.255
 timers bgp 10 120
 neighbor 10.10.0.1 remote-as 99
 neighbor 10.10.0.1 update-source Loopback10
 !
access-list 10 deny 10.111.0.0 0.0.0.255
access-list 10 permit any
access-list 11 permit 10.111.0.1
access-list 11 deny 10.111.0.0 0.0.0.255
access-list 11 permit any
access-list 102 deny eigrp any any
access-list 102 permit ip any any
 !
dialer-list 1 protocol ip list 102
 !
end
```

LISTING 5-13. *Called router—one of two targets*

We start with the definition of three loopback interfaces, one for advertising a route over the Frame Relay link (10.111.0.1), one for IP unnumbered identification of the ISDN link (10.111.0.2), and one for BGP exchanges (10.111.0.10). Since there could be other artificial loopback targets in use, we block the entire range of addresses 10.111.0.0/24 with access lists 10 and 11. We only let the Frame Relay target address 10.111.0.1 escape in access list 11; the list is only applied to EIGRP advertisements sent out the serial link to Los Angeles. In this example, we could just as easily have set up the filters with explicit blocks of 10.111.0.1 and 10.111.0.10; however, that approach can get unwieldy (and consequently error prone) when the router needs to support multiple callers with independent needs.

The definition of the Ethernet and serial interfaces is normal. The BGP configuration is the same we used for two-level dial backup. The key is to establish a peering so that keepalives will be flowing to force up the ISDN line when needed. Other than that, the configuration of the Chicago router is as a standard IP dial-on-demand ISDN target. Aside from the name and address differences, the New York router is identical to the Chicago router. Now that we have our targets set up to advertise the correct addresses over the desired links, we can turn our attention to the configuration of the Los Angeles router in Listing 5-14.

```
version 11.0
!
hostname LosAngeles
!
username Chicago password secretCLA
username NewYork password secretNYLA
ip subnet-zero
isdn switch-type basic-ni1
!
interface Loopback0
 description Source address for dial backup and BGP peering
 ip address 10.10.0.1 255.255.255.255
!
interface Ethernet0
 description Local user network(s)
 ip address 10.10.10.1 255.255.255.0
!
interface Serial0
 description Primary link to Chicago
 ip address 10.0.0.1 255.255.255.252
 bandwidth 128
 delay 2000
!
interface Serial1
 description Primary link to New York
 ip address 10.0.0.5 255.255.255.252
 bandwidth 128
 delay 2000
!
```

(continued)

```
interface BRI0
 description Dial backup to New York and Chicago
 ip unnumbered Loopback0
 encapsulation ppp
 bandwidth 128
 delay 3000
 no keepalive
 isdn spid1 80055512120101
 isdn spid2 80055512130101
 dialer idle-timeout 170
 dialer map ip 10.111.0.2 name Chicago broadcast 18775551234
 dialer map ip 10.222.0.2 name NewYork broadcast 18775556789
 dialer hold-queue 10
 dialer load-threshold 10 either
 dialer-group 1
 ppp authentication chap
 ppp multilink
!
router eigrp 1
 network 10.0.0.0
 no auto-summary
!
router bgp 99
 network 10.10.0.1 mask 255.255.255.255
 timers bgp 10 120
 neighbor 10.111.0.10 remote-as 99
 neighbor 10.111.0.10 update-source Loopback0
 neighbor 10.222.0.10 remote-as 99
 neighbor 10.222.0.10 update-source Loopback0
!
! Routing for BGP Keepalives to Chicago router
! Use frame relay if available
ip route 10.111.0.10 255.255.255.255 10.111.0.1 150
! Otherwise force up ISDN
ip route 10.111.0.10 255.255.255.255 10.111.0.2 160
! ISDN dial address
ip route 10.111.0.2 255.255.255.255 BRI0
!
! Routing for BGP Keepalives to New York router
! Use frame relay if available
ip route 10.222.0.10 255.255.255.255 10.222.0.1 150
! Otherwise force up ISDN
ip route 10.222.0.10 255.255.255.255 10.222.0.2 160
```

(continued)

```
! ISDN dial address
ip route 10.222.0.2 255.255.255.255 BRI0
!
access-list 102 deny    eigrp any any
access-list 102 permit ip any any
!
dialer-list 1 protocol ip list 102
!
end
```

LISTING 5-14. *Calling router with ISDN backup of two links*

Unlike the targets, which need multiple loopback interfaces in order to control routing advertisements, the Los Angeles router only needs a single loopback interface definition.

Like that of the Chicago and New York routers, the configuration of the Ethernet and serial interfaces here is arbitrary. The only special consideration is in assigning routing weights to the serial links relative to the ISDN backup links. We need to set these up so that traffic will flow across the ISDN lines when we want it to, but will cease to flow once the primary link that the ISDN line is protecting returns to service. In this case, we have assigned a delay of 2,000 to the serial link and of 3,000 to the ISDN (multilink PPP) link. That way, when the ISDN link between Los Angeles and Chicago comes up to replace the serial link between the two routers, traffic will flow across it rather then using the indirect route through the New York router. At the same time, as soon as the serial link returns to service, it will be preferred over the ISDN link and the ISDN link can drop.

Alternatively, if we were just bringing up the link to minimize recovery delay should the second primary link also fail, we could adjust routing weights so the roundabout path over the remaining primary links continued to be preferred. In that case we would not have a problem with EIGRP feasible successors and would not get hit with holddown delays. In this simplistic scenario, it would be easier to convert to OSPF so that holddown would not be a factor.

To improve performance while on dial backup, we use multilink PPP, under the assumption that only one serial link at a time will require ISDN coverage. We set the load threshold low, maximizing the probability that, under normal loading, we will get the second link up before traffic gets too backed up. Should the second primary link fail while both ISDN B-channels are in use for the first primary link, there is no problem. Cisco's implementation of multilink PPP will automatically drop the second channel so that the second backup call can be placed. Then, since multilink PPP will have been negotiated on both calls, as soon as one call is no longer needed, the other call can jump back up to using both channels.

Note that in this configuration, floating static routes are only used for the BGP keepalives. All other traffic is routed dynamically using the production routing protocol. If static routes are needed—for example, to define a default route—more can be added as long as they do not interfere with the routes defined for steering BGP keepalives. These routes are fairly simplistic and should not present a problem. BGP updates will not be sent via the default route (BGP will only send updates to a peer whose subnetwork is explicitly known). So we only need to worry about introducing a static route that explicitly includes a subnetwork range that includes the remote BGP peer address.

Proper operation requires that the Los Angeles router never learn through the dynamic routing protocol how to reach the BGP peer address. Otherwise, the route through the ISDN port will never float to the top and bring up the link. That is why the routers in New York and Chicago block the BGP address on all their ports, not just on the ports leading to the Los Angeles router.

Note that we route indirectly through the primary link, rather than simply advertising the BGP peer address out the serial port to the Los Angeles router. As mentioned in Chapter 2, distance-vector routing protocols like EIGRP may require holddown to ensure routing stability when a route is lost. When holddown is activated, new paths to a destination that has been declared invalid for any reason are temporarily ignored. This ensures that the new path is not dependent upon the path that disappeared.

While BGP-driven dial-on-demand routing is very powerful and flexible, it is not always suitable. Aside from conflicting with the use of BGP for interdomain routing (in which case it may be possible to substitute RIPv2 or EGP for driving the dial-on-demand requirements), it is limited to providing only a single relationship between any pair of routers. That is why we have to rely on RIPv2-directed updates to force up multiple paths when aggregating multilink PPP bundles. But with a little ingenuity, we can duplicate virtually any configuration requiring *dialer watch* without subjecting ourselves to the limitations in the current implementation of *dialer watch*.

WRAP-UP

Dial-on-demand has many applications beyond simply providing a cost-effective means to connect occasional users in a small office or home office to the central office. In this chapter, we built on the basic capabilities developed in Chapter 4 and explored some of the ways we can expand the utility and functionality of dial backup.

We started the chapter looking at the unique configuration and operational requirements introduced when using ordinary phone lines and analog modems for router-to-router backup. We showed how we could use an analog modem attached to the AUX maintenance port found on most Cisco routers to provide emergency communications while waiting for lines to be installed or when recovering from construction accidents.

We then explored how we can get more useful bandwidth from our backup solutions. Using multilink PPP, we found that combining multiple analog links could get us up to about 100 Kbps and that we could combine ISDN B-channels from an entire PRI to get 1.25 to 2.0 Mbps. We then looked at how we could get even more bandwidth on demand by forcing the setup of multiple ISDN PRI multilink bundles and using equal path load sharing.

We then took a diversion into the world of IPX to see how the techniques we had explored so far could work in an environment other than TCP/IP. In the process, we saw how we could use the superior responsiveness of a routing protocol for one network architecture to reduce the recovery time required by other network protocols.

We finished the chapter by looking at how we could combine BGP with dial-on-demand to recover from arbitrary link failures. This permits us to implement capabilities such as providing dial backup for dial backup or forcing up a dial backup link in a multiply connected environment while some primary links are still functioning.

NOTES

1. Be careful of variations in notation for IPX addresses. To the extent that there is a standard, Novell uses decimal digits for the 32-bit network ID and hexidecimal digits for the host ID portion, separating the two by a colon. Cisco uses hexidecimal notation for both halves, but confuses the issue by using a period between the two pieces, as well as between each 16-bit piece of the host ID portion. Both "standards" allow dropping any leading zeroes from the Network ID.

CHAPTER 6

Multiple Routers at a Single Site

Sites that require high network availability usually require more than just redundant communications links. It is common practice to place a second router at a site to eliminate the downtime associated with diagnosing a failed router and scheduling a replacement at a remote site. While routers do not fail very often, if the only router at a site fails, all network communications are lost and there is no way to determine whether the problem is a sitewide disaster, a major communications cable cut, or just a failed router. Then there is the time required to dispatch service to the site—this can be particularly problematic in a large network that spans multiple time zones or, even worse, continents. Even if the site is one on which service personnel and spare parts are readily available, having multiple routers online makes normal maintenance much easier. It means a router can be brought down to implement upgrades or perform other maintenance without interrupting production network traffic.

Generally, the primary challenge in implementing a multiple router site is not in configuring a second or third router on the LAN to support some additional WAN links. That part of the job could be done by any network administrator with a basic knowledge of IP addressing. Rather, the challenge is in designing the implementation so that the availability benefits of having two routers go beyond just simplifying routine maintenance and surviving random router failures. For the addition of a second router to really contribute to network availability, it is essential that all support systems either be equally reliable or be adequately redundant to ensure the availability of at least one router at all times.

Indeed, as we shall see in the rest of this chapter, the configuration of two routers so that one can handle the load of the other is frequently trivial. This is not surprising, as the whole philosophy of network design is centered around the concept of alternate routes and routers exchanging hello packets with one another to determine which routes are available at any given point in time.

The challenges arise from the inadequacy of other components—such as simple-minded IP hosts that only understand a single default gateway for access to other subnetworks—and from LAN component failures that can split the network, creating illegal topologies. We will also see how the specific protocols and applications being supported change the impact of various failure modes. As we have seen in our discussions on multiple communications paths, there is more to providing useful redundancy than simply installing a second router. Careful planning is required to minimize the number of common points of failure. In the effort to eliminate some single points of failure, it is quite common to introduce other single points of failure that are not as obvious.

For example, to minimize the danger of service disruption due to physical harm (such as a fire, burst pipe, or loss of air conditioning), a popular approach is to use two routers, each in a different part of the building. This is a good idea—particularly when there are two independent communications service entrances—since it minimizes the probability that a single incident will disconnect both routers from the WAN. But it also increases the likelihood that a single incident could physically split the site LAN into two disconnected networks sharing a common subnetwork ID. Such a broken topology cannot be supported by IP, IPX, and many other popular protocol suites, resulting in disrupted communications even though working links remain.

In this chapter, we will look at three major configuration concerns that are unique to a LAN with multiple routers providing WAN connectivity. These are

- Minimizing the disruption of normal user system connectivity should the router serving as their default gateway fail

- Having one router provide dial backup for a link serviced by another router

- Providing continued access to the WAN for as many users as possible when a LAN served by multiple routers is segmented into disconnected LANs

PROTECTING LAN USERS FROM ROUTER LOSS

Historically, routers have been very expensive network components. Most protocol suites were developed at a time when having more than one router accessible to a host system was rare. As a result, while most popular protocol suites have strong protocols for dynamic routing at the router-to-router level (intermediate-system-to-intermediate-system, or IS-IS, in OSI parlance), they still tend to have weak end-system-to-intermediate system (ES-IS) routing protocols.

TCP/IP is, perhaps, the worst offender in this regard. While it has the strongest and widest variety of IS-IS protocols available for any protocol suite (including OSPF, EIGRP, Integrated IS-IS, and BGP), most of its end-system implementations still depend upon the very weak default gateway approach to ES-IS routing. We covered TCP/IP ES-IS weaknesses from the viewpoint of router-to-end system routing, and ways to get around them, in Chapter 3's discussion on multihomed hosts. But we basically ignored the other direction, which is how an end system with a single LAN connection can find the appropriate router on that LAN to deliver IP packets to destinations that are not on the same physical LAN.

The original definition of TCP/IP pretty much assumed that routers never failed. Hosts were configured with a default gateway (remember that TCP/IP referred to routers as "gateways" until the late 1980s and still uses the old terminology in many places). When powered up, a TCP/IP end system knows its IP address, its subnetwork mask, and the IP address of a single local router. When sending a packet, the end system applies its subnetwork mask to both its own IP address and that of the destination. If the two results are identical, the destination is on the same subnetwork as the sender, and the packet is delivered directly to the destination end system using the appropriate protocols for that subnetwork. If, however, the results are not identical, then the destination is on a different subnetwork that cannot be reached directly.

Delivery of a packet to another subnetwork requires that the packet be sent to a router on the same subnetwork as the sender for forwarding to the ultimate destination. Since the only router known to the end system is the default gateway, this would be the router used. Routers, on the other hand, learn through their router-to-router routing protocols of all other routers that they can reach and that provide the best path to each possible destination. If another router on the same subnetwork as the sender has a better route to the desired destination, the router initially receiving the packet would forward the original packet along the best path available. It would also send an Internet Control Message Protocol (ICMP) re-direct packet back to the sending end system, informing it of the better router available for that destination. Depending upon the sophistication of the protocol implementation on the sending end system, that new router information might be remembered for future use with packets destined to the same destination, or it might be ignored. Either way, the off-network packets would be delivered correctly.

Effectively, routing from end system to local router is via static routes. Because IP is a connectionless protocol, there is no intrinsic mechanism for an end system to determine whether a router that used to be good has failed. ICMP re-directs assume that the initial poor-choice router is online to provide redirection to a better router. Once redirection has happened, there is no mechanism for falling back to the original router should the better router fail. Indeed, there are some protocol stack implementations in use wherein the only mechanism for removing an ICMP re-direct installed route is to reboot the system. Even implementations that support configuring multiple default gateways may have the same problem, because on some the first gateway that responds to an address resolution request is treated as the one and only default gateway.

IP implementations are supposed to protect themselves from routers that turn into black holes. The problem is that there is no standard mechanism at the IP level to determine whether or not an IP packet sent to an address on the same subnetwork arrived correctly. This is not a defect in the IP protocol. Rather, it is a fundamental property of the class of best-effort datagram protocols in which IP is included. The decision was made as part of the original design of the TCP/IP architecture that any recovery mechanism would be part of a protocol running above IP and not included in the IP protocol itself.

Unfortunately, although the need for black hole protection was recognized and indeed mandated by RFC 1122 back in 1989, proper detection is non-trivial and cannot be depended upon. Testing of specific implementations is essential if predictable response to router failure is required. This is true unless a protocol—such as Cisco's Hot Standby Router Protocol (HSRP, RFC 2281) or the recently standardized Virtual Router Redundancy Protocol (VRRP, RFC 2338), popular with Nortel and other vendors—is used on the routers to shield users from host implementation inconsistencies.

So let's look at some of the protocols designed to run above IP to provide router independence for end systems.

PASSIVE RIP

The original and still most popular technique for providing router independence for TCP/IP end systems is passive RIP. Historically, both IP and IPX networks used variations on the Routing Information Protocol (RIP) when dynamic routing was desired for intradomain routers. RIP depended upon LAN broadcasts for communications between routers on a LAN and had no security mechanisms. So it was easy for an end system on a LAN to eavesdrop on the router-to-router RIP exchanges and extract the appropriate routing entries for all reachable, advertised networks.

This approach has many advantages over the default gateway approach. First of all, it eliminates the need to include a default gateway definition on every end system. It also avoids the extra traffic and overhead of handling ICMP re-directs, as packets should always be sent to the optimal router to begin with. Most important, it allows end systems to dynamically adjust to local routers' coming online and going offline. A new router coming online will be installed in the end systems' routing tables when its first reachability broadcast is received. Similarly, failed routers will be removed from the end systems' routing tables when update packets stop arriving and the entries time out.

As with all networking capabilities, there are, of course, trade-offs to be made when using passive RIP. In general, these are the same trade-offs we discussed in Chapter 3 when we used RIP to support hosts with interfaces on more than one subnetwork. RIP is only useful on LANs that support broadcasting. By default, each router on the LAN supporting RIP broadcasts update packets every 30 seconds, requiring one update packet for every 25 destination subnetworks advertised.

Unless the end system RIP implementation supports setting RIP detection intervals to non-default values, passive RIP responds slowly to router failures. Using default timers, passive RIP requires at least 60 to 90 seconds to detect a dead router and remove it from the end system's routing table. Some implementations, designed to allow the end system to support routing between interfaces, will take even longer to respond due to route holddown. Even in the best case, passive RIP is slow enough to recover that router failure will be quite noticeable to users.

There is also the question of inefficiency in trying to map real route metrics into RIP's 15 available distance values. Attempting to do so almost invariably results in an unmaintainable morass of manually configured route metric conversions. Consequently, it is highly likely that ICMP re-directs will be required even in a well-connected network with many nearly equal routes. Combined with a lack of support for variable-length subnetwork masking, this makes passive RIP usually only suitable in simple networks—or when it is acceptable to limit advertisements to just the default route.

One final limitation is that not all end system IP protocol stacks support passive RIP, so it may not even be an available choice. But some end systems extend the concept beyond just listening in on RIP version 1 (RIPv1) broadcasts. They can detect routers and routes by eavesdropping on other routing protocols that use broadcasts or multicasts for router-to-router exchanges, such as RIPv2, OSPF, and EIGRP.

On the other hand, passive RIP does work, and, despite its limitations, it is still superior to alternatives such as using only a static definition of default gateway.

CONFIGURATION EXAMPLE: PASSIVE RIP

Because of the many limitations of RIP, even with the release of the RIPv2 protocol, large networks today generally depend upon more modern routing protocols and no longer routinely run any version of RIP. However, virtually all router implementations still support RIP and allow you to redistribute routes learned from one routing protocol into another routing protocol. This makes it easy to run a routing protocol chosen for fast and efficient routing between the routers and still provide RIP updates for end systems to eavesdrop on. Listing 6-1 shows a Cisco router configuration excerpt that simply broadcasts a default route using RIP version 1 (Cisco introduced their support for RIPv2 in IOS 11.1) if the routing table on the router has a path to 10.0.0.1. The mechanism used to determine the reachability of 10.0.0.1 is immaterial to the functioning of passive RIP.

```
version 11.0
!
interface Ethernet0
ip address 192.168.110.201 255.255.255.0
!
router rip
network 192.168.110.0
redistribute static metric 1
distribute-list 10 in Ethernet0
distribute-list 11 out Ethernet0
!
ip route 0.0.0.0 0.0.0.0 10.0.0.1
access-list 10 deny    any
access-list 11 permit 0.0.0.0
!
end
```

LISTING 6-1.   *Minimal passive RIP example*

Note the filter applied to RIP updates received from the Ethernet by the line *distribute-list 10 in Ethernet0*. The filter prevents the router from learning any routes via RIP. This prevents a malicious or misconfigured end system from creating routing problems for the routers. However, there is no way the router can prevent a malicious end system from broadcasting invalid RIP updates and confusing other end systems on the LAN.

There is no intent in this example to use passive RIP to optimize router selection. The line *distribution-list 11 out Ethernet0* filters RIP updates being sent out onto the Ethernet so that they only include the default route. This keeps the update packet size minimal. It also avoids confusing passive RIP listeners with updates based on routes to networks with subnetwork mask usage incompatible with RIP version 1. If this router has a path to the network default gateway 10.0.0.1, it will advertise the default route using RIP version 1. If this router does not have a path to 10.0.0.1 in its routing tables, it will stop sending RIP updates altogether—with no default route defined, it has no routes to advertise.

If we wanted to advertise a default route unconditionally, we could add the floating static route *ip route 0.0.0.0 0.0.0.0 Null0 250* to the configuration. That way, if we did not have a useful default route learned through the production routing protocol, we would still have one to advertise.

Listing 6-2 shows how the static default route used in Listing 6-1 can be replaced with a default route learned from the routing protocol actually used for router-to-router path determination. We still make no attempt to optimize router selection by distributing more detailed routes; there is poor resolution of the route metric and a lack of support for variable-length subnetwork masks in RIPv1. While RIPv2 does handle variable-length subnetwork masks, it still retains the crude zero-to-15 route metric of RIPv1. Plus, many passive RIP implementations are still based on the original Berkeley routed implementation of RIPv1. If router selection optimization is an objective, limited success may be possible using route-maps, as was done in the example in Chapter 3. But keep in mind that neither version of RIP is a good mechanism for the task. Accurate route selections are going to be very difficult, if not impossible, to achieve if the topology is at all complex.

Note that because there is no default gateway defined, it is essential that a default route be learned through OSPF if it is to be redistributed to passive RIP users. The assumption here is that the OSPF routing domain is a much better place to

```
version 11.0
!
interface Ethernet0
ip address 192.168.110.201 255.255.255.0
ip ospf authentication-key ospfSecret1
!
interface Serial0
ip address 172.19.254.5 255.255.255.252
ip ospf authentication-key ospfSecret2
!
router ospf 200
network 192.168.110.0 0.0.0.255 area 192.42.110.0
network 172.19.0.0 0.0.255.255 area 0
area 0 authentication
area 192.42.110.0 authentication
area 192.42.110.0 range 192.42.110.0 255.255.255.0
area 0 range 172.19.254.4 255.255.255.252
redistribute rip metric 1 subnets
!
router rip
network 192.168.110.0
redistribute ospf 200 metric 1
distribute-list 10 in ethernet0
distribute-list 11 out ethernet0
access-list 10 permit 192.168.0.198
access-list 10 permit 192.168.0.199
access-list 11 permit 0.0.0.0
!
end
```

LISTING 6-2. *Passive RIP support combined with active RIP and OSPF*

control the default route for the network as a whole, with the alternative being the configuration nightmare of a static default route definition on every router on every LAN.

In this second example, we also enable RIP to accept routing updates from the two hosts 192.168.0.198 and 192.168.0.199. These are dual homed hosts with multiple LAN connections for higher reliability (the second connection is not shown in the example). The example shows how we can combine the use of passive RIP and active RIP on the same LAN. But be extremely careful, as the lack of subnetwork mask specification in RIPv1 update packets can cause the incorrect interpretation of advertisements received. Plan on verifying correct redistribution of routes learned by RIPv1 every time any changes are made on the end system or the router, such as IOS upgrades. It may be necessary to define two loopback interfaces in the same major network used to identify the dual homed systems to force RIPv1 to assume the correct subnetwork mask. Check the routing table on another router that is not on the same LAN to verify that the routes are being learned and redistributed correctly into the primary routing protocol.

If possible, RIPv2 or another routing protocol should be used instead of RIPv1. Protocols like RIPv2 and OSPF not only provide much more efficient use of address space; they also allow cleaner, more maintainable designs. They achieve this through their use of multicasting rather than broadcasting of updates or hello packets, their support for security features that reduce the risk of accidental or intentional misroutes, and—in the case of OSPF and BGP—their ability to distribute accurate routing metrics and detect one-way link failures. However, as mentioned earlier, we are much less likely to find support for protocols other than RIPv1 available on all the platforms that need to be supported.

PROXY ARP

Those working with end systems that do not support passive RIP can get some of these benefits simply by using proxy Address Resolution Protocol (ARP). The proxy ARP protocol was designed to assist network management by reducing the need to reconfigure end systems every time the subnetwork mask changes or when moving from one subnetwork to another within a larger subnetwork address space. However, we can take advantage of the way it makes a large network divided into many subnetworks look like a single large network to reduce the vulnerability of the static default gateway definition on each end system.

Proxy ARP works by allowing a tighter subnetwork mask on the router than on the end system. For example, consider a network built around allocations of the 10.0.0.0/8 block for private networks. A LAN might be assigned the subnetwork 10.0.10.0/24. The end systems on that LAN are configured with addresses that are correctly contained in the subnetwork assigned to the LAN but that use a subnetwork mask of 255.0.0.0. Only the routers on the LAN are configured with the correct subnetwork mask for the LAN.

That way, when an end system on the LAN attempts to communicate with another system that is outside the local subnetwork of 10.0.10.0/24, but still within 10.0.0.0/8, the end system determines that the destination is local and simply issues an ARP request to get the destination's MAC address. With proxy ARP enabled on the router, when the router receives the ARP, it identifies it as one for a system that is not on the local LAN. It responds as if the router were the remote system addressed, with an ARP response associating the router's MAC address with the remote destination's IP address. The local end system believes it is directly connected to the destination, while in reality its packets are being forwarded from the local subnetwork toward the destination subnetwork by their local router.

The benefit of proxy ARP, from our viewpoint, comes when we define the default gateway to be an address outside the real local subnetwork but inside the overall address block (so it looks local to the end system). The default gateway known to the end system is like any other non-local IP address that the end system thinks is local. So when the end system ARPs on the LAN to reach the default gateway, the local router replies. Under normal conditions, operation is totally transparent—the effect is identical to the local router's having two IP addresses, its real one and the default gateway's.

When proxy ARP is configured on all local routers and the router that initially responded fail, the end system automatically gets another router the next time the IP address is ARPed. The two main drawbacks of depending on proxy ARP are the speed of recovery and the need to use only a subset of the assigned address space on the LAN (to leave room for the default gateway that is being proxied).

Recovery speed can be slow, as there is no commonly implemented standard for how long to keep ARP results locally cached. This results in wide variations among systems. Most systems routinely refresh their ARP cache whenever there is a significant gap in traffic to the IP address—but the definition of *significant* can range from seconds to hours. On many end systems, it is possible to manually flush the ARP cache to force discovery of the remaining router. But some systems may recover faster simply by being shut down and rebooted, which could make the 3-minute wait for passive RIP much more palatable.

The addressing requirements tend to be an either/or decision. Either the network address can be subdivided or the entire network address space must be assigned to a single LAN. In the latter case, proxy ARP is not useful. Note that the default gateway does not have to be in unused address space. It only needs to be outside the address space assigned to the LAN. For example, if the address space is split between two LANs, end systems on each LAN could use a default gateway definition from the address space of the other LAN. The address does not even need to be a router—as soon as a packet being sent via the default gateway reaches the router local to the end system, it is routed based on the real destination, not on what the end system thinks should be the next hop.

Since proxy ARP is enabled by default on Cisco and most other routers, there is no need for a configuration example. However, be aware that using secondary addresses may be incompatible with proxy ARP. Cisco routers will respond with a proxy ARP only to ARP requests that come from the primary address space defined on the LAN interface. ARP requests from addresses in the secondary address space will not generate proxy ARP responses. Since this constraint is not documented, it should not be depended on in a design.

Even when proxy ARP is not required for getting around default gateway assignment limitations, it is still worth using. In today's environment of tight IP address allocations, proxy ARP can be a great time saver. When a LAN segment's subnetwork address mask has to be modified to squeeze out a few more usable addresses, only the routers on the affected LAN segments need to be reconfigured—not every single device.

IRDP, BootP, and DHCP

ICMP Router Discovery Protocol (IRDP, RFC 1256), Boot Protocol (BootP), and Dynamic Host Configuration Protocol (DHCP) are all designed to eliminate the need to hard configure all systems on an IP LAN. IRDP was specifically designed to allow systems on a LAN to dynamically detect all available routers and make a real-time choice of the appropriate default gateway to use. It bases its choice on the routers available and their advertised priority. Unfortunately, IRDP does not provide an answer to the critical function of determining that a router currently in use to reach an IP address is no longer available. While RFC 1256 discusses this problem and suggests some alternative approaches, it leaves the solution up to the host system, with no support from the routers. Indeed, the basic conclusion reached in the alternatives discussion was that every alternative considered by the IRDP team had either significant defects or performance problems when it was scaled to large LANs. As a result, IRDP is neither widely nor consistently implemented, making its use problematic. As a solution to the multiple router problem, it automates the listing of default gateways to try. But it ignores the questions of which available router should be used for any specific IP packet and how to recover when an available router becomes unavailable without warning.

BootP and DHCP use MAC-level broadcasts on the LAN to contact a BootP or DHCP server on the LAN and get a valid IP address, subnetwork mask, and default gateway. This takes place during the initial system boot-load process. DHCP provides additional flexibility by incorporating the concept that the IP address information provided is leased rather than sold. That is, DHCP attaches a time-out to the information provided, allowing the same IP address to be shared among multiple systems. BootP, on the other hand, assumes that the address information is dedicated to that MAC address. It has no facilities for time sharing of address space.

What does this have to do with providing support for multiple routers on a LAN? While it is rarely the reason for using either, we can consider BootP or DHCP as an ES-IS of last resort. For example, the default configuration could assign half the users to one router and the other half to the other router, providing simple load sharing. A background process running on a local computer could periodically test the routers to verify that they were still alive. Should one of the routers fail to respond, the script could alert the help desk that there is a router problem at the location. It could modify the DHCP or BootP database so that only IP addresses for working routers are given out as default gateway values. While this would not immediately help the systems already running with the broken default gateway, a simple reboot would automatically reconfigure the isolated system to use the working default gateway, and work could resume.

Theoretically, this could even be fully automated with DHCP by making the lease times very short. However, short lease times rarely work in practice because there are many DHCP implementations currently in use that do not properly handle expiring leases. Given that there are better and more general solutions to this problem, the use of BootP or DHCP to provide a pseudo-dynamic ES-IS protocol does not make sense—unless there is no other choice available for a specific environment.

VRRP AND CISCO HSRP

Given the problem of end systems' inconsistent detection of routing black holes, Cisco developed the Hot Standby Router Protocol (HSRP, RFC 2281). This protocol runs only on the routers and is transparent to the end systems. It works by defining a virtual router IP and MAC address that is shared by multiple routers. One router acts as the active router and responds to the HSRP IP address and HSRP MAC address. Should this router fail to send timely keepalives to the other routers on the LAN, the next router reconfigures its interface and assumes the IP and MAC addresses of the virtual router. Since even the MAC address is constant, the existing ARP cache contents remain valid. The router swap is transparent to the IP protocol; but it can be a problem for IPX, OSI, DECnet, and other protocols.

Other router vendors provide similar protocols. Most follow the lead of Bay/Nortel and support the Internet standards track Virtual Router Redundancy Protocol (VRRP, RFC 2338). This and the HSRP protocol are very similar in function and performance, although the terminology used to define each is different. To minimize confusion, we will restrict this discussion to HSRP—but keep in mind that what we do here with HSRP on Cisco routers can be accomplished using the same philosophy (albeit different commands) on routers supporting VRRP.

HSRP and VRRP are not perfect, but they are quick. Using default timer settings, a standby router will take over for a failed active router in about 3 seconds. This is fast enough that most protocols will not even notice the downtime unless they are actively sending at the time. Even then, the lost packets will typically be recovered transparently by higher layer protocols.

The primary challenge with HSRP is the hardware limitation to a single MAC address in Cisco Ethernet interfaces based on the Lance chip set. These interfaces, used on Cisco 25xx series and other routers, can support only one MAC address at a time. This limits the number of HSRP virtual router definitions to no more than one per interface. More importantly, it causes the MAC address of the standby router to disappear without warning when the standby router must take over for a failed active router.

As a result, extreme care must be taken when designing HSRP capabilities into implementations using less capable routers. Consider Figure 6-1, in which we define the HSRP standby IP address to be 10.0.0.254 and the physical router IP addresses to be 10.0.0.1 and 10.0.0.2, respectively. Further assume that the MAC addresses are 00c0ab000001 for HSRP and 00c0ab111111 and 00c0ab222222 for physical Routers 1 and 2, respectively. When HSRP is enabled and Router 1 is the active router, the ARP table on the user system will look like Table 6-1.

When Router 1 fails, Router 2 takes over as active router, and the ARP tables look like Table 6-2 instead.

At this point, any applications attempting to reach Router 1 at IP address 10.0.0.1 will fail—but not as expected. The MAC address that delivered frames to Router 1 now delivers frames to the wrong router. This is not a problem, as Router 1 is dead anyway. However, consider systems that were communicating with Router 2. Even though Router 2 is alive and well, its MAC address has changed, making 10.0.0.2 inaccessible until the ARP cache times out and is renewed. All IP users on the LAN must be sure to use only the HSRP virtual router IP address, as it is the only IP address

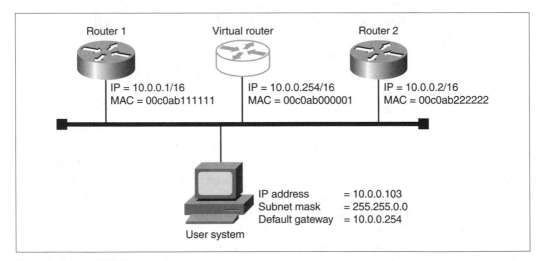

FIGURE 6-1. *HSRP operation*

TABLE 6-1. *ARP Table with Router 1 Active and Router 2 in Standby*

IP ADDRESS	MAC ADDRESS	PHYSICAL ROUTER
10.0.0.254	00c0ab000001	Router 1
10.0.0.1	00c0ab000001	Router 1
10.0.0.2	00c0ab222222	Router 2

TABLE 6-2. *ARP Table with Router 1 Dead and Router 2 Alive*

IP ADDRESS	MAC ADDRESS	PHYSICAL ROUTER
10.0.0.254	00c0ab000001	Router 2
10.0.0.1	N/A	Router 1 (dead)
10.0.0.2	00c0ab000001	Router 2

with a dependable, consistent MAC address. However, other protocol suites, such as IPX, do not have this luxury. They can be broken unless the routers are capable of maintaining their permanent MAC address, as well as the HSRP MAC address.

Even with fully capable routers, care must be taken to ensure that efficiency is preserved. Enabling HSRP on a LAN interface disables ICMP redirects for that interface. As a result, if one router on the LAN has better connectivity to some destinations than do other routers on the same LAN, it may be preferable to give that router priority for becoming the active HSRP router. In the worst case, virtually every packet sent to the default router would need to be resent over the LAN to get to the correct outbound router, doubling the traffic density on the LAN.

CONFIGURATION EXAMPLE: SIMPLE HSRP

The simple configuration in Figure 6-2, using HSRP on two routers to support IP and IPX, highlights many of these considerations. This example also illustrates some of the useful features provided by Cisco in its HSRP implementation.

Key to the configuration used for this example is that Router 1 has the only permanent link to the rest of the network. The dial backup link provided by Router 2 is only activated when the primary link via Router 1 is down. There is no need for load balancing because all traffic should go to the router with the active link. This is fortunate, as there is no way to provide load balancing when limited to only one HSRP virtual router. (In the next example, we will show how to achieve limited load balancing by defining two HSRP virtual routers.)

Starting with the configuration for Router 1 in Listing 6-3, we configure HSRP using *standby* statements under the interface definition of the LAN on which HSRP is

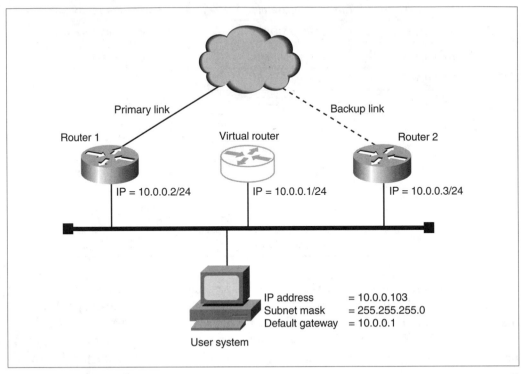

FIGURE 6-2. *Simple HSRP example*

```
version 11.0
!
hostname Router1
!
interface Ethernet0
description Remote Facility router 1
ip address 10.0.0.2 255.255.255.0
no ip redirects
ipx network 120251 encapsulation SAP
standby 1 priority 110
standby 1 preempt
standby 1 ip 10.0.0.1
standby 1 track serial0 20
!
end
```

LISTING 6-3. *Simple HSRP example, Router 1 configuration*

to be supported. The *no ip redirects* directive is technically unnecessary, as turning on HSRP automatically disables the issuing of ICMP redirect indications. If it is not included in the configuration, it will be automatically added by the router.

To ensure that the router with the active connection is the active router, we use a number of controls provided by Cisco as part of their HSRP implementation. This implementation determines which router will be the active router, which will be relegated to the standby mode, and when switching from one to the other will be permitted. The *standby priority* command sets the normal priority for the router. The router with the highest priority will become the active router and assume the identity of the virtual router. Listing 6-4 shows an example implementation with the goal of having whichever router is carrying the traffic be the active router. Normally that would be Router 1, so we give Router 1 a priority of 110 and Router 2 a priority of 95.

We use the *standby track* command to modify the relative priorities of the routers based on which links are up and which are down. In this case, should the primary link on Router 1 go down, the *standby 1 track serial0 20* command will reduce the priority of Router 1 by 20, giving Router 1 an effective priority of 90 for standby group 1. This is not enough to cause a change of active routers, however, as the default behavior of HSRP is only to change active routers when there is no choice. To get around this default behavior, we add the *standby 1 preempt* line, which tells each router to take over as active router any time it has the higher priority.

The best way to verify the priorities and tracking weights is to set up a truth table and ensure that for every combination of states of tracked interfaces, the desired router is active. Table 6-3 gives the truth table for HSRP with tracking and preemption enabled for this example.

```
version 11.0
!
hostname Router2
!
interface Ethernet0
description Remote Facility router 2
ip address 10.0.0.3 255.255.255.0
no ip redirects
ipx network 120251 encapsulation SAP
standby 1 priority 95
standby 1 preempt
standby 1 ip 10.0.0.1
standby 1 track bri0 10
!
end
```

LISTING 6-4. *Simple HSRP example, Router 2 configuration*

TABLE 6-3.   *Truth Table for Simple HSRP Configuration Example*

FRAME RELAY STATUS	ISDN LINK STATUS	ROUTER 1 BASE PRIORITY	ROUTER 1 FRAME STATE ADJUSTMENT	ROUTER 1 ADJUSTED PRIORITY	ROUTER 2 BASE PRIORITY	ROUTER 2 ISDN LINK ADJUSTMENT	ROUTER 2 ADJUSTED PRIORITY	ACTIVE ROUTER
UP	DOWN	110	0	110	95	10	85	ONE
DOWN	DOWN	110	20	90	95	10	85	ONE
DOWN	UP	110	20	90	95	0	95	TWO
UP	UP	110	0	110	95	0	95	ONE

We must be careful when interpreting the truth table to avoid being misled. It would appear that Router 1 is always active unless the only connection to the data center is the ISDN link on Router 2 (the third line where the Router 2 adjusted weight of 95 is greater than the Router 1 adjusted weight of 90). But this is not actually true. The problem is that the ISDN link, as a dial-on-demand link, will always appear to be up, whether or not a call is actually in progress. Whether the status is *UP* with the line dialed and active, or *UP (spoofing)* with the line ready to dial, the *standby tracking* command sees the link as being up.

As a result, the actual behavior of the configuration is that Router 1 is only the active router while the primary link is up. Unless the ISDN link is administratively shut down, Router 2 will preempt Router 1 regardless of the functional state of the ISDN link. In this example, such behavior is acceptable; it really makes no difference which router is active when both the primary link and the dial backup link are unavailable. In other scenarios, however, this could lead to undesired HSRP behavior if the mechanism is not understood.

Anomalous behavior can also occur due to the delay from the time the primary interface first comes back to life (changing the standby weights) until the link is fully connected and recognized by the routing protocol. (At this time traffic actually stops flowing out the ISDN link and resumes flowing over the Frame Relay link.) Since this is a temporary disturbance, it is only a minor inconvenience for IP users. However, it is potentially a critical window for failure for IPX (Novell) users.

It was mentioned earlier that HSRP can create problems for IPX users. This sample configuration provides an example of the kinds of problems HSRP can cause and shows how it is sometimes possible to work around the problems. The primary problem comes from the automatic inclusion of the LAN MAC address in the IPX network address of a device. IPX works in this configuration because there are only clients at the remote site; all servers are at the data center. When a Novell client comes to life, it locates the nearest server and the router providing the optimal path to the server. Since that router will be the one with the working link to the core, the router address will be based on the active router MAC address. This will work correctly except when both links are up from the viewpoint of HSRP, forcing the active router to switch to Router 1 while the traffic is still flowing via the ISDN link. It can take some time for IPXRIP to time out and discover the correct path to the data center.

But the real IPX problem comes when the Frame Relay link fails enough to force a routing change but not enough to take the Frame Relay interface down at the physical level. Under these conditions, the IPX routing protocol learns the correct route via Router 2, and clients start sending their packets straight to Router 2. IPX communications are lost when the Frame Relay link finally does fail enough to change the standby priority and Router 2 preempts. At this point, the MAC address used for Router 2 disappears and clients are sending their IPX packets into a black hole. HSRP and IPX should not be mixed if the routers are not capable of supporting multiple MAC addresses simultaneously.

CONFIGURATION EXAMPLES: LOAD BALANCING WITH HSRP

HSRP makes it possible to implement simple load-sharing schemes. With routers that can support more than one MAC address per interface, two or more default gateways can be defined as HSRP virtual routers on each LAN, and the users assigned randomly or based on need. Alternatively, users can be distributed across multiple LANs, and the HSRP configurations on each LAN independently adjusted to achieve load balancing at the router level.

Consider the network diagrammed in Figure 6-3. Rather than assign 10.0.0.1 and 10.0.0.2 as the real IP addresses of the two routers, we assign non-router addresses to the Ethernet interfaces and define the two router IP addresses as HSRP virtual routers. (Remember that this approach requires more than one MAC address per interface and therefore is not suitable for 25xx and other Lance chip-based Cisco routers.) We then configure half the users to use 10.0.0.1 as their default gateway and the other half to use 10.0.0.2. In addition to balancing the traffic between the two routers, we use *standby track* to force a switch over if one of the routers becomes significantly more disconnected from the rest of the enterprise than the other.

A realistic HSRP configuration implementing this policy for the two routers is given in Listings 6-5 and 6-6. Note that the tracking adjustments are assigned so that preemption will occur only if the standby router has at least two more serial links up than the active router. This minimizes flip-flopping of active and standby routers. But it still provides a high probability that by the time the network degrades to the point where the majority of the packets sent to the active router are being passed on to the standby router, the standby router will have taken over and eliminated the extra LAN bandwidth consumption.

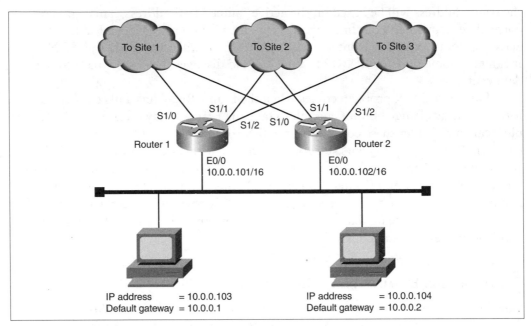

FIGURE 6-3. *Small-site load balancing with HSRP*

```
version 11.0
!
hostname Router1
!
interface Ethernet0/0
 description Remote Facility router 1
 ip address 10.0.0.101 255.255.0.0
 no ip redirects
 standby 1 priority 110
 standby 1 preempt
 standby 1 ip 10.0.0.1
 standby 1 track serial1/0 10
 standby 1 track serial1/1 10
 standby 1 track serial1/2 10
 standby 2 priority 95
 standby 2 preempt
 standby 2 ip 10.0.0.2
 standby 2 track serial1/0 10
 standby 2 track serial1/1 10
 standby 2 track serial1/2 10
!
end
```

LISTING 6-5. *Small-site load balancing with HSRP, Router 1 configuration*

```
version 11.0
!
hostname Router2
!
interface Ethernet0/0
 description Remote Facility router 2
 ip address 10.0.0.102 255.255.0.0
 no ip redirects
 standby 1 priority 95
 standby 1 preempt
 standby 1 ip 10.0.0.1
 standby 1 track serial1/0 10
 standby 1 track serial1/1 10
 standby 1 track serial1/2 10
 standby 2 priority 110
 standby 2 preempt
 standby 2 ip 10.0.0.2
 standby 2 track serial1/0 10
 standby 2 track serial1/1 10
 standby 2 track serial1/2 10
!
end
```

LISTING 6-6. *Small-site load balancing with HSRP, Router 2 configuration*

The degree of load balancing provided by the single LAN configuration will depend upon the user traffic characteristics. It also has the disadvantage of confusing users and administrators by establishing two default gateways on the LAN. Most important, if each router has different connectivity to the outside world, the loss of ICMP redirection could cause a significant performance hit as well as increasing the router loading.

Using multiple LANs to achieve simple load balancing in a configuration like that in Figure 6-4 is also a popular technique. Here we define only one HSRP active router per LAN, and distribute the load on a LAN-by-LAN basis. In Listings 6-7 and 6-8, we make Router 1 the active router for the left-hand LAN and Router 2 the active router for the right. Again, this assumes there are similar loads on each LAN and minimal performance variation between delivering to one router and to the other.

Note that we can still use interface tracking to force the active router to a specific real router if the external connectivity becomes skewed. And, of course, if one router should fail, the other will quickly take over all routing operations.

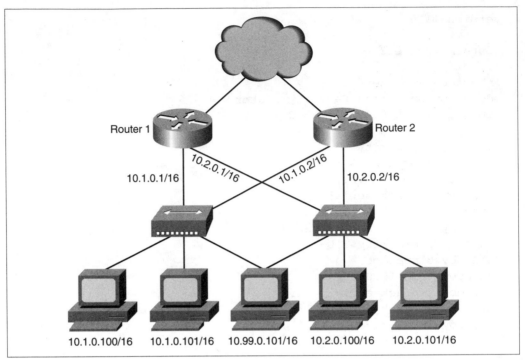

FIGURE 6-4. *Dual-LAN load balancing with HSRP*

```
version 11.0
!
hostname Router 1
!
interface Ethernet0/0
 description Remote Facility router 1
 ip address 10.1.0.101 255.255.0.0
 no ip redirects
 standby 1 priority 110
 standby 1 preempt
 standby 1 ip 10.1.0.1
 standby 1 track serial1/0 10
 standby 1 track serial1/1 10
 standby 1 track serial1/2 10
!
interface Ethernet0/1
 description Remote Facility router 1
 ip address 10.2.0.101 255.255.0.0
```

(*continued*)

```
 no ip redirects
 standby 2 priority 95
 standby 2 preempt
 standby 2 ip 10.2.0.1
 standby 2 track serial1/0 10
 standby 2 track serial1/1 10
 standby 2 track serial1/2 10
 !
end
```

LISTING 6-7. *Dual-LAN load balancing with HSRP, Router 1 configuration*

```
version 11.0
!
hostname Router2
!
interface Ethernet0/0
description Remote Facility router 2
ip address 10.1.0.102 255.255.0.0
no ip redirects
standby 1 priority 95
standby 1 preempt
standby 1 ip 10.1.0.1
standby 1 track serial1/0 10
standby 1 track serial1/1 10
standby 1 track serial1/2 10
!
interface Ethernet0/1
description Remote Facility router 1
ip address 10.2.0.102 255.255.0.0
no ip redirects
standby 2 priority 110
standby 2 preempt
standby 2 ip 10.2.0.1
standby 2 track serial1/0 10
standby 2 track serial1/1 10
standby 2 track serial1/2 10
!
end
```

LISTING 6-8. *Dual-LAN load balancing with HSRP, Router 2 configuration*

CONFIGURATION EXAMPLE: MEETING SPECIAL NEEDS WITH HSRP

To get an idea of the extent to which HSRP can support unique requirements, we will look at how HSRP is used to handle a number of special requirements in the production network configuration pictured in Figure 6-5. In this network, most users on the LAN communicate with local servers and random other sites, half of which connect to Router 1 and half of which connect to Router 2. A few special users communicate heavily with a unique service site that connects via a dedicated link to Router 1, with ISDN backup to Router 2.

Before we get to the HSRP configurations, we'll discuss the design of this site. It combines a number of redundancy features that have already been discussed, plus a few that are somewhat unusual. As is often the case in real life, this is due to a number of political and historical factors. All normal users are on the main LAN rather than being split equally between the two LANs at the site, as recommended earlier in this chapter. Originally, there was only one LAN, and a number of applications and

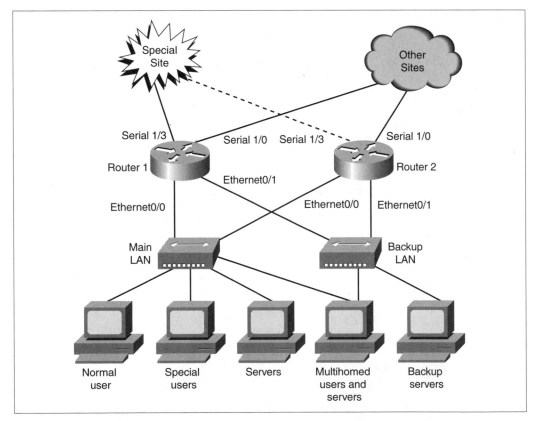

FIGURE 6-5. *Special needs HSRP example*

operational procedures were built around the assumption of a single LAN. The cost of upgrading the installed applications exceeds the estimated cost of the downtime that could be eliminated by moving half the users over to the backup LAN.

Similarly, cost considerations caused the lack of Frame Relay redundancy to other normal sites. The Frame Relay links at this site were highly oversubscribed; configuring redundant logical permanent virtual circuits (PVCs) to remote locations would have required bringing more high-speed lines into this site. Most remote sites have single routers with a single low-speed 56-Kbps access link. The added PVC, then, would provide only a minor reliability improvement—the majority of all Frame Relay failures experienced are physical layer problems with the low-speed access links. Not shown on this diagram, because it is irrelevant to HSRP configuration, are the provisions for ISDN backup of the Frame Relay connections.

A key design feature that is not obvious from the diagram is the ISDN backup for the leased line from Router 1, interface Serial1/3 to the Special Site. The ISDN call setup is handled by the DSU on Router 2's interface serial 1/3, rather than by an ISDN interface on the router. As a result, the ISDN link looks to the router like a leased line that is usually in the failed state but occasionally comes to life.

One unusual requirement here is the support of a secondary IP address, range 192.168.45.0/24, for users who have not yet been migrated to the 10.201.0.0/16 subnetwork. In today's tight IPv4 address space, the need to move LANs from one address space to another is becoming more common. The migration can be much less stressful if a controlled transition is implemented. This can be done by supporting both address schemes for a period of time while systems are modified to support the new addressing. Of course, it is essential to guard against the temptation to just leave the duplicate assignments in place.

Based on these conditions, the following HSRP loading plan is desired:

1. The normal users' default gateway (10.201.0.1) should be Router 2 unless Router 1 has the only active Frame Relay connection.

2. The special users' default gateway (10.201.0.6) should be the router that has the active special link.

3. The obsolete users' default gateway (192.168.45.1) should be the router that is not supporting special users.

4. If one router dies, the other router should take over for all user classes.

As it turns out, the third goal cannot be met, since Cisco does not provide the ability in HSRP to use negative adjustments as part of the *standby track* command. Instead, the obsolete subnetwork default gateway is unilaterally assigned to Router 2 as long as Router 2's Ethernet interface is alive. Should Router 2 become incapable of supporting IP on *interface Ethernet0/0*, control will transfer over to Router 1 until

Router 2 comes back to life, at which point Router 2 will preempt Router 1 and take back control.

Listings 6-9 and 6-10 show how we can meet goals 1, 2, and 4 using HSRP on the Ethernet interfaces to the main LAN. The authentication statements are not par-

```
version 11.0
!
hostname Router1
!
interface Ethernet0/0
 description Core Router 1 with link to Special
 ip address 10.201.0.9 255.255.0.0
 ip address 192.168.45.9 255.255.255.0 secondary
 no ip redirects
 ipx network 1234321 encapsulation SAP
 standby 1 priority 90
 standby 1 preempt
 standby 1 authentication Normal
 standby 1 ip 10.201.0.1
 standby 1 track Serial1/0 25
 standby 2 priority 110
 standby 2 preempt
 standby 2 authentication Special
 standby 2 ip 10.201.0.6
 standby 2 track Serial1/3 25
 standby 4 priority 90
 standby 4 authentication Obsolete
 standby 4 ip 192.168.45.1
!
end
```

LISTING 6-9. *Special needs HSRP example, Router 1 configuration*

```
version 11.0
!
hostname Router2
!
interface Ethernet0/0
 description Core Router 2 with backup link to Special
 ip address 10.201.0.2 255.255.0.0
 ip address 192.168.45.2 255.255.255.0 secondary
 no ip redirects
```
(continued)

```
ipx network 1234321 encapsulation SAP
standby 1 priority 110
standby 1 preempt
standby 1 authentication Normal
standby 1 ip 10.201.0.1
standby 1 track Serial1/0 25
standby 2 priority 90
standby 2 preempt
standby 2 authentication Special
standby 2 ip 10.201.0.6
standby 2 track Serial1/3 25
standby 4 priority 110
standby 4 preempt
standby 4 authentication Obsolete
standby 4 ip 192.168.45.1
!
end
```

LISTING 6-10. *Special needs HSRP example, Router 2 configuration*

ticularly useful from a security viewpoint, since the passwords are sent over the LAN as clear text, but they do serve two worthwhile purposes. They document the purpose of each standby group and they help prevent configuration errors from going unnoticed. A log entry is made for every HSRP packet exchange with mismatched passwords, which at one exchange per second tends to be hard to ignore.

DIAL BACKUP BY ONE ROUTER FOR A LINE ON ANOTHER

Another challenge introduced by having multiple routers at a site, particularly a small site, is using dial backup to adequately protect against line outages. While it is easy to set up dial backup for a single router using the *backup interface* approach, this approach only works when the primary link and the backup link are on the same router. It is generally not useful for dial backup when there are two or more routers at a site.

Backup interface is triggered by a router detecting that an interface has failed. There is no provision for one router to detect the failure of an interface on a second router so that the first router can initiate a backup call. Consider the minimum-cost, physically diverse site configuration in Figure 6-6. We put one router at each end of a large building and connect the two 10BaseT concentrators to create a single extended LAN.

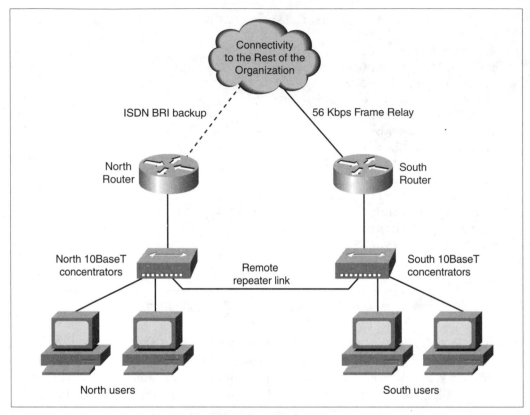

FIGURE 6-6. *Physical configuration of a two-router site with physical diversity and dial backup*

In a production network, we would replace the single link with physically diverse, redundant links using IEEE 802.1d transparent Spanning-Tree (TST) bridge protocol. But for now, we want to keep the configuration simple. For the same reason, we connect this site to a single router at a single data center site, as shown in Figure 6-7. We can generalize the concepts we will use to handle this basic configuration to support a site with an arbitrary number of routers connecting to an arbitrary mesh of other sites.

The key to success is to trigger the dialing of the backup link based on the inability of the South Router to reach the data center LAN rather than on the state of the Frame Relay interface on the South Router. In other words, we want to trigger the dial backup based on whether or not an IP address is in the routing tables of the North and South routers. Based on our survey of dial backup approaches in Chapter 4, we know that either *dialer watch* or dial-on-demand should be usable, so we will discuss examples of both approaches.

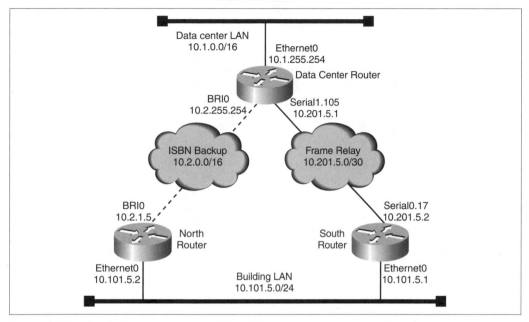

FIGURE 6-7. *Logical connectivity and IP addressing for two-router site example*

CONFIGURATION EXAMPLE: USING *DIALER WATCH*

The Cisco *dialer watch* feature introduced in IOS 12.0 is ideal for this application, provided we are comfortable with using EIGRP as our routing protocol.[1] *Dialer watch* works by taking a list of IP addresses (the *dialer watch-list*) and checking if any of them is still in the local routing table any time the routing table is modified to remove a watched IP address. If no valid route remains, the primary link is considered down and the backup link is forced to dial, regardless of the presence or absence of "interesting" traffic defined by the *dialer-list*. For example, if we enabled *dialer watch* on the address of the other end of the Frame Relay link, any time the Frame Relay link went down, the route to it would be removed from the routing table. We would immediately initiate a dial backup call.

Operation is more reliable if we do not depend upon the Frame Relay link to fail before initiating a dial backup call. Rather than watch the other end of the Frame Relay link, which will always be considered reachable—unless the Frame Relay link has failed to the extent that the local interface is down—we can watch the Ethernet address of the data center LAN. That way, regardless of the state of the serial interface on the South Router, we will dial as soon as any failure occurs that makes the data center LAN unreachable.

We will start our examination of the router configurations in Listing 6-11 with the South Router. The South Router supports the Frame Relay link from the remote

```
version 11.0
!
hostname South
! Router with primary link being backed up
interface Ethernet0
 ip address 10.101.5.1 255.255.255.0
!
interface Serial0
 no ip address
 encapsulation frame-relay
!
interface Serial0.17 point-to-point
 description Primary link to Data Center
 ip address 10.201.5.2 255.255.255.252
 frame-relay interface-dlci 17 broadcast
!
router eigrp 1
 network 10.0.0.0
 no auto-summary
!
end
```

LISTING 6-11. *South Router with primary (Frame Relay) link to data center*

site to the data center. From the viewpoint of *dialer watch*, it makes no difference what technology is used for this primary link. All that matters is that we use EIGRP for the routing protocol between this router and the North Router. If desired, we could use another routing protocol between this router and the data center. However, configuration is much easier if EIGRP is used between the North Router running *dialer watch* and the data center router, so we use EIGRP everywhere.

Note that although *dialer watch* requires running IOS 12.0 or better, that requirement applies only to the North Router. Other routers in the network only need to support EIGRP and any interfaces and protocols used. While here we show them running IOS 11.0—as is the convention when the IOS release is not significant—most practitioners would prefer to run the same IOS release on all routers in the network.

Running the same software release on all systems minimizes problems with incompatible changes to default parameters and other inconsistencies. Still, some prefer the more conservative route of deliberately mixing software releases and router vendors to reduce the number of systems affected when a major software defect surfaces. As we discussed in Chapter 1, the latter is a better approach for maximum availability, but the cost of the testing effort required is too high for most organizations. Most are better served by adequately testing a single release and restricting their configurations to use only well-tested features.

Turning our attention to the North Router, which is running the *dialer watch* code in Listing 6-12, we see a configuration very similar to the *dialer watch* example

```
version 12.0
!
hostname North
! Router with ISDN backup link
username DataCenter password SharedSecret
!
interface Ethernet0
 ip address 10.101.5.2 255.255.255.0
!
interface BRI0
! Secondary backup line
 ip address 10.2.1.5 255.255.0.0
 encapsulation ppp
! Dialer map for the IP network which is being watched
dialer map ip 10.1.0.0 name DataCenter speed 56 broadcast
 ➥ 18005551212
! Dialer map for the actual remote end address for routing
dialer map ip 10.2.255.254 name DataCenter speed
 ➥ 56 broadcast 18005551212
 dialer-group 1
! Enable dialer watch on this interface
 dialer watch-group 2
 ppp authentication chap
!
! Must use EIGRP or IGRP routing for dialer watch
router eigrp 1
 network 10.0.0.0
 no auto-summary
!
access-list 100 deny    eigrp any any
access-list 100 permit ip any any
! Watch IP network 10.1.0.0
dialer watch-list 2 ip 10.1.0.0 255.255.0.0
dialer-list 1 protocol ip list 100
!
end
```

LISTING 6-12.   *North Router using* dialer watch *to control backup ISDN link*

explored in Chapter 4. If anything, this example is simpler because there are no WAN links to configure other than the ISDN support. Note that we also support dial-on-demand to simplify testing of ISDN link functionality. This requires us to define "interesting" traffic in *access-list 100* so that EIGRP neighbor multicasts will not bring up or keep up the ISDN link.

Remember that for *dialer watch* to function, we must assign unique numbers across all *dialer-lists* and *dialer watch-list*s. That is, we must not use the same number to identify a *dialer watch-list* and a *dialer-list* on the same router. Since this is an undocumented limitation, it may or may not exist in any particular IOS release.

We also can use *dialer watch* with OSPF or some other routing protocol as our primary routing protocol, as long as we run EIGRP on this router and redistribute the watched routes from the primary routing protocol into EIGRP. However, we will then need to ensure that the watched routes cannot be learned across the dial link by any protocol other than EIGRP, or the dial backup will be unstable.

At the data center router in Listing 6-13, we have a standard dial-in router configuration. Again, there are no traces of *dialer watch* on this router, so any IOS release will work. We could even use a non-Cisco router if we chose to work around the EIGRP requirement by using route redistribution on the North Router.

```
version 11.0
!
hostname DataCenter
!
username North password SharedSecret
! Names and passwords for other callers go here
!
interface Ethernet0
 description Data center LAN
 ip address 10.1.255.254 255.255.0.0
!
interface Serial1
description Frame Relay to remote locations
no ip address
encapsulation frame-relay
!
interface Serial1.105 point-to-point
 description Primary link to South Router
 ip address 10.201.5.1 255.255.255.252
 frame-relay interface-dlci 105 broadcast
!
! Subinterfaces for other sites not shown...
!
```

(continued)

```
interface BRI0
 description This is where backups dial in.
 ip address 10.2.255.254 255.255.0.0
 encapsulation ppp
 dialer idle-timeout 300
 dialer map ip 10.2.1.5 name North speed 56 broadcast
! Dialer maps for other callers go here
 dialer-group 1
 ppp authentication chap
!
router eigrp 1
 network 10.0.0.0
 no auto-summary
!
access-list 100 deny    eigrp any any
access-list 100 permit ip any any
dialer-list 1 protocol ip list 100
!
end
```

LISTING **6-13.**   *Router backup using* dialer watch; *data center router with Frame Relay and ISDN links*

Even though this end of the ISDN link will never place a call, we still configure it with a 5-minute idle time-out and ignore the routing protocol hello packets that would otherwise keep the link up forever. We do this to catch some errors that would not be detected by a simple ping test of the ISDN test address using dial-on-demand. A series of ISDN calls in the router log, each exactly 5 minutes long, then becomes an immediate red flag. It indicates that there is a serious problem with ISDN dial backup that is not being detected by the router placing the call. Without the idle time-out at this end of the link, the remote would keep the link up even though no responses were coming back. The inability to communicate might not be noticed until users complained.

Clearly there are many improvements we would make to this example design before putting it into a production environment. We would dial into a different router in order to avoid that single point of failure, and we would use an ISDN PRI interface at the data center to allow more than two locations to be on ISDN at the same time. We might also want to consider enhancements such as strengthening authentication through the use of caller ID information or using multilink PPP for higher bandwidth. The exact configuration will obviously be highly dependent upon user and organizational requirements.

There is another possible improvement that is not as obvious. If there are multiple LANs at the data center site, we could "watch" a loopback interface address defined on the data center router so that dial backup would not be triggered unnecessarily by an inconsequential LAN failure. Similarly, if there were only one data center LAN (not very common in a high availability data center, but quite possible in a random mesh topology), we could "watch" a loopback address on a different router at the site. That way, we could not only recover from a primary link failure, but also attempt to dial around a LAN failure at the site. The key is to think through what we are trying to accomplish and look for ways to adapt our tools to enable us to get there.

CONFIGURATION EXAMPLE: USING DIAL-ON-DEMAND

While *dialer watch* provides an easy solution to multiple router site dial backup, it is not a solution for everyone. The following reiterates the three critical limitations to be considered in any potential application of *dialer watch*.

- The only routing protocols supported are IGRP and EIGRP.
- The only network protocol supported is IP.
- There is no support on IOS releases prior to 12.0.

Cisco may address the first two shortcomings in subsequent releases, but there are no plans to retrofit the *dialer watch* capabilities into prior IOS releases. It is also not clear when other router vendors will provide similar capabilities on their systems. So we need to look at how we can achieve the same functionality provided by *dialer watch* using any router supporting dial-on-demand and floating static routes. The trick is to use judiciously defined floating static routes rather than *dialer watch* to trigger the dial event.

We will start with the network design in Figures 6-6 and 6-7. Our discussion will use Cisco semantics, but, unlike *dialer watch,* our approach is not Cisco proprietary and could be implemented in a mixed-vendor environment. The key is to define floating static routes for the target destinations that will force the DDR activation anytime the primary link is unavailable. Then we must redistribute those routes to other local routers to attract the traffic necessary to activate the dial-on-demand.

In this example, we define the default route on both the North and South routers to be via the data center LAN. We then add to the North Router with the backup link, a floating static route that associates the address of the data center LAN with the BRI interface. When the primary link is connected, the route to the data center LAN is learned from the dynamic routing protocol, and both routers use the primary link as their best path to everywhere.

When the primary link fails, the route to the data center LAN via the primary link is removed from the routing tables. This allows the route to the data center via the backup link to float into action on the North Router. We configure the routing protocol on the North Router to redistribute the new route to the data center. The South Router then learns about it and forwards traffic to the North Router to be delivered to the data center.

This extra level of redirection is essential. We need the South Router to send all outbound traffic to the North Router in order to ensure that "interesting" traffic will be available to force up the dial link. But we must not put a floating static route on the South Router to do the job. Otherwise, we introduce a routing loop: the South Router would discover the primary link down and start to send traffic to the North Router for delivery. In the meantime, until the North Router learned of the failure through the routing protocol, it would continue to send all traffic to the South Router for delivery over the primary link.

Instead, the North Router activates the backup route only when it learns from the South Router of the loss of connectivity. At this point, the South Router has no route to the data center, and any traffic is discarded. As soon as the North Router activates the route, it informs the South Router; all traffic for the data center is then forwarded to the North Router for delivery.

The configuration of the South Router in Listing 6-14 is identical to the *dialer watch* configuration except for three added lines (in bold type). Two lines specify the bandwidth and delay of the primary link for use in routing metrics, and the third adds a floating static route defining a default route via an address on the data center LAN. In a real configuration, these lines probably would have been part of the *dialer watch* configuration as well—but now that we are using dial-on-demand, they become critical to efficient operation. Note also that while we continue to use EIGRP as the production routing protocol, to minimize the number of changes, our choice of routing protocol is no longer constrained.

```
version 11.0
!
hostname South
! Router with primary link being backed up
interface Ethernet0
 ip address 10.101.5.1 255.255.255.0
!
interface Serial0
 no ip address
 encapsulation frame-relay
!
```

(continued)

```
interface Serial0.17 point-to-point
 description Primary link to Data Center
 ip address 10.201.5.2 255.255.255.252
 bandwidth 56
 delay 2000
 frame-relay interface-dlci 17 broadcast
!
router eigrp 1
 network 10.0.0.0
 no auto-summary
!
! Default route is via learned path to data center LAN
ip route 0.0.0.0 0.0.0.0 10.1.255.254 150
!
end
```

LISTING 6-14. *South Router with primary (Frame Relay) link to data center, with dial-on-demand additions in bold*

The default route via the data center LAN *(ip route 0.0.0.0 0.0.0.0 10.1.255.254)* is required even if a default route is being advertised by the production routing protocol. The target of this default route must not be on any subnetwork physically attached to the local router. It must be an address that can only be learned through the production routing protocol so that it will disappear from the local routing tables when no links are up between this site and the data center.

The values used in the bandwidth and delay statements on the Frame Relay interface are arbitrary. The only requirement is that when the Frame Relay link and the ISDN link are both up, all traffic between the two sites be routed via Frame Relay, even if that means an extra hop across the LAN at each end. Otherwise the ISDN link could stay up forever even though it was no longer needed. With routing protocols other than IP, it is necessary to add statements guiding the path selection for any packets considered "interesting" in the dial-on-demand filter—such as *ipx delay* for IPX. This is true both here and on the backup and target routers.

Moving over to the North Router in Listing 6-15, note that all the extra lines for *dialer watch* are gone. In their place, we find a *bandwidth 56* and *delay 5000* under the BRI interface to ensure that the ISDN link not carry traffic when the primary link is available. There is also a redistribute static command under *router eigrp 1* (controlled by *distribute-list 11 out static*), and a pair of floating static routes to activate dial-on-demand.

```
version 11.0
!
hostname North
! Router with ISDN backup link
username DataCenter password SharedSecret
!
interface Ethernet0
 ip address 10.101.5.2 255.255.255.0
!
interface BRI0
! Secondary backup line
 ip address 10.2.1.5 255.255.0.0
 encapsulation ppp
 bandwidth 56
 delay 5000
 dialer map ip 10.2.255.254 name DataCenter speed 56 broadcast
   ➥ 18005551212
 dialer-group 1
 ppp authentication chap
!
! Can use any routing protocol desired!
router eigrp 1
 redistribute static
 network 10.0.0.0
 distribute-list 11 out static
 no auto-summary
!
! Default route is via best path to data center LAN
ip route 0.0.0.0 0.0.0.0 10.1.255.254 150
! If no known route to data center LAN, use ISDN backup
ip route 10.1.0.0 255.255.0.0 10.2.255.254 155
access-list 11 permit 10.1.0.0 0.0.255.255
access-list 100 deny   eigrp any any
access-list 100 permit ip any any
!
dialer-list 1 protocol ip list 100
!
end
```

LISTING 6-15. *North Router with ISDN backup link to data center, with dial-on-demand additions in bold*

As long as the primary link is up, the routing protocol running will announce the data center LAN, and the floating static route (*ip route 10.1.0.0 255.255.0.0 10.2.255.254 155*) will remain inactive. The floating static route defining the default route (*ip route 0.0.0.0 0.0.0.0 10.1.255.254 150*) may or may not be active, depending upon whether the routing protocol is distributing a default route. We block redistribution of the static route defining the default route to prevent its distribution outside the local site. Depending on other connectivity that may be in place, we may also find it beneficial to filter routing advertisements from the North and South routers on links leaving the site. This would remove the backup path to the data center LAN.

When the primary link fails, all routes learned through the link disappear and both of the North router's floating static routes are activated. The floating static route to the data center LAN activates the default route on the South Router when it arrives there via the production routing protocol. As soon as the dial backup link comes up, the routing protocol learns where everything really is, and the floating static routes float out of action.

At the data center in Listing 6-16, no configuration changes are required. However, if filtering of external routes is required to prevent the introduction of incorrect routing information from the redistributed static routes, it may be necessary to install the filters here. What can be filtered and where will depend upon the production routing protocol in use and the version of the router software.

```
version 11.0
!
hostname DataCenter
!
username North password SharedSecret
! Names and passwords for other callers go here
!
interface Ethernet0
  description Data center LAN
  ip address 10.1.255.254 255.255.0.0
!
interface Serial1
  description Frame Relay to remote locations
  no ip address
  encapsulation frame-relay
!
interface Serial1.105 point-to-point
  description Primary link to South Router
  ip address 10.201.5.1 255.255.255.252
  frame-relay interface-dlci 105 broadcast
```

(continued)

```
!
! Subinterfaces for other sites not shown...
!
interface BRI0
 description This is where backups dial in.
 ip address 10.2.255.254 255.255.0.0
 encapsulation ppp
 dialer idle-timeout 300
 dialer map ip 10.2.1.5 name North speed 56 broadcast
 ! Dialer maps for other dial ins go here
 dialer-group 1
 ppp authentication chap
!
router eigrp 1
 network 10.0.0.0
 no auto-summary
!
access-list 100 deny    eigrp any any
access-list 100 permit ip any any
!
dialer-list 1 protocol ip list 100
!
end
```

LISTING 6-16. *Router backup using dial-on-demand; data center router with Frame Relay and ISDN links*

CONFIGURATION EXAMPLE: USING BGP-DRIVEN DIAL-ON-DEMAND

We have mentioned numerous times that a critical requirement for successful use of dial-on-demand for backup purposes is having "interesting" traffic present at the router with the backup line to force the dial. When there is only one dial link, it is usually easy enough to ensure that some normal traffic (often the syslog event reporting that the primary link has gone down) will force the link up. If we want to provide a second dial backup link to improve the probability of a successful connection, it becomes much more difficult to ensure that there will be appropriate traffic to trigger the dialing.

The easy solution is to use IOS 12.0 and *dialer watch*. First, two unique loopback port addresses are defined at the target site. Next, route advertisement filters are configured so that a route to both addresses can be learned over the primary link, a route to only one can be learned over the preferred dial link, and no routes to either can be learned via the secondary dial link. We can then set up a *dialer watch* on the preferred dial link for the address that is only advertised over the primary link, and a *dialer watch* on the secondary dial link for the address that is advertised over both the primary and the preferred dial links. This is a trivial extension to the *dialer watch* example discussed at the beginning of this section.

Even if we are not in a position to use *dialer watch,* we can still get two levels of backup. To do so, we set up a pair of loopback addresses with restricted advertising—the same as if we were using *dialer watch* to do the job. But instead of *dialer watch,* we use the TCP keepalive packets between BGP neighbors to force up dial-on-demand. This is the same thing we did in the BGP-driven dial backup example in Chapter 5 to provide two levels of backup for a single router.

In this example, we build on the configuration we have been using so far and add a second backup link to the mix—an asynchronous modem off the Auxiliary port of the South Router with the primary link. Then, just to keep it interesting, we also add support for Novell NetWare IPX and configure the ISDN backup to use unnumbered addresses to conserve IP address space. We also get more realistic for a large site at the target by configuring a T1 for Frame Relay and a PRI for ISDN back at the data center. The resultant network is shown in Figure 6-8.

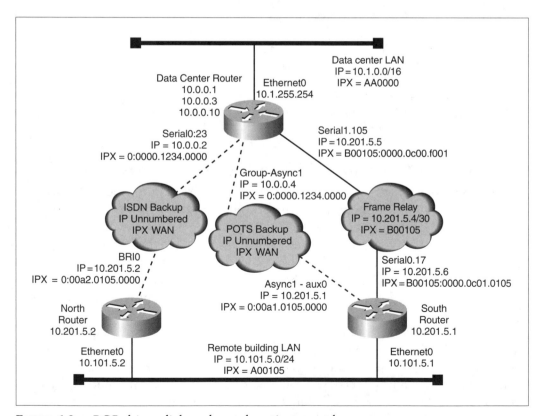

FIGURE 6-8. *BGP-driven dial-on-demand routing example*

The theory of operation here is identical to that in the single router example in Chapter 5. So we can move straight to the Cisco configurations—starting with the South Router with the primary link and asynchronous modem on its AUX port, from Listing 6-17—to see how the theory can be applied to practice.

```
version 11.0
!
hostname South
!
username DataCenter password SouthSecret
!
ipx routing 0000.0c01.0105
ipx internal-network A10105
chat-script courier ABORT ERROR ABORT "NO " ABORT BUSY ""
  ➥ "at" "" "at&f" OK "atl1m1&b1&h1&r2&c1&d3&m4&k1s0=2" OK
  ➥ "at dt \T" TIMEOUT 90 CONNECT \c
!
interface Loopback0
 description IP address for Async dial
 ip address 10.201.5.1 255.255.255.255
!
interface Ethernet0
 description Building LAN
 ip address 10.101.5.1 255.255.255.0
 ipx network A00105 encapsulation SAP
!
interface Serial0
 description 56Kbps frame relay link
 no ip address
 encapsulation frame-relay
!
interface Serial0.17 point-to-point
 description PVC to Data Center Router
 ip address 10.201.5.6 255.255.255.252
 bandwidth 56
 delay 2000
 ipx delay 7
 ipx network B00105
 frame-relay interface-dlci 17
!
interface Async1
 description Dial backup to data center just in case
```

(*continued*)

```
 ip unnumbered Loopback0
 encapsulation ppp
 bandwidth 33
 delay 15000
 ipx ipxwan 0 unnumbered South
 ipx delay 30
 async default routing
 async mode interactive
 dialer in-band
 dialer idle-timeout 300
 dialer map ipx 0.0000.1234.0000 name DataCenter broadcast
 ➡ 18885551212
 dialer map ip 10.0.0.4 name DataCenter modem-script courier
 ➡ broadcast 18885551212
 dialer hold-queue 10 timeout 60
 dialer-group 1
 ppp authentication chap
!
router eigrp 1
 network 10.0.0.0
 no auto-summary
!
ip host TestISDN 10.0.0.2
ip host TestAsync 10.0.0.4
! Default route via frame relay to avoid unnecessary calls
ip route 0.0.0.0 0.0.0.0 10.0.0.1 150
! If no default route via frame, use ISDN if available
ip route 0.0.0.0 0.0.0.0 10.0.0.3 155
! If no route exists, force up the async link
ip route 0.0.0.0 0.0.0.0 10.0.0.4 160
! Force ISDN test packets to the North router
ip route 10.0.0.2 255.255.255.255 10.101.5.2
! Asynchronous dial forcing address
ip route 10.0.0.4 255.255.255.255 Async1
access-list 102 deny   eigrp any any
access-list 102 permit ip any any
access-list 902 deny  1
access-list 902 deny  4
access-list 902 permit -1
!
dialer-list 1 protocol ip list 102
dialer-list 1 protocol ipx list 902
!
```

(continued)

```
line aux 0
 password mumble
 script dialer courier
 login
 modem InOut
 transport input all
 speed 38400
 flowcontrol hardware
 !
end
```

LISTING 6-17. *IP and IPX with BGP-driven ISDN, South Router*

The configuration of the South Router is standard point-to-point Frame Relay with Async dial backup through the AUX port. Refer to the discussion in Chapter 5 on the use of the AUX port for dial backup for operational considerations. Although this is an example of using BGP to drive dial-on-demand in a multiple router site, there is no BGP on this router. There is, however, one extra floating static default route, activated by knowledge of an address that can only be learned via the routing protocol running across the ISDN link. Otherwise, the only influence of the North Router's ISDN link is in the *ip host* and *ip route* definitions to support ISDN link testing.

Each pair of routers can have a unique shared secret. Here, data center and South use the shared password *SouthSecret,* while data center and North use the password *NorthSecret.* The *ipx routing* command turns on IPX so that Novell NetWare can be supported on the network. The IPX internal network assignment is critical, as it becomes part of the IPX host address identifying this router when IPXWAN is used. Note that in IOS 11.2 and later, the IPX definition of "interesting" traffic would read as follows:

access-list *902* *deny* *rip*

access-list *902* *deny* *sap*

access-list *902* *permit* *any*

Keep in mind that this configuration is the minimum needed to get ISDN and asynchronous dial support of IP and IPX, not a tuned production configuration. Typical commands useful when supporting IPX are not shown. These include custom queuing to provide better IPX responsiveness, use of NLSP rather than IPXRIP, inclusion of all the filters appropriate for keeping the link from coming up unnecessarily, suppression of advertisement of unnecessary addresses and services, and spacing out of RIP and SAP updates over slow WAN links. In particular, this IPX configuration will not function without the support of IP to bring up the dial links. If there is no outbound IP traffic present at the primary router when the Frame Relay link dies, it will never even attempt to bring up the asynchronous link. Indeed, as you can see from the dialer maps, IPX traffic is incapable of bringing up the dial link on this router, as only the IP dialer map has the necessary chat script specified.

The definition and weighting of the floating static routes is essential to successful multiple levels of backup operation. The static routes must have a higher distance specified than that used by the interior routing protocol. The routing advertisements from the data center router must filter its defined loopback addresses so that only the desired target addresses are advertised over each link. If multiple data center routers are used, all that is required is that the appropriate loopback interface addresses be defined on each. There is no problem with defining the same target addresses on multiple routers, as long as they are filtered out of any direct advertisements, such as over a common Ethernet (hence the advertisement filter on the Ethernet port in the data center router).

The forwarding of traffic via the ISDN link, when required, is handled automatically by the routing protocol. Under normal conditions, all traffic—including BGP keepalives—flows via Frame Relay. When the Frame Relay link goes down, the 10.0.0.1 target is no longer reachable and the router looks for an alternative route. Since the target address 10.0.0.3 is only advertised over ISDN, it will not be available. The only available route will be the default route via 10.0.0.4, the asynchronous link. Under the rules of dial-on-demand routing, dial links are always connected (whether they are physically connected or not), so the floating static route through the asynchronous port is activated, and a call is initiated.

At first glance, the North Router in Listing 6-18 also appears to be a standard IP and IPX dial-on-demand configuration. However, when we look at the hierarchy of floating static default routes, we find that all the traffic that would normally bring up the ISDN line is routed to the Async interface on the South Router. We need to take a closer look at the configuration of the North Router to see how ISDN calls are forced up by BGP.

Since BGP will only establish a connection to a neighbor that is explicitly in the routing tables, and the address 10.0.0.10 is not advertised over any links from the target router, we define two explicit static routes just for BGP. The preferred route is via the Frame Relay target address so that when Frame Relay is up, BGP will exchange keepalive packets using the Frame Relay link. However, whenever the primary route disappears, we fall back to the floating static route through the "always available" target address used for ISDN. This is why we need two ISDN target addresses. One is for routing production traffic in both routers when the ISDN is up

```
version 11.0
!
hostname North
!
username DataCenter password NorthSecret
ipx routing 0000.0c02.0105
ipx internal-network A20105
isdn switch-type basic-ni1
!
interface Loopback0
 description Source address for ISDN calls
 ip address 10.201.5.2 255.255.255.255
!
interface Ethernet0
 description Building LAN
 ip address 10.101.5.2 255.255.255.0
 ipx network A00105 encapsulation SAP
!
interface BRI0
 description Primary backup path for this site
 ip unnumbered Loopback0
 encapsulation ppp
 bandwidth 56
 delay 5000
 no keepalive
 ipx ipxwan 0 unnumbered North
 ipx delay 30
 isdn spid1 80055512120101
 isdn spid2 80055512130101
 dialer idle-timeout 170
 dialer map ipx 0.0000.1234.0000 name DataCenter speed
 ➥ 56 broadcast 18005551234
 dialer map ip 10.0.0.2 name DataCenter speed 56 broadcast
 ➥ 18005551234
 dialer hold-queue 10
 dialer-group 1
 ppp authentication chap
!
router eigrp 1
 network 10.0.0.0
 no auto-summary
!
```

(continued)

```
router bgp 99
 network 10.201.5.2 mask 255.255.255.255
 timers bgp 10 120
 neighbor 10.0.0.10 remote-as 99
 neighbor 10.0.0.10 update-source Loopback0
!
ip host TestISDN 10.0.0.2
ip host TestAsync 10.0.0.4
! Default route via frame relay to avoid unnecessary calls
ip route 0.0.0.0 0.0.0.0 10.0.0.1 150
! If no default route via frame, use ISDN if available
ip route 0.0.0.0 0.0.0.0 10.0.0.3 155
! If no route exists, force up the async link
ip route 0.0.0.0 0.0.0.0 10.0.0.4 160
! Use frame relay on other router for BGP if available
ip route 10.0.0.10 255.255.255.255 10.0.0.1 150
! Otherwise, have BGP force up the ISDN link
ip route 10.0.0.10 255.255.255.255 10.0.0.2 160
! ISDN dial address
ip route 10.0.0.2 255.255.255.255 BRI0
! Support for simplified Async testing
ip route 10.0.0.4 255.255.255.255 10.101.5.1
access-list 102 deny   eigrp any any
access-list 102 permit ip any any
access-list 902 deny  1
access-list 902 deny  4
access-list 902 permit -1
!
dialer-list 1 protocol ip list 102
dialer-list 1 protocol ipx list 902
!
end
```

LISTING 6-18. *IP and IPX with BGP-driven ISDN, North Router*

and running; the other is for use by the BGP on the North Router to force up the ISDN link when needed. So even if we are currently carrying all production traffic through the asynchronous link on the primary router, the secondary router will continue to try to bring up the ISDN link, due solely to BGP's exchange of keepalive messages.

Although it increases our overhead slightly, we adjust the timers on BGP to send a keepalive every 10 seconds rather than the default 60 seconds. This reduces the maximum delay before an ISDN dial attempt is forced. We need to make sure any modified timer values are matched on the remote-peer BGP configuration.

One other convenience feature that is easy to overlook is the definition of a static route to the asynchronous activation address. This allows for testing of the asynchronous port by pinging the activation address from any system on the LAN, eliminating the need for a telnet session to the South Router. We include a static route on the South Router pointing the ISDN activation address to the North Router for exactly the same reason.

```
version 11.0
!
hostname DataCenter
!
username North password NorthSecret
username South password SouthSecret
ipx routing 0000.0C00.F001
ipx internal-network 1234
isdn switch-type primary-dms100
chat-script courier ABORT ERROR ABORT "NO " ABORT BUSY "" "at"
 ➡ "" "at&f" OK "atl1m1&b1&h1&r2&c1&d3&m4&k1s0=2" OK
!
controller T1 0
 framing esf
 linecode b8zs
 pri-group timeslots 1-24
!
interface Loopback0
 description Unique Address for Network Management
 ip address 10.255.0.1 255.255.255.255
!
interface Loopback1
 description Primary target for frame relay users
 ip address 10.0.0.1 255.255.255.255
!
interface Loopback2
 description IP Address for ISDN Unnumbered
 ip address 10.0.0.2 255.255.255.255
!
interface Loopback3
 description Routing target for ISDN use
 ip address 10.0.0.3 255.255.255.255
!
```

(continued)

```
interface Loopback4
 description IP Address for Async Unnumbered
 ip address 10.0.0.4 255.255.255.255
!
interface Loopback10
 description Routing target for BGP keepalives
 ip address 10.0.0.10 255.255.255.255
!
interface Ethernet0
 description Data Center LAN
 ip address 10.1.255.254 255.255.0.0
 ipx network AA0000 encapsulation SAP
!
interface Serial0
 description Frame Relay (T1)
 no ip address
 encapsulation frame-relay
!
! Subinterfaces to support other sites go here
!
interface Serial0.105 point-to-point
 description Primary Link to Router "South"
 ip address 10.201.5.5 255.255.255.252
 bandwidth 56
 delay 2000
 ipx delay 7
 ipx network B00105
 frame-relay interface-dlci 105
!
interface Serial0:23
 description Call In Support for ISDN backup
 ip unnumbered Loopback2
 encapsulation ppp
 bandwidth 56
 delay 5000
 no keepalive
 ipx ipxwan 0 unnumbered DataCenter
 ipx delay 20
 dialer idle-timeout 300
 dialer map ipx 0.00A2.0105.0000 name North speed 56 broadcast
 dialer map ip 10.201.5.2 name North speed 56 broadcast
! Dialer maps to support other sites go here
 dialer-group 1
 ppp authentication chap
```

(continued)

```
!
interface Group-Async1
 description Call in support for POTS backup
 ip unnumbered Loopback4
 encapsulation ppp
 bandwidth 33
 delay 15000
 ipx ipxwan 0 unnumbered DataCenter
 ipx delay 30
 async default routing
 async mode dedicated
 dialer in-band
 dialer idle-timeout 300
 dialer map ipx 0.00A0.0105.0000 name South broadcast
 dialer map ip 10.201.5.1 name South broadcast
! Dialer maps to support other sites go here
 dialer-group 1
 ppp authentication chap
 pulse-time 3
 group-range 1 8
!
router eigrp 1
 network 10.0.0.0
 distribute-list 10 out Group-Async1
 distribute-list 11 out Ethernet0
 distribute-list 12 out Serial0.105
 distribute-list 13 out Serial0:23
 no auto-summary
!
router bgp 99
 network 10.0.0.10 mask 255.255.255.255
 timers bgp 10 120
 neighbor 10.201.5.2 remote-as 99
 neighbor 10.201.5.2 update-source Loopback10
!
ip classless
access-list 10 permit 10.0.0.4
access-list 10 deny   10.0.0.0 0.0.0.255
access-list 10 permit any
access-list 11 deny   10.0.0.0 0.0.0.255
access-list 11 permit any
access-list 12 permit 10.0.0.1
access-list 12 deny   10.0.0.0 0.0.0.255
access-list 12 permit any
```

(continued)

```
access-list 13 permit 10.0.0.2 0.0.0.1
access-list 13 deny   10.0.0.0 0.0.0.255
access-list 13 permit any
!
dialer-list 1 protocol ipx permit
dialer-list 1 protocol ip permit
!
line 1 8
 script startup courier
 script reset courier
 modem InOut
 transport preferred none
 transport input all
 speed 115200
 flowcontrol hardware
!
end
```

LISTING 6-19. *IP and IPX with BGP-driven ISDN, data center router*

Before we discuss the individual functions configured on the data center router in Listing 6-19, keep in mind that normally these functions would be distributed across two or more routers to eliminate the data center router as a single point of failure. Since routers that are the target of dial backup calls like this one will often be serving many callers, it is quite possible that all functions will be on each data center router. This is true even though each caller may use one data center router for its primary link and a different data center router for each mode of dial backup call. In Chapter 7 we will explore ways to make multiple independent call-accepting routers look and behave like a single router for dial backup purposes. This will further enhance redundancy without adding significant complexity to the remote router configurations.

Note the inclusion of an advertisement filter on the local Ethernet port in addition to those on the links to the remotes. This filter allows us to reuse the same loopback address targets on all routers in the data center without the routers' confusing each other. Just be careful when setting up this filter not to block a loopback address used to identify the real router to network management. The safest approach is to dedicate a block of addresses to these artificial needs and allocate router IDs from a different block of addresses.

The key to success is to map out what connectivity is available and which backups should be active under what conditions. Once the priorities are identified, the appropriate loopback addresses can be defined at the required target locations, and the required floating static routes sorted by administrative distance. In addition to checking that the operation will be what we want under the conditions we are trying to protect against, we should look for any failure modes that could cause an undesirable set of connections. We can then iterate, fixing our design by including the "bad scenario" in the set of protected conditions.

PROTECTING AGAINST LAN SEGMENTATION

While using two routers at each location eliminates the problem of losing a router or connecting link, it also introduces a new vulnerability. If the LAN shared by the two routers is split into two segments, as can occur if the LAN spans multiple hubs or switches, then users on one LAN segment or the other may be cut off from effective communications, even though they remain physically connected. Consider the simplified site IP network in Figure 6-9.

Under most failure conditions, the redundant components allow for continued operation. If a WAN link fails, the routers cooperate to shift all traffic transparently to the remaining link. Similarly, if one of the routers fails, the remaining router keeps all data moving. If a failure severs the link between a router and its supporting hub

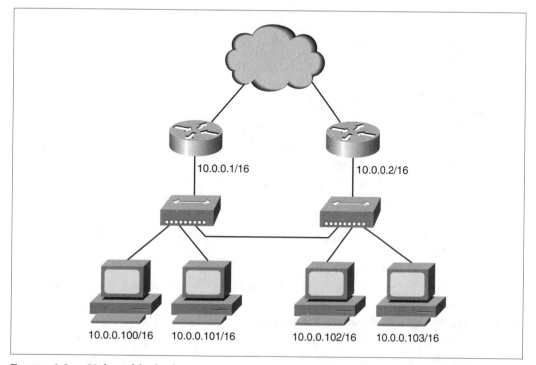

FIGURE 6-9.   *Vulnerable dual router network*

(or switch, as the case may be), the interface on the router fails, or the interface on the hub fails, that router will stop advertising reachability of the LAN. Again, the other router will carry all the traffic. Even if a hub fails and its users are left disconnected, the LAN interface on the router will go down and the router will send data back out across the WAN to the remaining router for those users still connected to a working hub.

Consider, however, what happens if the link between the two hubs is lost or disconnected. Both routers continue to advertise the entire subnetwork as reachable, even though each can now only reach the users on its half of the LAN. Although both routers still deliver packets from users on the LAN to the rest of the network, incoming packets may or may not be delivered to the router on the same piece of the LAN as the destination user. It depends on the routing weights on the WAN links and on the specific user.

The standard solution for this failure mode is to build the LAN using a mesh of switches that can address link failure with Spanning Tree recalculations. This allows us to support multiple physically diverse inter-switch links and eliminates the single point of failure in any one link between two different locations in the building.

While a redundant switched LAN design is necessary for high availability operation, it is not sufficient to eliminate all potential for LAN segmentation. The fundamental limitation is the single link at each router connecting it to the LAN. This means that each router must depend on a single switch for its connectivity to the rest of the LAN. Also, the physically diverse inter-switch links are no longer diverse where they come together at the switch, and there may be common paths shared inside the switch proper.

A similar failure mode also occurs when a hub, switch, or router interface fails in a way that makes the LAN port serving the router appear to the router to be alive—even though the router is no longer able to communicate with other devices on the LAN. Nor does it work to split the LAN into two independent subnetworks, each served by a single router, as then each router would again become a single point of failure. Nor is the problem limited to IP users—IPX users will suffer the same fate. Indeed, any network architecture that routes on the basis of an address containing reference to a specific physical network (as the subnetwork ID in IP and the network ID in IPX do) will fail if the physical network is split into two or more disconnected segments.

Only network architectures that do not include a level in the routing hierarchy corresponding to the physical network of attachment in the internetwork address are immune to this mode of failure. For example, the OSI Intermediate System-to-Intermediate System (IS-IS) routing protocol could theoretically recover from the failure automatically because the routing hierarchy embedded in an OSI network address skips directly from the intradomain routing area to the end system identifier.

A Workaround for IP Networks

One solution that will work with any protocol that supports dynamic routing is to connect each router to two or more shared LANs and install multihomed hosts, as described in Chapter 3, Multihomed Hosts. However, the cost of making all hosts multihomed just to counter a very low probability failure mode may be hard to justify. More powerful routers are required, the number of LAN components is doubled, and routers throughout the network are burdened with the extra networks being advertised.

If we cannot obtain all the availability we need by implementing a well-connected switched LAN from quality, high-reliability components, we can modify the network design at the router level to provide an extra layer of resistance to disruption due to LAN segmentation. Even though at this point we are assuming a well-designed, redundantly linked switched architecture, we will simplify the discussion by continuing to show two hubs connected by a single link. The actual connectivity is not relevant to the discussion as long as there is a potential for LAN segmentation that needs to be countered.

In the TCP/IP network architecture, we can stay with a single LAN and work around the problem by judicious use of variable length subnetwork masking (VLSM). To see how we can work around the LAN segmentation problem, we take the same physical configuration as in Figure 6-9 but modify the address assignments as shown in Figure 6-10. (Note that this approach will not work for IPX users, as the physical network ID in a Novell IPX network is always a fixed 32 bits, and each physical network can have only one network ID.)

At first glance, this addressing modification looks more like a step backward than an improvement. The trick is that both routers are configured to support the full range of user addresses, and each advertises the reachability of both subnetwork address ranges.

We accomplish this addressing sleight of hand by using a third, common subnetwork for routing between the two routers on the LAN (for example, 10.1.0.0/24). Each router then covers its preferred portion of the overall LAN address range using static routes pointing to the LAN interface. An additional static route on each router points to the LAN interface using a subnetwork address and mask that includes all users on the LAN (in this case 10.1.0.0/20). The static routes are then redistributed into the dynamic routing protocol with metrics that make the local LAN segment routes much more desirable than the overall route.

Normally, routers will always deliver packets to a directly connected network regardless of routing metrics. However, route specificity (prefix length) can take precedence over all other considerations. In order to deliver packets directly to the destination end-system on the LAN without first going to the router advertising that segment's IP subnetwork, we override the learned routes with a third set of static

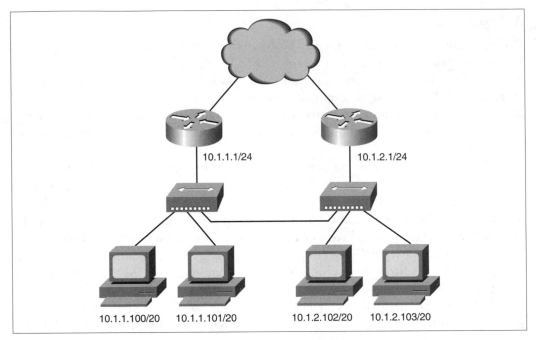

FIGURE 6-10. *Modified dual router network*

routes that have even longer prefixes. That way, routing on the LAN behaves like a single IP subnetwork rather than like multiple independent subnetworks requiring one-armed routing. Because these longer prefix routes would direct traffic from the outside to the wrong router during a LAN segmentation event, we must ensure that these more specific static routes are filtered from any routing advertisements leaving the router so that only the desired static routes are seen by the outside world.

When the LAN is operating normally, either router can send packets into the cloud from any source on the LAN and can deliver packets arriving from the cloud to any address on the LAN. Even if the two routers connect into the WAN at widely different locations or with different service quality, optimal routing is maintained. This occurs because each router advertises the other router's portion of the LAN subnetwork based on learning it via the routing protocol over the LAN, adding only a single LAN hop to the route metric. Should a router fail, the other router will continue to distribute reachability to the failed router's subnetwork, only now it will be based on the higher-cost static route for the overall LAN subnetwork pointing to the LAN interface. This route is ignored during normal operation because of its higher associated cost and lower specificity.

This means that even though each router is not "on" the other router's local subnetwork, each can still send packets to those users if one should happen to arrive. Similarly, Hot Standby Router Protocol is used to define a default gateway (or two, when load balancing) that can be reached by all user systems regardless of which routers are alive or connected to the LAN segment of the end-system.

This approach is not without its trade-offs. For example, using proxy ARP to simplify subnetwork mask independence can be problematic. Cisco routers will provide only a proxy ARP response to end-systems that have IP addresses in the subnetwork defined on the LAN interface. Our protected end-systems are all on subnetworks that are defined only by static routes, so proxy ARP is not usable. Instead, each end-system must have a correctly configured subnetwork mask (for the overall subnetwork) and use a default gateway in the much smaller "real" subnetwork shared by the routers' LAN interfaces. Consequently, use of HSRP or VRRP is usually mandatory to prevent the default gateway from being a single point of failure.

Probably the biggest drawback to this approach is that it does nothing to alleviate the inability of users on the LAN to communicate with other users who are on the same LAN but who happen to be on the other side of the split. Following LAN segmentation, local users can continue to communicate with the outside world, but they are cut off from local users on the other side of the break. The problem remains even though the routers may still have connectivity via other LANs at the site or via the WAN. Since this limitation is present in a normally configured environment as well, it might not be considered a significant issue.

Multihomed hosts implemented using routing to a third address inside the host—as described in Chapter 3—will continue to function correctly. But local users on other LANs supported by the same routers at the site could get confused as their ability to communicate with singly connected systems on the segmented LAN will depend upon their default gateway—potentially making the ability to connect seem random.

Two other considerations are the lack of IPX support and the configuration complexity. IPX will continue to fail the same way IP does in the typical single-subnetwork configuration discussed in the introduction. The complex configuration—particularly the use of selectively redistributed routes with selective adjustment of route metrics using route maps—can be problematic by exposing defects in, and implementation differences between, various router software releases.

CONFIGURATION EXAMPLE: SINGLE LAN WITH TWO WAN ROUTERS

In Figure 6-11, we take the simplified configuration of Figure 6-10 and attach a more practical LAN to it using layer 2 switches. We also add a third physical switch segment to the LAN. We show how we can configure a router attached to that switch so that it can continue to communicate following a LAN segmentation event, regardless of which piece of the LAN its switch remains a part of. The approach is easily extended to allow more routers to protect additional LAN segments and switches. Similarly, the individual subnetwork masks can be adjusted to make any of the protected LAN areas capable of supporting more (or fewer) end systems.

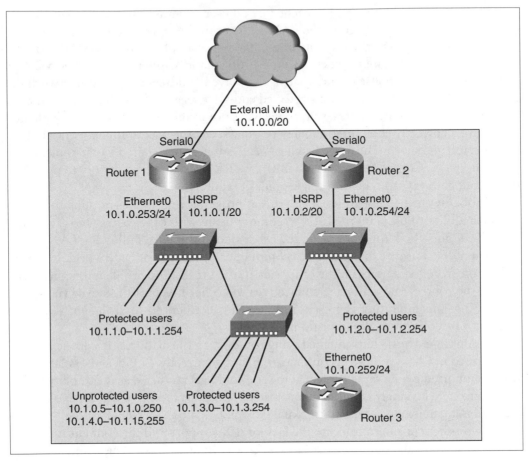

FIGURE 6-11. *LAN segmentation protection scenario*

While this approach does provide added resilience, it also stresses the routing protocols significantly. It becomes necessary to thoroughly test all possible failure modes—not just LAN segmentation—to ensure proper operation in any given environment.

Starting with the configuration for Router 1 in Listing 6-20, only a small portion of the overall subnetwork serviced by the LAN is configured on the Ethernet interface. For EIGRP or OSPF to establish a neighbor relationship and exchange routing information across the LAN, all routers must be configured so their Ethernet interface address is on the same subnetwork using the same subnetwork mask— 10.1.0.0/24 in this case. The definition of a second HSRP address on the interface is optional, but it allows us to provide some load balancing of outbound traffic.

```
version 11.0
!
hostname Router1
!
interface Ethernet0
 ip address 10.1.0.253 255.255.255.0
 no ip redirects
 standby 1 priority 110
 standby 1 preempt
 standby 1 authentication mumble
 standby 1 ip 10.1.0.1
 standby 2 priority 90
 standby 2 preempt
 standby 2 authentication mumble
 standby 2 ip 10.1.0.2
!
interface Serial 0
 description Link to the outside world
 ip address 10.255.1.6 255.255.255.252
!
router eigrp 1
 redistribute static route-map Local
 network 10.0.0.0
 no auto-summary
!
ip classless
! All destinations on the local LAN
ip route 10.1.0.0 255.255.240.0 Ethernet0
! LAN subnetworks attached to this router
ip route 10.1.1.0 255.255.255.0 Ethernet0
! Routes to avoid one-armed routing
ip route 10.1.2.0 255.255.255.128 Ethernet0
ip route 10.1.2.128 255.255.255.128 Ethernet0
ip route 10.1.3.0 255.255.255.128 Ethernet0
ip route 10.1.3.128 255.255.255.128 Ethernet0
!
! Static routes denied redistribution
access-list 20 permit 10.1.2.0 0.0.0.255
access-list 20 permit 10.1.3.0 0.0.0.255
! Static routes redistributed with low metrics
access-list 21 permit 10.1.1.0 0.0.0.255
```

(*continued*)

```
! Static routes redistributed with high metrics
access-list 22 permit 10.1.0.0 0.0.15.255
!
! Control redistribution of static routes into EIGRP
route-map Local deny 25
 match ip address 20
!
route-map Local permit 30
 match ip address 21
  set metric 10000 100 255 1 1500
!
route-map Local permit 35
 match ip address 22
  set metric 10000 10000 255 1 1500
!
end
```

LISTING 6-20. *Simple LAN segmentation resistant example, Router 1*

The configuration under *router eigrp 1* is deceptively simple, consisting of only three statements. The *redistribute static route-map Local* statement tells EIGRP to advertise any static routes available as specified by the route map Local. The *network 10.0.0.0* statement enables EIGRP routing on all interfaces on subnetworks in the major network 10.0.0.0/8. The *no auto-summary* statement is required only if this router has any interfaces not in 10.0.0.0/8. It keeps all the individual routes for subnetworks inside 10.0.0.0 from being combined into a single advertisement for the 10.0.0.0 major network when leaving the 10.0.0.0 network for another major network.

The static routes that follow are what allow the router to reach all destinations on the LAN. The first route tells the router that all systems in the overall subnetwork can be reached directly through interface Ethernet0. The second route then defines the subnetwork assigned to our local switch's LAN segment, the subnetwork that this router is protecting. The next four routes split each subnetwork protected by another router on this LAN into two smaller subnetworks. This allows this router to send packets arriving for end-systems on other routers' switches directly to the addressee rather than routing them to that segment's router first.

Redistribution of the static routes into EIGRP is controlled by the route map Local, which in turn is controlled by *access lists 20, 21* and *22. Access list 20* in configured to permit all static routes that we do not want to advertise that might otherwise match any tests for routes that we do want to redistribute. *Access list 21* is configured to pass only our local LAN segment subnetwork, the subnetwork we are trying to protect. Finally, *access list 22* needs to match the overall LAN subnetwork.

By the time we get to *access list 22,* all other routes in the overall subnetwork must have been matched by *access list 20* or *21.*

The route map Local is where the critical work is done. Route map Local first checks for the long prefix static routes used to prevent one-armed routing. All static routes that are permitted by *access list 20* are denied under the route-map Local deny 25 section.

Route map Local then checks for any static routes defining the local subnetwork LAN segment attached to this route runder route-map Local permit 30. These are determined by matching *access list 21* in the clause *match ip address 21.* In addition to permitting these routes to be redistributed, the clause *set metric 10000 100 255 1 1500* sets the EIGRP metric applied to the route. Because we want these routes to look like a normal subnetwork on a 10 Mbps Ethernet, we set the bandwidth to 10,000 Kbps, the delay to 100 tens of microseconds, the reliability to a perfect 255 (out of 255), the loading to the minimum of 1 (out of 255), and the maximum packet size to 1500 octets. These are the same metrics that are applied by default to the real Ethernet subnetwork 10.1.0.0/24. If the interface was a Fast Ethernet interface running at 100 Mbps, we would change the line to read *set metric 100000 10 255 1 1500.*

The short prefix static route for the overall LAN is then permitted by matching *access list 22* under route-map Local permit 35. Since we do not want this route to be used unless the router that should be advertising a shorter prefix is completely unavailable, we set the delay metric to 10,000 tens of microseconds. With Cisco routers, this is actually not required, as a longer prefix route will always be used over a less specific route. However, it does make it clear when looking at the routing tables on a remote router that this is not the preferred route. It also clearly identifies any routes missed by the previous two filters that are being improperly advertised.

The configuration of Router 2 in Listing 6-21 is a mirror image of Router 1's. The HSRP groups are set up to be the reverse of those on Router 1 to provide a degree of load balancing for locally sourced traffic. The static routes and the access lists used by the route map controlling their redistribution are adjusted to match the LAN segment that this router is protecting.

Unlike Routers 1 and 2, Router 3 in Listing 6-22 does not support any external connectivity. As a result, it should never process any production traffic. Router 3's only purpose is as a source of routing advertisements for its subnetwork (10.1.3.0/24) to whichever of Routers 1 and 2 has LAN connectivity to the Router 3 LAN segment. For example, if the Router 3 LAN segment should become disconnected from Router 1, traffic for 10.1.3.0/24 will be sent from outside sources to Router 2, which will continue to propagate the preferred route learned from Router 3. Router 1 will still advertise a route to the overall subnetwork but that route will be ignored because it is less specific and has a higher cost metric.

If Router 3 fails, traffic for its LAN segment will continue to be delivered to the site based on the redistributed static route on both Routers 1 and 2. This route covers

```
version 11.0
!
hostname Router2
!
interface Ethernet0
 ip address 10.1.0.254 255.255.255.0
 no ip redirects
 standby 1 priority 90
 standby 1 preempt
 standby 1 authentication mumble
 standby 1 ip 10.1.0.1
 standby 2 priority 110
 standby 2 preempt
 standby 2 authentication mumble
 standby 2 ip 10.1.0.2
!
interface Serial 0
 description Link to the outside world
 ip address 10.255.1.10 255.255.255.252
!
router eigrp 1
 redistribute static route-map Local
 network 10.0.0.0
 no auto-summary
!
ip classless
! All destinations on the local LAN
ip route 10.1.0.0 255.255.240.0 Ethernet0
! LAN subnetworks attached to this router
ip route 10.1.2.0 255.255.255.0 Ethernet0
! Routes to avoid one-armed routing
ip route 10.1.1.0 255.255.255.128 Ethernet0
ip route 10.1.1.128 255.255.255.128 Ethernet0
ip route 10.1.3.0 255.255.255.128 Ethernet0
ip route 10.1.3.128 255.255.255.128 Ethernet0
!
! Static routes denied redistribution
access-list 20 permit 10.1.1.0 0.0.0.255
access-list 20 permit 10.1.3.0 0.0.0.255
! Static routes redistributed with low metrics
access-list 21 permit 10.1.2.0 0.0.0.255
! Static routes redistributed with high metrics
access-list 22 permit 10.1.0.0 0.0.15.255
!
```

(*continued*)

```
! Control redistribution of static routes into EIGRP
route-map Local deny 25
 match ip address 20
!
route-map Local permit 30
 match ip address 21
 set metric 10000 100 255 1 1500
!
route-map Local permit 35
 match ip address 22
 set metric 10000 10000 255 1 1500
!
end
```

LISTING 6-21. *Simple LAN segmentation resistant example—Router 2*

```
version 11.0
!
hostname Router3
!
interface Ethernet0
 ip address 10.1.0.252 255.255.255.0
!
router eigrp 1
 redistribute static route-map Local
 network 10.0.0.0
 no auto-summary
!
ip classless
! All destinations on the local LAN
ip route 10.1.0.0 255.255.240.0 Ethernet0
! LAN subnetworks attached to this router
ip route 10.1.3.0 255.255.255.0 Ethernet0
!
! Static routes redistributed with low metrics
access-list 21 permit 10.1.3.0 0.0.0.255
!
! Control redistribution of static routes into EIGRP
route-map Local permit 30
 match ip address 21
 set metric 10000 100 255 1 1500
!
end
```

LISTING 6-22. *Simple LAN segmentation resistant example—Router 3*

the entire subnetwork assigned to the distributed LAN. Once at Router 1 or 2, traffic will be sent straight to the end system as long as the LAN is still fully connected.

The design of Router 3 can be replicated to support additional LAN segments. Since these isolated routers never carry production traffic, they will never introduce a performance bottleneck, and the cheapest, slowest router capable of handling the routing protocol can be used. Just remember to add the appropriate static routes to Routers 1 and 2 to avoid one-armed routing, and extend *access list 20* so they are not advertised.

For maximum robustness in a highly connected switched network, we can dispense with the local segment routes on the routers with external connectivity. Instead, we use a separate Router 3-like router on each switch. This protects the users on the "end" switches connecting to the external routers from being isolated because the external router on that switch developed a LAN connectivity problem.

CONFIGURATION EXAMPLE: PUTTING IT ALL TOGETHER

The following router configurations from a production network show how all the techniques discussed in this chapter have been applied in the real world. This example also demonstrates how network design can be influenced by history and user requirements.

The site is a critical spoke in the hub-and-spokes configuration shown in Figure 6-12. All the other spokes are single router sites using Frame Relay with ISDN backup. IP, Novell IPX, and IBM SNA communications are supported from the site to the data center at the hub site. IP is routed using EIGRP; IPX is routed using Novell IPXRIP; and IBM SNA is carried over TCP/IP using Data Link Switching (DLSw) on the site routers. The critical communications need driving the network availability requirements is SNA from controllers at the site to a central IBM system in the data center at the hub site. However, we will only look at the IP and IPX parts at this time. The IBM communications are supported by DLSw on the routers; the IBM SNA availability requirement therefore translates to a mandate that TCP/IP connections between routers at the data center and any router at the site that has an active LAN connection never go down. For now, we will focus on meeting this IP connectivity requirement and postpone further discussion of IBM SNA support until Chapter 10.

Other IP and IPX communications requirements were much less severe. The only Novell server accessed is at the data center, and that is required only for electronic mail support and Intel LANdesk for the help desk, neither of which was considered a critical function. Local personal computers were fully configured for stand-alone use of all personal productivity applications (other than e-mail, of course), minimizing the impact of network outages. Similarly, aside from DLSw support of SNA, the only IP usage was network management and limited access to

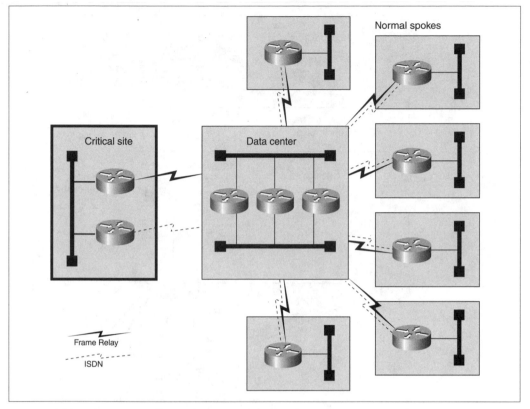

FIGURE 6-12. *Putting it all together—overview*

the site's UNIX server for processing time and attendance records. Since site time clocks did not depend upon the LAN for keeping real-time records, a network outage less than a few hours in duration would be merely an inconvenience rather than a major loss.

At the site, the two routers were about 500 m apart, connected as shown in Figure 6-13. Since they were at opposite ends of a large building, the probability of LAN segmentation was significant, despite the diversity provided by the extra connection via the shipping dock. The routers themselves were Cisco 2524 modular routers that support only a single LAN interface—which in turn supports only a single HSRP address. However, since normally only one of the routers would have a WAN connection to the data center, there was no benefit to defining multiple HSRP addresses for load balancing. Indeed, rather than being an impediment, the single HSRP address served as an effective way to automatically route LAN users to the router with the best external connectivity.

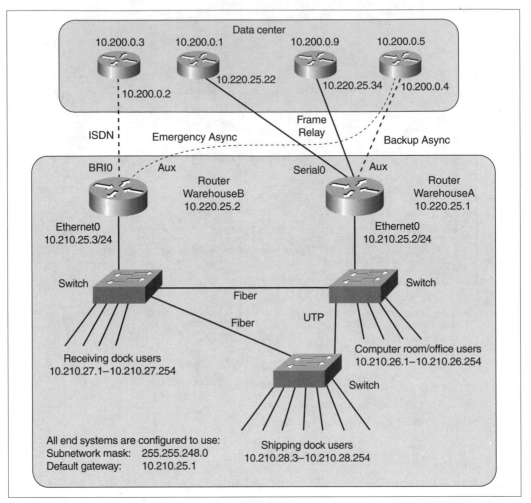

FIGURE 6-13. *Putting it all together—extended site detail*

To minimize communications costs, only one of the two routers had a permanent connection to the data center. Instead, we used multiple levels of dial backup with the primary path a T1 Frame Relay link from Router WarehouseA, with PVCs defined to two independent core routers. The preferred backup path was an ISDN BRI dialed from Router WarehouseB, and analog dial over a POTS line at Router WarehouseA is the final fallback. A second physical Frame Relay link to Router WarehouseB was considered, but the idea was rejected because the cost of providing adequate physical diversity exceeded the losses associated with network failure. In other words, it was cheaper to pay overtime or transport the data entry people to an alternate location than to buy the physical diversity required to reduce the potential for an extended outage.

Due to routing anomalies found during testing, there are also configuration items that may be unique to the specific IOS versions in use. For example, we found an interaction between IOS 11.0(11) running at the data center and IOS 11.2(15) at this site that prevented lost routes from being properly deleted from an adjacent router. The workaround for the problem was to limit EIGRP advertisements on each WAN link to only carry target addresses unique to the link. While this is appropriate for a spoke in a hub-and-spokes topology—where the only impact is the need to define some extra default routes—a different workaround (or better still, elimination of the defect causing the problem) would be required for a general mesh network, in which general routing must be performed at every site.

Note in the configuration of Router WarehouseA in Listing 6-23 that EIGRP is not used to route IPX traffic even though that is a supported feature. This, too, is historical. When the network was originally implemented, EIGRP did not reliably support IPX, and NLSP was yet to be announced. So the network was designed with EIGRP routing of IP and IPXRIP routing of IPX. This did slow down recovery of IPX sessions when network failures occured, since (depending upon the exact mode of failure) it could take several minutes for IPXRIP to identify the failure and switch over to a new route. The client had plans to phase out IPX usage altogether, so this unnecessary delay was not considered a problem. However, if the design were being done today, we would use NLSP or IPX EIGRP for the IPX routing protocol.

```
version 11.0
!
hostname WarehouseA
!
enable secret TopSecret
!
! Data Center router name and password for Async dial backup
username AsyncServer password AsyncSecret
no ip domain-lookup
! Configure IPX routing on this router
ipx routing 0000.0ADC.1901
ipx internal-network ADC1901
chat-script hayes ABORT ERROR ABORT "NO " ABORT BUSY
  ➡ "" "at" "" "at&f" OK "atl1m1&c1&d2&k3S0=2" OK "at dt \T"
  ➡ TIMEOUT 90 CONNECT \c
!
interface Loopback0
  description Address which is always up for management access
  ip address 10.220.25.1 255.255.255.255
!                                                    (continued)
```

```
interface Ethernet0
 description Computer Room end of the Warehouse LAN
 ip address 10.210.25.2 255.255.255.0
 no ip redirects
 ipx network AD21800 encapsulation SAP
 standby 1 priority 110
 standby 1 preempt
 standby 1 authentication OnlyOne
 standby 1 ip 10.210.25.1
!
interface Serial0
 description 2524 Integrated T1 CSU/DSU
 no ip address
 encapsulation frame-relay
!
interface Serial0.22 point-to-point
 description Backup PVC for frame relay (target 10.200.0.22)
 ip address 10.220.25.33 255.255.255.252
 bandwidth 1544
 delay 2500
 ipx delay 7
 ipx network ADC1920
 frame-relay interface-dlci 22
!
interface Serial0.23 point-to-point
 description Primary PVC for frame relay (target 10.200.0.21)
 ip address 10.220.25.21 255.255.255.252
 bandwidth 1544
 delay 2000
 ipx delay 1
 ipx network ADC1914
 frame-relay interface-dlci 23
!
interface Serial1
 description No interface installed in this slot
 no ip address
 shutdown
!
interface BRI0
 description No interface installed in this slot
 no ip address
 shutdown
!
```

(continued)

```
interface Async1
 description Analog backup for the ISDN backup on WarehouseB
 ip unnumbered Loopback0
 encapsulation ppp
 bandwidth 33
 delay 15000
 ipx ipxwan 0 unnumbered WarehouseA
 ipx delay 30
 ipx output-rip-delay 200
 ipx output-sap-delay 200
 ipx sap-interval 5
 async default routing
 async mode interactive
 dialer in-band
 dialer idle-timeout 300
 dialer map ipx 0.0AC8.00CC.0000 name AsyncServer broadcast
   ➥ 12125551111
 dialer map ip 10.200.0.4 name AsyncServer broadcast
   ➥ 12125551111
 dialer hold-queue 10 timeout 60
 dialer-group 1
 ppp authentication chap
!
router eigrp 1
 redistribute static route-map Protect
 network 10.0.0.0
 distribute-list 22 in Async1
 distribute-list 20 in Serial0.22
 distribute-list 21 in Serial0.23
 no auto-summary
!
! Simplify testing when logged in via telnet
ip host TestISDN 10.200.0.2
ip host TestAsync 10.200.0.4
ip classless
! Hierarchy of default routes
! Primary Frame Relay link
ip route 0.0.0.0 0.0.0.0 10.200.0.21 200
! Secondary Frame Relay link
ip route 0.0.0.0 0.0.0.0 10.200.0.22 201
! ISDN link if it is up and running
ip route 0.0.0.0 0.0.0.0 10.200.0.3 205
! Either Async link, but only if up and running
ip route 0.0.0.0 0.0.0.0 10.200.0.5 207
```

(continued)

```
! Force up Async link on this router
ip route 0.0.0.0 0.0.0.0 10.200.0.4 210
!
! Simplify ISDN testing
ip route 10.200.0.2 255.255.255.255 10.210.27.1
ip route 10.200.0.4 255.255.255.255 Async1
! Route to all LAN users, just in case
ip route 10.210.24.0 255.255.248.0 Ethernet0
! Route to protect our local segment
ip route 10.210.26.0 255.255.255.0 Ethernet0
! Routes to other LAN destinations to avoid one-armed
➥ routing
ip route 10.210.27.0 255.255.255.128 Ethernet0
ip route 10.210.27.128 255.255.255.128 Ethernet0
ip route 10.210.28.0 255.255.255.128 Ethernet0
ip route 10.210.28.128 255.255.255.128 Ethernet0
ip route 10.210.29.0 255.255.255.128 Ethernet0
ip route 10.210.29.128 255.255.255.128 Ethernet0
logging 10.201.0.119    ! Log to NOC
logging 10.210.26.30    ! Log to a very local system
!
! Static routes denied redistribution
access-list 10 permit 10.210.27.0 0.0.0.255
access-list 10 permit 10.210.28.0 0.0.3.255
! Static routes redistributed with low metrics
access-list 11 permit 10.210.26.0 0.0.0.255
! Static routes redistributed with high metrics
access-list 12 permit 10.210.24.0 0.0.7.255
!
! Don't let too many routes in
access-list 20 permit 10.200.0.22 ! Secondary target
access-list 20 permit 0.0.0.0
access-list 21 permit 10.200.0.21 ! Primary target
access-list 21 permit 0.0.0.0
access-list 22 permit 10.200.0.5  ! Async target
! Define interesting traffic for DDR
access-list 102 deny   eigrp any any
access-list 102 permit ip any any
access-list 902 deny 1         !RIP
access-list 902 deny 4         !SAP
access-list 902 permit -1      !any
!
```

(continued)

```
! Route map to control redistribution of statics
route-map Protect deny 25
 match ip address 10
!
route-map Protect permit 30
 match ip address 11
 set metric 10000 100 255 1 1500
!
route-map Protect permit 35
 match ip address 12
 set metric 10000 50000 255 1 1500
!
dialer-list 1 protocol ip list 102
dialer-list 1 protocol ipx list 902
!
line con 0
 password aSecret
 login
line aux 0
! Dual roles: dial out for backup and dial in for net
➥ management
 password aSecret
 script dialer hayes
 script reset hayes
 login
 modem InOut
 transport input all
 speed 38400
 flowcontrol hardware
line vty 0 4
 password aSecret
 login
!
end
```

LISTING 6-23.   *Multiple protocol complete configuration, Router WarehouseA*

Also note that the Auxiliary port is used for dual purposes. Not only does it support the second level of dial backup, it also supports dial-in access to allow network management to directly access the router if necessary. In many environments, this could be considered an unacceptable security risk, as it exposes the routers to dial in by crackers as well as by network management personnel. Any outside access to routers must be closely monitored and controlled.

Turning our attention to the configuration of Router WarehouseB in Listing 6-24, we discover that this router actually goes beyond the stated goal of two levels of backup communication to implement a third. Even though there is no modem attached to the Auxiliary port, it is still configured to support both DDR dial out and management dial in. In an emergency, a modem could be dispatched to the site and any functional phone line in the area could be used to restore communications until the data networking lines were repaired. Enabling dial in on the modem line is not a significant security risk here. There is no modem on-line to respond to an unfriendly dial access, except while emergency restoral or access is in active use.

```
version 11.0
!
hostname WarehouseB
!
enable secret TopSecret
!
username ISDNserver password ISDNsecret
username AsyncServer password AsyncSecret
no ip domain-lookup
ipx routing 0000.0ADC.1902
ipx internal-network ADC1902
isdn switch-type basic-ni1
chat-script hayes ABORT ERROR ABORT "NO " ABORT BUSY
  ➦ "" "at" "" "at&f" OK "atl1m1&c1&d2&k3S0=2" OK "at dt \T"
  ➦ TIMEOUT 90 CONNECT \c
!
interface Loopback0
 ip address 10.220.25.2 255.255.255.255
!
interface Ethernet0
 description Receiving Dock end of Warehouse LAN
 ip address 10.210.25.3 255.255.255.0
 no ip redirects
 ipx network AD21800 encapsulation SAP
 standby 1 priority 90
 standby 1 preempt
 standby 1 authentication OnlyOne
 standby 1 ip 10.210.25.1
!
interface BRI0
 description Primary backup for WarehouseA
 ip unnumbered Loopback0
```

(continued)

```
 encapsulation ppp
 bandwidth 56
 delay 5000
 no keepalive
 ipx ipxwan 0 unnumbered WarehouseB
 ipx delay 30
 isdn spid1 20155511110101
 isdn spid2 20155511120101
 dialer idle-timeout 170
 dialer map ipx 0.0AC8.00CB.0000 name ISDNserver speed
 ➥ 56 broadcast 12125551111
 dialer map ip 10.200.0.2 name ISDNserver speed 56 broadcast
 ➥ 12125551111
 dialer hold-queue 10
 dialer-group 1
 ppp authentication chap
!
interface Async1
 description No modem is attached, but be prepared
 ip unnumbered Loopback0
 encapsulation ppp
 bandwidth 33
 delay 15000
 ipx ipxwan 0 unnumbered WarehouseB
 ipx delay 30
 ipx output-rip-delay 200
 ipx output-sap-delay 200
 ipx sap-interval 5
 async default routing
 async mode interactive
 dialer in-band
 dialer idle-timeout 300
 dialer map ipx 0.0AC8.00CC.0000 name AsyncServer broadcast
 ➥ 12125554444
 dialer map ip 10.200.0.4 name AsyncServer broadcast
 ➥ 12125554444
 dialer hold-queue 10 timeout 60
 dialer-group 1
 ppp authentication chap
!
router eigrp 1
 redistribute static route-map Protect
 network 10.0.0.0
```

(continued)

```
 no auto-summary
!
! BGP is only used to force ISDN to dial
router bgp 25
 network 10.220.25.2 mask 255.255.255.255
 timers bgp 10 240
 neighbor 10.201.0.3 remote-as 25
 neighbor 10.201.0.3 update-source Loopback0
!
ip host TestISDN 10.200.0.2
ip host TestAsync 10.200.0.4
ip classless
ip route 0.0.0.0 0.0.0.0 10.200.0.21 200 ! Primary link
ip route 0.0.0.0 0.0.0.0 10.200.0.22 201 ! Secondary link
ip route 0.0.0.0 0.0.0.0 10.200.0.3 204  ! ISDN (if up)
ip route 0.0.0.0 0.0.0.0 10.200.0.5 207  ! Async (if up)
ip route 0.0.0.0 0.0.0.0 10.200.0.2 210  ! Force up ISDN
ip route 10.200.0.2 255.255.255.255 BRI0
ip route 10.201.0.3 255.255.255.255 10.200.0.1
ip route 10.201.0.3 255.255.255.255 10.200.0.2 190
ip route 10.200.0.4 255.255.255.255 Async1
ip route 10.210.24.0 255.255.248.0 Ethernet0
ip route 10.210.27.0 255.255.255.0 Ethernet0
ip route 10.210.26.0 255.255.255.128 Ethernet0
ip route 10.210.26.128 255.255.255.128 Ethernet0
ip route 10.210.28.0 255.255.255.128 Ethernet0
ip route 10.210.28.128 255.255.255.128 Ethernet0
ip route 10.210.29.0 255.255.255.128 Ethernet0
ip route 10.210.29.128 255.255.255.128 Ethernet0
logging 10.201.0.119   ! Log to NOC
logging 10.210.27.30   ! Log to local system
access-list 10 permit 10.210.26.0 0.0.0.255
access-list 10 permit 10.210.28.0 0.0.3.255
access-list 11 permit 10.210.27.0 0.0.0.255
access-list 12 permit 10.210.24.0 0.0.7.255
access-list 102 deny   eigrp any any
access-list 102 permit ip any any
access-list 902 deny 1
access-list 902 deny 4
access-list 902 permit -1
route-map Protect deny 25
 match ip address 10
!
```

(continued)

```
route-map Protect permit 30
 match ip address 11
 set metric 10000 100 255 1 1500
 !
route-map Protect permit 35
 match ip address 12
 set metric 10000 50000 255 1 1500
 !
dialer-list 1 protocol ip list 102
dialer-list 1 protocol ipx list 902
 !
line con 0
 password aSecret
 login
line aux 0
 password secret
 script dialer hayes
 script reset hayes
 login
 modem InOut
 transport input all
 speed 38400
 flowcontrol hardware
line vty 0 4
 password aSecret
 login
 !
end
```

LISTING 6-24. *Multiple protocol complete configuration, Router WarehouseB*

WRAP-UP

Improving the availability of network services at a site requires more than simply installing a second router. We started with an examination of how end systems on the network could best find a functional router when there is more than one to choose from. Although there are many protocols available that can serve better than a static default gateway assignment, the usual choice will be Cisco's Hot Standby Router Protocol (if Cisco routers are being used) or Virtual Router Redundancy Protocol (if other brands of routers are used). Another very popular approach, although it is slow to recover from failures unless tuned, is passive RIP.

We then diverged to look at the impact on dial backup when the dial backup link is on one router and the link being backed up is on another. While *backup interface* can no longer be used, we found that both *dialer watch* and dial-on-demand could easily adapt to the modified environment.

We finished our investigation by looking at the challenge of minimizing the impact of LAN failures that split a single LAN into disconnected segments. This mode of failure should be extremely rare in a well-designed, highly redundant switched LAN. However, when it does occur, the impact on IP and IPX communications is severe. While nothing can be done to help IPX—other than installing two or more independent LANs and multihoming all critical systems—non-standard assignment of IP subnetwork addresses can be combined with overlapping subnetwork masks to greatly reduce the impact on singly connected IP end systems. We showed a configuration in which the only IP communications disrupted would be those between local systems on opposite sides of the break in the LAN.

NOTE

1. While *dialer watch* can also be used with Cisco's IGRP, today we would only design a network based on IGRP for backwards compatibility with an existing IGRP implementation.

Hub-and-Spoke Topology

A very popular topology for many corporate networks is the star topology of Figure 7-1, commonly referred to as a hub-and-spoke network. These networks usually start small, with a handful of remote sites requiring access to headquarters resources, and then grow with the organization until there may be hundreds of spokes all linked to a common core. Frequently these networks start out as branch office users dialing into the headquarters systems, and evolve into Frame Relay or leased-line networks as a way to reduce long distance costs and improve performance.

Since the driving application is access to services provided by the headquarters, the design emphasis is on providing each location a solid connection to headquarters. Typically each branch will have a primary connection to one or two routers at headquarters and perhaps dial backup to yet another router at headquarters in case the primary link goes down. The only way one branch can communicate with another branch is to send data into the headquarters hub site to be routed back out to the correct branch.

Depending upon the needs of the organization, the hub-and-spoke with a single core will typically grow into either a hierarchical tree or a network of hubs, each with attached spokes. The hierarchical tree pattern in Figure 7-2 is the classical IBM SNA terminal network, which is easily optimized to minimize communications costs. The small circles could be branch offices or they could be regional offices. All communications are to and from systems at the headquarters hub; there is no significant traffic from one branch to another, and there is one path only between any two locations. Because of its singly connected nature and the impact of intermediate node failures in which a single failure can disconnect all branches connecting through an intermediate node, the hierarchical tree topology is not a good topology for high availability networking. If it is used, a frequent workaround for the sensitivity to node outages is to provide dial backup around the intermediate nodes. That way,

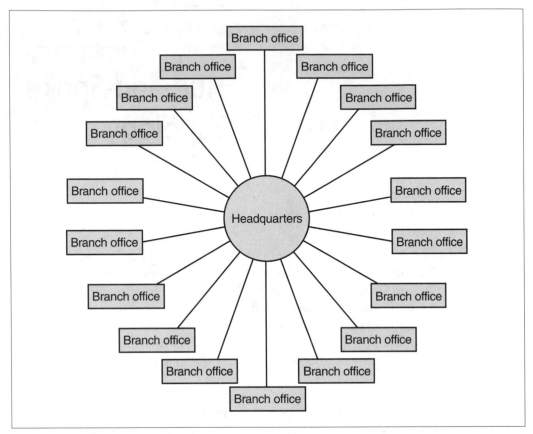

FIGURE 7-1. *Basic hub-and-spoke topology*

if a node fails, the branch offices that are cut off dial around the failed node directly into the headquarters hub.

The other popular growth pattern is the extended hub-and-spoke in Figure 7-3, where the hub expands to consist of multiple hub sites that are well connected. Spokes then attach to the nearest hub to minimize communications costs. The two topologies can also be combined, giving us an extended hub and then using hierarchical trees to consolidate the communications from multiple branch offices.

Because the primary reason for the popularity of hub-and-spoke architectures is the cost savings possible, in this chapter we will look at ways we can improve the connectivity and fault tolerance of a hub-and-spoke network with minimal impact on the implementation cost. We will start by looking at routing protocols for hubs with many spokes. The hub-and-spoke topology both stresses and simplifies the job of the

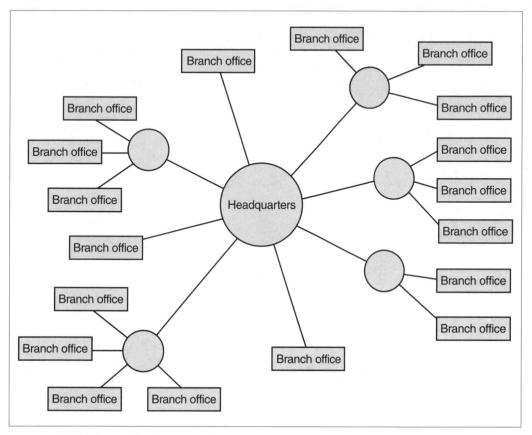

FIGURE 7-2. *Hierarchical tree topology*

routing protocol, and we can take advantage of the topology to dramatically reduce the routing overhead without affecting the network's ability to provide services despite failures.

We will then look at dial backup with multiple dial-access servers. We modify dial-on-demand routing for backing up our primary links so that all hub routers appear identical down to their IP address. That way, any spoke can dial into any available hub router without concern for which one answers. We finish this chapter by looking at the challenge of our network growing to the point where we physically are using more than one hub location. We show how we can adapt the spokes to continue functioning even when the overriding assumption that the hub is the one place to go for service is no longer true. In other words, we look at how to survive an event in which our one logical hub becomes two disconnected hubs.

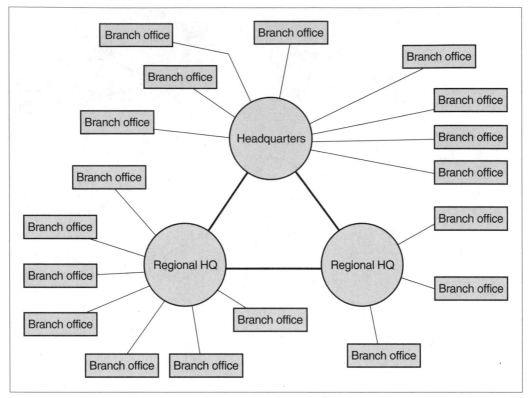

FIGURE 7-3. *Multiple hubs, multiply connected*

ROUTING PROTOCOLS FOR HUBS WITH MANY SPOKES

The popularity of the hub-and-spoke architecture resides in the ability to keep the complexity and cost of network support at each spoke location at a minimum. From the viewpoint of each spoke, no dynamic routing protocol is needed because the only route to anywhere is to send any packets that are not to local destinations to the hub. All complexity is contained in the hub, which, for reliability, is usually a cluster of routers (for a single headquarters data center) or a tightly knit backbone of critical sites (once the vulnerability of relying on a single location for business continuity is recognized).

This translates into significantly lower WAN costs because the vast majority of spokes can be adequately serviced by routers with just enough horsepower to fill the pipe to the hub site. Since a large organization could easily have thousands of spokes, the ability to use a low-end router such as a 2600, or even a 1600 or 1700, rather than a 3600 or 4700 can add up to substantial savings, even if high-end routers must be installed at the hub sites to handle all the spokes that are attached. There is no need to run a sophisticated routing protocol at each spoke because even though there may be thousands of networks in the organization to keep track of, each individual spoke only needs to keep track of which networks are local and what paths are available to the hub site connectivity services.

ROUTING REQUIREMENTS FOR HUB ROUTERS VERSUS SPOKE ROUTERS

At each spoke, we only need enough of a routing protocol to determine the best available path to the hub. Many hub-and-spoke networks are configured using static routes at each spoke and no dynamic routing protocol whatsoever. However, this is not adequate for high availability networking, as it is possible for the link to fail between spoke and hub in such a way that the physical link remains up (so that the static route using that link continues to be active) even though the link is incapable of carrying traffic. This is particularly true of Frame Relay, cell relay, and other network services that define a DTE/DCE interface between the router and the local switch that can be up even though the end-to-end network service is not functional. This is the same failure mode that forced us to abandon *backup interface* as a dial-backup solution and use either dial-on-demand or *dialer watch*.

What does work well for spokes is a simple routing protocol that can detect whether a link is functional. Overhead can be minimized by limiting the routing advertisements from the hub router to one or two target addresses while the spoke informs the hub of all subnetworks serviced by that spoke. Since the number of subnetworks advertised by a spoke is typically very limited, the routing overhead in either direction tends to be minimal even if a chatty routing protocol such as RIPv2 is used.

The key to performance for the spoke is not the quality of the routing protocol, as the routing decisions are trivial and the choices are few. Rather, it is the speed with which the routing protocol can detect that the link being used is no longer functional and then remove the link from the routing tables. Depending on the bandwidth available and the downtime permitted, we will normally use either EIGRP or RIPv2 between the hub-and-spoke. EIGRP has the advantage of simpler configuration in an all-Cisco environment, and RIPv2 allows support of routers from any vendor using an open standard. RIPv1 or IGRP are normally unsuitable because they will not scale up to handle very large networks due to their lack of variable length subnetwork masking (VLSM) support. OSPF or Integrated IS-IS are normally unsuitable because of the difficulty of supporting the huge numbers of peers on each hub router that occur in a hub-and-spoke topology.

The hub routers are where the routing gets complex in a hub-and-spoke topology. Between hub routers we need a routing protocol capable of handling multiple parallel paths to thousands of destinations quickly, efficiently, and robustly—limiting our choice of protocols to either EIGRP, OSPF, or Integrated IS-IS. The bottom line is that in a hub-and-spoke topology, we usually end up with either EIGRP everywhere in a Cisco-only network or with an OSPF core redistributing routes learned from the spokes through RIPv2.

Much more variation is seen in the choice of media providing the connectivity between the hub and the spokes. From the viewpoint of the routing protocols, the specific media chosen is immaterial. However, from the viewpoint of availability, the choice can be critical. The key, as always, is to maximize the physical diversity and minimize the common points of failure. For low-bandwidth applications, 56-Kbps Frame Relay might be used with ISDN backup. For higher data rates, T1 or DSL backed up by cable modems might be more appropriate. Relying on dial-on-demand for all connectivity is rarely acceptable because of its inability to detect link failure until after the link is needed for production traffic.

In addition to variations in the choice of media, we also see much variation in the endpoints for each primary and alternate route from spoke to hub. While the primary route is normally selected for optimal support of every day traffic, the alternate routes are usually chosen based on providing routing diversity and minimizing cost. For example, if ISDN backup is used, the call may be placed to another local spoke location to avoid long distance charges, or a cluster of local spokes may be connected through DSL to allow access to each others' T1 lines as required.

In the first two configuration examples that follow in the next section, we implement the same physical network differing only in the choice of routing protocols. In the first example, we use Frame Relay to one hub router with ISDN backup to a second hub router. In the second example, we implement the exact same structure providing the same link recovery performance using open protocols rather than EIGRP. In the third configuration example, we will add a second router at the spoke, supporting a second permanent link.

CONFIGURATION EXAMPLE: EIGRP EVERYWHERE

We will first look at a classic hub-and-spoke network. In this network, each spoke has a single router with a single 56-Kbps Frame Relay connection to a hub router. The Frame Relay link is backed up by a dial-on-demand ISDN link to a second hub router. Dual LANs are used to provide redundant communications between the hub routers. Figure 7-4 details the connectivity and configuration of the hub and one spoke.

As is essential in any hub-and-spoke network, we have an implicit IP addressing plan used to assign subnetworks from the 10.0.0.0 private address space. The hub takes all its addresses from the 10.0.0.0/16 subnetwork while each spoke takes all of its addresses from the subnetwork 10.XX.0.0/16, where XX is the number of the spoke. Based on this scheme, we are looking at spoke 101 and we can support at most 255 spokes before we need to revise the addressing plan. While this numbering plan makes life simple and easy while the network is small by providing an obvious

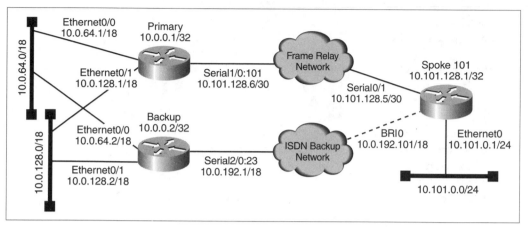

FIGURE 7-4. *Frame Relay spoke with ISDN backup*

mapping between IP address and location, it does not scale well when we need to expand to thousands of spokes and hierarchical addressing to support OSPF areas.

Many of the features of this network might seem to be arbitrary. For example, we treat each Frame Relay PVC as an independent point-to-point link on its own /30 network, while we treat the ISDN backup network as a single large subnetwork. Numbered point-to-point links are used to simplify monitoring of link status by typical SNMP network management systems. So let's start with the configuration for the router Spoke 101 in Listing 7-1.

The spoke configuration is simple dial-on-demand backup with no bells or whistles. Not obvious is the assumption in the spoke's configuration that the hub will

```
version 11.0
!
hostname Spoke101
!
username HubBackup password secret101
ip host TestISDN 10.0.192.1
isdn switch-type basic-ni1
!
interface Loopback0
 description Always Up IP Address for Spoke 101
 ip address 10.101.128.1 255.255.255.255
!
```

(*continued*)

```
interface Ethernet0
 ip address 10.101.0.1 255.255.255.0
!
interface Serial0
 no ip address
 encapsulation frame-relay
!
interface Serial0.1 point-to-point
 ip address 10.101.128.5 255.255.255.252
 bandwidth 56
 delay 2000
 frame-relay interface-dlci 17 broadcast
!
interface BRI0
 ip address 10.0.192.101 255.255.192.0
 encapsulation ppp
 bandwidth 56
 delay 5000
 no keepalive
 isdn spid1 20155501010000
 isdn spid2 20155512130000
 dialer idle-timeout 170
 dialer map ip 10.0.192.1 name HubBackup broadcast
   ➥ 12125551234
 dialer hold-queue 10
 dialer-group 1
 ppp authentication chap
!
router eigrp 1
 network 10.0.0.0
 no auto-summary
!
ip classless
ip route 0.0.0.0 0.0.0.0 10.0.0.1 200 ! Use frame if up
ip route 0.0.0.0 0.0.0.0 10.0.192.1 210 ! Otherwise, use ISDN
ip route 10.0.192.1 255.255.255.255 BRI0
access-list 102 deny   eigrp any any
access-list 102 permit ip any any
!
dialer-list 1 protocol ip list 102
!
end
```

LISTING 7-1. *Simple single router spoke using EIGRP Everywhere*

carefully filter all routing advertisements so that the spoke is shielded from any need to keep track of all the other subnetworks that are on the network. The assumption is that all packets to destinations other than those local to the spoke are routed by the appropriate default route. The hub routers must further filter their advertisements to ensure that only the target address appropriate for the link that is up can get through to the spoke. In this case, only the address 10.0.0.1 and the default route, if known, are advertised over the Frame Relay link, while no addresses are advertised over the ISDN link. Even though no addresses are advertised over the ISDN link to the spoke, EIGRP is still run over the ISDN link so that the hub can learn what subnetworks at the spoke can be reached through the ISDN link.

Turning our attention to the configuration of the primary hub router in Listing 7-2, we can see how the hub protects the individual spokes from the true complexity of the network. Keep in mind that we are not concerning ourselves here with standard hub configuration items on the LAN side, such as HSRP or routing to dual homed hosts, so we can concentrate on the requirements unique to a hub-and-spoke topology.

Our first challenge is the mismatch in data rates between the spoke end of the Frame Relay connection where the data rate and the Committed Information Rate (CIR) are both 56 Kbps, and the data rate at the hub end of the Frame Relay PVC is T1, even though the CIR remains 56 Kbps. To prevent the lost packets that could occur if the hub actually started to send data to a spoke at the full 1.544 Mbps data rate, we run at least IOS 11.2 at the hub site in order to use traffic shaping. The statement *frame-relay traffic-shaping* under *interface Serial1/0* enables traffic rate shaping on all channels of the Frame Relay interface and the statement *frame-relay class Spokes* sets the Frame Relay configuration default for all PVCs and SVCs to that specified by the *map-class frame-relay Spoke* section.

Since the CIR and the peak data rate at the spoke end are the same, we configure the *frame-relay class Spoke* traffic shaping to an average data rate of 56,000 bps and the peak data rate to the same. If the CIR is less than the data rate of the spoke end,

```
version 11.2
!
hostname HubPrimary
!
interface Loopback0
  description Target address for Frame Relay users
  ip address 10.0.0.1 255.255.255.255
!
interface Ethernet0/0
  description Primary data center LAN
  ip address 10.0.64.1 255.255.192.0
```

(continued)

```
!
interface Ethernet0/1
 description Secondary (backup) data center LAN
 ip address 10.0.128.1 255.255.192.0
!
interface Serial1/0
 no ip address
 encapsulation frame-relay
 frame-relay traffic-shaping
 frame-relay class Spokes
 frame-relay lmi-type ansi
!
interface Serial1/0.101 point-to-point
 description PVC to Spoke 101
 ip address 10.101.128.6 255.255.255.252
 bandwidth 56
 delay 2000
 frame-relay interface-dlci 101
!
! . . . Other Frame Relay subinterfaces go here
!
router eigrp 1
 network 10.0.0.0
 distribute-list 12 out Ethernet0/0
 distribute-list 12 out Ethernet0/1
 distribute-list 10 out Serial1/0.101
 distribute-list 10 out Serial1/0.102
 distribute-list 10 out Serial1/0.103
! . . . Filters for other Frame Relay subinterfaces go here
 no auto-summary
!
ip classless
!
map-class frame-relay Spokes
 frame-relay traffic-rate 56000 56000
access-list 10 permit 10.0.0.1
access-list 10 permit 0.0.0.0
access-list 10 deny   any
access-list 12 deny   10.0.0.1
access-list 12 permit any
!
end
```

LISTING 7-2. *Primary hub router using EIGRP Everywhere*

we would need to adjust the traffic shaping parameters to match the actual CIR, Committed Burst Size (Bc), and Excess Burst Size (Be) parameters of the virtual circuit.

Assuming the T1 Frame Relay links at the hub are oversubscribed, which is the normal case in a hub-and-spoke topology, this traffic shaping only prevents unnecessary packet loss in the traffic flow from hub to spoke. Should all the spokes start transmitting at their maximum data rate, there could be more data arriving at the hub than can fit through the T1 link at the hub end. This problem is much less common than the need to traffic shape the data going out the T1 and much more painful to cure. The choice is either to cut back on the number of spokes per hub interface or to play games with the CIR and traffic shaping from spoke to hub.

The first choice, reducing the number of spokes per hub interface so that the hub site links into the Frame Relay network are not oversubscribed, can significantly increase the cost to provision all spokes. However, it is the only choice that eliminates the risk of packet discards under worst case loading with no impact on performance.

The second choice, dynamically reducing the CIR in response to congestion notification generated by the Frame Relay network, requires us to also install traffic shaping at each spoke location. The risk with this approach is our dependence on responding to congestion before the Frame Relay service starts discarding frames. A variation on this approach is to misconfigure each spoke router's traffic-shaping with a lower than actual CIR and a higher peak data rate. Depending on the application mix we may be able to use priority queuing to minimize the impact of the reduced bandwidth on important traffic, or it may be appropriate to configure a second PVC to each spoke with a very low or zero CIR for the lower priority bulk traffic and use policy routing to segregate the data streams.

The other key to success in the hub-and-spoke topology is the filtering of routing updates out the Ethernet and Frame Relay interfaces. There are two filters required. The first filter is applied to all LAN interfaces and prevents other hub routers (and the dial backup router in particular) from learning of the Frame Relay target address 10.0.0.1. The second filter is then applied on all routing advertisements going out to the spokes and permits each spoke to learn only of the 10.0.0.1 preferred target address and the default route. Advertising the default route is optional; doing so speeds up the return of traffic flow to the primary link if the interface does not change state. Either way, we shield the spokes from all other details of how the organization is tied together and what subnetworks are up and which are not. This way, the routing burden on each spoke is independent of the number of spokes. Although not an issue in small networks, forgetting the routing filter for a spoke in a large hub-and-spoke network can overload the spoke so badly that the router crashes. Although not shown in Listing 7-1, we often include a redundant route filter at the spoke end, just in case.

Filtering the routing advertisements to the spokes is the key to the efficiency of the hub-and-spoke topology. Since the only route available from the spoke to any destination not local to the spoke is through the hub, there is no need for the spoke to be aware of how the hub connects to other destinations. In order to benefit from this routing simplification, however, there must be no way for the spoke to be exposed to the complexity handled by the hub no matter what link is used to reach the hub. Therefore, we see in Listing 7-3 an equivalent set of filters in the configuration for the dial-backup target router.

```
version 11.0
!
hostname HubBackup
!
username Spoke101 password secret101
username Spoke102 password secret102
username Spoke103 password secret103
username Spoke104 password secret104
! . . . Logins for other spokes which could call in
!
isdn switch-type primary-dms100
!
controller T1 2/0
 framing esf
 linecode b8zs
 pri-group timeslots 1-24
!
interface Ethernet0/0
 description Primary data center LAN
 ip address 10.0.64.2 255.255.192.0
!
interface Ethernet0/1
 description Secondary (backup) data center LAN
 ip address 10.0.128.2 255.255.192.0
!
!
interface Serial2/0:23
 description Dial backup call-in support
 ip address 10.0.192.2 255.255.192.0
 bandwidth 56
 delay 5000
 ip tcp header-compression passive
 encapsulation ppp
 no keepalive
 isdn caller 2015550101
```
(continued)

```
  isdn caller 2015550102
  isdn caller 2015550103
 ! . . . Other numbers from which calls will be accepted go here
  dialer idle-timeout 300
  dialer map ip 10.0.192.101 name Spoke101 broadcast
  dialer map ip 10.0.192.102 name Spoke102 broadcast
  dialer map ip 10.0.192.103 name Spoke103 broadcast
  dialer map ip 10.0.192.104 name Spoke104 broadcast
 ! . . . Dialer maps for other spokes which could call in
  dialer-group 1
  ppp authentication chap
 !
 router eigrp 1
  network 10.0.0.0
  distribute-list 11 out Serial2/0:23
  no auto-summary
 !
 ip classless
 access-list 11 permit 10.0.192.0 0.0.63.255
 access-list 11 deny    any
 access-list 102 deny    eigrp any any
 access-list 102 permit ip any any
 !
 dialer-list 1 protocol ip list 102
 !
 end
```

LISTING 7-3. *Backup hub router using EIGRP Everywhere*

Other than the routing advertisement filter on the ISDN interface (*distribute-list 11 out Serial2/0:23*), this is a standard configuration for a dial-backup target router. Here we have enhanced security by using the *isdn caller* command to only accept incoming calls from specific phone numbers. If you are using this extra level of security, take care to ensure that all locations that might place a call are configured to deliver calling number identification. Depending on the ISDN service provider and their BRI line configuration, it might also be necessary to include ISDN caller lines for all local directory numbers assigned to each BRI.

Similarly, although the subnetwork mask used for our ISDN IP addressing scheme can theoretically permit over 16,000 spokes, we will run out of configuration memory for all local user definitions, dialer maps, and calling number filters long before we hit that limit. At some point, we need to change our configuration to use external servers for handling caller authentication and authorization. Cisco supports both their own Terminal Access Controller Access Control System (TACACS) and the open standard Remote Authentication Dial-In User Services (RADIUS, RFC 2865). If we want to continue to use calling number identification for additional security, our only option will be RADIUS.

Those who do not wish to depend upon external authentication servers need not despair. Later in this chapter, we will show how we can use dialer profiles and virtual templates to eliminate the need for a dialer map for each spoke, and once we eliminate the dialer maps, we no longer need to define a unique login for each spoke either. That way, our scaling is only limited by the need to configure each calling number acceptable on each interface. This is 23 bytes of configuration memory per spoke per interface in North America, where phone numbers are 10 digits long, and should we decide to forego the extra security provided by caller ID, there is no configuration limit.

CONFIGURATION EXAMPLE: OSPF HUB WITH RIPv2 SPOKES

Should we choose to stay with open standards for routing rather than EIGRP, the configuration gets a bit more complex. The challenge is that the processor load imposed by the OSPF protocol increases greatly as the number of neighbors goes up, so configuration guidelines for even a high-end 7500-series router limits the number of OSPF neighbors to under 100 per router. This is clearly not an acceptable limit for a cost effective hub in a large hub-and-spoke configuration, so we need to use a less CPU-intensive routing protocol to handle all the spokes.[1]

At the same time, we want OSPF to handle the potentially severe routing requirements inside the hub complex. The answer is to run two routing protocols, one inside the hub complex (optimized for the sophisticated routing required there), and a different routing protocol between the hub and each spoke (chosen to minimize the processor load). This is not as bad a compromise at it appears because in a hub-and-spoke network, the only place where significant routing decisions are required is within the hub complex, and all that is required between the hub and any particular spoke is an ability for the hub to learn what addresses are serviced by that spoke and for the spoke to determine if any particular link to the hub site is up.

We run OSPF on all hub site routers but only over the links between the hub site routers. We then run RIPv2 between the hub routers and the spokes with advertisement filters to block all route advertisements from the hub except the hub target address. Note that in the same way as we did with EIGRP, we ensure the spoke routers have a default route through floating static routes pointing to the target addresses for the various available routes rather than depending on advertising the default route directly. This not only simplifies configuration of backup routes but also avoids problems ensuring the hub routers have a default route to advertise. We can also take advantage of the small number of routes that must be advertised to increase the frequency of RIP broadcasts over the hub to spoke links to improve responsiveness to link failures that are not detected immediately because they do not cause the link to fail. This leads us to the configurations in Listings 7-4, 7-5, and 7-6.

These example configurations implement the same, identical network that we used for the EIGRP example in Figure 7-4. The only difference is that rather than routing with the Cisco proprietary EIGRP protocol, we use the open routing protocols OSPF and RIPv2. While the complexity is higher (because of the use of two protocols and the redistribution of routes from RIPv2 into OSPF), the resulting performance is normally indistinguishable.

The spoke configuration in Listing 7-4 is almost identical to the EIGRP Everywhere spoke already discussed in Listing 7-1. Only four lines must change

```
version 11.2
!
hostname Spoke101
!
username HubBackup password secret
ip host TestISDN 10.0.192.1
isdn switch-type basic-ni1
!
interface Loopback0
 description Always Up IP Address for Spoke 101
 ip address 10.101.128.1 255.255.255.255
!
interface Ethernet0
 ip address 10.101.0.1 255.255.255.0
!
interface Serial0
 no ip address
 encapsulation frame-relay
!
interface Serial0.1 point-to-point
 ip address 10.101.128.5 255.255.255.252
 bandwidth 56
 delay 2000
 frame-relay interface-dlci 17 broadcast
!
interface BRI0
 ip address 10.0.192.101 255.255.192.0
 encapsulation ppp
 bandwidth 56
 delay 5000
```

(continued)

```
  no keepalive
  isdn spid1 20155501010000
  isdn spid2 20155512340000
  dialer idle-timeout 170
  dialer map ip 10.0.192.1 name HubBackup broadcast 12125551234
  dialer hold-queue 10
  dialer-group 1
  ppp authentication chap
!
router rip
  version 2
  timers basic 5 15 15 30
  network 10.0.0.0
  no auto-summary
!
ip classless
ip route 0.0.0.0 0.0.0.0 10.0.0.1 200 ! Use frame if up
ip route 0.0.0.0 0.0.0.0 10.0.192.1 210 ! Otherwise use ISDN
ip route 10.0.192.1 255.255.255.255 BRI0
access-list 102 deny   udp any any eq rip
access-list 102 permit ip any any
!
dialer-list 1 protocol ip list 102
!
end
```

LISTING 7-4. *Simple single router spoke using RIPv2 and OSPF*

to run RIPv2 as the routing protocol rather than EIGRP. Obviously, the line *router eigrp 1* changes to *router rip*. We then need to add the line *version 2* under *router rip* to specify RIP version 2 rather than RIP version 1. The other line added under *router rip, timers basic 5 15 15 30* changes the interval between advertisements from the default 30 seconds down to 5 seconds and reduces the invalid, hold down, and flush time-outs to 15, 15, and 30 seconds from the defaults of 3, 3, and 4 minutes, respectively. That way, worst case delay before a backup call is placed is reduced from 4 minutes to 1.5 minutes (30 seconds for RIP to detect the failure and one minute for the per minute update of floating static rates).

The only other change is in the definition of interesting traffic for the dialer in access list 102. Instead of ignoring EIGRP, we now must ignore RIP broadcasts so the dial-backup link is not dialed except when needed.

The changes to the hub site routers, starting with the primary hub router in Listing 7-5, are much more extensive. We now are running two routing protocols,

```
version 11.2
!
hostname HubPrimary
!
interface Loopback0
 description Network Management & OSPF Identification
 ip address 10.0.0.201 255.255.255.255
!
interface Loopback1
 description Target address for Frame Relay users
 ip address 10.0.0.1 255.255.255.255
!
interface Ethernet0/0
 description Primary data center LAN
 ip address 10.0.64.1 255.255.192.0
!
interface Ethernet0/1
 description Secondary (backup) data center LAN
 ip address 10.0.128.1 255.255.192.0
!
interface Serial1/0
 no ip address
 encapsulation frame-relay
 frame-relay traffic-shaping
 frame-relay class Spokes
 frame-relay lmi-type ansi
!
interface Serial1/0.101 point-to-point
 description Spoke 101
 ip address 10.101.128.6 255.255.255.252
 frame-relay interface-dlci 101
!
! . . . Other Frame Relay subinterfaces go here
!
router ospf 1
 redistribute rip metric 2000 subnets
 passive-interface Serial1/0.101
 passive-interface Serial1/0.102
 passive-interface Serial1/0.103
! . . . Hushing of other spoke subinterfaces go here
network 10.0.0.0 0.255.255.255 area 1
!
```

(continued)

```
router rip
 version 2
 timers basic 5 15 15 30
 passive-interface Ethernet0/0
 passive-interface Ethernet0/1
 network 10.0.0.0
 distribute-list 10 out Serial1/0.101
 distribute-list 10 out Serial1/0.102
 distribute-list 10 out Serial1/0.103
 ! ...Filters for other spoke subinterfaces go here
 no auto-summary
 !
 ip classless
 !
 map-class frame-relay Spokes
  frame-relay traffic-rate 56000 56000
 access-list 10 permit 10.0.0.1
 access-list 10 permit 0.0.0.0
 access-list 10 deny    any
 !
 end
```

LISTING 7-5. *Primary hub router using OSPF and RIPv2*

and we must ensure that each interface only transmits updates for the routing protocol active across each link. In addition, because OSPF will use the loopback port with the highest IP address as the source address for its link state advertisements, we must define a loopback interface with an address unique to this router. Since there is no facility for forcing OSPF to use a particular loopback address, we must ensure that any address range used for target addresses that will be filtered from advertisements is lower than any address range used for management addresses on the same router. In this example, we dedicate the address range 10.0.0.0 through 10.0.0.127 for targets, and then use the range 10.0.0.128 through 10.0.63.255 for router unique identifiers.

We then define every Frame Relay subinterface leading to a spoke as a *passive-interface,* to suppress the sending of OSPF hellos or link-state advertisements out to spokes that are not listening for them. Similarly, we prevent the transmission of RIP updates on the hub-to-hub interfaces by declaring them to be passive interfaces in the *router rip* section. Note that whether an interface should be declared passive for RIP or for OSPF is a function of what is at the other end of the link, regardless of the type of interface involved. For example, a Frame Relay subinterface providing connectivity to another hub system must have OSPF as active and RIP as passive.

One simplification introduced by the change in routing protocols is that we no longer need to filter the target address on the primary hub router to prevent it from being advertised by the dial backup hub router. Since no hub routers are redistributing OSPF routes into the RIP routes sent to the spokes, we can dispense with controls on the OSPF routes being propagated throughout the hub network.

The configuration changes required on the backup hub router providing dial backup services in Listing 7-6 are equivalent to those made to the primary hub router.

```
version 11.2
!
hostname HubBackup
!
username Spoke101 password secret101
username Spoke102 password secret102
username Spoke103 password secret103
username Spoke104 password secret104
! . . . Definition of other spokes which could call in
!
isdn switch-type primary-dms100
!
controller T1 2/0
 framing esf
 linecode b8zs
 pri-group timeslots 1-24
!
interface Loopback0
 description Network Management & OSPF Identification
 ip address 10.0.0.202 255.255.255.255
!
interface Ethernet0/0
 description Primary data center LAN
 ip address 10.0.64.2 255.255.192.0
!
interface Ethernet0/1
 description Secondary (backup) data center LAN
 ip address 10.0.128.2 255.255.192.0
!
!
interface Serial2/0:23
 ip address 10.0.192.1 255.255.192.0
 ip tcp header-compression passive
 encapsulation ppp
```

(continued)

```
 no keepalive
 isdn caller 2015550101
 isdn caller 2015550102
 isdn caller 2015550103
! . . . Other numbers from which calls will be accepted go here
dialer idle-timeout 300
 dialer map ip 10.192.0.101 name Spoke101 broadcast
 dialer map ip 10.192.0.102 name Spoke102 broadcast
 dialer map ip 10.192.0.103 name Spoke103 broadcast
 dialer map ip 10.192.0.104 name Spoke104 broadcast
! . . . Dialer maps for other spokes which could call in
 dialer-group 1
 ppp authentication chap
!
router ospf 1
 passive-interface Serial2/0:23
 redistribute rip metric 3000 subnets
 network 10.0.0.0 0.255.255.255 area 1
!
router rip
 version 2
 timers basic 5 15 15 30
 passive-interface Ethernet0/0
 passive-interface Ethernet0/1
 network 10.0.0.0
 distribute-list 11 out Serial2/0:23
 no auto-summary
!
ip classless
access-list 11 permit 10.0.192.0 0.0.63.255
access-list 11 deny    any
access-list 102 deny   udp any any eq rip
access-list 102 permit ip any any
!
dialer-list 1 protocol ip list 102
!
end
```

LISTING 7-6. *Backup hub router using OSPF and RIPv2*

The primary drawback of using OSPF and RIP rather than EIGRP is the higher sensitivity to IOS bugs and configuration errors. In particular, earlier releases of Cisco IOS had problems handling external routes in OSPF (which is how the routes redistributed from RIP are distributed in OSPF), which can lead to routes that were down not being properly removed from all routers. This in turn can lead to routing loops and black holes, exactly the sort of problem we sought to avoid by choosing OSPF in the first place. However, today this is less of an issue because we must use at least IOS 11.2 for RIPv2 support anyway.

CONFIGURATION EXAMPLE: DUAL CONNECTIONS TO EVERY SPOKE

While not as common, the simplifying assumptions we made for a hub-and-spoke topology apply equally well when the spokes are multiply connected to the hub. Indeed, even though standard RIP can detect only a single route to any particular destination, we can use our spoke technique of routing through a hierarchy of static routes to target addresses to provide load sharing of redundant full-time links. All we need to do is use a different target address (and an associated floating static route) on each available link from the spoke to the hub.

When planning a hub-and-spoke with dual permanent connections, we must be careful to maximize our link diversity. If the second connection is simply another PVC defined on a single Frame Relay access line, almost any failure that brings down the first PVC also takes down the second. In the high availability spoke in Figure 7-5, we use two routers at the spoke connecting through independent links to two different hub routers. Note that we also use two different Frame Relay networks to improve diversity in the WAN without resorting to dial backup.

For now we will ignore how the hub routers are connected and the details of connectivity between diverse hub sites and concentrate on configuring the connectivity between the two routers at the one spoke site and the two hub routers connecting them with core services and other spokes.

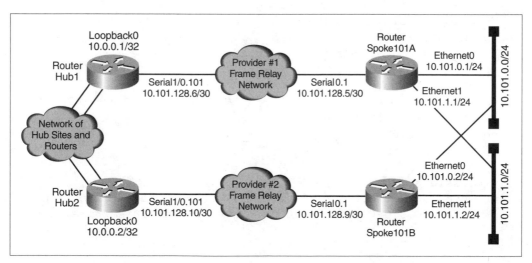

FIGURE 7-5. *Spoke with dual links and routers*

Listings 7-7 and 7-8 show how simple the configuration of each spoke router can be. The majority of the complexity is in the HSRP configuration of the two LANs at the spoke site. Although purely arbitrary, the router Spoke 101A is the preferred HSRP router for LAN 10.101.0.0/24, while the router Spoke 101B is the preferred

```
version 11.2
!
hostname Spoke101A
!
interface Ethernet0/0
 ip address 10.101.0.1 255.255.255.0
 standby priority 110
 standby preempt
 standby ip 10.101.0.254
 standby track Serial0.1 30
!
interface Ethernet0/1
 ip address 10.101.1.1 255.255.255.0
 standby priority 90
 standby preempt
 standby ip 10.101.1.254
 standby track Serial0.1 30
!
interface Serial0
 no ip address
 encapsulation frame-relay
!
interface Serial0.1 point-to-point
 description Link to router Hub1
 ip address 10.101.128.5 255.255.255.252
 frame-relay interface-dlci 17 broadcast
!
router rip
 version 2
 timers basic 5 15 15 30
 network 10.0.0.0
 no auto-summary
!
ip classless
ip route 0.0.0.0 0.0.0.0 10.0.0.1 200 ! Use direct frame if up
ip route 0.0.0.0 0.0.0.0 10.0.0.2 210 ! Spoke101B's frame link
!
end
```

LISTING 7-7.   *Dual router spoke using RIPv2 and OSPF router Spoke 101A*

HSRP router for LAN 10.1.1.0/24. Both are configured so that if their link to a hub router goes down, the router with the remaining link preempts to become the active HSRP router on both LANs, minimizing the need to send traffic bound for the core back across the local LAN to get to the spoke router that still has a working link to the hub site.

If the load balancing implemented using this split of default gateway assignments between the two LANs is not sufficient, as could occur if we only had a single LAN at the spoke, we could remove the weights on the floating static routes so that both are always active whenever their respective target is available. However, we must be very careful when we do this to ensure that routing will be stable under all conditions. For example, if we simply eliminated the distance metrics on the static routes on both Spoke 101A and Spoke 101B, we would introduce random routing loops.

This can be seen by tracing a packet from a user on LAN 10.1.0.0 to a system at the hub site. The user sends the packet to the default gateway of 10.1.0.254, which, with both links up, is determined by HSRP to be router Spoke 101A. Router Spoke 101A sees the two equally distant routes to 0.0.0.0 (since all activated static routes have identical metrics), and depending on the last routing decision, either sends the packet across the Frame Relay link to router Hub 1 or across the LAN to router Spoke 101B, because that is the route learned from RIP to get to 10.0.0.2. When the packet arrives at router Spoke 101B, the same situation exists and there is a 50-50 chance that router Spoke 101B will choose the path through router Spoke 101A to 10.0.0.1 to deliver the packet. Assuming per-destination load balancing is in effect, any packets that router Spoke 101B sends back to Spoke 101A would get sent right back in a classic routing loop.

One way to achieve load balancing is to leave the hierarchy of static routes in effect at router Spoke 101B and adjust the HSRP weights so that router Spoke 101A is the active gateway for both LANs. That way, all users will send to router Spoke 101A, which in turn will deliver half the packets through its direct connection and the other half through router Spoke 101B, which will deliver all packets it receives through its direct connection. Under these conditions, the routers would load balance between the two available routes. The disadvantage, of course, of doing load balancing this way is that the traffic level on the LAN will immediately increase by 50 percent. On the other hand, if the links back to the hubs are slow, this increase may not be significant compared to the performance improvement from load balancing on the WAN links.

The configuration of the second spoke router in Listing 7-8 is a mirror image of the first spoke router in Listing 7-7. Turning our attention to the hub routers, we find that the configuration for router Hub 1 is identical to that of the primary hub in Listing 7-5. The configuration of router Hub 2, in Listing 7-9, follows the same pattern; the only changes required are in bold print.

We could easily add dial backup to this configuration using the same approach as in Listings 7-5, 7-6, and 7-7. However, in the next section, we will look at a more expandable approach to dial backup in a large hub-and-spoke network.

```
version 11.2
!
hostname Spoke101B
!
interface Ethernet0/0
  ip address 10.101.0.2 255.255.255.0
  standby priority 90
  standby preempt
  standby ip 10.101.0.254
  standby track Serial0.1 30
!
interface Ethernet0/1
  ip address 10.101.1.2 255.255.255.0
  standby priority 110
  standby preempt
  standby ip 10.101.1.254
  standby track Serial0.1 30
!
interface Serial0/0
  no ip address
  encapsulation frame-relay
!
interface Serial0/0.1 point-to-point
  description Link to router Hub 2
  ip address 10.101.128.9 255.255.255.252
  frame-relay interface-dlci 17 broadcast
!
router rip
  version 2
  timers basic 5 15 15 30
  network 10.0.0.0
  no auto-summary
!
ip classless
! Use our frame link if up
ip route 0.0.0.0 0.0.0.0 10.0.0.2 200
! otherwise use Spoke1A's frame link
ip route 0.0.0.0 0.0.0.0 10.0.0.1 210
!
end
```

LISTING 7-8. *Dual router spoke using RIPv2 and OSPF router Spoke 101B*

```
version 11.2
!
hostname Hub2
!
interface Loopback0
 description Network Management & OSPF Identification
 ip address 10.0.0.202 255.255.255.255
!
interface Loopback1
 description Primary target for Frame Relay users
 ip address 10.0.0.2 255.255.255.255
!
interface Serial1/0
 no ip address
 encapsulation frame-relay
 frame-relay traffic-shaping
 frame-relay class Spokes
 frame-relay lmi-type ansi
!
interface Serial1/0.101 point-to-point
 description Spoke 101
  ip address 10.101.128.10  255.255.255.252
 frame-relay interface-dlci 101
!
! . . . Other Frame Relay subinterfaces go here
!
router ospf 1
 redistribute rip metric 2000 subnets
 passive-interface Serial1/0.101
 passive-interface Serial1/0.102
 passive-interface Serial1/0.103
! . . . Hushing of other spoke subinterfaces go here
 network 10.0.0.0 0.255.255.255 area 1
!
router rip
 version 2
 timers basic 5 15 15 30
 passive-interface Ethernet0/0
 passive-interface Ethernet0/1
! . . . Turn off RIP on interfaces to other hub routers
 network 10.0.0.0
 distribute-list 10 out Serial1/0.101
 distribute-list 10 out Serial1/0.102
```

(*continued*)

```
 distribute-list 10 out Serial1/0.103
 ! . . . Filters for other spoke subinterfaces go here
  no auto-summary
 !
 !ip classless
 !
 map-class frame-relay Spokes
  frame-relay traffic-route 56000 56000
 access-list 10 permit 10.0.0.2
 access-list 10 permit 0.0.0.0
 access-list 10 deny   any
 !
 end
```

LISTING 7-9. *Second hub router using OSPF and RIPv2 highlighting changes from primary hub router configuration*

DIAL BACKUP WITH MULTIPLE DIAL ACCESS SERVERS

In our discussion of hub-and-spoke topology considerations, we have already noted that dial backup is a common requirement. The classic router-to-router approach to dial backup, assigning an IP subnetwork to the ISDN connection, has problems when the need arises to scale the number of routers dialing in. Problems also arise as soon as an attempt is made to provide redundancy for the hub router being called.

The fundamental problem is that the IP subnetwork assigned must be unique to the dialer. While multiple PRI lines can be combined under a single dialer to provide one or two hundred lines on a single router, eventually we will need to expand to multiple routers to provide adequate access. When we expand dial-in access to include a second router, we need to use a different IP subnetwork for its dialer. The same applies even if we simply want a second dial-in access server to reduce the impact of a single router failure.

With traditional *backup interface* or dial-on-demand dial backup, we could only configure a single IP subnetwork on the BRI interface used at the spoke. It was not until the introduction of dialer profiles in IOS 11.2 that there was any mechanism available on Cisco routers to associate more than one configuration with a dialer rotary. Even with dialer profiles, support for multiple IP subnetworks for dial backup to equivalent sites is unnecessarily complex. It is much easier to use IP unnumbered and avoid the problem altogether.

ELIMINATING DIAL ACCESS SERVER DEPENDENCY

Using IP unnumbered for the ISDN link allows us to use a single dialer configuration at the spoke and dial any of several target routers simply by defining multiple dialer maps, one for each number to be dialed. If there are multiple PRIs on one router and we do not wish to combine them into a single rotary group with a single lead number, that is not a problem. We can simply define a dialer map on the spoke for each number, using the same IP address and router name.

We can actually go a step further and use an artificial loopback address defined solely for use with dial backup. This target address is defined on all hub routers that might be called by spokes dialing in. That way, a single, common dial-in configuration is possible on all spoke routers, which minimizes the potential for mistakes. Taken to its logical conclusion, we can also use common, shared target address definitions for our permanent links.

CONFIGURATION EXAMPLE: SINGLE SPOKE, TWO CORE TARGETS, IP ONLY

Consider the sample hub and spoke in Figure 7-6. This is identical to the example illustrated in Figure 7-4, except that we now have both hub routers configured for dial-in access and are using IP unnumbered rather than an explicit IP subnetwork for the ISDN communications. The duplicate IP address used by the ISDN link on both hub routers is deliberate and not an error. From the viewpoint of the spoke router, both hub routers have the same IP address when dialing in. We could take this same configuration and expand it to dial additional routers and the only change required on the spoke would be the addition of a dialer map and username/password for each new router. The floating static routes responsible for link recovery would be unchanged.

Any time the primary link fails, each dialer map to 10.0.0.2 is executed until one of them succeeds. That way, even if a hub router used for dial backup has failed, the call can be completed to any other hub router with an available incoming line.

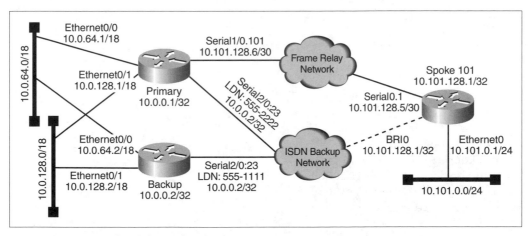

FIGURE 7-6. *Simple spoke with two ISDN targets*

Listing 7-10 shows the configuration necessary on the spoke to handle calling both hub routers. Compare this with Listing 7-1, which provides similar functionality except that the spoke is limited to dialing a single hub router. The few changes required at the spoke are bolded. The key is that all the difficult work is done at the hub routers.

```
version 11.0
!
hostname Spoke101
!
username HubBackup password secret101
username HubPrimary password secret101
! Add Logins for additional dial backup access servers
isdn switch-type basic-ni1
!
interface Loopback0
 description Always Up IP Address for Spoke 101
  ip address 10.101.128.1 255.255.255.255
 !
interface Ethernet0
  ip address 10.101.0.1 255.255.255.0
 !
interface Serial0
 no ip address
 encapsulation frame-relay
 !
interface Serial0.1 point-to-point
  ip address 10.101.128.5 255.255.255.252
 bandwidth 56
 delay 2000
 frame-relay interface-dlci 17 broadcast
 !
interface BRI0
 ip unnumbered Loopback0
 encapsulation ppp
 bandwidth 56
 delay 5000
 no keepalive
 isdn spid1 20155501010000
 isdn spid2 20155512130000
 dialer idle-timeout 170
```

(continued)

```
    dialer map ip 10.0.0.2 name HubBackup broadcast 5551111
    dialer map ip 10.0.0.2 name HubPrimary broadcast 5552222
  ! Add dialer maps for additional dial-in servers here
   dialer hold-queue 10
   dialer-group 1
   ppp authentication chap
  !
 router eigrp 1
  network 10.0.0.0
  no auto-summary
  !
 ip host TestISDN 10.0.0.2
 ip classless
 ip route 0.0.0.0 0.0.0.0 10.0.0.1 200 ! Use frame if up
 ip route 0.0.0.0 0.0.0.0 10.0.0.2 210 ! Get ISDN link up
 ip route 10.0.0.2 255.255.255.255 BRI0
 access-list 102 deny   eigrp any any
 access-list 102 permit ip any any
 !
 dialer-list 1 protocol ip list 102
 !
 end
```

LISTING 7-10. *Single router spoke with redundant IP dial backup*

Aside from the changes required to use IP unnumbered rather than an explicit subnetwork for the ISDN link, the only changes required are to define a username and password for each additional hub site router we can call and to add an appropriate dialer map to *interface BRI0*. Since the same IP address is used to define all ISDN targets, there is no need to define additional floating static routes.

The changes at the hub routers are equally minor. The configuration for Hub Primary in Listing 7-11 appears much more complex because it contains not only the original Frame Relay configuration, but also a complete ISDN backup configuration. The only change not obviously associated with the addition of ISDN backup support is the access-list applied to EIGRP advertisements out the Ethernet ports. Rather than blocking address 10.0.0.1, the filter has been changed to block all addresses in the range 10.0.0.0 through 10.0.0.127. What we are doing here is jumping ahead and blocking all IP addresses in the common advertisement range. Although not absolutely necessary, doing so minimizes the potential for mistakes or confusion when routers see advertisements for addresses that they have defined as loopback ports.

The ISDN configuration on all hub routers is essentially identical, so rather than worrying about the addition of ISDN support on router Hub Primary, we

```
version 11.2
!
hostname  HubPrimary
!
username  Spoke101 password secret101
username  Spoke102 password secret102
username  Spoke103 password secret103
username  Spoke104 password secret104
!  .  .  .  Logins for other spokes which could call in
!
ip subnet-zero
isdn switch-type primary-dms100
!
controller T1 2/0
 framing esf
 linecode b8zs
 pri-group timeslots 1-24
!
interface Loopback0
 description Target address for Frame Relay users
 ip address 10.0.0.1 255.255.255.255
!
interface Loopback1
 description Target address for ISDN Callers
 ip address 10.0.0.2 255.255.255.255
!
interface Ethernet0/0
 description Primary data center LAN
 ip address 10.0.64.1 255.255.192.0
!
interface Ethernet0/1
 description Secondary (backup) data center LAN
 ip address 10.0.128.1 255.255.192.0
!
interface Serial1/0
 no ip address
 encapsulation frame-relay
 frame-relay traffic-shaping
 frame-relay class Spokes
 frame-relay lmi-type ansi
!
interface Serial1/0.101 point-to-point
 description Spoke 101
```

(*continued*)

```
 ip address 10.101.128.6 255.255.255.252
 frame-relay interface-dlci 101
!
! . . . Other Frame Relay subinterfaces go here
!
interface Serial2/0:23
 ip unnumbered Loopback1
 ip tcp header-compression passive
 encapsulation ppp
 no keepalive
! Caller ID checking, if desired, would go here
 dialer idle-timeout 300
 dialer map ip 10.101.128.1 name Spoke101 broadcast
 dialer map ip 10.102.128.1 name Spoke102 broadcast
 dialer map ip 10.103.128.1 name Spoke103 broadcast
 dialer map ip 10.104.128.1 name Spoke104 broadcast
! . . . Dialer maps for other spokes which could call in
 dialer-group 1
 ppp authentication chap
!
router eigrp 1
 network 10.0.0.0
 distribute-list 12 out Ethernet0/0
 distribute-list 12 out Ethernet0/1
 distribute-list 10 out Serial1/0.101
 distribute-list 10 out Serial1/0.102
 distribute-list 10 out Serial1/0.103
! . . . Filters for other Frame Relay subinterfaces go here
 no auto-summary
 distribute-list 11 out Serial2/0:23
!
ip classless
!
map-class frame-relay Spokes
 frame-relay traffic-rate 56000 56000
access-list 10 permit 10.0.0.1
access-list 10 permit 0.0.0.0
access-list 10 deny   any
access-list 11 permit 10.0.0.2
access-list 11 permit 0.0.0.0
access-list 11 deny   any
access-list 12 deny   10.0.0.0 0.0.0.127
access-list 12 permit any
```

(continued)

```
access-list 102 deny    eigrp any any
access-list 102 permit ip any any
!
dialer-list 1 protocol ip list 102
!
end
```

LISTING 7-11. *Primary hub router using common IP unnumbered target*

concentrate just on the configuration changes necessary on router Hub Backup to support router independent ISDN backup. Changes from the original dial backup support configuration in Listing 7-3 are bolded in Listing 7-12. (What is not highlighted is the elimination of calling ID checking, which was removed to reduce clutter rather than to meet any requirements for supporting router-independent dial backup.)

Starting at the top, the first addition is the definition of a loopback interface to support IP unnumbered. We use a loopback port for two reasons. First we do not want the ability to use ISDN to be dependent on some other interface being up, such as one of the Ethernet interfaces. Second, since we will be duplicating the IP address of the ISDN routing target address on other routers, we cannot use a real interface

```
version 11.0
!
hostname HubBackup
!
username Spoke101 password secret101
username Spoke102 password secret102
username Spoke103 password secret103
username Spoke104 password secret104
!  . . . Logins for other spokes which could call in
!
isdn switch-type primary-dms100
!
controller T1 2/0
 framing esf
 linecode b8zs
 pri-group timeslots 1-24
!
interface Loopback1
 description Target address for ISDN Callers
 ip address 10.0.0.2 255.255.255.255
!
```

(*continued*)

```
interface Ethernet0/0
 description Primary data center LAN
 ip address 10.0.64.2 255.255.192.0
 !
interface Ethernet0/1
 description Secondary (backup) data center LAN
 ip address 10.0.128.2 255.255.192.0
 !
 !
interface Serial2/0:23
 ip unnumbered Loopback1
 bandwidth 56
 delay 5000
 ip tcp header-compression passive
 encapsulation ppp
 no keepalive
! Caller ID checking, if desired, would go here
 dialer idle-timeout 300
 dialer map ip 10.101.128.1 name Spoke101 broadcast
 dialer map ip 10.102.128.1 name Spoke102 broadcast
 dialer map ip 10.103.128.1 name Spoke103 broadcast
 dialer map ip 10.104.128.1 name Spoke104 broadcast
! . . . Dialer maps for other spokes which could call in
 dialer-group 1
 ppp authentication chap
 !
router eigrp 1
 network 10.0.0.0
 distribute-list 12 out Ethernet0/0
 distribute-list 12 out Ethernet0/1
 distribute-list 11 out Serial2/0:23
 no auto-summary
 !
ip classless
access-list 11 permit 10.0.0.2
access-list 11 deny   any
access-list 12 deny   10.0.0.0 0.0.0.127
access-list 12 permit any
access-list 102 deny   eigrp any any
access-list 102 permit ip any any
 !
dialer-list 1 protocol ip list 102
 !
end
```

LISTING 7-12. *Backup hub router using common IP unnumbered target*

that must have a unique IP address. We then change the PRI port from an explicit IP address to using IP unnumbered. As part of that change, we need to change the dialer maps to match the unnumbered IP addresses that are now being used by the spokes.

Finally, to avoid trouble from having the same IP address defined on multiple routers, we filter the routing advertisements leaving the Ethernet ports (or any other ports leading to other hub routers) to eliminate all artificial addresses. Note that although we only use the artificial address 10.0.0.2 on this router, we filter the entire range so that when a spoke that is running on dial backup reconnects its primary link, we do not advertise the Frame Relay target address 10.0.0.1. The distribution list applied to all ISDN connections similarly prevents other ISDN-connected spokes from learning of any addresses that could confuse their routing.

CONFIGURATION EXAMPLE: SINGLE SPOKE, TWO CORE TARGETS, IP AND IPX

We can take a similar approach with IPX by using IPXWAN. However, due to limitations in defining floating static routes for IPX, this approach can be used only in conjunction with IP where the IP routing protocol can force the dialing. The IP configuration is unchanged from that of the previous example in Figure 7-6. The IPX configuration is detailed in Figure 7-7.

As before, the spoke configuration in Listing 7-13 appears deceptively simple because all hard work is done on the hub routers. Indeed, the IP portion of the configuration is identical to the previous example and the IPX additions are virtually identical to those already presented in earlier chapters.

The only new feature in this spoke configuration is the addition of redundant remote system definitions and dialer maps. Now when the primary link goes down,

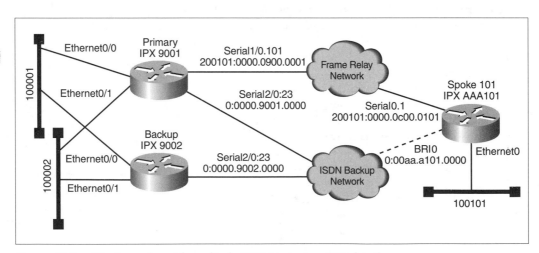

FIGURE 7-7. *Single spoke with multiple ISDN targets—IPX detail*

```
version 11.0
!
hostname Spoke101
!
username HubBackup password secret101
username HubPrimary password secret101
! Add Logins for additional ISDN targets here
ipx routing 0000.0c00.0101
ipx internal-network AAA101
isdn switch-type basic-ni1
!
interface Loopback0
 description Always Up IP Address for Spoke 101
 ip address 10.101.128.1 255.255.255.255
!
interface Ethernet0
 ip address 10.101.0.1 255.255.255.0
 ipx network 100101 encapsulation SAP
!
interface Serial0
 no ip address
 bandwidth 56
 encapsulation frame-relay
!
interface Serial0.1 point-to-point
 ip address 10.101.128.5 255.255.255.252
 bandwidth 56
 delay 2000
 ipx network 200101
 ipx delay 7
 frame-relay interface-dlci 17 broadcast
!
interface BRI0
 ip unnumbered Loopback0
 encapsulation ppp
 bandwidth 56
 delay 5000
 ipx ipxwan 0 unnumbered Spoke101
 ipx delay 30
 isdn spid1 20155501010000
 isdn spid2 20155512130000
 dialer idle-timeout 170
```

(continued)

```
 dialer map ipx 0.0000.9002.0000 name HubBackup broadcast
  5551111
 dialer map ip 10.0.0.2 name HubBackup broadcast 5551111
 dialer map ipx 0.0000.9001.0000 name HubPrimary broadcast
  5552222
 dialer map ip 10.0.0.2 name HubPrimary broadcast 5552222
 ! Add dialer maps for additional targets here
 dialer hold-queue 10
 dialer-group 1
 ppp authentication chap
 !
router eigrp 1
 network 10.0.0.0
 no auto-summary
 !
ip host TestISDN 10.0.0.2
ip classless
ip route 0.0.0.0 0.0.0.0 10.0.0.1 200 ! Use frame if up
ip route 0.0.0.0 0.0.0.0 10.0.0.2 210 ! Otherwise, get ISDN up
ip route 10.0.0.2 255.255.255.255 BRI0
access-list 102 deny   eigrp any any
access-list 102 permit ip any any
access-list 902 deny 1
access-list 902 deny 4
access-list 902 permit -1
 !
ipx route 100001 0.0000.9001.0000 floating-static
ipx route 100002 0.0000.9002.0000 floating-static
 !
dialer-list 1 protocol ip list 102
dialer-list 1 protocol ipx list 902
 !
end
```

LISTING 7-13. *Single router spoke with IP and IPX dial backup*

we have multiple dialer maps available to reach the ISDN target address of 10.0.0.2. Cisco dial-on-demand routing treats these redundant dialer maps as an outgoing rotary group, trying each in turn until a call completes. This allows us to order the IP dialer maps to specify which targets should be tried first. However, we need to be aware that the default behavior for dialers is to remember the last successful call and to start with that map the next time a call must be placed. More importantly, success or failure is a function of whether the call was answered, not whether a useful communications link was negotiated. Consequently, we not only need to regularly test each spoke to ensure that its dial backup still functions, but also test each dial-in number to ensure that it is properly answering calls, negotiating link parameters, and successfully exchanging routing and data traffic.

In a large hub-and-spoke network, the health of the dial-in ports can be determined by examining the logs. However, we must be careful, because sometimes an IOS failure—such as an inability to establish new routing neighbor relationships—allows existing calls to continue correctly but prevents new calls from setting up useful communications.

Testing of incoming ports can be greatly simplified by setting up a test spoke system at the network operations center solely for link testing. This system is built either without a permanent link or with filters on the permanent link so that test addresses are only reachable through the dial links so that successful communications can occur only if the dial link being tested is fully functional.

One trick we can use with this test system is to define artificial test addresses that are tied to specific dial-in targets. An example of how to do this is provided in Listing 7-14. In addition to defining the addresses 10.0.0.101, 10.0.0.102, etc., to force dialing of specific interfaces on HubBackup and HubPrimary, we define the loopback interface 10.255.255.2 and put the LAN in an address block that can be accessed only from the hub through a dial-in link. This way, we can test a specific dial-in PRI by Telneting to the test spoke at address 10.255.255.1, which is reachable through its primary link, and after verifying that no BRI channels are currently up (e.g., by using *show dialer* or *show isdn status*), we can bring up the link we want to test by using the *ping* command. If the addresses 10.255.255.2/32 and 10.255.255.128/25 then show up in the routing tables on the hub routers (easily verified by pinging or Telneting to 10.255.255.2 or any system on the TestSpoke LAN from any system on a hub network), that access port is functional and we can drop the call and try another port.

```
version 11.0
!
hostname TestSpoke
!
username HubBackup password testsecret
username HubPrimary password testsecret
! . . . Other hub routers to test go here
ipx routing 0000.0c00.0FFF
ipx internal-network AAAFFF
isdn switch-type basic-ni1
!
```

(continued)

```
interface Loopback0
 description IP Address for Management and Frame Access
 ip address 10.255.255.1 255.255.255.255
!
interface Loopback1
 description IP Address accessible only via dial-up
 ip address 10.255.255.2 255.255.255.255
!
interface Ethernet0
 ip address 10.255.255.129 255.255.255.128
 ipx network 100FFF encapsulation SAP
!
interface Serial0
 no ip address
 bandwidth 56
 encapsulation frame-relay
!
interface Serial0.1 point-to-point
 ip address 10.255.255.21 255.255.255.252
 ip access-group 199 in
 ip access-group 198 out
 bandwidth 56
 delay 2000
 frame-relay interface-dlci 17 broadcast
!
interface BRI0
 ip unnumbered Loopback0
 encapsulation ppp
 bandwidth 56
 delay 5000
 no keepalive
 ipx ipxwan 0 unnumbered Spoke101
 ipx delay 30
 isdn spid1 20155512340000
 isdn spid2 20155512350000
 dialer idle-timeout 170
 dialer map ipx 0.0000.9002.0000 name HubBackup broadcast
 ➥ 5551111
 dialer map ip 10.0.0.2 name HubBackup broadcast 5551111
! Test Router HubBackup PRI on Serial0:23
 dialer map ip 10.0.0.101 name HubBackup broadcast 5551111
! Test Router HubBackup PRI on Serial1:23
 dialer map ip 10.0.0.102 name HubBackup broadcast 5551131
```

(continued)

```
   dialer map ipx 0.0000.9001.0000 name HubPrimary broadcast
     ➥ 5552222
   dialer map ip 10.0.0.2 name HubPrimary broadcast 5552222
 ! Test Router HubPrimary PRI on Serial0:23
   dialer map ip 10.0.0.103 name HubPrimary broadcast 5552222
 ! Add dialer maps for additional targets here
   dialer hold-queue 10
   dialer-group 1
 ppp authentication chap
 !
router eigrp 1
 network 10.0.0.0
 distribute-list 99 out Serial0.1
 no auto-summary
 !
ip host TestISDN 10.0.0.2
ip classless
ip route 0.0.0.0 0.0.0.0 10.0.0.1 200 ! Use frame if up
ip route 0.0.0.0 0.0.0.0 10.0.0.2 210 ! Otherwise, get ISDN up
ip route 10.0.0.2 255.255.255.255 BRI0
ip route 10.0.0.101 255.255.255.255 BRI0
ip route 10.0.0.102 255.255.255.255 BRI0
ip route 10.0.0.103 255.255.255.255 BRI0
access-list 99 deny    10.255.255.2
access-list 99 deny    10.255.255.128 0.0.0.127
access-list 99 permit  any
access-list 102 deny   eigrp any any
access-list 102 permit ip any any
access-list 198 deny   ip host 10.255.255.2 any
access-list 198 deny   ip 10.255.255.128 0.0.0.127 any
access-list 198 permit ip any any
access-list 199 deny   ip any host 10.255.255.2
access-list 199 deny   ip any 10.255.255.128 0.0.0.127
access-list 199 permit ip any any
access-list 902 deny 1
access-list 902 deny 4
access-list 902 permit -1
!
dialer-list 1 protocol ip list 102
dialer-list 1 protocol ipx list 902
!
end
```

LISTING 7-14. *Test Spoke for simplified testing of hub dial-in ports*

For example, we could test the PRI on Serial0:23 of HubBackup by executing the following test process:

1. Log onto any system on a LAN other than the TestSpoke LAN.

2. Telnet to the router TestSpoke at IP address 10.255.255.1.

3. *Ping* 10.0.0.101.

4. Disconnect from the router by typing *exit*.

5. *Ping* any end system on the TestSpoke LAN 10.255.255.128/25.

IPX operation can be verified at the same time by using the *show ipx routes* and *show ipx services* commands on the TestSpoke router to see if the IPX route advertisements and service advertisements are making it across the link. These need to be verified at both TestSpoke and on a hub router, because unlike the case for IP, both RIP and SAP advertisements must function correctly in both directions for IPX communications to work.

The acid test for IPX functionality is to verify that an IPX system installed on the TestSpoke router LAN works correctly. Because the Frame Relay link is not even configured to support IPX traffic, IPX services can work only if the dial backup link is working correctly. We always must be on guard against falling into the trap of assuming that just because one protocol works, all other protocols must be working also. Each protocol must be tested independently.

The key point is that it is frequently possible to dramatically simplify the routine testing required to achieve high availability by adjusting the router configuration to support testing. Frequently, as is the case here, this can be done with minor impact on configuration complexity and major impact on the cost and effectiveness of automating the desired level of testing.

Turning our attention to the hub routers, only minor changes are required to add IPX support, and the configuration of the primary router in Listing 7-15 and the backup router in Listing 7-16 are otherwise identical to those in the preceding IP-only example. While these listings are generally self-explanatory, there is one new feature present. We define extra loopback interfaces (such as *interface Loopback2* on router HubPrimary) to support the IP addresses used by TestSpoke to force up specific links to the hub site routers. This allows the *ping* used to force up the link during hub interface testing to succeed rather than fail, which in turn speeds up testing. This eliminates the delay for all ping attempts to time out and provides immediate feedback to the tester that the link has come up. Notice how our default block in EIGRP for the Ethernet ports of 10.0.0.0/127 automatically prevents these new addresses from escaping.

```
version 11.2
!
hostname HubPrimary
!
username Spoke101 password secret101
username Spoke102 password secret102
username Spoke103 password secret103
username Spoke104 password secret104
! . . . Logins for other spokes which could call in
username TestSpoke password testsecret
!
ipx routing 0000.0900.0001
ipx internal-network 9001
isdn switch-type primary-dms100
!
controller T1 2/0
 framing esf
 linecode b8zs
 pri-group timeslots 1-24
!
interface Loopback0
 description Common target address for Frame Relay users
 ip address 10.0.0.1 255.255.255.255
!
interface Loopback1
 description Common target address for ISDN Callers
 ip address 10.0.0.2 255.255.255.255
!
interface Loopback2
 description Target address for individual ISDN line Testing
 ip address 10.0.0.103 255.255.255.255
!
interface Ethernet0/0
 description Primary Data Center LAN
 ip address 10.0.64.1 255.255.192.0
 ipx network 100001
!
interface Ethernet0/1
 description Secondary (backup) LAN
 ip address 10.0.128.1 255.255.192.0
 ipx network 100002
!
```

(continued)

```
interface Serial1/0
 no ip address
 encapsulation frame-relay
 frame-relay traffic-shaping
 frame-relay class Spokes
 frame-relay lmi-type ansi
!
interface Serial1/0.17 point-to-point
 description TestSpoke access
 ip address 10.255.255.22 255.255.255.252
 bandwidth 56
 delay 2000
 frame-relay interface-dlci 17
!
interface Serial1/0.101 point-to-point
 description Spoke 101
 ip address 10.101.128.6 255.255.255.252
 bandwidth 56
 delay 2000
 ipx network 200101 encapsulation SAP
 ipx delay 7
 frame-relay interface-dlci 101
!
! . . . Other Frame Relay subinterfaces go here
!
interface Serial2/0:23
 ip unnumbered Loopback1
 ip tcp header-compression passive
 bandwidth 56
 delay 5000
 encapsulation ppp
 no keepalive
 ipx ipxwan 0 unnumbered HubPrimary
 ipx delay 30
 dialer idle-timeout 300
 dialer map ipx 0.00aa.afff.0000 name TestSpoke broadcast
 dialer map ip 10.255.255.1 name TestSpoke broadcast
 dialer map ipx 0.00aa.a101.000 name Spoke101 broadcast
 dialer map ip 10.101.128.1 name Spoke101 broadcast
 dialer map ipx 0.00aa.a102.0000 name Spoke102 broadcast
 dialer map ip 10.102.128.1 name Spoke 102 broadcast
 dialer map ipx 0.00aa.a103.0000 name Spoke103 broadcast
 dialer map ip 10.103.128.1 name Spoke103 broadcast
```

(continued)

```
! . . . Dialer maps for other spokes which could call in
 dialer-group 1
 ppp authentication chap
!
router eigrp 1
network 10.0.0.0
 distribute-list 12 out Ethernet0/0
 distribute-list 12 out Ethernet0/1
 distribute-list 10 out Serial1/0.101
 distribute-list 10 out Serial1/0.102
 distribute-list 10 out Serial1/0.103
! . . . Filters for other Frame Relay subinterfaces go here
 distribute-list 11 out Serial2/0:23
 no auto-summary
!
ip classless
!
map-class frame-relay Spokes
 frame-relay traffic-rate 56000 56000
access-list 10 permit 10.0.0.1
access-list 10 permit 0.0.0.0
access-list 10 deny   any
access-list 11 permit 10.0.0.2
access-list 11 permit 0.0.0.0
access-list 11 deny   any
access-list 12 deny   10.0.0.0 0.0.0.127
access-list 12 permit any
access-list 102 deny   eigrp any any
access-list 102 permit ip any any
access-list 902 deny 1
access-list 902 deny 4
access-list 902 permit -1
!
dialer-list 1 protocol ipx list 902
dialer-list 1 protocol ip list 102
!
end
```

LISTING 7-15.   *Primary hub router for IP and IPX*

```
version 11.0
!
hostname HubBackup
!
username Spoke101 password secret101
username Spoke102 password secret102
username Spoke103 password secret103
username Spoke104 password secret104
!  . . . Logins for other spokes which could call in
username TestSpoke password testsecret
!
ipx routing 0000.0900.0002
ipx internal-network 9002
isdn switch-type primary-dms100
!
controller T1 2/0
 framing esf
 linecode b8zs
 pri-group timeslots 1-24
!
interface Loopback1
 description Common target address for ISDN Callers
 ip address 10.0.0.2 255.255.255.255
!
interface Loopback2
 description Target address for individual ISDN line Testing
 ip address 10.0.0.101 255.255.255.255
!
interface Loopback3
 description Target address for individual ISDN line Testing
 ip address 10.0.0.102 255.255.255.255
!
interface Ethernet0/0
 description Primary Data Center LAN
 ip address 10.0.64.2 255.255.192.0
 ipx network 100001
!
interface Ethernet0/1
 description Secondary (backup) LAN
 ip address 10.0.128.2 255.255.192.0
 ipx network 100002
!
!
```

(continued)

```
interface Serial2/0:23
 ip unnumbered Loopback1
 bandwidth 56
 delay 5000
 ip tcp header-compression passive
 encapsulation ppp
 no keepalive
 ipx ipxwan 0 unnumbered HubBackup
 ipx delay 30
 dialer idle-timeout 300
 dialer map ipx 0.00aa.afff.0000 name TestSpokebroadcast
 dialer map ip 10.255.255.1 name TestSpoke broadcast
 dialer map ipx 0.00aa.a101.0000 name Spoke101 broadcast
 dialer map ip 10.101.128.1 name Spoke101 broadcast
 dialer map ipx 0.00aa.a102.0000 name Spoke102 broadcast
 dialer map ip 10.102.128.1 name Spoke102 broadcast
 dialer map ipx 0.00aa.a103.0000 name Spoke103 broadcast
 dialer map ip 10.103.128.1 name Spoke 103 broadcast
! . . . Dialer maps for other spokes which could call in
 dialer-group 1
 ppp authentication chap
!
interface Serial2/1:23
 !
 ! Identical configuration to Serial2/0:23
 !
!
router eigrp 1
 network 10.0.0.0
 distribute-list 12 out Ethernet0/0
 distribute-list 12 out Ethernet0/1
 distribute-list 11 out Serial2/0:23
 no auto-summary
!
ip classless
access-list 11 permit 10.0.0.2
access-list 11 permit 0.0.0.0
access-list 11 deny   any
access-list 12 deny   10.0.0.0 0.0.0.127
access-list 12 permit any
access-list 102 deny   eigrp any any
access-list 102 permit ip any any
access-list 902 deny 1
```

(continued)

```
access-list 902 deny 4
access-list 902 permit -1
!
dialer-list 1 protocol ip list 102
dialer-list 1 protocol ipx list 902
!
end
```

LISTING 7-16. *Backup hub router for IP and IPX*

CONFIGURATION EXAMPLE: MULTIPLE ISDN AND ASYNC TARGETS

In this final dial backup configuration example for hub-and-spoke topology, we take advantage of the automatic combining of dialer maps into rotaries to provide a single configuration that can be used for either ISDN or POTS dial backup. The spoke configuration uses classical dialer maps, allowing support of older IOS releases (in the case of the client for which this was developed, hardware constraints limited many spokes to IOS 11.0). The hub routers supporting dial-in for backup use dialer profiles and virtual templates to minimize the configuration overhead for each spoke being supported. Local authentication is used to avoid the need for redundant RADIUS or TACACS servers. In the production configuration from which this example was derived, the hub PRI lines are also used for placing calls to service providers and for supporting incoming calls from telecommuters using home PCs. These additional capabilities are not shown in this example.

The general configuration is illustrated in Figure 7-8. There are three classes of dial backup numbers possible: those that support ISDN only (router ISDNonly), those that support Asynchronous POTS only (router AsyncOnly), and those that accept either ISDN or voice calls and that handle either appropriately (router ISDNorAsync).

This configuration assumes that any single spoke normally is using either ISDN or analog for backup, but not both. Although it will work with both connected, as configured, there will be no further attempts to dial an alternative mode backup call once the routing protocol announces that a dial backup connection has been made. As a result, if an ISDN call cannot be completed before an asynchronous connection is established, you must manually force the ISDN call to dial if you want to shift from analog mode to the higher performing ISDN mode of backup. Alternatively, we could use *dialer watch* or directed routing updates to continue attempts to force up the ISDN link once dial-on-demand routing has been satisfied by the asynchronous connection.

Before we get to the dial backup configuration, we should include a few words about the IP numbering scheme used, because the pattern is not as obvious as in previous examples.

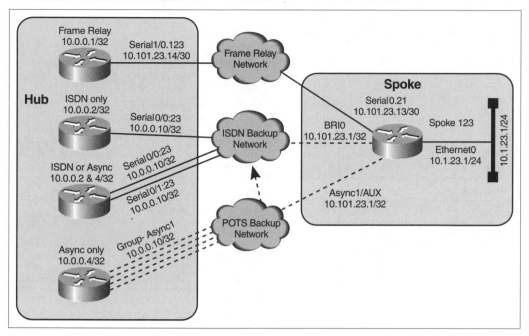

FIGURE 7-8.   *Spoke with both ISDN and Async backup*

IP addresses are assigned based on the spoke number and allow support for up to 9,999 spokes before requiring non-obvious address assignments. The basic pattern is that the LAN at each spoke is 10.*ss.ss*.0/24, where *ss.ss* is the four-digit spoke number. All other spoke related addresses, such as numbered links to hubs and loopback addresses, are assigned from the address range of 10.1*ss.ss*.0 through 10.1*ss.ss*.255. The hub sites can then use the remaining addresses.

In this example, we use 10.0.0.0/25 for artificial loopback addresses, 10.0.0.128/25 for router IDs, and 10.2*xx*.0.0/16 for LANs and other functional networks. These assignments are summarized in Table 7-1.

As is typical of an address scheme designed using RFC 1918 private address space, this addressing plan makes no attempt to minimize address consumption. Instead, it favors readability of dotted decimal addresses over efficiency. This scheme, like any other that ties IP address to organization units, also may turn out to be very difficult to aggregate efficiently as the network expands.

Unlike our previous examples, the spoke configuration in Listing 7-17 now is considerably more complex. However, that should not be surprising because the hub is now supporting two different modes of dial backup to five different phone numbers on three different hub routers. Even though support for dial backup testing is minimal, it doubles the number of dialer maps and adds more static routes to the mix. Making up for this added complexity is the simplification of configuration

TABLE 7-1. *Addressing Scheme for Figure 7-8*

STARTING IP ADDRESS	ENDING IP ADDRESS	DESCRIPTION
10.0.0.0	10.0.0.127	Target addresses not routinely advertised: 10.0.0.1 = Frame Relay target 10.0.0.2 = ISDN up routing target 10.0.0.3 = ISDN dialing test target 10.0.0.4 = Async up routing target 10.0.0.5 = Async dialing test target 10.0.0.10 = Generic dial backup dialing target
10.0.0.128	10.0.0.255	Hub router IDs for network management
10.0.128.0	10.0.255.255	Point-to-point links between hub routers
10.*ss.ss*.0	10.*ss.ss*.255	LAN at spoke number *ssss*
10.1*ss.ss*.1	Host ID	Router loopback at spoke *ssss*
10.1*ss.ss*.12	10.1*ss.ss*.15	Frame Relay link from spoke *ssss* to hub router 1
10.1*ss.ss*.20	10.1*ss.ss*.23	Frame Relay link from spoke ssss to hub router 2
10.2*xx*.0.0	10.2*xx*.255.255	Hub site LAN *xx* (255.255.0.0 subnet mask)

management because we now have a single configuration that remains unchanged as the primary and backup connectivity actually used by the spoke changes.

A spoke initially can be installed in a new location even before digital services are in place, using any available POTS line in the facility. Once both Frame Relay and ISDN service are installed, connected, and tested, the analog modem can be removed. At no time is it necessary to reconfigure the spoke router as communications services are added or deleted. If at some point in the future there is a double failure of digital services, or just a prolonged problem with either digital service, a modem can be dispatched and any available, still-functional POTS line can be pressed into service. If the spoke is important enough, even a cellular phone and compatible modem could be used to restore service while waiting for permanent repairs. To see how this works, we need to look at Listing 7-17.

The spoke configuration diverges from standard Frame Relay with dial backup when we get to the *interface BRI0* configuration. There we have four dialer maps for address 10.0.0.3, one for each of the two rotary numbers on each of the two hub routers supporting ISDN dial backup. If there were more routers or more rotaries per routers, we would include them here. The confusing part is that we then repeat the dialer maps using the IP address 10.0.0.10 in place of 10.0.0.3. A similar pattern occurs under *interface Async1*, except that the IP address 10.0.0.3 is replaced by the IP address 10.0.0.5. We also force per-packet load balancing with no *ip route-cache*.

The reasoning behind the extra dialer maps can be seen in the floating static routes further down the configuration. When the primary link goes down, the address

```
version 11.0
!
hostname Spoke123
!
username AsyncOnlyHub password Secret123A
username ISDNonlyHub password Secret123B
username ISDNorAsyncHub password Secret123C
!
isdn switch-type basic-ni1
chat-script courier ABORT ERROR ABORT "NO " ABORT BUSY "" "at"
➥ "" "at&f" OK "atl1m1&b1&h1&r2&c1&d3&m4&k1s0=2" OK
➥ "at dt \T" TIMEOUT 90 CONNECT \c
!
interface Loopback0
 description Network Management
 ip address 10.101.23.1 255.255.255.255
!
interface Ethernet0
 description Spoke 123 LAN
 ip address 10.1.23.1 255.255.255.0
!
interface Serial0
 no ip address
 bandwidth 56
 encapsulation frame-relay
!
interface Serial0.21 point-to-point
 ip address 10.101.23.13 255.255.255.252
 bandwidth 56
 delay 2000
 frame-relay interface-dlci 21 broadcast
!
interface BRI0
 ip unnumbered Loopback0
 encapsulation ppp
 no ip route-cache
 bandwidth 56
 delay 5000
 no keepalive
 isdn spid1 21255501230000
 isdn spid2 21255510100000
 dialer idle-timeout 170
```

(continued)

```
! Dialer maps for testing ISDN links at this site
 dialer map ip 10.0.0.3 name ISDNonlyHub speed 56 broadcast
 ➥ 18005551111
 dialer map ip 10.0.0.3 name ISDNorAsyncHub speed 56 broadcast
 ➥ 18005552222
 dialer map ip 10.0.0.3 name ISDNonlyHub speed 56 broadcast
 ➥ 18005553333
 dialer map ip 10.0.0.3 name ISDNorAsyncHub speed 56 broadcast
 ➥ 18005554444
! Dialer maps for backup protection
 dialer map ip 10.0.0.10 name ISDNonlyHub speed 56 broadcast
 ➥ 18005551111
 dialer map ip 10.0.0.10 name ISDNorAsyncHub speed
 ➥ 56 broadcast 18005552222
 dialer map ip 10.0.0.10 name ISDNonlyHub speed 56 broadcast
 ➥ 18005553333
 dialer map ip 10.0.0.10 name ISDNorAsyncHub speed
 ➥ 56 broadcast 18005554444
 dialer hold-queue 10
 dialer-group 1
 ppp authentication chap
!
interface Async1
 ip unnumbered Loopback0
 encapsulation ppp
 no ip route-cache
 bandwidth 30
 delay 15000
 async default routing
 async mode interactive
 dialer in-band
 dialer idle-timeout 300
! Dialer maps for testing Asynchronous links
 dialer map ip 10.0.0.5 name ISDNorAsyncHub modem-script
 ➥ courier broadcast 18005552222
 dialer map ip 10.0.0.5 name ISDNorAsyncHub modem-script
 ➥ courier broadcast 18005554444
 dialer map ip 10.0.0.5 name AsyncOnlyHub modem-script courier
 ➥ broadcast 18005559999
 dialer map ip 10.0.0.5 name AsyncOnlyHub modem-script courier
 ➥ broadcast 18005550000
! Dialer maps actually used to support communications
```

(*continued*)

```
  dialer map ip 10.0.0.10 name ISDNorAsyncHub modem-script
  ➥ courier broadcast 18005552222
  dialer map ip 10.0.0.10 name ISDNorAsyncHub modem-script
  ➥ courier broadcast 18005554444
  dialer map ip 10.0.0.10 name AsyncOnlyHub modem-script
  ➥ courier broadcast 18005559999
  dialer map ip 10.0.0.10 name AsyncOnlyHub modem-script
  ➥ courier broadcast 18005550000
  dialer hold-queue 10 timeout 45
  dialer-group 1
  ppp authentication chap
!
router eigrp 1
 network 10.0.0.0
 distribute-list 4 in Async1
 distribute-list 2 in BRI0
 no auto-summary
!
ip host TestISDN 10.0.0.3
ip host TestAsync 10.0.0.5
ip classless
ip route 0.0.0.0 0.0.0.0 10.0.0.1 200 ! Use frame if available
ip route 0.0.0.0 0.0.0.0 10.0.0.2 204 ! Otherwise, ISDN if up
ip route 0.0.0.0 0.0.0.0 10.0.0.4 207 ! Otherwise Async if up
ip route 0.0.0.0 0.0.0.0 10.0.0.10 210 ! Get a backup link up
ip route 10.0.0.3 255.255.255.255 BRI0
ip route 10.0.0.5 255.255.255.255 Async1
ip route 10.0.0.10 255.255.255.255 BRI0
ip route 10.0.0.10 255.255.255.255 Async1
!
logging trap debugging
logging 10.0.130.50
access-list 2 permit 0.0.0.0
access-list 2 permit 10.0.0.10
access-list 2 permit 10.0.0.2 0.0.0.1
access-list 2 deny   any
access-list 4 permit 0.0.0.0
access-list 4 permit 10.0.0.10
access-list 4 permit 10.0.0.4 0.0.0.1
access-list 4 deny   any
access-list 102 deny   eigrp any any
access-list 102 permit ip any any
!
```

(continued)

```
dialer-list 1 protocol ip list 102
!
line aux 0
 password NetMgmtSecret
 login
 modem InOut
 transport input all
 rxspeed 38400
 txspeed 38400
 flowcontrol hardware
!
end
```

LISTING 7-17.   *Spoke router with unified ISDN and Async dial backup*

10.0.0.1 (which can be learned only through the routing protocol over the primary link) disappears from the routing table. The address 10.0.0.2 can be learned only through the ISDN link while 10.0.0.4 can be learned only through the asynchronous dial link. If neither link is up, the default route will drop down to the last floating static route that points at 10.0.0.10. Because there are static routes pointing 10.0.0.10 to both the BRI0 and Async1 interfaces, both of which are always up whenever dial-on-demand routing is active, we now have two equal cost (static) routes active to the hub. The next packet to arrive at the router that needs the default route will force either an ISDN dial or an async dial, depending on the current state of load balancing between the two available routes to 10.0.0.10.

Because we don't know whether ISDN or Async will be available, we turn off route caching on both so that the load balancing functions on a per-packet basis rather than on a per-destination. The second outbound packet to be routed will then force dialing of whichever link was not prompted by the first packet. This is where the assumption that only one or the other dial backup paths will normally be available might become critical. If the first packet is routed through the Async port and we are depending on production traffic to force up the links, there might not be a second packet to force up the ISDN link until after the Async link is already up and all packets are routed through it. To avoid this situation, we configure logging on the spoke so that a syslog report of the Async interface coming up will be generated even if there is no other production traffic to provide a nudge to get the ISDN connected. The problem is that this cannot be guaranteed to make an ISDN connection, even with a hold queue to force us to keep trying for 30 seconds, because our initial ISDN dial attempts could all fail.

At this point, we could just say that the system is working as designed and the Async dial has provided the desired continuity of service in the face of a double (primary and ISDN backup) failure. We also could use our async dial connection to Telnet to the router (or any other system on the spoke LAN) and start pinging the ISDN test address 10.0.0.3. This forces the ISDN interface to dial continuously while production traffic continues to flow over the Async connection.

Once either the ISDN or the Async link is up, the floating static route through the target address that is learned through the routing protocol takes over and per-packet load balancing no longer applies. So even though we have turned off route caching, there is only one route, so we do not need to be concerned about the impact of potential out-of-order packet delivery on any of the applications supported.

The second set of dialer maps also helps us when it comes time to test the dial links at the spokes. By having addresses that are tied to a specific spoke interface, we can independently force an ISDN call to test the BRI line or an Async call to test the POTS line. We define test maps to all the target ports to minimize the probability that a spoke test will fail due to a router or link outage at the hub site. To facilitate testing of the hub site interfaces, we also want to set up a test spoke using the same approach of assigning a unique target address corresponding to each dial-in phone number that we used for the test spoke in Listing 7-14.

We need the ability to test each hub PRI individually, even if the numbers used by normal spokes are configured by the service provider as dial rotaries that span PRIs. Otherwise, we may not be aware of failures until they cripple an entire rotary group. Only a single test spoke is normally required, although geographically large networks with multiple hubs may set up a test spoke per region to reduce long distance charges for testing. There is usually no significant benefit to testing every combination of spoke-and-hub link unless a lack of configuration management makes unintended changes to user names or passwords likely, in which case, the problem is much larger than one that can be solved by brute force, dial backup testing.

Another new item is the routing filters on the spoke end of the dial links. These are required in this example because the use of local authentication on the dial-in servers limits us to a single, shared virtual template for both ISDN and asynchronous connections. This requires us to use the same routing advertisement filter for both ISDN and asynchronous connections at the hub site end. It is up to the spoke router to filter incoming routing advertisements so that only the addresses appropriate for the actual link in use are allowed through. These filters also would be needed if RADIUS or TACACS were used for authentication and the choice was made not to distinguish between ISDN and asynchronous calls in the authentication database.

Turning our attention to the configuration of the hub routers, we will ignore the configuration of the Frame Relay, ISDN-only and Async-only hubs because they are merely repeats of what we have looked at before. We will, however, review the combined ISDN and Async hub in Listing 7-18 to show one way we can support both ISDN and asynchronous calls on the same PRI interface.

```
version 12.0
!
hostname ISDNorAsyncHub
!
aaa new-model
aaa authentication login default local
aaa authentication login console enable
aaa authentication login vty local
aaa authentication login dialin local
aaa authentication ppp default local
aaa authentication ppp dialin if-needed local
!
username NetManager password MgmtSecret
username TestSpoke password testsecret
username Spoke101 password Secret101C
username Spoke102 password Secret102C
!  . . .
username Spoke122 password Secret122C
username Spoke123 password Secret123C
!  . . . Additional spokes defined here
ip subnet-zero
!
ip address-pool local
virtual-profile virtual-template 1
virtual-profile aaa
isdn switch-type primary-dms100
modemcap entry FasterMICA:MSC=&f&d2s52=1s54=26
!
!
controller T1 0/0
 framing esf
 linecode b8zs
 pri-group timeslots 1-24
!
controller T1 0/1
 framing esf
 linecode b8zs
 pri-group timeslots 1-24
!
interface Loopback0
 description Hub Router 5 Management ID
 ip address 10.0.0.205 255.255.255.255
!
interface Loopback2
 description ISDN "UP" target address for spoke routers
```

(continued)

```
 ip address 10.0.0.2 255.255.255.255
!
interface Loopback3
 description ISDN call forcing address for spoke routers
 ip address 10.0.0.3 255.255.255.255
!
interface Loopback4
 description Async "UP" target address for spoke routers
 ip address 10.0.0.4 255.255.255.255
!
interface Loopback5
 description Async call forcing address for spoke routers
 ip address 10.0.0.5 255.255.255.255
!
interface Loopback10
 description Actual address used for all spoke dialins
 ip address 10.0.0.10 255.255.255.255
!
interface FastEthernet0/0
 description Primary connection to other hub routers
 ip address 10.200.0.5 255.255.0.0
!
interface Serial0/0:23
 description ISDN PRI-LDN 800-555-2222
 no ip address
 encapsulation ppp
 dialer pool-member 11
 isdn incoming-voice modem
 ppp authentication chap
!
interface Serial0/1:23
 description ISDN PRI—LDN 800-555-4444
 no ip address
 encapsulation ppp
 dialer pool-member 11
 isdn incoming-voice modem
 ppp authentication chap
!
interface FastEthernet1/0
 description Backup connection to other hub routers
 ip address 10.201.0.5 255.255.0.0
!
interface Virtual-Template1
 description Dial-in by spoke routers
 bandwidth 56
```

(continued)

```
 delay 5000
 ip unnumbered Loopback10
 ip tcp header-compression passive
 no keepalive
 no peer neighbor-route
 no peer default ip address
 ppp authentication chap
!
interface Group-Async1
 ip unnumbered Loopback10
 encapsulation ppp
 no ip mroute-cache
 dialer in-band
 dialer pool-member 22
 async mode dedicated
 no cdp enable
 ppp authentication chap
 group-range 65 94
!
router eigrp 1
 network 10.0.0.0
 distribute-list 10 out FastEthernet0/0
 distribute-list 10 out FastEthernet1/0
 distribute-list 1 out Virtual-Template1
 no auto-summary
!
! Advertisement filter for spokes on dialup
access-list 1 permit 0.0.0.0
access-list 1 permit 10.0.0.2 0.0.0.1
access-list 1 permit 10.0.0.4 0.0.0.1
access-list 1 permit 10.0.0.10
access-list 1 deny   any
! DDR should ignore EIGRP on IP
access-list 100 deny   eigrp any any
access-list 100 permit ip any any
!
dialer-list 1 protocol ip list 100
!
line 65 94
 modem InOut
 modem autoconfigure type FasterMICA
 transport preferred none
 transport input all
!
end
```

LISTING 7-18. *Hub router for IP backup through ISDN and Async*

The combination ISDN and Async target hub routers take advantage of the ability of ISDN networks to interoperate with the analog public switched telephone network to carry voice calls end-to-end. When a voice call arrives at the combination router, the call is identified as a voice call and the router assigns it to a modem based on the line *isdn incoming-voice modem* in each PRI interface definition.

To scale to hundreds or thousands of spokes, it is not practical to define a unique dialer profile per spoke. Instead, we use virtual profiles that are created on demand when answering a call. Normally associated with RADIUS and TACACS, virtual profiles can be used also with local authentication as we do here. This allows us to take advantage of the line utilization flexibility benefits of dialer profiles without getting buried in a morass of dialer profiles. Since all we need to define a unique spoke is a unique user name and password for CHAP, we can easily support hundreds of spokes before we need to consider an external authentication server.

The *aaa* statements at the top of the configuration set this router up to handle all authentication using the local user name and password database. These are followed by the individual lines defining a login name and password for each spoke. As configured, login names and passwords are also required to permit network managers to access the router for maintenance purposes. In this example, we define a shared user name, *NetManager,* for router access. In a real network, logins that enforced individual accountability would be more appropriate.

The key to supporting a large number of callers are the lines *virtual-profile virtual-template 1* and *virtual-profile aaa*. The former line says to create virtual profiles based on the template in *virtual-template 1,* and the latter line instructs the router to use the information gathered by *aaa new-model* to complete the virtual profile during a login attempt.

Dialer profiles require that we also use PPP encapsulation and some form of PPP authentication on both the physical line and the profile because the physical lines (*Serial0/0:23* and *Serial0/1:23* in this example) must identity each caller so that they can determine which dialer profile should be used for the incoming call. In this case, the only dialer profiles defined are those created at call time from the virtual template, but in many real world applications, it is quite likely that there will be other users sharing the lines. If only a single real dialer profile is required in addition to the virtual profiles, a second dialer profile should be defined to prevent triggering a bug in many IOS releases where an incoming call to a router with exactly one defined *interface dialer* profile will be bound to that dialer profile before the caller is identified. This bypasses the desired creation of a virtual profile for the call.

The use of local authentication with virtual profiles limits us to a single virtual template. As a result, the same virtual template must be used for both ISDN and analog calls. Since both calling modes use the same real IP address, 10.0.0.10, this might not seem to be a problem. However, when we go to filter the EIGRP advertisements, the distribution list under *router eigrp 1* is tied to the virtual template (*distribute-list 1 out Virtual-Template1*), so all we can do is limit the advertisements to the five target addresses applicable to all dial up calls. We must make up for this lack of selectivity by installing incoming route advertisement filters on every spoke.

The incoming route filters are a good idea in a very large hub-and-spoke network even if they are not needed to support PRI lines with digital modems. Whether due to configuration errors or IOS bugs, routing leaks do happen, and hitting a typical low-end spoke router with a few thousand routes not only consumes all the bandwidth on the link, but also can overload the router to the point where it crashes and reboots. Be particularly wary of early releases of IOS 12.0, as they all suffered from a defect in which routing protocol *distribute-list* commands were not immediately applied to an incoming call that was creating a new virtual profile.

This approach of combining all available links into a single dialer is not suitable if multilink PPP is required for higher ISDN bandwidth. Because both Async and ISDN are using the same target address and share the same dialer rotary, an attempt could be made to bring up a multilink PPP bundle with one link running over ISDN and the other over asynchronous POTS. This is not an effective way to run multilink PPP, so we avoid the problem by not enabling multilink PPP.

If we want to use multilink PPP and do not wish to use BGP or dialer watch, we could do so by modifying the design slightly and configuring the hub routers to use a different IP address for ISDN and Async links (10.0.0.3 and 10.0.0.5 in this example). That way, although 10.0.0.10 could still be used to force up whatever mode of backup is available, once connected, the actual IP address would prevent attempts at multilink PPP across link types. We could also use the same technique to allow dialing multiple sites in a diversified hub. Giving each site its own IP address would force additional calls that were made to expand the multilink PPP bundle to be made only to the already-connected site.

USING MORE THAN ONE HUB

As an organization continues to grow, it soon outgrows the ability to locate all shared resources in a single location, and the "hub" location becomes a network of locations. This diversification typically arises not so much from an inability to support all applications at a single site, but in recognition that a single site hub is an unacceptable single point of failure.

A single site server can take advantage of the techniques discussed in Chapter 3 to provide higher availability to clients, and clustering can be used to scale to support an arbitrary number of users. The challenge lies in the expansion of core services to multiple sites. The common techniques used for high availability at a single site do not work when the server itself must be split across multiple sites and can no longer be identified by a single IP address.

In general, either the client must be capable of transparently dealing with multiple servers, or a layer of indirection must be inserted between the clients and servers so that clients can be directed to an appropriate available server. Application level solutions provide a better solution to the problem, since only the application is aware of any application specific constraints that might affect the ability to gracefully recover from a server failure. However, many mission critical applications that must be supported do not include the ability to deal with alternative servers, and we must enhance the network support for these applications so that they can be transparently redirected to different servers as necessary.

This must be done carefully, however, as many client-server applications maintain state information on the server, which may cease to be valid if a change of servers occurs at the wrong time. For many commercial applications, the client must abandon any work in progress at the time the primary server fails and start over when connecting to the backup server.

Due to the wide range of applications and their capabilities and requirements, a number of different techniques may be required. We must also consider the extent and mode of the failure. As it turns out, there are three different failure scenarios with which we must deal. A hub site could have failed, taking down both the server and all routers supporting the spoke. Alternatively, the server may still be alive, just no longer be reachable by the hub router serving the spoke. Finally, network connectivity could be intact, but the server still be down.

If the event is failure of the entire hub site, we are looking at a disaster recovery scenario. Hub-and-spoke requirements for disaster recovery are not unique, so we will defer the topic until we cover disaster recovery in general in Chapter 11. Similarly, if the server is down, it is not a network problem, although we may be able to help out using some of the disaster recovery tools discussed in Chapter 11. However, if the problem is a network problem and the server is still alive and just out of reach, if it is important enough, we can work around the problem.

DEALING WITH LOSS OF HUB NETWORK CONNECTIVITY

If the server is still alive and functional, and the problem is that the router serving the spoke has lost connectivity to the server, we have a networking problem, not a server problem. While a multiply connected full mesh network connecting all hub sites should be immune to this mode of failure, the reality is that full physical diversity for all links into a single building is frequently not cost effective and loss of connectivity, despite backups and alternate routes, should be included in network planning. Street work, flooded utilities, and other common incidents that can affect all communications to a site typically cut off all communications, but it is not safe to assume that this always will be the case.

The worst case for us is that the hub site used by a spoke is completely cut off from the rest of the hub network but is still connected to its spokes, as in Figure 7-9. Since the default for a spoke is to assume that the hub is fully connected and can be

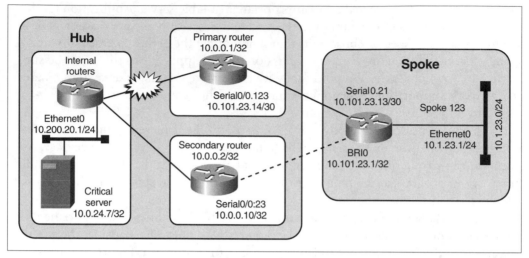

FIGURE 7-9. *Loss of internal connectivity scenario*

used as the default route to everywhere, we clearly have a problem. What we need is a way to force the spoke to dial the backup hub site even though it has a working connection to its primary hub site, without burdening the spoke with learning the full topology of the network (in which case, we would no longer achieve the efficiency benefits of the hub-and-spoke topology).

If only a few critical servers need be protected, we can expand the routing information sent to the spokes to include not only the target for the default route, but also the network addresses of the critical servers. Care must be taken to keep the number of servers advertised to a minimum when doing this, particularly if you are using RIPv2 for spoke routing, where every route advertised increases the size of the routine update broadcast packets.

CONFIGURATION EXAMPLE: SPOKE DIALING AROUND LOSS OF HUB INTERNAL CONNECTIVITY

Listings 7-19 and 7-20 show the changes required from a standard hub-and-spoke configuration to ensure that the backup number will be called not only when the primary link is unavailable, but also any time the critical server cannot be reached regardless of the state of the primary link. We need to recognize that if we take this approach, one of its side effects is that all spokes configured with critical server protection will bring up their ISDN links any time the critical server fails while it is in use. This could create some interesting corporate politics if the critical server is not as reliable as it should be and the networking budget is hit with excessive unnecessary ISDN call expenses.

```
version 11.0
!
hostname Spoke123
!
username Backup password Secret123
!
isdn switch-type basic-ni1
!
interface Loopback0
 description Network Management and ISDN source address
 ip address 10.101.23.1 255.255.255.255
!
interface Ethernet0
 description spoke 123 LAN
 ip address 10.1.23.1 255.255.255.0
!
interface Serial0
 no ip address
 bandwidth 56
 encapsulation frame-relay
!
interface Serial0.21 point-to-point
 ip address 10.101.23.13 255.255.255.252
 bandwidth 56
 delay 2000
 frame-relay interface-dlci 21 broadcast
!
interface BRI0
 ip unnumbered Loopback0
 encapsulation ppp
 bandwidth 56
 delay 5000
 no keepalive
 isdn spid1 21255501230000
 isdn spid2 21255510100000
 dialer idle-timeout 170
 dialer map ip 10.0.0.10 name Backup speed 56 broadcast
 ➥ 18005551111
 dialer hold-queue 10
 dialer-group 1
 ppp authentication chap
!
```

(continued)

```
router eigrp 1
 network 10.0.0.0
 no auto-summary
!
ip host TestISDN 10.0.0.10
ip classless
ip route 0.0.0.0 0.0.0.0 10.0.0.1 200 ! Use frame if up
ip route 0.0.0.0 0.0.0.0 10.0.0.10 210 ! Get a backup link up
ip route 10.0.0.10 255.255.255.255 BRI0
! Try ISDN if no route to critical server
ip route 10.0.24.7 255.255.255.255 10.0.0.10 210
!
logging 10.0.130.50
access-list 102 deny    eigrp any any
access-list 102 permit ip any any
dialer-list 1 protocol ip list 102
!
end
```

LISTING **7-19.** *Spoke router with ISDN backup driven by loss of hub or critical server*

On the spoke, only the one *ip route* line highlighted in bold print in Listing 7-19 needs to be changed to provide critical server protection. We have added a floating static route so that any time we do not receive an explicit advertisement over the primary link for a route to the critical server, we bring up the ISDN backup link to attempt to reach the critical server that way.

The changes are equally minor on the primary hub router. As can be seen in Listing 7-20, the only change is to the access-list used to filter routing advertisements on the primary link (*interface Serial0.123*), which we adjust to allow through advertisements pointing to the critical server. No changes are required on the backup target router, so its listing is not shown.

When we use this approach, we do need to be diligent in managing the network, because any time the critical server or the site supporting it fails, all locations configured to dial around a server disconnection will place ISDN calls, which could get expensive if the situation is not detected and corrected. Should this occur, we can configure a loopback port on a convenient router with the address of the critical server. That way, spokes see the required address in the routing tables and do not force up the ISDN link in vain. Of course we do have to remember to remove the definition once the real server returns to operation.

This approach can also be applied to the more robust hub-and-spoke configurations used earlier, which provided multiple levels of dial backup to multiple hub backup routers. However, we should modify the approach slightly so that only those backup target routers that provide an adequately diverse path to the critical server

```
version 11.0
!
hostname Primary
!
interface Loopback0
 description Routing target address for Frame Relay users
 ip address 10.0.0.1 255.255.255.255
!
interface Ethernet0/0
 description Hub side connectivity not illustrated
!
interface Serial1/0
 no ip address
 encapsulation frame-relay
 frame-relay lmi-type ansi
!
interface Serial1/0.123 point-to-point
 description PVC to Spoke 123
 ip address 10.101.23.14 255.255.255.252
 bandwidth 56
 delay 2000
 frame-relay interface-dlci 123
!
! . . . Other Frame Relay subinterfaces go here
!
router eigrp 1
 network 10.0.0.0
 distribute-list 12 out Ethernet0/0
 distribute-list 12 out Ethernet0/1
 distribute-list 10 out Serial1/0.121
 distribute-list 10 out Serial1/0.122
 distribute-list 10 out Serial1/0.123
 ! . . . Filters for other Frame Relay subinterfaces go here
no auto-summary
 !
ip classless
access-list 10 permit 0.0.0.0
access-list 10 permit 10.0.0.1
access-list 10 permit 10.0.24.7
access-list 10 deny   any
access-list 12 deny   10.0.0.0 0.0.0.127
access-list 12 permit any
!
end
```

LISTING 7-20. *Primary hub router modifications for critical server protection*

are called. This can be done by defining floating static routes for an arbitrary artificial address and adding dialer maps pointing to that address for only the routers that provide diverse routing. The essential modifications for the spoke in Listing 7-19 are highlighted in Listing 7-21.

```
    •
    •
    •
!
interface BRI0
 ip unnumbered Loopback0
 encapsulation ppp
 bandwidth 56
 delay 5000
 no keepalive
 isdn spid1 21255501230000
 isdn spid2 21255510100000
 dialer idle-timeout 170
! Dialer maps for diverse routing to the critical server
 dialer map ip 10.0.0.7 name BackupSite speed 56 broadcast
    ➥ 18005551111
 dialer map ip 10.0.0.7 name BackupSite speed 56 broadcast
    ➥ 18005552222
! Dialer maps for backup protection
 dialer map ip 10.0.0.10 name PrimarySite speed 56 broadcast
    ➥ 18005558888
 dialer map ip 10.0.0.10 name BackupSite speed 56 broadcast
    ➥ 18005551111
 dialer map ip 10.0.0.10 name PrimarySite speed 56 broadcast
    ➥ 18005559999
 dialer map ip 10.0.0.10 name BackupSite speed 56 broadcast
    ➥ 18005552222
 dialer hold-queue 10
 dialer-group 1
 ppp authentication chap
!
router eigrp 1
 network 10.0.0.0
 distribute-list 2 in BRI0
 no auto-summary
!
```

(continued)

```
ip host TestISDN 10.0.0.3
ip classless
ip route 0.0.0.0 0.0.0.0 10.0.0.1 200 ! Use frame if up
ip route 0.0.0.0 0.0.0.0 10.0.0.10 210 ! Get backup link up
! ISDN to critical server
ip route 10.0.24.7 255.255.255.255 10.0.0.7 210
! Alternate route to critical server
ip route 10.0.0.7 255.255.255.255 BRIO
! Default dial backup route
ip route 10.0.0.10 255.255.255.255 BRIO
!
logging trap debugging
logging 10.0.130.50
access-list 2 permit 0.0.0.0
access-list 2 permit 10.0.0.10
access-list 2 permit 10.0.24.7
access-list 2 permit 10.0.0.2 0.0.0.1
access-list 2 deny any
   •
   •
   •
```

LISTING 7-21. *Spoke router with ISDN backup driven by loss of hub or critical server*

Note that we do not adjust the routing filter to allow in the target address used to bring up the diverse ISDN link. As soon as the link comes up and the routing protocol peering is established, packets destined for the critical server will use the dynamic routing protocol to find the best path, and the link will be utilized as appropriate. The artificial trigger address does not need to exist, even on the target router. When the link comes up, the PPP negotiates the 10.0.0.10 address for the hub end of the link and that dialer map will take over.

WRAP-UP

The hub-and-spoke network topology allows us to build very large networks with very small routers, but we have to understand the impact of the topology to take advantage of its benefits.

In a hub-and-spoke network, the only path from the spoke to anywhere else is through the link to the hub site, so we normally use default route advertisements and floating static routes to actually pick a path. We still, however, need to run a routing protocol with each spoke. This can introduce scaling challenges because modern routing protocols such as OSPF and EIGRP are optimized for complex mesh networks, limiting their ability to handle very large numbers of routers connecting to a single router.

We started the chapter with a look at how we could use the Cisco proprietary EIGRP protocol with aggressive route distribution filters to allow support for large hub-and-spoke networks. Then we looked at the alternative of using one protocol between the hub and the spokes and another routing protocol between the routers making up the hub site network by using RIPv2 and OSPF, respectively. By limiting the routing information exchanged between the hub and each spoke, we could efficiently use a protocol such as RIPv2, which would not stress the hub routers, regardless of the number of spokes supported by each. Redistributing the routes learned from RIPv2 into OSPF then allows the routers making up the hub site to efficiently utilize the highly redundant paths typical in that part of the network.

We then looked at how we could improve the availability experienced in a hub-and-spoke network using either multiple permanent links or dial backup. We showed how we could configure dial backup so that we could use simple dial-on-demand for dialing into any of several routers using the same configuration for all. Other dial backup solutions considered included placing both ISDN and Async calls without any aids, such as *dialer watch* or BGP, and using a single hub router to support both ISDN and Async dial-in calls from other routers on the same PRI line using digital modems.

We finished the chapter with a look at how we could modify dial backup from a spoke location to bypass a loss of connectivity within the logical hub.

NOTE

1. In a small hub-and-spoke environment where this limitation is acceptable, we could use OSPF everywhere and configure each spoke as a stub area.

Connecting to Service Providers

S o far in this book, communications have been confined to our own network and we have had control over all aspects of routing. In this chapter, we look at the challenges that emerge when we connect to other people's networks, whether that is a simple network connection to a specialized service provider or access to the Internet through one or more Internet Service Providers (ISPs).

As soon as we need connectivity outside our own network, we are into the realm of interdomain routing. No longer can we efficiently use intradomain routing protocols such as OSPF and EIGRP to provide optimal routing. Just as we run our network, other organizations run theirs, and we can not expect them to use the same routing metrics we are using in our network. Indeed, in many cases, such as when connecting to the Internet, we cannot trust the other network at all and must validate everything sent to us to protect ourselves from denial of service attacks and cyber breakins.

In this chapter, we limit the discussion to TCP/IP because the only other network protocol architectures that even attempt to address interdomain routing are the OSI protocol suite and the IBM Systems Network Architecture (SNA). We ignore the former because the solutions are conceptually identical to those used for TCP/IP (but usually simpler because interdomain routing requirements are built into standard OSI network addresses). We ignore the latter because SNA solutions are unique to networks of multiple IBM mainframes.

If we are using private RFC 1918 IP addresses, we might also find that we need to use Network Address Translation (NAT) to successfully communicate. If security dictates the use of firewalls for protection, this function usually is provided by the firewall. However, it also can be implemented in the routers where it may also be called Port and Address Translation (PAT), a more accurate description of the full functionality normally required.

We will start this chapter looking at solutions appropriate for tying two independent networks together, such as when connecting to a specialized service provided by another organization. The assumption is that the routing requirements are simple enough that all routing in both directions can be handled with simple static routes.

We will then turn our attention to connecting to the Internet and the unique requirements for reliable connectivity to Internet Service Providers. We start with a single connection to a single ISP, and then add more connections to the same ISP. We finish the chapter by looking at multiple connections to multiple ISPs, with and without the use of BGP.

LINKING TO AN EXTERNAL NETWORK

We will look first at techniques to provide high availability connectivity to a single other routing domain. This is the challenge usually faced when an organization needs online access to the services provided by a specialized service provider. It also can occur during a corporate merger, in which the independently designed networks of the merging companies suddenly need to interconnect before a unified network can be designed and implemented.

In this environment, we will look at three different solution scenarios that deal with increasing levels of difficulty in providing reliable access through redundant communications links. We will start with the easiest mode of redundant operation, the use of redundant static routes. We will follow it with two additional scenarios, one for when we can not safely assume that link failures are reliably reported at the link level, and one for when the physical diversity at the user site can lead to segmentation of the internal network so that some users must use a specific link even though more than one is connected. In this situation, we need a way to force the service provider to return the packets through the same path used to reach them, even if it is not the "best" path available.

For the sake of providing an example, we will use the scenario in Figure 8-1, where a retail chain using a hub-and-spokes architecture has a leased line to the credit card approval service from their corporate headquarters. This is done in lieu of having each card reader independently dial an 800 number. This improves service and reduces costs by eliminating the 30-second delay per transaction while the call is placed and the modems negotiate a connection.

Although internal network redundancy is not illustrated, assume that the internal reliability and redundancy are adequate to meet all availability requirements. In this chapter, we will ignore the internal architecture except where it may affect external connectivity.

Our key assumption for now is that we are connecting to a domain with a limited number of well-defined network addresses from a domain that also features a well-defined range of addresses. Typically, these network connections are configured with static routes for simplicity, along with packet filters to block any traffic

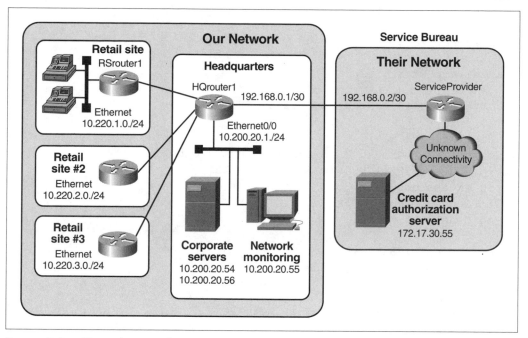

FIGURE 8-1. *Typical external service provider scenario*

that is not from a legitimate user and to an authorized destination. These blocks are not only to protect the service bureau, but also to isolate one client from another. After all, the service bureau is in business to provide their services, not to provide connectivity between their clients or to serve as a conduit for computer espionage.

By the same token, the user of the service should also implement filters for protection from traffic from the service bureau. In this example scenario, while we want to be able to monitor the status of the external credit card server from the internal network management system at IP address 10.200.20.55 on the corporate headquarters local area network (LAN), we do not want to expose our valuable trade secrets residing on other systems on the same LAN.

The configuration in Listing 8-1 for router HQrouter1 shows the crucial details of a typical implementation that might be used to meet this simple service scenario. Notice how both sides are totally independent of the other side's internal implementation details. The configuration of the interface itself is no different from an internal link, although we are more likely to use standard rather than proprietary link protocols and features. A quick count of configuration lines is revealing—four lines to define the interface, two lines to advertise it so we can use it, and fourteen lines to protect it.

```
version 12.0
!
hostname HQrouter1
!
ip subnet-zero
!
interface Ethernet0/0
 description HQ LAN
 ip address 10.200.20.1 255.255.255.0
!
interface Serial0/0
 description Credit Card Service Bureau Connection
 ip address 192.168.0.1 255.255.255.252
 ip access-group 101 out
 ip access-group 102 in
 bandwidth 56
!
router ospf 123
 redistribute static subnets
 network 10.200.20.0 0.0.0.255 area 1
!
ip route 172.17.30.55 255.255.255.255 Serial0/0
!
access-list 101 permit tcp 10.220.0.30 0.0.255.1 host
 ➡ 172.17.30.55 eq 3306
access-list 101 permit tcp 10.220.0.32 0.0.255.15 host
 ➡ 172.17.30.55 eq 3306
access-list 101 permit tcp 10.220.0.48 0.0.255.1 host
 ➡ 172.17.30.55 eq 3306
access-list 101 permit icmp host 10.200.0.55 host 172.17.30.55
access-list 101 permit udp host 10.200.0.55 host 172.17.30.55
access-list 101 deny    ip any any log
!
access-list 102 permit tcp host 172.17.30.55 eq 3306
 ➡ 10.220.0.30 0.0.255.1 established
access-list 102 permit tcp host 172.17.30.55 eq 3306
 ➡ 10.220.0.32 0.0.255.15 established
access-list 102 permit tcp host 172.17.30.55 eq 3306
 ➡ 10.220.0.48 0.0.255.1 established
access-list 102 permit icmp host 172.17.30.55 host 10.200.0.55
access-list 102 permit icmp 192.168.0.0 0.0.0.3 host
 ➡ 10.200.0.55
access-list 102 deny    ip any any log
!
end
```

LISTING 8-1.   *User router HQrouter1 configuration for the baseline service access scenario*

Although often neglected in the rush to get a new service up and running, this listing reflects a serious effort to provide real security at the interface with the service bureau. The application service is provided by a system at IP address 172.17.30.55 using TCP to port 3306. The application is used only by the cash registers at each retail site. Each retail site is assigned a 256-address subnetwork block from the 10.220.0.0 subnetwork, and all registers are assigned addresses between 10.220.xx.30 and 10.220.xx.49 inclusive. The first three lines of access-list 101 therefore prevent access to the credit card verification service from any systems with an IP address outside the range reserved at each store for cash registers. Then the access-list restricts even the cash register access to just the one application program on that service provider platform.

The next two lines of access-list 101 allow the network monitoring system to use *ping* and *traceroute* to the credit card verification server to verify that it is accessible. The final line of access-list 101 appears to duplicate the default clause appended to all Cisco access-lists, which is a denial of any access not explicitly permitted. We need to include it because the default *deny any* does not include the *log* keyword to cause any packets that meet the specified condition to be logged. In this access-list, we do not bother logging expected traffic, but we do want a record of any attempts to send traffic that is not authorized. This is an essential part of any security barrier, as otherwise perpetrators can just keep on trying until they find a weakness that can be exploited. By logging violations and routinely checking the log for any violations, we have a chance of detecting and deterring a breakthrough attempt before it succeeds.

Note that access-list 101 is on the outbound traffic and protects the service provider rather than us. This guards against our being used as a base for attacks on the service provider's systems. Since we can not expect the service provider to be privy to our internal addressing conventions, we can assign a much tighter filter without fear of interfering with production traffic.

We protect ourselves from the service provider (and their other clients) with access-list 102. This access-list is a mirror image of access-list 101 with one exception. Unlike access-list 101, the *established* keyword appended to the first three lines of this access-list allows only the TCP connection establishment handshake to be initiated by the cash registers. This protects our cash registers from attacks from a compromised system at the service provider pretending to be the credit card verification server. It does not, however, protect the cash registers from attacks that come in the form of packets that appear to be part of the data stream in a correctly initiated credit card verification transaction. That requires appropriate software checks, such as boundary checking to prevent buffer overflows, in the application software.

Even though some versions of *traceroute* send UDP packets, and others send ICMP packets, all versions depend on ICMP packets coming back to show the route taken. Therefore there is no need to expose our network monitor to incoming UDP traffic, but we do want to see the ICMP packets coming back from the router on the other side of the link so that we can verify that the link is functional. We cannot simply *ping* the service bureau's router because its address is not advertised as reachable from our internal network. However, we can always Telnet to router HQrouter1 and *ping* from there if we need to, since packets sourced by a router are not subject to outbound filters. As with the outgoing access-list, we also add to the end of the list an explicit deny with logging of everything not already permitted to warn us of invalid access attempts.

The actual communications are handled by the static route, which says to send any packets for the credit card server out the serial port connecting to the service provider. Because this is the only route to the credit card service bureau, the inflexibility of a static route is not a problem. To avoid the need to install static routes everywhere in order to communicate with the remote server, we redistribute the static route into OSPF.

The service bureau side of the link in Listing 8-2 is much simpler, but it also illustrates some common challenges. Notice that the service bureau is running an old release of Cisco's IOS in a class-based environment. This is common because there is strong reluctance to upgrade or replace functional systems, particularly when the

```
version 10.3
!
hostname ServiceProvider
!
ip subnet-zero
!
interface Ethernet0/0
 description Service Distribution LAN
 ip address 172.18.0.1 255.255.0.0
!
!... links to other clients
!
interface Serial3/4
 description Link to client: Example Retail
 ip address 192.168.0.2 255.255.255.252
 ip access-group 101 in
 bandwidth 56
!
router rip
 redistribute static
 network 172.18.0.0
```
                                                        (continued)

```
!
ip route 10.0.0.0 255.0.0.0 Serial3/4
!
access-list 101 permit ip 10.0.0.0 0.255.255.255 172.17.0.0
 ➥ 0.0.255.255
!
end
```

LISTING 8-2.   *Service bureau router ServiceProvider configuration for the baseline service access scenario*

expertise required to do so is not maintained in house. The lack of security filtering also might be considered distressing, because the only check made is to verify that incoming traffic is from a network that is supposed to be on the other end of the link and that is destined to the service provider's service network.

On the other hand, remember that we have no knowledge of the service provider's internal connectivity, and it is just as likely that this router, and the LAN to which it attaches, is dedicated to us and merely serves as a front end to the firewall that provides the real protection of the service provider's assets. The only thing we can say for certain regarding the security or the level of sophistication of this service provider is that it does not care about the security of our network and it assumes that to the extent that we do care, we will configure our end of the link accordingly (which, in this example, is exactly the situation).

The challenge we face with this configuration is the lack of redundancy in our connection with the service provider. In many ways, the situation is very similar to what we faced in the previous chapter when we looked at hub-and-spoke networks, except now the headquarters router is the spoke and the service provider is the hub. The key is that both ends of the link service well-defined address communities with no useful alternate paths available. Just as we did with the spokes in a hub-and-spoke network, we can provide alternate redundant paths between us and the service provider without implementing a fully integrated routing protocol.

CONFIGURATION EXAMPLE: REDUNDANT STATIC ROUTES

If we can assume that the physical state of the link at each end of the link accurately reflects the end-to-end status of the link, we can provide high availability redundancy using simple static routes. This mode of operation is normally possible only if the communications are provided by dedicated point-to-point leased lines. If a network service such as ATM or Frame Relay is used for the communications link, this approach often will seem to function initially, but as we have discussed in previous chapters, the fact that not all failure modes are immediately signaled to both ends

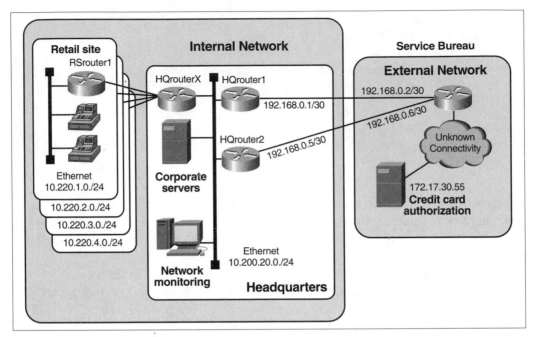

FIGURE 8-2. *Redundant connectivity to service provider*

of every virtual circuit affected will ultimately lead to erratic operation and unnecessary downtime.

To see how it works, consider the connectivity in Figure 8-2, where we have expanded the scenario of Figure 8-1 to provide redundant links from the corporate headquarters to the external service provider. We terminate the links on independent routers on the internal network but leave them both on the same router on the external network so that we can see both modes of configuration. The actual choice of one versus two routers would depend on their reliability and the availability goals for the connection. However, keep in mind that a second router makes life much easier for the network support staff when they need to maintain and upgrade the equipment.

The configuration of router HQrouter1 in Listing 8-3 is identical to the single link configuration in Listing 8-1 with one exception. Instead of using the default

```
version 11.0
!
hostname HQrouter1
!
ip subnet-zero
!
```
                                                                    (continued)

```
interface Ethernet0/0
 description HQ LAN
 ip address 10.200.20.1 255.255.255.0
!
interface Serial0/0
 description Credit Card Services Primary Connection
 ip address 192.168.0.1 255.255.255.252
 ip access-group 101 in
 ip access-group 102 out
 bandwidth 56
!
router ospf 123
 redistribute static metric 20 metric-type 2 subnets
 network 10.200.20.0 0.0.0.255 area 1
!
ip route 172.17.30.55 255.255.255.255 Serial0/0
!
access-list 101 permit tcp host 172.17.30.55 eq 3306
 ➥ 10.220.0.30 0.0.255.1 established
access-list 101 permit tcp host 172.17.30.55 eq 3306
 ➥ 10.220.0.32 0.0.255.15 established
access-list 101 permit tcp host 172.17.30.55 eq 3306
 ➥ 10.220.0.48 0.0.255.1 established
access-list 101 permit icmp host 172.17.30.55 host
 ➥ 10.200.20.55
access-list 101 permit icmp 192.168.0.0 0.0.0.3 host
 ➥ 10.200.20.55
access-list 101 deny   ip any any log
!
access-list 102 permit tcp 10.220.0.30 0.0.255.1 host
 ➥ 172.17.30.55 eq 3306
access-list 102 permit tcp 10.220.0.32 0.0.255.15 host
 ➥ 172.17.30.55 eq 3306
access-list 102 permit tcp 10.220.0.48 0.0.255.1 host
 ➥ 172.17.30.55 eq 3306
access-list 102 permit icmp host 10.200.20.55 host 172.17.30.55

access-list 102 permit udp host 10.200.20.55 host 172.17.30.55
access-list 102 deny   ip any any log
!
end
```

LISTING 8-3. *Router HQrouter1 configuration for redundant service access using static routing*

metric assignment for redistributing the route to the credit card network into OSPF, we explicitly define the metric to be used for the distribution. We do this even when we are setting the metric to the values set by default for two reasons. Why? First, it makes it clear what the values are so that we can easily see how the network is designed to operate. Second, and more important, it protects us from future problems if the primary router is upgraded or replaced and the replacement IOS uses a different default value. In an emergency replacement scenario, this can make the difference between a simple swap and a change that takes hours to debug and fix.

The router HQrouter2 configuration in Listing 8-4 is very similar. The addresses on the Ethernet and serial interfaces must change to match the addresses used for the new connections. We must also modify the access-list entries used for network monitoring, which allow access to the link.

We also need to make a choice regarding load balancing when both links are operational. As configured, both links have identical metrics, so router HQrouterX connecting to the retail sites could choose either connecting router for forwarding packets destined for the service provider. By default, a Cisco router will use fast-switching, which load balances on a per destination basis. Since there is only a single target IP address, only one of the two routes would be used and the other would sit idle. If we wanted packet-by-packet load balancing, we would need to disable fast-switching on the headquarters LAN side of the router using the *no ip route-cache* statement on all interfaces connecting to routers HQrouter1 and HQrouter2. The tradeoff is that this would cause all store traffic headed to other systems on the LAN, including the corporate servers, to be process-switched. Process-switching is much more processor intensive and may not be supportable, depending on the router and possible peak traffic loading.

Another alternative available on high-end Cisco router models equipped with route-switch processors (and in lower end models in newer IOS releases) is Cisco Express Forwarding (CEF). Enabling CEF with the *ip cef* command allows us to enable per-packet load balancing on desired interfaces using the *ip load-sharing per-packet* command. This can provide the benefits of per-packet load sharing without giving up the efficiency of route caching. Remember, however, that load sharing does not work if it requires sending packets back out the same interface from which they arrived.

We can also achieve a degree of load balancing while using fast switching by connecting the retail sites directly to the outbound routers.

```
version 11.0
!
hostname HQrouter2
!
```
(continued)

```
interface Ethernet0/0
 description HQ LAN
 ip address 10.200.20.2 255.255.255.0
!
interface Serial0/0
 description Credit Card Services Secondary Connection
 ip address 192.168.0.5 255.255.255.252
 ip access-group 101 in
 ip access-group 102 out
 bandwidth 56
!
router ospf 123
 redistribute static metric 20 metric-type 2 subnets
 network 10.200.20.0 0.0.0.255 area 1
!
ip route 172.17.30.55 255.255.255.255 Serial0/0
!
access-list 101 permit tcp host 172.17.30.55 eq 3306
➥ 10.220.0.30 0.0.255.1 established
access-list 101 permit tcp host 172.17.30.55 eq 3306
➥ 10.220.0.32 0.0.255.15 established
access-list 101 permit tcp host 172.17.30.55 eq 3306
➥ 10.220.0.48 0.0.255.1 established
access-list 101 permit icmp host 172.17.30.55 host
➥ 10.200.20.55
access-list 101 permit icmp 192.168.0.4 0.0.0.3 host
➥ 10.200.20.55
access-list 101 deny    ip any any log
!
access-list 102 permit tcp 10.220.0.30 0.0.255.1 host
➥ 172.17.30.55 eq 3306
access-list 102 permit tcp 10.220.0.32 0.0.255.15 host
➥ 172.17.30.55 eq 3306
access-list 102 permit tcp 10.220.0.48 0.0.255.1 host
➥ 172.17.30.55 eq 3306
access-list 102 permit icmp host 10.200.20.55 host
➥ 172.17.30.55
access-list 102 permit udp host 10.200.20.55 host 172.17.30.55
access-list 102 deny    ip any any log
!
end
```

LISTING 8-4. *Router HQrouter2 configuration for redundant service access using static routing*

Shifting our attention over to the service bureau end of the link, the critical aspects of that configuration are provided in Listing 8-5. Even though we have a single point of failure in using a single router, we reduce our exposure slightly by configuring each link on a different serial interface card.

```
version 10.3
!
hostname ServiceBureau
!
ip subnet-zero
!
interface Ethernet0/0
 description Service Distribution LAN
 ip address 172.18.0.1 255.255.0.0
!
... links to other clients
!
interface Serial2/7
 description Link 1 of 2 to client: Example Retail
 ip address 192.168.0.6 255.255.255.252
 ip access-group 101 in
 bandwidth 56
!
interface Serial3/4
 description Link to 2 of 2 client: Example Retail
 ip address 192.168.0.2 255.255.255.252
 ip access-group 101 in
 bandwidth 56
!
router rip
 redistribute static
 network 172.18.0.0
!
ip route 10.0.0.0 255.0.0.0 Serial2/7
ip route 10.0.0.0 255.0.0.0 Serial3/4
!
access-list 101 permit ip 10.0.0.0 0.255.255.255 172.17.0.0
➥ 0.0.255.255
!
end
```

LISTING 8-5. *Service provider side router configuration for redundant service access using static routing*

```
ip route 10.0.0.0 255.0.0.0 Serial3/4
ip route 10.0.0.0 255.0.0.0 Serial2/7 200
```

LISTING 8-6.   *Adjustment to router ServiceProvider to use backup link only if primary link is down*

Load balancing, if desired, is much easier for this side because there are many different IP addresses accessing the server. As a result, per-destination load balancing will normally be sufficient.

If we have one fast link and one slow link, we would not use load balancing. Instead, we would change the static route pointing to the slow link into a floating static route to prevent it from being used while the better link is up. For example, if the link to *Serial2/7* was for backup use only, we would change the static routes associating our retail network with that interface to read as in Listing 8-6.

It takes more effort to make the links primary and secondary on the internal network configuration. If all store packets heading for the service bureau come through the third headquarters router, we need only to adjust the metric used in the redistribution statement into OSPF to direct other routers to send their traffic to the router with the primary path. However, we need to be careful because if any links from the stores connect directly to the router with the backup link, the static route defining access through the connected link will override any OSPF alternate route selection, because a static route to a connected link in the up state is considered a connected destination and available indirect routes are not even considered before the packet is forwarded.

We can get around this limitation by using a floating static route on the backup router with an administrative distance greater than the OSPF external route learned from the primary router. That way, the backup route is activated only if no route to the credit card server is learned from OSPF. Once activated, the backup route will itself be redistributed into OSPF so that other systems on the network can learn of its presence.

CONFIGURATION EXAMPLE: STATIC ROUTES DRIVEN BY AN IGP

If the primary link in Figure 8-2 is through a Frame Relay, DSL, or ATM network rather than a direct point-to-point leased line connection, we can no longer depend on the link level going down at both ends whenever the link is incapable of carrying traffic. Under these conditions, we can use a routing protocol to detect link failure so that the alternate route can be used. It is not sufficient to merely have two equal static routes, because the link that fails can become a black hole, preventing traffic from reaching the service provider (or returning, depending on the mode of failure).

The specific routing protocol used is usually not a significant factor, because we do not want to use it for routing. We want only to be able to determine the state of the links so that we can activate the appropriate static routes. This allows us to select any routing protocol that provides sufficient configuration options to meet our needs and with which all parties responsible for the configuration at each end of the link can feel comfortable.

As a general rule, the choice will usually come down to either Routing Information Protocol version 2 (RIPv2) or EIGRP, for the reasons we preferred these two protocols when setting up a hub-and-spoke configuration. Both provide the ability to filter advertisements to minimize overhead, and neither is CPU-intensive in this application.

In this case, since the service provider network is already using RIP, we must be careful to avoid undesired redistribution of routing information, so our preference is to use EIGRP. While it would be possible to use RIP, it would be much more difficult because Cisco supports only a single RIP process on a router. So we would have to depend on distribution list filters to keep the two routing domains separated. In the scenario we have selected, the difficulty would be compounded by the lack of support for RIPv2 in IOS release 10.3 (RIPv2 requires at least IOS release 11.2).

The configuration of the interfaces (other than changing the mode of operation of *Serial0/0* from point-to-point to Frame Relay) and the configuration of the internal OSPF routing is untouched. The definition of packet filters for protection is also unchanged except for an added permit line to open up the inbound access-list (101) to allow routing exchanges to get in. The critical change is in the target address used to trigger the static route that is to be redistributed by OSPF. Rather than aiming it at the serial interface, we aim it at an IP address that will be known only if we can learn of it from the router on the other end of the link. It is essential that it not be associated with any interface on the local router, since we cannot depend on the local interface going down when the link is not operational. In Listing 8-7, we base our route to the service provider on the advertisement for 192.168.0.8, a loopback port on the remote router. Similarly, we define a loopback port locally that we can advertise to the service provider over EIGRP so that it will know that the link to us is operational.

EIGRP network statements use class-based address boundaries to decide what addresses to advertise. Consequently, the configuration line *network 192.168.0.0* is sufficient to both enable EIGRP on the serial link and include the loopback interface address in routing advertisements sent over that link. If there were other interfaces assigned addresses in the same class C address range, we would need to filter the advertisements with *distribute-list out* statements and prevent running EIGRP where not desired with *passive-interface* statements. We leave the EIGRP hello interval and hold time at their default values of 5 and 15 seconds to minimize overhead. If availability requirements dictated, these could be reduced to detect link failure more quickly, but since static routes are only updated once per minute unless an interface changes state, the overall impact would be negligible.

```
version 11.0
!
hostname HQrouter1
!
ip subnet-zero
!
interface Loopback1
 description Target for Service Provider Routing
 ip address 192.168.0.10 255.255.255.255
!
interface Ethernet0/0
 description HQ LAN
 ip address 10.200.20.1 255.255.255.0
!
interface Serial0/0
 no ip address
 encapsulation frame-relay
!
interface Serial0/0.1 point-to-point
 description Credit Card Services Primary Connection
 ip address 192.168.0.1 255.255.255.252
 ip access-group 101 in
 ip access-group 102 out
 bandwidth 56
 frame-relay interface-dlci 111 broadcast
!
router eigrp 321
 network 192.168.0.0
!
router ospf 123
 redistribute static metric 20 metric-type 2 subnets
 network 10.200.20.0 0.0.0.255 area 1
!
ip route 172.17.30.55 255.255.255.255 192.168.0.8
!
access-list 101 permit tcp host 172.17.30.55 eq 3306
 ➥ 10.220.0.30 0.0.255.1 established
access-list 101 permit tcp host 172.17.30.55 eq 3306
 ➥ 10.220.0.32 0.0.255.15 established
access-list 101 permit tcp host 172.17.30.55 eq 3306
 ➥ 10.220.0.48 0.0.255.1 established
access-list 101 permit eigrp host 192.168.0.2 any
access-list 101 permit icmp host 172.17.30.55 host
 ➥ 10.200.20.55
```

(*continued*)

```
access-list 101 permit icmp 192.168.0.0 0.0.0.3 host
➡ 10.200.20.55
access-list 101 deny    ip any any log
!
access-list 102 permit tcp 10.220.0.30 0.0.255.1 host
➡ 172.17.30.55 eq 3306
access-list 102 permit tcp 10.220.0.32 0.0.255.15 host
➡ 172.17.30.55 eq 3306
access-list 102 permit tcp 10.220.0.48 0.0.255.1 host
➡ 172.17.30.55 eq 3306
access-list 102 permit icmp host 10.200.20.55 host
➡ 172.17.30.55
access-list 102 permit udp host 10.200.20.55 host 172.17.30.55
access-list 102 deny    ip any any log
!
end
```

LISTING 8-7. *Router HQrouter1 configuration for redundant service access using dynamically driven static routing*

The backup router (Listing 8-8) gets the same modifications. In this version, we configure for equal-cost-path load sharing, and there is no problem reusing the same target address at the service provider because we do not redistribute it into OSPF. In terms of load balancing and configuring for primary/standby routes, this dynamically driven configuration behaves exactly like the static configuration in the previous example. The only difference is that we drive the static routes using addresses learned through the dynamic routing protocol running between the two sites rather than the state of the interfaces themselves.

The loopback addresses that serve as our routing targets, as well as the interface addresses, are not part of the network domain of either the internal or external networks. However, as was the case with the interface addresses when we used simple static routes, we may choose to advertise the interface addresses internally to simplify network management, in which case we also would need to modify the access-lists to allow access. Since we are using OSPF for our internal network, all we need to do is add the line *network 192.168.0.4 0.0.0.3 area 1* under *router ospf 123*.

The changes on the server side in Listing 8-9 are somewhat more extensive because the subnetworks used for the links and targets are from the same class C network used for other clients. As a result, the service provider should filter outgoing advertisements (because we do not care about the status of any links or loopbacks other than ours) and must filter incoming advertisements to protect their other clients from any routes we inadvertently advertise that belong to other clients.

```
version 11.0
!
hostname HQrouter2
!
interface Loopback1
 description Target for Service Provider Routing
 ip address 192.168.0.11 255.255.255.255
!
interface Ethernet0/0
 description HQ LAN
 ip address 10.200.20.2 255.255.255.0
!
interface Serial0/0
 no ip address
 encapsulation frame-relay
!
interface Serial0/0.1 point-to-point
 description Credit Card Services Secondary Connection
 ip address 192.168.0.5 255.255.255.252
 ip access-group 101 in
 ip access-group 102 out
 bandwidth 56
 frame-relay interface-dlci 111 broadcast
!
router eigrp 321
 network 192.168.0.0
!
router ospf 123
 redistribute static metric 20 metric-type 2 subnets
 network 10.200.20.0 0.0.0.255 area 1
!
ip route 172.17.30.55 255.255.255.255 192.168.0.8
!
access-list 101 permit tcp host 172.17.30.55 eq 3306
  ➥ 10.220.0.30 0.0.255.1 established
access-list 101 permit tcp host 172.17.30.55 eq 3306
  ➥ 10.220.0.32 0.0.255.15 established
access-list 101 permit tcp host 172.17.30.55 eq 3306
  ➥ 10.220.0.48 0.0.255.1 established
access-list 101 permit eigrp host 192.168.0.6 any
access-list 101 permit icmp host 172.17.30.55 host
  ➥ 10.200.20.55
```

(continued)

```
access-list 101 permit icmp 192.168.0.0 0.0.0.3 host
➡ 10.200.20.55
access-list 101 deny    ip any any log
!
access-list 102 permit tcp 10.220.0.30 0.0.255.1 host
➡ 172.17.30.55 eq 3306
access-list 102 permit tcp 10.220.0.32 0.0.255.15 host
➡ 172.17.30.55 eq 3306
access-list 102 permit tcp 10.220.0.48 0.0.255.1 host
➡ 172.17.30.55 eq 3306
access-list 102 permit icmp host 10.200.20.55 host
➡ 172.17.30.55
access-list 102 permit udp host 10.200.20.55 host
➡ 172.17.30.55
access-list 102 deny    ip any any log
!
end
```

LISTING 8-8. *Router HQrouter2 configuration for redundant service access using dynamically driven static routing*

```
version 10.3
!
hostname ServiceProvider
!
ip subnet-zero
!
interface Loopback1
 description Target for Retail Client Routing
 ip address 192.168.0.8 255.255.255.255
!
interface Ethernet0/0
 description Service Distribution LAN
 ip address 172.18.0.1 255.255.0.0
!
interface Serial2/7
 no ip address
 encapsulation frame-relay
!
interface Serial2/7.1 point-to-point
 description Link to client: Example Retail
 ip address 192.168.0.6 255.255.255.252
```

(continued)

```
  ip access-group 101 in
  bandwidth 56
  frame-relay interface-dlci 271 broadcast
!
interface Serial3/4
 no ip address
 encapsulation frame-relay
!
interface Serial3/4.1 point-to-point
 description Link to client: Example Retail
 ip address 192.168.0.2 255.255.255.252
 ip access-group 101 in
 bandwidth 56
 frame-relay interface-dlci 341 broadcast
!
router eigrp 321
 network 192.168.0.0
 distribute-list 1 out Serial2/7.1
 distribute-list 1 in Serial2/7.1
 distribute-list 1 out Serial3/4.1
 distribute-list 1 in Serial3/4.1
!
router rip
 redistribute static
 network 172.18.0.0
!
ip route 10.0.0.0 255.0.0.0 192.168.0.10
ip route 10.0.0.0 255.0.0.0 192.168.0.11
!
access-list 1 permit 192.168.0.0 0.0.0.7
access-list 1 permit 192.168.0.8 0.0.0.3
!
access-list 101 permit ip 10.0.0.0 0.255.255.255 172.17.0.0
 ➡ 0.0.255.255
access-list 101 permit eigrp 192.168.0.0 0.0.0.255 any
!
end
```

LISTING 8-9. *Service bureau router configuration for redundant service access using dynamically driven static routing*

CONFIGURATION EXAMPLE: PRIMARY PATH WITH DIAL BACKUP

We mentioned that routing changes are required to set up the links as a primary and a secondary rather than as two equal links. The same changes allow us to make the secondary link a dial backup rather than an idle dedicated link. The network picture remains identical, so let's look at the configuration changes required to make it happen.

The configuration of the primary client router that has the preferred link to the service provider is unchanged. If its link is up to the service provider, then the router advertises the service address into OSPF. All changes required to provide dial backup (or for that matter, any less preferred backup route) are on the secondary router in Listing 8-10. Note that we do not show the access-lists for security protection in the listing because they are unchanged.

```
version 11.2
!
hostname HQrouter2
!
username ServiceProvider password sharedsecret
isdn switch-type basic-ni1
!
interface Loopback1
 description Target for Service Provider Routing
 ip address 192.168.0.11 255.255.255.255
!
interface Ethernet0/0
 description HQ LAN
 ip address 10.200.20.2 255.255.255.0
!
interface BRI0
 no ip address
 encapsulation ppp
 isdn spid1 21255512120101
 isdn spid2 21255512130101
 dialer pool-member 11
 ppp authentication chap
!
interface Dialer1
 description Dial Out to Service Provider
 ip 192.168.0.5 255.255.255.252
 ip access-group 101 in
 ip access-group 102 out
```

(continued)

```
 encapsulation ppp
 no ip route-cache
 dialer remote-name ServiceProvider
 dialer string 19735551212
 dialer hold-queue 10
 dialer pool 11
 dialer-group 1
 ppp authentication chap
!
router ospf 123
 redistribute static metric 100 metric-type 2 subnets
 network 10.200.20.0 0.0.0.255 area 1
!
ip route 172.17.30.55 255.255.255.255 192.168.0.6 200
!
! access-lists for security (101 and 102) go here
!
dialer-list 1 protocol ip permit
!
end
```

LISTING 8-10. *Router HQrouter2 configuration for access with dial backup to a private service provider*

There are three key modifications aside from those required to physically change the Frame Relay link into a dial-up link. Two are in the static route, which defines the path to the credit card authorization server. The route is now a floating static route, so if a route to the server is learned through OSPF (which will be the case anytime the primary link is available), this route will be suppressed and this router will not advertise a route to the server into OSPF. In addition, we target the static route to the physical interface on the other side of the link rather than to the learned address because we need the route to be activated for traffic to be sent to this router to bring up the dial link.

Finally, we increase the metric on the static route we inject into OSPF. That way, as soon as the primary router's circuit is restored and it resumes advertising its route to the service bureau, other routers will start sending all traffic to it. This can speed up convergence in the OSPF area because other routers will start sending their traffic to the primary link without waiting for the secondary link to disappear. However, in a large OSPF network, we may prefer to keep the metrics the same so that the routing updates do not need to be propagated outside the area.

IOS 11.2 is required because we chose to use dialer profiles in this example implementation. We disable fast-switching (*no ip route ??due?*) to work around an

IOS implementation defect that causes erratic forwarding delays when a dialer is used without a virtual interface.

The router at the service bureau similarly requires minor adjustments in addition to adding dial-in support. The configuration in Listing 8-11 assumes an ISDN Basic Rate Interface (BRI) line is used at this end as well. As we have seen in the chapters on dial backup, the changes for a Primary Rate Interface (PRI) or even an analog line are minor and irrelevant to the functioning of our solution.

```
version 10.3
!
hostname ServiceProvider
!
username HQrouter2 password sharedsecret
isdn switch-type basic-5ess
ip subnet-zero
!
interface Loopback1
 description Target for Retail Client Routing
 ip address 192.168.0.8 255.255.255.255
!
interface Ethernet0/0
 description Service Distribution LAN
 ip address 172.18.0.1 255.255.0.0
!
interface Serial2/7
 no ip address
 encapsulation frame-relay
!
interface Serial2/7.1 point-to-point
 description Primary Link to client: Example Retail
 ip address 192.168.0.2 255.255.255.252
 ip access-group 101 in
 frame-relay interface-dlci 271 broadcast
!
interface BRI3/0
 description Dial Backup Link to client: Example Retail
 ip 192.168.0.6 255.255.255.252
 ip access-group 101 in
 encapsulation ppp
 dialer map ip 192.168.0.5 name HQrouter2 broadcast
 dialer hold-queue 10
 dialer-group 1
```

(continued)

```
   isdu caller 2125551212
   ppp authentication chap
 !
router eigrp 321
 passive-interface BRI3/0
 network 192.168.0.0
 distribute-list 1 out Serial2/7.1
 distribute-list 1 in Serial2/7.1
 !
router rip
 network 172.18.0.0
 redistribute static
 !
ip route 10.0.0.0 255.0.0.0 192.168.0.10 190
ip route 10.0.0.0 255.0.0.0 192.168.0.5 200
 !
access-list 1 permit 192.168.0.0 0.0.0.7
access-list 1 permit 192.168.0.8 0.0.0.3
 !
access-list 101 permit ip 10.0.0.0 0.255.255.255 172.17.0.0
 ➥ 0.0.255.255
access-list 101 permit eigrp 192.168.0.0 0.0.0.255 any
 !
dialer-list 1 protocol ip permit
 !
end
```

LISTING 8-11. *Service bureau router configuration for dial backup support*

Since we are running IOS 10.3, we must use legacy dialer maps rather than the dialer profiles used on the calling side. We verify also the calling phone number (the *isdn caller* line) before we even answer an incoming call. As is typical in security considerations, we must trade off protection (only accept calls from a specific number) with convenience (temporarily fixing an ISDN line problem at the headquarters site by swapping the current line with a functional line will not work until the configuration is also changed on the service bureau end).

Because EIGRP network statements use default IP class assignments, we disable EIGRP exchanges on the dial-up link using the *passive interface* command. Although not mandatory, it does prevent the addition of EIGRP overhead to the traffic on the ISDN line.

Like the headquarters side, the routing decision for selecting the link to use for return traffic is done by the floating static routes. If the primary link is up and EIGRP has established a neighbor relationship with HQrouter1 and learned a route to 192.168.0.10, that route becomes the active static route for all traffic to 10.0.0.0.

Any time that there is no route to 192.168.0.10, that static route will be disabled and the static route through 192.168.0.5, the ISDN link, will float to the top and become the active route to 10.0.0.0. Since there is no number to dial in the dialer map, we must wait for the incoming call to provide the physical connection.

CONFIGURATION EXAMPLE: USING NAT TO ROUTE RETURN TRAFFIC

When we progress to the point where we need greater physical diversity in our internal network connections to outside services, we can run into a problem. Consider what happens when we move the router with the backup connection from the headquarters building to another site, as in Figure 8-3. While this provides us with continued services even if we lose the headquarters building, it can also introduce new problems against which we must guard.

For example, assume the configuration of the retail sites to be a classic hub-and-spoke network in which the spokes have no knowledge of the topology of the hubs. An infrastructure failure that completely disrupted connectivity between the headquarters data center and the backup data center (shown as a single link in our diagram even though it is almost certainly multiple, diverse links) would effectively split our internal network into two independent, disconnected networks, one centered around the headquarters building and one centered around the backup data center.

In this environment, a failure of the link between any retail site and the headquarters, which would force the store to resort to its backup data center link, would

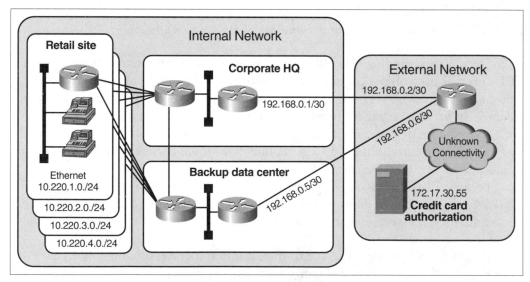

FIGURE 8-3. *Allowing independent use of alternate paths*

result in an environment in which stores still had physical connectivity to the credit card service bureau but an inability to complete transactions. To see why this is the case, consider the situation in Figure 8-4, where we break the link between the two hub sites and the link between the top store (IP network 10.220.1.0/24) and the headquarters data center.

In this situation, the cash register at IP address 10.220.1.40 sends its connection request to IP address 172.17.30.55 to the local store router. That router has no connection to the headquarters data center, so it sends the packet to the backup data center. At the backup data center, the packet is then forwarded across the backup link to the service provider, where it is delivered to the credit card verification server at 172.17.30.55.

The problem arises on the return trip. At the service center router, the preferred path to 10.0.0.0/8 is through the link to the headquarters data center router, so the packet is sent there. But the headquarters data center router has no path to the store and can only discard the packet. The result is that communications are impossible even though a physical link is available.

One solution is to eliminate the isolation between the internal and external networks and exchange full routing information between the two domains. This may not be an acceptable solution because the primary reason we chose static routing in the first place was to eliminate the need for such an exchange. It also makes the security more difficult as the set of allowable paths becomes a moving target. If our network is large, we may also find that the router on the other end of the link does not have the capacity to handle all needed routes.

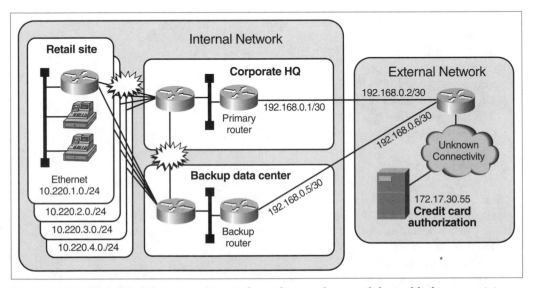

FIGURE 8-4. *Multiple failures resulting in loss of internal network logical hub connectivity*

An alternative solution, which often can be used, is to keep the simple static routing approach, but use NAT to make our internal network look like an entirely different network at the other end of the backup link. This allows us to continue to provide functional connectivity without increasing the routing complexity. There are two primary limitations to this approach. First, none of the applications that must be supported over the link can maintain TCP connections for an extended period of time (or if they do, they must be able to easily and automatically recover if the connection is broken). Second, none of the applications can include IP addressing information as part of the application protocol.

Listing 8-12 shows the modifications required to the dial backup solution we just looked at to support NAT. Each connection opened to the remote server will have the source address of the cash register translated to an address in the subnetwork 10.230.0.0/24 before it is sent over the link. If only a small number of users

```
version 11.2
!
hostname BackupRouter
!
username ServiceProvider password sharedsecret
!
interface Ethernet0/0
 description Backup Data Center LAN
 ip address 10.200.40.1 255.255.255.0
 ip access-group 103 in
 ip nat inside
!
interface BRI0
 no ip address
 encapsulation ppp
 isdn spid1 21255512120101
 isdn spid2 21255512130101
 dialer pool-member 11
 ppp authentication chap
!
interface Dialer1
 description Dial Out to Service Provider
 ip address 192.168.0.5 255.255.255.252
 ip access-group 101 in
 ip access-group 102 out
 ip nat outside
 encapsulation ppp
 dialer remote-name ServiceProvider
```

(continued)

```
   dialer string 19735551212
   dialer hold-queue 10
   dialer pool 11
   dialer-group 1
   ppp authentication chap
!
router ospf 123
   redistribute static metric 100 metric-type 2 subnets
   network 10.200.40.0 0.0.0.255 area 1
!
ip nat pool creditcard 10.230.0.2 10.230.255.254 netmask
➥ 255.255.0.0
ip nat inside source static 10.200.0.55 10.230.0.1
ip nat inside source list 99 pool creditcard
ip route 172.17.30.55 255.255.255.255 192.168.0.6 200
!
! Define addresses to be dynamically NATed
access-list 99 permit 10.220.0.30 0.0.255.1
access-list 99 permit 10.220.0.32 0.0.255.15
access-list 99 permit 10.220.0.48 0.0.255.1
access-list 99 deny    any
! Define traffic permitted back from the service bureau
access-list 101 permit tcp host 172.17.30.55 eq 3306
➥ 10.230.0.0 0.0.255.255 established
access-list 101 permit icmp host 172.17.30.55 host 10.230.0.1
access-list 101 permit icmp 192.168.0.0 0.0.0.3 host
➥ 10.230.0.1
access-list 101 deny    ip any any log
! Define traffic permitted out to the service bureau
access-list 102 permit icmp host 10.230.0.1 host 172.17.30.55
access-list 102 permit udp host 10.230.0.1 host 172.17.30.55
access-list 102 deny    ip host 10.230.0.1 any log
access-list 102 permit tcp 10.230.0.0 0.0.255.255 host
➥ 172.17.30.55 eq 3306
access-list 102 deny    ip any any log
! Prevent spoofing of NATed addresses
access-list 103 deny    ip 10.230.0.0 0.0.255.255 any log
access-list 103 permit any any
!
dialer-list 1 protocol ip permit
!
end
```

LISTING 8-12. *Backup router configuration using NAT*

needed access, we would probably use static NAT for all of them, as we do for the network management system. However, in this case, we assume that we have too many users to keep track of and instead set up a dynamic translation in which each connection is assigned an address at the time the first packet from that source is seen by this router.

While NAT keeps the routing simple and dynamic translation makes the assignment of NAT addresses easier, they do complicate our security filters. Whereas a single access-list on the outbound link to the service provider was sufficient to prevent us from sending bogus packets, we now need three access-lists to provide the same degree of protection: one for the outbound link to the service provider, one to define the NAT translations allowed, and one applied to all inbound links that already have filters in place.

Access-list 99 allows network address translation to be applied only to the cash register addresses. This replaces the source address range checks provided by the first three lines of access-list 102 in Listing 8-7. Only packets from cash register addresses get dynamic addresses assigned from the 10.230.0.0/16 range. The static NAT configuration similarly assures that only the network management system at 10.200.0.55 will be translated to 10.230.0.1.

Because it is relatively easy to spoof the source address in a packet, we also need to ensure that the only source of packets with return addresses in 10.230.0.0/16 is the network address translation on this router. This requires every interface on this router to have an input filter that blocks that address range. Access-list 101 on the inbound link to the service provider already provides that restriction on the service provider link as a side effect of restricting inbound packets to explicitly allowed IP addresses. However, we must add access-list 103 to the Ethernet interface (and any other interfaces, not shown, that also lack inbound IP filters) to provide protection from inside abusers.

Having constrained the translated addresses with inbound filters and NAT specifications, we then can apply the application-specific filtering desired with access-lists 101 and 102. The enforcement of the TCP socket restriction and server address restrictions on the cash registers is complicated by the assignment of the network management systems to the same subnetwork address range. As a result, we must either use a complicated sequence of filters to specify the address range assigned to the cash registers or postpone testing for the most likely traffic sources by testing for exceptions and then blocking all possible invalid addresses. After that, we would use a broader address definition that includes the invalid addresses already filtered out. Because there is only one address range that is special and the tests required for it are simple, we choose the latter approach.

Thus, in access-list 102, we first test for the special case of ICMP or UDP traffic from the network management systems to the credit card authorization server. If we match either case, the packet is passed and no further filters are applied. Then, in the third line, we block all traffic from the network management system. Since acceptable traffic will have already matched one of the two previous lines, this serves to block only unauthorized traffic from the network management server. Because there are no other sources of addresses in the 10.230.0.0/16 subnetwork address space other than translated cash register addresses, we can safely use a one-line test of a source address anywhere in the entire subnetwork for the destination and TCP socket check in the fourth line. Finally, in the fifth and final line of access-list 102, we add an explicit *deny ip any any log* to provide logging of any invalid packets blocked by the filter.

When working with access-lists and network address translation, we must always keep in mind that access-lists on an outside interface (*ip nat outside*) are applied on the "outside" translated addresses, after the NAT function for outbound packets and before the NAT function for inbound packets. Similarly, access-lists on an inside interface apply to the "inside" addresses before translation of inbound packets (coming into the interface from the inside network) destined to outside destinations and after translation of outbound packets (going from the router interface out to the inside network) from outside destinations; that is, the order of processing for packets coming into a router interface are packet filters and then network address translation. For outbound packets, the filtering comes after any address translation.

For the return path on the link (access-list 101), we open a small chink in our defenses to allow our most common traffic to get through on the first test, minimizing the processing overhead. We take advantage of the *established* keyword to block attempts to set up a TCP connection to the network management system, assuming the network management system can protect itself from the TCP packets that could get through without degrading performance. If necessary, or just to have higher confidence, we could check the corner cases first and add deny blocks for addresses 10.230.0.0, 10.230.0.1, and 10.230.255.255 before the statement that allows normal transaction traffic along the lines of the access-list in Listing 8-13. We

```
! Define traffic permitted back from the service bureau
access-list 101 permit icmp host 172.17.30.55 host 10.230.0.1
access-list 101 permit icmp 192.168.0.0 0.0.0.3 host
➡ 10.230.0.1
access-list 101 deny    ip any 10.230.0.0 0.0.0.1 log
access-list 101 deny    ip any host 10.230.255.255 log
access-list 101 permit tcp host 172.17.30.55 eq 3306
➡ 10.230.0.0 0.0.255.255 established
access-list 101 deny    ip any any log
!
end
```

LISTING 8-13. *A tighter access-list for incoming traffic that affords more protection*

also should make this change if we want to have log entries warn us of a probe of our defenses.

The disadvantage of the tighter access-list is that the normal traffic on the link will not be recognized until the fifth line of the access-list. Although not a significant issue on a 56-Kbps link or an access-list with only six lines, the CPU cycles consumed by inefficient ordering of access-lists can be significant as the data rate rises and the length of the access-list increases to hundreds of entries.

Shifting our attention to the service provider end of the connection in Listing 8-14, there is no network address translation required. From the viewpoint of

```
version 11.2
!
hostname ServiceProvider
!
username BackupRouter password sharedsecret
isdn switch-type basic-5ess
ip subnet-zero
!
interface Loopback1
 description Target for Retail Client Routing
 ip address 192.168.0.8 255.255.255.255
!
interface Ethernet0/0
 description Service Distribution LAN
 ip address 172.18.0.1 255.255.0.0
!
interface Serial2/7
 no ip address
 encapsulation frame-relay
!
interface Serial2/7.1 point-to-point
 description Primary Link to client: Example Retail
 ip address 192.168.0.2 255.255.255.252
 ip access-group 101 in
 bandwidth 56
 frame-relay interface-dlci 271 broadcast
!
interface BRI3/0
 description Dial Backup Link to client: Example Retail
 ip address 192.168.0.6 255.255.255.252
 ip access-group 101 in
 encapsulation ppp
                                              (continued)
```

```
      isdn caller 2125551212
      dialer map ip 192.168.0.5 name BackupRouter broadcast
      dialer hold-queue 10
      dialer-group 1
      ppp authentication chap
     !
    router eigrp 321
     passive-interface BRI1/0
     network 192.168.0.0
     distribute-list 1 out Serial2/7.1
     distribute-list 1 in Serial2/7.1
     !
    router rip
     redistribute static
     network 172.18.0.0
     !
    ip route 10.0.0.0 255.0.0.0 192.168.0.10
    ip route 10.230.0.0 255.255.0.0 192.168.0.5
    !
    access-list 1 permit 192.168.0.0 0.0.0.7
    access-list 1 permit 192.168.0.8 0.0.0.3
    !
    access-list 101 permit eigrp 10.0.0.0 0.255.255.255 any
    access-list 101 permit ip 10.0.0.0 0.255.255.255 172.17.0.0
     ➡ 0.0.255.255
    !
    dialer-list 1 protocol ip permit
    !
    end
```

LISTING 8-14. *Service bureau router configuration for dial backup with client NAT*

the service bureau, the backup link is a completely different client. The impact of this on any internal firewalls and configuration of the service applications will also need to be considered.

In this example, we also take advantage of the preference of longer matching prefixes when selecting a route to use. Rather than tighten the addressing of the original static route to 10.0.0.0/8, we merely add a more specific static route for 10.230.0.0/16. Routers that do not automatically give preference to a more specific route would need to have the alternate path removed from the primary route. In this example, it would be sufficient to change the primary static route to cover only 10.220.0.0/16, but then we would also need to change the redistribution of routes into the local routing protocol.

CONNECTING TO AN INTERNET SERVICE PROVIDER

Even though theoretically we could use the techniques already discussed to connect to an Internet Service Provider (ISP) to get access to the Internet, we will normally find that our choice of routing protocols is not an option. Instead, we typically will be given a choice of using either static routing or Border Gateway Protocol (BGP) version 4 for our connections. While at first glance this might seem restrictive, we will see that once we get over the hurdle of learning BGP, it is incredibly flexible and a far better solution for controlling routing between domains any time there are more than two domains involved—which is always the case when we are connecting to the Internet with its thousands of routing domains.

Security considerations when connecting to the Internet are also very different. Connecting to another private network implies a certain degree of trust, and once the bugs are worked out of the connection, any invalid traffic logged by the filters in place should trigger an immediate alarm. On the other hand, the Internet is a hostile environment where defenses are constantly being probed for weaknesses, and we can expect to see continuous reporting of attempted invalid traffic. Instead, we must elevate the analysis of bad traffic so that the alarm is only sounded when a potentially successful attack is detected. Otherwise, the alarm will never be silent.

Of course the organization's connection to the Internet is not the only network portal that must be zealously guarded, and a solid security policy is essential for survival. Most organizations will need to guard many back door routes, from system administrators who leave a modem attached to one of their systems for emergency maintenance to telecommuters who also have Internet connections of their own. Nor is the risk limited to the telecommuter with a full-time DSL or cable modem connection. While penetration of the organization's defenses is more difficult when the organization and Internet connections are not in place simultaneously, the exposure is still there. Some corporations have decided that telecommuters should do their personal Internet surfing through their corporate connection so that protection can be kept in place at all times.

Today's routers provide many extra features to enhance security. Our preference, however, is to keep the logical configuration simple and use independent firewalls for protection. Dedicated firewalls tend to have easier configuration of security features, better auditing tools to ensure that the protection we have configured matches the protection we desire, and better reporting tools for detecting attempted and successful breakins and denial of service attacks. The security features on the router can then be dedicated to protecting the router itself and the firewall. This allows a much simpler configuration and reduces the probability of making configuration errors (either in design or in implementation) that could leave the organization exposed.

We will also use the security features on the router to reduce the potential of our organization being used as a base for launching attacks on others. Unfortunately, far too many networks connecting to the Internet neglect to take adequate steps to protect themselves, and they fail to protect others from attacks by their internal users or from internal systems taken over by outsiders.

As we did with our private service provider, let's look first at a typical Internet connection so that we have a baseline for comparing the benefits and weaknesses of various approaches to improving availability. Consider the organization in Figure 8-5 with a single Internet connection. We will assume a configuration based on the following four-point security policy:

1. Systems in "no man's land" are assumed to have been taken over and are not to be trusted. Access to them will be subject to the same rules that apply to all other external Internet services.

2. All access to systems in the demilitarized zone (DMZ) is filtered by proxies in the firewall(s) to ensure that all service requests are directed only to servers designed to handle those requests.

3. All service requests (as distinguished from responses to service requests) by systems in the DMZ to systems outside the DMZ (such as to internal organizational databases) must be directed only to specific services on trusted servers that validate all fields before responding.

4. Except as provided under Point 3, no services will be provided by internal systems to any external request. In other words, internal systems can access the Internet but cannot be accessed from the Internet.

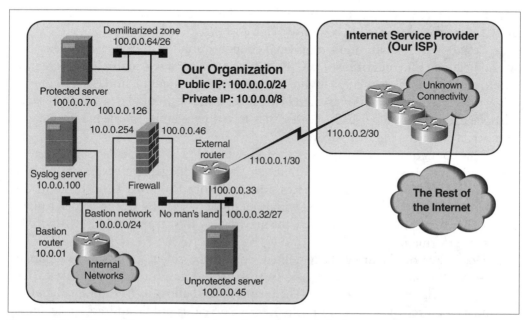

FIGURE 8-5. *Typical Internet connection through a single link to an ISP*

In this configuration, our public IP address, a 24-bit prefix assigned to us by the ISP, is further subnetted to provide address space for our external systems (100.0.0.33 through 100.0.0.62 on 100.0.0.32/27), our publicly accessed servers (100.0.0.66 through 100.0.0.126 on 100.0.0.64/26), static NAT assignments for management systems on the inside monitoring and controlling no man's land and DMZ systems (100.0.0.8 through 100.0.0.15 as /32 host addresses), and dynamic NAT for internal users accessing the Internet (100.0.0.16 through 100.0.0.31 as /32 host addresses using port and address translation to allow multiple systems to share each individual address). Addresses 100.0.0.128 through 100.0.0.255 remain available for future expansion as needs dictate.

The address used on the link to the ISP is usually assigned by the ISP, not us, and is usually from the ISP's public address space rather than ours. Even though using a globally unique address might seem a waste of public network address space, it makes problem detection and troubleshooting much easier. Using unnumbered links makes network monitoring much more difficult, while using private addresses turns the link into a black hole not only for *traceroute*, but also for any error or event that is normally reported through ICMP because packets with private source addresses are not permitted through the Internet.

Even though RFC 1918 strongly recommends that "routing information about private networks shall not be propagated on inter-enterprise links, and packets with private source or destination addresses should not be forwarded across such links,"[1] you may still receive ICMP packets with private source addresses. There are quite a few sites and a number of ISPs that use RFC 1918 private IP addresses for internal links and you may discover them being delivered unfiltered in the source address in an ICMP packet generated in response to a *traceroute* or other probe.

Based on this background, a minimal configuration for the external router would be along the lines of Listing 8-15. Even though we have access-lists preventing external access to the router, password discipline is still essential, and hard-to-guess passwords resistant to dictionary and brute force attacks should be always be used. Also, be careful with older IOS releases; they have lower limits on the maximum number of characters in a password.

This configuration also assumes the following NAT assignments for management and control: Syslog server to 100.0.0.9, SNMP management access (monitoring only) from 100.0.0.10, and Telnet access required from 100.0.0.10 and 100.0.0.11. The actual inside systems associated with each of these services would be determined by configuration of the firewall where the network address translation and service filtering is performed.

Depending on the firewall capabilities, we may be able to point all these public addresses at the same inside address or use a single public address and translate each service to a different inside address. The former would allow us to start small and expand as required. The latter can help preserve precious public address space. Some

```
version 11.0
!
hostname ExternalRouter
!
no service finger ! "no ip finger" in later IOS releases
service timestamps debug datetime msec localtime
service timestamps log datetime msec localtime
no service udp-small-servers    ! 12.0 default
no service tcp-small-servers    ! 12.0 default
!
enable secret <UseAStrongPassword>
no ip bootp server
ip subnet-zero
no ip source-route
no ip domain-lookup
!
interface Ethernet0/0
 description No Man's Land LAN
 ip address 100.0.0.33 255.255.255.224
 ip access-group 193 in
 no ip directed-broadcast
!
interface Serial0/0
 description Link to the Internet via ISP
 ip address 110.0.0.1 255.255.255.252
 ip access-group 191 in
 ip access-group 192 out
 no ip unreachables
 no ip directed-broadcast
 no ip proxy-arp
 bandwidth 1544
 ntp disable
!
no ip http server  ! Add for IOS releases with HTTP access
ip classless
ip route 100.0.0.8 255.255.255.248 100.0.0.46
ip route 100.0.0.16 255.255.255.240 100.0.0.46
ip route 100.0.0.64 255.255.255.192 100.0.0.46
ip route 100.0.0.0 255.255.255.0 Null0
ip route 0.0.0.0 0.0.0.0 110.0.0.2
no logging console
logging trap debugging
logging 100.0.0.9
```
                                                    (continued)

```
!
! Filter to block all access
access-list 90 deny    any
! Filter defining systems in 100.0.0.8/29 allowed telnet access
access-list 91 permit 100.0.0.10
access-list 91 permit 100.0.0.11
! Filter defining systems in 100.0.0.8/29 allowed SNMP access
access-list 92 permit 100.0.0.10
! Definition of Acceptable traffic from the Internet
access-list 191 deny    ip 192.168.0.0 0.0.255.255 any log
access-list 191 deny    ip 172.16.0.0 0.15.255.255 any log
access-list 191 deny    ip 10.0.0.0 0.255.255.255 any log
access-list 191 deny    ip 127.0.0.0 0.255.255.255 any log
access-list 191 deny    ip 255.0.0.0 0.255.255.255 any log
access-list 191 deny    ip 224.0.0.0 31.255.255.255 any log
access-list 191 deny    ip host 0.0.0.0 any log
access-list 191 deny    ip 100.0.0.0 0.0.0.255 any log
access-list 191 permit ip host 110.0.0.2 100.0.0.8 0.0.0.7
access-list 191 deny    ip 110.0.0.0 0.0.0.3 any log
access-list 191 deny    ip any host 100.0.0.33 log
access-list 191 deny    ip any 100.0.0.8 0.0.0.7 log
access-list 191 permit ip any 100.0.0.0 0.0.0.255
access-list 191 deny    ip any any log
! Definition of acceptable traffic to the Internet
access-list 192 deny    ip any 192.168.0.0 0.0.255.255 log
access-list 192 deny    ip any 172.16.0.0 0.15.255.255 log
access-list 192 deny    ip any 10.0.0.0 0.255.255.255 log
access-list 192 deny    ip host 100.0.0.33 any log
access-list 192 permit ip 100.0.0.8 0.0.0.7 host 110.0.0.2
access-list 192 deny    ip 100.0.0.8 0.0.0.7 any log
access-list 192 permit ip 100.0.0.0 0.0.0.255 any
access-list 192 deny    ip any any log
! Definition of acceptable traffic from the inside
access-list 193 permit ip 100.0.0.8 0.0.0.7 host 100.0.0.33
access-list 193 deny    ip any 100.0.0.0 0.0.0.255 log
access-list 193 permit ip 100.0.0.8 0.0.0.7 host 110.0.0.1
access-list 193 permit ip 100.0.0.8 0.0.0.7 host 110.0.0.2
access-list 193 deny    ip any 110.0.0.0 0.0.0.3 log
access-list 193 deny    ip 100.0.0.8 0.0.0.7 any log
access-list 193 permit ip 100.0.0.0 0.0.0.255 any
access-list 193 deny    ip any any log
!
```

(continued)

```
no cdp run
!
snmp-server community AccessCommunity RO 92
snmp-server trap-authentication
snmp-server enable traps
snmp-server host 100.0.0.11 TrapCommunity
!
line aux 0
 access-class 90 in
 transport input all
line vty 0 4
 access-class 91 in
 password PickAGoodOne
 login
!
end
```

LISTING 8-15. *Single connection to the Internet with router protection configured*

designers will even choose to extend the private inside addresses out to the DMZ and no man's land subnetworks, thus eliminating the need for NAT. However, that approach makes it easier for errors in protection to slip by undetected.

The complexity of the configuration comes from security considerations. The actual communications are fairly simple. In this baseline example, we have a single external serial connection (*interface Serial0/0*) leading to the Internet and a single interior LAN connection (*interface Ethernet0/0*) leading to the firewall and unprotected systems. All routing is through static routes or to connected subnetworks. If the destination for a packet is not on a connected network, we check the static routes. The first three routes to 100.0.0.8/29, 100.0.0.16/28, and 100.0.0.64/26 force traffic for us, other than any to the no man's land, directly to the firewall to be evaluated and forwarded as appropriate.

The next line, directing our entire public address space to the bit bucket, normally is never used. Its purpose is to prevent any packets to destinations in our assigned address space that are on networks that have yet to be defined to be forwarded on the default route. The next line defines the default route and sends all packets to unknown destinations out the link to our ISP. The assumption is that if the destination is not one we know, it must be on the Internet.

The remainder of the configuration is for security purposes: protecting our network, the router itself, and the Internet at large. Examining the configuration line by line, we start on line five by disabling services that have the potential to be abused or that unnecessarily reveal configuration information that can be used to better direct an attack against us.

The finger service allows an external user to probe who is logged in, display the message of the day banner, and possibly reveal internal management system addresses and login names. While this should not materially help an attacker, there is no benefit to providing the information, so we turn the service off.

The UDP and TCP "small servers" are services such as *daytime, echo, chargen,* and *discard.* Although these can be useful in a small TCP/IP network for testing, they are not particularly useful in a production environment and have potential as avenues for creating excess traffic resulting in denial of services to real traffic. While they default to *disabled* in IOS 12.0, in earlier IOS releases, they defaulted to *on.*

Similarly, we turn off BootP services and all other services that could be used to generate IP broadcasts. Source routing can be used to override configured routing decisions and has no place in our network where the only benefits it provides are to attackers. Turning off DNS lookups when executing local commands is done not because of any known exposure, but as a part of the policy of turning off unneeded capabilities so that defects in the software do not create gratuitous vulnerabilities.

Skipping ahead, although some network administrators like the Web management interface provided on newer Cisco IOS releases, it exposes too much of our router to outsiders. Rather than trying to protect the service, we turn it off. We will leave Telnet and SNMP access enabled in this configuration, protecting each by strict access filters. Another option in high risk environments would be to disable all network-based access to the router and require a physical connection to the console or auxiliary port. However, that can make router management so difficult as to negate the uptime benefit of the added security.

Turning off logging to the console prevents a flood of system log messages from consuming the router. Remember that on Cisco routers the console port, although slow, has a very high CPU priority. In environments in which the console is routinely connected to a display, many network managers will change this command so that critical and emergency messages continue to be displayed on the console.

We turn off the Cisco Discovery Protocol (CDP) on all interfaces using the command *no cdp run.* CDP is a proprietary Cisco protocol used to exchange device information for network management purposes. There is no benefit to running the protocol, which issues broadcasts out each interface, if we are not using it. If we actually were using CDP internally, we could shut it off on the external interface only by using the command *no cdp enable on interface Serial1/0.*

Returning to the inside connection defined by *interface Ethernet0/0,* the last two lines are part of our security plan. The packet filter (*ip access-group 193*) on this interface protects the router from inside attacks (which are not likely if the firewall is well managed) and from attacks launched from unprotected systems in no man's land. The disabling of IP broadcast propagation (*no ip directed-broadcast*) does *not* protect us but does prevent hackers from using us as a broadcast amplifier and should be the default on all interfaces throughout the network unless there is a known requirement for the service.

Skipping down to *access-list 193,* we can see how the router attempts to protect itself from attacks launched from local platforms. The first two lines limit access to the public address of the router's Ethernet interface to only the network management systems. This is required for normal access to the router for monitoring and control. Only the network management systems are permitted to communicate with the router; no other systems are allowed to send anything but transit packets for forwarding to other destinations to the router. The second line of this pair reinforces the topology that the only 100.0.0.0/24 address that should be a destination for a packet coming in through the Ethernet port is the router itself.

The next three lines provide similar protection for the addresses associated with the serial link to the ISP. Only the network management systems are allowed to send packets to the link addresses, and even those are limited to packets that are sent to one or the other of the endpoint addresses. There is no reason for other inside users to access the link other than in transit mode, so we can block all packets to any of the link's addresses regardless of source.

The final three lines block the network management system from reaching any addresses not explicitly permitted, allow all other inside addresses to reach the Internet, and block and log any attempts from addresses other than ours to get to this router or beyond.

We return to the interface definition for the link to the ISP, *interface Serial0/0.* Although the disabling of proxy ARP and network time protocol on this interface is not essential, it is included anyway, along with disabling of directed broadcasts, as part of the general policy of disabling any service that it is not essential to expose. Disabling the generation of ICMP destination-unreachable packets is a bit more controversial, because it prevents the router from informing legitimate users that they are using an invalid address or attempting to reach a service that is disabled.

We include the line because even though disabling the generation of ICMP destination-unreachable packets is a non-fatal inconvenience to legitimate users, it can dramatically slow down address and port scans by illegitimate users and other potential attackers. By not immediately returning an ICMP destination-unreachable for each attempt at a bad port or address, the prober must wait for each probe to time out before going on to test the next address or port. Although this will not stop determined attackers, it could slow them down enough to provide us time to detect the attack and to take protective measures before a compromise occurs.

Our primary protection is in the access-list number 191 filtering incoming IP packets on the interface. We start by filtering out any packets with invalid source addresses. These include the three RFC 1918 private address ranges in the first three lines, the local host loopback address range in the fourth line, and any broadcast, multicast, or null addresses that might be used by an attacker. If we want to be able to *traceroute* through links that use private addresses and our ISP does not automatically filter them from us, we might choose to open up the RFC 1918 filter just enough to let ICMP time-to-live-expired packets through.

In the eighth line of the filter, we reject any packets coming from our public address range. Packets from us should be going out this interface only and should never be coming in. Any packets coming in with our source address are either forgeries or caught in a routing loop. In either case, the only appropriate action is to discard them. For the same reason, we discard any packets coming in with an address indicating they originated from our external serial interface unless they are from the interface on the far end and destined to an internal network management system. This is another filter in which we might choose to open a hole to allow the ISP's router to show up in a *traceroute*.

In the final lines of the filter, we test the destination address of the packet. First we check for forbidden targets in our public address block (the Ethernet interface of this router and the network management systems, although for the latter we did open a hole for access to the far end of the link as part of the source address checks), and then we block all packets with destination addresses not in our public network range. This intrinsically protects our external interface as well.

We log all attempts at access violations here just as we did on the inside Ethernet interface. However, unlike the inside interface, we can expect to see large numbers of packets logged since port probing has become a routine nuisance on the Internet. Scanning and tracking events in the logs is all the more critical as a result because security depends on discovering a real attack before it succeeds so that preventive measures can be taken. Even with automated tools, it takes time and effort to check the logs for events and patterns that might indicate a new approach, which might lead to a potentially successful attack.

Unlike the inbound access-list, the outbound access-list 192 attempts to protect the Internet community from attacks based from or relayed through our site. The basic philosophy of the filter is to let out only traffic that has a source address from our public network. However, within that class of acceptable traffic, we block out unacceptable destinations (any RFC 1918 private address) and our few public addresses that are forbidden Internet access (such as our internal Ethernet interface and the network management systems, except for access to the other end of the link).

CHALLENGES FOR HIGHER INTERNET AVAILABILITY

Security is not the only challenge when it comes to Internet availability. We also have multiple single points of failure in our prototype configuration. We will start by adding a second link to our ISP and then add redundant routers at each end of the redundant link. We will conclude this chapter by looking at the implications of connecting to two independent ISPs, which provides redundancy all the way to the system on the other side of the Internet. In the next chapter, we will then work backwards to extend the redundancy to include the firewalls, which eliminates all single points of failure from end to end.

Before we start looking at alternate paths, however, we need to recognize two very different sets of Internet connectivity requirements. There is Internet connectivity for the purpose of accessing services available on the Internet, and there is Internet connectivity for the purpose of providing services to others on the Internet.

There are many cost-saving short cuts that are possible when meeting the needs of service users, but that are not useful for service providers. For example, a user surfing the Web is not concerned with what IP address is used to identify his or her system out on the Internet, and if it changes from time to time in response to a link going up or down, the impact is only a minor inconvenience, if it is noticed at all. In contrast, a Web server must service a specific public address so that it can be reached from users elsewhere on the Internet.

We will ignore security configuration in the remainder of this chapter in order to focus on the configuration requirements for providing redundancy. This is not to imply that security does not remain a vital concern with redundant connections. Rather, it merely recognizes that the security needs are constant and there is nothing to be gained by repeating the same configuration advice over and over. We will, however, point out where changes in the "standard" approach are required to support the higher availability design.

CONFIGURATION EXAMPLE: STATIC ROUTING WITH TWO INTERNET LINKS

We will start by adding a second link between our external router and the ISP, as in Figure 8-6. The changes in our configuration, shown in Listing 8-16, are minimal. We simply defined both ISP serial interfaces as equivalent routes to allow load balancing.

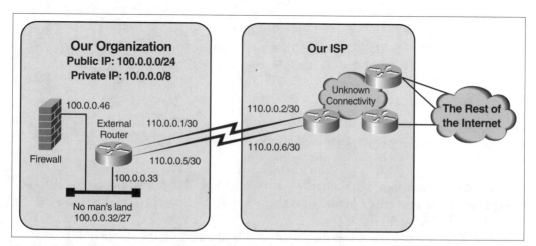

FIGURE 8-6. *Simple Internet connectivity with redundant links*

```
version 11.0
!
hostname ExternalRouter
!
ip subnet-zero
!
interface Ethernet0/0
 description No Man's Land LAN
 ip address 100.0.0.33 255.255.255.224
 ip access-group 193 in
 no ip directed-broadcast
!
interface Serial0/0
 description Link to the Internet via ISP
 ip address 110.0.0.1 255.255.255.252
 ip access-group 191 in
 ip access-group 192 out
 no ip unreachables
 no ip directed-broadcast
!
interface Serial0/1
 description Second Link to the Internet via ISP
 ip address 110.0.0.5 255.255.255.252
 ip access-group 191 in
 ip access-group 192 out
 no ip unreachables
 no ip directed-broadcast
!
ip route 0.0.0.0 0.0.0.0 Serial0/0
ip route 0.0.0.0 0.0.0.0 Serial0/1
ip route 100.0.0.8 255.255.255.248 100.0.0.46
ip route 100.0.0.16 255.255.255.240 100.0.0.46
ip route 100.0.0.64 255.255.255.192 100.0.0.46
ip route 100.0.0.0 255.255.255.0 Null0
!
end
```

LISTING 8-16.   *Single external router with two links to the same ISP*

From the viewpoint of security, we also would need to adjust the access-lists to reproduce the protection in place for the original ISP link (110.0.0.0/30) on the second link (110.0.0.4/30).

From the viewpoint of routing, operation is identical to the single link configuration except that we now have two static routes defining the default route rather than one. We then have zero, one, or two default routes available, depending on the state of the two serial links. If both links are up, outbound traffic will be load-balanced between the two links on a per destination or packet-by-packet basis, depending on whether fast packet-switching or CEF is enabled. Load balancing for inbound traffic depends on the configuration used by the ISP at their end of the links, and we have no way to influence that except through our sales representative.

Superior resilience to router failure can be attained by using two routers and two LANs for the external no man's land network, as in Figure 8-7. This example scenario takes our basic static routing approach to Internet connectivity about as far as it can go.

Load balancing is provided on the other side of the firewalls. Each firewall translates inside private addresses to an independent range of public addresses and uses a different external LAN to reach the external routers. The firewalls, in turn, send their outbound packets to an HSRP-defined address on the external LAN, which in turn is prioritized based on the status of each external router's link to the ISP. Return traffic from the Internet gets routed to the correct firewall based on the address range used for the network address translation. The configuration of router External #1 in Listing 8-17 shows how this works. The configuration of router External #2 in Listing 8-18 is a mirror image of the configuration of router External #1.

Router External #1 is the preferred router for HSRP on LAN #1, so its HSRP priority is set to 110 on LAN #1 and to 90 on LAN #2. Router External #2, as the preferred router for HSRP on LAN #2, uses just the opposite priorities: 90 on LAN #1 and 110 on LAN #2. The *standby track* command is used on the router with higher priority on each LAN to drop its priority to 80 anytime its link to the ISP goes down. So, for example, if the link between router External #2 and the ISP should fail,

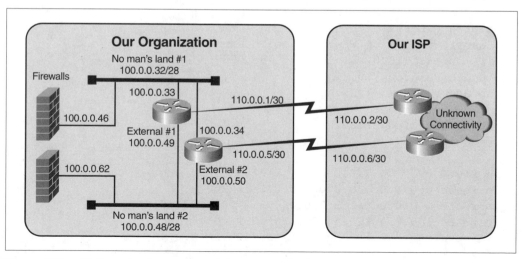

FIGURE 8-7. *Fully redundant connectivity to a single ISP*

```
version 11.0
!
hostname External_1
!
ip subnet-zero
!
interface Ethernet0/0
 description No Man's Land LAN #1
 ip address 100.0.0.33 255.255.255.240
 ip access-group 193 in
 no ip redirects
 no ip directed-broadcast
 standby 1 priority 110
 standby 1 preempt
 standby 1 authentication External
 standby 1 ip 100.0.0.35
 standby 1 track Serial0/0 30
!
interface Ethernet0/1
 description No Man's Land LAN #2
 ip address 100.0.0.49 255.255.255.240
 ip access-group 193 in
 no ip redirects
 no ip directed-broadcast
 standby 2 priority 90
 standby 2 preempt
 standby 2 authentication External
 standby 2 ip 100.0.0.51
!
interface Serial0/0
 description First link to the Internet via ISP
 ip address 110.0.0.1 255.255.255.252
 ip access-group 191 in
 ip access-group 192 out
 no ip unreachables
 no ip directed-broadcast
 bandwidth 1544
!
ip route 0.0.0.0 0.0.0.0 Serial0/0
ip route 0.0.0.0 0.0.0.0 100.0.0.34 200
ip route 100.0.0.8 255.255.255.252 100.0.0.46
ip route 100.0.0.12 255.255.255.252 100.0.0.62
ip route 100.0.0.16 255.255.255.248 100.0.0.46
```

(continued)

```
ip route 100.0.0.24 255.255.255.248 100.0.0.62
ip route 100.0.0.64 255.255.255.224 100.0.0.46
ip route 100.0.0.96 255.255.255.224 100.0.0.62
ip route 100.0.0.0 255.255.255.0 Null0
ip route 110.0.0.4 255.255.255.252 100.0.0.34
!
end
```

LISTING 8-17. *Router External #1 with first link to the same ISP using static routing*

```
version 11.0
!
hostname External_2
!
ip subnet-zero
!
interface Ethernet0/0
 description No Man's Land LAN #1
 ip address 100.0.0.34 255.255.255.240
 ip access-group 193 in
 no ip redirects
 no ip directed-broadcast
 standby 1 priority 90
 standby 1 preempt
 standby 1 authentication External
 standby 1 ip 100.0.0.35
!
interface Ethernet0/1
 description No Man's Land LAN #2
 ip address 100.0.0.50 255.255.255.240
 ip access-group 193 in
 no ip redirects
 no ip directed-broadcast
 standby 2 priority 110
 standby 2 preempt
 standby 2 authentication External
 standby 2 ip 100.0.0.51
 standby 2 track Serial0/0 30
!
interface Serial0/0
 description Second Link to the Internet via ISP
 ip address 110.0.0.5 255.255.255.252
```

(continued)

```
 ip access-group 191 in
 ip access-group 192 out
 no ip unreachables
 no ip directed-broadcast
 bandwidth 1544
!
ip classless
ip route 0.0.0.0 0.0.0.0 Serial0/0
ip route 0.0.0.0 0.0.0.0 100.0.0.49 200
ip route 100.0.0.8 255.255.255.252 100.0.0.46
ip route 100.0.0.12 255.255.255.252 100.0.0.62
ip route 100.0.0.16 255.255.255.248 100.0.0.46
ip route 100.0.0.24 255.255.255.248 100.0.0.62
ip route 100.0.0.64 255.255.255.224 100.0.0.46
ip route 100.0.0.96 255.255.255.224 100.0.0.62
ip route 100.0.0.0 255.255.255.0 Null0
ip route 110.0.0.4 255.255.255.252 100.0.0.49
!
end
```

LISTING 8-18. *Router External #2 with second link to the same ISP using static routing*

its priority as HSRP router for LAN #2 will drop to 80 and router External #1 will become the default router on both LANs, doing its best to handle all Internet traffic from both firewalls.

We also need to add a static route for the other router's ISP link to provide continued access to the ISP links for the network management systems. Otherwise, packets addressed to either end of the other router's ISP link would be routed through the default route and out to the ISP, a path that is configured to discard them.

ROUTING WITH BGP

We can do a lot with static routing and HSRP to provide redundancy for our Internet connection, but as we saw when connecting to other service providers, unless each link includes an end-to-end keepalive protocol, we need to run a routing protocol over the links to detect failures that do not take down the link at the physical level.

The protocol of choice for this purpose is BGP version 4 (BGP4). Generally, when we ask an ISP to provide routing over our link to them, we will have our choice of any routing protocol we desire, as long as it is BGP4.

While talk of using BGP may evoke images of high-end routers with 128 MB or more of memory, the truth is that BGP is flexible enough that we may be able to get all the routing that we need by using a pair of 2500 routers with minimal RAM. The key is that as long as we are connecting only to a single ISP, we need BGP only to determine if the link is up. There is no need to carry all the routes in the Internet when there will be no difference in reachability regardless of which path we take.

Most ISPs will offer us our choice of three modes of BGP routing when connecting:

1. A single route (usually the default route to make redistribution easier) that we can use to determine if the link is up or down

2. Local networks only (just the IP addresses in the routing domain of the ISP) so that we can send traffic heading to other subscribers of that ISP directly to the correct ISP

3. Everything (their path to every destination they know on the Internet) so that we can make our own routing decisions and attempt to choose the best path

As a general rule, when connecting to a single ISP, regardless of the number of independent connections we have to that ISP, there is no advantage to advancing beyond mode one. However, some providers offer the option of advertising just the IP addresses of their network backbone interconnection points. If this option is available, we can use those routes to determine our default route and avoid sending packets to an ISP router that has been cut off from the rest of the world.

Configuration Example: Using BGP for Link Fault Detection

Returning to the example scenario in Figure 8-7, in which we have two routers at our site with two independent connections to the same ISP, we can adapt the static routing used in Listing 8-17 to use BGP to detect link outages and force outbound traffic away from a down link to the link that is still operational.

For this configuration to function, we need our ISP to configure BGP on the router at their end of the link to speak to us and advertise a default route to us. As part of their configuration, the ISP also should filter the advertisements from us so that they only accept routes for addresses that belong to us. However, we should not depend on the ISP to protect us from any configuration errors that we happen to make as some will accept anything we give them so that they do not need to reconfigure every time a customer changes an address space. The ISP also may need to filter the routes being sent to us so that we are sent only the default route. This will depend on how BGP is used on their router for other purposes.

The BGP commands required to safely support us on a Cisco router are shown in Listing 8-19. The first line, *router bgp 54321*, enables BGP processing on the

```
version 11.0
!
router bgp 54321
 neighbor 110.0.0.1 remote-as 65000
 neighbor 110.0.0.1 default-originate
 neighbor 110.0.0.1 distribute-list 1 in
 neighbor 110.0.0.1 distribute-list 2 out
!
access-list 1 permit 100.0.0.0 0.0.0.255
access-list 2 permit 0.0.0.0
!
end
```

LISTING 8-19. *ISP side of the BGP configuration to support router External #1*

router for Autonomous System Number (ASN) 54321. (In real life, the ISP would substitute their assigned ASN for the 54321.) The ASN 65000 used to refer to us would be replaced by an ASN chosen from the range of ASN values reserved for private use (64512 through 65535). The four *neighbor* lines that follow instruct the BGP process on the router to speak with the BGP on our router, advertise a default route to us, and filter all advertisements received from us and sent to us through access-lists 1 and 2, respectively.

The inbound distribution list using access-list 1 is a precaution to ensure that speaking BGP with us does not inject any routes into the ISP's routing tables that do not belong to us. The outbound distribution list using access-list 2 prevents the ISP's router from sending us all other routes known to BGP on that router.

Not shown are the configuration lines required to redistribute our address into the local intradomain routing protocol and to prevent our public address (and those of other clients who will be aggregated into larger address advertisements from the ISP's address space) from being distributed by BGP to other IBGP or EBGP neighbors. These aspects of the configuration are too variable because they depend on the specific topology, configuration, and approach to interior routing used by the ISP.

Note that it is just as important for the ISP to learn our public address from us as it is for us to learn the default route dynamically from the ISP. Failure of the link must be detected at both ends in order for any alternate routes to be useful. We can test this by executing a *traceroute* or *ping* from a system elsewhere on the Internet to one of our public addresses. Note that the test sequence described here will disrupt production traffic, so it should be scheduled accordingly.

First we verify that we can reach our system from the remote system. Then we simulate line failure by installing an access-list blocking inbound TCP packets on one of our ISP links. This will stop the exchange of BGP keepalive hello packets across the link without affecting the link-level status of the link. The easiest way to do this is to define a new access-list that takes the existing inbound access-list on the interface and adds a *deny tcp any any* statement as the first line. Then we can change the access-list used on the interface simply by changing the access-list number in the *ip access-group in* line for the interface.

Next we verify that our public address still can be reached. Keep in mind that using default keepalive and hold times, it will take up to 3 minutes for BGP to determine that the link is no longer useable. If our default path was through the disabled link, we should see from *traceroute* the switchover to the remaining path when the BGP hold time expires. Executing *traceroute* from internal systems out to any destination on the Internet, if allowed by our security policy, also should show the change of route to the one remaining link, regardless of the default path.

Then we use the same technique of modifying the access filter to disable BGP on the second router. The ping or trace route should start to fail when the BGP hold time expires on the second link. It should continue to fail even if we add a static route to either external router to restore a default route out to the ISP. Once we are confident that BGP is controlling routing in both directions, we delete the static route.

Depending on the ISP's internal configuration and route aggregation strategy, the remote system may start to get back ICMP destination unreachable messages. Make sure that the *ping* or *traceroute* being used can be configured to display any ICMP destination unreachable packets received, because not all implementations include that capability. If necessary, a protocol analyzer can be used to detect them.

Now that we have verified that link failures have been correctly recognized, we restore the original inbound access-list on the first router on which BGP was disabled. At this point, BGP will have lost its TCP connection to the ISP router and will be retrying to establish the connection every few minutes. As soon as a connection retry succeeds, the two BGP speakers should reestablish their conversation, and the public address should become reachable once again. We have now confirmed that either link alone can be used to carry traffic as long as the other link fails in a way that is detectable by BGP. Finally, we restore the production inbound access-list on the second router so its BGP can re-enable use of the second link.

When failure testing BGP, we do need to be careful to minimize the number of times we change our routes being advertised into the Internet. Any link that is changing state too frequently will be *dampened,* which causes it to be treated as down even though it is up, until it has been up long enough to no longer be considered flapping. Depending on the ISP and whether our address range is being advertised by itself or aggregated with other subnetworks, dampening may be activated for up to an hour on any of our links that drop and return to life more than once an hour.

Returning to the side of the link that is under our control, router External #1 in Listing 8-20 shows a typical configuration (minus the standard Internet connection protections) that takes advantage of BGP to detect ISP link failure while retaining

```
version 11.0
!
hostname External_1
!
ip subnet-zero
!
interface Ethernet0/0
 description No Man's Land LAN #1
 ip address 100.0.0.33 255.255.255.240
 ip access-group 193 in
 no ip redirects
 no ip directed-broadcast
 standby 1 priority 110
 standby 1 preempt
 standby 1 authentication External
 standby 1 ip 100.0.0.35
 standby 1 track Serial1/0 30
!
interface Ethernet0/1
 description No Man's Land LAN #2
 ip address 100.0.0.49 255.255.255.240
 ip access-group 193 in
 no ip redirects
 no ip directed-broadcast
 standby 2 priority 90
 standby 2 preempt
 standby 2 authentication External
 standby 2 ip 100.0.0.51
!
interface Serial1/0
 no ip address
 encapsulation frame-relay
!
interface Serial1/0.1
 description Link to the Internet via ISP
 ip address 110.0.0.1 255.255.255.252
 ip access-group 191 in
 ip access-group 192 out
 no ip unreachables
 no ip directed-broadcast
 bandwidth 1544
 frame-relay interface-dlci 123
!
```

(continued)

```
router bgp 65000
 network 100.0.0.0 mask 255.255.255.0
 neighbor 110.0.0.2 remote-as 54321
 neighbor 110.0.0.2 distribute-list 1 in
!
ip classless
ip route 0.0.0.0 0.0.0.0 100.0.0.34 200
ip route 100.0.0.8 255.255.255.252 100.0.0.46
ip route 100.0.0.12 255.255.255.252 100.0.0.62
ip route 100.0.0.16 255.255.255.248 100.0.0.46
ip route 100.0.0.24 255.255.255.248 100.0.0.62
ip route 100.0.0.64 255.255.255.224 100.0.0.46
ip route 100.0.0.96 255.255.255.224 100.0.0.62
ip route 100.0.0.0 255.255.255.0 Null0
ip route 110.0.0.4 255.255.255.252 100.0.0.34
!
access-list 1 permit 0.0.0.0
!
end
```

LISTING 8-20. *Router External #1 using BGP to detect ISP link status*

the simplicity of the previous static routed example. Any router capable of handling a T1 and two Ethernet interfaces would have the CPU power to handle this configuration. However, we need to check first, because not all low-end routers capable of handling the traffic include the software to support BGP. For example, while we could have used a pair of Cisco 1605 routers with pure static routing, the smallest dual-Ethernet Cisco routers with BGP support included in IOS 11.2 are 2514s.

The configuration is almost identical to the static routed version, because we are still using static routes everywhere except across the link to the ISP. As a result, the Ethernet configurations are identical, and if the ISP link does go down at the link level, the HSRP configuration will route the firewall directly to the correct router. We also still have a routing loop due to the use of static routes for backup. If both ISP links go down, outbound packets will loop between the two external routers until the time-to-live expires. This is not as bad as it seems because the packets are not going to go anywhere regardless, and there is no other traffic on the external LAN that is being delayed. If, due to other factors, this was a problem (for example, the two routers were at alternate sites and connected through a WAN link), we would need to enable a routing protocol between them and propagate the default route information that way.

Similarly, the WAN link configuration is unchanged, other than to explicitly show a Frame Relay link rather than a point-to-point link. Unlike the pure static route configuration, however, we can use this BGP-based configuration over any permanent type of link to the ISP, including point-to-point, Frame Relay, DSL, or ATM. If we enabled a routing protocol between the external routers, we also could support dial backup just as we did with a private service provider earlier in this chapter. One change we should make, however, is to lengthen the idle timer so that a worst case flapping primary link would not cause the backup link to cycle on and off fast enough to trigger route dampening on the backup link as well as on the primary link. We also would need to adjust the definition of "interesting" traffic to exclude BGP packets.

The actual BGP configuration, while at first glance appearing more complex than an equivalent intradomain routing protocol configuration (such as those used with a private service provider in the beginning of this chapter), is actually somewhat simpler. The illusion of complexity is due to the inclusion of a first-level of outbound advertisement filtering and explicit variable length subnet masking in the routing configuration, as opposed to requiring definition of access-lists to achieve the same effect. The configuration is more demanding in some ways, however, as parameters that are arbitrary when configuring other protocols now have explicit meaning and each peer must be explicitly defined.

Starting with the definition of the BGP configuration section with *router bgp 65000,* the number used must be the private ASN assigned to us by the ISP. It is not an arbitrary process ID the way it is in OSPF and EIGRP.

We must explicitly define the networks that we will be advertising to the ISP using *network* statements. If we had more than one public network address range, we would use a network statement for each. BGP will advertise a network only if there is an exact match to the network statement, including the subnet mask, in the router's routing table. In this case, we already have a static route for 100.0.0.0/24 pointing to Null0 to prevent routing of unused portions of our subnet back out to the Internet. Even if all subnetworks within our assigned address space were used, we would still need this statement for BGP because it needs an entry (even if never used for actual routing) in the routing table that exactly matches the network statement address and subnetwork mask.

The third BGP line defines with whom we will exchange BGP routes. The destination must be an address on a network connected to the router, like it is here. The final line duplicates the advertisement filter already on the ISP end of the link. While this should not be needed, we include it so that if the ISP makes a configuration error and attempts to send us all known routes, we will reject them so that our router will not run out of memory and crash while trying to process all routes in the Internet. On the other hand, since we have no other BGP peers, there is no need for an output filter because there are no other sources of routes aside from the network statements.

The static routes that conclude this configuration extract are also unchanged, with one exception. We no longer need or want a static route defining the link to the

ISP as the preferred default route. That route is now provided by BGP. The backup to that route, however, remains the floating static route to the other external router.

CONFIGURATION EXAMPLE: BGP TO ISP WITH DYNAMIC INTERNAL ROUTING

The previous example gives us full immunity to single faults, but the use of static routes to access the fallback path to the Internet leaves us unnecessarily exposed to service disruption due to double faults. If the LAN connection used by router External #1 to reach the ISP link on router External #2 should be unusable at the time that the ISP link from router External #1 fails, traffic for the Internet delivered to router External #1 by either firewall will fail, even though a perfectly functional LAN connection still exists between the two routers.

While the initial response to this concern might be to add another floating static route through the other LAN with a higher administrative distance, this second backup route would not be used when it was needed. The challenge is that the LAN interface can be up even though the destination desired is not accessible.

Our backup static routing minimized the potential for service disruption by taking advantage of the HSRP configuration. If the entire LAN failed, only traffic delivered on the second LAN would need to be routed, and that goes directly to the other router because that router has the HSRP priority on the second LAN. Similarly, any LAN failure severe enough to be detectable by the first router and to deactivate the static route through the LAN (allowing the backup route to be activated) would certainly remove this router as the active HSRP router. In this case, all traffic from the firewalls would be going to the second router anyway.

The only scenario the single static route combined with HSRP does not handle is the one in which the LAN interface on the second router fails and the rest of the LAN continues to function normally. Again, a natural response would be to add a second static route through the second LAN and give it the same administrative distance as the static route through the first LAN. This actually makes the configuration more sensitive to LAN failure, because the two routes would be load balanced and an undetected problem in either LAN would cause packets to be lost. This also would be a nasty problem to troubleshoot because the symptoms would be erratic. If the load balancing were packet-by-packet, traffic coming from Firewall #1 would start seeing 50% packet loss while traffic from Firewall #2 would function normally. If the load balancing were per-destination, users coming through Firewall #1 would be able to reach some destinations but not others.

The solution is to dynamically route between the two external routers. However, this is not as easy as it sounds because most interior routing protocols are not designed to operate in a hostile environment. Remember, these routers are communicating over external networks, and any systems on these external unprotected networks could be taken over by hostile forces, including the other router.

Our primary concern is the threat of attack through any computers on the external LAN. It is trivial for an attacker who has taken over a computer on the LAN to convert it into a protocol analyzer, capture all LAN traffic passing by, and generate packets with arbitrary source and destination IP and MAC addresses. Consequently, our choice of an interior routing protocol is limited to those that support strong authentication. We also remove the HSRP configuration to eliminate our exposure because of the lack of strong authentication in that protocol.

Strong authentication support may require an IOS upgrade because the need for support of strong security has been only recently recognized. On Cisco routers, the choice of routing protocols with strong authentication are limited to OSPF (IOS 11.0 or later), RIPv2 (IOS 11.1[3] or later), EIGRP (11.2[4]F or later), and BGP (11.0 or later). If using IOS 11.0 or 11.1, there are also constraints on the maximum key length for OSPF. The EIGRP and RIPv2 message digests include time stamps, so if we are using either of these protocols, we also would need to configure the routers to have functional clocks.

Listing 8-21 shows how we can add OSPF between the two external routers to minimize our exposure to attack while still maximizing our ability to communicate. Protection against an attacker spoofing incorrect link state updates to divert traffic is provided by configuring OSPF to include Message Digest 5 (MD5) authentication in each packet sent, effectively signing each packet with a digital signature based on the

```
version 11.0
!
hostname External_1
!
ip subnet-zero
!
interface Ethernet0/0
 description No Man's Land LAN #1
 ip address 100.0.0.33 255.255.255.240
 ip access-group 193 in
 no ip redirects
 no ip directed-broadcast
 ip ospf message-digest-key 100 md5 LongStrongKey
!
interface Ethernet0/1
 description No Man's Land LAN #2
 ip address 100.0.0.49 255.255.255.240
```
                                                      (*continued*)

```
 ip access-group 193 in
 no ip redirects
 no ip directed-broadcast
 ip ospf message-digest-key 100 md5 LongStrongKey
!
interface Serial1/0
 no ip address
 encapsulation frame-relay
!
interface Serial1/0.123
 description Link to the Internet via ISP
 ip address 110.0.0.1 255.255.255.252
 ip access-group 191 in
 ip access-group 192 out
 no ip unreachables
 no ip directed-broadcast
 bandwidth 1544
 frame-relay interface-dlci 123
!
router ospf 321
 redistribute connected
 redistribute bgp 65000
 network 100.0.0.32 0.0.0.31 area 666
 default-information originate
 area 666 authentication message-digest
!
router bgp 65000
 network 100.0.0.0 mask 255.255.255.0
 neighbor 110.0.0.2 remote-as 54321
 neighbor 110.0.0.2 distribute-list 1 in
!
ip route 100.0.0.0 255.255.255.0 Null0
ip route 100.0.0.8 255.255.255.252 100.0.0.46
ip route 100.0.0.12 255.255.255.252 100.0.0.62
ip route 100.0.0.16 255.255.255.248 100.0.0.46
ip route 100.0.0.24 255.255.255.248 100.0.0.62
ip route 100.0.0.64 255.255.255.224 100.0.0.46
ip route 100.0.0.96 255.255.255.224 100.0.0.62
!
access-list 1 permit 0.0.0.0.0.0.0
!
end
```

LISTING 8-21. *Router External #1 using fully dynamic routing toward the Internet*

secret shared between the routers on the subnetwork. This secret is set as part of each interface's configuration using the *ip ospf message-digest-key* command.

Both the text of the secret and the numeric key ID must match at each end of the network connection for OSPF to function. The use of a key ID allows for an orderly change of passwords, without disruption of OSPF functionality during the transition period when the password is changed on one router and not on the other. Normally only one key ID is defined on any single interface except while in the process of changing secrets. Aside from defining the shared secret, no other changes are required to the interface definitions.

Moving on to the OSPF definitions in the *router OSPF* section, the process ID is arbitrary, as is the area number used. We continue to use static routes for all routing through the firewalls because our security policy mandates that we not send anything to or through a firewall that is not absolutely essential. The *network* command includes both Ethernet interfaces and nothing else, enabling OSPF routing on just those two interfaces. The *area authentication message-digest* command turns on strong authentication in the area, using the shared secrets defined on each interface in the area.

The *redistribute connected* line is optional. It tells OSPF to advertise all subnetworks that are physically attached to any interfaces that are not included in a network statement. This extends the same degree of resilience implemented for the Internet to network management's need to reach the serial link to the ISP. Alternatively, we could have left the static route providing that redirection in place, but by routing it dynamically, we improve the chances of being able to communicate during multiple failure conditions.

The *redistribute bgp* line allows the default route learned by BGP to be shared with the other external router. Because an OSPF autonomous system boundary router does not, by default, generate a default route into the OSPF routing domain, we need to explicitly enable its redistribution with the *default-information originate* line. Unlike the same command in BGP, the OSPF default-information origination is conditional on a default route being available. Unlike static routes, which also may be used for this function, OSPF is smart enough to use whichever LAN is currently available. LAN availability is determined by OSPF through bidirectional exchange of hello packets, rather than by the detection of failure at the link level.

Note that although we can adjust load balancing for outbound traffic by selecting which firewall is used, any load balancing for inbound traffic is up to the ISP. The tools that are available to us for influencing inbound routing are generally not appropriate when connecting through a single ISP. As a general rule, any inbound load balancing will be on a per-destination basis. If the two links we have to the ISP are physically diverse enough to provide resilience to local ISP problems, packet-by-packet load balancing not only will be difficult, but also could be counter-productive because it is highly likely that the delays associated with the two paths will differ enough to cause excessive out-of-sequence packet delivery.

For the same reason, any load balancing for outbound packets also should be per destination rather than on a per packet basis. So far, our load balancing for outbound traffic has been on a per-source basis, based on which firewall the inside system is using. This approach has the added benefit of providing symmetric routing, where outbound packets follow the same path through the network as inbound packets.

CONFIGURATION EXAMPLE: DETECTING ISP FAILURES WITH BGP

If our ISP is cooperative, we can significantly improve our ability to detect routing and connectivity problems if we have the ISP configure BGP to advertise their upstream provider addresses to us rather than a default route. We can then generate our default route locally, based on receiving advertisements for one or more of the addresses on the other side of our ISP. We can have a high degree of confidence that the route will be good.

Consider the situation in Figure 8-8, in which we have two links to a U.S. service provider. Rather than advertising a default route, we have the ISP instead send us their routes to two of the major North American Network Access Points (NAPs): MAE-East and MAE-West. We then assume that any access router of our ISP that can reach at least one of these two key exchange points is adequately connected for our use.

On the ISP router, the configuration would include the statements in Listing 8-22. This is only a slight change from our previous ISP BGP configuration for advertising a default route. The *default-originate* line is removed and the outbound (to us) distribution list is modified to let out only the paths to the MAE-East and MAE-West networks.

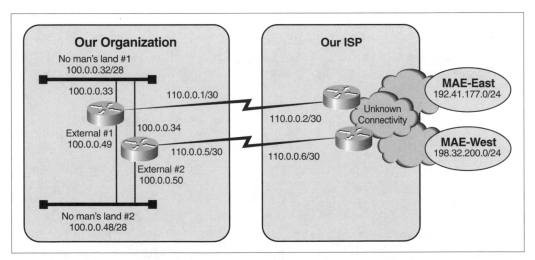

FIGURE 8-8. *Using BGP to determine ISP connectivity to NAPs*

```
router bgp 54321
 neighbor 110.0.0.1 remote-as 65000
 neighbor 110.0.0.1 distribute-list 1 in
 neighbor 110.0.0.1 distribute-list 2 out
 !
access-list 1 permit 100.0.0.0 0.0.0.255
access-list 2 permit 192.41.177.0 0.0.0.255
access-list 2 permit 198.32.200.0 0.0.0.255
 !
end
```

LISTING 8-22. *ISP side of the filtered BGP configuration*

On our side of the link, the critical configuration lines for router External #1 are shown in Listing 8-23. The BGP section is identical to when we were accepting an ISP generated default route, but the access-list referenced in our inbound distribution filter has changed. Rather than allowing in only the default route, we now allow in only the same NAP-status indicating routes that the ISP router has been configured to send us.

```
version 11.0
!
hostname External_1
!
ip subnet-zero
!
interface Ethernet0/0
 description No Man's Land LAN #1
 ip address 100.0.0.33 255.255.255.240
 ip access-group 193 in
 no ip redirects
 no ip directed-broadcast
 ip ospf message-digest-key 100 md5 LongStrongKey
!
interface Ethernet0/1
 description No Man's Land LAN #2
 ip address 100.0.0.49 255.255.255.240
 ip access-group 193 in
 no ip redirects
 no ip directed-broadcast
 ip ospf message-digest-key 100 md5 LongStrong Key
!
```

(*continued*)

```
interface Serial1/0
 no ip address
 encapsulation frame relay
!
interface Serial1/0.123
 description Link to the Internet via ISP
 ip address 110.0.0.1 255.255.255.252
 ip access-group 191 in
 ip access-group 192 out
 no ip unreachables
 no ip directed-broadcast
 bandwidth 1544
 frame-relay interface-dlci 123
!
router ospf 321
 redistribute connected
 redistribute bgp 65000
 network 100.0.0.32 0.0.0.31 area 666
 default-information originate
 area 666 authentication message-digest
!
router bgp 65000
 network 100.0.0.0 mask 255.255.255.0
 neighbor 110.0.0.2 remote-as 54321
 neighbor 110.0.0.2 distribute-list 1 in
!
ip classless
ip default-network 192.41.177.0
ip default-network 198.32.200.0
!
ip route 100.0.0.0 255.255.255.0 Null0
ip route 100.0.0.8 255.255.255.252 100.0.0.46
ip route 100.0.0.12 255.255.255.252 100.0.0.62
ip route 100.0.0.16 255.255.255.248 100.0.0.46
ip route 100.0.0.24 255.255.255.248 100.0.0.62
ip route 100.0.0.64 255.255.255.224 100.0.0.46
ip route 100.0.0.96 255.255.255.224 100.0.0.62
!
access-list 1 permit 192.41.177.0 0.0.0.255
access-list 1 permit 198.32.200.0 0.0.0.255
!
end
```

LISTING 8-23. *Router External #1 with Frame Relay link to the same ISP using BGP-driven static routing with indirect determination of the default route*

The key is in the two *ip default-network* statements specifying the two NAP indicator networks. Our router will inject a default route into the local routing table if any network specified in an *ip default-network* statement is in the local routing table. In other words, if the ISP router to which we attach has access to the Internet core, we will use it as our default route. If it does not have access, we will fall back on our floating static default route and hope that the other external router's ISP connection is still good. If we use OSPF for routing between the external routers, we would no longer need to redistribute BGP into OSPF but we would still need the *default-information originate* line.

An alternate approach is for the ISP to conditionally advertise a default route to us based on the same conditional routing information. This can be done using a configuration like that in Listing 8-24. When using this approach, we would use the same configuration on our end as when the ISP was using an unconditional default-originate to generate the default route for us. However, unlike before, the default route would only be advertised when it would truly be useful.

A fringe benefit of this approach is that when the ISP changes their connectivity so that an alternate trigger address is appropriate, the configuration changes affect only their routers and not ours. On the other hand, we have no way of knowing (until it is too late) whether the ISP is tracking meaningful targets as its condition for generating the default route.

```
version 11.0
!
router bgp 54321
 neighbor 110.0.0.1 remote-as 65000
 neighbor 110.0.0.1 default-originate route-map default-map
 neighbor 110.0.0.1 distribute-list 1 in
 neighbor 110.0.0.1 distribute-list 2 out
!
access-list 1 permit 100.0.0.0 0.0.0.255
access-list 2 permit 0.0.0.0 0.0.0.0
access-list 3 permit 192.41.177.0
access-list 3 permit 198.32.200.0
!
route-map default-map permit 10
 match ip address 3
!
end
```

LISTING 8-24. *ISP with conditional advertisement of the default route*

CONNECTING THROUGH MULTIPLE ISPs

Protection from ISP-wide failures requires that we connect to more than one ISP, rather than having more than one link to different sites of the same ISP. Although particularly important when working with smaller ISPs with limited or only indirect connectivity to any Internet NAPs, even major providers have run into systemwide troubles from time to time, usually due to configuration errors or exposing software defects.

When selecting a second ISP, we also need to be careful that the second ISP does not share facilities or upstream providers with our current ISP. For example, it does little good to tie into two independent service providers if both rely on UUNet for their backbone connectivity. A UUNet disaster would disconnect both providers from the rest of the Internet, and leave us isolated despite our costly redundant connections. It wouldn't be much better to make our second connection directly to UUNet, as that still leaves us vulnerable to the same failure mode.

Since the connectivity of the Internet is constantly evolving, and is vastly different in different regions of the world, we need to understand both the current state and any current trends to make an appropriate choice.

We also need to be aware that there are three different classes of public internet addresses: provider-independent, portable, and non-portable. Portable and non-portable address space assignments are requested by ISPs for provisioning their customers. The portable option indicates that the ISP enables its customer to keep the IP address space in case the customer changes providers. Non-portable address space must be returned to the ISP if changing providers, which would require the customers to renumber their networks.

Provider-independent address space is obtained directly rather than going through an ISP. Due to the scarcity of IP address space and the routing burden for the Internet for supporting fragmented address assignments, provider-independent address space is increasingly hard to obtain. Unless our requirement is enough to justify at least a 19-bit prefix (a Classless InterDomain Routing [CIDR] block equivalent to 32 class C addresses), we could find ourselves with an address that is poorly routed or that cannot be reached at all from some areas of the Internet. There are service providers who have a routing policy of excluding all routes for prefixes longer than a certain length (so that all routes can still fit in the memory their routers can support), and the smaller our block, the more likely we are to be excluded.

Obtaining portable address space from one of our ISPs could be considered a way of subcontracting to the ISP the effort of procuring an assignment of provider-independent address space. While the ability to take our business and go elsewhere might give us some leverage when negotiating contract renewal, the address space could have the same problems we faced with a provider-independent address space, even if we stay with our original ISP. After all, we are not the only client assigned portable space from the ISP's block, and if enough clients with space in the block move to other ISPs, the remaining pieces being advertised by our ISP might not be a large enough block to get carried through networks with prefix reduction policies.

Non-portable address space, although it does not have the cachet of provider-independent address space, does ensure us of acceptable route propagation as part of the larger block of addresses assigned to our ISP. Because of the routing benefits of non-portable addresses and the ability to propagate large CIDR blocks representing many independent networks as a single path advertisement to a specific ISP, there is good reason to use non-portable addresses wherever possible. Fortunately, with a good ISP, we can get all the routing benefits of a provider-independent address space from a non-portable address space as long as we remain a customer of the ISP that owns it.

CONFIGURATION EXAMPLE: USING NAT FOR AN ALTERNATE ISP PATH

If the Internet connectivity availability requirement that has forced us to use two ISPs is driven by internal users seeking access to Internet services, we may be able to make some dramatic simplifications in implementing redundant connectivity. We can assign half the users to the non-portable address space assigned to us by one provider and the other half to the non-portable address space assigned to us by the second provider. We then set up our topology to route each outbound packet to the router connecting to the correct ISP. While it is not needed in this example, we can use policy routing based on the source address of each outbound packet to ensure correct routing. The trick is that if one of the ISP links should fail, we not only forward the packet on to the router with the remaining link to the "wrong" ISP, but also use network address translation to change the source address to one in the address space of the remaining functional ISP.

This approach is generally acceptable for outbound access only, because any services offered to the public such as Web sites that have a public address from the ISP with the failed link, will be inaccessible from the outside. Even for outbound access, any connections that were active will be dropped every time the ISP link in use changes. However, for Web browsing and many other interactive applications, the changeover may not even be noticed.

BGP is not required unless a routing protocol is necessary to detect link failure. If BGP is needed, a simple default route setup is sufficient, like the one we used in our example of two links to the same ISP. We do not even need to worry about the ISP properly responding to our BGP advertisements, because there will be no traffic for our addresses served by that link until the link returns to life.

The basic connectivity being implemented is shown in Figure 8-9, where public addresses 100.0.0.0/24 and 110.0.0.0/30 are non-portable addresses allocated to us by one ISP, and 101.0.0.0/24 and 120.0.0.0/30 are non-portable addresses allocated to us by the other ISP.

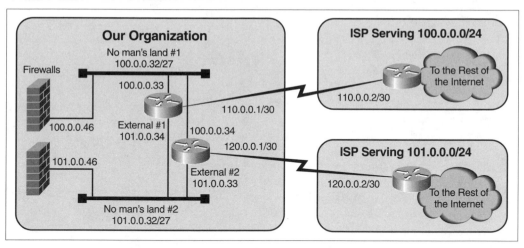

FIGURE 8-9. *Simple configuration for redundant ISPs using NAT*

In normal operation, systems using the top firewall are assigned addresses 100.0.0.0/24, which sends outbound packets to router External #1, which then sends the packets unmodified to the top ISP serving 100.0.0.0/24. All packets from Internet sources addressed to 100.0.0.0/24 will be delivered through the top ISP link to router External #1. Systems assigned addresses from 101.0.0.0/24 similarly come through the lower firewall to router External #2 and out to the lower ISP.

If the ISP link serving 100.0.0.0 fails, all services offered from that address range will no longer be reachable from the Internet. However, just as we did with two links to the same ISP, internal users' outbound packets will be rerouted from router External #1 over the 100.0.0.32/27 LAN to router External #2, to be sent out through the alternate ISP. The problem is, if we just forward the packet to the ISP, even if it gets to the Internet destination, there is no way for the response to get back to us because the link serving 100.0.0.0/24 is down.

In order for bidirectional communications to occur, when a packet for the 100.0.0.0 ISP comes into router External #2, we must NAT the 100.0.0.0 source address to an unused address in the 101.0.0.0/24 address space. Although the changed source address means that any active connections will need to be reestablished, it also means that the destination out on the Internet will be able to send a response back that will go through our second ISP to get delivered across the ISP link that is still functioning.

Listings 8-25 and 8-26 show how we can configure a pair of small Cisco routers to implement this functionality.

Before we discuss the details of the routing and NAT functions, keep in mind that the access-lists required for protection that are not shown will require modifications to reflect the addressing changes. In particular, the Ethernet interfaces connecting

```
version 11.2
!
hostname External_1
!
ip subnet-zero
ip nat pool net-100 100.0.0.128 100.0.0.143 netmask
  ➥ 255.255.255.240
ip nat inside source list 1 pool net-100 overload
!
interface Ethernet0
 description No Man's Land LAN #1
 ip address 100.0.0.33 255.255.255.224
 ip access-group 193 in
 no ip redirects
 no ip directed-broadcast
 ip nat inside
 standby 1 priority 110
 standby 1 preempt
 standby 1 authentication External
 standby 1 ip 100.0.0.35
 standby 1 track Serial0 30
!
interface Ethernet1
 description No Man's Land LAN #2
 ip address 101.0.0.34 255.255.255.224
 ip access-group 194 in
 no ip redirects
 no ip directed-broadcast
 ip nat inside
 standby 2 priority 90
 standby 2 preempt
 standby 2 authentication External
 standby 2 ip 101.0.0.35
!
interface Serial0
 description Link to the Internet via ISP serving 100.0.0.0/24
 ip address 110.0.0.1 255.255.255.252
 ip access-group 191 in
 ip access-group 192 out
 no ip unreachables
 no ip directed-broadcast
 ip nat outside
 bandwidth 1544
```

(continued)

```
!
ip route 0.0.0.0 0.0.0.0 Serial0
ip route 0.0.0.0 0.0.0.0 100.0.0.34 200
ip route 100.0.0.0 255.255.255.0 Null0
ip route 100.0.0.8 255.255.255.248 100.0.0.46
ip route 100.0.0.16 255.255.255.240 100.0.0.46
ip route 100.0.0.64 255.255.255.192 100.0.0.46
ip route 100.0.0.128 255.255.255.240 101.0.0.46
ip route 120.0.0.0 255.255.255.252 100.0.0.34
!
access-list 1 permit 101.0.0.0 0.0.0.127
!
end
```

LISTING 8-25. *Router External #1 with link to the ISP serving 100.0.0.0/24, using static routing and NAT*

```
version 11.2
!
hostname External_2
!
ip subnet-zero
ip nat pool net-101 101.0.0.128 101.0.0.143 netmask
 ➡ 255.255.255.240
ip nat inside source list 1 pool net-101 overload
!
interface Ethernet0
 description No Man's Land LAN #1
 ip address 100.0.0.34 255.255.255.224
 ip access-group 193 in
 no ip redirects
 no ip directed-broadcast
 ip nat inside
 standby 1 priority 90
 standby 1 preempt
 standby 1 authentication External
 standby 1 ip 100.0.0.35
!
interface Ethernet1
 description No Man's Land LAN #2
 ip address 101.0.0.33 255.255.255.224
 ip access-group 194 in
```

(continued)

```
   no ip redirects
   no ip directed-broadcast
   ip nat inside
   standby 2 priority 110
   standby 2 track Serial0 30
   standby 2 preempt
   standby 2 authentication External
   standby 2 ip 101.0.0.35
  !
 interface Serial0
   description Link to the Internet via ISP serving 100.0.0.0/24
   ip address 120.0.0.1 255.255.255.252
   ip access-group 191 in
   ip access-group 192 out
   no ip unreachables
   no ip directed-broadcast
   ip nat outside
   bandwidth 1544
  !
  !
 ip route 0.0.0.0 0.0.0.0 Serial0
 ip route 0.0.0.0 0.0.0.0 101.0.0.34 200
 ip route 101.0.0.0 255.255.255.0 Null0
 ip route 101.0.0.8 255.255.255.248 101.0.0.46
 ip route 101.0.0.16 255.255.255.240 101.0.0.46
 ip route 101.0.0.64 255.255.255.192 101.0.0.46
 ip route 101.0.0.128 255.255.255.240 100.0.0.46
 ip route 110.0.0.0 255.255.255.252 101.0.0.34
  !
 access-list 1 permit 100.0.0.0 0.0.0.127
  !
 end
```

LISTING 8-26. *Router External #2 with link to the ISP serving 101.0.0.0/24, using static routing and NAT*

to the 101.0.0.32/27 LAN require new access-list entries for the 101 subnetwork. Equally important, but not as apparent, the access-lists on the serial link to the ISP on router External #2 are not the same as the access-lists identified by the same list numbers on router External #1.

The LAN configurations for this example are functionally identical to the LAN configurations for dual connections to a single ISP and function exactly the same way to use HSRP to route outbound data to the external router with a functional ISP link. Aside from the use of different address ranges on each LAN, the only real change is the addition of an *ip nat inside* statement to each interface.

In the same way, the serial link to the ISP is identical in function to the single ISP configuration except for two changes. We add an *ip nat outside* statement, and make the obvious addressing change due to the use of two different ISP's address space.

Configuring the NATs takes only three lines. On router External #1 these lines are:

> *ip nat pool net-100 100.0.0.128 100.0.0.143 netmask 255.255.255.240*
> *ip nat inside source list 1 pool net-100 overload*
> *access-list 1 permit 101.0.0.0 0.0.0.127*

The first line sets aside a range of IP addresses that are serviced by the ISP accessed by router External #1 for use by NAT. This must be from a range of addresses not used by real systems. All packets from 101.0.0.0-based systems will have their addresses translated into a 100.0.0.0 address in this range. We also must ensure that any packets coming back from the Internet addressed to systems in this address range are routed through an *inside* interface to allow the destination address to be translated back to the correct 101.0.0.0 address.

The second line says that each packet coming in an inside interface with a destination that requires it to go out an outside interface, with a source address "permitted" by access-list 1, will have its source address translated to an available address contained in the address pool *net100*. The *overload* keyword allows us to translate multiple inside addresses onto the same pool address, translating the source port to another value, if necessary, to ensure that each pairing of inside to outside system is unique. Once a dynamic association is established by an outgoing packet, the translation will be remembered so that an inverse translation can be applied to incoming packets destined to a translated address.

The third line is the access-list, which specifies the inside addresses we will translate. In this case, we will translate any address from 101.0.0.0 to 101.0.0.127, so a one line access-list is sufficient to specify any real system that should be using the alternate ISP on router External #2.

The static routes are the same as we used before with two exceptions:

- The addresses on router External #2 reflect the address space provided by the second ISP.

- There is an added route sending any packets with a destination address, which corresponds to the address space used for NAT, to the other firewall for users with the other ISP's addresses.

Note that neither external router is configured to route towards internal addresses defined by the other external router's ISP address space (other than for testing of the links to the ISPs). There is no need to do so since there are no valid routes that would direct inbound packets to the other external router.

We could adapt this configuration to use simple BGP to detect link failures and to use OSPF or another interior routing protocol to provide better resilience to pathological LAN failure modes. The bottom line, however, is that this approach to ISP redundancy is rarely satisfactory for the long term. We noted in our introduction that this approach does not protect services we provide to the Internet and disrupts access to Internet services by internal users every time they are forced from one link to the other. It is also difficult to achieve load balancing and route optimization over the redundant ISP links.

This approach can be useful when transitioning from one ISP to another. By using NAT, we can separate the transition of the ISP from the transition of user configurations. That way, we can concentrate our real time efforts on the systems providing external services and schedule user reconfiguration for less hectic times.

Achieving transparent access to and from our organization, regardless of which ISP link is working, requires full cooperation from both ISPs and procurement of a globally unique ASN for our organization. Load balancing and route optimization might also require an upgrade of our external routers to systems capable of handling the complete Internet routing table.

INTERDOMAIN ROUTING WITH BGP

Maximum availability of Internet connectivity requires us to have fully redundant, physically and logically diverse routes to all destinations on the Internet. In pursuing this goal we must be realistic, because there is no guarantee that the system we wish to connect to on the Internet has similar connectivity. If the other system connects through an ISP that has failed, and the system has no alternate path, we will not be able to connect with it.

However, we can maximize the probability that other systems still connected to the Internet will be able to reach us. To do this, we must participate in routing over the Internet as an independent Autonomous System (AS) so that the IP addresses we use can be identified in the routing paths as ours rather than those of a specific ISP. As an AS, we can then be reached by virtually any other end system that has a path to any of the ISPs we use.

Note that the critical requirement is not that we own our own IP address space. As we mentioned before, provider independent address space is only an advantage if the prefix is broad enough not to be filtered by resource strapped service providers. The challenge is that different providers have different filtering policies and may be address specific. For example, one major provider uses the filter parameters in Table 8-1 to reduce the size of their routing tables.

From the viewpoint of maximizing availability, there are two schools of thought. One is to go for non-portable provider address space, which is part of the provider's largest advertised CIDR block. That way, even if our specific advertisements get blocked, we can hope that as the packet gets closer to our provider, it will reach less resource-constrained service providers, who will be able to route it to us even if our link to the provider owning the address is down. This choice depends on the service provider having enough capability always available to at least advertise its full CIDR block even if not all addresses inside it are available. It also depends on the provider recognizing when its link to us is down and routing packets to our portion of its address space out of its network to the service provider who still can communicate with us.

The other choice is to use provider-independent address space and hope that anyone who desires to communicate with us will use a service provider that recognizes and supports the fragmentation of the provider-independent address space. For organizations large enough to justify and obtain a full Class B network or the CIDR block equivalent, provider independent is an obvious choice. On the other hand, an organization that cannot even justify a full Class C of address space would be better served by a piece of provider-dependent address space, as they are very likely to be filtered otherwise.

However, as the Internet continues to expand and the core routing tables grow, there is going to be increasing pressure to force users to use addresses that allow hierarchical routing. This means that the pressure for users to get IP addresses from a block assigned to their ISPs, and for those ISPs to get their blocks of addresses from a block assigned to their service providers, and so on up the chain, is only going to

TABLE 8-1. *Path Address Filtering Used by One Major ISP*

ADDRESS RANGE	MAX PREFIX LENGTH	COMMENT
0.0.0.0–23.255.255.255	8	Class A networks
24.0.0.0–24.255.255.255	19	Cable modem ISPs
25.0.0.0–126.255.255.255	8	Class A networks
128.0.0.0–191.255.255.255	16	Class B networks
192.0.0.0–194.255.255.255	24	Provider-independent Class Cs
195.0.0.0–195.255.255.255	19	European ISPs
196.0.0.0–205.255.255.255	24	Provider-independent Class Cs
206.0.0.0–223.255.255.255	19	ISP CIDR blocks

increase. As the cost of routing provider-independent networks continues to rise, we may see the day when it is a given that changing service providers means changing address space.

In order to continue operation despite failure of an ISP, we need to connect to at least two independent ISPs and do so in such a way that knowledge of how to reach us will reach others on the Internet even if the ISP who has the address block containing our address space is not functional. The mechanism for doing that is the BGP.

A major challenge in setting up BGP is its requirement that every routed address space be associated with a specific ASN, referred to as the origin of the route. Consequently, our backup ISP can not simply start advertising our addresses for us, because those addresses currently originate from our primary ISP's ASN. The backup ISP also cannot use the ASN of our original ISP, because that would cause the packet to be routed to that ISP rather than through our backup ISP. In order for our address space to be multihomed, we must obtain an ASN for ourselves.

This is not as easy as it should be because ASNs are only 16-bit unsigned integers, so there are only 65,536 unique values possible and over 20% of them are already allocated. Consequently, there are fairly strict guidelines governing assignment of new ASNs with the goal of conserving as many as possible. For example, to use BGP for multiple connections to a single provider, a "reserved for private use" ASN is mandatory. Today, global ASNs are only issued to organizations that connect to more than one service provider and that require a significantly different routing policy that can not be satisfied by using the ASN of one of the organization's providers.

Because, unlike our service providers, we do not provide transit routing for other Autonomous Systems, we will normally qualify for our own ASN until such time as the growth rate in ASN number assignments mandates a policy change. By that time, the market for high availability Internet access could be large enough that high availability providers will be available to meet the needs of most organizations currently requiring their own ASN for multihoming.

Another challenge we face is the plethora of BGP mechanisms to determine which of two routes is better. This is not surprising because the role of BGP is to provide routing across an Internet of networks in which each network has its own set of routing metrics and policies, but the result for us is that we often will need to use a different approach with each service provider, adding to the complexity of our configuration.

Perhaps more important from our viewpoint as a multihoming organization is that, in the same manner as internal routing protocols, BGP normally will use the most specific route available, regardless of metrics; that is, if, out on the Internet, a router sees our specific IP address range advertised with a poor path through our backup supplier, and the CIDR block of our primary supplier contains our address range with a much better path, the path through the backup provider will be taken despite its quality. Preventing this behavior requires our primary ISP to advertise our specific address block in addition to their larger CIDR block. That way, more reasonable metrics such as AS path length can be used to route traffic for us. However, this not only requires our primary ISP to propagate our more specific route, but also extends through their service providers all the way up to whatever tier of the Internet at which the primary and backup paths converge. Because our goal in selecting service providers is to maximize path diversity, that convergence of connectivity should not occur until our specific paths have propagated all the way to the major exchange points forming the backbone of the Internet.

An alternative approach (which may be acceptable for some applications) is to treat the path through the backup ISP as the primary path. We would then consider the aggregate-only path advertised by the primary ISP as a backup that normally will be used only by other subscribers of the primary ISP. This approach should be avoided in high inbound traffic (many Mbps) or delay-sensitive applications due to the higher potential for using inappropriate routes for inbound traffic.

CONFIGURATION EXAMPLE: MULTIHOMED ORGANIZATION SPEAKING BGP

We look first at the scenario in Figure 8-10 and configure a multihomed BGP speaker using a single external router. Although this does represent a single point of failure in the one router, it is a common configuration, particularly when getting started, because it requires only one router capable of handling full Internet routing tables. It also allows us to focus our attention initially on the issues of running BGP with other Autonomous Systems. In the example configuration that follows, we will add

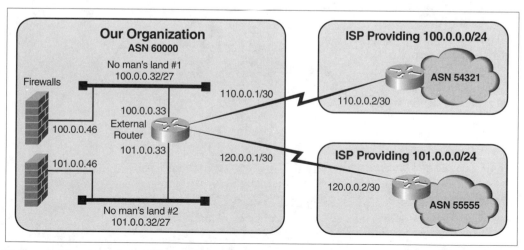

FIGURE 8-10. *Simple multihomed organization speaking BGP to redundant ISPs*

the second external router and deal with the additional complexity of running BGP between routers within our own AS. We will continue to ignore the challenge of providing adequate redundancy through the firewalls into the rest of the organization until our discussion of firewalls in the next chapter.

The key to this configuration is that all of our public addresses are equally well-served by either ISP, both inbound and outbound. We no longer need to route outbound packets based on their source address, or use network address translations to make an address reachable despite loss of the ISP that assigned us that address. Part of the negotiations with each ISP when setting up BGP connections includes ensuring that each will honor our advertisements and open any routing and packet filters in place to all of our public addresses.

Listing 8-27 shows the relevant parts required by the Cisco configuration. Configuration of the LAN and serial port are similar to what we have seen before, although we would want to adjust the packet filters, which are referenced but not shown, to minimize the address windows left open to attackers.

```
version 11.0
!
hostname External
!
ip subnet-zero
!
interface FastEthernet0/0
 description No Man's Land LAN #1
 ip address 100.0.0.33 255.255.255.224
 ip access-group 193 in
 no ip directed-broadcast
!
interface FastEthernet0/1
 description No Man's Land LAN #2
 ip address 101.0.0.33 255.255.255.224
 ip access-group 194 in
 no ip directed-broadcast
!
interface Serial1/0
 no ip address
 encapsulation frame-relay IETF
!
interface Serial1/0.1 point-to-point
 description Link to the ISP providing 100.0.0.0/24
 ip address 110.0.0.1 255.255.255.252
 ip access-group 191 in
 ip access-group 192 out
```

(continued)

```
 no ip unreachables
 no ip directed-broadcast
 no arp frame-relay
 frame-relay interface-dlci 500 IETF
 bandwidth 1500
!
interface Serial2/0
 description Link to the ISP providing 101.0.0.0/24
 ip address 120.0.0.1 255.255.255.252
 ip access-group 195 in
 ip access-group 196 out
 no ip unreachables
 no ip directed-broadcast
 bandwidth 1500
!
router bgp 60000
 network 100.0.0.0 mask 255.255.255.0
 network 101.0.0.0 mask 255.255.255.0
 aggregate-address 110.0.0.0 255.255.255.252 summary-only
 aggregate-address 120.0.0.0 255.255.255.252 summary-only
 redistribute connected
 neighbor 110.0.0.2 remote-as 54321
 neighbor 110.0.0.2 version 4
 neighbor 110.0.0.2 filter-list 10 out
 neighbor 120.0.0.2 remote-as 55555
 neighbor 120.0.0.2 version 4
 neighbor 120.0.0.2 filter-list 10 out
 no auto-summary
!
ip classless
ip route 0.0.0.0 0.0.0.0 Serial2/0
ip route 0.0.0.0 0.0.0.0 Serial1/0.1 200
ip route 100.0.0.0 255.255.255.0 Null0
ip route 100.0.0.8 255.255.255.248 100.0.0.46
ip route 100.0.0.16 255.255.255.240 100.0.0.46
ip route 100.0.0.64 255.255.255.192 100.0.0.46
ip route 101.0.0.0 255.255.255.0 Null0
ip route 101.0.0.8 255.255.255.248 101.0.0.46
ip route 101.0.0.16 255.255.255.240 101.0.0.46
ip route 101.0.0.64 255.255.255.192 101.0.0.46
ip as-path access-list 10 permit ^(_60000)*$
!
end
```

LISTING 8-27. *Single router providing multihoming through BGP*

Many BGP users like to get just the ISP's local routing tables, a popular option for providing outbound route optimization without the overhead of taking full routes. However, our purpose in running BGP is to determine not only that the link to the ISP is up, but also that the ISP is itself linked to the rest of the Internet, so we have each ISP provide us with full routing tables.

This option is often referred to as running "defaultless" because we do not use a default route to the Internet. Theoretically, if we do not have an explicit route to a destination from one of our service providers, we can assume that destination does not exist. The danger is that this assumes that our service providers are not filtering out any routes to limit the size of their routing tables. If either of our providers routes internally with a default route to their service provider, we must do the same. In this case our best approach is to use a conditional default route based on their advertising routes to key backbone sites, the same approach we took when using multiple paths to a single ISP. We could also use this shortcut to avoid carrying full routes, but then we would lose the ability to avoid poor routes.

We see the first significant difference in the *router bgp 60000* line. Unlike before, when we were using an ASN assigned by the service provider, we now must use our globally unique ASN assigned in response to our request to the authority for assigning Internet numbers for our region of the world.

The next two lines are the familiar *network* lines that define what networks we will advertise. In this case, we are advertising a /24 prefix from the CIDR block of each ISP. These networks must be present in our routing tables with the designated prefix for the networks to be advertised. We ensure this by adding a static route for each pointing to the null interface.

The next three lines are optional, but will be desirable later when we replace the one external router with a pair of external routers for redundancy. They also illustrate an alternate way to control the routes being advertised by BGP. The *aggregate-address* command tells BGP to advertise the entire subnetwork specified if any portion of it is known. The *summary-only* modifier further restricts that advertisement to just the one summary prefix for the entire subnetwork.

In order for the aggregate addresses to be generated, BGP must be able to learn about the existence of the routes. This knowledge is provided by the *redistribute connected* line. Cisco routers consider static routes pointing to an interface to be connected, so this line also provides the route information required by the *network* lines to advertise our production network ranges. The final *no auto-summary* line stops BGP from advertising a summary route for every major network containing a subnetwork being advertised.

There are two potentially significant differences between using *network* and *aggregate-address*. The *network* keyword will originate an advertisement for the specified network only if there is an exact match known to BGP. For example, the line *network 192.168.52.0 mask 255.255.255.0* will advertise a route only if there is an entry for 192.168.52.0/24 in the router's routing table. If there are two entries, one for 192.168.52.0/25 and one for 192.168.52.128/25, no advertisement will be generated even though the entire subnetwork is known. Similarly, no advertisement is generated if the routing table contains 192.168.48.0/20. An exact match is required.

The *aggregate-address* command, on the other hand, will generate an advertisement for the entire subnetwork as long as any portion of it is known through a more specific route. It will also flag the advertisement as an atomic aggregate. Routes marked as atomic aggregates may traverse autonomous systems not included in the AS path of the route, and may not be de-aggregated by other BGP speakers, which may have more specific routes to some portion of the aggregate; that is, a BGP speaker with an atomic aggregate route to 192.168.52.0/24 and another route to 192.168.52.128/25 cannot choose to advertise the route for 192.168.52.0/24 as a route for the 192.168.52.0/25 portion of it.

The two sets of neighbor statements, one per BGP peer, are familiar except for the line *neighbor . . . filter-list 10 out.* This line is critical, since the AS path filter specified makes us a stub area rather than a transit area. By default, BGP will advertise to other AS all the routes that it learns from any other AS. Depending on the connectivity between our two service providers, we could wind up being the shortest path between them. To prevent that, we add a filter that limits our advertisements to only those that we originate. The AS path filter is defined by the line *ip as-path access-list 10 permit ^(_60000)*$.*

AS path filters on Cisco routers use regular expressions to allow flexibility in testing an AS path. Our AS path filter allows to pass any advertisement whose AS path contains our ASN repeated any number of times and blocks from passage any advertisements that contain any ASN other than ours. The carat symbol matches the beginning of the line, the dollar sign matches the end of the line, and the underscore matches any delimiter that can begin or end an ASN, including beginning or end of line. The parentheses say to treat the pattern contained inside them as a single item, while the asterisk says match the preceding item zero or more times.

The pattern *^(_60000)*$* could be written also as *^(60000_)*$* or as *^(_60000_)*$*. Both say to match any path that contains the AS number 60000 zero or more times. Any ASN other than 60000 will not match.

We use this pattern in case we need to influence the selection of routes back to us. Padding with multiple copies of our ASN the route to be avoided is often necessary for load balancing, to steer traffic toward a faster link if not all ISP links are equivalent in performance, or to steer traffic away from a lower performing ISP.

Because we are not using AS path padding in this example, we could have used the empty regular expression of *permit ^$.* This regular expression, specifying the beginning of path and the end of path with nothing between them, will match only routes that we originate with no path modifications. (Our ASN is inserted by the BGP speaker at the ISP receiving our advertisements.)

CONFIGURATION EXAMPLE: MULTIHOMED BGP WITH REDUNDANT ROUTERS

Now that we have covered the external routing portion of a multihomed BGP configuration, we can look at the requirements for internal BGP routing to go along with the external BGP routing so that we can eliminate the single point of failure inherent in using only one external router.

We will use the same connectivity we used with dual routers and static routing, and the same ASNs used in the single router example just discussed. Figure 8-11 shows how all the pieces come together.

The critical conceptual change required to support multiple external routers is the need to exchange external routing information between the external routers so that each can determine the best route to all external destinations. This requires each external router to run BGP with all ISP routers to which it has links and with all other external routers in our AS. The general rule is that all BGP speakers in an AS must be fully meshed; that is, every BGP speaker must have a neighbor relationship set up with every other BGP speaker in the AS.

In this example, with only two BGP speakers to worry about, full mesh connectivity is not an issue. In larger networks with large numbers of BGP speakers, such as in a major ISP network, a BGP feature called Route Reflection is available to reduce the burden of the BGP full-mesh connectivity requirement. However, even in our small two router environment, we use an interior routing protocol to maximize the ability of BGP to communicate between the two routers.

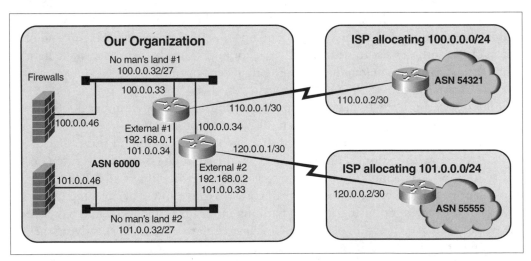

FIGURE 8-11. *Multihomed organization using BGP with redundant ISPs and redundant external routers*

Listing 8-28 gives the routing definitions required on router External #1. To minimize the potential for confusion, all other configuration details, including security, are omitted. As before, we temporarily ignore the details of operational redundancy between the external routers and internal systems because redundancy is dependent on the firewalls and security policy.

```
version 11.0
!
hostname External_1
!
ip subnet-zero
!
interface Loopback0
 description Target address for IBGP neighboring
 ip address 192.168.0.1 255.255.255.255
!
interface FastEthernet0/0
 description No Man's Land LAN #1
 ip address 100.0.0.33 255.255.255.224
 ip ospf message-digest-key 100 md5 LongStrongKey
!
interface FastEthernet1/0
 description No Man's Land LAN #2
 ip address 101.0.0.34 255.255.255.224
 ip ospf message-digest-key 100 md5 LongStrongKey
!
interface Serial2/0
 description Link to the ISP providing 100.0.0.0/24
 ip address 110.0.0.1 255.255.255.252
!
router ospf 1
  network 100.0.0.32 0.0.0.31 area 666
  network 101.0.0.32 0.0.0.31 area 666
  network 110.0.0.0 0.0.0.3 area 666
  network 192.168.1.0 0.0.0.0 area 666
  area 666 authentication message-digest
!
router bgp 60000
 no synchronization
 network 100.0.0.0 mask 255.255.255.0
 network 101.0.0.0 mask 255.255.255.0
```

(continued)

```
 aggregate-address 110.0.0.0 255.255.255.252 summary-only
 redistribute connected
 neighbor 110.0.0.2 remote-as 54321
 neighbor 110.0.0.2 version 4
 neighbor 110.0.0.2 filter-list 10 out
 neighbor 192.168.0.2 remote-as 60000
 neighbor 192.168.0.2 update-source Loopback0
 neighbor 192.168.0.2 version 4
 neighbor 192.168.0.2 password SamePasswordAsOnPeer
 default-information originate
 no auto-summary
!
ip classless
ip default network 192.41.177.0    !MAE-East
ip default-network 198.32.200.0    !MAE-West
!
ip route 100.0.0.0 255.255.255.0 Null0
ip route 100.0.0.8 255.255.255.248 100.0.0.46
ip route 100.0.0.16 255.255.255.240 100.0.0.46
ip route 100.0.0.64 255.255.255.192 100.0.0.46
ip route 100.0.0.0 255.255.255.0 Null0
ip route 101.0.0.8 255.255.255.248 101.0.0.46
ip route 101.0.0.16 255.255.255.240 101.0.0.46
ip route 101.0.0.64 255.255.255.192 101.0.0.46
!
ip as-path access-list 10 permit ^(_60000)*$
!
end
```

LISTING 8-28. *Router External #1 speaking EBGP to one ISP and IBGP to an external*

This configuration is very similar to the single router case except that now we have configured both OSPF and IBGP across the "no man's land LAN" between the two external routers. The OSPF configuration is identical to the OSPF configuration used for two external routers connected to a single ISP, but with one crucial exception. Because of the huge number of entries in the BGP routing database when it takes full Internet routes, we do not redistribute BGP routes into OSPF like we did before. Instead, we let IBGP decide the best route to the outside world and limit OSPF to selecting the best route between the two routers.

Ordinarily, BGP will insert routes it learns from other IBGP speakers into the local routing table only if they are known from the interior routing protocol. This function is called synchronization. It prevents the situation in which a packet could get forwarded to a router that is not running IBGP and that router not having any idea of where to send the packet next because the destination was not known to the interior routing protocol.

Since all our routers on any path that IBGP could select to the Internet are running IBGP, we do not need to synchronize, and indeed will never synchronize, because we are not redistributing BGP routes into OSPF, our interior routing protocol. To avoid waiting indefinitely for a route to appear in the OSPF routing tables, we turn off synchronization with the *no synchronization* command under *router bgp*.

We configure the Interior part of BGP using loopback interfaces rather than physical interfaces so that LAN instability will not affect the BGP routing tables. Because these loopback addresses are not used anywhere other than to support routing between the two external routers, we can use private RFC 1918 addresses and preserve our public address for applications that require an externally accessible address.

The peering with router External #2 at 192.168.0.2 is interior BGP because the peer is in the same AS. We use MD5 authentication when exchanging routes with router External #2 because we are communicating over LANs, and we do not want to risk having BGP misled by bogus packets generated by a system on the LAN that has been taken over by hostile forces. Remember that we did the same with OSPF as well. For the same reason, we also might consider using authenticated OSPF or some equally robust means to direct traffic from the firewalls to the external routers. HSRP, with its clear text authentication string, easily could be fooled into yielding the active role to a system spoofing a router running HSRP with a high priority.

Finally, we define a default path based on either ISP advertising a route to MAE-East or MAE-West. That way, we can handle any addresses that have too long a prefix to propagate through our service providers. Using a conditional, rather than a static, default route minimizes the potential of our having a black hole for our default gateway.

If our firewalls used static routing rather than OSPF to locate the external routers, we would need to enable HSRP on the no man's land LANs. In this case, security considerations would forbid using the LANs to support any systems other than routers and firewalls.

Listing 8-29 shows the matching configuration for the other external router. This time we leave in all the standard security protections we have already discussed in the context of a static connection to a single ISP. We still leave out boiler plate additions such as user definitions and an appropriate banner of the day. Our security policy remains identical to that in our original security discussion. The changes are due to the addition of support for a second link, a second public address space, and dynamic internal routing, which could cause inbound packets to take a roundabout path through both external routers on their way out to the Internet or when returning.

```
version 11.0
!
no service finger
service password-encryption
no service udp-small-servers
no service tcp-small-servers
!
hostname External_2
!
enable secret <UseAStrongPassword>
!
no ip bootp server
ip subnet-zero
no ip source-route
no ip domain-lookup
!
interface Loopback0
 description Target address for IBGP neighboring
 ip address 192.168.0.2 255.255.255.255
!
interface FastEthernet0/0
 description No Man's Land LAN #1
 ip address 100.0.0.34 255.255.255.224
 ip access-group 193 in
 no ip redirects
 no ip directed-broadcast
 ip ospf message-digest-key 100 md5 LongStrongKey
!
interface FastEthernet1/0
 description No Man's Land LAN #2
 ip address 101.0.0.33 255.255.255.224
 ip access-group 193 in
 no ip redirects
 no ip directed-broadcast
 ip ospf message-digest-key 100 md5 LongStrongKey
!
interface Serial2/0
 description Link to the ISP providing 101.0.0.0/24
 ip access-group 191 in
 ip access-group 192 out
 no ip unreachables
 no ip directed-broadcast
```

(*continued*)

```
 no ip proxy-arp
 bandwidth 1544
 ntp disable
!
router ospf 1
  network 100.0.0.32 0.0.0.31 area 666
  network 101.0.0.32 0.0.0.31 area 666
  network 120.0.0.0 0.0.0.3 area 666
  network 192.168.0.0 0.0.0.255 area 666
  area 666 authentication message-digest
!
router bgp 60000
 no synchronization
 network 100.0.0.0 mask 255.255.255.0
 network 101.0.0.0 mask 255.255.255.0
 aggregate-address 120.0.0.0 255.255.255.252 summary-only
 redistribute connected
 neighbor 120.0.0.2 remote-as 55555
 neighbor 120.0.0.2 version 4
 neighbor 120.0.0.2 filter-list 10 out
 neighbor 192.168.0.1 remote-as 60000
 neighbor 192.168.0.1 update-source Loopback0
 neighbor 192.168.0.1 version 4
 neighbor 192.168.0.1 password SameLongStrongPasswordAsOnPeer
 default-information originate
 no auto-summary
!
ip classless
ip default-network 192.41.177.0    !MAE-East
ip default-network 198.32.200.0    !MAE-West
!
ip route 100.0.0.0 255.255.255.0 Null0
ip route 100.0.0.8 255.255.255.248 100.0.0.46
ip route 100.0.0.16 255.255.255.240 100.0.0.46
ip route 100.0.0.64 255.255.255.192 100.0.0.46
ip route 101.0.0.0 255.255.255.0 Null0
ip route 101.0.0.8 255.255.255.248 101.0.0.46
ip route 101.0.0.16 255.255.255.240 101.0.0.46
ip route 101.0.0.64 255.255.255.192 101.0.0.46
!
no ip http server ! 11.2.default
ip as-path access-list 10 permit ^(_60000)*$
no logging buffered
```

(continued)

```
no logging console
logging trap debugging
logging 100.0.0.9
logging 101.0.0.9
!
! Filter to block all access
access-list 90 deny    any
! Filter defining internal systems allowed telnet access
access-list 91 permit 100.0.0.10
access-list 91 permit 101.0.0.10
! Filter defining systems in 100.0.0.8/29 allowed SNMP access
access-list 92 permit 100.0.0.11
access-list 92 permit 101.0.0.11
! Definition of Acceptable traffic from the Internet
access-list 191 deny    ip 192.168.0.0 0.0.255.255 any log
access-list 191 deny    ip 172.16.0.0 0.15.255.255 any log
access-list 191 deny    ip 10.0.0.0 0.255.255.255 any log
access-list 191 deny    ip 127.0.0.0 0.255.255.255 any log
access-list 191 deny    ip 255.0.0.0 0.255.255.255 any log
access-list 191 deny    ip 224.0.0.0 3.255.255.255 any log
access-list 191 deny    ip host 0.0.0.0 any log
access-list 191 deny    ip 100.0.0.0 0.0.0.255 any log
access-list 191 deny    ip 101.0.0.0 0.0.0.255 any log
access-list 191 deny    ip 110.0.0.0 0.0.0.3 any log
access-list 191 permit ip host 120.0.0.2 100.0.0.8 0.0.0.7
access-list 191 permit ip host 120.0.0.2 101.0.0.8 0.0.0.7
access-list 191 deny    ip 120.0.0.0 0.0.0.3 any log
access-list 191 deny    ip any host 100.0.0.34 log
access-list 191 deny    ip any host 101.0.0.33 log
access-list 191 deny    ip any 100.0.0.8 0.0.0.7 log
access-list 191 deny    ip any 101.0.0.8 0.0.0.7 log
access-list 191 permit ip any 100.0.0.0 0.0.0.255
access-list 191 permit ip any 101.0.0.0 0.0.0.255
access-list 191 deny    ip any any log
! Definition of acceptable traffic to the Internet
access-list 192 deny    ip any 192.168.0.0 0.0.255.255 log
access-list 192 deny    ip any 172.16.0.0 0.15.255.255 log
access-list 192 deny    ip any 10.0.0.0 0.255.255.255 log
access-list 192 deny    ip host 100.0.0.34 any log
access-list 192 deny    ip host 101.0.0.33 any log
access-list 192 permit ip 100.0.0.8 0.0.0.7 host 110.0.0.2
access-list 192 permit ip 101.0.0.8 0.0.0.7 host 110.0.0.2
```

(continued)

```
access-list 192 deny    ip 100.0.0.8 0.0.0.7 any log
access-list 192 deny    ip 101.0.0.8 0.0.0.7 any log
access-list 192 permit ip 100.0.0.0 0.0.0.255 any
access-list 192 permit ip 101.0.0.0 0.0.0.255 any
access-list 192 deny    ip any any log
! Definition of acceptable traffic from the inside
access-list 193 permit ip 100.0.0.8 0.0.0.7 host 100.0.0.34
access-list 193 permit ip 100.0.0.8 0.0.0.7 host 101.0.0.33
access-list 193 permit ospf host 100.0.0.33 host 224.0.0.5
access-list 193 permit ospf host 101.0.0.34 host 224.0.0.5
access-list 193 permit ospf host 100.0.0.33 host 100.0.0.34
access-list 193 permit ospf host 101.0.0.34 host 101.0.0.33
access-list 193 permit tcp host 192.168.0.1 host 192.168.0.2
➡ eq 179
access-list 193 permit tcp host 192.168.0.1 eq 179 host
➡ 192.168.0.2 established
access-list 193 deny    ip any 100.0.0.0 0.0.0.255 log
access-list 193 deny    ip any 101.0.0.0 0.0.0.255 log
access-list 193 permit ip 100.0.0.8 0.0.0.7 host 120.0.0.1
access-list 193 permit ip 101.0.0.8 0.0.0.7 host 120.0.0.1
access-list 193 permit ip 100.0.0.8 0.0.0.7 host 120.0.0.2
access-list 193 permit ip 101.0.0.8 0.0.0.7 host 120.0.0.2
access-list 193 deny    ip any 110.0.0.0 0.0.0.3 log
access-list 193 deny    ip any 120.0.0.0 0.0.0.3 log
access-list 193 deny    ip 100.0.0.8 0.0.0.7 any log
access-list 193 deny    ip 101.0.0.8 0.0.0.7 any log
access-list 193 permit ip 100.0.0.0 0.0.0.255 any
access-list 193 permit ip 101.0.0.0 0.0.0.255 any
access-list 193 deny    ip any any log
no cdp run
!
snmp-server community AccessCommunity RO 92
snmp-server trap-authentication
snmp-server enable traps
snmp-server host 100.0.0.11 TrapCommunity
snmp-server host 101.0.0.11 TrapCommunity
!
line con 0
 transport input none
!
line aux 0
access-class 90 in
transport input none
```

(continued)

```
!

line vty 0 4
login
password PickAGoodOne
access-class 91 in
!
end
```

LISTING 8-29. *Router External #2 configuration including typical protective features and access lists for an external router that is attaching to the Internet*

WRAP-UP

Connecting to other networks introduces another level of complexity into the internetworking arena. Interdomain routing requires us to exert more explicit control over the routing protocols because we can no longer assume compatible configuration of internal routing protocols, or even support for any specific protocol. The challenges of connecting to an ISP often have more to do with security than with routing, but the routing protocols can be formidable as well due to the huge number of networks that make up the Internet.

We started this chapter by looking at some simplifications that could be made when connecting to an isolated, trusted service provider by using the example of a retail chain connecting to a credit card authorization service. Our emphasis was on providing dynamic detection of link failures without having to trust our routing exchanges with the other party by using floating static routes driven by a mutually acceptable intradomain routing protocol such as EIGRP, OSPF, or RIP.

We then looked at the impact of connecting to an ISP, and ended the chapter with an example of using Border Gateway Protocol version 4 as a full partner in Internet routing exchanges. BGP is a "proper" way to connect with any service provider, but is usually not considered unless both parties are already familiar with BGP and running it for other purposes.

Along the way, we looked at techniques we could use for maximizing availability whether we used one ISP or multiple ISPs. We also looked at various levels of BGP usage, from simply determining if a link to an ISP was functional to carrying all routes on the Internet known to our ISPs. In the process, we saw that we could get most of the benefits of carrying full routes—without requiring a high end router—by using BGP to check for reachability of two or three key indicator routes.

As might be expected when discussing connections to the Internet, we also spent considerable time discussing security considerations. Keep in mind that security is not static, but a constantly changing requirement as new weaknesses are discovered and attacks get more sophisticated. The recommendations here should be considered only a starting point. It is essential to keep up to date with the latest security fixes and workarounds for the products and applications in use in your environment and adapt your configurations as required.

NOTE

1. Rekhter, Y., et al. *Address Allocation for Private Internets, Request for Comments: 1918,* February 1996.

Connecting Through Firewalls

Any time we have a connection between networks with differing security policies, we need to provide protection, usually in the form of a firewall. Depending upon the degree of protection required and the security policies of the organizations, the firewall can be implemented in any of several ways. Traditionally, a firewall is a stand-alone box. The box can be anything from a dedicated appliance—such as a Cisco PIX or Sonicwall firewall—to a general purpose NT, UNIX, or Linux system running filtering software. In between are "hardened" general-purpose systems dedicated to running firewall software, like Check Point's popular Firewall-1. Many router vendors also provide firewall capabilities on their routers, which may be suitable in cost-conscious environments with moderate security requirements.

We saw examples of both approaches in the previous chapter when we connected with external networks. When connecting to a trustworthy service supplier we defined access filters on our router, allowing it to serve as a firewall. For our Internet connections, we used dedicated firewalls.

But firewalls can be beneficial even between internal networks. In many organizations, firewalls are underutilized, and sensitive areas such as personnel and finance share common network resources with other functional areas. Appropriately placed and configured firewalls can protect sensitive systems and increase the probability of detecting harmful activities before they have a chance to cause loss or damage.

We will start this chapter with a look at how firewalls work and the terminology used to describe their operation. In the normal treatment of firewalls the emphasis is on security considerations. But we will assume the firewalls are capable of enforcing the desired security policy and instead focus on those firewall properties that affect the network design.

We will then look at various approaches for providing continued operation when a firewall fails. In a review of firewall-based solutions commonly provided by high availability firewall vendors, we will look at some of the tradeoffs between hot standby backup and load sharing solutions. We will also see how certain failures can prevent correct operation while not being detectable by the firewalls themselves.

We will finish the chapter by showing how routers can use BGP to detect the loss of a firewall. By using BGP to control the static routes used to actually forward packets to the firewalls, we can provide load sharing and automatic routing around firewall failures without sacrificing security.

FIREWALL CONCEPTS

The Internet Firewall FAQ[1] defines a firewall as "a system or group of systems that enforces an access control policy between two networks." Some firewall designs focus on what traffic to block and others focus on what traffic to permit; but the key function of all firewalls is to implement an access control policy.

Regardless of the firewall architecture chosen, it is critical to remember that the firewall is only a piece of the overall security solution, and overall security is only as strong as the weakest link in its implementation. In particular, firewalls provide no protection against attacks that do not go through the firewalls. They will not stop an employee from walking out of the building with crucial data on a floppy disk, nor protect the data on the hard drive of a laptop computer that is stolen from a traveling executive, nor block attacks through unmanaged modem dial-in access.

A firewall is only effective as part of an overall organizational security architecture implementing a realistic and meaningful security policy. The challenge of developing an appropriate security policy is non-trivial, since any security policy must recognize the following critical limitations in security implementation:

- Perfect security is impossible. We can only raise the cost of unauthorized access so that it is greater than the value of the asset being protected.

- Security has a price. Implementing security mechanisms will make access more difficult and more expensive for legitimate users. ·

Firewalls also provide no protection against attackers using social engineering to extract passwords and other access information from users, allowing an attacker to penetrate the firewall in the guise of a legitimate user. Also, a firewall cannot protect against application weaknesses that can be exploited through legitimate service requests, such as a Web interface to a database that does not perform validity checks on all requests.

How Firewalls Are Used

What firewalls can do, and do very well, is provide enforcement of access controls between networks, simplifying and strengthening the access controls already in place on services and user systems. For example, a firewall may be configured to allow only Web requests to get to the Web server, and only DNS requests to get to the domain name server, and yet provide inside users unhindered access to outside resources. That way, Web administrators can devote more time to strengthening Web services and less time to hardening their system to protect services not provided to the outside network.

When discussing firewall implementations, we will frequently use the terms *inside* and *outside,* as in Figure 9-1. We can think of the purpose of the firewall as protecting the users and services on the inside from the evil influences on the outside. While most firewall discussions associate the outside with the Internet and the inside with the organizational intranet, the concepts of inside and outside can get blurred when using firewalls to partition a network into secure compartments or when multiple networks are served from a single firewall.

Consider a firewall between a network serving the personnel department and a network serving the finance department. Depending upon the specific information that needs to be accessed, who holds the data, and who is driving the transaction, either network could be considered the outside or the inside. Neither side is inherently more trustworthy or more evil than the other. This can create confusion when configuring the firewall, as most firewall software has a strong inside-versus-outside bias in its configuration, requiring different commands or syntax depending upon the direction of the trust relationship.

Another potential confusion factor when discussing firewalls is that the security community has a very different conception of the term *single point of failure*. We have been using the term in the sense of service availability and the need for redundant communications paths to maintain network uptime. When security analysts refer to a single point of failure, they mean that a single lost component could allow a breach of the security policy desired. Compare the two Internet connection architectures in Figure 9-2.

In Figure 9-2(a), a breach of either firewall would allow direct access to the organization's intranet from the Internet, so a security analyst would consider the network architecture to have single points of failure. Yet from the availability perspective, the architecture with the single points of failure is the redundant security architecture of Figure 9-2(b). When discussing single points of failure

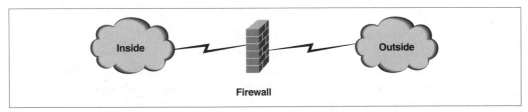

FIGURE 9-1. *Firewall terminology*

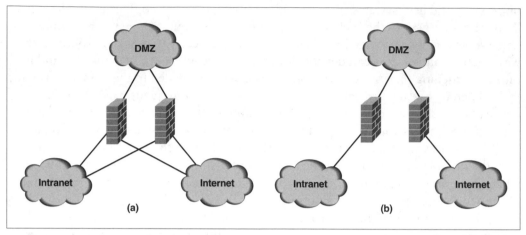

FIGURE 9-2.   *Single point of failure between Internet and intranet: (a) single point of failure from the security perspective; (b) single point of failure from the availability perspective*

and redundant solutions with security analysts, it is essential to understand which perspective is being used, because both definitions are correct within their associated context.

Finally, the DMZ network in Figure 9-2(a) shows another way a network can be both inside and outside. The DMZ is an outside network relative to the inside intranet, yet is an inside network relative to the outside Internet. Although not shown here, a common technique in production designs is the use of multiple DMZ networks. With this approach, when a DMZ system is lost to attackers, DMZ systems on other DMZ networks are still protected from a direct assault.

There are many styles of firewall operation, from simple address and socket filters to transparent application proxies. There are just as many conflicting claims as to which is better, which provides higher security, and which provides superior performance or transparency. Rather than get involved in the arguments and marketing claims, we will make only two distinctions regarding redundant connectivity through the firewalls. From the viewpoint of the network design, all we care about is whether the path through the firewall is state sensitive and whether the firewall appears to our routers as an end-system or as another router.

The former distinction is referred to as *stateless* versus *state sensitive* firewalls. The latter distinction is usually ignored by security experts, since it has no impact on firewall operation or effectiveness. It does, however, have considerable impact on the design of the networks supporting the firewalls, as will be seen in our configuration examples. Since there is no formal lexicon to describe the two modes, we will refer to them as router mode and end-system mode.

STATE SENSITIVE VERSUS STATELESS FIREWALLS

In a stateless firewall, each packet is independently evaluated, with no reference to any preceding packets that may have passed in either direction. A stateless firewall may also be referred to as a static NAT or a passive screening firewall. Fully transparent redundancy and load sharing are easily achieved when using stateless firewalls.

In a state sensitive firewall, the decision of whether to pass a packet will depend upon packets that have been seen before. Examples of state sensitive firewalls are stateful inspection and application proxy. State sensitive firewalls monitor the exchange of packets, opening holes in the firewall as needed for each allowed communication—such as when an inside user opens a TCP connection to an outside service. The firewall closes the holes it creates as soon as they are no longer needed for authorized traffic.

Transparent proxies depend heavily on state tracking so that protocols like FTP can work through the firewall without diminishing overall security. Our challenge with state sensitive firewalls is that the correct behavior of the firewall depends upon its state, and transparent redundancy is not possible unless the firewall can share that state information with its backup unit. This limits our ability to provide transparent redundancy for state sensitive firewalls to those which include proprietary synchronization mechanisms. If there is no synchronization of the state information between the firewalls, we can still automate the failover to a backup firewall. But all open communications requiring state information for support will be dropped and need to be reestablished through the replacement firewall before we continue.

When using state sensitive firewalls, we must ensure that our routing schemes always route packets between any communicating pair of users through the same firewall in both directions. Otherwise, the filter that was opened based on the inside connection request might not be on the firewall used to return the response from the outside system. For minimum service disruption, this firewall selection must be maintained despite failures in supporting routers or connected networks.

Even if the firewalls provide state synchronization, per-packet load balancing should normally only be used through stateless firewalls to minimize timing dependencies on state information updates. Load balancing with state sensitive firewalls, while possible, is difficult even on a per-destination basis. Many firewalls do a combination of stateless and state sensitive filtering. For our purposes, if there is any state sensitivity on the firewall, we will treat all use of the firewall for the affected users or subnetworks as state sensitive. To the extent that a particular communications session happens to be stateless, switch over to a backup firewall will still be transparent. Only load sharing will be affected by treating stateless sessions as state sensitive.

The choice of stateless versus state sensitive can impact the transparency of firewall failure recovery and may influence our approach to load balancing or route selection. However, we will ignore the distinction in our designs. Any design that will work with state sensitive firewalls will, by default, also work with stateless firewalls. Consequently, we will assume state sensitive firewall constraints in all our designs. This is often a good idea even with stateless firewalls because it minimizes the potential of delivering packets out of order on any specific data flow.

ROUTER MODE VERSUS END-SYSTEM MODE FIREWALLS

The distinction between router mode firewalls and end-system mode firewalls has a major impact on our network design. This may come as a surprise, given that the impact on a conventional network is so minimal that the distinction is usually ignored by the firewall specialist. Indeed, router mode versus end-system mode considerations are often confused with proxy-mode versus pass-through mode considerations, which can impact security but have no impact on network design.

Consider the situation in Figure 9-3. We have an outside user at address 110.1.2.3 who is authorized access to the inside server at 10.0.0.1. To the outside user, the server appears to have the address 100.0.0.99, a valid outside address on the same LAN as the outside interface of the firewall. Similarly, to the inside server, the outside user appears at address 10.1.2.99. The inside server sees the outside user as a normal inside user who happens to be on the same LAN segment as the firewall. The firewall provides the address translations, responding to the outside address of the inside server on its outside interface and to the inside address of the outside user on its inside interface.

When configured this way, the firewall acts as an end-system, serving as the end point for all connections requiring communications between the inside and the outside. From the viewpoint of the inside network, the firewall is the outside user, while from the viewpoint of the outside network, the firewall is the inside server. The firewall examines each packet coming from the outside user to the inside server to

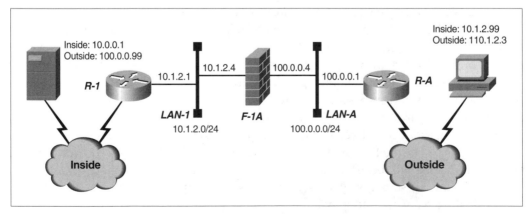

FIGURE 9-3. *Firewall running in end-system mode*

determine whether it meets the security policy in effect for that pairing of systems. Those requests that are allowed by the policy are then passed on to the internal server to be executed. The server's responses are then checked by the firewall to verify that they too are in accordance with the implemented security policy before the firewall sends them on to the outside user.

End-system mode firewall usage is compatible with any addressing scheme on either network because neither the inside nor the outside network has any visibility into the existence of the other network. There is no need for the IP addresses used on either side of the firewall to be unique. This allows the firewall to effectively link networks with overlapping address space, a common requirement when two organizations are using RFC 1918 private addresses. Communications can proceed safely and securely as long as there is address space in each network to be used by its side of the firewall. The application being supported must also use a protocol that the firewall knows how to proxy (or one that does not need to be proxied because no addressing information is carried as part of the protocol payload).

Consider Figure 9-4. The inside server at IP address 10.0.0.1 is now identified on the outside with address 100.9.9.99, while the outside user is translated to an inside address of 10.7.8.99. The firewall and surrounding networks are unchanged, but now the outbound packets have a destination address that is not associated with any inside LAN. Similarly, the outside address of the server is not associated with the outside LAN serving the firewall. These associations must now be provided by configuring the real routers on the network to associate the translated addresses with a path whose next hop is the firewall's interface. Correct routing will no longer occur automatically by virtue of the addresses assigned to the firewall services.

Another way to see the difference between end-system mode and router mode operation is to follow a packet from the inside server to the outside user. In either mode of operation, the packet is routed through the inside network until it arrives at

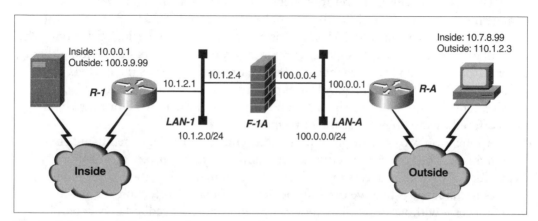

FIGURE **9-4.**   *Firewall running in router mode*

Router R-1. When running in end-system mode, Router R-1 will recognize the destination in the packet as an address on LAN-1 and use the Address Resolution Protocol (ARP) to get the Ethernet Medium Access Control (MAC) address to use for the IP address 10.1.2.99. The firewall will recognize the IP address as one of its service addresses and respond with the MAC address of the firewall's interface. All services and the management and control IP address of 10.1.2.4 share the same interface and the same MAC address, but only the firewall knows that. The end result is that Router R-1 sends the packet to the MAC address of the firewall's interface with an IP destination address of 10.1.2.99. On the other side of the firewall, the packet (assuming it passes all security tests) will be sent to Router R-A with a return address of 100.0.0.99 for delivery to the user system at 110.1.2.3.

When running in router mode, many aspects of end-system mode must be performed manually. To begin with, since there is no IP subnetwork containing 10.7.8.99 in the inside, we need to distribute knowledge of the correct path to use throughout the inside network. In a small network, we might include a static route on every inside router associating 10.7.8.99 with the IP address 10.1.2.4. In larger networks, this quickly becomes impractical, and we usually configure Router R-1 to redistribute its static route for 10.7.8.99 into the inside routing domain.

Once the packet arrives at Router R-1 (following the same route as in end-system mode), Router R-1 forwards the packet to the firewall at 10.1.2.4 as the next hop on the way to 10.7.8.99. To do so, it uses ARP to get the MAC address associated with 10.1.2.4, and gets back the MAC address of the firewall's interface. Just as with end-system mode, the end result is that Router R-1 sends the packet to the MAC address of the firewall's interface with an IP destination address of 10.7.8.99. From the viewpoint of the firewall, there is no difference between the packets delivered when it is running in end-system mode and when it is in router mode. What changes is how the real routers find the firewall.

This identity is even clearer if we keep all addresses as in Figure 9-3 but change the subnetwork mask on the access LANs to 255.255.255.192 so that they are /26 LANs rather than /24 LANs. In this case, the packets entering and leaving the firewall are identical even though the configuration of the routers surrounding them is very different. There is no change in how the firewall processes the packets passing between inside and outside, regardless of the mode of operation. There is also no requirement that the mode be the same on both sides of the firewall or that all services offered by the firewall use the same mode.

Application proxy firewalls in particular tend to be implemented using end-system mode. This makes the network configuration for the proxy an automatic byproduct of providing access to the firewall for configuration and management.

Our challenge is that we can only achieve automatic protection against firewall failures—without depending upon proprietary firewall redundancy capabilities—when the firewalls are treated by the routers as routers. The problem is that we cannot support two end-systems with the same IP address (which is what would be required for one end-system mode firewall to duplicate a specific service provided by another end-system mode firewall). With router mode, there is no problem having multiple IP addresses available as a route to a single IP address.

We will see in the last configuration example in this chapter that we actually can provide automatic failover for firewalls in end-system mode. But be forewarned: the solution is not pretty. We will use multiple tricks to make the firewalls appear to our routers as router mode firewalls, and then NAT the addresses used by the firewalls to present a consistent address appearance to users. The resultant configuration works, but it is complex and places strict constraints on address assignments.

FIREWALLS IN A FULLY REDUNDANT NETWORK

Figure 9-5 illustrates a classic redundant firewall configuration supporting two different connections between inside and outside. One connection uses static network address translation to support access by a specific outside user to a specific inside server using Firewall F-1A in end-system mode. The other uses dynamic network address translation with port remapping to support access by an internal Web surfer to any outside Web server. Firewall F-2B supports that service using router mode on the inside and end-system mode on the outside.

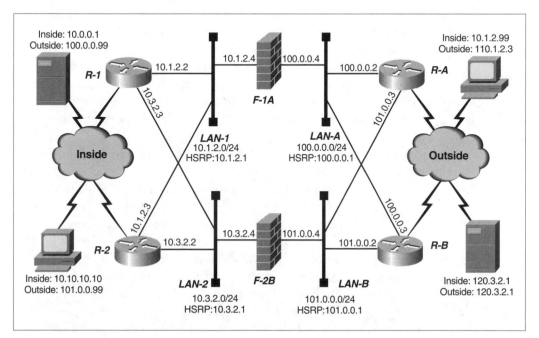

FIGURE 9-5. *Redundant firewalls with manual failure recovery*

Destinations reached through the upper firewall (Firewall F-1A) are transparent to the routers, as the firewall is configured to respond to the inside addresses to which the outside systems are translated. If an outside address is not translated to a valid address on LAN-1, it is invisible to the inside network. As a result, while it would be possible to introduce bad packets by penetrating the firewall, potential damage would be limited to a denial of service. This is true unless the penetration is complete enough to also provide a useable return address.

In the lower firewall (Firewall F-2B), it is not practical to specify a unique translation for every possible Internet destination. Instead, we must make a choice. If the application protocol is a popular one, such as Web access, we can force the inside user to access the outside service through a proxy interface on the firewall. Today's Web browsers are capable of sending all requests to a proxy server while maintaining the look and feel of a direct connection. Since using an explicit proxy server would only illustrate another implementation of end-system mode firewall usage, we instead will assume the use of a transparent proxy accessed as the default route for unknown addresses.

Using a default route rather than an explicit proxy address may be more convenient to the user, but it makes the job of providing protection more difficult for the firewall. It also makes it much more difficult to define and support multiple firewall paths to the outside. When using firewall proxies, we can advertise each outbound path separately and provide backup for each as required. But there is only one default route, so we must carefully adjust our routing to ensure that all packets to the outside from any specific authorized source will go to the same firewall.

Any inside router or link failures that change the available paths could cause the optimum default route for an inside user to change to a different firewall. This would shut down all open connections and interrupt application use. Typically, we would use policy routing on the inside to define different default routes for different inside users. We must use care in the policy routing design. It is important not only to ensure that the routing will work correctly, regardless of what fails, but also to ensure that we do not consume all available CPU cycles. Some modes of policy routing will force process switching on the interfaces involved.

In this book, our emphasis is on high availability. Any security problems that result in a denial of service (or a need to shut down networking to reduce exposure while a security breach is being repaired) could prevent us from attaining our availability goals. As a result, our examples of firewall usage will tend to be very conservative from a security as well as from a network design viewpoint.

For example, we assume that administration of the security policy and administration of the network are handled independently. Even though Cisco and other router vendors offer a wide range of firewall features on their routers, our designs always use stand-alone firewalls. This is not meant to imply that the router configurations should ignore security. Rather, it recognizes that the greater challenge that occurs when the firewalls are not under our control and we need to support them regardless.

The routers must protect themselves from hostile forces, particularly those on outside networks. Security is best served when the network and security are designed to reinforce and enhance each other. Just as we use multiple levels of redundancy for critical services—to keep the network functioning despite failures—we want to have the security design provide multiple layers of protection. Not only is it desirable to have a barrier that will control the damage when our first layer of protection is overcome, it is also more efficient to stop illicit traffic before it gets into our network.

Typically, we provide a first layer of defense at the outside routers. Denial of service attacks targeting the network protocols themselves, such as smurf and TCP Syn-flood, should be stopped before they have a chance to consume network resources. This also reduces the number of nuisance hits on the protection provided by the firewalls. When a firewall reports an attack that should have been stopped by the router feeding it, we know we need to get to work quickly and repair the router configuration before the firewall succumbs as well. By the same token, if we start getting security violation reports from the inside router, it means that our firewall has been penetrated by evil forces. We are now potentially less than one layer of protection away from exposing everything we are trying to protect. Our normal response at this point is to immediately disconnect the firewall from the network to prevent further encroachment and to allow us to analyze and isolate the break-in. Once we understand the attack and know which vulnerability was exploited, we can adjust our defenses and return to normal operation.

CONFIGURATION EXAMPLE—REDUNDANT NETWORK WITH FIREWALLS

Security philosophy is easy to talk about, but how do we configure the routers to support the firewalls and end-systems of Figure 9-5?

In this baseline dual redundant network design, we use a separate LAN for each firewall and dedicate it to the firewall. Any local users at the site supported by the same routers are put on their own LAN segments. This keeps the traffic patterns simple and eliminates any unnecessary processing demands on the firewalls. It also ensures that any attacks must get past all three security barriers with no support before reaching vulnerable systems. Filters and firewall features are more easily added on the routers, allowing for reinforcement of the security policy implemented in the firewalls.

Firewall F-1A is assumed to be configured to support the communications between the inside server and the outside user using the values in Table 9-1. The conduit through the firewall is configured so that the outside user appears to the inside server as an inside user at address 10.1.2.99. Similarly, the outside user sees the inside server as an outside server at address 100.0.0.99. This is a classic end-system mode

TABLE 9-1. *Assumed Configuration for Firewall F-1A in Figure 9-5*

SERVICE	CONFIGURATION
IP address of inside firewall interface for management and control .	10.1.2.4/24
IP address of outside firewall interface for management and control	100.0.0.4/24
Default gateway for inside firewall interface (outside to inside traffic)	10.1.2.1
Default gateway for outside firewall interface (inside to outside traffic)	100.0.0.1
Inside firewall address for conduit from inside server to outside user @ 110.1.2.3	10.1.2.99
Outside firewall address for conduit from outside user to inside server @ 10.0.0.1	100.0.0.99

firewall configuration for a dedicated application. It could be used not just for communications with the outside world, as implied here, but also for support of applications accessed via a corporate intranet. After all, not all areas of the organization are at the same security level. Consider access to headquarters' payroll information by the human resources manager at a branch office.

Firewall F-2B is assumed to be configured as a hybrid of router mode on the inside and end-system mode on the outside, using the specifications in Table 9-2. Outbound packets from the Web-surfing user at 10.10.10.10 are addressed to the actual outside IP address of the servers being accessed, although the outside servers think the requests are coming from a browser at 101.0.0.99 rather than 10.10.10.10. No routing is done by the firewall. It is therefore up to the inside access routers to generate a default route for the organization pointing to the service address on this firewall. Since this is the only application requiring a default route, we will not worry about supporting and controlling multiple default routes in this example.

HSRP (or VRRP with routers other than Cisco's) is used on the routers to allow the firewalls to use a single static default gateway for all traffic leaving the firewall. Normally, Firewall F-1A sends its packets through Routers R-1 and R-A, while Firewall F-2B sends its packets through Routers R-2 and R-B, providing a degree of router load balancing. However, should a router fail, the default gateway will automatically and transparently switch over to the remaining router.

Many security policies will not allow HSRP or VRRP to be used if there are any systems on the access LAN than firewalls and routers. This is because the weak authentication in these protocols makes it too easy for a corrupted system to capture all traffic by asserting a high priority and taking over as the active router. This is a

TABLE 9-2. *Assumed Configuration for Firewall F-2B in Figure 9-5*

SERVICE	CONFIGURATION
IP address of inside firewall interface for management and control	10.3.2.4/24
IP address of outside firewall interface for management and control	101.0.0.4/24
Default gateway for inside firewall interface (outside to inside traffic)	10.3.2.1
Default gateway for outside firewall interface (inside to outside traffic)	101.0.0.1
Inside firewall address for conduit from inside surfer to outside world @ any address	10.3.2.12
Outside firewall address for conduit from outside world back to surfer @ 10.10.10.10	101.0.0.99

tradeoff, as the use of HSRP or VRRP makes the configuration of the firewall much easier. It also eliminates the need to run a routing protocol on the firewall in order to take advantage of the availability of a backup router.

Now that we understand how the firewalls are configured to perform their security function, we can turn our attention to the router configurations required to support those functions. We will start with Router R-1, the top inside router, in Listing 9-1. Keep in mind that the listings in this example only include the configuration required to support communications through the firewalls. They do not include

```
version 11.0
!
hostname R-1
!
ip subnet-zero
!
interface Loopback0
 description Management and Routing Identifier
 ip address 10.200.123.1 255.255.255.255
!
interface Ethernet0
 description LAN-1 link to firewall F-1A
 ip address 10.1.2.2 255.255.255.0
 no ip redirects
```
                                                        (continued)

```
  standby priority 200
  standby preempt
  standby ip 10.1.2.1
 !
interface Ethernet1
  description LAN-2 link to firewall F-2B
  ip address 10.3.2.3 255.255.255.0 secondary
  no ip redirects
  standby priority 100
  standby ip 10.3.2.1
 !
interface Serial0
  description T1 Link to inside backbone (area 0)
  ip address 192.168.0.2 255.255.255.252
  bandwidth 1500
 !
interface Serial1
  description Alternate Link to inside backbone (area 0)
  ip address 192.168.0.6 255.255.255.252
  bandwidth 1500
 !
router ospf 123
  network 10.1.2.0 0.0.0.255 area 1.2.3.4
  network 10.3.2.0 0.0.0.255 area 1.2.3.4
  network 10.200.123.1 0.0.0.0 area 1.2.3.4
  network 192.168.0.0 0.0.0.7 area 0.0.0.0
  default-information originate
  area 1.2.3.4 range 10.200.123.0 255.255.255.192
 !
 ! Route Internet to F-2B web proxy
 ip route 0.0.0.0 0.0.0.0 10.3.2.12
 !
end
```

LISTING 9-1. *Inside Router R-1 supporting firewalls to the outside*

any of the access filters or other protection essential to protect each router's integrity. They also do not include filtering that duplicates that expected from the firewall, as would normally be used to provide redundant security protection.

While we show connections from this router into the OSPF backbone area, we have omitted support for any LANs servicing local users. Remember that only access routers and the firewalls are allowed on the access networks. If there were local users to be supported, we would define additional LAN interfaces to support them. Any other use of the access LANs would weaken our security, as well as making the configuration of redundant security barriers on the access routers much more complex.

We start with a loopback address to identify this router to network management and to provide a stable router ID for OSPF advertisements. We then define our two interfaces for the access LANs. Filters for self-protection and redundant security barriers are not shown because they would depend upon the security policy being enforced. Depending upon our load balancing goals, we might also add OSPF routing weights to the access LAN definitions. This would steer incoming traffic from the inside network to the preferred router, if it is available.

On the other hand, since we have configured this router as an OSPF area border router, we would be better served if we summarized as many of the LANs as possible into our OSPF advertisements. We do this for the loopback addresses in the *area* command under *router ospf*. This is a common practice in OSPF LANs; it minimizes the size of all routing tables on all routers in the domain. It also eliminates the need for routers outside the area to recalculate the routing tables every time a link or router in the area goes up or down.

We can see that our choice of addresses for the access LANs was not good from an OSPF viewpoint. They were chosen for this example to minimize the potential for confusion when reading the configurations, not for efficient area route summarization. In a production network, we would have different priorities.

One quirk of Cisco's implementation of OSPF worth noting is that even though the default route is defined by a static route, we must use the command *default-information originate* rather than *redistribute static* to get OSPF to advertise a default route. This is a side effect of the way the OSPF protocol handles default routes.

The configuration of the other inside router, Router R-2, in Listing 9-2 is a mirror image of that of Router R-1.

```
version 11.0
!
hostname R-2
!
interface Loopback0
 description Management and Routing Identifier
 ip address 10.200.123.2 255.255.255.255
!
interface Ethernet0
 description LAN-1 link to firewall F-1A
 ip address 10.1.2.3 255.255.255.0
 no ip redirects
```
(continued)

```
   standby priority 100
   standby ip 10.1.2.1
 !
interface Ethernet1
  description LAN-2 link to firewall F-2B secondary
  ip address 10.3.2.2 255.255.255.0 secondary
  no ip redirects
  standby priority 200
  standby preempt
  standby ip 10.3.2.1
 !
interface Serial0
  description T1 Link to inside backbone (area 0)
  ip address 192.168.0.10 255.255.255.252
  bandwidth 1500
 !
interface Serial1
  description Alternate Link to inside backbone (area 0)
  ip address 192.168.0.14 255.255.255.252
  bandwidth 1500
 !
router ospf 123
  network 10.1.2.0 0.0.0.255 area 1.2.3.4
  network 10.3.2.0 0.0.0.255 area 1.2.3.4
  network 10.200.123.2 0.0.0.0 area 1.2.3.4
  network 192.168.0.8 0.0.0.7 area 0.0.0.0
  default-information originate
  area 1.2.3.4 range 10.200.123.0 255.255.255.192
 !
 ! Route Internet to F-2B web proxy
ip route 0.0.0.0 0.0.0.0 10.3.2.12
 !
end
```

LISTING 9-2.   *Inside Router R-2 supporting firewalls to the outside*

Listings 9-3 and 9-4 provide the critical parts of the configurations of the routers outside the firewalls. Again, the access-lists, packet filters, and other configuration items essential to protect the routers in a hostile environment are not shown but would need to be included in a production configuration. This is particularly important when the routers are connected directly to the Internet, as they are in this example.

```
version 11.0
!
hostname R-A
!
!  WARNING!! Self defense configuration statements not shown
!
ip subnet-zero
!
interface Loopback0
 description Target address for IBGP neighboring
 ip address 192.168.0.1 255.255.255.255
!
interface Serial0/0
 description T1 to ISP #1
 ip address 110.0.0.1 255.255.255.252
!
interface Ethernet1/0
 description LAN-A link to firewall F-1A
 ip address 100.0.0.2 255.255.255.0
 no ip redirects
 standby 6 priority 200
 standby 6 preempt
 standby 6 ip 100.0.0.1
!
interface Ethernet1/1
 description LAN-B link to firewall F-2B
 ip address 101.0.0.3 255.255.255.0
 no ip redirects
 standby 7 priority 100
 standby 7 ip 101.0.0.1
!
router ospf 60000
 passive-interface Serial0/0
 network 100.0.0.0 0.0.0.255 area 1.2.3.4
 network 101.0.0.0 0.0.0.255 area 1.2.3.4
 network 110.0.0.0 0.0.0.3 area 1.2.3.4
 network 192.168.0.1 0.0.0.0 area 1.2.3.4
!
router bgp 60000
 network 100.0.0.0 mask 255.255.255.0
 network 101.0.0.0 mask 255.255.255.0
```

(*continued*)

```
  neighbor 110.0.0.2 remote-as 54321
  neighbor 110.0.0.2 filter-list 10 out
  neighbor 192.168.0.2 remote-as 60000
  neighbor 192.168.0.2 update-source Loopback0
!
ip classless
!
ip as-path access-list 10 permit ^(_60000)*$
!
end
```

LISTING 9-3. *Outside Router R-A supporting firewall access to the inside*

```
version 11.0
!
hostname R-B
!
!  WARNING!! Self defense configuration statements not shown
!
ip subnet-zero
!
interface Loopback0
 description Target address for IBGP neighboring
 ip address 192.168.0.2 255.255.255.255
!
interface Serial0/0
 description T1 to ISP #2
 ip address 120.0.0.1 255.255.255.252
!
interface Ethernet1/0
 description LAN-A link to firewall F-1A
 ip address 100.0.0.3 255.255.255.0
 no ip redirects
 standby 6 priority 100
 standby 6 ip 100.0.0.1
!
interface Ethernet1/1
 description LAN-B link to firewall F-2B
 ip address 101.0.0.2 255.255.255.0 secondary
 no ip redirects
 standby 7 priority 200
 standby 7 preempt
```

(continued)

```
   standby 7 ip 101.0.0.1
 !
router ospf 60000
 passive-interface Serial0/0
 network 100.0.0.0 0.0.0.255 area 1.2.3.4
 network 101.0.0.0 0.0.0.255 area 1.2.3.4
 network 120.0.0.0 0.0.0.3 area 1.2.3.4
 network 192.168.0.2 0.0.0.0 area 1.2.3.4
 !
router bgp 60000
 network 100.0.0.0 mask 255.255.255.0
 network 101.0.0.0 mask 255.255.255.0
 neighbor 120.0.0.2 remote-as 54321
 neighbor 120.0.0.2 filter-list 10 out
 neighbor 192.168.0.1 remote-as 60000
 neighbor 192.168.0.1 update-source Loopback0
 !
ip classless
 !
ip as-path access-list 10 permit ^(_60000)*$
 !
end
```

LISTING 9-4. *Outside Router R-B supporting firewall access to the inside*

The configurations of the firewall access LANs are a mirror image of those of the inside router configuration. HSRP is again used to simplify outbound routing from the firewalls themselves. If the firewalls were being used internally for the isolation of sensitive areas, there might be no significant difference in the router configurations. However, in this example, we assume that the outside connects to the Internet. We include BGP routing statements required to connect to redundant Internet service providers, as in the example configurations in Chapter 8.

This example differs slightly from those in Chapter 8: the firewalls are configured so that all services look like end-systems on the LAN. As we mentioned earlier, whether the firewalls run in end-system mode or in router mode, the data packets sent are identical.

The only functional difference here is in the way the router determines what MAC address to use for a packet heading toward the firewall. In Chapter 8, where we used a static route pointing to the IP address of the firewall's interface, the router would ARP for the address of the firewall port and forward the packet there. In this configuration, the router ARPs for the MAC address associated with the outside address of the inside destination. It is up to the firewall to respond with the MAC address of its interface. Either way, the bits going over the wire will have the MAC address of the firewall interface and the outside IP address of the inside destination.

The only configuration difference between this example and those in Chapter 8 is that the path to the destination may be defined by a static route or by virtue of being on a connected subnetwork. This, in turn, changes how we distribute paths to outside destinations through the interior routing protocol. We may need to redistribute static routes, redistribute connected networks, or do nothing (if the advertisements happen automatically as a result of running a routing protocol on the interface to coordinate with other routers on the same access LAN).

One simplification that results from configuring the firewall to look like endsystems is the elimination of the static routes for all the inside networks. Because the access LANs are configured to include the entire range of the public network address space, there is no need for aggregate routes pointing to the null interface. BGP can now get the correct routes from the Ethernet interfaces.

One problem we have not yet addressed is that while our configuration may have no single points of failure in the router or network portions of the design, each firewall is a single point of failure for the services it is providing. Even though we have two firewalls with fully redundant cross connects, each firewall provides its own distinct set of services and neither can substitute for the other.

REDUNDANT FIREWALLS WITH AUTOMATIC SWITCHOVER

The bottom line is that even though all components on both networks are fully redundant, the firewalls only look redundant—neither firewall is capable of filling in for the other. Firewalls are designed to be an exclusive choke point in the path of the traffic they are intended to control. Providing alternate paths that do not go through a firewall is generally not going to help maintain a protected environment.

We could solve our availability dilemma by keeping the configuration essentially unmodified and using extremely reliable firewalls. This usually means using a clustered firewall implementation that presents a single system image to the network. StoneBeat FullCluster from Stonesoft is a popular product supporting this approach. It interconnects multiple Check Point FireWall-1 systems, running on standard NT or Solaris systems, to create a scalable firewall cluster. By providing transparent failover of individual systems and continuity of IP addresses, the cluster is seen as one firewall from the viewpoint of the network.

Other vendors provide equivalent approaches to provision high availability firewalls. We need to be careful in selecting our implementation though, as many do not preserve state information, which causes all open connections to be lost. State synchronization is particularly difficult in a Virtual Private Network (VPN) application environment providing secure tunnels. Generally, solutions will either be based on a hot standby approach or a load sharing approach.

The hot standby firewall approach in Figure 9-6 is the easiest approach to implement. The failover is invisible to the network infrastructure, and there is no reduction in capacity when running in backup mode. However, this approach is not without its weaknesses. The standby firewall does not contribute to production capacity while in standby state. And some mechanism is needed to routinely test the standby firewall to ensure that it will function properly when required. Plus, we need to be aware of the mechanism provided by the manufacturer for accessing the backup firewalls while in standby mode. We also need to know if it changes when the standby goes active.

The load sharing backup approach in Figure 9-7 lacks the simplicity of the standby firewall approach and is only supported by a few firewall vendors, usually in the form of a proprietary firewall cluster architecture. The key benefit of this approach is that it allows us to utilize the full capacity of all installed firewalls. At the same time, we may need even more complexity in order to provide stable service throttling if a firewall should fail during peak loading, when we are in need of full capacity.

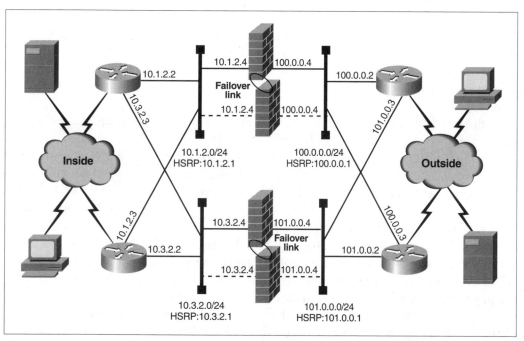

FIGURE 9-6. *Redundant firewalls with hot standby failover*

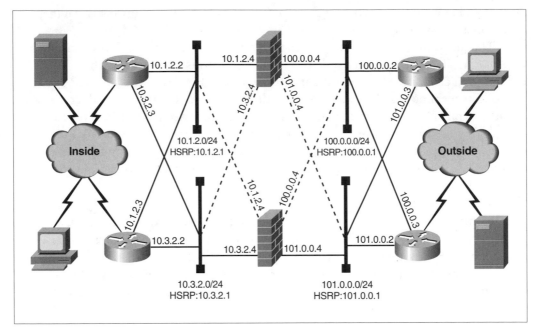

FIGURE 9-7. *Redundant firewalls with load sharing failover*

Regardless of the mode of redundancy, we need to consider how the backup returns control to the primary firewall when that system returns to service. This is particularly critical if the firewalls in use have no provision for synchronizing state information. The return to normal operation would then also cause a service disruption for users.

Either of these approaches is far better than no redundancy at all; but we are still exposed to single points of failure due to our reliance on the firewalls to detect any problems that might require a failover. After all the problem that requires us to switch to a backup firewall may not be in the firewall at all but in the router or the LAN components required to access the firewall. Consider the impact of a LAN failure that prevents an access router from reaching the access LAN but does not cause the LAN interface on the router to go down. The router would have no way of detecting the need to switch to a backup path, because its LAN interface would still be up. Traffic would be forwarded to oblivion rather than to the other access router, which could still reach the firewalls. We cannot expect a protocol running between the primary and backup firewalls to detect this mode of failure.

This is another manifestation of the same problem we encountered in earlier chapters when connecting routers over a Frame Relay, cell relay, or any other network service link. Loss of connectivity between the two communicating end points may occur with no indication of problems at the physical or link level. The solution is the same. We need to run a routing protocol end to end through the link to continuously test for proper connectivity.

The problem is that, in a security-conscious environment, routing and firewalls do not mix. The purpose of putting in a firewall in the first place is that the systems on either side of the firewall are unwilling to trust one another. Even if we have compatible addressing schemes on either side of the firewall, we dare not accept a potentially untrustworthy routing update. Such an update could cause us to route packets into a black hole or, even worse, deliver sensitive information into the hands of someone not authorized to see it.

Nor is it desirable to run a routing protocol between the access routers and the firewall. One of the cardinal rules of firewall design is to keep the number of services and protocols running on the firewall to the absolute minimum. Each service or protocol supported opens up the firewall to one more avenue of attack and distracts it from its primary role of providing protected traffic flows.

However, what we can do with minimal impact on security is exchange very well-defined packets between an inside router and an outside router. This will serve solely to determine whether the path between them through a particular firewall is functional. If we determine that the path is good, then we can enable the appropriate static routes to utilize that path for production traffic. If more than one path is available, we can adjust our static routes to use the preferred path. The key is to make the packets easy for the firewall to test and validate—minimizing the size of the hole which must be opened through the firewall to support the exchange—and to not depend upon the correctness of the packets received, except in determining that the path appears useable.

In this way, even if the other side is taken over by hostile forces, the worst they can do is either convince us to shut down the link (which is now under their control anyway, and consequently no loss) or to continue to use it as usual (which we would have been doing regardless if we had taken the conservative approach of routing only via static routes).

The ability to automatically determine if a particular firewall is up or down, while interesting, does not provide us with an automatic fallback capability. That requires some additional effort. We will look at two scenarios. In one, for router mode firewalls, the addresses used to identify systems on the other side of the firewall are independent of the addresses assigned to the firewall interface. The other is for end-system mode firewalls; in it, the firewalls directly respond to all destination addresses assigned to the other side.

For the router mode firewall environment, we can configure our firewalls with different interface addresses but otherwise mirror all provided services. We then use our dynamically driven static routes to select the best firewall available, automatically choosing a functional firewall and router combination regardless of any firewall, LAN, or router failure.

Working with end-system mode firewalls is more challenging. Any time it is not possible to define the services on both firewalls to use the same inside and outside addresses, we will need to be more creative. Success will require using network address translation on the routers. The different addresses required to use each firewall will then appear as a single IP address to the end-systems actually communicating. We will also need to play games with the IP subnetwork masks when using end-system mode firewalls to get around routing limitations.

Before we get into the details of automating failover between alternative end-system mode firewalls, we will examine automating failover when using mirrored router mode firewalls. Even if all your firewalls run in end-system mode, it is necessary to understand how the router mode configuration works. Theoretically, router controlled switchover to a backup firewall is impossible with end-system mode firewalls. Our end-system mode configuration only works because we trick the routers at each end into thinking they are working with router mode firewalls.

ROUTER CONTROLLED FAILOVER USING MIRRORED ROUTER MODE FIREWALLS

The most common use of router mode firewalls, when the address of the firewall and the address of the destination on the other side of the firewall are independent, is to support general purpose Internet access. We will consider the application scenario in

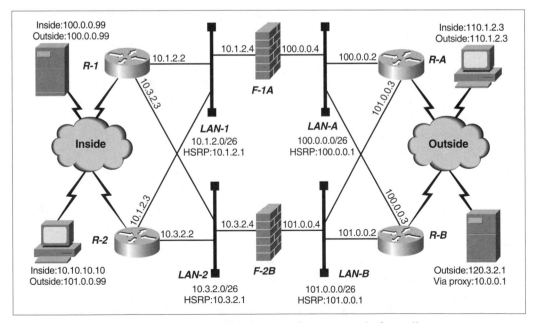

FIGURE 9-8. *Router controlled firewall failover with router mode firewalls*

Figure 9-8. While we show only a single user reaching out to the Internet and a single Web server being accessed from the Internet, the solution is easily scaled to support as many systems as the firewalls can handle. We just need to keep in mind that, while in normal operations we can split the load across both firewalls, that is not the case here. We need to size the firewalls to be able to continue operations with adequate performance when just one of the two remains functional.

The firewalls in this scenario are assumed to be configured identically in terms of the user services provided. That means that all addresses used for network address translation or proxy access are independent of the addresses used to identify the physical ports on the firewall. From the viewpoint of the logical operation of the network, the security policy implemented on the firewalls and the mechanisms used to enforce security are irrelevant.

We assume each firewall will pass any legitimate Web traffic between any valid Internet address and our Web server at 100.0.0.99. (We also assume it will block any traffic other than correctly formatted Web requests—or Web requests directed to, or responses returning from, any server on the inside other than 100.0.0.99.) On this network, we route to the public address of the Web server and establish a default route that takes us back out to the outside world via a firewall. In the context of our Internet connection examples in Chapter 8, when we discuss access to the Web server, the entire inside network is one of our DMZ networks.

The inside user access to the World Wide Web, on the other hand, is more typical of an internal network in the context of Chapter 8's examples. The inside user is configured to use a proxy server for access to the outside world. The user's Web browser makes all of its requests indirectly, sending them in packets addressed to the proxy server at 10.0.0.1 rather than to the ultimate destination. From the viewpoint of routing on the internal network, all we need is a route to the proxy server. Since our firewalls are running in router-like mode, they appear as the final hop on the way to 10.0.0.1, allowing us to define the same proxy on both firewalls.

Note that we need to configure the routing so that any specific user's requests will always be delivered to the same firewall's proxy server. Otherwise, the state information will be unavailable and the user's browsing will be disrupted. While this service disruption is considered acceptable if the alternative is no service—as when switching firewalls to recover from a firewall or access failure—it is not something we want as part of normal operation.

If we were using a transparent firewall configuration rather than one with an explicit proxy address, the inside router configuration would duplicate the configuration used to support the inside Web server. In a high-traffic environment, routing toward a default address makes it more difficult to load share. With a service proxy, we can easily load share by defining multiple proxy addresses and prioritizing each to use a different firewall under normal (all firewalls functional) operating conditions. When running transparent, however, we would need to use policy routing and artificial target addresses to distribute the outgoing traffic based on the inside source address.

The key to recovering from firewall failure here is our use of BGP to detect when a path through a firewall is available. By advertising a unique target address for each available path, we can trigger the appropriate floating static route to direct our production traffic. At a minimum, we need two paths between the inside and the outside that share no common components. For example, we could use one path consisting of Router R-1 to Router R-A via Firewall F-1A and a second of Router R-2 to Router R-B via Firewall F-2B. These two paths are all that would be required for a fully redundant solution with no single point of failure.

To provide protection against as many double faults as possible, we define four paths rather than two, using the paths in Table 9-3. Defining eight paths—to protect against all survivable triple failures that leave one inside router, one firewall, and one outside router still working—is normally not worth the effort. BGP configuration is much more complex if we try to support two firewalls connecting the same pair of routers. Plus, no matter how many paths we define, some double failures—including both inside routers, both outside routers, or both firewalls—are impossible to protect against without adding a third level of redundancy. Also, keep in mind that failure of any access LAN is equivalent to failure of the firewall served by that LAN.

The primary disadvantage of using four paths rather than two is the added configuration complexity. There are more BGP peerings to set up (and for the routers to maintain) and twice the number of static routes. However, in a state-sensitive firewall environment, this is a small price to pay for eliminating the need to change firewalls when a router fails.

For the example configurations that follow, we will assume the firewalls are configured to support the ports, routes, and user services in Table 9-4. The configuration is the same as that of a conventional firewall setup supporting the given applications and subject to the given desired security policies. The only difference is the duplication of the application support services on both firewalls using identical addressing.

The critical concept behind our design is in the shift from using static routes pointing to a specific firewall service address to direct incoming and outgoing traffic

TABLE 9-3. *Path Selection for Maximum Double Fault Tolerance Using Four Paths*

PATH	INSIDE ROUTER	FIREWALL OR LAN	OUTSIDE ROUTER
1	Router R-1	Firewall F-1A	Router R-A
2	Router R-1	Firewall F-2B	Router R-B
3	Router R-2	Firewall F-1A	Router R-B
4	Router R-2	Firewall F-2B	Router R-A

TABLE 9-4.   *Firewall Configuration for Simple Firewall Redundancy Example*

SERVICE	CONFIGURATION
IP address of inside firewall interface for management and control	10.1.2.4/26 for Firewall F-1A 10.3.2.4/26 for Firewall F-2B
IP address of outside firewall interface for management and control	100.0.0.4/26 for Firewall F-1A 101.0.0.4/26 for Firewall F-2B
Default gateway for inside firewall interface (outside to inside traffic)	10.1.2.1 for Firewall F-1A 10.3.2.1 for Firewall F-2B
Default gateway for outside firewall interface (inside to outside traffic)	100.0.0.1 for Firewall F-1A 101.0.0.1 for Firewall F-2B
Inside route from DMZ to all outside addresses (default route)	Primary: 0.0.0.0/0 via 10.1.2.4 Secondary: 0.0.0.0/0 via 10.3.2.4
Outside route from all addresses to DMZ servers	Primary: 100.0.0.96/28 via 100.0.0.4 Secondary: 100.0.0.96/28 via 101.0.0.4
Web services offered by DMZ server	Any public address to 100.0.0.99 asking for services provided by server
Inside route from inside users to WWW and FTP proxy	Primary: 10.0.0.1/32 via 10.1.2.4 Secondary: 10.0.0.1/32 via 10.3.2.4
Outside route from all addresses to firewall proxy server	Primary: 101.0.0.99/32 via 100.0.0.4 Secondary: 101.0.0.99/32 via 101.0.0.4
World Wide Web access from internal network users	Proxy access from inside at 10.0.0.1. Outside proxy uses address 101.0.0.99

to one firewall only. Instead, we use floating static routes that point to loopback interface addresses on the other side of the firewalls. The addresses are learned via BGP. When a path fails, the target address associated with that path becomes unreachable and a backup route using a different path floats into effect. By careful selection of the route weights and sharing of local route information between routers, we minimize the potential for unnecessary changing of firewalls for any traffic flow.

Table 9-5 gives the definitions of the conduits for exchanging BGP routing information. These conduits are the key to automating firewall failover. Note that we only provide a conduit for the BGP speaker on the inside to contact the BGP speaker on the outside. If the BGP speakers on the outside routers do not support a passive (listen-only) option, this will cause false alarms during connection setup as the outside BGP speakers attempt to connect to their neighbors on the inside. The connection attempts will stop as soon as the inside speaker establishes a connection to the outside speaker but could be annoying if an inside speaker failed.

TABLE 9-5. *Firewall Configuration for Simple Firewall Redundancy Example*

SERVICE	CONFIGURATION
BGP Conduit for R-1 with R-A via F-1A (TCP to Port 179, inside to outside)	10.1.2.2 NAT to 100.0.0.65 100.0.0.2 NAT to 10.1.2.65
BGP Conduit for R-1 with R-B via F-2B (TCP to Port 179, inside to outside)	10.3.2.3 NAT to 101.0.0.65 101.0.0.2 NAT to 10.3.2.66
BGP Conduit for R-2 with R-B via F-1A (TCP to Port 179, inside to outside)	10.1.2.3 NAT to 100.0.0.66 100.0.0.3 NAT to 10.1.2.66
BGP Conduit for R-2 with R-A via F-2B (TCP to Port 179, inside to outside)	10.3.2.2 NAT to 101.0.0.66 101.0.0.3 NAT to 10.3.2.65

In this example, we prefer to have Firewall F-1A handle the DMZ Web server traffic and Firewall F-2B handle interior Web surfers. So we define two target addresses on each of the four routers, one for each path to that router using the assignments in Table 9-6. We can then use address filters on our BGP advertisements to allow only the correct targets to be learned over each peering associated with any path.

We then define our floating static routes so that DMZ traffic will use Path 1 or 3 before using Path 2 or 4, while surfers will use Path 2 or 4 if available and only use Path 1 or 3 if they have no choice. Note that in order for failure recovery to work, the routers must only be able to learn a route to the target addresses on the other side of the firewall through BGP.

Since BGP includes the address of the next hop to take as part of the route advertisement, we will need to configure our BGP speakers to override that address with the correct address on the firewall. The specific technique used will depend upon the BGP implementation. For example, with Cisco routers we use route maps, while with the Merit GateD routing daemon for UNIX and Linux, we would configure a gateway address as part of the peer definition. The critical requirement is that we do not accept the next hop specified by the router on the other side of the firewall.

TABLE 9-6. *Target Addresses for Each Path from Each Router*

PATH	INSIDE ROUTER ADVERTISES	FIREWALL	OUTSIDE ROUTER ADVERTISES
1: R-1⇔F-1A⇔R-A	10.255.255.1 (on R-1)	Firewall F-1A	10.255.255.11 (on R-A)
2: R-1⇔F-2B⇔R-B	10.255.255.2 (on R-1)	Firewall F-2B	10.255.255.13 (on R-B)
3: R-2⇔F-1A⇔R-B	10.255.255.3 (on R-2)	Firewall F-1A	10.255.255.14 (on R-B)
4: R-2⇔F-2B⇔R-A	10.255.255.4 (on R-2)	Firewall F-2B	10.255.255.12 (on R-A)

CONFIGURATION EXAMPLE: AUTOMATIC FAILOVER WITH ROUTER MODE FIREWALLS

As with all the example configurations in this chapter, router configuration for self defense and to reinforce firewall restrictions (for redundant security protection) is not shown. This allows us to focus on the routing aspects of the implementation. In a real world implementation, particularly one connecting to the Internet, neglecting router security can be expected to have a major adverse impact on availability.

Listing 9-5 shows the essential parts of the configuration of Router R-1. We set up our static routes so that Firewall F-1A is the preferred path to the general outside world. We use the direct path from this router if BGP indicates that the path through Firewall F-1A to Router R-A is up. Otherwise, we take the longer path via Router R-2 if it is advertising (via BGP) a path through Firewall F-1A to Router R-B. Only if neither inside router has a path via Firewall F-1A will we fall back to a path through Firewall F-2B.

```
version 11.2
!
hostname R-1
!
ip subnet-zero
!
interface Loopback0
 description Management ID for this Router
 ip address 10.0.0.101 255.255.255.255
!
interface Loopback1
 description Target IP for outside to inside via firewall F-1A
 ip address 10.255.255.1 255.255.255.255
!
interface Loopback2
 description Target IP for outside to inside via firewall F-2B
 ip address 10.255.255.2 255.255.255.255
!
interface Ethernet0
 description Firewall Access LAN-1
 ip address 10.1.2.2 255.255.255.192
 standby 1 priority 200
 standby 1 preempt
 standby 1 ip 10.1.2.1
!
```

(continued)

```
interface Ethernet1
 description Firewall Access LAN-2
 ip address 10.3.2.3 255.255.255.192
 standby 2 priority 100
 standby 2 ip 10.3.2.1
!
router ospf 123
 redistribute static subnets route-map advertise
 network 10.0.0.101 0.0.0.0 area 59
 network 10.1.2.0 0.0.0.63 area 59
 network 10.3.2.0 0.0.0.63 area 59
! . . . network definitions for other interfaces go here
 default-information originate
!
router bgp 65111
 no synchronization
 network 10.255.255.1 mask 255.255.255.255
 network 10.255.255.2 mask 255.255.255.255
 timers bgp 5 15
 neighbor 10.0.0.102 remote-as 65111
 neighbor 10.0.0.102 description IBGP with router R-2
 neighbor 10.0.0.102 update-source Loopback0
 neighbor 10.0.0.102 route-map map_here out
 neighbor 10.1.2.65 remote-as 60000
 neighbor 10.1.2.65 description Peering with R-A via F-1A
   ➥ (10.255.255.11)
 neighbor 10.1.2.65 ebgp-multihop
 neighbor 10.1.2.65 distribute-list 11 in
 neighbor 10.1.2.65 distribute-list 1 out
 neighbor 10.1.2.65 route-map map_hop_11 in
 neighbor 10.3.2.66 remote-as 60000
 neighbor 10.3.2.66 description Peering with R-B via F-2B
   ➥ (10.255.255.13)
 neighbor 10.3.2.66 ebgp-multihop
 neighbor 10.3.2.66 distribute-list 13 in
 neighbor 10.3.2.66 distribute-list 2 out
 neighbor 10.3.2.66 route-map map_hop_13 in
!
ip classless
! Direct to F-1A
ip route 0.0.0.0 0.0.0.0 10.255.255.11 1
! To F-1A through R-2
ip route 0.0.0.0 0.0.0.0 10.255.255.14 2
```

(continued)

```
! Direct to F-2B
ip route 0.0.0.0 0.0.0.0 10.255.255.13 3
! To F-2B through R-2
ip route 0.0.0.0 0.0.0.0 10.255.255.12 4
! Direct to F-2B
ip route 10.0.0.1 255.255.255.255 10.255.255.13 1
! To F-2B through R-2
ip route 10.0.0.1 255.255.255.255 10.255.255.12 2
! Direct to F-1A
ip route 10.0.0.1 255.255.255.255 10.255.255.11 3
! To F-1A through R-2
ip route 10.0.0.1 255.255.255.255 10.255.255.14 4
! Real route to F-1A
ip route 10.1.2.65 255.255.255.255 10.1.2.4
! Real route to F-2B
ip route 10.3.2.66 255.255.255.255 10.3.2.4
!
access-list 1 permit 10.255.255.1
access-list 2 permit 10.255.255.2
access-list 10 permit 10.0.0.1
access-list 11 permit 10.255.255.11
access-list 13 permit 10.255.255.13
!
route-map advertise permit 10
 match ip address 10
!
route-map map_here permit 15
 match ip address 11
 set ip next-hop 10.0.0.101
!
route-map map_here permit 25
 match ip address 13
 set ip next-hop 10.0.0.101
!
route-map map_hop_11 permit 10
 match address 11
 set ip next-hop 10.1.2.4
!
route-map map_hop_13 permit 10
 match address 13
 set ip next-hop 10.3.2.4
!
end
```

LISTING 9-5. *Router R-1 supporting redundant firewalls in routing mode*

Interface Loopback0 is our standard host IP definition for the router to provide a constant IP address independent of the state of any real interfaces. We need this address defined for the IBGP peering between the two inside routers used to share reachability of the outside routers via the firewalls.

There is no benefit to distributing the external or internal target addresses defined by *interface Loopback1* and *interface Loopback2* (all addresses in this configuration starting with prefix 10.255.255) into OSPF (or whatever intradomain routing protocol we choose to use). There should never be any traffic to or from those IP addresses. We do need to share any outside target addresses we can reach with Router R-2, but that will occur naturally with the IBGP session we must set up between the two routers.

The access LAN interfaces are configured the same as before, when we were not supporting firewall fallback. We use HSRP to make this router (R-1) the preferred default gateway for Firewall F-1A and the backup default gateway for Firewall F-2B. We do not show any interfaces configured to support local users, but if there are any local access requirements, we would put them on their own LANs and not compromise our security by sharing the firewall access LANs (unless allowed by our security policy).

We show OSPF as the inside routing protocol and configure it to distribute the access LANs and the management loopback address. This ensures that the two inside access routers can find each other to exchange BGP routing information. They can also provide paths for each other to reach the firewalls if necessary. One access router may advertise reachability through the firewalls when the other router needs to use that path. We must ensure that the other router routes the packet through the router that has the path, rather than directly to the firewall. Otherwise, if the path goes down because of a problem with the access LAN, we risk a black hole in our routing.

The production paths through the firewall are conditionally advertised based on a route through the firewall being available. The default route is redistributed by the *default-information originate* line, while the Web proxy interface at 10.0.0.1 is picked up by the *redistribute static* line. We add a route map to the static redistribution so that only the globally useful static routes are introduced into the OSPF routing domain. In particular, we do not want our static routes to the BGP conduits on the firewall to be advertised. The *subnets* keyword is required to permit advertising only the host route for 10.0.0.1.

The key to failure recovery is that when a packet gets to this router, it will use the best static route through the firewalls available for that destination. This route could go directly to the preferred firewall, indirectly to the preferred firewall via the other access router, or directly or indirectly to the backup firewall. All the possible routes are determined by BGP exchanges between the inside and the outside routers.

In order for the static routes to work correctly, it is essential that the addresses used for targets be unique in the domain of the side using them. If some other inside router were to advertise a route to 10.255.255.11, for example, we could wind up sending data intended for the outside to that location instead.

We also need to define a pair of static routes so that BGP can get to the speakers on the other side of the firewalls. These routes are only used locally on the router and are not advertised by any protocols to other systems.

The key to the failover function is the BGP setup under *router bgp 65111*. We use EBGP across the firewalls and IBGP between the access routers on each side of the firewalls. This router provides the two targets 10.255.255.1 and 10.255.255.2, so BGP is configured by the two *network* statements to source only those two routes.

We also adjust the hello and keepalive timers from their default values of 1 minute and 3 minutes down to 5 and 15 seconds, respectively. These timers should be adjusted based on experience with the firewalls, the criticality of the traffic being supported, and its sensitivity to switching firewalls. With state sensitive firewalls, we do not want to switch to the backup firewall unless we have no other choice. When adjusting the BGP timers, we must ensure that they are consistent across all peers. We will see when we get to the outside routers how we can adjust the timers for each individual peer to meet differing requirements. There is no benefit to being overly aggressive with the BGP timers because we will still need to wait an average of 30 seconds for the next per-minute update of the floating static routes.

The first peer configured (*neighbor 10.0.0.102*) is the IBGP peering with the other inside router, Router R-2. This serves a dual purpose. First of all, the rules of BGP configuration require all BGP speakers in an AS to be fully meshed. Second, the peering allows us to share any routes through the firewalls that we detect with Router R-2 and to learn of any routes Router R-2 has detected from its BGP peerings through the firewalls. This peering has the fringe benefit of allowing us to keep all the artificial addresses used for steering firewall traffic out of the OSPF routing domain. The route map applied to advertisements forces Router R-2 to send packets to Router R-1 rather than directly to the firewall when using Router R-1's paths.

The next peer (*neighbor 10.1.2.65*) is the first of our two peers going through the firewalls to an outside router. The static route vectors our packets to this peer via the IP address 10.1.2.4 on Firewall F-1A. The firewall tests the packet for validity and translates the destination address from 10.1.2.65 to the actual address of Router R-A, 100.0.0.2. It then changes the source address from our local address—10.1.2.2—to the IP address of the firewall conduit on the outside—100.0.0.65. The firewall is not required to understand the BGP protocol and does not need to adjust any of the addresses contained in the data fields of the packet. We will configure BGP to ignore the addresses it cannot use. In keeping with our philosophy that you can not include too much documentation in a router configuration, our first line for this peer is a description line explaining who the remote peer really is, the firewall used to reach it, and the route we expect to learn from it.

Since the remote peer is not on a common subnetwork with this router, we need to add the *ebgp-multihop* line. Otherwise, BGP would never speak to the remote because it would be waiting for that subnetwork to be configured. Even if the BGP link were using an end-system mode firewall configuration for this conduit, we would still need to specify *ebgp-multihop*. Without it, the IP time-to-live setting in all BGP packets to the peer would be set to one, which could cause the firewall to discard rather than forward the BGP packets.

The next two lines define distribution lists for input and output. These limit the BGP session with this peer to accepting a route to the target address only for this path and to sharing only the one route we want associated with this path on the outside. While this might appear to be overkill—we will be applying identical filters on the other side of the firewall—we really do want both filters on both sides. We want to limit what we advertise to minimize what information we expose about our internal configuration. More important, we must limit what we accept, as we cannot trust the other side to not send us potentially confusing or misleading routes.

In the last line for this peer, we compensate for the untranslated IP address included as the next hop for this route. Even if the next hop information provided were the correct IP address to use on this side of the firewall (or the firewall understood BGP well enough to do the translation for us), we dare not trust it. The key to our security while using BGP is that we do not trust the protocol to tell us anything other than whether a particular path between the inside and the outside appears to be functional. On a Cisco router, we use the route-map function to detect the desired target route and set the next hop to the correct value. In this case, the route *map map_hop_11* looks for any addresses in the incoming updates that match those in access-list 11. It then sets the next hop value to 10.1.2.4, the port for this path through Firewall F-1A.

The remainder of the BGP section is the configuration of the BGP peering for the alternate route from this router. This peering is configured the same as the primary route; the only modifications are those required to match the addresses appropriate for this route. To minimize the potential for confusion, the access-lists and route maps are numbered to match the target address with which they are to be used.

We then define a set of floating static routes for each service supported (in this case, a default route and the proxy at 10.0.0.1). This is done with an explicit weighted route for each potential path through the firewalls. These target IP addresses are only reachable when BGP learns of them—at which time the next hop values will be included in the routing table and can be seen using the *show ip route* command. We set up the default route to use our direct path through Firewall F-1A if available, falling back to the path through the same firewall as advertised (and reached) from Router R-2. If there is no path available through Firewall F-1A, we will use a path through Firewall F-2B, again preferring our direct path over the indirect path via Router R-2. If there are no paths available, none of the static routes will be active, and OSPF will cease to advertise the availability of a route.

The last two static routes tell BGP how to get to its peers on the other side of the firewalls. The access-lists are used by BGP to control routes advertised and routes accepted. Lists 11 and 13 are also used by the route maps to determine which advertisements need to get their next hop field adjusted.

Keep in mind that this configuration is the minimum required to support the failover function and does not include any of the self defense, management, or redundant security that would be part of a production configuration.

Proceeding on to the configuration for Router R-2 in Listing 9-6, we see a configuration almost identical to that of Router R-1. The loopback interfaces have addresses appropriate for this router (it provides targets 10.255.255.3 and 10.255.255.4), and the access LANs are configured so that this router is the preferred default gateway on access LAN 2.

```
version 11.2
!
hostname R-2
!
ip subnet-zero
!
interface Loopback0
 description Management ID for this Router
 ip address 10.0.0.102 255.255.255.255
!
interface Loopback3
 description Target IP for outside to inside via firewall F-1A
 ip address 10.255.255.3 255.255.255.255
!
interface Loopback4
 description Target IP for outside to inside via firewall F-2B
 ip address 10.255.255.4 255.255.255.255
!
interface Ethernet0
 description Firewall Access LAN-1
 ip address 10.1.2.3 255.255.255.192
 standby 1 priority 100
 standby 1 ip 10.1.2.1
 !
```

                                                        (*continued*)

```
interface Ethernet1
 description Firewall Access LAN-2
 ip address 10.3.2.2 255.255.255.192
 standby 2 priority 200
 standby 2 preempt
 standby 2 ip 10.3.2.1
!
router ospf 123
 redistribute static subnets route-map advertise
 network 10.0.0.102 0.0.0.0 area 59
 network 10.1.2.0 0.0.0.63 area 59
 network 10.3.2.0 0.0.0.63 area 59
! . . . network definitions for other interfaces go here
 default-information originate
!
router bgp 65111
 no synchronization
 network 10.255.255.3 mask 255.255.255.255
 network 10.255.255.4 mask 255.255.255.255
 timers bgp 5 15
 neighbor 10.0.0.101 remote-as 65111
 neighbor 10.0.0.101 description IBGP with router R-1
 neighbor 10.0.0.101 update-source Loopback0
 neighbor 10.0.0.101 route-map map_here out
 neighbor 10.1.2.66 remote-as 60000
 neighbor 10.1.2.66 description Peering with R-B via F-1A
  ➥ (10.255.255.14)
 neighbor 10.1.2.66 ebgp-multihop
 neighbor 10.1.2.66 distribute-list 14 in
 neighbor 10.1.2.66 distribute-list 3 out
 neighbor 10.1.2.66 route-map map_hop_14 in
 neighbor 10.3.2.65 remote-as 60000
 neighbor 10.3.2.65 description Peering with R-A via F-2B
  ➥ (10.255.255.12)
 neighbor 10.3.2.65 ebgp-multihop
 neighbor 10.3.2.65 distribute-list 12 in
 neighbor 10.3.2.65 distribute-list 4 out
 neighbor 10.3.2.65 route-map map_hop_12 in
!
ip classless
! Direct to F-1A
ip route 0.0.0.0 0.0.0.0 10.255.255.14 1
! To F-1A through R-1
ip route 0.0.0.0 0.0.0.0 10.255.255.11 2
```

(continued)

```
! Direct to F-2B
ip route 0.0.0.0 0.0.0.0 10.255.255.12 3
! To F-2B through R-1
ip route 0.0.0.0 0.0.0.0 10.255.255.13 4
! Direct to F-2B
ip route 10.0.0.1 255.255.255.255 10.255.255.12 1
! To F-2B through R-1
ip route 10.0.0.1 255.255.255.255 10.255.255.13 2
! Direct to F-1A
ip route 10.0.0.1 255.255.255.255 10.255.255.14 3
! To F-1A through R-1
ip route 10.0.0.1 255.255.255.255 10.255.255.11 4
! Real route to F-1A
ip route 10.1.2.66 255.255.255.255 10.1.2.4
! Real route to F-2B
ip route 10.3.2.65 255.255.255.255 10.3.2.4
!
access-list 3 permit 10.255.255.3
access-list 4 permit 10.255.255.4
access-list 10 permit 10.0.0.1
access-list 12 permit 10.255.255.12
access-list 14 permit 10.255.255.14
!
route-map advertise permit 10
 match ip address 10
!
route-map map_here permit 15
 match ip address 12
 set ip next-hop 10.0.0.102
!
route-map map_here permit 25
 match ip address 14
 set ip next-hop 10.0.0.102
!
route-map map_hop_14 permit 10
 match address 12
 set ip next-hop 10.3.2.4
!
route-map map_hop_12 permit 10
 match address 14
 set ip next-hop 10.1.2.4
!
end
```

LISTING 9-6. *Router R-2 supporting redundant firewalls in routing mode*

The BGP configuration is also identical to that of Router R-1, except that the addresses and filters are changed to reflect the use of paths that share as little commonality as possible with those tested by Router R-1.

The static routes are also the same as Router R-1's, except they are floated with weights so that the direct routes from this router to the firewall will be preferred over those which must be relayed through Router R-1. But, as on Router R-1, we prefer an indirect route to the primary firewall for a service over a direct route to the backup firewall.

The configuration of Router R-A in Listing 9-7 also starts out looking like a carbon copy of the inside router configurations, with only the expected addressing modifications. Further on, however, additional changes appear. These are due to inclusion of a BGP routed link to the first ISP. Unlike the inside routers, which used BGP strictly for firewall control, the outside routers also run BGP as an independent autonomous system, dual-homed to the Internet via two different ISPs.

```
version 11.2
!
hostname R-A
!
!  WARNING!! Self defense configuration statements not shown
!
ip subnet-zero
!
interface Loopback0
 description Management ID for this Router
 ip address 100.0.0.201 255.255.255.255
!
interface Loopback11
 description Target IP for outside to inside via firewall F-1A
 ip address 10.255.255.11 255.255.255.255
!
interface Loopback12
 description Target IP for outside to inside via firewall F-2B
 ip address 10.255.255.12 255.255.255.255
!
interface Serial0/0
 description T1 to ISP #1
 ip address 110.0.0.1 255.255.255.252
!
interface Ethernet1/0
 description Firewall Access LAN-A
```

(continued)

```
 ip address 100.0.0.2 255.255.255.192
 no ip redirects
 standby 1 priority 200
 standby 1 preempt
 standby 1 ip 100.0.0.1
!
interface Ethernet1/1
 description Firewall Access LAN-B
 ip address 101.0.0.3 255.255.255.192
 no ip redirects
 standby 2 priority 100
 standby 2 ip 101.0.0.1
!
router ospf 123
 network 100.0.0.201 0.0.0.0 area 59
 network 100.0.0.0 0.0.0.63 area 59
 network 101.0.0.0 0.0.0.63 area 59
 network 110.0.0.0 0.0.0.3 area 59
!
router bgp 60000
 no synchronization
 network 10.255.255.11 mask 255.255.255.255
 network 10.255.255.12 mask 255.255.255.255
 network 100.0.0.0 mask 255.255.255.0
 network 101.0.0.0 mask 255.255.255.0
 network 110.0.0.0 mask 255.255.255.252
 redistribute connected
 neighbor 100.0.0.202 remote-as 60000
 neighbor 100.0.0.202 description IBGP with Router R-B
 neighbor 100.0.0.202 timers 5 15
 neighbor 100.0.0.202 update-source Loopback0
 neighbor 100.0.0.202 route-map map_here out
 neighbor 100.0.0.65 remote-as 65111
 neighbor 100.0.0.65 description Peering with R-1 via F-1A
   ➥ (10.255.255.1)
 neighbor 100.0.0.65 ebgp-multihop
 neighbor 100.0.0.65 timers 5 15
 neighbor 100.0.0.65 distribute-list 1 in
 neighbor 100.0.0.65 distribute-list 11 out
 neighbor 100.0.0.65 route-map map_hop_1 in
 neighbor 101.0.0.66 remote-as 65111
 neighbor 101.0.0.66 description Peering with R-2 via F-2B
   ➥ (10.255.255.4)
```

(continued)

```
neighbor 101.0.0.66 ebgp-multihop
neighbor 101.0.0.66 timers 5 15
neighbor 101.0.0.66 distribute-list 4 in
neighbor 101.0.0.66 route-map map_hop_4 in
neighbor 101.0.0.66 distribute-list 12 out
neighbor 110.0.0.2 remote-as 54321
neighbor 110.0.0.2 description ISP Routes
neighbor 110.0.0.2 distribute-list 10 out
neighbor 110.0.0.2 filter-list 9 out
no auto-summary
!
ip classless
! Direct to F-1A
ip route 100.0.0.99 255.255.255.255 10.255.255.1 1
! F-1A through R-B
ip route 100.0.0.99 255.255.255.255 10.255.255.3 2
! Direct to F-2B
ip route 100.0.0.99 255.255.255.255 10.255.255.4 3
! F-2B through R-B
ip route 100.0.0.99 255.255.255.255 10.255.255.2 4
! Direct to F-2B
ip route 101.0.0.99 255.255.255.255 10.255.255.4 1
! F-2B through R-B
ip route 101.0.0.99 255.255.255.255 10.255.255.2 2
! Direct to F-1A
ip route 101.0.0.99 255.255.255.255 10.255.255.1 3
! F-1A through R-B
ip route 101.0.0.99 255.255.255.255 10.255.255.3 4
! Route to R-1
ip route 101.0.0.65 255.255.255.255 100.0.0.4
! Route to R-2
ip route 101.0.0.66 255.255.255.255 101.0.0.4
! Summaries for BGP
ip route 100.0.0.0 255.255.255.0 null0
ip route 101.0.0.0 255.255.255.0 null0
!
! Router R-1 through F-1A
access-list 1 permit 10.255.255.1
! Router R-2 through F-2B
access-list 4 permit 10.255.255.4
! Keep internal routes out of BGP
access-list 10 deny   10.0.0.0 0.255.255.255
access-list 10 permit any
```

(continued)

```
! Router R-1 through F-1A
access-list 11 permit 10.255.255.11
! Router R-2 through F-2B
access-list 12 permit 10.255.255.12
!
route-map map_here permit 15
 match ip address 1
 set ip next-hop 100.0.0.201
!
route-map map_here permit 25
 match ip address 4
 set ip next-hop 100.0.0.201
!
route-map map_hop_1 permit 10
 match address 1
 set ip next-hop 100.0.0.4
!
route-map map_hop_4 permit 10
 match address 4
 set ip next-hop 101.0.0.4
!
ip as-path access-list 10 permit ^(_60000)*$
!
end
```

LISTING 9-7. *Router R-A supporting redundant firewalls in routing mode*

We can no longer globally adjust the network statements for our two public network ranges and ISP link; nor can we globally adjust the BGP timers to speed up convergence. Instead, we set the timers on each internal peer individually and leave the ISP peering at default values. We also need to add static routes pointing to *null0* for our public networks so that BGP will be able to advertise them to the ISP. Unlike with our previous ISP connections, we must include a distribution list on our output here so that we do not advertise our internal target addresses to the ISP.

The remainder of the BGP configuration—along with the static routes, access-lists, and route maps—are all identical in function to the inside routers', albeit modified in address particulars.

The configuration for Router R-B in Listing 9-8 is functionally almost identical to that for Router R-A. The only differences are addressing changes required to reflect connection to a different ISP, and different paths to test through the firewalls to the inside routers. Just keep in mind that security and management are not shown in these sample configurations but must not be neglected in the real world.

```
version 11.2
!
hostname R-B
!
!  WARNING!! Self defense configuration statements not shown
!
ip subnet-zero
!
interface Loopback0
 description Management ID for this Router
 ip address 100.0.0.202 255.255.255.255
!
interface Loopback13
 description Target IP for outside to inside via firewall F-1A
 ip address 10.255.255.13 255.255.255.255
!
interface Loopback14
 description Target IP for outside to inside via firewall F-2B
 ip address 10.255.255.14 255.255.255.255
!
interface Serial0/0
 description T1 to ISP #2
 ip address 120.0.0.1 255.255.255.252
!
interface Ethernet1/0
 description Firewall Access LAN-A
 ip address 100.0.0.3 255.255.255.192
 no ip redirects
 standby 1 priority 100
 standby 1 ip 100.0.0.1
!
interface Ethernet1/1
 description Firewall Access LAN-B
 ip address 101.0.0.3 255.255.255.192
 no ip redirects
 standby 2 priority 200
 standby 2 preempt
 standby 2 ip 101.0.0.1
!
router ospf 123
 network 100.0.0.202 0.0.0.0 area 59
 network 100.0.0.0 0.0.0.63 area 59
```

(continued)

```
 network 101.0.0.0 0.0.0.63 area 59
 network 120.0.0.0 0.0.0.3 area 59
 ! . . . network definitions for other interfaces go here
 !
router bgp 60000
 no synchronization
 network 10.255.255.13 mask 255.255.255.255
 network 10.255.255.14 mask 255.255.255.255
 network 100.0.0.0 mask 255.255.255.0
 network 101.0.0.0 mask 255.255.255.0
 network 120.0.0.0 mask 255.255.255.252
 redistribute connected
 neighbor 100.0.0.201 remote-as 60000
 neighbor 100.0.0.201 description Firewall routes through R-A
 neighbor 100.0.0.201 update-source Loopback0
 neighbor 100.0.0.201 route-map map_here out
 neighbor 100.0.0.66 remote-as 65111
 neighbor 100.0.0.66 description Peering with R-2 via F-1A
   ➡ (10.255.255.3)
 neighbor 100.0.0.66 ebgp-multihop
 neighbor 100.0.0.66 timers 5 15
 neighbor 100.0.0.66 distribute-list 3 in
 neighbor 100.0.0.66 distribute-list 14 out
 neighbor 100.0.0.66 route-map map_hop_3 in
 neighbor 101.0.0.65 remote-as 65111
 neighbor 101.0.0.65 description Peering with R-1 via F-2B
   ➡ (10.255.255.2)
 neighbor 101.0.0.65 ebgp-multihop
 neighbor 101.0.0.65 timers 5 15
 neighbor 101.0.0.65 distribute-list 2 in
 neighbor 101.0.0.65 route-map map_hop_2 in
 neighbor 101.0.0.65 distribute-list 13 out
 neighbor 120.0.0.2 remote-as 55555
 neighbor 120.0.0.2 description Peering with ISP #2
 neighbor 120.0.0.2 distribute-list 10 out
 neighbor 120.0.0.2 filter-list 9 out
 no auto-summary
 !
ip classless
ip route 100.0.0.99 255.255.255.255 10.255.255.3 1
ip route 100.0.0.99 255.255.255.255 10.255.255.1 2
```

(continued)

```
ip route 100.0.0.99 255.255.255.255 10.255.255.2 3
ip route 100.0.0.99 255.255.255.255 10.255.255.4 4
ip route 101.0.0.99 255.255.255.255 10.255.255.2 1
ip route 101.0.0.99 255.255.255.255 10.255.255.4 2
ip route 101.0.0.99 255.255.255.255 10.255.255.3 3
ip route 101.0.0.99 255.255.255.255 10.255.255.1 4
ip route 100.0.0.66 255.255.255.255 100.0.0.4
ip route 101.0.0.65 255.255.255.255 101.0.0.4
ip route 100.0.0.0 255.255.255.0 null0
ip route 101.0.0.0 255.255.255.0 null0
!
access-list 2 permit 10.255.255.2
access-list 3 permit 10.255.255.3
access-list 10 deny   10.0.0.0 0.255.255.255
access-list 10 permit any
access-list 13 permit 10.255.255.13
access-list 14 permit 10.255.255.14
!
route-map map_here permit 15
 match ip address 2
 set ip next-hop 100.0.0.202
!
route-map map_here permit 25
 match ip address 3
 set ip next-hop 100.0.0.202
!
route-map map_hop_2 permit 10
 match address 2
 set ip next-hop 101.0.0.4
!
route-map map_hop_3 permit 10
 match address 3
 set ip next-hop 100.0.0.4
!
ip as-path access-list 9 permit ^(_60000)*$
!
end
```

LISTING 9-8. *Router R-B supporting redundant firewalls in routing mode*

ROUTER-CONTROLLED FAILOVER OF ALTERNATE END-SYSTEM MODE FIREWALLS

Providing automatic failover when the firewalls are running in end-system mode is significantly more difficult than when they are running in router mode. Consider the scenario in Figure 9-9, in which we take the proxy address used by the internal Web-browsing user and move it from 10.0.01 to an end-system mode address of 10.1.2.99. We leave the outside address of the browser proxy to Firewall F-1A's LAN at 100.0.0.99, but we expand the subnetwork mask on the outside LAN to include all IP addresses from 100.0.0.1 through 100.0.0.255. Now both sides of the firewall are in end-system mode.

We keep this example configuration manageable by limiting ourselves to supporting the one service and using only two paths through the firewalls. A four-path configuration in end-system mode is much more complex and requires at least one more LAN at each site to provide dual failure redundancy. (Limitations on router network address translation currently prevent us from defining two different static address translations to the same IP address using the same ports.)

We use the same BGP conduits we used in router mode, except that now our access LAN subnetwork masks have been expanded so they are in end-system mode as well. Overall, the firewall configuration is assumed to be that shown in Table 9-7.

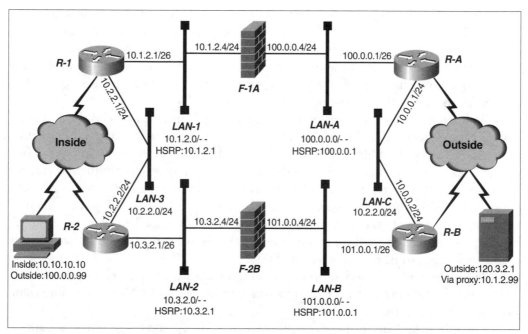

FIGURE 9-9. *Router-controlled firewall failover with end-system mode firewalls*

TABLE 9-7. *Firewall Configuration for End-System Mode Firewall Backup*

SERVICE	CONFIGURATION
IP address of inside firewall interface for management and control	10.1.2.4/24 for Firewall F-1A 10.3.2.4/24 for Firewall F-2B
IP address of outside firewall interface for management and control	100.0.0.4/24 for Firewall F-1A 101.0.0.4/24 for Firewall F-2B
Default gateway for inside firewall interface (outside to inside traffic)	10.1.2.1 for Firewall F-1A 10.3.2.1 for Firewall F-2B
Default gateway for outside firewall interface (inside to outside traffic)	100.0.0.1 for Firewall F-1A 101.0.0.1 for Firewall F-1B
Inside addresses of firewall proxy server	Firewall F-1A: 10.1.2.99 Firewall F-2B: 10.3.2.99
Outside addresses of firewall proxy server	Firewall F-1A: 100.0.0.99 Firewall F-2B: 101.0.0.99
BGP conduit for R-1 with R-A via F-1A (TCP to port 179, in to out)	10.1.2.1 NAT to 100.0.0.65 100.0.0.1 NAT to 10.1.2.65
BGP conduit for R-2 with R-B via F-2B (TCP to port 179, in to out)	10.3.2.1 NAT to 101.0.0.65 101.0.0.2 NAT to 10.3.2.65

Our first challenge is to allow control of the path used by the floating static routes. The problem is that as long as an interface on the router is up, all destinations on the subnetwork that interface attaches to are assumed to be directly reachable. There are no checks made of the routing tables. So even if BGP determines that a firewall is no longer a useful path, we have no way to stop advertising the services offered by that firewall, because the LAN is still accessible.

As long as there are no systems other than routers and firewalls on the access LANs, we can get around this problem fairly easily. We can deliberately misconfigure the routers so that the addresses used by the firewall for services do not appear to be on the LAN subnetwork, even though the firewall is configured to put them there. In this case, even though the access LANs all have a subnetwork mask of 255.255.255.0, we configure the routers with subnetwork masks of 255.255.255.192 so that the firewall services appear to the routers to be on different networks. This way, we can use the same technique we used for router mode firewalls: we can have the choice of path made by floating static routes driven by BGP.

This deliberate misconfiguration breaks IP broadcasting. As a result, the need to strictly limit what devices are allowed to attach to the access LANs is now more than just a security concern.

The other challenge is not so easily overcome. We can no longer duplicate the same services on both firewalls, as we would then have end-systems with duplicate IP addresses. With extreme care we can sometimes get this to work by defining overlapping address ranges. For example, we could define the inside access LAN on both firewalls as 10.0.0.0/24, assign the management port of Firewall F-1A as 10.0.0.12, assign the management port of Firewall F-2B as 10.0.0.20, and assign the services as addresses 10.0.0.33 through 10.0.0.254. On the routers we could then configure LAN-1 as 10.0.0.8/29 and LAN-2 as 10.0.0.16/29, and use a router mode firewall configuration.

This approach can create problems with firewall configuration management tools, as it will be (quite properly) flagged as a configuration error. Consequently, we may need to develop a configuration that can be used without mirroring the same configuration on multiple firewalls.

When the backup services must be configured as alternative service provisions at different IP addresses, we can still automate the failover. Network address translation can be used on the routers to convert the addresses expected by users to the addresses actually used by the firewall.

CONFIGURATION EXAMPLE: AUTOMATIC FAILOVER WITH END-SYSTEM MODE FIREWALLS

In this example, we have two firewalls configured so that the service required is duplicated using a different service address on each firewall. To make the two service addresses appear as one to the users, we use NAT on the routers providing the path through the backup firewall. It translates the service addresses to the addresses expected by the users.

We will show only the inside router configurations, as the outside routers are a mirror image as far as the routing through the firewalls is concerned. In this configuration, the combination of Router R-2, Firewall F-2B, and Router R-B is treated as a unit. If any part along the path fails, the alternative path of Router R-1, Firewall F-1A, and Router R-A will be used to replace it. In place of the cross connects in the previous configuration, we must dedicate the second Ethernet port to connecting the access routers. This substitution allows us to strictly control on which ports packets will arrive when using the alternate path, allowing their addresses to be correctly translated.

Even if the firewalls are stateless, the network address translation will break any existing connections whenever switching from one firewall to the other. As a result, the switchover is not transparent. However, it is automatic and the downtime averages only 45 seconds with a worst-case delay of 75 seconds as configured here.

Since the primary route in this example is through Router R-1 and Firewall F-1A to Router R-A, the configuration of Router R-1 in Listing 9-9 only needs to detect the working route to use. If the path through Firewall F-1A is available, it will be used. Otherwise, the fallback route via Router R-2 will be taken (if available).

```
version 11.2
!
hostname R-1
!
ip subnet-zero
!
interface Loopback0
 description Management ID for this Router
 ip address 10.0.0.101 255.255.255.255
!
interface Loopback1
 description Target IP for outside to inside via firewall F-1A
 ip address 10.255.255.1 255.255.255.255
!
interface Ethernet0
 description Firewall Access LAN-1
 ip address 10.1.2.1 255.255.255.192
!
interface Ethernet1
 description Link to router R-2
 ip address 10.2.2.1 255.255.255.0
!
router ospf 123
 redistribute static subnets route-map advertise
 network 10.0.0.101 0.0.0.0 area 59
 network 10.1.2.0 0.0.0.63 area 59
 network 10.2.2.0 0.0.0.255 area 59
! . . . network definitions for other interfaces go here
!
router bgp 65111
 no synchronization
 network 10.255.255.1 mask 255.255.255.255
 timers bgp 5 15
 neighbor 10.2.2.2 remote-as 65111
 neighbor 10.2.2.2 description IBGP with Router R-2
 neighbor 10.2.2.2 update-source Loopback0
 neighbor 10.1.2.65 remote-as 60000
 neighbor 10.1.2.65 description Peering with R-A via F-1A
   ➥ (10.255.255.11)
 neighbor 10.1.2.65 ebgp-multihop
 neighbor 10.1.2.65 distribute-list 11 in
```

(continued)

```
   neighbor 10.1.2.65 distribute-list 1 out
   neighbor 10.1.2.65 route-map map_hop_11 in
 !
 ip classless
 ! Direct to F-1A
 ip route 10.1.2.99 255.255.255.255 10.255.255.11 1
 ! To F-2B through R-2
 ip route 10.1.2.99 255.255.255.255 10.255.255.12 2
 ! Real route to F-1A
 ip route 10.1.2.65 255.255.255.255 10.1.2.4
 !
 access-list 1 permit 10.255.255.1
 access-list 9 permit 10.1.2.64 0.0.0.63
 access-list 10 permit 10.1.2.0 0.0.0.255
 access-list 11 permit 10.255.255.11
 !
 route-map advertise deny 10
  match ip address 9
 !
 route-map advertise permit 15
  match ip address 10
 !
 route-map map_hop_11 permit 10
  match ip address 11
  set ip next-hop 10.1.2.4
 !
 end
```

LISTING 9-9.   *Router R-1 supporting redundant firewalls in end-system mode*

Because this is the primary route that users expect to see, there is no network address translation required and the configuration follows the same logic as the previous example. The only differences are a simpler configuration due to the lack of redundancy in connectivity, and the elimination of double fault tolerance by the support of two paths rather than four.

The configuration of Router R-2 in Listing 9-10 shows the critical addition of network address translation, which is required to support automated failover. All router interfaces except the link to the firewall are labeled as inside interfaces. The firewall interface is declared an outside interface. Network address translation can only be used when transitioning between an inside and an outside interface (in either direction).

The *ip nat outside source static 10.3.2.99 10.1.2.99* statement instructs the router to change the source address in a packet going from the outside to the inside

```
version 11.2
!
hostname R-2
!
ip subnet-zero
!
interface Loopback0
 description Management ID for this Router
 ip address 10.0.0.102 255.255.255.255
!
interface Loopback1
 description Target IP for outside to inside via firewall F-2B
 ip address 10.255.255.2 255.255.255.255
!
interface Ethernet0
 description Link to router R-1 through LAN-3
 ip address 10.2.2.2 255.255.255.0
 ip nat inside
!
interface Ethernet1
 description Firewall Access LAN-2
 ip address 10.3.2.1 255.255.255.192
 ip nat outside
!
! ADD "ip nat inside" statements to all interfaces other than
  Ethernet1
!
router ospf 123
 redistribute static subnets route-map advertise
 network 10.0.0.102 0.0.0.0 area 59
 network 10.2.2.0 0.0.0.255 area 59
 network 10.3.2.0 0.0.0.63 area 59
! . . . network definitions for other interfaces go here
!
router bgp 65111
 no synchronization
 network 10.255.255.2 mask 255.255.255.255
 timers bgp 5 15
 neighbor 10.2.2.1 remote-as 65111
 neighbor 10.2.2.1 description IBGP with Router R-1
 neighbor 10.2.2.1 update-source Loopback0
```

(continued)

```
    neighbor 10.3.2.65 remote-as 60000
    neighbor 10.3.2.65 description Peering with R-B through F-2B
     ➥ (10.255.255.12)
    neighbor 10.3.2.65 ebgp-multihop
    neighbor 10.3.2.65 distribute-list 12 in
    neighbor 10.3.2.65 distribute-list 2 out
    neighbor 10.3.2.65 route-map map_hop_12 in
    !
    ! Fix inside address if using F-2B
    ip nat outside source static 10.3.2.99 10.1.2.99
    ip classless
    ! Un-NATed through R-1
    ip route 10.1.2.0 255.255.255.0 10.255.255.11 1
    ! Backup through F-2B
    ip route 10.1.2.0 255.255.255.0 10.255.255.12 2
    ! Route for BGP
    ip route 10.3.2.65 255.255.255.255 10.3.2.4
    !
    access-list 2 permit 10.255.255.2
    access-list 10 permit 10.1.2.0.0.0.0.255
    access-list 12 permit 10.255.255.12
    !
    route-map advertise permit 10
     match ip address 10
    !
    route-map map_hop_12 permit 10
     match address 12
     set ip next-hop 10.3.2.4
    !
    end
```

LISTING 9-10. *Router R-2 supporting redundant firewalls in end-system mode*

from the outside value of 10.3.2.99 to the inside value of 10.1.2.99. Since the mapping is static, it will also change the destination address in an outbound packet from the normal proxy address of 10.1.2.99 to the backup proxy address of 10.3.2.99. A similar mapping on Router R-B is not needed, as the return packets must be directed back to Firewall F-2B's source address of 101.0.0.99 rather than back to Firewall F-1A at 100.0.0.99.

If we were providing outside access to an inside service, then we would need to have address translation on the outside routers perform an equivalent role.

WRAP-UP

Firewalls play a critical role in modern networks, and their importance is increasing as organizations recognize the vulnerabilities of internetworking. We can no longer be satisfied merely to communicate. The challenge now is to communicate safely and efficiently.

The strict security requirements associated with a firewalled environment make high availability networking particularly challenging, as we are constrained in what can be done from a security standpoint. Vocabulary can also be a challenge when communicating with security analysts, as the security concept of redundancy and the networking concept of redundancy are not the same.

Firewall vendors have responded to the availability needs of their customers with high reliability and redundant firewall products. But there is sometimes still a need for network design to provide greater resilience than can be provided by a stand-alone firewall. Although dynamic routing protocols and firewall security are normally considered an incompatible mix, we have shown how, with careful use of BGP, we can get many of the failure detection and recovery benefits of a dynamic routing protocol without sacrificing security. Nor have we depended upon any additional trust across the firewall boundary or significantly increased the complexity of the firewall itself.

NOTE

1. Curtin, Matt & Ranum, Marcus J. "Internet Firewalls: Frequently Asked Questions." http://www.interhack.net/pubs/fwfaq/, 1999/11/25 17:34:19, Revision: 9.4. Copyright © 1995–1996, 1998 Marcus J. Ranum. Copyright © 1998, 1999 Matt Curtin. All rights reserved. This document may be used, reprinted, and redistributed as is providing this copyright notice and all attributions remain intact.

IBM SNA and DLSw

M any organizations need to support IBM SNA over IP networks, and a popular way to do this is by using Data Link Switching (DLSw). If you don't need to support SNA services, you can skip to the next chapter. But if you do need to support SNA, you need to understand how DLSw behaves in an IP network with multiple routers running DLSw on the same LAN.

We will start with redundant DLSw support on Token Rings, where DLSw support for redundancy is automatic and fully functional. Then we will look at providing support for redundant DLSw connections when the local attachment network is Ethernet rather than Token Ring. We will finish the chapter with a look at running DLSw through firewalls, where we'll discuss what we must do to keep network address translation from interfering with DLSw operation.

DATA LINK SWITCHING (DLSw)

The integration of LAN-attached workstations with traditional IBM host systems has been an ongoing challenge since the invention of the local area network. Supporting diverse protocols on a single LAN is rarely a problem, and it is not unusual to find SNA, NetBEUI, IPX, and TCP/IP all running on the same Token Ring or Ethernet LAN.

The challenge arises when the scope of the network expands beyond a single LAN or local cluster of bridged LANs. Mainframe-oriented SNA WANs, based on Synchronous Data Link Control (SDLC), are highly sophisticated and effective supporters of SNA traffic for the large enterprise. But they are generally poor for support of LAN-to-LAN traffic, other than IBM SNA. This has led many organizations into the frustrating position of supporting two independent WAN networks to interconnect their scattered LANs—a dedicated 37xx-based SNA WAN for SNA application access, and a routed network for non-SNA inter-LAN traffic.

While many IBM shops expected the problems to be resolved by the introduction of Local Entry Networking (LEN) with the IBM Token Ring technology, their hopes were not realized. SNA instead became split into two separate camps—the new LAN-oriented LEN, using Logical Link Control Type 2 (LLC2), for reliable communications within a single LAN, and the traditional mainframe-oriented front-end-based SNA over WAN links. The fundamental problem is that the LAN-oriented architecture of LEN was designed for efficiency and performance with low-end equipment, and it does not include the network and transport layers required to make the protocols routeable.

As the popularity of LAN-based SNA grew over the years, these limitation became more and more problematic. Source route bridging helps for Token Rings, but the bottom line remains that the protocols are LAN based and have problems dealing with the propagation delays, bandwidth limitations, and alternate routing needs of large wide area networks.

Router vendors and others have tried to find ways to work around the problem, and there are many large networks still dependent on proprietary solutions such as Cisco's Remote Source Route Bridging (RSRB). However, these solutions are not only proprietary; they are also generally unsatisfactory in terms of performance and robustness. The basic problem is that they try to make the WAN look like a LAN to the SNA applications, which is impossible when the WAN gets heavily loaded.

How DLSw Works

In 1993, IBM introduced Data Link Switching as a mechanism for integrating support for SNA and NetBIOS protocols (as used in IBM LAN architectures) into other network architectures. DLSw was published in RFC 1434 as an open protocol that all vendors could use. DLSw does not provide full routing but instead provides switching at the data link layer to encapsulate SNA and NetBIOS frames in suitable packets for transport over a routed network. While we will only look at using DLSw over TCP/IP, other transport connections capable of providing guaranteed, sequenced delivery of packets may also be used.

DLSw version 1, as defined in RFC 1795, is designed to support SNA Physical Unit (PU) 2, PU 2.1, and PU 4 systems. Optionally, it can support NetBIOS systems attached via IEEE 802.2-compliant LANs, as well as SNA PU 2 (primary or secondary) and PU 2.1 systems attached via point-to-point and multipoint SDLC links. DLSw version 2, defined in RFC 2166, adds a number of backwards compatible enhancements, improving scaleability for networks with large numbers of end-systems requiring SNA services.

SDLC attached systems are converted to have a LAN appearance to other DLSw attached systems (each SDLC PU is presented to the DLSw Switch-to-Switch Protocol [SSP] as a unique MAC/SAP address pair). Token Ring LAN attached systems see DLSw as a source-routing bridge. Token Ring remote systems that are accessed through DLSw appear as systems attached to an adjacent ring. This ring is a virtual ring that is manifested within each data link switch.

DLSw addresses a number of issues with LLC2 and NetBIOS. The primary concern is the assumption in the design of LLC2 that the network transit delay would be predictable. The LLC2 procedures use a fixed timer to detect lost frames. The problem is that when remote bridging is used over wide area lines, the network delay is not only larger, but it can also vary greatly depending upon congestion. Since the time-outs are normally set fairly short to provide quick response to normal lost frames, a link may be taken down whenever the WAN is temporarily congested.

Flow and congestion control also create problems because appropriate settings for a local LAN connection are rarely appropriate for a WAN connection. Adding to the challenge, NetBIOS services also make use of connectionless and broadcast frames.

While DLSw may look like a bridge to the end system, it does not act like a bridge. Unlike a bridge, DLSw terminates LLC2 connection-oriented data flow at the local DLSw switch, as shown in Figure 10-1.

In traditional bridging, the LLC protocol exchanges are end to end. DLSw terminates each LLC2 connection locally. This means that the LLC2 acknowledgments, keepalives, and flow control frames are not carried over the WAN. DLSw multiplexes the information frames for all link layer communications onto a single TCP connection to the DLSw service at the destination LAN.

Because LLC2 acknowledgments are kept local, time-out values appropriate for the local LAN remain valid and delays in the WAN portion of the network are not a

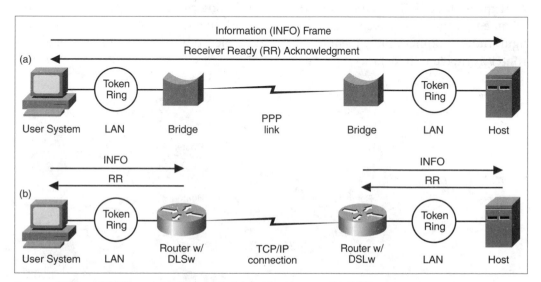

FIGURE 10-1. *LLC2 termination with (a) bridges versus (b) DLSw*

factor. SDLC links are handled in a similar manner, with polling and poll responses performed locally to keep responsiveness high and overhead for the WAN low. Net-BIOS overhead is further reduced by having the local DLSw switch respond to search frame broadcasts once the location of an end-system is known.

CONFIGURATION EXAMPLE: REDUNDANT DLSW BETWEEN TOKEN RINGS

Because DLSw looks like a source route bridge to Token Ring attached devices, we can provide redundancy in a DLSw configuration by using two routers on each ring and configuring DLSw on both, as in Figure 10-2. The DLSw peers used will depend upon the routing of information frames returned to the initiating system by the DLSw systems on its ring. DLSw implementations by different vendors provide different means of influencing load balancing. We will ignore this detail in our pursuit of availability, but the compatibility of the techniques to be used should be checked before a multivendor solution is chosen.

Since the user and host systems are running SNA or other IBM proprietary protocols, the handling of multiple Token Rings and Token Ring interfaces is beyond the scope of this discussion. Assumed but not shown is the redundant connectivity inside the LAN, which minimizes the impact of LAN infrastructure failures. The SNA and NetBIOS protocols we are supporting function at the MAC layer. This means that splitting of the ring into two rings will not affect operation, as long as at least one of the routers running DLSw can still communicate with the end-system.

Cisco router configurations to support this scenario are provided in Listings 10-1 through 10-4. The structure of the IP networking cloud is not shown, but we do assume that the local Token Rings are serving both IP and SNA traffic. All four configurations are functionally identical in this example, so we will only discuss one router at each end in detail.

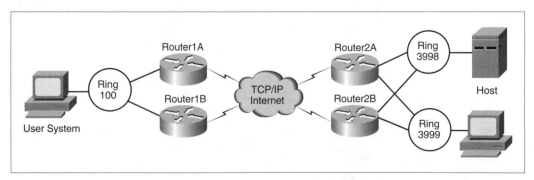

FIGURE 10-2. *Redundant DLSw between Token Ring attached devices*

```
version 11.0
!
hostname Router1A
!
source-bridge ring-group 4084
dlsw local-peer peer-id 10.1.128.1
dlsw remote-peer 0 tcp 10.2.128.1
dlsw remote-peer 0 tcp 10.2.128.2
!
interface Loopback1
 description Always up address for DLSw
 ip address 10.1.128.1 255.255.255.255
!
interface TokenRing0
 ip address 10.1.0.2 255.255.128.0
 ring-speed 16
 source-bridge 100 10 4084
 source-bridge spanning
!
interface Serial0
 ip address 10.1.129.1 255.255.255.252
!
router ospf 123
 network 10.1.0.0 0.0.255.255 area 1
!
end
```

LISTING 10-1. *Token Ring redundant DLSw configuration—Router 1A*

Router 1A in Listing 10-1 is a standard Cisco DLSw configuration. The *source-bridge ring-group* statement provides the bridging infrastructure to allow DLSw to be linked to the local Token Rings. By default, DLSw requires explicit specification of peers for each end of the DLSw connection. This requirement can be avoided by enabling promiscuous mode. However, promiscuous mode is considered a security risk in many environments, because it allows any other DLSw device to establish a peer relationship with the router in promiscuous mode, opening the router up to denial-of-service attacks. Promiscuous mode can also make network management more difficult. Failed peers are merely absent from the peer tables at the promiscuous end, rather than retained with a down status.

The local peer ID is used to identify this system to other DLSw switches and will be used as the source address in all DLSw TCP/IP connections. All remote peers must use our local peer ID to connect to us or the DLSw peering will not function.

```
version 11.0
!
hostname Router1B
!
source-bridge ring-group 4084
dlsw local-peer peer-id 10.1.128.2
dlsw remote-peer 0 tcp 10.2.128.1
dlsw remote-peer 0 tcp 10.2.128.2
!
interface Loopback1
 description Always up address for DLSw
 ip address 10.1.128.2 255.255.255.255
!
interface TokenRing0
 ip address 10.1.0.3 255.255.128.0
 ring-speed 16
 source-bridge 100 11 4084
 source-bridge spanning
!
interface Serial0
 ip address 10.1.129.5 255.255.255.252
!
router ospf 123
 network 10.1.0.0 0.0.255.255 area 1
!
end
```

LISTING 10-2. *Token Ring redundant DLSw configuration—Router 1B*

This is different from Remote Source Route Bridging (RSRB), in which any IP address on the router can be used by a remote peer to establish a bridge connection. We want to be certain that any router peering with numerous other routers uses a stable address for its local ID, since any change would require modifying the configuration on every peer router.

We have multiple options for the local peer ID. We normally prefer to use a loopback address not only for configuration stability but also so that the peering is not dependent upon a specific interface being up. We could also safely use the Token Ring address for peering in a situation—like this example—in which we have only a single LAN interface. After all, if the Token Ring interface goes down, there is no benefit to have DLSw up and running. Another option would be to use the IP address of our only WAN connection. That way, a WAN failure would force SNA traffic over to the other DLSw peer. It would not continue the current peerings by sending the

DSLw TCP/IP packets back out over the LAN to get to the router with the working WAN connection. The viability of this option would depend upon the SNA communications being supported. If an SNA session needs to be restarted for us to learn the alternate route, as is the case for some products, then it would be more efficient to keep the DSLw peer functional despite the suboptimal routing. Regardless, this option should only be considered if there is a single WAN interface and a single LAN interface, leaving no other alternate routes. Otherwise, in a double fault scenario, we could wind up disabling DLSw on the only router with a functioning LAN interface on a particular LAN. We would then unnecessarily shut down SNA communications for that LAN.

The remote peers are defined by the *dlsw remote-peer tcp* statements. The zero parameter for the *list-group* specification associates the remote peer with the default set of local users. In some cases we need to provide segregation of traffic in a multi-ring environment. We could use the *dlsw ring-list* or *dlsw port-list* command, limiting the systems allowed to communicate with this remote peer to those on a specific set of rings (logical or physical)—or to those connected to specific ports (which allows control of SDLC-attached devices as well as LANs).

The IP address specified in each remote peer statement must match the IP address specified in the local peer statement on the remote peer. In this configuration example, we peer to both routers at the remote site. This way, as long as at least one router running DLSw is working at each location, SNA communications will be able to continue.

In large hub-and-spoke configurations, we may need to eliminate the cross peerings (so that Router 1A only peers with Router 2A, and Router 1B only peers with Router 2B). This will keep the number of peers supported on each hub router at a reasonable level. It also cuts in half the number of TCP connections each hub router must support, while still providing single fault tolerance. We are not able to continue operations under as many combinations of double router faults than as before; we also lose the ability to continue load sharing at the location with both routers still operational.

The Token Ring configuration on each router is also standard. The only requirement that is unique to DLSw is the need to configure source route bridging on each ring. This allows us to bridge the ring to the internal router ring defined by the *source-bridge ring-group* statement. On Router 1A this is done by the *source-bridge 100 10 4084* statement, which configures the router as bridge number 10 between ring 100 (the real Token Ring) and ring 4084 (the virtual ring inside the router used by DLSw).

Unlike with RSRB, the virtual ring number used by DLSw is only locally significant and does not need to be identical on all routers connecting as DLSw peers. It should, however, be identical on all DLSw systems in the same bridged domain, to allow for the efficient detection of bridge routing loops.

The *source-bridge spanning* line concluding the *TokenRing0* interface definition is optional but highly recommended, as it greatly reduces broadcast explorer frame traffic as the network of source route bridged rings grows to include more rings and more links between rings.

In Listing 10-3, we turn our attention to Router 2A, at the other end of the DLSw communications link. We find a mirror image of the DLSw configuration of Router 1A. Our local peer ID is the IP address used in the remote peer ID statement on Router 1A, while Router 1A's local peer ID is configured here as one of the remote peer IDs.

```
version 11.0
!
hostname Router2A
!
source-bridge ring-group 4084
dlsw local-peer peer-id 10.2.128.1
dlsw remote-peer 0 tcp 10.1.128.1
dlsw remote-peer 0 tcp 10.1.128.2
!
interface Loopback1
 description Always up address for DLSw
 ip address 10.2.128.1 255.255.255.255
!
interface TokenRing0/0
 ip address 10.2.0.2 255.255.192.0
 ring-speed 16
 source-bridge 3998 10 4084
 source-bridge spanning
!
interface TokenRing0/1
 ip address 10.2.64.2 255.255.192.0
 ring-speed 16
 source-bridge 3999 10 4084
 source-bridge spanning
!
interface Serial1/0
 ip address 10.2.129.1 255.255.255.252
!
router ospf 123
 network 10.2.0.0 0.0.255.255 area 2
!
end
```

LISTING 10-3. *Token Ring redundant DLSw configuration—Router 2A*

While the ring numbers must be unique, we can reuse the bridge ID. We continue to use the same identifier for the internal ring (a good idea even if not mandatory) but identify the local ring at this site with ring number 3998 rather than 100. Bridge IDs are only required to be unique on each real ring.

We do not show HSRP in this example because it is not relevant to the operation of DLSw. But we would normally include it in all our configurations to maximize availability whenever two routers service one LAN. We do, however, configure a second Token Ring with ring number 3999 on each router (see Listing 10-4 for

```
version 11.0
!
hostname Router2B
!
source-bridge ring-group 4084
dlsw local-peer peer-id 10.2.128.2
dlsw remote-peer 0 tcp 10.1.128.1
dlsw remote-peer 0 tcp 10.1.128.2
!
interface Loopback1
 description Always up address for DLSw
 ip address 10.2.128.2 255.255.255.255
!
interface TokenRing0/0
 ip address 10.2.0.3 255.255.192.0
 ring-speed 16
 source-bridge 3998 11 4084
 source-bridge spanning
!
interface TokenRing0/1
 ip address 10.2.64.3 255.255.192.0
 ring-speed 16
 source-bridge 3999 11 4084
 source-bridge spanning
!
interface Serial1/0
 ip address 10.2.129.5 255.255.255.252
!
router ospf 123
 network 10.2.0.0 0.0.255.255 area 2
!
end
```

LISTING 10-4. *Token Ring redundant DLSw configuration—Router 2B*

Router 2B) to show that that has no impact on the DLSw configuration. Note that while each router must use a different bridge number on each physical ring, the same bridge number can be reused for each physical ring.

DLSw FOR ETHERNET-ATTACHED DEVICES

DLSw is a popular approach for supporting Ethernet-attached SNA devices as well as those on Token Rings. However, successful use of DLSw with Ethernet in a high availability design requires us to pay close attention to the limits of the DLSw protocol and its underlying design assumptions.

As we have seen, redundant configuration of DLSw between Token Rings is automatic. Unfortunately, this approach to DLSw redundancy does not work when the LANs are Ethernet rather than Token Ring. The problem is that DLSw emulates a source route bridge, and Ethernet-attached systems do not support source route bridging. Consequently, when configuring DLSw in an Ethernet environment, we must follow the rules for classical learning bridges. We must configure DLSw so there are no loops formed in the DLSw connectivity network.

This can be a nasty surprise for the network designer, because no errors are reported when more than one DLSw peer is configured between two Ethernets. Even worse, the design may initially appear to work correctly, as DLSw peerings are set up and SNA sessions are established. However, the success is illusory. With time, performance will deteriorate and SNA sessions will fail.

The problems are not unique to Ethernet, but will arise any time we have two or more DLSw routers in the same transparent bridged domain capable of reaching the same MAC address. Standard DLSw can only support redundant connections in a source routed environment.

REDUNDANT DLSw VERSUS TRANSPARENT BRIDGING

Consider the connectivity in Figure 10-3. We have two routers on an Ethernet, both peered with DLSw to a router on a Token Ring. Connected this way, DLSw will ultimately fail due to unreliable local reachability information and circuit contention.

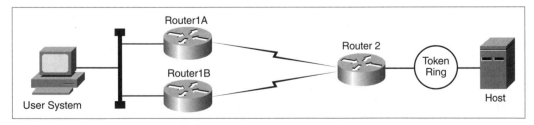

FIGURE 10-3. *Faulty network design with redundant DLSw to an Ethernet*

Local reachability information is incorrectly gathered because DLSw normally depends upon the Token Ring routing information field (RIF) to detect loops. Consider what can happen when the host and the user system initiate a connection.

- The host sends out a TEST frame with its source MAC address and the MAC address of the user system as the destination.

- Router 2 will remember that the frame from the host came in from the Token Ring and treat that address as a local entry.

- Since Router 2 does not yet recognize the MAC for the user, it sends DLSw explorer frames to the DLSw peers on Router 1A and Router 1B, looking for reachability of the user system.

- Router 1A receives the DLSw explorer frame and sends a TEST frame out on the Ethernet LAN looking for the user system. It also notes that it can reach the host via the WAN.

- Router 1B receives the TEST frame from Router 1A. It inserts the host MAC address in its table of local systems because it cannot distinguish this TEST frame from one generated by a local end-system.

- Router 1B sends a DLSw explorer frame to Router 2 looking for the user system.

At this point, Router 1A has valid data regarding the location of the host, while Router 1B has incorrectly identified the host's location as the local LAN. Meanwhile, the DLSw explorer frame originally sent from Router 2 finally arrives at Router 1B. Router 1B now knows it has a problem because the host MAC addresses appears as reachable through both the LAN and the WAN interfaces. Depending upon the implementation, the router may ignore the inconsistent update, replace the old location with the new location, or discard all location information. No matter which approach is taken, there will be a combination of arrival times and delivery delays that will result in invalid reachability information in at least one of the three routers.

For example, we could always use the location provided by the last frame processed. This is the normal approach for transparent bridges, allowing automatic recovery from a system being moved from one LAN to another. But if both DLSw explorer frames arrive and are processed at Routers 1A and 1B before either receives a TEST frame from the other, both routers will believe that the host is on the local LAN. They will ignore any attempts by the user system to respond to the TEST frame, preventing communications between the two.

Since the results are timing dependent, communications failure can appear to be a random error. But the bottom line is that even though it may work initially, communications with DLSw are not going to be reliable.

If, by some quirk of timing, we actually achieve correct entries in the reachability tables on all DLSw peers, there are still problems. We are guaranteed a communications failure due to circuit contention if the user system initiates the SNA session and sends an XID frame to the host MAC address. Both Ethernet DLSw routers will pick up the frame and send circuit setup requests to Router 2. Assume the setup packet from Router 1A arrives first. Router 2 processes the setup request and responds to Router 1A with an acceptance. Then the setup request arrives from Router 1B. This is interpreted as a duplicate circuit. In accordance with the protocol specification, the duplicate is rejected and the original is canceled, so no data can flow.

Changing the Token Ring to an Ethernet does not help. If both ends are Ethernet, and we make the mistake of putting redundant DLSw peers on both ends, we produce unreliable reachability information and circuit contention. We also consume WAN bandwidth and router CPU cycles with looping explorer packets. With no source routing information, the DLSw bridges have no way to determine that they have already processed a TEST frame or explorer frame; they continue to pass each on indefinitely.

Attempting to implement redundant DLSw on an Ethernet can also cause problems for correctly configured Ethernet switches on the LAN. But that point is moot—the bottom line is that it simply does not work.

REDUNDANT DLSw WITHOUT SOURCE ROUTE BRIDGING

Standard RFC 1795 DLSw does not provide for redundant operation outside of a source route bridged environment, but there are two general approaches available to achieve this goal: transparent redundancy and backup peers. Both approaches are proprietary, so we will only consider the Cisco implementations.

Cisco's proprietary approach to transparent redundancy for Ethernet-attached DLSw is called *DLSw+ Ethernet Redundancy*. The capability was first made available in IOS release 12.0(5T) and will not be available in a General Deployment IOS release before IOS 12.1.

DLSw+ Ethernet Redundancy works by having the DLSw routers on the Ethernet use a proprietary protocol to identify and elect a master router for the Ethernet (or other transparent bridged domain). All DLSw routers on the LAN use a multicast MAC address to identify themselves on the LAN and handle the election.

The DLSw router elected to be master router then maintains a database of all DLSw circuits with an endpoint in the transparent bridged domain. Each DLSw router in the domain maintains an LLC2 connection to the master and must have the master router's agreement before initiating or accepting a new DLSw circuit for the domain. Using its database of all DLSw circuits being handled, the master router ensures that only one circuit is set up for each SNA session.

One disadvantage of Cisco's approach is that a single MAC address identifying a remote SNA system can appear from multiple DLSw routers, if there are multiple local users with sessions to the same remote system. This can create problems for switches in the local LAN that expect to be running in a properly configured transparent Spanning-Tree (TST) environment. The feature implementation includes configuration capabilities that allow the equivalent of network address translation at the MAC level (so that the remote system has a different MAC address from each DLSw router on the local LAN). But it requires manual configuration of all translations. This makes the scaling of a configuration difficult, particularly in a data center environment in which switches are almost certain to be required.

The alternative approach for redundant DLSw peers on an Ethernet LAN uses the *backup* modifier on the *dlsw remote-peer* command, available in IOS 11.2 and later. DLSw backup peers allow us to configure alternate DLSw peers that remain inactive until they are needed to replace a failed peer. This approach is proven and it allows for minimizing the number of DLSw circuits that any router must support at any given instant. Since all the rules for transparent bridging are followed, and there is never more than one path active at any instant, there are no problems using backup peers in a switched environment.

On the down side, backup peers do not allow for load sharing, as they are not even connected until the primary peering fails. All SNA connections on the primary peer are dropped when the primary fails, and those established on the backup peer must be dropped when the primary returns to service.

As is usual in most network decisions, the best approach depends on the user requirements and the application environment. We will start our configuration examples with one using backup to provide a "no single point of failure" DLSw implementation between two Ethernet LANs.

CONFIGURATION EXAMPLE: REDUNDANT ETHERNET PEERS USING BACKUP PEERS

Backup peers allow us to configure a DLSw+ router to bring up a new peer if an existing peer should fail. The challenge is to set up the primary and backup peers to ensure that, no matter which DLSw router fails, there will always be exactly one active path between the two LANs. We will configure the scenario in Figure 10-4, which is identical to the Token Ring scenario in Figure 10-2 except that the Token Rings have been replaced with Ethernets.

We will configure DLSw so that all traffic normally is carried by a peering between Router 1A and Router 2A. Each of these is then configured with a backup peer to the B router on the other LAN. The different router failure modes and the associated impact on DLSw connectivity are summarized in Table 10-1.

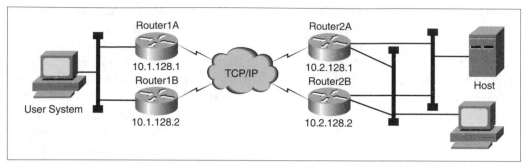

Figure 10-4. *Redundant DLSw peers in an Ethernet environment*

One key to the success of this approach is that the TCP/IP Internet must be well connected. We must never have a situation in which Router 1A and Router 2A cannot communicate to keep their DLSw peer relationship up, but can communicate with their backup peers and bring up a DLSw connection to them. That would put us in the position of having two DLSw peers running between the two Ethernets, which is not acceptable.

The DLSw configuration for Router 1A is given in Listing 10-5. This is a standard DLSw configuration for an Ethernet LAN except for the backup statement. Since we have not yet looked at an Ethernet DLSw configuration, we will examine this one line by line.

The first major difference in this configuration is that we don't use a *source-bridge ring-group* definition to start the list of DLSw peers. Instead, we have a *dlsw bridge-group* line at the end of the list to bind the DLSw process to a transparent bridge group. Contrary to the many published Cisco examples, there is no need for a *source-bridge ring-group* line when using Ethernet rather than Token Ring. Including one, however, will not interfere with DLSw operation.

Next, we see that the local-peer statement has an *lf 1500* modifier added to it. This is to ensure that we never try to negotiate a frame size larger than will fit on Ethernet. In some earlier IOS versions, the global use of the qualifier on the local-peer statement is not supported and we would need to add it to each *remote-peer*

Table 10-1. *DLSw Peers Active During Router Failures*

ROUTER FAILED	ACTIVE PEERING	TRAFFIC IMPACT
Router 1A	Router 2A to Router 1B	All sessions drop and reestablish
Router 1B	Router 1A to Router 2A	No impact—default peering
Router 2A	Router 1A to Router 2B	All sessions drop and reestablish
Router 2B	Router 1A to Router 2A	No impact—default peering

```
version 11.2
!
hostname Router1A
!
dlsw local-peer peer-id 10.1.128.1 lf 1500
dlsw remote-peer 0 tcp 10.2.128.1
dlsw remote-peer 0 tcp 10.2.128.2 backup-peer 10.2.128.1
 ➡ linger 0
dlsw bridge-group 5
!
interface Loopback1
 description Always up address for DLSw
 ip address 10.1.128.1 255.255.255.255
!
interface Ethernet0
 ip address 10.1.0.2 255.255.128.0
 bridge-group 5
 bridge-group 5 spanning-disabled
!
interface Serial0
 ip address 10.1.129.1 255.255.255.252
!
router ospf 123
 network 10.1.0.0 0.0.255.255 area 1
!
bridge 5 protocol ieee
!
end
```

LISTING 10-5. *Backup peer configuration for Router 1A*

line. Explicitly setting the maximum frame length to a value compatible with Ethernet should not be necessary in a pure Ethernet environment. It will, however, protect us in a mixed LAN environment in which not all end-systems properly negotiate maximum frame size.

Note that we normally only peer with Router 2A. The peering with Router 2B at 10.2.128.2 is only activated when the peering to Router 2A at 10.2.128.1 is down. The added *linger 0* modifier is essential if the far end is an Ethernet as well. Otherwise the backup peer would remain up to support open SNA connections at the same time as the primary link. This would result in frames from the same MAC address arriving via two different paths on the remote network. While a Token Ring with source routing would not be confused, an Ethernet would.

Moving down to the definition of the Ethernet interface, we link the interface to the DLSw bridge through the line *bridge-group 5*. The numeric argument must match the bridge group specified in the *dlsw bridge-group* line in the DLSw configuration. Unless we are actually providing transparent bridge services, there is no need to run the Spanning-Tree protocol on the LAN. We eliminate the unnecessary traffic overhead by turning off the Spanning-Tree negotiation protocol with the *bridge-group 5 spanning-disabled* command.

Finally, to prevent confusion, we also specify that the Ethernet mode of bridging will be IEEE TST. This will cause the router to broadcast IEEE-format Spanning-Tree bridge hello frames rather than using the original DECnet format. Since IEEE Spanning Tree is the default, this line will be inserted for us should we neglect to specify it.

The configuration of Router 1B in Listing 10-6 is identical to that of our previous examples except for the configuration of the DLSw peers. In the definition of the local

```
version 11.2
!
hostname Router1B
!
dlsw local-peer peer-id 10.1.128.2 lf 1500 passive
dlsw remote-peer 0 tcp 10.2.128.1
dlsw bridge-group 5
!
interface Loopback1
  description Always up address for DLSw
  ip address 10.1.128.2 255.255.255.255
!
interface Ethernet0
  ip address 10.1.0.3 255.255.128.0
  bridge-group 5
  bridge-group 5 spanning-disabled
!
interface Serial0
  ip address 10.1.129.5 255.255.255.252
!
router ospf 123
  network 10.1.0.0 0.0.255.255 area 1
!
bridge 5 protocol ieee
!
end
```

LISTING 10-6. *Backup peer configuration for Router 1B*

peer capability, we have added the option *passive* to the specification of the largest frame size. This prevents the DLSw state machine on the router from actively trying to establish DLSw connections to the specified remote peers. Instead, it will wait for the remotes to connect to it. Since this router is a backup peer for Router 1A, our connection attempts would only be rejected anyway, so there is no benefit to sending them.

The implementation of the backup and switchover for the reverse direction can be seen by looking at the configuration of Router 2A in Listing 10-7. This

```
version 11.2
!
hostname Router2A
!
dlsw local-peer peer-id 10.2.128.1 1f 1500
dlsw remote-peer 0 tcp 10.1.128.1
dlsw remote-peer 0 tcp 10.1.128.2 backup-peer 10.1.128.1
  linger 0
dlsw bridge-group 5
!
interface Loopback1
 description Always up address for DLSw
 ip address 10.2.128.1 255.255.255.255
!
interface FastEthernet0/0
 ip address 10.2.0.2 255.255.192.0
 bridge-group 5
 bridge-group 5 spanning-disabled
!
interface FastEthernet0/1
 ip address 10.2.64.2 255.255.192.0
 bridge-group 5
 bridge-group 5 spanning-disabled
!
interface Serial1/0
 ip address 10.2.129.1 255.255.255.252
!
router ospf 123
 network 10.2.0.0 0.0.255.255 area 2
!
bridge 5 protocol ieee
!
end
```

LISTING 10-7. *Backup peer configuration for Router 2A*

configuration is a mirror image of the configuration of Router 1A in Listing 10-5. Just as Router 1A will fall back to a peering with Router 2B if Router 2A should fail, Router 2A will set up a peering with Router 1B if Router 1A should fail.

In the same way, the configuration of Router 2B in Listing 10-8 mirrors that of Router 1B, providing a target for Router 1A to connect to should Router 2A fail.

While this use of backup peers will protect us from router or DLSw failure, it still leaves us exposed to other failures. Consider what happens if Router 1A loses its Ethernet connection but otherwise remains online. Router 1A will still be able to

```
version 11.2
!
hostname Router2B
!
dlsw local-peer peer-id 10.2.128.2 1f 1500 passive
dlsw remote-peer 0 tcp 10.1.128.1
dlsw bridge-group 5
!
interface Loopback1
 description Always up address for DLSw
 ip address 10.2.128.2 255.255.255.255
!
interface FastEthernet0/0
 ip address 10.2.0.3 255.255.192.0
 bridge-group 5
 bridge-group 5 spanning-disabled
!
interface FastEthernet0/1
 ip address 10.2.64.3 255.255.192.0
 bridge-group 5
 bridge-group 5 spanning-disabled
!
interface Serial1/0
 ip address 10.2.129.5 255.255.255.252
!
router ospf 123
 network 10.2.0.0 0.0.255.255 area 2
!
bridge 5 protocol ieee
!
end
```

LISTING 10-8. *Backup peer configuration for Router 2B*

function as a DLSw peer, and a backup peering will not be forced to Router 1B. As a result, all SNA and IBM NetBIOS sessions will fail.

We could protect against most instances of Ethernet connection failure on Router 1A by using the Ethernet address rather than a loopback address for the local peer address. However, that change would still not protect us against a failure that was not detected at the link level on the Ethernet interface, nor would it protect more than one LAN interface supporting DLSw—so we could not use it effectively on Router 2A or Router 2B.

CONFIGURATION EXAMPLE: BACKUP PEERS ON A SEGMENTABLE LAN

Providing protection against all modes of DLSw failure in an Ethernet environment requires that we are able to bring up backup peers any time the Ethernet LAN is segmented, preventing frames from traveling between the two DLSw routers across the LAN. This could be considered the same problem that we saw when providing continued IP access via multiple routers on a single LAN, despite the LAN's being split into multiple disconnected LANs. Though we can detect that the two routers are no longer connected via the LAN, we cannot detect where the break is, and there could be systems on either side of the split.

Fortunately, addressing with DLSw is at the MAC layer. Frames will be correctly directed to the appropriate LAN segment—no matter where the split occurs—once the router that can no longer reach the end-system ages out its MAC address entry. However, we still need a means to detect that the preferred DLSw peers are no longer useful so that we can bring up the backup peering on the backup router.

One way we can detect link loss is to use a DLSw peering between the two local routers that can only be maintained through the LAN. We have the backup router backup that peering with a useful peering to the remote site. By using that peering rather than a backup peer on the remote site, we can cover virtually all the failure modes protected by the previous example. We also cover failure of the LAN connection of the primary local router or other segmentation of the LAN.

The trick is to configure the local test peering so that it does not confuse the production DLSw. We can achieve this through the use of selective bridge groups or port lists on the primary router. In Listing 10-9, we can see the changes to Router 1A required to support this approach. Instead of using the default value of zero for the bgroup-list number in our remote peer statements, we define two bgroup-lists, one that associates with the real bridge group (*dlsw bgroup-list 7*) and one that associates with a non-existent bridge group (*dlsw bgroup-list 11*).

By using the bridge group-list associated with the real bridge group used on the Ethernet, we can continue running DLSw with the remote LAN routers as in the previous example. However, the DLSw peer on Router 1B will only be able to communicate with systems in bridge group-list 11—which defines a bridge group that does not

```
version 11.2
!
hostname Router1A
!
dlsw local-peer peer-id 10.1.128.1 lf 1500
dlsw bgroup-list 7 bgroups 5
dlsw bgroup-list 11 bgroups 6
dlsw remote-peer 7 tcp 10.2.128.1
dlsw remote-peer 7 tcp 10.2.128.2 backup-peer 10.2.128.1
 ➥ linger 0
dlsw remote-peer 11 tcp 10.1.128.2
dlsw bridge-group 5
dlsw bridge-group 6
!
interface Loopback1
 description Always up address for DLSw
 ip address 10.1.128.1 255.255.255.255
!
interface Ethernet0
 ip address 10.1.0.2 255.255.128.0
 bridge-group 5
 bridge-group 5 spanning-disabled
!
interface Serial0
 ip address 10.1.129.1 255.255.255.252
 ip access-group 150 out
 ip access-group 151 in
!
router ospf 123
 network 10.1.0.0 0.0.255.255 area 1
!
access-list 150 deny    tcp host 10.1.128.1 host 10.1.128.2
 ➥ eq 2065
access-list 150 permit ip any any
access-list 151 deny    tcp host 10.1.128.2 host 10.1.128.1
 ➥ eq 2065
access-list 151 permit ip any any
!
bridge 5 protocol ieee
bridge 6 protocol ieee
!
end
```

LISTING 10-9. *Backup peer configuration for Router 1A*

exist. This prevents any communications from occurring but leaves the peer relation-ship intact, which is what we want.

We ensure that the test peering over the LAN occurs only via the LAN inter-faces by applying the DLSw-specific packet filters defined by access-lists 150 and 151 to all interfaces except the Ethernet one. With these filters in place on both Router 1A and Router 1B, we will be able to keep the test peering alive only if both routers have working LAN interfaces. Extended access-lists are essential to prevent interference with production DLSw traffic, which is also going to and from the same local peer ID address and port.

We shift our focus in Listing 10-10 to Router 1B, examining how to take advantage of this new peering. Rather than passively waiting for a connection from

```
version 11.2
!
hostname Router1B
!
dlsw local-peer peer-id 10.1.128.2 1f 1500
dlsw remote-peer 0 tcp 10.1.128.1
dlsw remote-peer 0 tcp 10.2.128.1 backup 10.1.128.1 linger 0
dlsw bridge-group 5
!
interface Loopback1
 description Always up address for DLSw
 ip address 10.1.128.2 255.255.255.255
!
interface Ethernet0
 ip address 10.1.0.3 255.255.128.0
 bridge-group 5
 bridge-group 5 spanning-disabled
!
interface Serial0
 ip address 10.1.129.5 255.255.255.252
 ip access-group 150 out
 ip access-group 151 in
!
router ospf 123
 network 10.1.0.0 0.0.255.255 area 1
!
access-list 150 deny   tcp host 10.1.128.2 host 10.1.128.1
  ➥ eq 2065
access-list 150 permit ip any any
```

(continued)

```
access-list 151 deny   tcp host 10.1.128.1 host 10.1.128.2
  ➥ eq 2065
access-list 151 permit ip any any
!
bridge 5 protocol ieee
!
end
```

LISTING 10-10. *Backup peer configuration for Router 1B*

Router 2A, we now control recovery from Router 1A failure at Router 1B. This establishes a peering with Router 2A any time our peering with Router 1A fails. To ensure that our peering with Router 1A is actually through the LAN interfaces and not through any other path, we also need to install packet filters that block all DLSw traffic between 10.1.128.1 and 10.1.128.2 except via the LAN. These filters are defined in access-lists 150 (for outbound packets) and 151 (for inbound packets) and installed on every interface except the LAN we are protecting.

The configuration at the remote site of Router 2A, shown in Listing 10-11, must also be modified to reflect the change in backup peering strategy. There is actually only one change required, which is to specify that the original backup peering to Router 1B be a passive peer.

```
version 11.2
!
hostname Router2A
!
dlsw local-peer peer-id 10.2.128.1 1f 1500
dlsw remote-peer 0 tcp 10.1.128.1
dlsw remote-peer 0 tcp 10.1.128.2 passive
dlsw bridge-group 5
!
interface Loopback1
 description Always up address for DLSw
 ip address 10.2.128.1 255.255.255.255
!
interface FastEthernet0/0
 ip address 10.2.0.2 255.255.192.0
 bridge-group 5
 bridge-group 5 spanning-disabled
!
interface FastEthernet0/1
```

(continued)

```
  ip address 10.2.64.2 255.255.192.0
  bridge-group 5
  bridge-group 5 spanning-disabled
 !
interface Serial1/0
  ip address 10.2.129.1 255.255.255.252
 !
router ospf 123
  network 10.2.0.0 0.0.255.255 area 2
 !
bridge 5 protocol ieee
 !
end
```

LISTING 10-11. *Backup peer configuration for Router 2A*

There are no changes made to the configuration of Router 2B, so Listing 10-8 still applies.

Note that while we are now immune to all typical failure modes on the LAN 1 side, we have not fixed the other side. Providing equivalent robustness on Routers 2A and 2B is not possible using backup peers; there are two LANs at that site and DLSw will only allow a single remote peer to be configured per remote IP address.

CONFIGURATION EXAMPLE: REDUNDANT PEERS USING DLSW+ ETHERNET REDUNDANCY

As we saw in our previous example, using backup peers for redundant DLSw to a multiple LAN site leaves us undesirably vulnerable to LAN connection failures. Until recently, our only choice if we required incremental availability was to use Token Ring for the LANs so that DLSw could be configured with all possible peers active all the time. Cisco's proprietary DLSw+ Ethernet Redundancy feature gives us the ability to configure an Ethernet topology like Figure 10-5 with full redundancy as well.

We will assume that the user system can initiate a connection, and that the LANs at the host site are switched while the LAN at the user site is not. We will look at the user site configuration first, as it is simpler, with a single LAN and no switches to worry about. We'll start with Router 1A in Listing 10-12.

The first thing we notice in the configuration is that there is no *dlsw bridge* statement tying DLSw to the Ethernet or any other ports. Unlike normal DLSw Ethernet connections, which are based on translational bridging from the Ethernet to DLSw, DLSw+ Ethernet Redundancy provides its own connection through the *dlsw transparent redundancy-enable* line in the interface configuration.

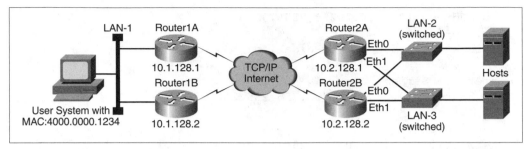

FIGURE 10-5. *Redundant DLSw with dual Ethernet LANs*

DLSw+ Ethernet Redundancy is incompatible with Ethernet translational bridging. Only one or the other may be used on a router to support DLSw. Similarly, if DLSw+ Ethernet Redundancy is configured on an Ethernet interface, the interface level *bridge-group* command is no longer available to support other Ethernet interfaces.

```
version 12.1
!
hostname Router1A
!
dlsw local-peer peer-id 10.1.128.1
dlsw remote-peer 0 tcp 10.2.128.1
dlsw remote-peer 0 tcp 10.2.128.2
!
interface Loopback1
 description Local Peer address for DLSw
 ip address 10.1.128.1 255.255.255.255
!
interface Ethernet0
 ip address 10.1.0.2 255.255.128.0
 dlsw transparent redundancy-enable 9999.9999.9999
    ➥ master-priority 10
!
interface Serial0
 ip address 10.1.129.1 255.255.255.252
!
router ospf 123
 network 10.1.0.0 0.0.255.255 area 1
!
end
```

LISTING 10-12. *DLSw+ Ethernet Redundancy configuration for Router 1A*

DLSw+ Ethernet Redundancy is enabled on each desired Ethernet interface by adding the *dlsw transparent redundancy-enable* command to the interface configuration. An appropriate Ethernet multicast MAC address must then be specified. Multicast MAC addresses have the high-order bit set to one. The second bit should be set to zero to indicate a privately administered address. This means that, expressed in hexadecimal, the first digit of the address should be an 8, 9, A, or B. The remaining digits are arbitrary. The address simply must be unique on the Ethernet LAN and not in use by any other applications.

Specification of the master priority is optional. It defaults to 64, with the lowest value on each Ethernet becoming the master DLSw connection assignor. The router with the most resources available (CPU cycles and memory) should be preferred for use as the master. If there is a tie at the priority level, the DLSw master will be selected based on the interface MAC addresses.

Router 1B in Listing 10-13 is configured almost identically. There are obvious modifications reflecting the need for unique IP addresses on each shared LAN. The

```
version 12.1
!
hostname Router1B
!
dlsw local-peer peer-id 10.1.128.2
dlsw remote-peer 0 tcp 10.2.128.1
dlsw remote-peer 0 tcp 10.2.128.2
!
interface Loopback1
 description Local Peer address for DLSw
 ip address 10.1.128.2 255.255.255.255
!
interface Ethernet0
 ip address 10.1.0.3 255.255.128.0
 dlsw transparent redundancy-enable 9999.9999.9999
 ➥ master-priority 101
!
interface Serial0
 ip address 10.1.129.5 255.255.255.252
!
router ospf 123
 network 10.1.0.0 0.0.255.255 area 1
!
end
```

LISTING 10-13. *DLSw+ Ethernet Redundancy configuration for Router 1B*

only significant change though is the specification of a higher master priority value for the DLSw+ Ethernet Redundancy feature to ensure that Router 1A will be elected master whenever a choice must be made. We specify the priority explicitly on interfaces because of variations that occur in the default value with different releases.

Rather than take chances, we specify non-default values any place where we might have a concern about the results of an election. This is a good practice in general, as it prevents surprises when default values change.

Moving over to the site with multiple switched LANs, we see a similar configuration in Listing 10-14 for Router 2A. Before we get to the impact of layer-2 switching on the configuration, note the use of the master priority here. It distributes the normal load of monitoring connections between the two routers at the site. Router 2A is the preferred router for the first LAN (10.2.0.0/18 on interface Ethernet0/0) and Router 2B (see Listing 10-15) is the preferred router on the second LAN (10.2.64.0/18 on interface Ethernet0/1).

```
version 12.1
!
hostname Router2A
!
dlsw local-peer peer-id 10.2.128.1
dlsw remote-peer 0 tcp 10.1.128.1
dlsw remote-peer 0 tcp 10.1.128.2
dlsw transparent switch-support
!
interface Loopback1
 description Always up address for DLSw
 ip address 10.2.128.1 255.255.255.255
!
interface Ethernet0/0
 mac-address 402a.0000.0001
 ip address 10.2.0.2 255.255.192.0
 dlsw transparent redundancy-enable 9999.9999.9999
   ➥ master-priority 50
 dlsw transparent map local-mac 402a.0000.1234 remote-mac
   ➥ 4000.0000.1234 neighbor 402b.0000.0001
!
interface Ethernet0/1
 mac-address 402a.0100.0001
 ip address 10.2.64.2 255.255.192.0
 dlsw transparent redundancy-enable 9999.9999.9999
   ➥ master-priority 150
```
                                                              (continued)

```
  dlsw transparent map local-mac 402a.0100.1234 remote-mac
    ➥ 4000.0000.1234 neighbor 402b.0100.0001
  !
interface Serial1/0
  ip address 10.2.129.1 255.255.255.252
  !

router ospf 123
  network 10.2.0.0 0.0.255.255 area 1
  !
end
```

LISTING 10-14. *DLSw+ Ethernet Redundancy configuration for Router 2A*

```
version 12.1
!
hostname Router2B
!
dlsw local-peer peer-id 10.2.128.2
dlsw remote-peer 0 tcp 10.1.128.1
dlsw remote-peer 0 tcp 10.1.128.2
dlsw transparent switch-support
!
interface Loopback1
  description Local peer address for DLSw
  ip address 10.2.128.2 255.255.255.255
!
interface Ethernet0/0
  mac-address 402b.0000.0001
  ip address 10.2.0.3 255.255.192.0
  dlsw transparent redundancy-enable 9999.9999.9999
    ➥ master-priority 150
  dlsw transparent map local-mac 402b.0000.1234 remote-mac
    ➥ 4000.0000.1234 neighbor 402a.0000.0001
!
interface Ethernet0/1
  mac-address 402b.0100.0001
  ip address 10.2.64.3 255.255.192.0
  dlsw transparent redundancy-enable 9999.9999.9999
    ➥ master-priority 50
  dlsw transparent map local-mac 402b.0100.1234 remote-mac
    ➥ 4000.0000.1234 neighbor 402a.0100.0001
```

(continued)

```
 !
 interface Serial1/0
  ip address 10.2.129.5 255.255.255.252
 !
 router ospf 123
  network 10.2.0.0 0.0.255.255 area 1
 !
 end
```

LISTING 10-15.   *DLSw+ Ethernet Redundancy configuration for Router 2B*

Our challenge in a switched LAN is the appearance of the remote MAC address on circuits established through both switches. Layer-2 switches and other transparent bridges are designed assuming that each MAC address can be associated with only one port. If the remote system connects to more than one SNA controller on the local LAN, it is possible that each router on the local LAN will support one of the connections. This will generate inconsistent forwarding tables in any switch that sees the two routers as being on separate ports. It can lead to inconsistent operation and the potential loss of frames destined to the remote system.

DLSw+ Ethernet Redundancy gets around the apparent duplicate MAC address problem by including a facility to perform the equivalent of network address translation at the MAC address level. This facility is turned on by the global command *dlsw transparent switch-support*. Unfortunately, it only supports static MAC address translations, so we need to define what local MAC address this router should use for each real remote MAC address it may need to support. We also need to define which other local system will be handling this remote MAC address.

The DLSw+ Ethernet Redundancy feature has tremendous potential to improve DLSw availability in an Ethernet environment, but this potential is tempered by a number of operational issues. Switch support in particular can be a major challenge. It is not a major issue in a NetBIOS environment in which MAC addresses are dynamically assigned to named services. But its use in an SNA environment in which devices are configured based on their MAC address may not be practical. Each remote controller would need to be configured multiple times, once for each possible local MAC address.

Limiting its use to simple hub-based Ethernets means that DLSw+ Ethernet Redundancy cannot be applied to the larger networks where its availability enhancement is most needed. Those may continue to require Token Ring based designs for some time to come.

DLSw THROUGH FIREWALLS

DLSw peers may also be set up through firewalls. While there are a few critical considerations, DLSw is generally a firewall-friendly protocol. We can use backup peers to provide reliable failover to backup firewalls. We can even use a firewall at each end of the connection, providing a conduit for sensitive traffic through less security-conscious portions of the organization's intranet, or across the Internet.

There are two key requirements for successful DLSw operation through firewalls. These are: preservation of the source and destination address value relationship, and maintenance of low average- and peak-transit delay.

The former requirement tends to be the most common stumbling block when firewalls incorporating network address translation are used. DLSw is a NAT clean protocol, in that no IP addresses are carried inside packets. There is no need for the firewall doing NAT to check and adjust the contents of packets based on the NAT in place.

The challenge is that DLSw does use the IP addresses of the source and destination peers as part of the protocol. When establishing a peer relationship, each peer will attempt to contact the other by initiating a TCP connection request to port 2065 on the other peer. This brings up a pair of TCP/IP connections, only one of which is needed. The DLSw protocol determines which connection to tear down by comparing the IP address of the local peer with the IP address of the remote peer. The peer with the lower local peer address then tears down its TCP/IP connection, and all further communications proceed over the remaining connection.

The numeric value of the IP address is otherwise ignored. There is no problem changing the IP address with network address translation, as long as both peers reach the same conclusion when comparing the two IP addresses. If the network address translation changes the results of the comparison, making both peers think the other has the higher address, they will both tear down their TCP connections. This will result in no communications. If both think the other is lower, the problem is more subtle. Both connections will remain active, and failure will not occur until an SNA connection attempt is made. At this point the destination peer will receive duplicate requests and recover by closing both links. In either case, DLSw will not function properly.

Consistent network performance with low delays, the second requirement for DLSw success, is a factor whether or not firewalls are involved. However, in the context of firewalled environments establishing virtual private networks (VPNs) over the Internet, adequate support for DLSw will usually mean procurement of Internet services from a single provider specializing in delivery of consistent quality of service.

DLSw Backup Peers for Firewall Redundancy

We addressed the challenges of achieving transparent redundancy through firewalls in Chapter 9. DLSw can be configured to protect itself from firewall failure through the use of backup peers even if the firewalls do not support transparent redundancy for TCP/IP. We do this by configuring one set of network address translations through one firewall and a backup set through the backup firewall.

Consider the scenario of Figure 10-6. We have redundant routers on an inside Token Ring (Routers R-1 and R-2) that we want to support using redundant peerings through the firewalls to Routers R-C and R-D on the outside Token Ring. The key is that we define a different inside address to each outside peer depending upon which firewall it came through. We do the same with the outside addresses of each inside peer.

In terms of security, we will normally need to allow through the firewall any TCP connections between the appropriate peers that are started with a connection request to port 2065. Since both DLSw peers may initiate a TCP connection, we should allow connection requests through in either direction. Be careful, however, since which port is used will depend upon the DLSw version and the specific implementation. For example, if we need to use an early version 1 DLSw implementation that does not support bidirectional TCP usage, we must configure the firewall to allow TCP connection requests to port 2067 rather than port 2065. Version 2 DLSw will also try to use port 2067 but should fall back to port 2065 if it fails. Version 2 DLSw peers also send UDP packets to port 2067. Some version 2 implementations also use multicasts, but support of multicasting is usually not mandatory. Cisco's DLSw+ uses only port 2065 and TCP by default, but if the priority support feature is enabled, we also need to open ports 1981, 1982, and 1983.

From our viewpoint, the key to the firewall configuration is the setup of the network address translations. For our scenario, we need the firewalls configured with the inside-to-outside translations specified in Table 10-2 and the outside-to-inside translations specified in Table 10-3. These provide one path through each firewall for

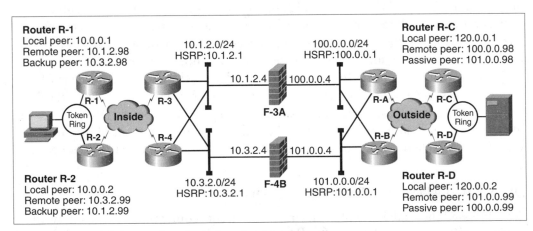

FIGURE 10-6. *DLSw peering through redundant firewalls*

TABLE 10-2. *Firewall Inside-to-Outside Address Translations and Routing*

FIREWALL	INSIDE PORT IP ADDRESS	ALLOWED SOURCE IP	OUTSIDE SOURCE IP	OUTSIDE DESTINATION	NEXT HOP
F-3A	10.1.2.98	10.0.0.1	100.0.0.98	120.0.0.1	100.0.0.1
F-3A	10.1.2.99	10.0.0.2	100.0.0.99	120.0.0.2	100.0.0.1
F-4B	10.3.2.98	10.0.0.1	101.0.0.98	120.0.0.1	101.0.0.1
F-4B	10.3.2.99	10.0.0.2	101.0.0.99	120.0.0.2	101.0.0.1

TABLE 10-3. *Firewall Outside-to-Inside Address Translations and Routing*

FIREWALL	OUTSIDE PORT IP ADDRESS	ALLOWED SOURCE IP	INSIDE SOURCE IP	INSIDE DESTINATION	NEXT HOP
F-3A	100.0.0.98	120.0.0.1	10.1.2.98	10.0.0.1	10.1.2.1
F-3A	100.0.0.99	120.0.0.2	10.1.2.99	10.0.0.2	10.1.2.1
F-4B	101.0.0.98	120.0.0.1	10.3.2.98	10.0.0.1	10.3.2.1
F-4B	101.0.0.99	120.0.0.2	10.3.2.99	10.0.0.2	10.3.2.1

Router R-1 to peer with Router R-C and for Router R-2 to peer with Router R-D—for a total of four paths, two primary and two backup.

If we wanted to support active peers between R-1 and R-D and between R-2 and R-C, we would expand our filters to allow either source address to use either destination address in both directions on both firewalls.

CONFIGURATION EXAMPLE: TOKEN RING DLSW THROUGH DUAL NAT FIREWALLS

By using the firewall NATs specified in Tables 10-2 and 10-3, we can achieve complete single fault tolerance. Keep in mind that our examples include only the essential aspects of the configuration on each router. Other considerations—such as filters on the routers interfacing with the firewalls, for added protection, or any of the details of internal connectivity—would need to be included in a production configuration.

When setting up DLSw (or any other services) through firewalls, strict attention to documentation is essential. There is no way to determine that the DSLw configurations on Routers R-1 and R-C are in any way related just by looking at the routers' running configurations. Adding comments to the configuration, as is done for Router R-2 in Listing 10-17, can be very helpful, but they will not be included in the running configuration. They will all be lost the first time the startup configuration is updated by copying the running configuration to it rather than making changes in the file copy and updating the startup configuration using TFTP.

Monitoring, troubleshooting, and error recovery can also be challenging. ICMP, SNMP, Telnet, and all the other protocols used for routine network management require their own holes punched through the firewall before they can be used. These considerations are all a natural side effect of using firewalls and are part of the cost of security.

Now we'll turn our attention back to DLSw and the configuration of Router R1 in Listing 10-16. The configuration appears to be a standard Token Ring configuration with a backup peer definition. However, closer examination gives a hint that something strange is going on. The backup peer is on a completely different IP subnetwork from the peer it is backing up. What is not obvious is that the backup peer and the primary peer are the same DLSw router accessed via different firewalls.

```
version 11.0
!
hostname R-1
!
ip subnet-zero
!
source-bridge ring-group 1234
dlsw local-peer peer-id 10.0.0.1
dlsw remote-peer 0 tcp 10.1.2.98
dlsw remote-peer 0 tcp 10.3.2.98 backup-peer 10.1.2.98
!
interface Loopback1
  description Local peer address for DLSw
  ip address 10.0.0.1 255.255.255.255
!
interface TokenRing0
  ip address 10.100.0.2 255.255.128.0
  ring-speed 16
  source-bridge 100 10 1234
  source-bridge spanning
  .
  .
  .
router ospf 123
  network 10.0.0.1 0.0.0.0 area 10.100.0.0
  network 10.100.0.0 0.0.255.255 area 10.100.0.0
!
end
```

LISTING 10-16. *DLSw through dual firewalls—inside DLSw Peer Router R-1*

The configuration of Router R-2 in Listing 10-17 is a mirror image of that of Router R-1. The only difference is that here we have included comments to remind us how the configuration is really working.

Routers R-3 and R-4, in Listings 10-18 and 10-19, service the firewalls and must advertise the firewall LANs so that other routers on the inside can find these firewalls. We use HSRP on these routers so that the firewalls can use static routing and still automatically survive the loss of an access router.

```
version 11.0
!
hostname R-2
!
ip subnet-zero
!
source-bridge ring-group 1234
! Our local peer address on the inside.
! NATs to 100.0.0.99 on the outside via Firewall F-3A
! NATs to 101.0.0.99 on the outside via Firewall F-4B
dlsw local-peer peer-id 10.0.0.2
! Remote peer router R-D at outside address 120.0.0.2
! via Firewall F-3A
dlsw remote-peer 0 tcp 10.1.2.99
! via Firewall F-4B
dlsw remote-peer 0 tcp 10.3.2.99 backup-peer 10.1.2.99
!
interface Loopback1
 description Local inside peer address for DLSw
 ip address 10.0.0.2 255.255.255.255
!
interface TokenRing0
 ip address 10.100.0.3 255.255.128.0
 ring-speed 16
 source-bridge 100 11 1234
 source-bridge spanning
 .
 .
 .
router ospf 123
 network 10.0.0.2 0.0.0.0 area 10.100.0.0
 network 10.100.0.0 0.0.255.255 area 10.100.0.0
!
end
```

LISTING 10-17. *DLSw through dual firewalls—inside DLSw Peer Router R-2*

```
version 11.0
!
hostname R-3
!
interface FastEthernet0/0
 ip address 10.1.2.2 255.255.255.128
 standby 1 priority 110
 standby 1 preempt
 standby 1 ip 10.1.2.1
!
interface FastEthernet0/1
 ip address 10.3.2.2 255.255.255.128
 standby 2 priority 90
 standby 2 ip 10.3.2.1

 .

 .

 .


router ospf 123
 network 10.1.2.0 0.0.0.127 area 1.2.3.4
 network 10.3.2.0 0.0.0.127 area 1.2.3.4
!
end
```

LISTING 10-18.   *DLSw through dual firewalls—inside Firewall Router R-3*

```
version 11.0
!
hostname R-4
!
interface FastEthernet0/0
 ip address 10.1.2.3 255.255.255.128
 standby 1 priority 90
 standby 1 ip 10.1.2.1
!
interface FastEthernet0/1
 ip address 10.3.2.3 255.255.255.128
 standby 2 priority 110
 standby 2 preempt
 standby 2 ip 10.3.2.1

 .

 .

 .
```

(continued)

```
router ospf 123
 network 10.1.2.0 0.0.0.127 area 1.2.3.4
 network 10.3.2.0 0.0.0.127 area 1.2.3.4
!
end
```

LISTING **10-19.** *DLSw through dual firewalls—inside Firewall Router R-4*

We will turn our attention now to the routers outside the firewalls. The Firewall Access Routers R-A and R-B in Listings 10-20 and 10-21 are standard configurations mirroring the inside Firewall Access Routers R-3 and R-4. Since the inside and outside networks are completely independent of one another, there is no need for them to be consistent. For example, here we show the outside network using Enhanced Interior Gateway Routing Protocol (EIGRP) for its intradomain routing, while the inside network uses Open Shortest Path First (OSPF).

```
version 11.0
!
hostname R-A
!
ip subnet-zero
!
interface Ethernet0
 ip address 100.0.0.2 255.255.255.0
 standby 1 priority 110
 standby 1 preempt
 standby 1 ip 100.0.0.1
!
interface Ethernet1
 ip address 101.0.0.2 255.255.255.0
 standby 2 priority 90
 standby 2 ip 101.0.0.1
   .
   .
   .
router eigrp 1
 network 100.0.0.0
 network 101.0.0.0
!
end
```

LISTING **10-20.** *DLSw through dual firewalls—outside Firewall Router R-A*

```
version 11.0
!
hostname R-B
!
ip subnet-zero
!
interface Ethernet0
 ip address 100.0.0.3 255.255.255.0
 standby 1 priority 90
 standby 1 ip 100.0.0.1
!
interface Ethernet1
 ip address 101.0.0.3 255.255.255.0
 standby 2 priority 110
 standby 2 preempt
 standby 2 ip 101.0.0.1
 .
 .
 .
router eigrp 1
 network 100.0.0.0
 network 101.0.0.0
!
end
```

LISTING 10-21. *DLSw through dual firewalls—outside Firewall Router R-B*

Similarly, the configuration of the outside DLSw peers in Listings 10-22 and 10-23 is a mirror image of the inside DLSw peers. The key difference is that the outside peers use the outside addresses rather than the inside addresses in their configuration.

```
version 11.0
!
hostname R-C
!
ip subnet-zero
!
source-bridge ring-group 321
! local inside NAT is 10.1.2.98 via Firewall F-3A
! local inside NAT is 10.3.2.98 via Firewall F-4B
dlsw local-peer peer-id 120.0.0.1
```

                                                              (*continued*)

```
! Peer with router R-1 via Firewall F-3A
dlsw remote-peer 0 tcp 100.0.0.98
! Backup peering with R-1 via Firewall F-4B
dlsw remote-peer 0 tcp 101.0.0.98 passive
!
interface Loopback1
 description Local peer address for DLSw
 ip address 120.0.0.1 255.255.255.255
!
interface TokenRing2/0
 ip address 120.100.0.2 255.255.255.0
 ring-speed 16
 source-bridge 120 10 321
 source-bridge spanning
 .
 .
 .
router eigrp 1
 network 120.0.0.0
!
end
```

LISTING 10-22.   *DLSw through dual firewalls—outside DLSw Peer Router R-C*

```
version 11.0
!
hostname R-D
!
ip subnet-zero
!
source-bridge ring-group 321
! local inside NAT is 10.1.2.99 via Firewall F-3A
! local inside NAT is 10.3.2.99 via Firewall F-4B
dlsw local-peer peer-id 120.0.0.2
! Peer with router R-2 via Firewall F-3A
dlsw remote-peer 0 tcp 101.0.0.99
! Backup peering with R-2 via Firewall F-4B
dlsw remote-peer 0 tcp 100.0.0.99 passive
!
interface Loopback1
 description Local peer address for DLSw
 ip address 120.0.0.2 255.255.255.255
!
```

(*continued*)

```
interface TokenRing2/0
 ip address 120.100.0.3 255.255.255.0
 ring-speed 16
 source-bridge 120 11 321
 source-bridge spanning
 .
 .
 .
 .
router eigrp 1
 network 120.0.0.0
 !
end
```

LISTING 10-23. *DLSw through dual firewalls—outside DLSw Peer Router R-D*

Note that each router peering has four separate pairs of peer addresses associated with it; an inside and an outside pairing for each firewall. A good idea for verifying the design is to summarize all possible combinations in a single table, as in Table 10-4. The critical check is that, for each peer relationship to be used, the same peer has the higher IP address whether the inside addresses or outside addresses are being compared. In this example, the inside peer has the lower address in all comparisons, so we have no problems. Sometimes it can be quite a challenge coming up with firewall addresses and local peer addresses that will all compare consistently.

For example, consider what would have happened if we wanted to set up the inside peers using their Token Ring interface addresses of 10.100.0.2 and 10.100.0.3, rather than defining loopback addresses at 10.0.0.1 and 10.0.0.2. This would shift the inside address comparison to favor the inside peer, while leaving the outside peer the winner on the outside—a combination of addresses that would not work.

We could restore the proper address relationships using appropriate modifications of any of the four addresses involved: by either lowering the inside peer inside address, raising the outside peer inside address, raising the inside peer outside address,

TABLE 10-4. *DLSw Peer Addressing Summary and Checklist*

PEERING	FIREWALL	INSIDE PEER INSIDE IP	OUTSIDE PEER INSIDE IP	INSIDE PEER OUTSIDE IP	OUTSIDE PEER OUTSIDE IP
R-1—R-C	F-3A	10.0.0.1	10.1.2.98	100.0.0.98	120.0.0.1
	F-4B	10.0.0.1	10.3.2.98	101.0.0.98	120.0.0.1
R-2—R-D	F-3A	10.0.0.2	10.1.2.99	100.0.0.99	120.0.0.2
	F-4B	10.0.0.2	10.3.2.99	101.0.0.99	120.0.0.2

or lowering the outside peer outside address. We may be able to adjust both inside or both outside addresses in order to get enough change to restore consistent comparisons. The key is that neither the magnitude nor the direction of the difference is important, only that both peers agree on which has the higher address in each peer relationship.

CONFIGURATION EXAMPLE: ETHERNET DLSW THROUGH DUAL NAT FIREWALLS

If supporting Ethernets rather than Token Rings, the configuration gets more challenging; we now have two competing requirements for backup peer relationships. If we can use Cisco's DLSw+ Ethernet Redundancy capability, we do not need to use backup peers for Ethernet recovery. We can then use the Token Ring approach, suitably modified to enable Ethernet peers and DLSw+ Ethernet Redundancy. The firewall configuration considerations and the DLSw+ Ethernet Redundancy configuration considerations are independent and do not impact one another.

On the other hand, if we want to use backup peers for Ethernet redundancy as well as firewall redundancy, we need to be careful that the needs of one do not interfere with the configuration needs of the other. We also must not end up with more than one link between the two Ethernets. Consider the scenario in Figure 10-7. There are eight different, independent modes of failure we would like to protect against.

Being immune to one of our DLSw peer routers' failing is not our only concern. We also need to protect against the loss of either firewall (which includes the loss of the access LAN on either side of the firewall) and against segmentation of either SNA Ethernet so that both DLSw peers on the LAN need to be active.

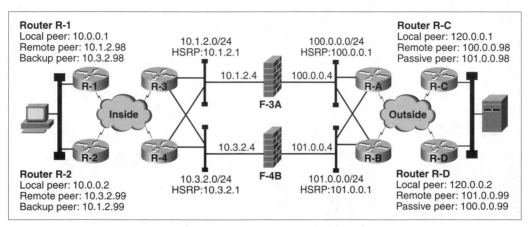

FIGURE 10-7. *Ethernet DLSw through redundant firewalls*

Using the same technique we used for detecting LAN failure on Ethernet peers when we were not using firewalls, we set up three sets of DLSw peers, each with its own backup peer. Their descriptions follow:

- Router R-1 to Router R-C via Firewall F-3A, backed up by the same peering via Firewall F-4B

- Router R-2 to Router R-1 via LAN only, backed up by Router R-2 to Router R-C via Firewall F-3A

- Router R-D to Router R-C via LAN only, backed up by Router R-D to Router R-2 via Firewall F-4B

Using these three sets of peers, the reaction to each of our critical failures is summarized in Table 10-5. While sessions may drop and need to be reestablished, depending upon the SNA and NetBIOS applications being supported, recovery from any single failure is complete and stable.

As is the case with any high availability design, network monitoring to quickly recognize failures and dispatch repair efforts is critical to success. This requirement is no less critical in a firewalled environment, even though firewalls make it much more difficult to achieve using traditional centralized management approaches. DLSw makes it easier in some ways because we can detect many crucial problems on the other side of the firewall simply by monitoring which peers are active. However, failure recovery is based on a standby backup basis. This means that functionality of the backup paths is not automatically tested as part of normal operation the way it is when Token Rings or DLSw+ Ethernet Redundancy are used. Suitable testing of

TABLE 10-5. *DLSw Peers Active During Router Failures*

FAILURE	ACTIVE PEERING	COMMENTS
Router R-1	R-2 to R-C via F-3A	Backup of R-2 to R-1 via LAN
Router R-2	R-1 to R-C via F-3A	No impact—default peering
Router R-C	R-D to R-2 via F-4B	Backup of R-D to R-C via LAN
Router R-D	R-1 to R-C via F-3A	No impact—default peering
Firewall F-3A	R-1 to R-C via F-4B	All sessions drop and reestablish
Firewall F-4B	R-1 to R-C via F-3A	No impact—default peering
Inside DLSw LAN	R-1 to R-C via F-3A R-2 to R-C via F-3A	Sessions on portion of LAN serviced by Router R-2 drop and reestablish
Outside DLSw LAN	R-1 to R-C via F-3A R-D to R-2 via F-4B	Sessions on portion of LAN serviced by Router R-D drop and reestablish

backup capabilities would need to be developed as part of the design solution, in addition to routine monitoring of proper functionality.

The firewall configurations (see Table 10-6 and Table 10-7) are the same as in the previous Token Ring example, with one exception—the allowed connection between Router R-2 and Router R-D via Firewall F-3A is replaced with an allowed connection between Router R-2 and Router R-C. While this may seem unbalanced, it is essential in order to avoid potentially activating two simultaneous DLSw peerings between the same two routers.

If we left the route connecting Router R-2 and Router R-D, then a failure of the inside LAN or Router R-1 at the same time as a failure of the outside LAN or Router R-C would bring up two peerings between Router R-2 and Router R-D, one through each firewall. While this would require a double failure, the impact of such a loop could affect more than just DLSw and so must be avoided.

The configurations of the firewall access routers are identical to those in the previous Token Ring examples (see Listings 10.18, 10.19, 10.20, and 10.21). The DLSw peers, however, bear little resemblance to the Token Ring versions of the same firewall setup. We must convert the DLSw bridging from source-routed Token Ring to translating-bridged Ethernet. Plus, the whole logic of the backup peers must be changed to prevent us from having more than one peer at a time between any two Ethernets.

TABLE 10-6. *Firewall Inside-to-Outside Address Translations and Routing*

FIREWALL	INSIDE PORT IP ADDRESS	ALLOWED SOURCE IP	OUTSIDE SOURCE IP	OUTSIDE DESTINATION	NEXT HOP
F-3A	10.1.2.98	10.0.0.1	100.0.0.98	120.0.0.1	100.0.0.1
F-3A	10.1.2.98	10.0.0.2	100.0.0.99	120.0.0.1	100.0.0.1
F-4B	10.3.2.98	10.0.0.1	101.0.0.98	120.0.0.1	101.0.0.1
F-4B	10.3.2.99	10.0.0.2	101.0.0.99	120.0.0.2	101.0.0.1

TABLE 10-7. *Firewall Outside-to-Inside Address Translations and Routing*

FIREWALL	OUTSIDE PORT IP ADDRESS	ALLOWED SOURCE IP	INSIDE SOURCE IP	INSIDE DESTINATION	NEXT HOP
F-3A	100.0.0.98	120.0.0.1	10.1.2.98	10.0.0.1	10.1.2.1
F-3A	100.0.0.99	120.0.0.1	10.1.2.98	10.0.0.2	10.1.2.1
F-4B	101.0.0.98	120.0.0.1	10.3.2.98	10.0.0.1	10.3.2.1
F-4B	101.0.0.99	120.0.0.2	10.3.2.99	10.0.0.2	10.3.2.1

Router R-1 in Listing 10-24 is the most complex configuration of the four DLSw routers. It provides a peer for use by Router R-2 to detect LAN problems. The peer must be defined so as not to share any production SNA or NetBIOS reachability information. At the same time, this configuration provides backup for the production peering with Router R-C—should there be a problem with Firewall F-3A—with a backup peer defined to Router R-C through Firewall F-4B.

```
version 11.2
!
hostname R-1
!
ip subnet-zero
!
dlsw local-peer peer-id 10.0.0.1 lf 1500
! 10.0.0.1 inside      = 100.0.0.98 outside via F-3A
!                      = 101.0.0.98 outside via F-4B
dlsw bgroup-list 7 bgroups 5
dlsw bgroup-list 11 bgroups 6
! Production peer with router R-C via firewall F-3A
dlsw remote-peer 7 tcp 10.1.2.98
! Peer to router R-C via F-4B if problems with F-3A
dlsw remote-peer 7 tcp 10.3.2.98 backup-peer 10.1.2.98
! Dummy peer so R-2 can see that we are alive and well
dlsw remote-peer 11 tcp 10.0.0.2
dlsw bridge-group 5    ! Production Traffic
dlsw bridge-group 6    ! Dummy for router R-2
!
interface Loopback1
 description Local peer address for DLSw
 ip address 10.0.0.1 255.255.255.255
!
interface Ethernet0
 ip address 10.100.0.2 255.255.128.0
 bridge-group 5
 bridge-group 5 spanning-disabled
  .
  .
  .
! Add the following two lines to all interfaces except
  Ethernet0
 ip access-group 150 out
 ip access-group 151 in
```

(continued)

```
    .
    .
router ospf 123
 network 10.0.0.1 0.0.0.0 area 10.100.0.0
 network 10.100.0.0 0.0.255.255 area 10.100.0.0
 !
access-list 150 deny    tcp host 10.0.0.1 host 10.0.0.2 eq 2065
access-list 150 permit ip any any
access-list 151 deny    tcp host 10.0.0.2 host 10.0.0.1 eq 2065
access-list 151 permit ip any any
 !
bridge 5 protocol ieee
bridge 6 protocol ieee
 !
end
```

LISTING 10-24. *Ethernet DLSw through dual firewalls—inside DLSw Peer Router R-1*

While the configuration may look complex, it is just a combination of the LAN-problem-detection capabilities discussed in the configuration example Backup Peers on a Segmentable LAN with the firewall recovery logic in the configuration example Token Ring DLSw through Dual NAT Firewalls. The only modification is the use of a numbered bgroup-list for the production peers. This distinguishes them from the Ethernet failure detection peer bgroup-list.

In this configuration, bgroup-list 7, which consists solely of bridge group 5, provides DLSw connectivity to the Ethernet. Bgroup-list 11 contains only the unused bridge group 6. This allows the backup Router R-2 on the LAN to determine that our peer is up and communicating over the LAN. But it doesn't confuse the production link with a duplicate view of the SNA and NetBIOS systems on the LAN.

It is the responsibility of Router R-1 to protect against failure of the primary path through Firewall F-3A. It does this by backing up its peering with Router R-C. It uses the inside address of Router R-C via Firewall F-3A with a backup peer that is still router R-C, but it uses the inside address when accessed through Firewall F-4B.

Router R-2 (see Listing 10-25) provides protection against failures affecting either Router R-1 or the Ethernet LAN that they are both entrusted to support. Any time Router R-2 is unable to communicate over the LAN with Router R-1, it will bring up a peering with Router R-C on the far network using the inside address of Router R-C when accessed via Firewall F-3A. As before, all interfaces on Router R-1 and Router R-2, other than the LAN being serviced, must include the IP packet filters. These filters block the establishment of a DLSw peering between the two routers

```
version 11.2
!
hostname R-2
!
dlsw local-peer peer-id 10.0.0.2 1f 1500
! 10.0.0.2 inside    = 100.0.0.99 outside via F-3A
!                    = 101.0.0.99 outside via F-4B
! Peer via LAN to bit-bucket on R-1
dlsw remote-peer 0 tcp 10.0.0.1
! Any problems with R-1 or LAN, bring up peer to R-C via F-3A
dlsw remote-peer 0 tcp 10.1.2.98 backup-peer 10.0.0.1
! Allow R-D to peer with us via F-4B if problems with R-C
dlsw remote-peer 0 tcp 10.3.2.99 passive
dlsw bridge-group 5
!
interface Loopback1
 description Local peer address for DLSw
 ip address 10.0.0.2 255.255.255.255
!
interface Ethernet0
 ip address 10.100.0.3 255.255.128.0
 bridge-group 5
 bridge-group 5 spanning-disabled
 .

 .
! Add the following lines to all interfaces except Ethernet0
 ip access-group 150 out
 ip access-group 151 in
 .

 .
router ospf 123
 network 10.0.0.2 0.0.0.0 area 10.100.0.0
 network 10.100.0.0 0.0.255.255 area 10.100.0.0
!
access-list 150 deny   tcp host 10.0.0.2 host 10.0.0.1 eq 2065
access-list 150 permit ip any any
access-list 151 deny   tcp host 10.0.0.1 host 10.0.0.2 eq 2065
access-list 151 permit ip any any
!
bridge 5 protocol ieee
!
end
```

LISTING 10-25. *Ethernet DLSw through dual firewalls—inside DLSw Peer Router R-2*

without blocking any other DLSw traffic. If necessary, the deny statements of access-lists 150 and 151 can be added to any other access-lists that are required for the interfaces.

One change in this router configuration (from the version with no fire-walls) is the passive peer defined for Router R-D using the inside address of Router R-D when accessed via Firewall F-4B. This peering is used by Router R-D to recover from any problems it detects with Router R-C or the LAN it is servicing.

Router R-C in Listing 10-26 is very similar to Router R-1, except it is on the receiving end of two backup peerings: through the alternate firewall with Router R-1 and through the primary firewall with Router R-2. Unnecessary (and futile) peer setup traffic is avoided by making the peer definitions for the backup circuits passive peers.

Under normal operating conditions, this configuration does not send any traffic through Firewall F-4B. If there are no other applications continuously verifying the availability of that firewall, it is essential that network management routinely test its functionality. Otherwise, the probability that the backup firewall will be available when needed would ultimately approach zero.

```
version 11.2
!
hostname R-C
!
dlsw local-peer peer-id 120.0.0.1 1f 1500
!  120.0.0.1 outside   = 10.1.2.98 inside via F-3A
!                      = 10.3.2.98 inside via F-4B
dlsw bgroup-list 7 bgroups 5  ! Real users
dlsw bgroup-list 11 bgroups 6 ! /dev/null
! Normal production peering with router R-1 via F-3A
dlsw remote-peer 7 tcp 100.0.0.98
! Allow router R-1 to bring up peer via F-4B
dlsw remote-peer 7 tcp 101.0.0.98 passive
! Allow R-2 to peer with us via F-3A if problems with R-1
dlsw remote-peer 7 tcp 100.0.0.99 passive
! Provide a harmless peer for R-D to use to test our health
dlsw remote-peer 11 tcp 120.0.0.2
dlsw bridge-group 5
dlsw bridge-group 6
!
```

(*continued*)

```
interface Loopback1
 description Local peer address for DLSw
 ip address 120.0.0.1 255.255.255.255
!
interface Ethernet1/0
 ip address 120.0.1.2 255.255.255.0
 bridge-group 5
 bridge-group 5 spanning-disabled
 .
 .
! Add the following to all interfaces except Ethernet1/0
 ip access-group 150 out
 ip access-group 151 in
 .
 .
router eigrp 1
 network 120.0.0.0
!
access-list 150 deny    tcp host 120.0.0.1 host 120.0.0.2
➥ eq 2065
access-list 150 permit ip any any
access-list 151 deny    tcp host 120.0.0.2 host 120.0.0.1
➥ eq 2065
access-list 151 permit ip any any
!
bridge 5 protocol ieee
bridge 6 protocol ieee
!
end
```

LISTING 10-26. *Ethernet DLSw through dual firewalls—outside DLSw Peer Router R-C*

Router R-D in Listing 10-27 is a mirror image of Router R-2. Any time its
peering with Router R-C fails, it automatically brings up the backup peering to
Router R-2 through firewall F-4B. Now we see why Router R-2 had to make its
backup peering to Router R-C rather than to here. We dare not take a chance that
both ends should suffer simultaneous failures and define two identical backup
peers—one through each firewall—between the two routers. In that case, we would
have two Ethernet-to-Ethernet peers active, and DLSw could wind up with routing
loops loading down the firewalls and the WAN.

While our design is not intended to survive double failures, it is essential that it
not cause more harm than good in any attempt to recover from failures.

```
version 11.2
!
hostname R-D
!
!  120.0.0.2 outside = 10.3.2.99 inside via F-4B
!   (No access defined via F-3A)
dlsw local-peer peer-id 120.0.0.2 lf 1500
! Peer via LAN to bit-bucket on R-C
dlsw remote-peer 0 tcp 120.0.0.1
! Any problems with R-C or LAN, bring up peer to R-2 via F-4B
dlsw remote-peer 0 tcp 101.0.0.99 backup-peer 120.0.0.1
dlsw bridge-group 5
!
interface Loopback1
 description Local peer address for DLSw
 ip address 120.0.0.2 255.255.255.255
!
interface Ethernet0/1
 ip address 120.0.1.3 255.255.255.0
 bridge-group 5
 bridge-group 5 spanning-disabled
 .
 .
! Add the following to all interfaces except Ethernet0/1
 ip access-group 150 out
 ip access-group 151 in
 .
 .
router eigrp 1
 network 120.0.0.0
!
!
access-list 150 deny   tcp host 120.0.0.2 host 120.0.0.1
 ➡ eq 2065
access-list 150 permit ip any any
access-list 151 deny   tcp host 120.0.0.1 host 120.0.0.2
 ➡ eq 2065
access-list 151 permit ip any any
!
bridge 5 protocol ieee
!
end
```

LISTING 10-27.   *Ethernet DLSw through dual firewalls—outside DLSw Peer Router R-D*

WRAP-UP

Support of IBM SNA communications is a frequent requirement in TCP/IP networks. When an IBM shop migrates from Token Ring to Ethernet networks to reduce costs, providing high availability redundant connectivity becomes much more difficult. Adding redundancy in a source-routed Token Ring environment is simply a matter of defining more DLSw peers. But the same approach does not work when Ethernets or other LAN technologies that do not support source-route bridging are involved.

While we cannot achieve the same ease of redundancy in Ethernet that we get automatically in Token Rings, we can get good protection for many applications through the use of the backup peer capability in DLSw. Cisco also recently introduced a proprietary DLSw+ Ethernet Redundancy capability which can be useful in some environments.

DLSw backup also allows us to automate recovery from firewall failures without depending upon complex or proprietary firewall failover mechanisms. This capability can be used with Token Rings or Ethernets.

Disaster Recovery Considerations

Fire, flood, hurricane, earthquake, terrorism, tornado—these natural and unnatural disasters commonly come to mind when disaster recovery for computer networks is discussed. Added to this list are the more mundane events that can take an entire data center out of action—broken pipes, extended power failure, construction accidents, faulty climate controls, and cut communications cables.

So far we have explored a wide variety of techniques for enabling continued operations when individual network or service component failures occur. Compensating for the failure of an entire facility requires a different approach. A site-wide or regional failure event, while less common than a simple router or link failure, can still occur, and we should include the possibility in our network availability planning.

Strategies for continuing operations when a site hosting critical services goes down have always been an essential part of any disaster recovery or business continuation plan. In a high availability environment, however, we cannot afford to take a traditional approach to disaster recovery. The downtime associated with getting a classical cold site turned on and loaded with current data—and the supporting communications changes implemented by our service providers—would be unacceptable.

At the same time, duplicating all services in a disaster recovery site with live data and with all supporting communications continuously online is a very expensive undertaking, especially for a capability that may never be needed. What we want to do instead is expand the concept of a clustered LAN server solution into that of an extended cluster capable of functioning with its individual components spread across the WAN. By using the WAN to spread our processing across geographically diverse sites, we translate the critical site disaster scenario into a capacity reduction scenario. The key is that we implement our clustering and sharing on tools capable of working over the extended WAN.

DISASTER RECOVERY REQUIREMENTS

Disaster recovery planning has been a way of life for the information systems departments of businesses and organizations that need to provide ongoing service unaffected by local occurrences—whether that service is a mainframe database or a bank of phone lines for a call center. Large-scale failures and other disasters will occur, and we need to plan for them in advance.

Traditionally, disaster recovery planning is based on backup sites that are ready to take over should a primary site fail. These backup sites can be inside an organization or can be contracted from another organization (either through a mutual support agreement or with an organization whose business is to provide backup facilities). The backup site can be an empty space with power where we rebuild our data center using whatever equipment we can salvage from our original data center and buying or leasing the rest. Or it can be a cold site where the necessary equipment is already installed, and we need only come in with our latest tape backups, install our systems, and go back online.

While the traditional cold site approach is more than adequate for classical back-end processing, its acceptability lies in the assumption that services can be down for hours or even days. When high availability applications must be supported, this assumption is no longer valid. However, cold sites and other offline backup solutions often still have a role in high availability disaster planning. They are used not just for support of back-end processing, but also as a way to minimize the cost of online redundancy. They do this by reducing the level of service required from the online backup solution to a level lower than would be acceptable long term.

DISASTER RECOVERY PLANNING

Planning in advance is essential to ensure that the downtime caused by a disaster will be acceptable to the end users. Advanced planning should be done not only for the network—or even information systems—requirements, but for all aspects of the business.

The first step in developing a disaster recovery plan is a risk assessment based on an inventory of all information systems resources and an assessment of how various disaster scenarios could impact those resources. The focus should be on the business impact. More important than the individual resources are the applications and business processes being supported by those resources. The best approach is to think of the disaster recovery plan as a mechanism for capturing the state of the ongoing Business Continuity Life Cycle in Figure 11-1, rather than as a finished document.

We start at the top of the circle with the current state of the business, the processes that keep it going, the applications that support those processes, and the systems and networks required to run those applications. We then look at the various

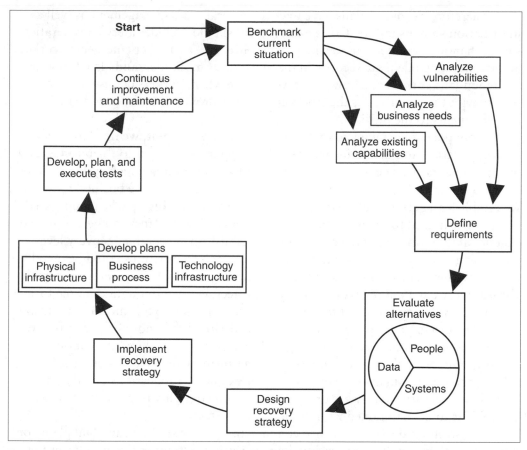

FIGURE 11-1. *Business Continuity Life Cycle © 1996 Comdisco, Inc., all rights reserved. Modified and reprinted with permission.*

ways that systems can fail, the impact those failures can have on the business, and our ability to cope. As always, before planning our disaster recovery strategy, we need to understand the real business requirements. Otherwise—as we have seen before—we are liable to develop plans that solve the easy or interesting problems rather than the important ones.

Once we have agreement on what is truly important to the business, we can look at the alternatives available for dealing with disaster. While the natural tendency of networkers is to focus on the systems, business continuity requires that the data and the people who use it are also available. This is why it is so important to focus on business continuity rather than just network or information systems availability. Systems, data, and people all need to come together before disaster recovery can be considered complete.

Therefore, recovery plans have to cover general crisis management as well as information systems failure. Crisis management should include safety considerations such as handling evacuations; dealing with police, fire, and other emergency workers; and maintaining adequate security in the midst of turmoil. It should also deal with such mundane concerns as how to get work done when workers choose to evacuate or stay with their families as the storm approaches or who is authorized to make official statements to the media.

From the networking and information systems viewpoint, we need to look at each application and determine what level of support is essential to the business and in what time frame. The goal is to develop guidelines detailing which systems can be down, and for how long, without excessive adverse impact on the business. Typically, we establish an acceptable recovery time for each system. This may be complicated if there is also a need to recover data before the replacement system can be considered functional. In terms of data, we again must establish an acceptable recovery level. Depending upon the application, the loss of one day's transactions could be merely an inconvenience or it could mean the difference between solvency and bankruptcy. Clearly, we are willing to invest far more in protecting the latter data than the former.

Once we have translated the business requirements into technical requirements, we can start to look at how best to provide the desired level and speed of recovery. This is frequently interpreted as having nightly tape backups shipped to out-of-town vaults or mirroring the transaction journal over the network to a remote site. But other tradeoffs should also be considered. For example, applications could be supported on alternative hardware or with reduced functionality to permit the critical capabilities to be maintained without breaking the bank.

The strategic decisions reached can then be translated into individual plans for implementation. Finally, an occasional disaster drill is essential. It is important not just to test the validity of the plans and ensure that they work as expected, but also to allow personnel to gain experience with them. The plans, then, won't be completely new when disaster strikes.

Even if all our plans work perfectly during testing, it is essential to keep them up to date. The business and the systems required to support the business will evolve, as will the technical tools available to help keep the business running. We then begin the cycle all over again. Except this time we start from a newly implemented level of disaster recovery capability and with knowledge of how those capabilities work when tested.

Development of appropriate plans can be particularly challenging in smaller organizations. Sometimes the network managers asked to generate the plans object to the implication that they are being tested on their ability to recover all essential systems in the event of a disaster. After all, they know exactly what they have to do to get services back online.

The network manager may need to be reminded that the disaster recovery plan is being written for the people who will need to do the job if the network manager is unavailable at the time of the disaster. A test exercise in which the experts are forced to stand aside and watch others struggle to implement their disaster recovery plans can be enlightening. While the experts may know every key component and configuration parameter that needs tweaking, others in the organization will be dependent upon what is written down and will waste hours tracking down details the experts thought were common knowledge.

In the process of developing the disaster recovery plan, it is also essential to verify all assumptions. If systems are to be restored from backup tapes, will those tapes be accessible if the original building is closed due to unsafe conditions? How will data and other changes entered since the last accessible backup be recovered? And what if that backup is flawed and not useable? Is there a copy of the list of all circuit numbers and service provider contact points other than in the network administrator's desk?

A review of others' experiences of major disasters can be sobering. During Hurricane David, power was cut off for over a week and emergency generators ran out of fuel. The rupture of a utility tunnel under the Chicago river flooded building basements all around the Loop, cutting off all communications dependent upon wires or fiber optic cable. Fire in the Illinois Bell Hinsdale switching center cut off all long distance service from multiple carriers serving the Chicago area. After the World Trade Center bombing, where evacuation was immediate and without warning, there was no access to the data or systems left behind for days. Measuring how your disaster recovery plan would stand up to any of these events can be enlightening and frightening.

The disaster recovery plan itself can also present a security dilemma. In order to be complete and useful, it must contain such sensitive information as which processes the business considers most important; access phone numbers for remote devices; license numbers for applications and systems; where to find names and passwords for admin, root, or equivalent access to all systems; as well as personal information such as the CEO's unlisted home phone number. Yet if the only copy is locked up in a safe inside the building and that building becomes a smoldering pile of ashes, the crucial information it contains will not help those struggling to restore service. The time to consider access alternatives is before access is needed.

Timeliness can also present a challenge. For example, to be useful, the plan must contain many phone numbers, including those for all support personnel, home phones numbers of key employees and management, and numbers for critical equipment and service vendors. A process must be in place to keep these numbers up to date in all copies as key managers are promoted or transferred, employees come and go, new vendors are engaged, and old vendors are let go.

DISASTER RECOVERY APPROACHES

The traditional approach to disaster recovery is based on the premise that in the event of a disaster, we can assemble an alternative data center facility and set up communications with that facility before the organization suffers inordinate losses. While this is frequently a cost effective approach, particularly for duplicating classical mainframe batch processing, it will rarely meet the needs of distributed interactive applications.

Whether the task is a Web-driven e-business or a retailer verifying credit cards, there are many networked applications today for which any downtime means lost revenue or increased risk. For these kinds of applications, we need a disaster recovery solution that is already online and functional, ready to take over when disaster strikes. Our choice in this case would be either an online, hot standby backup facility or continuous load sharing among multiple facilities. Each approach has its advantages and disadvantages, summarized in Table 11-1, and each has a place in the panoply of network design choices.

In a large organization, we may see all three approaches being used. Each application may be supported in the manner most consistent with the needs and budget of the organization and the cost of downtime associated with that application. For example, we might find a traditional cold site used for payroll processing, a hot backup site used for engineering collaboration, and load sharing used to keep e-business flowing at the corporate Web site (with server sites in Europe, North America, and Asia minimizing communications costs and maximizing performance during day-to-day operations). We may also see some business processes continued

TABLE 11-1. *Disaster Recovery Approaches for Networked Applications*

DISASTER RECOVERY APPROACH	KEY STRENGTHS	KEY WEAKNESSES
Traditional cold site	Lowest cost, particularly for mainframe class computing needs	Hours to days of downtime while site is being activated
Hot (online) backup site	Minimal, but non-zero, downtime	Highest cost for a given level of capability
	Only one copy of database is in use at any time	Lack of off-the-shelf tools for implementation
Load sharing among multiple sites	Disaster recovery is transparent to users	Pushing the state of the art in database if any of the applications do extensive updating
	Highest performance during normal operation	

through the use of alternate technologies, such as using telephone and fax in place of interoffice e-mail.

A hot backup site eliminates delays in staffing the backup site and restoring all data from tape. But a hot backup solution will not eliminate the disruption in service whenever switching takes place between the primary and the backup site. This will occur not only when the primary fails—forcing transfer over to the backup site—but also when the time comes to shift operations back to the restored primary site. This is because all active sessions to the backup site must be terminated and the databases synchronized before the primary site can be reactivated. This usually means that the hot backup site must be enabled and disabled manually to ensure that there is no overlap in services that could introduce database inconsistency.

Load sharing is normally preferable to hot backup if the applications can support it. There is no service disruption, other than to those transactions in progress at the failed site at the time of failure, and there is minimal wasted server capacity. As a general rule, load sharing should always be used, unless the application is one that cannot support a load sharing approach cost-effectively (usually due to the complexity of maintaining database consistency across diverse servers).

When comparing disaster recovery approaches, we do need to be careful, as the terminology is not standardized. Plus, we must distinguish between the capability being used and how it is being used. Consider an online backup site that is normally only used when the primary site fails. But it can continue to be used until transactions in progress have completed, even after the primary site has returned to service and started processing new transactions. The backup site would need to be implemented using load sharing tools, even though it is sized and run as a backup site and not a load sharing site.

TRADITIONAL APPROACHES

The traditional disaster recovery approach is to make a full tape backup at the end of each day and ship the tapes to a site far enough away (at least 100 miles) to make it highly unlikely that any disaster would affect both locations. Common sense must be used, of course, because even a location 200 miles upstream on the same river could be affected by the same flood. The theory is that when a disaster strikes, the tapes will survive and can be shipped to an alternative site, loaded on replacement systems, and used to get the business running again.

This approach can lose over 24 hours worth of data if the disaster occurs when the tapes are about to be shipped to off-site storage. We can also expect it to take 1 or 2 days to get the data loaded on the replacement systems, get all our service providers to turn on network access to the alternate site, and adjust all the network and system parameters to get everything to work once again. This assumes that the alternate site is a "hot" alternate site with all computer systems and network infrastructure installed and waiting to be turned on. Recovery can take considerably longer if the plan calls for purchasing replacement systems and getting them shipped to the alternate site.

The key from the network planning viewpoint is that the alternate site and the primary site will never be active at the same time. Therefore, there is no problem bringing up the alternate site using the same network addresses used for the primary site, and there is no need to modify other sites in the network to resume operations once the alternate site is operational. This duplication can be carried down to the physical layer. Service providers can re-map ATM, frame relay, and X.25 permanent virtual circuits to the correct endpoints at the alternate site, and they can forward ISDN and POTS calls placed to the original numbers. Even leased lines can be rerouted to terminate at the alternate site rather than the failed original site.

These are all routine networking changes that have been part of disaster recovery plans for decades. As long as they are arranged in advance, there is usually no problem getting quick turnaround in a real disaster. So while there may be a need for some emergency reconfiguration to work around mistakes made by the service provider, the network is typically not the critical path for bringing up the disaster recovery alternate site. We also need to plan for when the scope of the disaster is such that many organizations are seeking emergency changes and the service providers are overwhelmed and unable to meet their service commitments.

Many businesses cannot afford the loss of up to 24 hours of data. One popular enhancement is to use journaling to record all changes since the last tape backup and regularly copy the journal files across the network to an off-site repository. This may be done using network file copy or even by journaling directly to a remote file system to minimize the data loss when failure occurs.

However, we must recognize that even though journaling can eliminate the data recovery gap, it does not get the alternate system up and running any faster. In fact it slows us down. After the alternate system is restored from tape and working, we still must apply the journal files to recover the data up to the time of failure.

Reducing the recovery time to under one to two days requires electronic vaulting, with which we back up over the network rather than to tape. Electronic vaulting can be used in place of nightly backups, or the vaulting can be done even more frequently. Typically, the electronic vault will be at the alternate system site, eliminating any delay in getting the data from the storage site to the alternate site. This also eliminates problems if the disaster is one that disrupts normal transportation, such as a flood.

Using electronic vaulting typically reduces the system recovery time to between 2 and 12 hours. Further reductions are made possible by having a computer at the vaulting site running with the essential applications loaded, ready to take over as soon as the data can be loaded. Sometimes the system accepting the data updates is the same system that will be used to step in and take over the applications.

Depending upon the power of the backup system and its network connectivity, there may be a loss of capacity and performance when the disaster recovery site takes over. This is a common tradeoff made to keep the price of disaster recovery reasonable. It merely recognizes that many of the applications and processes running under normal conditions are not as time critical as others, and their recovery can be delayed.

We can combine our standby system and electronic vault and move to continuous updating by journaling in real time so that the standby system is always ready to step in and take over. Thus, recovery will take only as much time as is needed to reconfigure the network so that requests for service are delivered to the standby system at the alternate site, rather than to the primary system. At this point, further improvement in recovery time requires a different approach to the network connection, and we need to move to a hot backup facility approach.

HOT BACKUP FACILITY APPROACHES

From a networking viewpoint, the fundamental problem we face on an IP network when supporting a backup server facility is the one-to-one nature of normal IP-based communications. There is no *anycast* mechanism available in IP to allow a client to address requests to any capable server. IP version 6 does define an *anycast* service in RFC 1546, Host Anycasting Service, so there is hope for the future. In the meantime, we must devise a way to allow the client to address requests to either the primary or the backup server.

Using the traditional cold site approach, we would reconfigure the network so that the IP addresses associated with the services being backed up were at the backup data center facility. Thus, we would duplicate the out-of-order data center right down to the IP addresses used by the individual servers.

We cannot do this when using a hot standby data center, because the primary data center and the backup data center are both connected to the network at the same time. Both must have their own unique IP addresses so that the primary and the backup servers can communicate to keep the backup server data up to date.

ONE IP ADDRESS FOR TWO SITES

What we can do, however, is use three IP addresses for each service, as in Figure 11-2. We show a single server and its backup. One address is used to identify the physical server at the primary site, one address is used to identify the physical server at the backup site, and a third address is used by the client. In other words, the client uses a virtual server address, which the network then translates to the appropriate IP address to reach whichever real server is currently online.

While the network address translation could theoretically be done at either end of the connection at the client's router or the server's router, it is usually easier to do

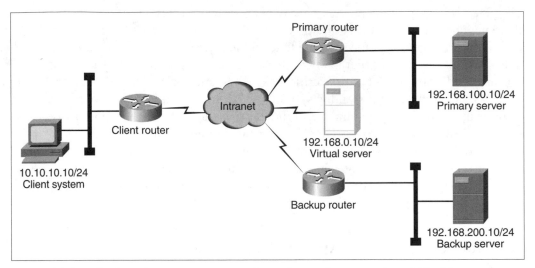

FIGURE 11-2. *Backup data center support through use of a server virtual IP address*

it at the server end. That way, the number of routers that need to be reconfigured to effect a changeover is minimized.

Since we are doing network address translation for addressing purposes rather than security, there is no need for active filters or any other firewall techniques commonly associated with network address translation. Consequently, unless the application requires network address translation to adjust the contents of packets, there is no need to ensure that packets between client and server always follow the same path.

Server synchronization is unaffected by the network address translation because no matter which server is active, both retain their real addresses at all times and can communicate using them. Only the clients use the virtual server address. However, if the router doing the network address translation is also traversed by these packets, we may need to install an alternate path or otherwise adjust our translation parameters. This will ensure that server-to-server traffic is not subjected to network address translation.

The switch from one site to the other can then be performed either manually—by reconfiguring the routers—or automatically, in the event that a site becomes disconnected. If we're automating the switchover, we must construct our solution with extreme care so that only one site at a time is identified with the virtual address. Moreover, we must ensure that the switch back to the primary server does not occur before the primary server has had a chance to synchronize its database with any changes made while the backup was active.

As long as we are using dynamic routing protocols, we can implement the site change merely by injecting a route to the desired virtual server location into the routers at the active site. If we tell the primary router that the next hop on the way to the virtual server is the real primary server, that route can be advertised throughout the network to all clients through the routing protocol. The only constraint is that only the primary or the backup server can be configured as the next hop at any instant in time. Otherwise both could end up receiving service requests, leading to inconsistent data and incorrect results.

CONFIGURATION EXAMPLE: BACKUP SERVER AND NETWORK ADDRESS TRANSLATION

Before we look at a useful configuration, let's look at a simple configuration that illustrates how the switchover can be handled by routers. This configuration is only suitable for implementation in an isolated test environment. However, it does demonstrate the concept of how routers can use dynamic routing and network address translation to move an IP address from one physical network to another, without being reconfigured. It also highlights the problems we must guard against to safely use dynamic IP address changes. In the next example, we will address the challenge of controlling the switch over from one site to the other.

In this example, we control the hot standby switchover by using floating static routes on the routers at the server sites. The configuration of the primary router in Listing 11-1 shows how the concept can be made to work. Assume that we start with only the primary site functional. There will be no route to the virtual server address, so the floating static route will be activated.

```
!!!!!! WARNING
!!!!!! WARNING    For concept demonstration only
!!!!!! WARNING             See text.
!!!!!! WARNING
!
version 12.0
!
hostname PrimaryRouter
!
ip subnet-zero
!
interface Loopback0
 description Management and Tunnel ID
 ip address 10.0.0.100 255.255.255.255
!
interface Tunnel0
 description Outside<->outside tunnel for server updates
 ip address 192.168.55.1 255.255.255.252
 tunnel source Loopback0
```
(continued)

```
  tunnel destination 10.0.0.200
 !
interface Ethernet0
 description Primary Server LAN
 ip address 192.168.100.1 255.255.255.0
 ip nat outside
 !
interface Serial0
 description Link to the Intranet
 ip address 10.0.100.1 255.255.255.252
 ip nat inside
 !
router ospf 123
 redistribute static subnets route-map virtual
 network 10.0.0.100 0.0.0.0 area 100
 network 10.0.100.0 0.0.0.3 area 100
 network 192.168.100.0 0.0.0.255 area 100
 !
ip nat outside source static 192.168.100.10 192.168.0.10
ip classless
ip route 192.168.0.10 255.255.255.255 192.168.100.10 200
ip route 192.168.200.0 255.255.255.0 192.168.55.2
 !
access-list 10 permit 192.168.0.10
route-map virtual permit 25
 match ip address 10
 !
end
```

LISTING 11-1. *Primary router configuration for primary server using a virtual server address*

Once activated, the route to 192.168.0.10 via 192.168.100.10 (the real primary server) will be redistributed into the routing protocol (OSPF in this case), and all clients will be able to reach the server. As packets come in from the intranet, the network address translation from inside to outside will adjust the IP addresses so that the real primary server can service the requests. As the packets go back out, the primary server address is translated back into the virtual server IP address.

When the backup router in Listing 11-2 comes online, it sees the advertisements from the primary site through the dynamic routing protocol, and its floating static route to the virtual server via the backup server is suppressed. To allow the backup server to communicate with the primary server, we define *Tunnel0*, a generic routing encapsulation (GRE) tunnel between the two sites (remember, to the rest of the network, both sites appear as LAN 192.168.0.0/24).

```
!!!!!! WARNING
!!!!!! WARNING    For concept demonstration only
!!!!!! WARNING             See text.
!!!!!! WARNING
!
version 12.0
!
hostname BackupRouter
!
ip subnet-zero
!
interface Loopback0
 description Management and Tunnel ID
 ip address 10.0.0.200 255.255.255.255
!
interface Tunnel0
 description Outside<->outside tunnel for server updates
 ip address 192.168.55.2 255.255.255.252
 tunnel source Loopback0
 tunnel destination 10.0.0.100
!
interface Ethernet0
 description Backup Server LAN
 ip address 192.168.200.1 255.255.255.0
 ip nat outside
!
interface Serial0
 description Link to the Intranet
 ip address 10.0.200.1 255.255.255.252
 ip nat inside
!
router ospf 123
 redistribute static subnets route-map virtual
 network 10.0.0.200 0.0.0.0 area 100
 network 10.0.200.0 0.0.0.3 area 100
 network 192.168.200.0 255.255.255.0 area 100
!
ip nat outside source static 192.168.200.10 192.168.0.10
ip classless
ip route 192.168.0.10 255.255.255.255 192.168.200.10 200
ip route 192.168.100.0 255.255.255.0 192.168.55.1
!
```

(continued)

```
access-list 10 permit 192.168.0.10
route-map virtual permit 25
 match ip address 10
!
end
```

LISTING 11-2. *Backup router configuration for backup server using a virtual server address*

The tunnel is required because any packets, sent by either server, that cross an outside-to-inside boundary—as would be required to communicate directly across the intranet—will have the return address translated to 192.168.0.X on the way out. We provide a tunnel that keeps the packets logically on the outside network as they are carried over the inside network. We therefore bypass the address translation, allowing the two servers to communicate and keep each other up to date. Note that although IOS 11.2 supports all the NAT commands required, we must use IOS 12.0 and put the servers on the outside network to avoid spurious translations.

The communications problems between servers could also be solved by configuring each server to respond to two IP addresses. One address would be used for production access and be translated as before; the other address would be dedicated to inter-server communications and not be subject to translation.

When the primary site fails, the primary site router is no longer online to advertise its route to the virtual server LAN. As soon as the OSPF service on the backup router detects the failure, the static route pointing the virtual server to the backup server can float into action. All further requests are then routed to the backup site and operations can proceed.

The backup router will continue to advertise the virtual server addresses based on its floating static routes as long as the real LAN is available. When the primary site returns to operation, the tunnel can be used to update the primary server. The backup servers can be taken offline and operation switched back to normal.

While this approach looks good on paper, it is fraught with potential problems. In particular, if either site loses external connectivity but not local connectivity, it will activate the floating static route for the virtual server. When external connectivity is restored, which site remains active will depend upon the timing of OSPF and floating static route updates and will be unpredictable.

While the network can be designed so that this scenario will never occur in normal operation, correct routing is not guaranteed in the presence of failures. For example, any time a site (or even just the router at a site) returns to life after a failure, and the LAN interfaces come up before the WAN interfaces, the active server will be unpredictable. Clearly this is not acceptable. Safe operation requires that an external mechanism be in place to prevent unintended switchovers.

CONFIGURATION EXAMPLE: BACKUP SERVER USING NAT AND HOST ROUTING

The difficulty with using routers to control which location advertises the virtual server IP address space is our inability to control the switchover under all possible sequences of failure conditions. Advertising the wrong site could cause loss-of-synchronization problems such as database inconsistency or lost data. The critical assumption here is that if we could safely send transactions to both sites simultaneously, we would be using a load sharing approach rather than trying to force an all-or-nothing cutover.

Controlling the switchover cleanly and accurately, while beyond the scope of what we can reasonably expect from a generic router, is not that difficult to achieve. For example, we can control which site is advertised using a custom script running on a Linux system running *GateD*. The script can make whatever tests are appropriate in the specific environment to determine whether the other site is online, whether this site is reasonably connected to users, and whether either site should be prevented from being the active server. Then, if the server at this site should be active, it can add the necessary routes to the local system routing table so that *GateD* can advertise the virtual servers using the desired routing protocol.

Since the control system conditionally generating the routing advertisements does not have to physically route any packets, it need not be capable of high performance routing. Any incoming traffic to a virtual address will have its address translated by the router to the real server address at that site, so the control system will never see it. Consequently, unlike the routers, the route controller does not impact the service capacity of the site. It may even be possible to run the tests and route generation on the servers themselves, although that can complicate testing and troubleshooting.

Since the route controller is a potential single point of failure, we should use at least two at each site. This does not create a problem for the routers, as they can easily handle the availability of multiple routes through the LAN to get to any particular destination. Since the routers are no longer responsible for determining the correct location of the active server, we also can use multiple routers at each site without impacting the stability of the switching mechanism.

The router configuration required to support the control system is much easier to implement than in the previous example. This is because the routers only propagate the address location change and do not try to control it. Take a look at the primary router's configuration in Listing 11-3. Superficially, this configuration appears identical to that in the previous example, in which the routers controlled the address mapping of the virtual server. Indeed, the configuration is identical except for the deletion of the floating static route and the associated lines required to control redistribution of that route into the dynamic routing protocol. In Listing 11-3, the virtual server route is learned from the control system. The control system is assumed here to speak the same routing protocol (OSPF) as the real routing, so no redistribution is required at the router.

```
version 12.0
!
hostname PrimaryRouter
!
ip subnet-zero
!
interface Loopback0
 description Management and Tunnel ID
 ip address 10.0.0.100 255.255.255.255
!
interface Tunnel0
 description Outside<->outside tunnel for server updates
 ip address 192.168.55.1 255.255.255.252
 tunnel source Loopback0
 tunnel destination 10.0.0.200
!
interface Ethernet0
 description Primary Server LAN
 ip address 192.168.100.2 255.255.255.0
 ip nat outside
!
interface Serial0
 description Link to the Intranet
 ip address 10.0.100.1 255.255.255.252
 ip nat inside
!
router ospf 123
 network 10.0.100.0 0.0.0.3 area 100
 network 10.0.0.100 0.0.0.0 area 100
!
ip nat outside source static 192.168.100.10 192.168.0.10
!
ip classless
ip route 192.168.200.0 255.255.255.0 192.168.55.2
!
end
```

LISTING 11-3. *Primary router configuration for primary server using a virtual server address provided by an external source*

We still continue to provide a tunnel so that communications can occur between active and standby servers to maintain database synchronization. The tunnel also supports communications between the control systems at each location so that they can determine which should be the active site and whether the standby system is capable of taking over.

The actual tests used by the control systems to determine which site should be the active site will depend upon the services provided by a site, the staffing available, acceptable failure modes, and sensitivity of the application to mistakes. For example, when a controller first comes online, it could test whether or not to activate a site by checking the distance to the virtual server address. If the virtual server is local, it means that the site is active through the efforts of another redundant control system at the site. If the virtual server address is being advertised but is at a distance indicating that the other site is active, then the server at this site should stay in standby mode, and the two servers should be working at getting synchronized. This would be normal startup mode for the backup site. It would also be a normal recovery for the primary site from any failure that caused a switchover to the backup site.

If the virtual server address is not being advertised, the controller should determine why before it starts advertising. This is another reason why we use a control system rather than depend upon the routers. It not only verifies that the remote site is not reachable, but also checks with the local servers to see if they are able to serve. Further, the control system checks the routing tables to see if this site appears to be connected to the rest of the organization. The critical contribution here to stability and data integrity is that physical servers default to inactive and only move to the active state when all tests (or systems management personnel) conclude that it is appropriate to do so.

An alternative way to automatically switch services to a backup site—assuming the client uses a directory service to find the servers—is to modify the directory service entries. They can be manipulated so that when the client asks for the network address associated with a particular server, the response will be the currently operational server. Before we can explore this approach, we need to understand how the TCP/IP Domain Name System (DNS) functions.

DOMAIN NAME SYSTEM OPERATION

We look first at the normal DNS mode of operation. Consider the scenario in Figure 11-3: a client, *client.xxx.com,* in domain *xxx.com* seeks to connect to the server *server.yyy.com* in domain *yyy.com.*

The DNS resolver in the client system starts by making a recursive DNS query to the local DNS server *dns.xxx.com* at the hard coded IP address 10.10.10.254. Recursive queries require the DNS server to return an absolute address even if the information is not available locally. The server *dns.xxx.com* will typically provide

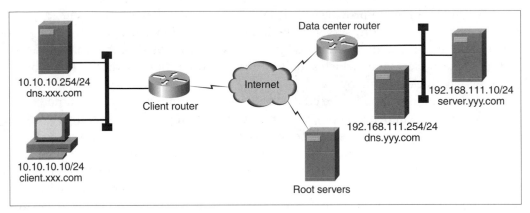

FIGURE 11-3. *Conventional use of static domain name services*

answers for the *xxx.com* domain, but for other domains it must seek out a server that may have the answers. In this example, it would send an iterative request to one of the root servers on the Internet.

Iterative requests allow return of either the absolute address or a list of alternative servers that should be checked for the information. In this case, the root server would return the location of the authoritative primary and alternate servers for the domain *yyy.com*. Based on that information, server *dns.xxx.com* would send a request to *dns.yyy.com* to get the address of *server.yyy.com*. If no response was received, *dns.xxx.com* would try each of the alternate IP addresses provided until it either got a response or ran out of authoritative servers to try. The first address obtained—or a failure message if no address could be mapped to the name—would then be returned to answer the recursive query of *client.xxx.com*.

Most DNS resolvers and servers maintain a cache of addresses obtained this way to minimize the need to continually probe for name-to-address mappings. Each response obtained includes a lifetime indicating how long the address mapping can be kept in cache. However, it should be noted that many implementations of DNS ignore the lifetime parameter, particularly if it is either very short or very long. This can create unnecessary downtime when alternate DNS mappings are used to direct service requests away from a down server.

In a larger organization, the domain names are organized in a hierarchy, and the DNS protocol is designed to support an arbitrary number of hierarchical levels. This makes the domain name system both efficient and resistant to failure. A corporation might choose to provide separate name spaces for each of its divisions, while within a large division, the name space might be further divided into departments. The corporation might also choose to define some top-level names such as a corporate Web site. The resulting hierarchy might look like Figure 11-4.

Each domain and subdomain should have at least two DNS servers in order to avoid having a single point of failure in a critical resource. Each domain

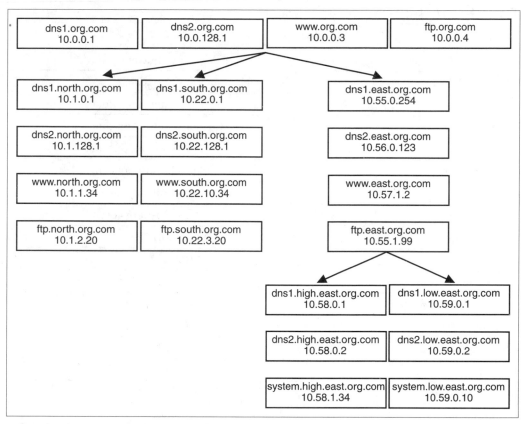

FIGURE 11-4. *Example DNS naming hierarchy*

or subdomain can also have defined end-systems—in this case an FTP server and a Web server. A look at the critical lines in the DNS database used by the corporate DNS servers in Table 11-2 shows how the system works. Here we show two different kinds of records: *NS* records defining name servers for parts of the domain, and *A* records associating IP addresses with names in the domain.

The different divisions of org.com must keep their DNS servers at the IP addresses contained in the DNS databases above them. Otherwise, the divisions are free to define and move systems as they see fit. Any request for an address of the form *xxx.north.org.com* will be answered with the names and IP addresses of the two DNS servers in that subdomain: *dns1.north.org.com* at 10.1.0.1 and *dns2.north.org.com* at 10.1.128.1.

Keep in mind that we only show here the two classes of DNS records required to illustrate the IP address lookup process in a DNS hierarchy. We do not show any of the other defined records that would be found in a production DNS database, such as aliases, mail exchange records, host information, and other descriptive data.

TABLE 11-2. *DNS Database for* dns1.org.com *and* dns2.org.com

NAME	RECORD TYPE	DATA
org.com	NS	dns1.org.com
org.com	NS	dns2.org.com
north.org.com	NS	dns1.north.org.com
north.org.com	NS	dns2.north.org.com
south.org.com	NS	dns1.south.org.com
south.org.com	NS	dns2.south.org.com
east.org.com	NS	dns1.east.org.com
east.org.com	NS	dns2.east.org.com
dns1.org.com	A	10.0.0.1
dns2.org.com	A	10.0.128.1
dns1.north.org.com	A	10.1.0.1
dns2.north.org.com	A	10.1.128.1
dns1.south.org.com	A	10.22.0.1
dns2.south.org.com	A	10.22.128.1
dns1.east.org.com	A	10.55.0.254
dns2.east.org.com	A	10.56.0.123
www.org.com	A	10.0.0.3
ftp.org.com	A	10.0.0.4

Now consider what happens when the client at *client.xxx.com* seeks the address of *system.high.east.org.com*. The client's local DNS server, *dns.xxx.com,* receives the recursive lookup request from the client. It then sends an iterative request to the root DNS server seeking an authoritative server for *system.high.east.org.com*.

The root server responds with a referral to *dns1.org.com* and *dns2.org.com* as the DNS servers for the *org.com* domain that might have the answer. It also gives their IP addresses. Based on this response, the client's local DNS server tries again, this time asking for *dns1.org.com*.

Server *dns1.org.com* looks in its database (Table 11-2), and does not find an entry for *system.high.east.org.com*. However, it does find name server entries for the domain *east.org.com*. Based on those entries, *dns1.org.com* responds with a referral to *dns1.east.org.com* and *dns2.east.org.com*—as DNS servers for the *east.org.com* domain that might have the answer—along with their IP addresses. Based on this response, the client's local DNS server tries again, this time asking *dns1.east.org.com*.

Server *dns1.east.org.com* looks in its database (Table 11-3), and does not find an entry for *system.high.east.org.com;* however, there are entries for name servers for the domain *high.east.org.com.* So *dns1.east.org.com* responds with a referral to *dns1.high.east.org.com* and *dns2.high.east.org.com*—the DNS servers for the *high.east.org.com* domain—along with their IP addresses. Based on this response, the client's local DNS server tries again, this time asking for *dns1.high.east.org.com.*

To find an answer, *dns1.high.east.org.com* looks in its database (Table 11-4) and finds an entry for the requested name *system.high.east.org.com.* The results of this successful lookup are returned to *dns.xxx.com* as an address answer that can be passed on to *client.xxx.com.*

TABLE 11-3.　*DNS Database for* dns1.east.org.com

NAME	RECORD TYPE	DATA
east.org.com	NS	dns1.east.org.com
east.org.com	NS	dns2.east.org.com
high.east.org.com	NS	dns1.high.east.org.com
high.east.org.com	NS	dns2.high.east.org.com
low.east.org.com	NS	dns1.low.east.org.com
low.east.org.com	NS	dns2.low.east.org.com
dns1.east.org.com	A	10.55.0.254
dns2.east.org.com	A	10.56.0.123
dns1.high.east.org.com	A	10.58.0.1
dns2.high.east.org.com	A	10.58.0.2
dns1.low.east.org.com	A	10.59.0.1
dns2.low.east.org.com	A	10.59.0.2

TABLE 11-4.　*DNS Database for* dns1.high.east.org.com

NAME	RECORD TYPE	DATA
high.east.org.com	NS	dns1.high.east.org.com
high.east.org.com	NS	dns2.high.east.org.com
dns1.high.east.org.com	A	10.58.0.1
dns2.high.east.org.com	A	10.58.0.2
system.high.east.org.com	A	10.58.1.34

DOMAIN NAME SYSTEM REDIRECTION

We can take advantage of the normal operation of DNS by using it to return an address based on which systems are available to serve at any given time. For example, an IP client might issue a DNS request for the address of the server. Normally, the DNS server would return the IP address of the primary server. However, if the primary server were determined to be down, the IP address of the backup server would be returned. (The ability to make this determination is what distinguishes one dynamic DNS implementation from another.)

Depending upon the client's protocol stack, we can frequently perform this server name-to-IP address change automatically, using no special hardware or software. The DNS has been a critical resource since the earliest days of networking, and most client implementations allow definition of more than one default name server.

We can use the ability of standard DNS to support backup DNS servers as a way to provide automatic failover using standard, static DNS servers. We install our primary DNS server in the primary data center and our alternate DNS server in the backup data center, as in Figure 11-5. The DNS server in the primary data center is configured to return the IP addresses of the server in the primary data center, while the DNS server in the backup data center is configured to return the IP addresses of the server in the backup data center. DNS is then configured to use the primary server, with the backup server as an alternate if needed.

As long as queries go to the primary DNS server, all client connections will go to IP addresses in the primary data center. But if the primary data center goes offline, clients will no longer be able to reach the DNS server there. At that point, DNS queries will be made to the DNS server at the backup data center, which is still accessible. That DNS server will return an IP address that takes traffic to the server in the backup data center.

While this approach can work, it suffers from a number of shortcomings. One problem is that once a client establishes a connection through the network to the backup IP address, that IP address will be used until the connection is broken. We might need to take the backup data center offline to get clients to stop accessing the backup server and go back to the primary server. Consequently, we would lose transactions not only when the primary failed, but also when the secondary was deliberately disabled to return service to normal.

We may also find that once the primary DNS server fails, no further attempts will be made to reach it. So we may need to disable the DNS server at the backup site to force client systems to go back to using the primary DNS server for resolving names. This will depend upon the client protocol stack implementation or the implementation of the client's local DNS server (if the queries are recursive).

Finally, the switchover is an all-or-nothing switch. If a single server fails, the backup server can only be used if all primary services are switched to the backup site.

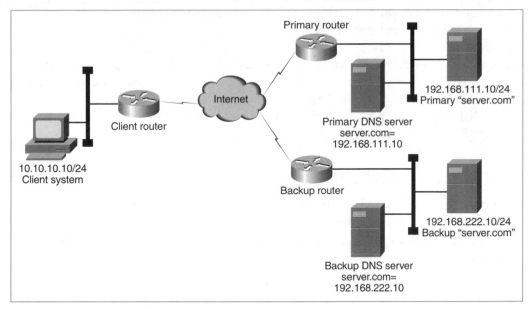

FIGURE 11-5. *Simple backup data center using alternate DNS*

Plus, if the primary DNS server fails, all services will be unnecessarily redirected to the backup site, since there is no way to distinguish between a DNS server failure and a site failure.

A better solution is to use DNS servers designed to automatically respond to each request with the appropriate address based on the status of the primary server. There are a number of products designed to do this, such as Cisco's DistributedDirector, F5 Networks' 3DNS Controller and RADWare's Web Server Director for Distributed Sites. These are usually marketed as load sharing solutions, but many can be programmed to serve as all-or-nothing fallback solutions as well.

When using proprietary load sharing devices, it can still be challenging to configure the switchover so that the inactive server can be brought back into synchronization before going active. But by choosing a load sharing solution that uses SNMP or other query capabilities, and configuring the servers to provide appropriate status responses to queries, we can build a robust and stable solution. Meanwhile, we do not have the problem we faced with static DNS servers—that of forcing users to access the correct DNS server. All will respond with the same, currently active IP address for each server name.

We can also often adapt the configuration to provide transfer on an individual server basis, providing not only disaster recovery but also protection from server failures. However, no matter how carefully we configure the DNS servers, we still have the gap in coverage—and potential of lost transactions—caused by stopping all transactions before switching servers and by ensuring the databases are synchronized before enabling the replacement to take over.

Regardless of the DNS redirection tools used, adequate application and platform testing is essential. We may still see requests to the wrong IP address due to intermediate DNS servers that ignore our lifetime limits on name-to-address mappings. This is usually not a problem on intranets, on which we can control the DNS servers. But it can be a headache when we attempt to use DNS redirection with Internet applications accessed by the general public.

LOAD SHARING APPROACHES

For non-stop availability, the only real choice for disaster recovery is geographically distributed load sharing. When the load sharing is implemented using multiple, geographically distributed load sharing devices, resilience in a disaster is a natural result of having no single site as a critical resource. Disaster recovery then becomes a question of capacity planning. Most of the products on the market for load sharing are targeted at the Web server market, and some of their techniques only work when the clients are Web browsers. But the fact that we cannot take full advantage of all their Web-oriented features does not mean that we can't use them to load balance other services.

However, we must recognize that load sharing of Web requests is much simpler than load sharing of other services. In particular, database applications requiring consistency across multiple sites being independently updated is theoretically impossible to do correctly under all possible failure conditions. This requires the application developers to make hard choices about which failure modes will be automatically recovered and how inconsistencies will be resolved when automatic recovery is not possible. Issues such as the handling of incomplete transactions, partial updates, and lost locks are outside the scope of network design, but must be resolved if the overall solution is to be useful to the organization.

One approach to load sharing is to apply the same philosophy we used for hot backup, and define a single IP address for the service. The difference is that the IP address is assigned to the load sharing device, as shown in Figure 11-6. The client sends its requests (1) to the IP address of the virtual server, 192.168.0.10, which is actually an address on the load sharing device. The load sharing device then does a double network address translation, changing the destination address in each packet to send the transaction to the selected real server (2) and changing the source address to another address on the load sharing device. This forces the response from the server (3) to be routed back through the load sharing device. The IP addresses then can be restored to their original values to return the response to the client (4).

This double network address translation approach suffers from several critical limitations—aside from those inherent in any application of NAT. When used

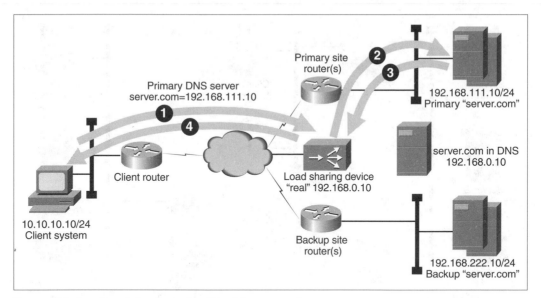

FIGURE 11-6. *Load sharing using IP address mangling*

in a WAN environment, not only does the double address translation impose an added traffic burden, but the load sharing device itself becomes a single point of failure.

While many of the load sharing devices available provide redundancy features that allow one load sharing device to back up another, these are normally limited to single-site solutions. This is because both load sharing devices must be on the same physical subnetwork so that they can use the same IP address. Their role in disaster recovery is therefore limited. Nonetheless, they can solve the challenge of routing around individual server failures, even when the backup server is at an alternate site.

While we may not be able to use this approach for multisite disaster recovery, load sharing devices using this approach can be a powerful tool within a single site. For a single site LAN, we might instead choose to use a layer-2 switch-based product that does the address translations at the MAC level rather than the IP level. This would minimize the impact of address translations on supported protocols. But these MAC layer devices are even less appropriate for a WAN-based disaster recovery solution.

LOAD SHARING USING DOMAIN NAME SERVICE REDIRECTION

DNS redirection is a popular approach to load sharing. We can take advantage of the hierarchical nature of DNS to provide a degree of fault tolerance in mapping server addresses to users. Consider the dual data center network in Figure 11-7. Each data center supports two servers and a DNS-based load sharing device.

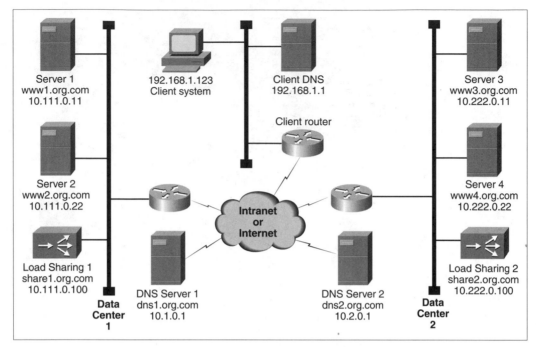

FIGURE 11-7. *Load sharing using DNS redirection*

For this example, all four Web servers are assumed to be equivalent, and each contains all the data for the corporate Web site, *www.org.com*. That is, queries to any of the four will return the same data and contain identical pointers to other pages. This is not an essential constraint in a production system, but it does keep the configuration much simpler, with no loss of validity.

Consider the DNS configuration of the corporate name servers (*dns1.org.com* and *dns2.org.com* in Table 11-5) and in the load sharing devices (*share1.org.com* in Table 11-6 and *share2.org.com* in Table 11-7). The key to load sharing can be seen in the different definitions of the corporate Web site name *www.org.com*. On the corporate DNS servers, the name *www.org.com* is configured as a subdomain of *org.com*, but on the load sharing devices, the name *www.org.com* returns the best available Web server for the client at the time of the request.

When the client's DNS server queries the corporate name server for the address of the corporate Web site *www.org.com*, the response is a referral to the two load sharing devices as the name servers for the subdomain *www.org.com*. But when the client's DNS server queries one of the load sharing devices, it will get back the address of whichever of the real corporate Web servers is the best available to service the client.

In a load balancing and performance-maximizing environment we would be interested in basing our choice of server on parameters that would optimize performance.

TABLE 11-5.   *DNS Entries on Corporate DNS Servers* dns1.org.com *and* dns2.org.com

NAME	RECORD TYPE	DATA
org.com	NS	dns1.org.com
org.com	NS	dns2.org.com
www.org.com	NS	share1.org.com
www.org.com	NS	share2.org.com
dns1.org.com	A	10.1.0.1
dns2.org.com	A	10.2.0.1
share1.org.com	A	10.111.0.100
share2.org.com	A	10.222.0.100

TABLE 11-6.   *DNS Entries on Load Sharing Device* share1.org.com

NAME	RECORD TYPE	DATA
www.org.com	NS	share1.org.com
share1.org.com	A	10.111.0.100
www.org.com	A	best available of 10.111.0.11, 10.111.0.22, 10.222.0.11 or 10.222.0.22.

TABLE 11-7.   *DNS Entries on Load Sharing Device* share2.org.com

NAME	RECORD TYPE	DATA
www.org.com	NS	share2.org.com
share2.org.com	A	10.222.0.100
www.org.com	A	best available of 10.111.0.11, 10.111.0.22, 10.222.0.11 or 10.222.0.22.

Such parameters might include routing metrics so that the client is directed to the server closest to the client, current server loading so that requests are sent to servers with the capacity to handle them, and perhaps even the identity of the client so that high priority clients go to the fastest servers.

For maximizing availability, however, we are most concerned with the ability of the load sharing device to determine which servers have failed. This will mean that clients are always sent to working systems that can meet their needs. Unlike with NAT, we can no longer check the return traffic from the server to ensure that requests are generating timely and appropriate responses. Instead, a variety of techniques can be used to try to make this determination, ranging from simple *ping* tests to verify that the IP address is still alive to creating test requests to verify that the server still responds appropriately and in a timely manner. Adjusting the polling frequency to improve responsiveness to failure may be desirable, depending on the specific load sharing system used.

We may also be able to use routing table changes in the routers to speed detection of down or disconnected sites. Some load sharing devices can communicate with nearby routers to detect, through the routing protocol, when routes to servers cease to be available. This allows for immediate removal of servers on the disconnected networks from DNS responses. Some load sharing devices query routers near the servers to determine the routing distance to the client, choosing the server closest to the client for their response.

For high performance sites, load sharing devices may be moved to the first line. They can serve as the corporate name servers, eliminating the delay of the extra level of indirection.

Another approach, DNS mangling, leaves the database on the DNS server static. Instead, the load sharing device acts as a proxy for incoming DNS queries. For queries to destinations being load shared, the proxy will "fix" the DNS server's response to direct the client to the correct server. This approach can simplify administration, as the load sharing adjustments are transparent to the real DNS server.

As always, there are many tradeoffs to be made among overhead, accuracy, server selection algorithms, failure detection methods, and cost. Care must also be taken if applications are supported that require persistence, although it is usually safe to assume that a client will continue to use the address originally provided until done.

HTTP REDIRECTION

HTTP redirection is another technique that is popular in load sharing devices designed for Web-serving applications. It takes advantage of a Web server's ability to respond to a request with a redirection indicator telling the client browser to get the requested information from a different server. The same technique can be used to determine which server to use; the fundamental difference is that the load sharing device is identified by the DNS as the IP address to use rather than the actual Web server.

There are two critical disadvantages to using HTTP redirection. First, it only works with Web-based services. Second, it puts the load sharing device into a mode where it becomes a single point of failure. On the other hand, for many applications, such as e-commerce, the only services that need to be supported are Web based.

HTTP redirection can make configuration of large server farms much simpler than with a pure DNS redirection approach, reducing the probability of downtime due to configuration errors. Typically, we would combine the two techniques. We would use DNS redirection to selected DNS load sharing systems, which would then deliver the addresses of our HTTP redirection load sharing systems rather than of the actual servers. This would allow us to retain the disaster recovery capability of DNS redirection while still benefiting from the lower-level flexibility of HTTP redirection.

WRAP-UP

The needs of disaster recovery transcend the scope of network design and must cover all information technology services and other business-critical functions. Traditional information technology disaster recovery is based on recreating the data center at a backup facility from tape backups. But the downtime associated with this approach is usually measured in days, and depending upon the mode of failure, all data since the last usable backup may be lost. Even if nightly backups are made and stored off-site, a full day of transactions could still be lost.

Data loss and the time required to cut over to the backup data center can be reduced by keeping the backup data center running continuously, with updates constantly being provided from the primary data center over the network. This can reduce the downtime associated with a major disaster to hours or even minutes. On the other hand, this strategy also requires maintaining a full-time backup data center, as well as potentially more complex applications, to allow for real-time updates of the backup site.

From the networking point of view, the same techniques can be used to support either backup data centers or load sharing data centers. While there are multiple possible approaches, the most useful ones for meeting high availability requirements are based on specialized DNS devices. These devices modify the address returned for a given name based on the ability of the server at that IP address to provide the requested function. We also noted that there are significant limitations inherent in every available approach, including DNS devices, that must be considered when developing a disaster recovery solution.

In large-scale service environments, we will usually need to utilize a range of solutions, maximizing the benefits each has to offer while minimizing the impact of its shortcomings.

Management Considerations

Network management is not optional if there is any expectation of meeting long-term availability targets. The more redundant and failure-proof we design the network, the greater the need for network management to keep it running correctly. We can divide critical management requirements into three general areas: network monitoring, configuration management, and total quality control.

Network monitoring is essential for long term availability. In a resilient, highly redundant network design, typical failures have no visible impact on network operation. If we are not constantly monitoring for failures, we may not discover them until enough other components have failed that functional availability is affected.

Network monitoring can also be a critical contributor to network security. Even when network management and security management are independent functions, they should still support one another. After all, the sooner an attack can be detected, the sooner countermeasures can be implemented.

While close monitoring minimizes the impact of random and externally caused failures, it does not protect us from ourselves. We use configuration management to control the potential for introducing failures through routine maintenance and upgrades. By controlling when and how the network can be altered, we reduce our potential to introduce errors and maximize our ability to correct mistakes by backing out of changes.

Finally, we can apply total quality control principles to the management of the network, thereby refining our design and procedures to maximize availability. By investigating anomalies detected by network monitoring and investigating any changes that do not behave exactly as predicted, we can track down design errors, incorrect procedures, and other oversights before they have a chance to adversely affect operations. Our attitude should be "the failure is not corrected until we understand what really happened and have put in place procedural changes to avoid similar problems in the future." This can go a long way toward preventing the surprises that would pop up if the originally masked defect were to appear again.

It is essential to note that while we will be discussing technical issues in this chapter, the most critical aspect of network management is human management. If proper network management at the technical level is not a priority of the organization's management chain, then the resources required to do the job right will not be available long term and network availability will be at risk.

NETWORK MONITORING

Maximizing availability requires maximizing the mean time between failures (MTBF) and minimizing the mean time to repair (MTTR). Even though the network may continue to function despite failures, this does not mean we can ignore failures. Instead, we must think of the failure as a ticking time bomb. If we are unable to repair a failed component before the component backing it up fails, we will suffer an outage. If there are multiple components backing it up, that may buy us additional time, but it is still just a matter of time before enough components fail that service is disrupted. And this ignores the potential for degraded performance.

In a normal network, a failure will prevent users from getting their work done and generate a flood of telephone calls. In a high availability network, however, users will rarely even be aware that a failure has occurred. The more transparent the recovery mechanism, the more important it is that we have adequate monitoring tools in place to detect any failure.

This requires monitoring of much more detailed network status indicators than is common in many organizations. For example, it is no longer adequate to merely *ping* a server periodically and page the system administrator if no response is received. Instead, we must check the status of each interface on the server; its backup if using a hot standby (to ensure we are communicating with the primary server and not an activated standby); and every router, switch, and other network component along the path to the server.

This generally means that all networking components must be manageable at the individual interface level. We can then use standard Simple Network Management Protocol (SNMP) tools to query all devices and provide indications of the status of lines and interfaces. While this is conceptually simple, the level of detail required can be a severe challenge for many SNMP tools, and the traffic burden to support all the polling of status information can be substantial.

NETWORK MANAGEMENT WITH SNMP

There is a vast array of SNMP-based network management tools available. These range from "point solution" tools like CiscoView—for managing Cisco routers and switches—to "enterprise management" suites like Computer Associates' Unicenter TNG—which tries to include every function under the sun. These tools range in price from the "free for the download" Multi Router Traffic Grapher (MRTG) to the "if you have to ask, you can't afford it" top-of-the-line products.

The key to success with all these tools is that the staff using them have the skills and the time to customize them to gather, filter, and report pertinent information. This customization is an ongoing process, not a one-shot event. Not only do networks grow and evolve with time, but so does the understanding of what is important in the specific environment. Like the proverbial boy who cried wolf, a network management system that pages everyone in the middle of the night to report events that can wait until morning is going to be ignored when it actually does report a critical failure.

What most sales representatives ignore while making their pitches is that SNMP is not just a protocol, or even a series of protocols. SNMP is an entire architecture for communications among network components and network managers. As such, it can be likened to a mechanic's tool kit. SNMP provides standard definitions for parameters that can be read on each network component (the Management Information Base, or MIB). It also provides a mechanism that a network manager can use to access or change items in the MIB (the SNMP protocol itself).

Note that SNMP does not provide any guidance as to which MIB entries are important or which values should be considered good or bad for any particular entry. These will all depend upon the application. The requirements regarding which MIB definitions must be implemented on any specific device are also minimal. This is deliberate, as any management capability is usually better than no management capability. One of the challenges when setting up network monitoring and management is to determine how the MIB data that is available can be evaluated to infer the information that we actually need to know.

We need our network management systems to be functional contributors to managing our network. We don't need "credenza ware" that sits in a prominent place in the computer room displaying a beautiful graphical rendition of the network, bearing little relation to reality. While such a system may impress visitors, it does not contribute to the availability of the network. It is essential that the network management tools chosen be ones that the staff is capable of using and maintaining as the network evolves.

Another challenge with SNMP is that there are three different versions of the protocol. The original SNMP version 1 (SNMPv1), published in 1987, was a quick hack intended to buy time until some real tools could be developed. Its popularity surprised even its most ardent supporters, as the protocol provided only minimal capabilities and was inefficient, depending upon polling for status updates and iterative requests for reading tabular data. SNMP also lacked such critical management capabilities as a security model, a standard way to manage itself, and an ability to determine the relationship among managed objects.

These shortcomings were recognized, and a second version (SNMPv2) was developed. Unfortunately, this second version fell victim to political squabbles, and its most important feature, provision of a security model capable of supporting authenticated and secure communications, was dropped. However, a compromise version, SNMPv2c, was ultimately published to allow use of the efficiency and object management improvements in the standard.

Useful security was finally added to SNMP in SNMPv3. SNMPv3 prototypes were first demonstrated at Network World/Interop in May 1998, and the new version reached draft standard status in 1999. However, both SNMPv1 and SNMPv2 continue to be widely used, since not every vendor immediately started shipping SNMPv3 in its products, and even for those that did, older products and software releases remain in service.

All versions of the SNMP standards are published as RFCs and available free of charge on the Internet. Some of the more important SNMP RFCs are listed in Table 12-1. All current Internet Engineering Task Force (IETF) RFCs are available from the IETF Web site at http://www.ietf.org/home.html. While on the home page, check the standards document (STD1) for the current RFC defining the standard for each protocol.

TABLE 12-1. *Core SNMP RFCs for Versions 1, 2, and 3*

RFC #	SNMP VERSION	STANDARD DEFINED
1155	1	Structure of Management Information Version 1 (SMI)
1157	1	Simple Network Management Protocol (Version 1)
1212	1	Concise MIB Definitions
1213	1	Management Information Base for TCP/IP (MIB-II)
1901	2	Introduction to Community-Based SNMPv2 (SNMPV2CB)
1909	2	Administrative Infrastructure for SNMPv2 (SNMPV2AI)
1910	2	User-Based Security Model for SNMPv2 (SNMPV2SM)
2571	3	Architecture for SNMP Management (ARCH-SNMP)
2572	3	Message Processing and Dispatching for SNMP (MPD-SNMP)
2573	3	SNMP Applications (SNMP-APP)
2574	3	User-Based Security Model for SNMPv3 (USM-SNMPV3)
2575	3	View-Based Access Control for SNMP (VACM-SNMP)
2578	3	Structure of Management Information Version 2 (SMIv2)
2579	3	Textual Conventions for SMIv2 (CONV-MIB)
2580	3	Conformance Statements for SMIv2 (CONF-MIB)

More important than the SNMP protocol is the definition of what can be managed by the protocol. The MIBs define which parameters can be read on the device and which can be adjusted. If we were tuning a car engine, SNMP would be the readouts on the sensors we use to measure the performance and the screwdriver we use to adjust the settings. But the MIBs define which sensors are available to be read by SNMP and which adjusting screws are available for us to turn with our screwdriver.

There is a wide range of standard MIBs defined, some of which are listed in Table 12-2. However, other than the original MIB-II defined for SNMPv1, support for MIBs can vary widely by platform. Fortunately, the situation is improving with

TABLE 12-2. *Some SNMP MIBs and Their Standards Status (as of RFC 2600, May 2000)*

RFC #	STATUS	STANDARD DEFINED
1213	Standard	Management Information Base for TCP/IP (MIB-II)
1643	Standard	MIB for Ethernet-Like Interfaces (ETHER-MIB)
2115	Draft Standard	Frame Relay DTE MIB Using SMIv2 (FRAME-MIB)
1908	Draft Standard	Coexistence Between Version 1 and Version 2 (COEX-MIB)
1907	Draft Standard	MIB for Version 2 of SNMP (SNMPv2-MIB)
1850	Draft Standard	OSPF Version 2 MIB (OSPF-MIB)
1757	Draft Standard	Remote Network Monitoring MIB (RMON-MIB)
1657	Draft Standard	Border Gateway Protocol Version 4 MIB (BGP-4-MIB)
1724	Draft Standard	RIP Version 2 MIB Extension (RIP2-MIB)
2742	Proposed Standard	Definitions of Managed Objects for Extensible SNMP Agents
2737	Proposed Standard	Entity MIB (Version 2)
2594	Proposed Standard	Definitions of Managed Objects for WWW Services
2564	Proposed Standard	Application Management MIB (APP-MIB)
2515	Proposed Standard	Managed Objects for ATM Management (ATM-MIBMAN)
2494	Proposed Standard	Managed Objects for DS0 and DS0 Bundle
2495	Proposed Standard	Managed Objects for DS1, E1, DS2, and E2
2496	Proposed Standard	Managed Objects for DS3/E3 (DS3-E3-MIB)
2465	Proposed Standard	Management Information Base for IP Version 6 (see also 2452, 2454, and 2466 for v6 TCP, UDP, and ICMP)
2127	Proposed Standard	ISDN MIB Using SMIv2 (ISDN-MIB)
2128	Proposed Standard	Dial Control MIB Using SMIv2 (DC-MIB)
2021	Proposed Standard	Remote Network Monitoring MIB Version 2 Using SMIv2

time. Access to the parameters required for adequate management may be part of proprietary MIBs that differ on each device. Although SNMP defines a standard way to read these proprietary MIBs, the meaning of the values returned will depend upon the vendor.

The situation in which the data required for effective management may or may not be available on every platform is a constant challenge for network managers. The introduction of Web-based network management, while it may free us from being tied to the console of a network management platform, does not significantly change what data is available to monitor and control the network.

MONITORING FUNCTIONS THAT DO NOT REPORT STATUS

We will often discover that there are critical functions that we cannot effectively monitor with SNMP. These may require the development of customized scripts to query the routers or other devices via Telnet (or whatever mechanism the product provides for "human" access), extract the desired status information via "screen scraping," and report the results to the management system. Just as with SNMP, we must always be careful of the impact of our monitoring on network overhead and system loading.

Another technique is to monitor the system log (syslog) in real time, continuously checking for pertinent reports. However, like SNMP traps, syslog monitoring by itself is not sufficient. Syslog events are generated, transmitted over the network, and recorded on a best-effort basis only. Just because a failure is not reported does not mean that a failure has not occurred. After all, the failure may have been one that blocked the ability to report the failure. Consequently, while we can take advantage of the syslog and SNMP traps to provide early warning, we cannot depend on them as our only mechanism. Nevertheless, using them may allow us to reduce the frequency of our SNMP or scripted polls to a more tolerable level.

Sometimes, we can get critical status information to be sent to the syslog by turning on debugging of some aspect of the facility we wish to monitor. For example, on a Cisco router we might use the debug command *debug dlsw* peer to allow us to track the status of DLSw peers. This is easier than Telnetting to the router, issuing the *show dlsw peers* command, and parsing the response for the desired status. However, we must be careful that we do not create so much noise traffic that we do more harm than good.

Generally, we will use a combination of techniques to gather our status information, concentrating on the parameters that are most likely to fail or have the highest impact when they do fail.

We can monitor for side effects as well as failure events. For example, if an ISDN line comes up, we know that something is amiss to have triggered the need for a backup call. This is true even if a circuit down report was never received regarding the line being backed up by the ISDN link.

SECURITY

In today's hostile network environment, it is essential that network management assist security management by constantly being on the lookout for any signs that could indicate an attempted security policy violation. For example, any invalid packets detected by an access-list on an inside router should be cause for immediate concern. It could mean that a path has been found through the outside routers and firewalls, and we are currently depending upon our last line of defense. Just as dangerous, it might be someone on the inside who is seeking revenge and testing our defenses.

While good security practices dictate that security administration be independent of other modes of administration, that does not mean that the security team should be kept in isolation. Any signs of potential security problems must be immediately shared with the security team to allow coordinated investigation and resolution. We must never forget that we need to work together to survive.

No matter what security measures we take, and particularly if we are connected to the Internet, we can expect to be attacked. The time to determine how to respond to an attack, whether from an anonymous Internet hacker or an inside job, is before the fact. Planning is always better when tempers are cool and there is time to think through the consequences of actions. In the heat of battle, it is all too easy to make mistakes. After all, the appropriate response could range from doing nothing to calling in the police in order to pursue criminal remedies. This is the time to put together the emergency response team and track down information such as whom to contact at our ISPs should we need their assistance in dealing with an attack.

Normally, the best response to attacks from the outside is to ensure that the defenses in place can handle the attack, to monitor the attack for any evidence that the defenses are not adequate, and otherwise to ignore it. Most attacks are from script kiddies trying out the latest exploit posted on the Internet and are best regarded as a verification that the defenses in place are working correctly. Particularly malicious attacks or ones that appear to be a new exploit should be reported to the appropriate computer security agencies. These agencies specialize in tracking hacker exploits and publicizing defense measures.

One such agency is the Carnegie Mellon University Software Engineering Institute's Computer Emergency Response Team (CERT). CERT collects data about hack attacks and lets the general community know about any trends it detects. Their Web site at http://www.cert.org contains a wealth of information. It also contains forms for submitting information on your attack so that others can be made aware of the danger without exposing your organization to undesired publicity. The SANS (System Administration, Networking, and Security) Institute at http://www.sans.org is another excellent source of timely information. They run the Global Incident Analysis Center (GIAC), which provides a rapid-response program wherein new and reemergent attacks are recorded, analyzed, and reported back to the community for immediate action.

Indefensible attacks, such as a distributed denial of service attack flooding our servers or access links with legitimate (but useless) traffic, may require help from our ISPs or their upstream providers. Depending upon the exploit and the real or potential damage, it may also be appropriate to call in law enforcement agencies. However, this requires preplanning if the necessities of preserving evidence for a criminal prosecution are to be met. Besides, many companies prefer to avoid seeking legal remedies due to the potential for adverse publicity.

If the problem is an employee or other inside job, it may be beneficial to bring in computer forensic experts to help find evidence and prepare it for use in a trial. In serious matters of theft or destruction, a report should be filed with police, who can then conduct their own investigation. Do not attempt to do the work of the police. In a criminal action, issues such as warrants and rightful search and seizure become very real, and any failure to follow due process will be exploited by the defense team. Vigilantism may not only allow the criminal to go free but could put you on the losing side of a civil counter suit.

Once the incident is over, perform a post mortem. Take the time to review all the events, actions, and reactions during the incident one more time. Security will always need to evolve and adapt, and hacking incidents can provide impetus to make necessary repairs and changes to defenses and procedures.

In terms of network availability, our primary concern will be denial of service attacks. After all, from the availability perspective, "denial of service" is just another name for "network not available." We will need to be tuned in to the security community so that we can learn of vulnerabilities and close them off before they are exploited against our network. Team members should be assigned to keep track of developments in the security arena. In addition to CERT and SANS, monitoring the BugTraq mailing list should be considered essential. Subscribe by sending an e-mail message to LISTSERV@SECURITYFOCUS.COM with a message body of: SUBSCRIBE BUGTRAQ Lastname, Firstname. Also check for and subscribe to any specialized versions of the BugTraq mailing list that apply to systems in use. For example, there is an NT version of BugTraq as well as manufacturers' mailing lists.

Keeping up to date can be time consuming, so most organizations delegate the responsibility to a small number of individuals. These individuals then are responsible for dissemination of useful information to those affected. Hot items such as newly discovered critical vulnerabilities should be immediately communicated by phone or pager, with follow-up to ensure the message gets through. It can also be challenging to make sure that someone is always staying on top of the latest happenings despite vacations, illness, and job changes.

There needs to be agreement between the security team and the network management team regarding who is responsible for monitoring the network for any signs of attack. This task is independent of the job of monitoring the firewalls, scanning for viruses, and tracking application server performance and security logs. Here we are looking for traffic patterns on the network that look like denial of service attacks and we are monitoring router and switch logs for any evidence of illicit activity.

Intrusion detection systems are becoming a standard part of high availability networks. These tools are available from several vendors and provide varying degrees of sensitivity and accuracy for the task. We can also take advantage of capabilities introduced into the routers and switches to help protect the network from various attacks, such as *ip tcp intercept* on Cisco routers to protect servers from TCP SYN-flood attacks. As always, the goal is to push detection and protection as close to the source of the trouble as possible.

Nor is our concern merely with denial of service attacks. After all, if the security manager pulls the plug on the firewalls to stop a successful hacker from exporting sensitive data to the competition, network access is disrupted for everyone. From the viewpoint of all other users, all network services reached through the firewalls are down. Anything we can do from a network design perspective to make the security team more effective will make our job easier as well.

We always need to keep in mind that security is an ongoing arms race; and just as there is no such thing as an absolutely failure-proof network, there is no such thing as perfect security. Everyone with an insight into network and systems operations needs to be constantly vigilant, looking for any signs of an attack and working together to thwart those detected before they can do harm.

ROUTINE TESTING OF BACKUP FACILITIES

Just as important as monitoring components in operation is detecting when currently idle backup components or communications facilities fail. This means that routine testing is essential for all backup facilities, from uninterruptible power supplies (UPS) to ISDN lines and switched virtual circuits.

Network testing of backup functionality is not limited to dial backup circuits, although those tend to be the most crucial to be tested regularly. The frequency of the testing will depend on the predicted failure rate of the backup function, the availability of the primary provision, and the required overall availability. Daily to weekly testing is usually sufficient for ISDN and analog lines. But other backup facilities also need to be routinely tested. For example, if we're using redundant firewalls with router controlled backup, we should test that all configuration changes made have been correctly duplicated on both firewalls. This is done by disabling one firewall and then the other, and verifying that all routes are correctly switched and that all firewalled applications continue to work properly.

We will frequently be challenged to strike a balance between frequency of testing and the cost of testing. This is particularly true if the test is, or has the potential to be, overly disruptive. For example, testing a UPS by disconnecting it from the power mains is easy, but if the UPS has failed, we have just pulled the plug on whatever devices the UPS was supposed to be protecting. We need to schedule this test at a time when downtime is acceptable (or at least minimally unacceptable) and prepare all systems potentially affected for a power cycle.

In the case of a UPS test, preparation for typical network components like a switch or a router is minimal. But a computer system may need to be shut down so that disk data is not inadvertently corrupted if the power winds up being cycled. Plus there is always the potential when a system is shut down that it will not start up again, further increasing the risk.

Another option is to use systems with redundant power supplies. That way, should the UPS for one power supply fail when tested, the system will continue operating from its redundant supply. Just make sure that the system has truly redundant power supplies first. There are systems with dual power supplies that are not redundant, and loss of a power supply to them will turn off half the box.

Although testing a UPS carries some risk, if we don't test it and unknown to us it has failed, when we need it the impact will be far greater. Unlike in our test scenario, the system will not be properly prepared for power loss. Plus, we will not have the option of resuming operation without the UPS while waiting for repairs or a replacement.

If at all possible, routine tests should be completely automated. This is particularly important for those that must be executed more frequently than once a month, or for those that are complex, time consuming, or otherwise difficult to perform. Without automation, the temptation to skip a test will be extremely hard to resist—especially when no failures have been detected for awhile or there are problems with the primary communications facilities that must be fixed quickly. If the tests are important enough to perform frequently they are important enough for us to ensure that they are executed routinely.

We can often make minor design modifications that dramatically reduce the difficulty of testing. By keeping the need for testing in mind from the very beginning of the design phase, we may be able to make the automation of testing possible where it would not have been so otherwise. This is similar to the impact on application design of starting out with a need to function effectively in a low bandwidth, high-delay environment. Many organizations have been burned by applications designed for a network environment with unlimited bandwidth and negligible delivery delay. These applications may perform phenomenally on an isolated single segment LAN, but slow down dramatically on a busy switched campus LAN—and become unusable when faced with the speed-of-light propagation delays and bandwidth limits of a typical WAN.

CONFIGURATION MANAGEMENT

Maintaining high network availability requires that all network components adequately implement the protocols and functions the network is depending on for proper operation. It also requires that no configuration errors be made that interfere with that operation. This translates into a need for configuration management, both of the process by which the network is designed and of the process by which changes are made to the network. When annual downtime must be limited to minutes or even seconds to reach availability goals, there is no longer room for uncontrolled and untested modifications to the network.

This does not mean that the network will not change and evolve. Change is inevitable in a useful, functional network that is satisfying real needs. If nothing else, the network will need to grow as the business grows, handling more traffic from the same applications as well as expanding to handle new applications. However, those changes must be implemented using a process that minimizes the potential for introducing errors or disrupting service.

Often the hardest task when introducing configuration management is capturing the complete current configuration. We normally would not expect that obtaining router and switch configurations would be a problem—virtually all routers and switches support the ability to copy configurations from the running device to a file server. Even for those few that do not, the configuration can be captured by connecting a computer running a terminal emulation program to the console port of the device, then stepping through the configuration while recording the session.

The challenge tends to be with hardware in stable applications that do not demand routine configuration changes. We may need to find and identify the proper cable required to connect to the console port. Vendors have used everything from standard 25-pin RS-232 connectors and 9-pin PC serial interfaces to 6-pin RJ-11 jacks and custom connectors only used by that vendor on that particular model. Even when the same connector is used on two different devices, we may find that different cables are required due to wiring differences. Depending on the existing documentation, we may also discover that the management password is no longer known (after all, how often do you need to reconfigure a 10BaseT hub?).

The time to locate the appropriate connectors and recover lost passwords is now, not in the panic of a network-down emergency. There should be established locations and procedures for maintaining passwords, product documentation, and infrequently used—but potentially critical—accessories like adapters for connecting a notebook PC to the control port of each device. It is also a good idea to identify a notebook computer or two with the appropriate software loaded to provide working terminal emulation. These will be needed if there are any devices that do not have a permanently attached console terminal.

There may be a terminal server at each equipment location already attached to the console port on each device. But do not neglect the devices that were not considered important enough to have terminal server access to the console port. For example, it is quite common to simply swap out a hub or workgroup switch if there is a hardware failure. These devices do not require any configuration to restore the network to normal operation. However, while users will immediately be back on-line, the device will still need its management module configured so that it can be monitored and maintained without another visit to the location.

Once the configuration of every device is known, the real work of configuration management can begin. Effective configuration management is founded on two critical assumptions:

1. The configuration documentation matches reality.

2. The configuration documentation can be understood.

A common fallacy is to concentrate on the first requirement and neglect the second. It is not enough just to document how a router is configured. How that router is expected to work in the overall design must also be included. In particular, all assumptions made on the behavior and configuration of interacting devices must be clearly identified.

CONFIGURATION DOCUMENTATION MATCHES REALITY

The configuration, once captured, must be maintained every time the network changes. This requires that a process be in place to control all changes. It is not enough to have the network management system poll every router every night and download a fresh copy of its configuration. While this keeps a running record of changes, it does not record any of the reasoning behind the changes or how those changes can be expected to impact network operation or management.

This does not mean that automated tools to track the actual running configurations are not appropriate. The contrary is true; they are extremely valuable, particularly when configured to allow for returning to any previous configuration if needed. However, their main value is as a verification tool to ensure that only planned changes are made—rather than as the primary tool to keep track of those changes.

Since all configuration changes should be designed, reviewed, and tested before installation is even scheduled, the changes detected should be verified against the changes expected to ensure that no mistakes were made. The automated online tool provides a second check to catch errors, just as accountants use double-entry book-keeping to minimize the potential for mistakes to slip by undetected.

CONFIGURATION IS UNDERSTOOD

The more difficult part of good configuration management is documenting the design assumptions behind the configurations that are installed. At one level, this requires documenting such niceties as address assignment policies and standard routing metrics for different link types. While not always formalized, this level of documentation is usually available in organizations that have any formalized documentation.

The challenge comes in documenting all the assumptions made in the currently running design. This is where an access filter that blocks a specific service is documented in terms of the intent of the filter—in addition to its IP address and port number. That way, as applications are modified or their connectivity is changed, the rationale behind the original design is not lost. Less dependence is placed on individuals' recognizing when a configuration modification might conflict with existing operations.

The overall design of the network should be documented, with explanations of such choices as: routing protocols in use, connectivity requirements, addressing schemes, any redistribution of routes, the use of additional capabilities such as DLSw or bridging, protocols and how they're supported, and application support requirements. Any other global requirements on the network—such as third-party service providers, typical traffic flows, expectations of resiliency, and firewall boundaries—should also be included. A clear overview of the functional design and its objectives provides a context for the details of the network design and the configuration of the individual components.

Once the overall design is well documented, every line in every router and switch configuration should be documented with an explanation of why that line is required and how it contributes to the overall design. All parameters left at their default value should also be documented, as defaults have been known to change with new software releases.

This exercise also serves as a reality check, because sometimes designers configure routers by copying an existing configuration without really understanding how it works. While a few extra statements may have no impact on the current configuration, they could conflict with future requirements, leading to confusion and a risk that inappropriate decisions will be made.

In the process of developing this level of configuration documentation, it is common to uncover previously undetected errors and identify desirable enhancements. It is also very common to find remnants left over from services that are no longer in use, access filters that could be implemented more efficiently, and bits and pieces of testing that were used to troubleshoot a problem and not removed after the solution was found.

Rarely do what is implemented and what the design says should be implemented turn out to be identical. Whether the correction should be made to the implementation or to the design documentation will depend upon the discrepancy. Normally, unless the error is one that threatens network stability, the design documentation should be modified to match reality, and the changes required to move to the desired configuration added to the list of modifications to be considered.

MANAGING CONFIGURATION CHANGES

Once we have a documented baseline configuration, we can proceed to maintenance mode and actually manage our configurations. Router configuration changes are no different from other maintenance activities, and all should be managed using a tightly controlled process.

The goal is not to introduce red tape into routine activities, but rather to recognize that any change has the potential to cause problems and must be carefully controlled. This starts with a formal peer review of all desired changes before implementation is scheduled. Any changes that are non-trivial or that add or delete functionality should also be thoroughly tested in a test environment. This will ensure that they work as expected and do not expose undocumented defects in operating system software or the network design.

The normal process is to develop each change as a formal configuration change document. At a minimum, this document should contain the following:

- A brief description of what will be done, who will do it (including contact information), and the reasons for doing it

- The expected impact on the rest of the network and supported applications

- Any known risk factors in the design (particularly if the changes could not be completely tested in a laboratory setting)

- All critical assumptions behind the design, including any capabilities that others might assume to be supported, but that are not part of the design (the non-objectives)

- Implementation instructions with an emphasis on critical sequencing and intermediate tests that can be used to verify correct implementation

- Final test requirements to verify that the change is completely implemented and working as designed

- Procedures to undo all changes and return to the previously working configuration with minimal disruption should problems occur

The change documentation should be reviewed by all parties who may be impacted by the changes before any of the changes proposed are implemented. This review is critical for a number of reasons. It gives others a chance to raise "What if?" and "Did you consider?" questions that can expose errors and oversights before they impact operations. These questions may also uncover superior approaches not thought of by the original designer. The review makes other parties aware of the changes being made so that they can be on the lookout for unexpected side effects.

This can dramatically reduce the troubleshooting time required. By involving those potentially affected—so they understand what has changed and how the changes are supposed to work—the review also reduces the tendency to automatically credit any network or application failures to the recent changes.

Care must be taken that the configuration change process, with its accompanying documentation, continues to function as a quality control mechanism. It should not be viewed and executed as an obstacle to getting the job done. The goal of the review process must be to maximize the probability of successful change by finding and correcting errors and oversights before they impact network operation. This means that reviewers must take their role seriously and spend the time required to completely understand any proposed changes and their potential impact on the network and the applications supported.

Another major obstacle to success in configuration management is the need for adequate verification testing. Few organizations have formal, automated test plans that can quickly and non-disruptively determine whether all critical functions are still working correctly. We want to avoid the scenario in which we implement a change, test that the change enables the desired new functionality, and only later discover that previously working systems are failing because of the change. Not only does this impact functional availability, but the subsequent emergency repairs are likely to introduce further errors and other undesirable side effects.

Finally, once the configuration change is implemented and tested, the master documentation should be updated to reflect all changes made both to the individual configurations and to the overall design. The changes should be part of the original configuration change documentation, but there may be corrections required that were not caught in the laboratory test or peer review stages.

There is a strong temptation to short cut this final step and merely file the individual change documents with the original design. The problem with this approach is that the current design soon becomes distributed across a large number of documents and it becomes increasingly difficult to determine exactly what is in place and how all the pieces fit together.

RECOVERING FROM EMERGENCY REPAIR EFFORTS

Sometimes we do not have the luxury of making changes as part of a controlled process. This usually happens when an emergency repair is triggered by the discovery of a software defect, security weakness, or design error that has a major impact on network viability. In these situations, it may be necessary to fix first and document later.

The key is to follow the normal configuration change process, with the exception of the timing of the changes already implemented. This is critical, as there are often better ways to resolve the weaknesses that only come to light when there is time to reflect on the overall design and requirements. It is also essential to test the changes that have been made to ensure that other services or functions were not impaired in the process of responding to the emergency.

Executing the configuration change process for changes already implemented does more than just update the documentation. It provides an opportunity to learn from the experience, consider other potential manifestations of the same or similar problems, and look for ways to improve process or testing to avoid repeat occurrences. It also allows us to verify the correctness of the changes made and back out any unnecessary changes remaining as part of the emergency repairs.

TOTAL QUALITY CONTROL

Maximizing network availability ultimately requires applying the principles of total quality control. The first level of availability improvement comes from using reliable components and eliminating single points of failure. The second level comes from maximizing the availability of the components and links we cannot control, by minimizing the time required to detect and repair failures through close monitoring and predictive analysis.

As the network components and design become more reliable, we need to improve availability by detecting failures before they occur. In many cases this is not as impossible as it sounds. For example, many classes of communications link failure can often be predicted on the basis of deteriorating bit error rates. This will not protect us from a cable cut by a construction crew, but it will avoid unnecessary downtime by allowing us to dispatch repair efforts before the line degrades to the point of disrupting service.

Routine monitoring of link performance can have other benefits as well. If we take the time and effort to collect and analyze detailed records, we may start to see patterns in the data. Higher error rates after heavy rains could indicate that an underground cable is flooding, increasing the probability of failure if the cable is left unrepaired. Duplication of error patterns in supposedly independent links indicates that the links may share a common failure mode, a situation that must be tracked down and fixed if we are depending upon the affected lines to back each other up.

What we are doing is using the routine variations in everyday performance to help us see failure modes before they become visible to our network management monitors. Note that to do so, we need to have the tools in place not only to measure these parameters, but also to collect and analyze the data in a productive way. Most important, we need to take the time to look at what we have and develop an understanding of what it means. We can usually divide our analysis into two modes—design verification and error analysis.

DESIGN VERIFICATION

As we continue to refine component reliability, predictive failure analysis, and network monitoring, our next critical challenge becomes one of ensuring design correctness. Design errors have the potential to cause massive downtime. Except in the most rigorous of design environments, in which alternate paths are designed by different teams using completely different hardware and software, the network design can be a single point of failure affecting the entire network. A single error, such as incorrect redistribution of routes between protocols, resulting in a routing loop, could cause a widespread inability to communicate and unacceptable downtime.

The challenge with design errors is that they do not always affect normal operation. An error that prevents proper recovery from a specific failure mode will not be noticed until that failure scenario occurs. An error that renders the network unstable given a specific combination or sequence of events could take down the entire network without warning.

Total quality control means verifying that the network is functioning as designed at all levels. This means looking at the routing tables to verify that the routes being used match what we think the optimal routes should be, that all critical EIGRP routes have the expected feasible successors, that OSPF is selecting the desired designated router on each LAN, that the correct routes are being advertised and selected by BGP, that each interface has the correct neighbor relationships active, and so on. It means checking each box to ensure that line utilization levels are as expected, the CPU loading on the processors is where it belongs, and memory consumption is correct.

Note that it is not sufficient to merely check that CPU and memory utilization are at acceptable levels. If we really understand our design (and that is essential if we are to safely make changes in the future), we should be able to predict the normal and peak loads on each router, the CPU loading and memory utilization under those conditions, the number of routes in the routing table, load sharing percentages on parallel links, traffic levels, and all other aspects of operation.

The key is that the network should be predictable, as should its response to various traffic loads, failure modes, and other stimuli. As we refine our understanding, we can apply that knowledge to improve our models of network operations, and then apply those models to other-than-normal conditions. We do not want to wait until a major failure occurs to discover that a key location can't handle the load required to continue service uninterrupted.

Our ultimate goal is to refine our network design to eliminate the need for emergency repairs, regardless of the mode of failure. While perfection is impossible to achieve in real life—particularly when we're faced with resource constraints— there is always room for improvement. As we push availability to higher and higher levels, we lose the luxury of waiting for failures to occur before we react.

ERROR ANALYSIS

The other key aspect of total quality control is to follow up on every failure detected to verify that the network response was correct. Any incident that is not routine should be investigated to determine what happened, what caused the event, and the appropriateness of the network response. In this way, we take advantage of each incident and use it as a test of network correctness.

In many ways, we are really defining an attitude toward the unknown. Whenever something out of the ordinary occurs, rather than trying to explain it away, we try to learn from the event. We use the glitches that occur in day-to-day operations to further test the correctness of our network design and identify additional improvements that may be possible.

Consequently, every failure drives multiple processes. First of all, it triggers an immediate response to fix the failure (assuming it is not self correcting). Second, it triggers an investigation of the network's response to the failure, verifying that the network design is correctly handling this failure and will properly handle others of the same nature.

Third, any failure that does not require an immediate repair response should be analyzed to determine whether a future repair response may be needed. For example, a leased line that drops for a few seconds and then returns to operation is probably all right and just needs to be watched. (The drop could have been a side effect of other repairs within the service provider's network.) But if the leased line starts to fail repeatedly for brief periods, complete failure in the near future is probable. We should start working right away to get it repaired.

Finally, we seek to determine why the failure occurred, with the objective of preventing the same failure from occurring elsewhere (or recurring here). This can be particularly valuable if the cause is one that can affect entire classes of components, as our predicted availability is predicated on all failures being independent. Any indication of a common failure mechanism should be analyzed and appropriate protective action taken.

WRAP-UP

Networks can be designed to be very reliable and highly resilient in response to those failures that do occur—all it takes is time and effort. But the job is just beginning when the network is installed. It takes continuous effort to keep the design functioning properly so that all the assumptions of MTTR and MTBF remain valid. Effective network management requires a substantial and continuous investment not only in equipment and software, but also in personnel. From the frontline network administrators—who must be skilled enough to use their tools effectively—to the network designers—who must integrate effective and efficient management into their designs—network management is part of everyone's job. This includes upper management, who need to recognize the payoff from good network management and ensure that the support is in place to make it happen.

Consequently, successful network management implementations usually include not only the technical activities required to keep the network functioning, but also the recording and reporting tools needed to clearly document how the investment in network design and management is paying off. There is nothing like a chart of all the downtime that did not occur (and the downtime that did occur but could have been avoided if better processes, tools, and training had been available) to provide ammunition for the perpetual battle for budgetary funds and upper-management support.

Glossary

1Base5—IEEE 802.3 StarLAN, 1 Mbps over unshielded twisted pair.

2B+D—*See* Basic Rate Interface (BRI).

10Base2—IEEE 802.3 CheaperNet, 10 Mbps over low-cost coaxial cable.

10Base5—IEEE 802.3 Ethernet, 10 Mbps over baseband coaxial cable.

10BaseF—IEEE 802.3 standard for 10 Mbps over multimode fiber optic cable.

10BaseT—IEEE 802.3 standard for Mbps over unshielded twisted-pair cable.

10Broad36—IEEE 802.3 standard for 10 Mbps over broadband cable systems.

23B+D—*See* Primary Rate Interface.

24×7—24 hours a day, 7 days a week.

30B+D—*See* Primary Rate Interface (PRI).

100BaseF—IEEE 802.3 standard for 100 Mbps over multimode fiber.

100BaseT—IEEE 802.3 standard for 100 Mbps over unshielded twisted-pair.

802—*See* IEEE 802.

1000BaseT—IEEE 802.3 standard for 1 Gbps over unshielded twisted-pair.

AAA—Authentication, Authorization, and Accounting.

AAL—ATM Adaptation Layer.

ABR—*See* Area Border Router (OSPF) or Available Bit Rate (ATM).

Access Control List (ACL)—Rules for packet filters that define which packets to pass and which to block.

Access Server—Router or other communications processor that connects asynchronous devices to a LAN or WAN through network or terminal emulation software.

Acknowledgment (ACK)—An indication that a "message" was received without error.

ACK—*See* Acknowledgment (ACK).

ACL—*See* Access Control List (ACL).

Address—A coded representation of the origin or destination of data.

Address Resolution Protocol (ARP)—Internet standard protocol used to map an IP address to a MAC address on a LAN (RFC 826).

Addressing—Specifying the source and/or destination.

Adjacent—Nodes that can communicate directly over a physical channel.

Administrative Distance—Cisco router parameter defining the trustworthiness of a routing information source. It is expressed as a numerical value between 0 and 255, where the higher the value, the lower the trustworthiness rating.

ADSL—*See* Asymmetric Digital Subscriber Line (ADSL).

AGREE—Advisory Group for the Reliability of Electronic Equipment.

Aggregate Bandwidth—The total bandwidth of a channel carrying a multiplexed data stream.

Analog—Signal encoding by means of continuously variable physical quantities.

Analog Channel—Communications path that uses analog signaling.

Application Layer—The top layer of the ISO OSI reference model where services useful to user applications are provided.

Application-Level Firewall—A firewall system in which service is provided by processes that maintain complete TCP connection state and sequencing.

Area—Logical set of network segments and their attached devices whose detailed internal connectivity is hidden from outside view to reduce routing complexity in networks routed by IS-IS or OSPF.

Area Border Router (ABR)—Router located on the border of one or more OSPF areas that connects those areas to the backbone network. ABRs are considered members of both the OSPF backbone and the attached areas.

ARP—*See* Address Resolution Protocol (ARP).

ARPANET—Advanced Research Projects Agency Network. Landmark packet-switching network established in 1969 that evolved into the Internet we know today.

AS—*See* Autonomous System (AS).

ASBR—*See* Autonomous System Boundary Router (ASBR).

ASCII—American Standard Code for Information Interchange.

ASN—*See* Autonomous System Number (ASN).

ASN.1—Abstract Syntax Notation One.

Asymmetric Digital Subscriber Line (ADSL)—DSL technology designed to deliver more bandwidth downstream (from the central office to the customer site) than upstream.

Downstream rates range from 1.5 to 9 Mbps, while upstream bandwidth ranges from 16 to 640 Kbps at distances up to 18,000 feet over a single copper twisted-pair cable.

Async—*See* Asynchronous Transmission.

Asynchronous Transfer Mode (ATM)—A connection-oriented high-speed network technology based on switching very small (48-octet payload) frames called cells.

Asynchronous Transmission—Having an arbitrary time between characters, with each character individually framed by a start bit and one to two stop bits. Popular for low-cost communications on PCs and workstations.

ATM—*See* Asynchronous Transfer Mode (ATM).

ATM Forum—International organization formed to speed the acceptance of ATM by providing timely interoperability specifications.

Authentication—The process of determining the identity of a user who is attempting to access a system.

Authorization—The process of determining what types of activities are permitted for a particular user.

Autonomous System (AS)—IP network sharing a common routing policy.

Autonomous System Boundary Router (ASBR)—An OSPF router located between an OSPF autonomous system and another network. ASBRs run both OSPF and the routing protocol of the other network, usually BGP4.

Autonomous System Number (ASN)—Globally unique ID used to identify a specific autonomous system in interdomain routing.

Availability—The percentage of time a device or service is functional over a measurement interval.

Available Bit Rate (ABR)—ATM network service category providing best-effort services for use by connections that do not require guarantees in terms of cell loss or delay (ATM Forum).

B-Channel—ISDN 64-Kbps full-duplex communications channel for user traffic in the form of digitized voice or a digital data stream.

Backbone—A network used to connect other networks.

Backup Interface—Cisco command name for the dial backup function that places a call because a specific router interface has gone down.

Backward Explicit Congestion Notification (BECN)—Indicator set by a Frame Relay network to inform the destination DTE that congestion is being experienced in the path from the destination back to the source. *See* also Forward Explicit Congestion Notification (FECN).

Bandwidth—The information capacity of a channel. For a digital channel, bandwidth is defined in bits/second. For an analog channel, it is dependent on the type and method of modulation.

Baseband—Transmission of a signal at its original frequency, without modulation.

Baselining—Setting initial network performance/traffic parameters against which subsequent parameters will be measured.

Basic Encoding Rules (BER)—Protocol for translating ASN.1 into an octet stream for transmission.

Basic Rate Interface (BRI)—Standard ISDN service providing two 64-Kbps bearer channels for voice or data and one 16-Kbps channel for low-speed data and signaling. Also referred to as 2B+D.

Bastion Host—A system that has been hardened to resist attack and installed in such a position on a network that it is expected to come under attack.

Bathtub Curve—Hardware failure probability characterized by a long period of reliable operation bounded by high failure rates during initial infant mortality and final wear out phases.

Baud Rate—The number of discrete conditions or signal events per second (not necessarily the same as bits per second).

Bc—*See* Committed Burst (Bc).

Be—*See* Excess Burst (Be).

BECN—*See* Backward Explicit Congestion Notification (BECN).

BER—*See* Bit Error Rate (BER) and Basic Encoding Rules (BER).

BGP—*See* Border Gateway Protocol (BGP).

BGP4—BGP Version 4. *See* Border Gateway Protocol (BGP).

Binary Exponential Backoff—Algorithm used to reschedule transmissions after an Ethernet collision.

Bit—A binary unit of information that can have a value of either zero or one (contraction of *binary digit*).

Bit Error Rate (BER)—Ratio of the number of bits received in error to the total number of bits sent.

Bit Transfer Rate—The number of bits transferred per unit of time.

Black Hole—An area or device in a network that packets may enter but from which they never emerge. Usually due to misconfiguration of a router or other device, but may also be caused by failure of a routing protocol to converge after a topology change, creating a routing loop.

BONDING—Bandwidth ON Demand INteroperability Group. A method for combining multiple B-channels into a single data channel.

BootP—Boot Protocol. A simple protocol used by diskless workstations to determine configuration parameters.

Border Gateway Protocol (BGP)—Internet standard interdomain routing protocol that replaced EGP. Version 4, supporting CIDR and other enhancements, is the preferred interdomain routing protocol for use on the Internet (RFC 1771).

Bps—Bits per second. A common convention is to use lower case, *bps,* for bits per second and upper case, *Bps,* for bytes per second, but not everyone follows it.

BRI—*See* Basic Rate Interface (BRI).

Bridge—Device used to connect segments of a LAN at the Data Link level.

Broadcast—Transmission of a message to all addresses.

Broadcast and Unknown Server (BUS)—Part of LANE that handles all MAC level broadcasts and multicasts, and the first unicast.

Browser—Hypertext client application, such as Microsoft Internet Explorer or Netscape Navigator, used to access hypertext documents and other services located on the WWW or Intranet servers.

Buffer—A block of memory for temporary storage.

Bug—Euphemism for a software defect.

Burn-in—Hardware device stressing intended to expose infant mortality failures before a device is placed into service.

Burst Errors—Several sequential bits in error.

Bus—A shared communications channel.

BUS—*See* Broadcast and Unknown Server.

Byte—Technically, the smallest addressable unit of data in a machine architecture, but commonly used as a synonym for *octet,* an 8-bit unit of data.

Cable—A transmission medium consisting of one or more conductors or optical fibers within a protective sheath.

Caching—Keeping information learned from a previous transaction for use in later transactions.

Caller ID—POTS service that delivers the telephone number of the calling telephone to the called party.

Calling ID—ISDN service that delivers the directory number of the calling station to the called station.

Campus—A group of buildings—a university campus, business office park, or collection of buildings—that reside in relatively close proximity to one another.

Carrier Sense Multiple Access—Listening before sending on a shared medium.

Carrier Signal—The underlying frequency that is modulated to carry information.

Category *X*—Grades of UTP cabling. Category 1 through Category 5 are described in the EIA-568 standard. The higher the number, the higher the data rate supported.

For example, ISDN requires Category 1, 10BaseT requires Category 3, and 100BaseT requires Category 5.

CBR—*See* Constant Bit Rate (CBR).

CCIE—Cisco Certified Internetwork Expert.

CCITT—International Consultative Committee on Telegraph and Telephony (Comité Consultatif Internationale de Télégraphique et Téléphonique) which is the predecessor of the International Telecommunications Union-Telecommunications Standardization Sector.

CDP—*See* Cisco Discovery Protocol (CDP).

CEF—*See* Cisco Express Forwarding (CEF).

Cell—Fixed length unit of information in an ATM network, consisting of a 48-octet payload and a 5-octet header.

Cell Relay—Network technology based on the use of small, fixed-size packets called cells. Because all cells are the same length, they can be processed and switched in hardware at high speeds. Cell relay is the basis for ATM, IEEE 802.6, and SMDS.

Central Office (CO)—The telephone company's local facility that provides telephone service for an area. It is the termination point of the telephone company's end of local loops.

CEPT1—*See* E1.

Challenge Handshake Authentication Protocol (CHAP)—Standard security protocol for PPP applications used to identify the remote end of the link (RFC 1994).

Channel—A path along which signals can be sent.

Channel Service Unit (CSU)—Interface for digital lines that provides line conditioning and loopback testing. Usually combined with a Data Service Unit (DSU).

CHAP—See Challenge Handshake Authentication Protocol (CHAP).

Character—A transmission symbol (usually 7 or 8 bits).

Chargen—Character generator service for TCP/IP that responds to a TCP connection request with a continuous stream of printable characters.

Chat Script—Cisco name for a command response sequence used to communicate with a modem.

Checksum—A form of error check.

Choke Packet—A flow/congestion control mechanism.

CIDR—*See* Classless InterDomain Routing (CIDR).

CIR—*See* Committed Information Rate (CIR).

Circuit-Switching—Providing a fixed path for messages.

Cisco Discovery Protocol (CDP)—Proprietary link level protocol that runs by default on all Cisco routers and switches to determine the identity of neighboring Cisco devices.

Cisco Express Forwarding (CEF)—Cisco name for a router operating mode that allows many functions commonly performed at process level to be handled at interrupt level.

Class of Service (CoS)—Indication of how an upper-layer protocol requests a lower-layer protocol to handle its messages.

Classless Interdomain Routing (CIDR)—Internet IP addressing plan that eliminates the concept of Class A, Class B, etc. Instead, IP addresses and their subnet masks are written as 4 octets, separated by periods, and followed by a forward slash and a 2-digit number that represents the subnet mask (RFC 1519).

Clear—To close a connection.

CLNS (also CL NS)—ISO ConnectionLess Network Service.

Close—To terminate a connection.

CO—*See* Central Office (CO).

Coaxial Cable—A cable consisting of one conductor surrounded by an insulated shield.

Collision—When two systems send at the same time.

Committed Burst (Bc)—The amount of data (in bits) that a Frame Relay network is committed to accept and transmit at the CIR. This parameter determines the time interval over which the CIR is averaged. Frames that exceed the Committed Burst may be marked Discard Eligible (DE).

Committed Information Rate (CIR)—Maximum average data rate at which a Frame Relay network agrees to transfer information under normal conditions.

Communications—The transfer of information between the origin and receiver.

Conduit—A defined path through a firewall to permit a specific traffic exchange.

Congestion Control—Any mechanism for relieving excess traffic in the network.

Connection—A logical relationship between two end points.

Connectionless—Message transmission without establishing a logical relationship first.

Connection-Oriented—Message transmission requiring establishing a logical relationship first; often (incorrectly) used to describe sequenced, error-free delivery.

Connectivity—A characteristic of systems meaning that they have the ability to pass data from one to the other.

Constant Bit Rate (CBR)—ATM network service category providing a guaranteed rate to transport services such as voice or video.

Contention—An attempt by two or more devices to gain control of a shared communications channel at the same time.

Convergence—Reaching agreement on what paths to use for routing through a network across all routing devices running a specific routing protocol after a change in the network topology.

Coordinated Universal Time (UTC)—International standard for time specifications, formerly called Greenwich Mean Time (GMT).

CRC—*See* Cyclic Redundancy Check (CRC).

Cryptographic—Security protection by encryption.

CSMA—*See* Carrier Sense Multiple Access (CSMA).

CSMA/CA—CSMA with Collision Avoidance.

CSMA/CD—CSMA with Collision Detection (used by Ethernet and IEEE 802.3).

CSU—*See* Channel Service Unit (CSU).

Cut-Through Switching—Switching approach that starts sending the incoming frame or packet out the outgoing port while it is still arriving on the incoming port, reducing the delays inherent in store-and-forward switching.

Cyclic Redundancy Check (CRC)—An error checking method commonly used in Data Link layer protocols.

D-Channel—Signalling channel on an ISDN interface that may be 16 Kbps (on a BRI) or 64 Kbps (on a PRI).

Data Circuit-Terminating Equipment (DCE)—The functional unit of a data station that establishes, maintains, and releases connections and otherwise interfaces data terminal equipment to a data transmission line (ITU-T).

Data Compression—A way of reducing the number of bits required to represent digital information; may or may not be lossless (where the uncompressed data are identical to the starting data).

Datagram—A unit of data that is handled in the network independent of any units that may have come before or that may come after it between the same end systems.

Data Link—A logical connection between two stations on the same circuit.

Data Link Connection Identifier (DLCI)—Logical index used in the Data Link protocol header to identify a particular end-to-end virtual circuit at the DTE/DCE interface of a Frame Relay network.

Data Link Layer—Layer two of the OSI reference model, responsible for node-to-node communications between adjacent nodes.

Data Service Unit (DSU)—Interface to attach Digital Terminal Equipment (DTE) to a public network. Usually combined with a Channel Service Unit (CSU).

Data Terminal Equipment (DTE)—Subscriber equipment that serves as a message source or message sink (ITU-T).

Data Units—*See* Protocol Data Unit (PDU).

Daytime—Test service for TCP/IP that responds to a TCP connection request or UDP query with a text string giving the date and time on the local system.

DCE—*See* Data Circuit-Terminating Equipment (DCE).

DDR—*See* Dial-on-Demand Routing (DDR).

DE—*See* Discard Eligible (DE).

Deadlock—Two processes (or more) not being able to progress because each holds resources required by the other and is waiting to finish before releasing those resources already acquired.

DECnet—Legacy network architecture developed by Digital Equipment Corporation (DEC).

Default Route—Path that is used for packets being routed toward a destination address not in the routing table.

Demarc—The demarcation point that signifies where the telephone company's wiring stops and the user's wiring starts.

Demilitarized Zone (DMZ)—Network behind a firewall where publicly accessible services are provided to users on the Internet.

Demodulation—Reconstructing information content from a modulated signal.

Denial-of-Service Attack—An intrusion in which a server or other devices is purposely overwhelmed or corrupted to the point where its operations are degraded or stopped altogether.

Designated Bridge—The TST bridge that is chosen to carry all traffic because it has the lowest path cost for forwarding a frame from a segment to the root bridge.

Designated Router—The router selected to generate LSAs for a multiaccess network (which also implies other responsibilities) when running OSPF.

DF—Do Not Fragment flag on an IP packet indicating the packet must not be fragmented.

DHCP—*See* Dynamic Host Configuration Protocol (DHCP).

Dial Backup—The backup of a network link through a dial-up connection.

Dial-on-Demand—Dial-up connections that are brought up and dropped as required to satisfy traffic demands.

Dial-on-Demand Routing (DDR)—Cisco's implementation of dial-on-demand in which the router spoofs keepalives so that end stations do not see the impact of the link being dropped when not needed for real traffic.

Dialer watch—Cisco command name for the dial backup function that places a backup call based on the absence of a specific address from the router's local routing table.

Diffusing Update Algorithm (DUAL)—A modified distance-vector routing algorithm providing immediate access to available alternate routes under certain conditions; used by Cisco's EIGRP protocol.

Digital—The use of a discrete code to represent information; compare with Analog.

Direct Memory Access (DMA)—Technique for transferring data within a computing system that bypasses handling by the central processing unit.

Directory Services (DS)—Network system function to provide required addressing given a global name.

Discard—Test service for TCP/IP that accepts TCP connections and UDP packets and discards them.

Discard Eligible (DE)—Frame Relay indication that the sender is exceeding the committed information rate on the PVC and frame loss may occur.

Distance-Vector—Class of routing algorithms that exchanges distance metrics to all known destinations with adjacent routers to find the shortest-path. Distance vector routing algorithms can be prone to routing loops but are computationally simpler than link-state routing algorithms.

DLC—Data Link Control.

DLCI—*See* Data Link Connection Identifier (DLCI).

DLSw—Data Link Switching. Standard protocol for forwarding SNA and NetBIOS traffic over TCP/IP networks using Data Link layer switching and encapsulation (RFC 1434).

DMZ—*See* Demilitarized Zone (DMZ).

DNS—*See* Domain Name System (DNS).

Domain—The physical devices and resources under the control of a network management entity.

Domain Name System (DNS)—Hierarchical directory services standard used to provide human readable names for IP addresses (RFC 1035).

DS1—North American digital signaling protocol multiplexing 24 64-Kbps bearer channels and an 8-Kbps control channel into a 1.544-Mbps data stream.

DS3—North American standard for data transmission at 44.736 Mbps; equivalent to 28 T1 links.

DSL—Digital Subscriber Line. Public network technology that delivers high bandwidth over conventional copper wiring at limited distances. *See also* Asymmetric Digital Subscriber Line (ADSL), High-Data-Rate Digital Subscriber Line (HDSL), ISDN

Digital Subscriber Line (IDSL), Single-Line Digital Subscriber Lane (SDSL), and Very-High-Data-Rate Digital Subscriber Line (VDSL) for more on the variations available.

DTE—*See* Data Terminal Equipment (DTE).

DUAL—*See* Diffusing Update ALgorithm (DUAL).

Dual Homing—Attaching a device to a network by way of two independent access points. *See also* Multihomed Host. The concept also applies to organizations connecting to multiple ISPs and is not restricted to only a single end-system.

Duplex Transmission—Data transmission over a circuit capable of transmitting in both directions at the same time.

Duplicate—A (usually unintended) second copy of a protocol data unit.

Dynamic Host Configuration Protocol (DHCP)—Standard for allocating IP addresses dynamically so that addresses can be reused when hosts no longer need them (RFC 2131).

Dynamic Routing—Using routing protocols that adjust automatically to network topology changes; also called *adaptive routing*. Contrast to routing based on static routes.

E1—The European standard for multiplexing 32 64-Kbps channels (30 for voice data, 1 for signaling, and 1 for framing and maintenance) into a 2.048-Mbps data stream. Also known as *CEPT1*.

E3—Wide-area digital transmission scheme used predominantly in Europe that carries data at a rate of 34.368 Mbps.

E-Commerce—Electronic Commerce.

EBGP—*See* Exterior BGP.

Echo—Test service for TCP/IP that accepts TCP connections and UDP packets and returns their content to the sender.

EFCI—*See* Explicit Forward Congestion Indication (EFCI).

EGP—*See* Exterior Gateway Protocol (EGP).

EIA—Electronic Industries Association.

EIA 568—Standard that describes the characteristics and applications for various grades of UTP cabling.

EIGRP—*See* Enhanced Interior Gateway Routing Protocol (EIGRP).

Encapsulation—Wrapping of data in a particular protocol header; often associated with tunneling.

Encryption—Making data unreadable except by those authorized to receive it.

End-System (ES)—A node on a network that is the source or destination of a communications. Note that an intermediate system is also an end-system from the viewpoint of traffic that terminates on the intermediate system, such as queries from a network management system.

End User—The source or destination of data sent through a network.

Enhanced Interior Gateway Routing Protocol (EIGRP)—Cisco proprietary distance-vector routing algorithm using a distributed update algorithm to reduce overhead and speed convergence without sacrificing stability.

Entity—An abstract or concrete thing in the universe of discourse (ITU-T).

Error—One or more bits of a message being wrong.

Error Control—The part of a protocol controlling the detection, and sometimes the correction, of errors. *See also* Error Correction and Error Recovery.

Error Correction—Encoding of information so that the original value can be restored despite errors in transmission by the receiving system; also called *Forward Error Correction*.

Error Recovery—Protocol function that corrects flawed transmissions by retransmitting the data.

ES—*See* End-System (ES).

ES-IS—End-System-to-Intermediate System.

Ethernet—A LAN standard for CSMA/CD networks. The term is also commonly used to refer to IEEE 802.3 networks, even though they are different standards.

Excess Burst—The number of bits that a Frame Relay network will attempt to transmit in excess of the Committed Burst. Frames that exceed the Excess Burst value may be discarded immediately by the DCE.

Exchange—*See* Central Office (CO).

Exchange Identification (XID)—Request and response packets exchanged by SNA devices prior to establishing a session.

Explicit Forward Congestion Indication (EFCI)—In ATM, one of the congestion feedback modes allowed by ABR service.

Explorer Frame—Frame sent out by an end-system in a source route bridged environment to determine a route to another end system.

Exterior BGP—BGP routing between different autonomous systems, where BGP is being used as an Exterior Gateway Protocol (EGP) for interdomain routing.

Exterior Gateway Protocol (EGP)—General Internet term for an interdomain routing protocol and the name of an obsolete protocol for exchanging routing information between autonomous systems (RFC 904).

Failover—To switch from a failed hardware/software component to a working component.

FAQ—Frequently Asked Questions.

Fast Ethernet—Any of a number of 100-Mbps Ethernet-like specifications offering a speed 10 times that of 10BaseT while preserving such qualities as frame format, MAC mechanisms, and MTU for backwards compatibility.

Fast-Switching—Cisco router mode of operation in which a route cache is used so that the router CPU needs to handle only the first packet in any stream going to a specific destination.

Fault Tolerant—Able to continue operation despite failure of some individual components.

FCC—Federal Communications Commission. The U.S. regulatory agency for communications providers.

FCS—*See* Frame Check Sequence (FCS).

FD—*See* Feasible Distance (FD).

FDDI—*See* Fiber Distributed Data Interface (FDDI).

Feasible Distance (FD)—Route metric value that determines if an alternate EIGRP-determined path can be considered a feasible successor. The distance from the neighbor to the destination must be less than the feasible distance for the neighbor to be a feasible successor for that destination.

Feasible Successor—Next hop for an EIGRP-determined path to a destination that, while not currently the optimal path, can be used if needed without fear of introducing a routing loop. *See also* Feasible Distance (FD).

FECN—*See* Forward Explicit Congestion Notification (FECN).

FEP—*See* Front End Processor (FEP).

Fiber Distributed Data Interface (FDDI)—A 100-Mbps ring network specification frequently used with fiber optic cabling but capable of supporting copper cable as well.

Fiber Optics (FO)—An alternative medium for communications that uses optical rather than electrical signals.

File Transfer Protocol (FTP)—Internet standard protocol for transferring files from one machine to another (RFC 959).

Finger—Software tool and standard protocol for determining whether a person has an account on a TCP/IP host (RFC 1288).

Firewall—A hardware/software barrier that protects networks from traffic on connected networks. Firewalls can serve a range of security purposes.

Flag—A character that indicates the occurrence of some condition, or the indicator that identifies the start or end of a frame in bit-oriented link protocols.

Flapping—Routing problem in which an advertised route between two nodes alternates (flaps) back and forth between two paths due to a network problem that causes intermittent interface failures.

Flat Addressing—Addressing scheme in which there is no useful relationship between the address and the location of the destination to simplify routing. IEEE 802 MAC addresses are an example of a flat-addressing scheme.

Floating Static Route—A static route that is only activated if no route is available to a destination subnetwork from a preferred source.

Flooding—Routing by sending out on all paths.

Flow Control—Procedure for regulating the flow of data between two points.

Foreign Exchange—Provision of telephone service at one central office of services (usually a local phone number) provided by another central office.

Forward Error Correction—*See* Error Correction.

Forward Explicit Congestion Notification (FECN)—Indicator set by a Frame Relay network to inform the destination DTE that congestion was experienced in the path from source to destination. *See also* Backward Explicit Congestion Notification (BECN).

Fragmentation—Splitting a message into pieces.

Frame—Common name for a Link layer PDU, the unit of information at the Data Link layer.

Frame Check Sequence (FCS)—The error check on a frame.

Frame Relay—ITU-T standard network service interface providing virtual circuits at the Data Link layer between connected devices.

Front End Processor (FEP)—Device or board that provides network interface capabilities for a networked device; in IBM SNA networks, a PU 4, typically an IBM 37xx.

FTP—*See* File Transfer Protocol (FTP).

Full Duplex—Capable of simultaneous transmission in both directions on a connection.

Functional Availability—Measure of the availability of particular functions where the impact of failure is scaled by the number of systems affected.

Gateway—Protocol Conversion Gateway (OSI RM) or an IP router.

Gbps—Gigabits per second; one billion (1,000,000,000) bits per second.

Generic Routing Encapsulation (GRE)—Internet standard protocol for carrying packets of an arbitrary network protocol in the packets of another arbitrary network protocol (RFC 2784).

Get Nearest Server (GNS)—Request packet sent by a client on an IPX network to locate the nearest active server of a particular type.

GNS—*See* Get Nearest Server (GNS).

GRE—*See* Generic Routing Encapsulation (GRE).

Half Duplex—Two-way communications through a channel that supports transmission in only one direction at a time. *See also* Simplex *and* Duplex.

Handshaking—Exchange of predetermined signals during communications to synchronize states or parameters.

Hardware Address—*See* MAC Address.

HDLC—*See* High-Level Data Link Control (HDLC).

HDSL—*See* High-Data-Rate Digital Subscriber Line (HDSL).

Header—The control portion at the start of a message.

Hello Packet—Packet transmitted to determine if a link is still alive, usually by a routing protocol to neighboring routers.

Hierarchical Addressing—Scheme of addressing that uses a logical hierarchy to determine location. For example, IP addresses consist of network numbers, subnet numbers, and host numbers.

Hierarchical Routing—The complex problem of routing on large networks can be simplified by reducing the size of the networks by breaking a network into a hierarchy of networks in which each level is responsible for its own routing.

High Availability—Describes the ability of computers, networks, and applications to maintain operations with minimal downtime. Implies a system designed with multiple redundant components that can continue to operate even when a failure exists in the system and/or is implemented with components with higher than average reliability; should always be quantified when used in a product or procurement specification. *See also* Availability *and* Reliability.

High-Data-Rate Digital Subscriber Line (HDSL)—DSL technology delivering 1.544 Mbps of bandwidth each way over two copper-twisted pairs at distances up to 12,000 feet.

High-Level Data Link Control (HDLC)—An ISO link-layer protocol that forms the basis for many other link-level protocols including 802.2, LAPB (X.25), LAPD (ISDN), and PPP.

Hit—A transient disturbance to a communications medium.

Holddown—State into which a route is placed so that routers will neither advertise the route nor accept advertisements about the route for a specific length of time. Holddown is used to allow old routing information to expire from all routers in the network before calculating a new path.

Hop—Forwarding of a data packet from one network node to another.

Host—Computer system on a network. Similar to a node, except that the host usually implies a computer system, whereas node generally applies to any networked system, including access servers and routers; *See also* Host Computer.

Host-Based Security—The technique of securing an individual system from attack.

Host Computer—A computer primarily providing services such as computation or database access.

Host Number—The part of an IP address that designates which node on the subnetwork is being addressed; also called a *host address*.

Host-to-Host Protocol—End-to-end (OSI RM Transport layer or above) protocol.

Hot Standby Router Protocol (HSRP)—Cisco-developed protocol that allows one router to take over the duties of another. Described in RFC 2281.

Hot Swapping—The act of replacing hardware modules without powering down active equipment or processes.

HSRP—*See* Hot Standby Router Protocol (HSRP).

HTML—*See* Hypertext Markup Language (HTML).

HTTP—*See* Hypertext Transfer Protocol (HTTP).

Hub—Any device that serves as the center of a star-topology network, or in IEEE 802.3 and Ethernet, a multiport repeater (sometimes called a *concentrator*).

Hypertext Markup Language (HTML)—Standard document formatting language that uses tags to indicate how a given part of a document should be interpreted by a viewing application, such as a Web browser.

Hypertext Transfer Protocol (HTTP)—The protocol used between Web browsers and Web servers to transfer content.

IAB—*See* Internet Architecture Board (IAB).

IANA—*See* Internet Assigned Numbers Authority (IANA).

IBGP—*See* Interior BGP.

ICMP—*See* Internet Control Message Protocol (ICMP).

ICMP Router Discovery Protocol (IRDP)—Protocol that enables a host to determine the address of a router that it can use as a default gateway (RFC 1256).

IDSL—*See* ISDN Digital Subscriber Line (IDSL).

IEEE—Institute of Electrical and Electronic Engineers.

IEEE 802—Project to develop LAN standards.

IEEE 802.1—High-level interface (architecture, internetworking, and management).

IEEE 802.2—Logical link control.

IEEE 802.3—CSMA/CD networks.

IEEE 802.4—Token bus networks.

IEEE 802.5—Token Ring networks.

IEEE 802.6—Metropolitan area networks (MANs).

IEEE 802.7—Broadband technical advisory group.

IEEE 802.8—Fiber optics technical advisory group.

IEEE 802.9—Integrated data and voice networks.

IEEE 802.10—LAN and MAN security.

IEEE 802.11—Wireless LANs.

IEEE 802.12—Demand Priority Access Method (also called *100VG-AnyLAN*).

IEEE 802.13—Not Used (was 100Base-X, which has been integrated into 802.3).

IEEE 802.14—Cable Modems.

IEEE 802.15—Wireless Personal Networks.

IEEE 802.16—Broadband Wireless Networks.

IESG—*See* Internet Engineering Steering Group (IESG).

IETF—*See* Internet Engineering Task Force (IETF).

IGP—*See* Interior Gateway Protocol (IGP).

IGRP—*See* Interior Gateway Routing Protocol (IGRP).

IMP—Interface Message Processor.

In-Band Control—Sending control messages over the same channel as data.

Information Frame—An HDLC or SDLC frame containing data or other higher-layer protocol data units.

Inside Wiring—Communications wiring on the customer side of the demarc.

Insider Attack—An attack on a protected network or system originating from a legitimate user.

Integrated IS-IS—Standard routing protocol that adds support for IP and other protocols to the OSI routing protocol IS-IS (RFC 1195).

Integrated Services Digital Network (ISDN)—A network in which the same digital switches and paths are used to establish connections for voice and data (ITU-T).

Interdomain Routing Protocol—Protocol used to exchange routing information between routing domains; also called an *Exterior Gateway Protocol (EGP)* on the Internet.

Inter-exchange Carrier (IXC)—Common carrier providing long distance connectivity between LATAs.

Interface—Connection between two systems or devices, a network connection on a router, or a boundary between adjacent layers of the OSI model.

Interior BGP—BGP routing within the same AS, where BGP is being used as an interior gateway protocol for intradomain routing.

Interior Gateway Protocol (IGP)—Protocol used to exchange routing information within an Internet autonomous system. Common IGPs are Interior Gateway Routing Protocol (IGRP), Open Shortest Path First (OSPF), and Routing Information Protocol (RIP).

Interior Gateway Routing Protocol (IGRP)—Cisco proprietary distance-vector routing protocol.

Intermediate-System-to-Intermediate System (IS-IS)—OSI link-state routing protocol based on DECnet Phase V routing. Routers exchange routing information for up to four metrics to the determine best available path for the quality of service requested.

International Organization for Standardization (ISO)—Voluntary coordinating group for development of standards in any field for international use, including networks.

International Telecommunications Union-Telecommunication Standardization Sector (ITU-T)—International body that develops worldwide standards for international telecommunications, replacing CCITT.

Internet—Interconnection of two or more networks. The international IP network that has evolved from the original ARPAnet (when capitalized—Internet), and a network of networks (when lower case—internet).

Internet Architecture Board (IAB)—Organization of researchers appointed by the trustees of the ISOC who discuss issues pertinent to Internet architecture. They are responsible for appointing a variety of Internet-related groups such as the IANA, IESG, and IRSG.

Internet Assigned Numbers Authority (IANA)—Organization that delegates authority for IP address-space allocation and domain-name assignment to other organizations. IANA maintains a database of assigned protocol identifiers used in the TCP/IP stack, including autonomous system numbers.

Internet Control Message Protocol (ICMP)—Network layer protocol that provides error reporting and other critical functions not included in the IP protocol specification (RFC 792).

Internet Engineering Steering Group (IESG)—Organization, appointed by the IAB, that manages the operation of the IETF.

Internet Engineering Task Force (IETF)—Volunteer task force consisting of almost 100 working groups responsible for developing Internet standards.

Internet Operating System (IOS)—Cisco's proprietary operating system that provides common functionality, scalability, and security for all Cisco products under the CiscoFusion architecture.

Internet Protocol (IP, IPv4, IPv6)—The Network layer protocol in the TCP/IP suite, currently at version 4 (RFC 791), hopefully to be superseded by version 6 (RFC 2460) before IPv4 addresses run out completely.

Internet Research Steering Group (IRSG)—Group that is part of the IAB and oversees the activities of the Internet Research Task Force.

Internet Service Provider (ISP)—Company that provides Internet access to other companies and individuals.

Internet Society (ISOC)—International non-profit organization, founded in 1992, that coordinates the evolution and use of the Internet. ISOC delegates authority to other groups related to the Internet, such as the IAB.

Internetwork—Between networks.

Internetwork Packet Exchange (IPX)—Network layer protocol used on Novell NetWare and other networks.

Intradomain Routing Protocol—Protocol used to exchange routing information within a routing domain; also called an *Interior Gateway Protocol (IGP)* on the Internet.

Intranet—Marketing buzzword for a private IP network.

Intranetwork—Within a single network.

Intrusion Detection—Detection of breakins or breakin attempts either manually or through software expert systems that analyze logs and other information available on the network.

IOS—*See* Internet Operating System (IOS).

IP—*See* Internet Protocol (IP, IPv4, IPv6).

IPC—InterProcess Communication.

IPL—Initial Program Load.

IP Address—32-bit address (IPv4) assigned to hosts using TCP/IP that is also called an *Internet address*. An IP address is commonly written as the decimal value of each octet, separated by periods (dotted decimal format). Each address consists of a subnetwork number and a host number. The subnetwork number is used for routing, while the host number is used to identify an individual host on the physical subnetwork. A subnetwork mask is used to extract subnetwork information from the IP address. Note that CIDR introduces a new way of representing IP addresses and subnetwork masks. IPv6 uses 128-bit addresses and CIDR notation.

IP Datagram—Fundamental unit of information passed across the Internet. Contains source and destination addresses along with data and a number of fields that define such things as the length of the datagram, the header checksum, and flags to indicate whether the datagram can be (or was) fragmented.

IP Spoofing—An attack in which a system attempts to illicitly impersonate another system by using its IP address.

IPv4—*See* Internet Protocol (IP, IPv4, IPv6).

IPv6—*See* Internet Protocol (IP, IPv4, IPv6).

IPX—*See* Internetwork Packet Exchange (IPX).

IPXRIP (also IPX RIP)—A simple distance-vector protocol for use with IPX.

IPXWAN—Standard protocol that negotiates end-to-end options for WAN links supporting IPX (RFC 1362).

IRDP—*See* ICMP Router Discovery Protocol (IRDP).

IRSG—*See* Internet Research Steering Group (IRSG).

IS—Information Systems; Intermediate System.

IS-IS—*See* Intermediate-System-to-Intermediate System (IS-IS).

ISDN—*See* Integrated Services Digital Network (ISDN), Basic Rate Interface (BRI), *and* Primary Rate Interface (PRI).

ISDN Digital Subscriber Line (IDSL)—Alternative to DSL used when the distance from the central office is too far to support any form of DSL; uses ISDN signalling on the local loop to provide 144-Kbps full duplex.

ISO—*See* International Organization for Standardization (ISO).

ISOC—*See* Internet Society (ISOC).

ISP—*See* Internet Service Provider (ISP).

IT—Information technology.

ITU-T—*See* International Telecommunications Union Telecommunication Standardization Sector (ITU-T).

IXC—*See* Inter-exchange Carrier (IXC).

Jitter—Analog link distortion caused by the variation of a signal from its reference timing positions.

Kbps—One thousand bits per second.

Keepalive—Message exchange used to verify that a communications channel is still functional.

Kermit—Computer program providing terminal emulation and file transfer over an asynchronous link.

L2F—*See* Layer 2 Forwarding Protocol (L2F).

LAN—*See* Local Area Network (LAN).

LAN Emulation (LANE)—A specification for providing protocol translations between LANs and ATM networks.

LAN Emulation Client—Part of LANE in end-systems that does data forwarding, address resolution, and other functions.

LAN Emulation Configuration Server (LECS)—Part of LANE that assigns individual LAN emulation clients to the appropriate LES.

LAN Emulation Server (LES)—Part of LANE that implements the control coordination functions such as resolving MAC to ATM addresses.

LANE—*See* LAN Emulation (LANE).

Last Mile—*See* Local Loop.

LES—*See* LAN Emulation Server (LES).

LATA—*See* Local Access and Transport Area (LATA).

Layer—The overall networking architecture defined by the OSI reference model is subdivided into "layers"; each layer provides a set of network-related services to the layer above.

Layer-2 Forwarding Protocol (L2F)—One of several protocols that support the creation of secure, virtual private dial-up networks over the Internet.

Layer-2 Switch—Multiport bridge with the potential for each user system to be on its own LAN segment.

Layer-2/3 Switch—A layer-2 switch with integrated routing capabilities to provide communications between VLANs.

Layer-3 Switch—A router with multiple LAN ports and presumed to be capable of making forwarding decisions at wire speeds.

Layer-3/4 Switch—A layer-3 switch that makes routing decisions based on the content of the packets being routed (usually the source or destination port).

Layer-4 Switch—*See* Layer-3/4 Switch.

Learning Bridge—Bridge that remembers the source address in received frames and filters frames that are known not to require forwarding to reduce traffic on the network.

Leased Line—A dedicated telephone channel.

Least Privilege—Designing operational aspects of a system to operate with a minimum amount of system privilege.

LEC—*See* LAN Emulation Client (LEC).

LECS—*See* LAN Emulation Configuration Server (LECS).

LEN—*See* Low-Entry Networking (LEN).

LES—*See* LAN Emulation Server (LES).

Level 1 Router—Intermediate system that routes traffic only within a single DECnet or OSI area.

Level 2 Router—Intermediate system that routes traffic between DECnet or OSI areas.

Line—A point-to-point link, usually in a WAN.

Link—The communications channel between two nodes on a network.

Link Aggregation—The grouping of physical links of the same media type and speed that can be treated as a single link.

Link State—Class of routing algorithms that flood all routing information to all routers so that each router can independently determine the best path to all destinations. Thereafter, only changes in link status are propagated, reducing overhead and speeding convergence.

Link-State Advertisement (LSA)—Packet used by link-state protocols to share routing information with neighbors.

LLC—*See* Logical Link Control (LLC).

LLC1—*See* Logical Link Control type 1 (LLC1).

LLC2—*See* Logical Link Control type 2 (LLC2).

Local Access and Transport Area (LATA)—A geographic territory that defines when communications within the U.S. can be the sole responsibility of the local telephone company.

Local Area Network (LAN)—A network small enough that the cost of interfaces is more important than efficient utilization of media bandwidth. LAN standards (such as Ethernet, FDDI, and Token Ring) specify cabling and signaling at the Physical and Data Link layers of the OSI RM.

Local Loop—The physical cable from a subscriber to the telephone company central office.

Logging—The process of receiving and storing information reported about events that occurred on a firewall, router, or other system.

Logical Link Control (LLC)—Link-layer protocol defined by IEEE 802.2.

Logical Link Control Type 1 (LLC1)—Subset of the IEEE 802.2 Logical Link Control protocol providing connectionless datagram service.

Logical Link Control Type 2 (LLC2)—Subset of the IEEE 802.2 Logical Link Control protocol providing a connection-oriented, reliable, sequenced delivery service.

Logical Unit (LU)—Definition of the services provided by a network addressable unit (NAU) that enables end users to communicate with each other and gain access to SNA network resources (IBM SNA).

Logical Unit 6.2 (LU 6.2)—The SNA LU that provides peer-to-peer communication between programs in a distributed computing environment (IBM SNA).

Low-Entry Networking (LEN)—SNA subset for a PU 2.1 node that supports LU protocols but must have a statically defined image of the APPN network (IBM SNA).

LSA—*See* Link-State Advertisement (LSA).

LU—*See* Logical Unit.

MAC—*See* Medium Access Control (MAC).

MAC Address—Standardized MAC layer address that is required for every port or device that connects to a LAN. Other devices in the network use these addresses to locate specific stations on the network. MAC addresses are 6 octets long and are controlled by the IEEE. Also known as a *hardware address, MAC-layer address,* or *physical address.*

MAN—*See* Metropolitan Area Network (MAN).

Management Information Base (MIB)—Definition of management items on a network node that can be accessed by SNMP.

Manchester Encoding—A signaling method used for transmission of data.

MAU—*See* Medium Attachment Unit (MAU) (Ethernet/802.3) *and* Multistation Access Unit (MAU or MSAU) (Token Ring/802.5).

Maximum Transmission Unit (MTU)—Maximum packet size that a particular transmission channel can handle (in octets).

Mbps—One million bits per second.

MD5—*See* Message Digest 5 (MD5).

Mean Time Between Failures (MTBF)—Statistical measure of the expected failure rate of a device during its useful life.

Mean Time to Repair (MTTR)—Statistical measure of the expected time required to restore a device to service after a failure occurs.

Media Access Unit (MAU)—Another name for a Medium Attachment Unit (MAU).

Medium Access Control (MAC)—Methodology by which a node gains access to the network medium to transmit a message (also called *Media Access Control*).

Medium Attachment Unit (MAU)—Device used in IEEE 802.3 networks to interface between the AUI port of a station and the shared medium of the network. The same device is called a *transceiver* in the Ethernet specification.

Message—A collection of data considered a single logical unit.

Message Digest 5 (MD5)—Standard message authentication algorithm used to verify the integrity of a communication, authenticate the origin, and check for timeliness (RFC 1321).

Metric—Measure of the cost of a route used by a routing protocol to determine the best available route.

Metropolitan Area Network (MAN)—A communications network too large to use standard LAN technology but small enough that standard WAN technology is not essential.

MIB—*See* Management Information Base (MIB).

Microcom Networking Protocol (MNP)—A series of protocols for error recovery and data compression designed for asynchronous modems.

MLP—*See* Multilink PPP.

MNP—*See* Microcom Networking Protocol.

Modem—Contraction for MOdulator-DEModulator, a device that converts digital signals to analog (and back) for transmission.

Modulation—Converting signals from one form (digital) into another (analog).

MSAU—*See* Multistation Access Unit (MAU, MSAU).

MTBF—*See* Mean Time Between Failures (MTBF).

MTTR—*See* Mean Time to Repair (MTTR).

MTU—*See* Maximum Transmission Unit (MTU).

Multicast—Single packets entering the network that are delivered to a specific subset of network stations.

Multicast Address—A single address that refers to a set of network devices; also called a *group address*.

Multidrop—*See* Multipoint.

Multihomed Host—End system attached to multiple physical network segments.

Multilink PPP—Standard protocol for combining multiple PPP connections into a single logical channel.

Multimode Fiber—Optical fiber supporting propagation of light entering over a range of angles. The resulting modal dispersion limits the data rate possible over a given distance.

Multiplexing—Division of a transmission channel into two or more independent communications channels.

Multiplexor (Mux)—A standalone device that performs multiplexing for a (typically point-to-point) channel.

Multipoint—Having several units sharing a line, usually with a master controlling access.

Multistation Access Unit (MAU, MSAU)—Wiring concentrator to which all end stations in a Token Ring network connect.

Multivendor Network—Network using equipment from more than one vendor, which can lead to challenges with compatibility and support.

NAK—Negative AcKnowledgment.

Name Resolution—The process of associating a network address with a given name.

NAP—Network Access Point.

NAT—*See* Network Address Translation (NAT).

National ISDN-1—A specification for a "standard" ISDN phone line to allow multi-vendor interoperability.

NETBEUI—*See* NetBIOS Extended User Interface (NETBEUI).

NetBIOS Extended User Interface (NETBEUI)—Implementation of the NetBIOS protocol used by network operating systems such as LAN Manager, LAN Server, Windows for Workgroups, and Windows NT. NetBEUI uses the 802.2 LLC2 protocol for its transport.

NetBIOS—*See* Network Basic Input/Output System (NetBIOS).

NetWare—Network operating system developed by Novell that provides transparent remote file access and numerous other distributed network services.

NetWare Link Services Protocol (NLSP)—Link-state routing protocol based on IS-IS developed by Novell for IPX networks.

Network—Set of computers, printers, routers, and other devices that are able to communicate with each other.

Network Address Translation (NAT)—Mechanism for translating addresses from one address space into another; normally associated with firewalls and reducing the demand for globally unique IP addresses, but can have other uses as well.

Network Basic Input/Output System (NetBIOS)—API defined by IBM for their PC LAN products, which became the standard for networked application portability in the PC world.

Network Interface—The modern name for the Demarc.

Network Interface Card (NIC)—A module that connects PCs, WSs, servers, and other computers to their networks.

Network Layer—The OSI reference model layer covering the services across a network.

Network-Level Firewall—A firewall in which traffic is examined at the network protocol packet level.

Network Management—The facility by which a network communication or device is observed and controlled.

Network Management System (NMS)—System responsible for managing at least part of a network; normally communicates with agents on network devices to keep track of performance statistics and resources.

Network Manager—The consciousness of the network management facility.

Network Operating System (NOS)—Generic term used to refer to distributed file systems such as LAN Manager, NetWare, NFS, and VINES.

Network Service Access Point (NSAP)—OSI global internetwork address.

Network Termination-1 (NT-1)—Device that converts an ISDN-U interface (the two-wire local loop used to provide ISDN service) to an ISDN S/T interface (used by subscriber equipment to allow sharing a single ISDN line).

NI-1—*See* National ISDN-1.

NIC—*See* Network Interface Card (NIC).

NLSP—*See* NetWare Link Services Protocol (NLSP).

NMS—*See* Network Management System (NMS).

Node—The processor component of a network.

Node Address—A unique address identifying each machine on a physical subnetwork.

NOS—*See* Network Operating System (NOS).

NSAP—*See* Network Service Access Point (NSAP).

NT-1—*See* Network Termination-1 (NT-1).

Null Modem—A device or cable that allows two DTEs to directly communicate without going through a service provider network.

Octet—An 8-bit data unit.

Open Shortest Path First (OSPF)—Link state routing protocol for IP (RFC 2328).

Open System Interconnection (OSI)—Connecting systems from different manufacturers by having all follow public published standards.

OSI—*See* Open System Interconnection (OSI).

OSI Reference Model—A layered protocol model defining a standard language for describing network functions and protocols.

OSI RM—*See* OSI Reference Model.

OSPF—*See* Open Shortest Path First (OSPF).

Out of Band—Using a separate channel for control systems.

Pacing—*See* Flow Control.

Packet—Common name for a network PDU, the unit of information at the Network layer.

Packet Internet Groper—*See* Ping.

Packet Switching—A mode of data transmission in which messages are broken into smaller units called packets and each packet is transmitted independently.

Packet Switching Network (PSN)—A network using packet switching for communications.

Parity—A simple 1-bit error check.

Passive RIP—Technique in which end systems listen in on RIP broadcasts between routers to determine what routers are available for relaying data to remote destinations.

Payload—Portion of a protocol data unit that contains the PDU of the layer above that layer of the OSI RM.

PDN—*See* Public Data Network (PDN).

PDU—*See* Protocol Data Unit (PDU).

Peer Protocol—A protocol for interaction between network nodes between entities within the same layer.

Perimeter-Based Security—The technique of securing a network by controlling access to all entry and exit points of the network.

Permanent Virtual Circuit (PVC)—A predefined communications path through a network of multiple connection alternatives.

Physical Layer—The lowest layer of the OSI reference model.

Physical Unit (PU)—SNA component that manages and monitors the resources of a node.

Ping—Common name for a software utility to send an ICMP echo request to a remote system and report any ICMP echo response received.

Pipelining—Having several messages in transit without acknowledgment.

Plain Old Telephone Service (POTS)—Traditional analog telephone service.

PNNI—*See* Private Network-to-Network Interface (PNNI) *and* Private Network Node Interface (PNNI).

Point of Presence (POP)—Location where the customer's responsibility begins and the service provider's ends.

Point-to-Point—A link usable for communication between two and only two data stations.

Point-to-Point Protocol (PPP)—Internet standard Data Link layer protocol for router-to-router and host-to-network connections over synchronous and asynchronous circuits. Unlike SLIP, PPP is designed to simultaneously support multiple Network Layer protocols (RFC 1661).

Poison Reverse—Routing updates used by distance-vector protocols that explicitly indicate that a network or subnet is unreachable to minimize the potential for routing loops.

Policy—Organization-level rules governing acceptable use of computing resources, security practices, and operational procedures.

Policy Routing—Forwarding packets based on user-configured policies. For example, traffic sent from a particular network might be forwarded out one interface, while all other traffic should be forwarded out another interface.

Polling—Link control by a master station inviting data stations to transmit one at a time.

POP—*See* Point of Presence (POP).

Port—A logical entry-exit point from a software process, or an identifier of the application process in a TCP or UDP packet.

Post, Telegraph, and Telephone (PTT)—Obsolete term for a government telecommunications agency.

POTS—*See* Plain Old Telephone Service (POTS).

PPP—*See* Point-to-Point Protocol (PPP).

Presentation Layer—The OSI reference model layer that converts the representation of the data.

PRI—*See* Primary Rate Interface (PRI).

Primary Rate Interface (PRI)—ISDN provision of 23B+D (T1) or 30B+D (E1). *See* B-Channel *and* D-Channel.

Priority Queuing—Router feature that allows sorting of an output queue by characteristics of the contents such as packet size or protocol.

Private Line—Same as a leased line.

Private Network Node Interface (PNNI)—Specification for signaling to establish point-to-point and point-to-multipoint connections across an ATM network (ATM Forum).

Private Network-to-Network Interface (PNNI)—A dynamic routing protocol for ATM networks (ATM Forum).

Process-Switching—Cisco router mode of operation that provides full route evaluation and per-packet load balancing across parallel WAN links. It requires the transfer of each packet to be routed to the router CPU, where the packets are repackaged for delivery to a WAN interface, with the router making a route selection for each packet.

Propagation Delay—The delay caused by the finite speed of electronic transmission.

Protocol—A set of rules and formats for communications.

Protocol Conversion Gateway—Devices to connect different network architectures using different protocols by providing protocol translation.

Protocol Data Unit (PDU)—Information that is delivered as a unit between peer entities. Contains control information and address information and may contain data.

Proxy—One entity serving for another entity.

Proxy ARP—Router service that has the router respond to ARP requests from end-systems looking for an IP address not on the local subnetwork.

PSTN—Public Switched Telephone Network (PSTN).

PTT—*See* Post, Telegraph, and Telephone (PTT).

PU—*See* Physical Unit (PU).

Public Data Network (PDN)—A network established and operated to provide data transmission services to the public.

Public Switched Telephone Network (PSTN)—A network established and operated to provide voice transmission (telephone) services to the public.

PVC—*See* Permanent Virtual Circuit; also an acronym for *PolyVinyl Chloride,* a common insulator used for cable construction.

Q Series Standards—ITU-T specifications for signaling on ISDN, Frame Relay, and other network connections.

QAM—*See* Quadrature Amplitude Modulation (QAM).

QoS—*See* Quality of Service (QoS).

Quadrature Amplitude Modulation (QAM)—Method of modulating digital signals onto a carrier signal involving both amplitude and phase coding; used in high-performance radio and voice channel modems.

Quality of Service (QoS)—Performance metric for a transmission system that reflects its performance and service availability.

Query—Message sent to find the value of some variable or set of variables. A query and a response make up a transaction.

Queue—An ordered set of elements waiting to be processed by a facility with limited capacity.

Queuing Delay—Amount of time that a frame or packet must wait before it can be processed or forwarded.

Queuing Theory—Mathematical principles describing the behavior of congestion in networks.

RADIUS—*See* Remote Authentication Dial-In User Services (RADIUS).

Rapid Reconfiguration—Enhanced TST algorithm defined by IEEE 802.1w for faster TST convergence in constrained topologies.

RARP—*See* Reverse Address Resolution Protocol (RARP).

Redistribution—Sharing routing information between routing protocols; sometimes called *route redistribution*.

Redundancy—Systems: the presence of multiple units of critical components combined so that in the event of a failure, the redundant components can perform the work of those that failed; communications theory: the portion of the total information contained in a message that can be eliminated without loss of essential information or meaning.

Redundancy Check—A check for errors using extra data inserted for that purpose.

Redundant System—Computer, router, network, or other system that contains two or more of any critical subsystems required for proper functioning, such as two disk drives, two links, or two power supplies.

Registered Jack (RJ)—Connector standards originally designed for telephone lines. Now used not only for telephone connections, but also for 10BaseT and other types of network connections.

Reliability—The probability of failure free operation over a period of time.

Remote Authentication Dial-In User Services (RADIUS)—A standard protocol for providing third-party authentication and authorization services (RFC 2865).

Remote Bridging—Connecting physically separate network segments at the Data Link layer via a dedicated or logical point-to-point link.

Remote Source Route Bridging (RSRB)—Remote bridging approach for source route networks that makes the WAN look like just another Token Ring LAN to the source routing end systems.

Repeater—A signal regenerator, normally used to propagate electrical signals between two (or more) network segments.

Request for Comments (RFC)—A series of documents serving as the official means for communicating information about the Internet. Most RFCs define protocols for use on the Internet, but some are humorous or historical. RFCs are available online at http://www.ietf.org and many other locations.

Resilient Links—Switches or NICs that can automatically detect loss of link pulse and can failover to designated backup ports or NICs.

Response—Message returned as a result of a query. It will normally contain the information requested or an error message. A query and a response make up a transaction.

Reverse Address Resolution Protocol (RARP)—Protocol in the TCP/IP suite that provides a method for finding IP addresses based on MAC addresses (RFC 903).

RFC—*See* Request for Comments (RFC).

Ring Network—A LAN with a ring topology consisting of a series of repeaters connected to one another by simplex transmission links to form a closed loop.

RIP—*See* Routing Information Protocol (RIP).

RIPv1—The original RIP version 1. *See* Routing Information Protocol (RIP).

RIPv2—RIP version 2. *See* Routing Information Protocol (RIP).

RJ—*See* Registered Jack (RJ).

RMON—Remote Monitoring MIB for SNMP that defines functions for the remote monitoring of networked devices (RFC 1271).

RMON2—New and improved version of RMON (RFC 2021).

RNR—Receiver not Ready frame used for flow control in HDLC, SDLC, and LLC2.

Robust—System design that minimizes the impact of typical failures.

Root Bridge—Bridge in a TST LAN that serves as the base for building the minimal Spanning Tree of connectivity used to eliminate forwarding loops.

Route Map—Method of controlling the redistribution of routes between routing domains.

Routeing—British spelling of the function of a router, which is the language used in international standards. Pronounced as "root-ing" (what you do at a football match) rather than the American "rout-ing" (what you do in a woodworking shop).

Router—Device that connects compatible networks at the network layer of the OSI reference model; technically, an intermediate system that makes routing decisions.

Routing—Finding a path across interconnected links or networks.

Routing Domain—A set of end systems and intermediate systems operating under the same set of administrative rules. In particular, a routing protocol may safely compare routing metrics received from other systems within the routing domain.

Routing Information Field (RIF)—Field in the IEEE 802.5 header that specifies the sequence of Token Ring network segments and source route bridges a packet must take to reach the destination.

Routing Information Protocol (RIP)—Very popular distance-vector routing protocol for IP networks defined by RFC 1058. Version 2 (RIPv2) added authentication and VLSM for CIDR (RFC 2453). The IPX variant is usually referred to as IPXRIP.

Routing Metric—Measure used by a routing algorithm to determine that one path is better than another. Metrics may be based on bandwidth, communication cost, delay, hop count, load, MTU, path cost, or other factors; sometimes referred to as a *metric*.

Routing Table—Data array in a networking device that specifies the next hop to use for specific network addresses or address ranges.

RR—Receiver Ready frame used for acknowledgments and flow control in HDLC, SDLC, and LLC2.

RS-232—Very popular standard for connecting DTE to DCE at data rates up to 19.2 Kbps; commonly used (for very short distances) at rates up to 115 Kbps.

RS-422—Balanced signaling method developed for RS-449 to support data rates up to several megabits per second (depending upon distance).

RS-423—Unbalanced signaling method developed for RS-449 to support backwards compatibility with RS-232.

RS-449—Follow-up standard intended to replace RS-232 in high-data rate applications, which never really caught on. It was superseded by EIA-530, which uses the same signaling for high speed (up to 10 Mbps) on the popular RS-232D connector.

RSA—Popular public-key cryptographic system (acronym for Rivest, Shamir, and Adelman, its inventors) (RFC 2437).

RSRB—*See* Remote Source Route Bridging (RSRB).

SAN—*See* Storage Area Network (SAN).

SAP—*See* Service Access Point (SAP) (IEEE 802) *and* Service Advertising Protocol (SAP) (IPX).

SAR—Segmentation and Reassembly.

Screened Twisted-Pair (ScTP)—Interconnection cable consisting of pairs of wires twisted together and protected by a less effective metallic shield; a compromise between the noise immunity of STP and attenuation characteristics of UTP.

Screening Router—A router configured to permit or deny traffic based on a set of permission rules installed by the administrator.

SDH—*See* Synchronous Digital Hierarchy (SDH).

SDSL—*See* Single-Line Digital Subscriber Line (SDSL).

Secondary—The subordinate end of a HDLC or SDLC link.

Secure Socket Layer (SSL)—Encryption technology providing secure transactions over the Web.

Segment—Section of a network that is bounded by bridges, routers, or switches; extent of a bus network bounded by repeaters; a Transport layer protocol data unit.

Sequenced Packet Exchange (SPX)—NetWare transport protocol providing reliable, connection-oriented service.

Serial Line Internet Protocol—Original standard protocol for point-to-point serial connections supporting TCP/IP (RFC 1057), but superseded by PPP.

Serial Transmission—Sending digital data as a sequence of individual bits.

Server Clustering—Linking together multiple servers in order to share resources in a loosely coupled configuration.

Server Message Block (SMB)—File-system protocol used in LAN manager and similar network operating systems.

Service Access Point (SAP)—The access means by which a pair of communicating entities in adjacent layers use or provide services. Field defined by the IEEE 802.2 LLC specification that identifies the network protocol carried in the frame.

Service Advertising Protocol (SAP)—IPX protocol that provides a means of informing network clients of available network resources and services.

Service Level Agreement (SLA)—A document for establishing and reporting various computing criteria—from application performance, response time, and availability metrics to general performance trends—that are affected by network performance and availability.

Service Profile Identifier (SPID)—A number assigned to an ISDN line by the service provider used by the ISDN switch to determine where to send calls and signals.

Services—The functions offered by an OSI reference model layer to communicating entities in the layer above.

Session Layer—Fifth layer of the OSI reference model.

Shielded Twisted-Pair (STP)—Interconnection cable consisting of pairs of wires twisted together and protected by one or more metallic shield layers.

Signal—Waves propagated along a transmission channel that convey some meaning to the receiver.

Simple Mail Transfer Protocol (SMTP)—Internet protocol providing e-mail services (RFC 821).

Simple Multicast Routing Protocol (SMRP)—Specialized multicast network protocol for routing multimedia data streams on enterprise networks.

Simple Network Management Protocol (SNMP)—Network management protocol providing a means to monitor and control network devices (RFC 1157 and many others).

Simplex—Transmission in a single predetermined direction only.

Single-Line Digital Subscriber Line (SDSL)—DSL technology delivering 1.544 Mbps both downstream and upstream over a single copper-twisted pair of up to 10,000 feet.

Single-Mode Fiber (SMF)—Fiber optic cabling with a very small core that allows light to enter only at a single angle. Required for very high speed over long distances.

SLA—*See* Service Level Agreement (SLA).

Sliding Window—A mechanism that indicates the frames that currently can be sent.

SLIP—*See* Serial Line Internet Protocol.

Slotted Ring—A LAN architecture in which a constant number of fixed-length slots circulate around a ring.

SMB—*See* Server Message Block (SMB).

SMDS—*See* Switched Multimegabit Data Service (SMDS).

SMF—*See* Single-Mode Fiber (SMF).

SMI—*See* Structure of Management Information (SMI).

Smoothing—See Traffic Shaping.

SMTP—See Simple Mail Transfer Protocol (SMTP).

SNA—*See* Systems Network Architecture (SNA).

SNA Network Interconnection (SNI)—IBM architecture for connecting multiple SNA networks.

SNI—*See* SNA Network Interconnection (SNI).

SNMP—*See* Simple Network Management Protocol (SNMP).

Social Engineering—An attack based on deceiving users or administrators at the target site, typically carried out by telephone.

Socket—A networkwide name for an entry or exit point at a process, or the conceptual interconnection point in the BSD UNIX network API.

SONET—*See* Synchronous Optical Network (SONET).

Source-Route Bridging (SRB)—Method of bridging popularized by IBM for Token Ring networks in which the entire route to a destination is predetermined prior to the sending of data to the destination.

Source-Route Translational Bridging (SR/TLB)—Method of bridging in which source-route stations can communicate with transparent bridge stations with the help of an intermediate bridge that translates between the two bridge protocols.

Source-Route Transparent Bridging (SRT)—IBM bridging scheme that merges the SRB and TST bridging technologies in one device.

Source Routing (SR)—Determining the path (route) at the source of the message.

Spanning-Tree Algorithm—*See* Transparent Spanning Tree (TST).

SPID—*See* Service Profile Identifier (SPID).

Split-Horizon Updates—Routing technique in which information about routes is blocked from advertisements sent out the router interface through which that information was received; used to prevent routing loops.

Spoofing—Scheme used by routers to cause an interface to appear as if it were up and supporting a session; the act of a packet illegally claiming to be from an address from which it was not actually sent. Spoofing is designed to foil network security mechanisms, such as filters and access-lists.

SPX—*See* Sequenced Packet Exchange (SPX).

SQL—*See* Structured Query Language (SQL).

SR—*See* Source Routing (SR).

SRB—*See* Source-Route Bridging (SRB).

SRT—*See* Source-Route Transparent Bridging (SRT).

SR/TLB—*See* Source-Route Translational Bridging (SR/TLB).

SSL—*See* Secure Socket Layer (SSL).

Star—Type of tree network in which there is exactly one intermediate node.

Start-Stop—Character asynchronous transmission.

Static Route—A route that is manually entered into the routing table rather than learned through a dynamic routing protocol.

Statistical Multiplexor—Sharing a link by only sending data when it is available.

Storage Area Network (SAN)—High-speed network that logically connects storage to servers.

Store and Forward—Store the message (or packet) before sending it on.

Store and Forward Switching—Switching approach that waits until the entire incoming frame has been received and the CRC has been verified before starting to send the frame out the outgoing port; eliminates the potential of unnecessarily forwarding a corrupted frame; contrast to Cut-Through Switching.

STP—*See* Shielded Twisted-Pair (STP).

Structure of Management Information (SMI)—Rules used to define managed objects in a MIB (RFC 1155).

Structured Query Language (SQL)—Standard for accessing relational databases.

Stub Area—OSPF area that carries a default route and intra-area routes only.

Subnetwork—A physical network.

Subnetwork Address—Portion of an IP address that indicates the physical network to which the device is attached.

Subnetwork Mask—Mask used in IP to indicate the portion of an IP address that specifies the subnetwork rather than the host on the subnetwork.

SVC—*See* Switched Virtual Circuit (SVC).

Switch—A popular networking term whose meaning must be determined from context as it can range from a device used for controlling the function of an electric light to a device in a telephone exchange handling thousands of calls simultaneously; a multiport bridge used to segment a LAN for higher performance.

Switch Type—The brand of equipment and software revision level used by the telephone company to provide ISDN service. *See* National ISDN-1.

Switched Connection—A mode of operating a data link in which a dedicated circuit is established between data stations.

Switched Multimegabit Data Service (SMDS)—High-speed WAN access technology offered by U.S. telephone companies.

Switched Virtual Circuit (SVC)—A temporary communications path through a network of multiple connection alternatives that is established on demand.

Synchronous Data Link Control (SDLC)—IBM SNA bit-oriented Data Link layer protocol.

Synchronous Digital Hierarchy (SDH)—ITU-T standard that defines a set of rate and format standards that are transmitted using optical signals over fiber. SDH is similar to SONET, with a basic SDH rate of 155.52 Mbps, designated as STM-1. *See also* SONET *and* STM-1.

Synchronous Optical Network (SONET)—North American standard for providing high-speed shared data communications at up to 2.5 Gbps to customers over fiber optic links.

Synchronous Transmission—Communication in which the sender and receiver share a common clock to delimit data bits.

Systems Network Architecture (SNA)—IBM's proprietary network architecture introduced in 1974.

T1 Carrier—A U.S. and Japanese telephone facility for transmitting DS-1-formatted data at 1.544 Mbps.

T3 Carrier—A telephone facility that transmits DS-3-formatted data at 44.736 Mbps through the telephone network.

TACACS—*See* Terminal Access Controller Access Control System (TACACS).

TCP—*See* Transmission Control Protocol (TCP).

TCP/IP—*See* Transmission Control Protocol/Internet Protocol (TCP/IP).

TEI—*See* Terminal Equipment ID (TEI).

Telecommunications Industry Association (TIA)—U.S. organization that develops standards relating to telecommunications technologies; evolved from the Electronics Industry Association.

Telnet—Virtual terminal protocol in the TCP/IP protocol suite (RFC 854).

Terminal Access Controller Access Control System (TACACS)—Authentication protocol that provides remote access authentication and related services, such as event logging. User passwords are administered in a central database.

Terminal Adapter—Equipment used to adapt ISDN BRI channels to existing DTE standards (usually RS-232 or V.35).

Terminal Equipment ID (TEI)—ID dynamically allocated when an ISDN user device is attached to the ISDN network to address the device over the D-channel.

Terminator—Electrical resistance at the end of a transmission line to absorb signals on the line and keep them from bouncing back.

TFTP—*See* Trivial File Transfer Protocol (TFTP).

Three-Way Handshake—Process used by the TCP protocol during connection establishment to synchronize sequence numbers.

Throughput—Rate of information transfer through a network system.

TIA—*See* Telecommunications Industry Association (TIA).

Time to Live (TTL)—IP protocol header field that serves to prevent looping packets from living forever.

Time-out—Waiting for a timer to expire before taking action.

Token—A recognizable control mechanism used to control access to a network.

Token Bus—A network architecture based on a bus topology and using a token-based media access method.

Token Ring—A network architecture using a ring topology and a token-based media access method. IEEE 802.5 and FDDI are two popular Token Ring standards.

Topology—The connectivity structure of a network.

Traceroute—Common program that traces the path a packet takes to a destination (RFC 1393).

Traffic Analysis—Determining the traffic level of a network.

Traffic Shaping—Limiting traffic surges that can congest an ATM, a Frame Relay, or another type of network. Data is buffered and then sent into the network in regulated amounts to ensure that the traffic will fit within the desired traffic envelope for the particular connection; also known as *metering, shaping,* and *smoothing.*

Transaction—Request and response unit of communication interaction.

Transceiver—Transmitter-receiver. *See also* Medium Access Unit (MAU).

Transmission Control Protocol (TCP)—Connection-oriented Transport layer protocol that provides reliable full-duplex data transmission (RFC 793).

Transmission Control Protocol/Internet Protocol (TCP/IP)—Common name for the suite of protocols developed for the ARPAnet in the 1970s that is now the foundation for the Internet.

Transparency—In applications, the mechanism providing the function is hidden from the user; in communications, allowing all bit patterns, including control patterns such as flags and controls, to be carried as data.

Transparent Bridging—Any bridging scheme in which the bridges require no support from end-systems, making their operation invisible to the MAC protocol.

Transparent Spanning-Tree (TST)—Protocol implementing the Spanning-Tree Algorithm to eliminate forwarding loops in bridged LANs with multiple parallel links (IEEE 802).

Trap—Unsolicited message sent by an SNMP agent to indicate the occurrence of a significant event or condition.

Trivial File Transfer Protocol (TFTP)—Standard protocol designed to require an absolute minimum of system capability to implement that allows files to be transferred from one computer to another over a network (RFC 1350).

Trojan Horse—A software entity that appears to do something normal but which contains a a trap-door or attack program.

Trunk—Physical and logical connection between two central offices across which network traffic travels; contrast to local loop.

TST—*See* Transparent Spanning-Tree (TST).

TTL—*See* Time to Live (TTL).

Tunneling—Protocol service that implements any standard point-to-point encapsulation scheme.

Tunneling Router—A router or system capable of routing traffic by encrypting it and encapsulating it for transmission across an untrusted network.

Twisted-Pair Cable—Interconnection cable consisting of pairs of wires twisted together.

Type 1 LLC—*See* Logical Link Control Type 1 (LLC 1).

Type 2 LLC—*See* Logical Link Control Type 2 (LLC 2).

U-Interface—A two-wire ISDN circuit that connects an ISDN line to the central office.

UA—Unnumbered Acknowledgment.

UBR—*See* Unspecified Bit Rate (UBR).

UDP—*See* User Datagram Protocol (UDP).

UI—Unnumbered Information.

UNI—User-Network Interface for ATM networks (ATM Forum).

Unicast—Message sent to a specifically identified network destination.

Uniform Resource Locator (URL)—Standardized addressing scheme for accessing hypertext documents and other services (RFC 1738).

Unshielded Twisted-Pair (UTP)—Interconnection cable consisting of pairs of wires twisted together with no protective metallic shielding.

Unspecified Bit Rate (UBR)—Service category for ATM networks that allows any amount of data up to a specified maximum to be sent across the network, but with no guarantees in terms of cell loss rate and delay (ATM Forum).

Uplink—In a hierarchy of hubs or switches, the link connecting a lower level hub or switch to a port on the hub or switch at the next level up.

UPS—Uninterruptible Power Supply.

URL—*See* Uniform Resource Locator (URL).

Useful Life—Period of time between burn-in and end-of-life wearout where a hardware device exhibits a constant, low failure rate. Note that the MTBF defined by the failure rate during the useful life period has no relation to the expected useful life and could be much longer than the device is expected to last in service.

User Address—A unique address for each communicating entity on the LAN where local control of addressing is maintained.

User Datagram Protocol (UDP)—Connectionless Transport layer protocol in the TCP/IP architecture (RFC 768).

User Friendly—A system that has desireable usability characteristics (e.g., easy to use, easy to learn, and intuitive).

User Program—A computer program running in a processor that performs information processing for some specific use.

UTC—*See* Coordinated Universal Time (UTC).

UTP—*See* Unshielded Twisted-Pair (UTP).

V Series Standards—ITU-T recommendations (international standards) for the connection of digital equipment to public telephone (analog voice) networks.

V.34—Modem standard supporting data rates up to 28.8 Kbps.

V.34 bis—Standard enhancements to V.34 that allow modem operation at speeds up to 33.6 Kbps (ITU-T) over POTS.

V.35—Standard Physical layer protocol for a synchronous DTE/DCE interface.

V.42—Modem standard providing error detection and recovery between analog modems.

V.42 bis—Modem standard that builds on V.42 to provide lossless data compression for analog modem communications.

V.90—Modem standard that can provide up to 56 Kbps from a digital interface to the analog modem, provided that the only digital to analog conversion in the path is at the CO serving the analog modem user's local loop.

V.92— Modem standard that builds on V.90 to provide faster call setup times and up to 48 Kbps in the analog-to-digital path.

Variable Bit Rate (VBR)—ATM service category for data traffic with average and peak traffic parameters (ATM Forum).

Variable Length Subnetwork Mask (VLSM)—Ability to specify a different subnetwork mask for the same network number on different subnetworks.

VC—*See* Virtual Circuit.

VDSL—*See* Very-High-Data-Rate Digital Subscriber Line (VDSL).

Very-High-Data-Rate Digital Subscriber Line (VDSL)—DSL technology delivering 13 to 52 Mbps downstream and 1.5 to 2.3 Mbps upstream over a single twisted-copper pair less than 1,000 to 4,500 feet long.

VINES—*See* Virtual Integrated Network Service (VINES).

Virtual Circuit—Network service providing sequenced, error-free delivery.

Virtual Connection—DTE-to-DTE connection that has a defined route and end-points. *See* Permanent Virtual Circuit (PVC) *and* Switched Virtual Circuit (SVC). In ATM, a virtual connection is called a *virtual channel.*

Virtual Integrated Network Service (VINES)—Banyan Systems network operating system.

Virtual LAN (VLAN)—Group of devices on one or more LANs that are configured (using management software) so that they can communicate as if they were attached to the same wire.

Virtual Network Perimeter—A network that appears to be a single protected network behind firewalls, but which actually encompasses encrypted virtual links over untrusted networks.

Virtual Router Redundancy Protocol (VRRP)—Standard protocol that allows one router to take over the identity of another router, hiding any router failures from end-systems (RFC 2338).

Virtual Telecommunications Access Method (VTAM)—The set of programs that controls communications between LUs in IBM SNA.

Virus—A replicating code segment that attaches itself to a program or data file.

VLAN—*See* Virtual LAN (VLAN).

VLSM—*See* Variable Length Subnetwork Mask (VLSM).

Voice Grade Line—The standard analog telephone channel (also called *POTS*).

Voice over IP (VoIP)—Providing telephone-style voice services over an IP-based network.

VoIP—*See* Voice over IP (VoIP).

VRRP—*See* Virtual Router Redundancy Protocol (VRRP).

VTAM—Virtual Telecommunications Access Method (IBM).

VTY—Virtual type terminal, but commonly used as virtual terminal lines (Cisco).

WAN—*See* Wide Area Network (WAN).

Web—*See* World Wide Web (WWW).

Web Browser—*See* Browser.

Weighted Fair Queuing—Congestion management algorithm that identifies conversations and ensures that capacity is shared fairly between these individual conversations (Cisco).

Wide Area Network (WAN)—A data communications capability serving users over an extended geographic area. Design is driven by the need to maximize the utilization of media bandwidth.

Window—The allowable messages (sequence numbers) that can be sent.

Wiring Closet—Central junction point for the wiring and wiring equipment that is used for interconnecting devices in a building.

Workgroup—Collection of workstations and servers on a LAN that are designed to communicate and exchange data with one another.

Workstation—A computer system designed for use by an individual; often connected to other workstations and hosts by a LAN.

World Wide Web (WWW)—Global community of servers providing hypertext and other services to Internet browsers.

Worm—A standalone program that copies itself from one host to another and then runs itself on each new host.

Wrap—Action taken by an FDDI network to recover in the event of a failure. The stations on each side of the failure reconfigure to create a single logical ring out of the primary and secondary rings.

WWW—*See* World Wide Web (WWW).

X Series Standards—ITU-T recommendations (international standards) for the connection of digital equipment to a public data network.

X.25—ITU-T recommendation defining the connection of a computer to a packet-switched network.

xDSL—Generic term used to refer to ADSL, HDSL, SDSL, and VDSL.

Xerox Network Systems (XNS)—Protocol suite originally designed at the Xerox Palo Alto Research Center. Many PC networking companies, such as 3Com, Banyan, Novell, and UB Networks, used or currently use a variation of XNS as their primary transport protocol.

XID—*See* Exchange Identification (XID).

XNS—*See* Xerox Network Systems (XNS).

Xmodem—Personal computer protocol for file transfer over an asynchronous channel.

INDEX

DATE DUE

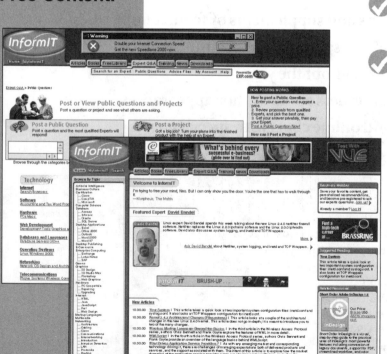

Register
Your Book

at www.aw.com/cseng/register

You may be eligible to receive:

- Advance notice of forthcoming editions of the book
- Related book recommendations
- Chapter excerpts and supplements of forthcoming titles
- Information about special contests and promotions throughout the year
- Notices and reminders about author appearances, tradeshows, and online chats with special guests

Contact us

If you are interested in writing a book or reviewing manuscripts prior to publication, please write to us at:

Editorial Department
Addison-Wesley Professional
75 Arlington Street, Suite 300
Boston, MA 02116 USA
Email: AWPro@aw.com

Addison-Wesley

Visit us on the Web: http://www.aw.com/cseng